The Collection of Wardā

Gorgias Eastern Christian Studies

70

Gorgias Eastern Christian Studies brings to the scholarly world the underrepresented field of Eastern Christianity. This series consists of monographs, edited collections, texts and translations of the documents of Eastern Christianity, as well as studies of topics relevant to the world of historic Orthodoxy and early Christianity.

The Collection of Wardā

A Contextual and Christological Analysis

By

Dahlia Khay Azeez

2024

Gorgias Press LLC, 954 River Road, Piscataway, NJ, 08854, USA

www.gorgiaspress.com

2024 ,

ISBN
Hardback 978-1-4632-4589-4
eBook 978-1-4632-4590-0

ISSN 1539-1507

Library of Congress Cataloging-in-Publication Data

A Cataloging-in-Publication Record is available at the Library of Congress.

Printed in the United States of America

To my beloved church
the Church of the East (The Ancient/Assyrian)
to those who shed their blood for your name
I present this book.
for all that you have to endure through centuries
persecutions and golden ages
glorious times and fails
but you could raise many times from ashes
how can I not see this as a miracle?
my little and simple church
I see you are always great in what you give,
maybe it is seen as crumbs
but it feeds the hunger of whom did not see the bread.

إلى كنيستي الحبيبة
كنيسة المشرق (القديمة/ الآشورية)
إلى كل من سكب دمه من أجل اسمك
أهدي هذا الكتاب.
لأجل كل ما تحمّلتِه خلال قرون
من اضطهادات وعصور ذهبية
أزمنة مجيدة وانكسارات
ولكن استطعتِ أن تقومي من الرماد عدة مرات
كيف لا يمكنني رؤية هذا كمعجزة؟
كنيستي الصغيرة والبسيطة
أراكِ دائماً عظيمة فيما تعطيه
وقد يُرى ما تعطيه هو كالفُتات
ولكنه يُشبع جوع من لم يرَ الخبز.

TABLE OF CONTENTS

ACKNOWLEDGMENTS

First of all, I want to thank God who accompanied me in every step in my life. Without Him I would have never arrived at this moment.

I want to give special thanks and honor to His Holiness, Patriarch Mar Addai II of the Ancient Church of the East (+2022), His Holiness, Patriarch Mar Gīwargīs III Ṣlīḇā, and His Holiness, Patriarch Mar Awa Royal, both of the Assyrian Church of the East, who all of them helped me with books, manuscripts and documents.

I want to thank my parents, whose love has strengthened me each time I felt weak, especially through the prayers of my mother. Without the help of my siblings and cousins I would not have had inner peace while working: Vienna, Noor, deacon Yousip and Youbil and my cousins Sister Agnes Daniel and Youneel Goryal.

My sincere thanks to father Vincent Van Vossel, who encouraged me to continue my studies in theology; he watched over me as a father guards his daughter who is taking her first steps in life, and he offered far more support than expected. He provided me not just with books I needed but also with encouragement when I was in trouble. I want to thank him, too, for all the years that he spent in Iraq teaching and working for all churches. I was blessed to have him as my teacher and friend during my studies in the Center for Eastern Studies in Baghdad. I experienced firsthand the wealth of his knowledge and the depth of his publications that are fundamental for anyone who wishes to enter more fully into the theology and spirituality of the Syriac tradition. He is a unique treasure for me and for all Iraqi Christians. Besides all of this, Fr. Van Vossel's family adopted me as one of their own. Their love and care sustained me during my studies in Belgium and in Rome, especially Aunt Danny and Uncle Andre, Uncle Johan and Aunt Mileen, Aunt Vera and Uncle Willi, Father Ben and Aunt Godelieve.

I am happy to have this opportunity to say thanks to everyone at the Pontifical Oriental Institute (PIO), all of whom made me feel at home, starting with Father Rector David Nazar, who was always ready to support me in times of need. I am also grateful to Father Philippe Luisier, SJ, and Father Massimo Pampaloni, SJ, who helped me to enroll at the PIO. I am especially indebted to my two dear friends who supported me academically and personally during my stay in Rome, Father Vincenzo Ruggieri, SJ, and Professor Gaga Shurgaia, who were most generous with their time and energy and who helped me understand many German, French and Russian texts. My thanks also to Professor Bishara Ebeid, my second moderator, and Father Wafiq

Nasri, both of whom helped me from the very beginning of this work, and to professor Emidio Vergani who was so gentle in answering my questions about S. Ephrem with a lot of expertise and preciseness. I want to show my gratitude also to the Secretary of the PIO, Maurizio Domenicucci and Varoujan Aharonian, who resolved all of my questions and doubts about practical matters. I am grateful, too, for all of the professors and staff of the PIO, both Jesuits and lay coworkers who always encouraged me when they saw me spending long hours in the library; it was their encouragement that kept me sustained my enthusiasm for the work I was doing. I am especially indebted to Simone D'Ambrosi, one of the librarians at the PIO who helped me often when I was in Baghdad by finding and forwarding articles to me. May thanks to Ndjimbidy Felix Florent, one of the librarians at the university of Urbaniana who helped me in searching for the thesis of P. Bachi. My thanks also to Bishop Najib Michael, OP, the Dominican who provided me with many manuscripts that I used in my book, and the Hill Manuscript Museum and Library that makes so many precious manuscripts available to all. My thanks to the Bishops of Erbil, Mar Abris Youkhanna and Mar Bashar Warda, who supported me very generously, and to Mar Youkhannan Yousip from India who sustained me with his prayers. I also need to thank Father Khoshaba Isho, and Deacon Roni Petros from Duhok, Deacon Oughin Azizian from Urmi for providing me with sources and their encouragement. Many thanks also to Bassam Sabri, administrator of the magazine *Naǧm al Mašriq* in Baghdad, who provided articles about Gīwargīs Wardā. Anton Pritula was very gentle in answering my questions about Gīwargīs and about his critical edition of the poetry of Gīwargīs Wardā that was immensely helpful in my work. I want also to thank Yaʿqūb ʾAfrām Manṣūr for his precious friendship and valuable help in translating some Arabic poems; I grieve deeply that he passed away on the 13th of July in 2020 before seeing my book, and I am very sad that I cannot now fulfil his wish to meet with him again in Erbil. My thanks also to Maroš Nicák, who sent to me many of his articles about Gīwargīs Wardā, and for my dear friend, Martina Korytiaková, who among many other kindnesses helped me with Slovak language. I want to thank the Assyrian Church of the East Relief Organization, USA Chapter ACERO-Us for supporting my academic research. I also want to thank Gorgias press for publishing this humble work, and the Hugoye group that shared with me many books and articles that I needed. I want to thank Mark Dickens who helped me a lot in correcting the English language.

Finally, my sincere thanks to Professor Herman Teule, who was the moderator of my academic studies abroad while I earned my preliminary undergraduate and graduate degrees at KuLeuven university and continued as the moderator for my doctorate at the PIO. He helped me to do the best I could in my studies, a great blessing for which I thank God every day. I want to show my gratitude for all the years that he dedicated in studying the tradition and history of the Church of the East and for this he merits to be called the Great Teacher ܡܠܦܢܐ ܪܒܐ.

SIGLA AND ABBREVIATIONS

AB	Analecta Bollandiana.
AOB	Acta Orientalia Belgica.
CSCO	Corpus Scriptorum Christianorum Orientalium.
EB	Eichstätter Beiträge.
EVO	Egitto Vicino Oriente.
ECS	Eastern Christian Studies.
GECS	Gorgias Eastern Christian Studies.
GEDSH	Gorgias Encyclopedic Dictionary of The Syriac Heritage.
HJSS	Hugoye Journal of Syriac Studies.
JA	Journal Asiatique.
JAAS	Journal of Assyrian Academic Studies.
JCSSS	Journal of the Canadian Society for Syriac Studies.
JECS	Journal of Eastern Christian Studies.
JSS	Journal of Semitic Studies.
MCPI	Medieval Christian Perceptions of Islam.
OC	Orienatalia Christiana.
OC	Oriens Christianus.
OCA	Orientalia Christiana Analecta.
OCP	Orientalia Christiana Periodica.
OLA	Orientalia Lovaniensia Analecta.
OPO	Orientalia Patristica Oecumenica.
PCAC	Patrimonio Culturale Arabo Cristiano.
PG	Patrologia Graeca.
PDO	Parole de l'Orient.
PO	Patrologia Orientalis.
RM	Ressembler Au Monde.
RSO	Rivista degli Studi Orientali.
SEECS	Syriac Encounters: Eastern Christian Studies.
SEERI	St. Ephrem Ecumenical Institute
SPM	Studia Patristica Mediolanensia.
SSA	Series Syro-Arabica.
TSEC	Texts and Studies in Eastern Christianity.
TT	Testimonia Theologica.
ZDMG	Zeitschrift der Deutschen Morgenländischen Gesellschaft.

ZWT	Zeitschrift für Wissenschaftliche Theologie.
ВГ	Волшебная гора.
fn.	footnote.
Cf.	compare.

System of Transliteration

Syriac[1]

Consonants								Vowels	
ܐ	ʾ	ܗ	h	ܠ	l	ܩ	q	ܐܳ	ā
ܒ	b	ܘ	w/o*	ܡ	m	ܪ	r	ܐܰ	a
ܒ݂	w/ḇ*	ܙ	z	ܢ	n	ܫ	š	ܐܶ	e
ܓ	g	ܚ	ḥ	ܣ	s	ܬ	t	ܐܷ	ē
ܓ̇	ġ	ܛ	ṭ	ܥ	ʿ	ܬ݂	ṯ	ܝܼ	ī
ܓ̰	ǧ	ܝ	y/i*	ܦ	p			ܘܼ	ū
ܕ	d	ܟ	k	ܦ̇	ṗ			ܘܿ	ō
ܕ݂	ḏ	ܟ݂	ḫ	ܨ	ṣ				

Arabic

Consonants			Vowels
ء ʾ	ر r	ف f	ة -a(h) -at
ا ā	ز z	ق q	ى ā
ب b	س s	ك k	أَ a
ت t	ش š	گ g	إِ i
ث ṯ	ص ṣ	ل l	أُ u
ج ǧ	ض ḍ	م m	اً -an*
ح ḥ	ط ṭ	ن n	إٍ -in*
خ ḫ	ظ ẓ	ه h	
د d	ع ʿ	و w/ū/o*	
ذ ḏ	غ ġ	ي y/ī	

[1] The marked letters with * were added by me to have a complete system for transliteration that has all the types of vocalization.

INTRODUCTION

The Hymns contained in the *Book of Wardā* are one of the glories of the Church of the East. To this day they are sung in the liturgies of the three branches that together constitute the East Syriac tradition: The Ancient Church of the East, the Assyrian Church of the East and the Chaldean Church.

Despite its popularity in the East Syriac tradition, this collection of hymns has only received limited scholarly attention. In part this reflects its relatively late date, written as it was during the Syriac Renaissance, still largely understudied in comparison to the Syriac literature from earlier authors such as Ephrem, Narsai or Isaac of Nineveh. Only in recent years have we witnessed the publication of a number of systematic studies of the hymns that go under the name of Wardā. One of the difficulties involved in the study of the *Book of Wardā* is that most of the hymns have not been critically edited, let alone translated into a modern language.

The present study focuses on an analysis of the Wardā-Christology, a lacuna in modern research. This is somewhat strange, since the Syriac Renaissance is recognized as a period which saw new and creative approaches to the ancient divide between the two main branches of Syriac Christianity: the Church of the East (called 'Nestorian' by others) and the Syriac Orthodox Church (called 'Jacobites' by others). Two important examples of Syriac theologians from this period are ʿAbdīšōʿ bar Brīḫā in the Church of the East and Gregory Bar ʿEbrāyā in the Syriac Orthodox Church. An important question that the present study seeks to answer is: Does Wardā's Christology somehow reflects new approaches or does it follow classical lines?

In order to answer to this question, it is important to make more Wardā material available. The number of hymns edited so far is insufficient for systematic analysis. For this reason, we have selected twenty hymns from the collection which have a more or less prominent focus on Christological issues and prepared a critical edition of them based on eleven manuscripts. This edition is accompanied by a translation into English (Chapter 3). Other hymns are also taken into consideration. The present study is based on the newly-edited hymns, as well as other unedited material and the *ʿŌnyāṯā* which have been recently published by scholars such as Pritula and Hood.

In order to understand 'Gīwargīs the theologian' it is necessary to contextualize him. Theology is not written in a vacuum. The first problem to be addressed concerns the identity of the author. Was Wardā the name of a historical person, Gīwargīs Wardā, or rather the designation of a compilation of hymns, the *Book of Wardā*? This issue is discussed in Chapters 1 and 2, but is not generally considered to be of major importace. After all, we have a collection of hymns, possibly composed by a certain Gīwargīs Wardā (according to tradition), possibly by various poets (according to some modern interpretations). However, it is clear that the Sitz im Leben of the collection is the 13th century, as is clear by various historical allusions, especially the upheaval caused by the emergence of the Mongol dynasty and the end of the Abbasid Caliphate. This historical context is the subject of Chapter 1.

One of the characteristics of the Syriac Renaissance is its openness to the Islamicate world. Islamic cultural patterns and sometimes philosophical, scientific and even spiritual ideas were taken over by Christian authors. Here we may mention again Bar Brīḫā and Bar ʿEbrāyā. This aspect is investigated in Chapter 1, which discusses the relationship between the Wardā-hymns and contemporary Islamic Arabic poetry. Chapter 2 discusses various general characteristics of the hymns, such as style, meter, the use of Greek loanwords and the place of the hymns in modern scholarship. Chapters 1 and 2 are thus introductions to the critical edition and translation in chapter 3 and the commentary in Chapter 4, which discusses the Wardā-Christology, the use of technical terms (such as ܩܢܘܡܐ 'qnōmā' and ܐܝܬܘܬܐ 'essence'), as well as specific Christological themes. The focus in this latter chapter is on understanding these Christological views against the background of the East Syriac tradition and appreciating that the hymns do not constitute a systematic theological treatise but rather Christology expressed in poetry and musical language, in which elegance of expression, rhyme, meter and biblical imagery are as important as the theological views themselves.

CHAPTER ONE

Part I:
Historical Context:
The East-Syriac Church During the 11th-13th Centuries

INTRODUCTION

In order to understand the hymns attributed to Gīwargīs Wardā, it is necessary to consider their historical context, placing the poet as best as we can into the most probable time period. This chapter will sketch the situation of the Church in Iraq/Mesopotamia, especially the East-Syriac branch, providing a short overview of East-Syriac Catholicoi, as well as the political chaos and natural disasters that affected the region, resulting in many famines and plagues. It is evident that these events affected all people in Iraq/Mesopotamia, for we see many ideas similar to those of Gīwargīs in the works of Muslim poets. Despite differences in religion, both Christians and Muslims interpreted these events in similar ways. It is not enough then to read the poetry that was written in a minority Christian community; it is also necessary to understand how the majority Muslims looked at these events. Indeed, it was impossible for Muslims to imagine that one day pagans would abolish the Abbasid Caliphate. Sometimes poetry whispers realities to us that are beyond our ordinary expectations.

1. SITUATING GĪWARGĪS WARDĀ IN HISTORY

Before discussing the context of ܟܬܒܐ ܕܘܪܕܐ the *Book of Wardā*, a preliminary remark is necessary. According to recent scholarship, it is uncertain whether a person called Gīwargīs Wardā ever existed. Wardā may rather refer to the title of a collection of hymns, namely the *Book of Wardā*; this issue will be discussed further in chapter 2. In the present chapter, the focus is on the historical setting of the book called Wardā, attributed to a poet named Gīwargīs Wardā.

The difficulty of determining the existence of a historical Gīwargīs Wardā is already apparent when we discuss his life dates. This is a riddle which faces every scholar dealing with the subject. Thus, Baumstark did not date his birth, suggesting only that Gīwargīs died before 1300.[1] By contrast, Paul H. Bachi,[2] in his thesis on Mariology of Gīwargīs Wardā, states that our poet might have born in the year 1175.[3] The same date is mentioned by the Chaldean Patriarch Emmanuel III Delly (1927-2004), who proposes that Gīwargīs was born in Erbil, without providing further sources.[4] Bachi and Delly dated the death of the poet to 1236 or 1237; Since Gīwargīs did not mention the attacks on Erbil in 1237, it is assumed that he died in that year or shortly before. In any event, we may be sure that he lived through the calamities that he wrote about.[5]

Table (1) outlines the history of the East-Syriac Church, from 1175 until 1300, based in part on an outline by Jean M. Fiey.[6]

(1) The first column contains the names of Catholicoi during the era when Gīwargīs may have lived or the *Book of Wardā* May have been compiled. Gīwargīs' life potentially overlapped the administrations of eight or nine Catholicoi. Information on the relevant Catholicoi of the East comes from ʿAbdīšōʿ bar Brīḫā's[7] and Bar ʿEbrāyā[8] and the book of أسفار الأسرار/*I libri dei misteri.*[9]

(2) The second column indicates some of the Caliphs who governed the country during this era. Information for this column, is based on the work of Fiey[10] and the Iraqi scholar Ḥusayn ʾAmīn.[11]

(3) The third column shows the foreign rulers who occupied Iraq: the Seljuks, Khwarazmians, Atabegs and Mongols. For information on the Mongols I will rely on Ḥusayn ʾAmīn and Cristopher Baumer.[12]

(4) The fourth column lists the Crusades,[13] in order to deepen our awareness of the historical context.

Echoes of these persons and events may be detected in the hymns of Gīwargīs.

---

[1] A. Baumstark, *Geschichte der syrischen Literatur*, pp. 304-306.

[2] Paul H. Bachi is an Iraqi Chaldean priest born in Telkef near Mosul in 1931. He was ordained priest in 1954. He studied in the Saint Peter Seminary of the Chaldean Patriarchate and continued his studies in the university of Propaganda fide in Rome in 1957, He died in Marseille, France in 2020.

[3] Paul H. Bachi, "Marie dans la doctrine de Ghiwarghis Warda," p. 94.

[4] E. Delly, "كيوركيس الملقب وردا" [Gīwargīs the so-called Wardā], pp. 515-522.

[5] The poet's year of birth proposed by modern scholars is not here considered a definitive fact, due to the lack of ancient sources.

[6] J.M. Fiey, *Jalons pour une historie de l'église en Iraq*, pp. 108-110.

[7] ʿAbdīšōʿ B. Brīḫā, ܡܪܓܢܝܬܐ [The Pearl], p. 72.

[8] B. ʿEbrāyā, ܡܟܬܒܢܘܬܐ ܕܐܩܠܝܣܝܣܛܝܩܝ [The Ecclesiastical Chronicle], pp. 512-513.

[9] Ṣalībā B. Yōḥannā, كتاب أسفار الأسرار, *I libri dei misteri*.

[10] J.M. Fiey, *Chrétiens syriaques sous les Abbassides*; J.M. Fiey, *Chrétiens syriaques sous les Mongols*.

[11] Ḥusayn ʾAmīn is an Iraqi historian who was born in 1925 in Baghdad and died in 2013. He was the first Arabic student who received a Ph.D. degree from the University of Alexandria in Egypt. He lectured in many European universities and wrote many publications on history. See Ḥ. ʾAmīn, تاريخ العراق في العصر السلجوقي [The History of Iraq in the Seljuks' Era], p. 323.

[12] C. Baumer, *The Church of the East*, p. 320.

[13] On which, see K.M. Setton ed., *A History of the Crusades* (6 vols).

Table (1):
Key individuals and events affecting the life of Gīwargīs Wardā

	Catholicoi	Caliphs	Foreign rulers	Crusades
1050			The Seljuks (1055-1157)	
1060				
1070			The Khwarazmians 1077-1220	
1080				
1090				First Crusade 1096-1099
1100				
1110				
1120			The Atabegs (1127-1233)	
1130				
1140	I. Īšōʿyāhb V (1149-1175)			Second Crusade 1146-1149
1150				
1160				
1170	II. Ēlīā III ʾAbū Ḥalīm (1176-1190)	al-Mustaḍīʾ (1170-1179)		
1180		an-Nāṣir (1179-1225)		Third Crusade 1189-1192

	Catholicoi	Caliphs	Foreign rulers	Crusades
1190				
1200	III. Yahḇālāhā II (1190-1222)			Fourth Crusade 1202-1204
1210			Ğengīz Ḫān (1206-1227)	
1220	IV. Sabrīšōʿ IV (1222-1225) V. Sabrīšōʿ V bar Mšīḥāyā (1226-1256)	aẓ-Ẓāhir (1225-1226) al-Mustanṣir (1226-1242)		Fifth Crusade 1217-1221 Sixth Crusade 1228-1229
1230				
1240		al-Mustaʿṣim (1242-1258)	Mōngki (1251-1259)	
1250	VI. Makkīḫā II (1257-1265)		Hūlāgū (1256–1265)	Seventh Crusade 1248-1254
1260	VII. Denḥā I (1265-1281)		Abāqā (1265–1282)	Eighth Crusade 1269-1272
1270				
1280			Taqūdār (Sultan ʾAḥmad) (1282–1284)	
1290			ʾArgūn (1284–1291)	
1300	VIII. Yahḇālāhā III (1281-1317)		Gayḫātū (1291–1295) Baydū (1295) Gāzān (1295–1304)	
1310	IX. Timothy II			
1320	(1318-1328)			

2. A COMMUNITY IN THE MIDDLE OF CHAOS

2.1 First Period: Catholicos Īšōʿyāhb V (1149-1175)

We have little information about Catholicos Īšōʿyāhb V except that he was a pious old man from Balad and that foreign influence on the church during his lifetime caused a great deal of chaos.[14] In the period before the Mongols, Iraq was under the occupation of the Seljuks, who originated in Turkestan; their rule started in 1055 with the capture of Baghdad and ended in 1157 with the death of Sanjar, the last Great Seljuk ruler.[15] The Abbasid Caliphs in Baghdad played a fundamental role in Iraq during this period. The Seljuks and the Abbasid Caliphs worked together to govern the region. The army and local government were controlled by the Seljuks, with the permission of and within limits set by the Caliphs. The Seljuks and Abbasids all Sunni Muslims, which helped them to preserve and protect the power of the caliphate together.[16] Nevertheless, the Seljuks wanted to restrict the rule of the Caliph to religious matters, in order that the Seljuks could control secular matters. The people suffered from disease, plagues and other natural disasters during the Seljuk era[17] (see Table 2). Seljuk rule ultimately came to an end because of internal corruption and internal opponents who sought the favor of the Caliph. Additionally, the Atabegs, who were responsible for raising the children of Seljuk rulers and had considerable influence over them, divided the Seljuks and gradually gained power, ruling from 1127 until 1233. There were also many battles that took place between the Crusaders and the Seljuks or the Atabegs.[18]

The Khwarazmian dynasty, which originated in Persia in 1077, also fought the Seljuks for control of territory, especially in Central Asia had Persia. However, they were unable to stand up before the Mongol invasion, which began in 1219 and put an end to the Khwarazmian. Caliph an-Nāsir (1179-1225) had conspired with the Khwarazmians in order to get rid of the Seljuks, but when tension increased between the Khwarazmians and the Caliph, he allied with the Mongols to get rid of the Khwarazmians.[19]

2.2 Second Period: Catholicos Ēlīā III ʾAbū Ḥalīm (1176-1190)

In 1176, Ēlīā III ʾAbū Ḥalīm became Catholicos. In his day, the patriarchal See was still in Baghdad. Bar ʿEbrāyā praised him for his knowledge, especially of languages and religious subjects, and also for his modesty and independence.[20] Ēlīā was able to consecrate many bishops and to rebuild some churches.[21] At this time, after much turmoil and many battles, Erbil and Mosul came under the control of the Atabegs. Erbil suffered a great deal, with many trying to take control of it in an effort to gain the favor of the Caliph, who through his oratory *al-Ḫiṭābat*[22] spread his political and

---

[14] Ṣalībā B. Yōḥannā, *كتاب أسفار الأسرار*, *I libri dei misteri*, p. 503.
[15] Ḥ. ʾAmīn, *تاريخ العراق في العصر السلجوقي* [The History of Iraq in the Seljuks' era], pp. 78-87.
[16] Ḥ. ʾAmīn, *تاريخ العراق في العصر السلجوقي* [The History of Iraq in the Seljuks' era], p. 72.
[17] Ğ.Ḥ. Ḫaṣbāk, *العراق في عهد المغول الأليخانيين* [Iraq in the time of the Il-Ḫānate Mongols], p. 210.
[18] Ḥ. ʾAmīn, *تاريخ العراق في العصر السلجوقي* [The History of Iraq in the Seljuks' era], p. 249; Ḥ.D.Ḫ. Al-Arbalī, *القال والقيل في سلطان أربيل* [Tittle-tattle about the Sultan of Erbil], p. 73, fn. 9.
[19] S. ʾĪsā, *العراق في التاريخ* [Iraq in History], p. 457.
[20] B. ʿEbrāyā, ܡܟܬܒܢܘܬܐ ܕܥܕܬܢܝܐ [The Ecclesiastical Chronicle], p. 432.
[21] Ṣalībā B. Yōḥannā, *كتاب أسفار الأسرار*, *I libri dei misteri*, p. 507.
[22] This is a speech used in the early days of Islam to promulgate the new religion; later on it was used during feasts or to encourage soldiers during war. Š. Ḍayf, *تاريخ الأدب العربي* [History of Arabic Literature], vol. II, pp. 106-129, 405.

religious views throughout the Muslim world. The ongoing internal battles among Muslims, as well as external strife with the Crusaders, made the whole region vulnerable to the Mongol conquest.[23] In addition, the people were weakened by the taxes that were levied on them and by a cruel administrative system that showed no mercy to anyone.[24] In 1187, the conquest of Jerusalem by Ṣalāḥ ad-Dīn al-Ayyūbī shocked all Christians, especially those in Baghdad. As a sign of the Muslim victory, a cross was given to the Caliph by Ṣalāḥ ad-Dīn, it was subsequently embedded in front of the gate of Baghdad so that everyone who passed by could spit on it and trample it underfoot.[25] As a result, great bitterness was created between Muslims and Christians at that time. A hymn about the fall of Jerusalem can be found in the *Book of Wardā*.[26]

From 1190 to 1233, the Atabeg Muẓaffar ad-Dīn Gukbūrī, ruled in Erbil. His relations with the Caliph in Baghdad improved, especially during the time of Caliph al-Mustanṣir (1226-1242), when Gukbūrī himself gave the keys of Erbil to the Caliph when he visited Baghdad in 1230. After the death of Gukbūrī, Erbil submitted to the Caliph after losing in battle.[27] Under Gukbūrī, Erbil had prospered, receiving new schools and hospitals, on top of its geographic and economic advantages. Although Gukbūrī had a reputation for being charitable toward the citizens of Erbil, even apponting Christians to many important positions in the government,[28] some authors portrayed him as an unjust oppressor.[29]

2.3 Third Period: Catholicos Yahḇālāhā II (1190-1222)

Prior to the Mongol assault on Iraq, the East-Syriac Church had able to preach the gospel and reach as far as China and India, a missionary movement which helped strengthen the Church. In 1190 Mar Yahḇālāhā II (1190-1222) became Catholicos. Bar ʿEbrāyā alleges that he bribed the Muslim governors in order to be appointed as Catholicos.[30] He was so effective against his opponents that the church enjoyed peace in his day.[31]

Other Patriarchs may also have engaged in bribery. An allusion to this situation may be found in a hymn attributed to our poet Gīwargīs Wardā, although it does not

---

[23] S. ʾĪsā, العراق في التاريخ [Iraq in History], pp. 457-461.
[24] ʿA.T. Al-ʿAbūd, الشعر العربي في العراق [Arabic Poetry in Iraq], p. 30.
[25] J.M. Fiey, *Chrétiens syriaques sous les Abbassides*, p. 259; H. Zayāt, الصليب في الإسلام [The Cross in Islam], pp. 10, 80.
[26] A. Mengozzi, "A Syriac Hymn on the Crusades," pp. 187-203; M. Nicák, "Zeugenschaft und Emotion," pp. 126-127.
[27] M.M. Ḥusayn, أربيل في العهد الأتابكي [Erbil during the Atabeg Era], p. 156; Ḥ.D.Ḫ. Al-Arbalī, القال والقيل في سلطان أربيل [Tittle-tattle about the Sultan of Erbil], pp. 233-239; Ḥ.D.Ḫ. Al-Arbalī, إربل تحت الأنظار [Erbil under the Spotlight], pp. 87-97; Ḥ.D.Ḫ. Al-Arbalī, المفصّل في تاريخ إربل [The History of Erbil in Detail], pp. 203-208.
[28] Ḥ.D.Ḫ. Al-Arbalī, المفصّل في تاريخ إربل [The History of Erbil in Detail], pp. 164-165.
[29] ʿA.A. Ṣāliḥ, أربيل مدينة الأدب والعلم والحضارة [Erbil, the City of Literature, Science and Civilization], p. 54; Ḥ.D.Ḫ. Al-Arbalī, القال والقيل في سلطان أربيل [Tittle-tattle about the Sultan of Erbil], pp. 247-290.
[30] B. ʿEbrāyā, ܡܟܬܒ ܕܥܕܬܢܝܘܬܐ [The Ecclesiastical Chronicle], p. 432.
[31] Ṣalībā B. Yōḥannā, كتاب أسفار الأسرار, *I libri dei misteri*, p. 511.

name any particular religious authority that had made such payments. The poet here criticizes the church authorities and their oppression of the community, which had lost its way because of their corrupt leadership. This hymn is for the fifth Sunday during the Fast (Hymn 8.(75),[32] Table 6):

'ܠܥܢܝܬܐ 8.(75). <u>ܘܝܠܗ ܠܙܒܢܢ ܕܒܝܫܐ ܛܒ</u>[33]

[18] ܬܘ ܚܙܘ ܪ̈ܥܘܬܐ. ܕܐܠܨܘ ܓܝܪ ܠܡܕܒܪܢܘܬܐ.
ܘܐܪܦܝܘ ܗܠܝܢ ܦܘܠܚܢܐ. ܛܥܘ ܥܢ̈ܐ ܘܪ̈ܚܠܬܐ܀

[19] ܬܘ ܚܙܘ ܟܗܢܘܬܐ ܙܒܝܢܐ. ܘܦܛܪܝܪܟܘܬܐ ܕܗܘܬ ܡܙܒܢܢܝܬܐ.
ܘܝܠܗ ܗܘܐ ܠܗ ܡܙܒܢܢܐ. ܡܫܝܚܝܐ ܐܝܟ ܙܒܘܢܐ܀'

'Hymn 8.(75). <u>Woe to our time how wicked it is</u>
[18] Come and see the shepherds,
who oppressed the communities,
and ignored these duties,[34]
so the sheep and ewes were deluded.
[19] Come and see the priesthood purchased,
the pontificate sold,
woe to that one who sold it,
a Christian who bought it.'[35]

During the time of Yahḇālāhā II, Ğengīz Ḫān created the Mongol Empire, ruling it from 1206 to 1227. The Mongols were willing to cooperate with Christians, Muslims, or any other religion so long as they remained obedient to the empire; those who did not surrender would be attacked and killed.[36] In the early days of the Mongol invasion, there was no religious motivation, but rather a concern with world domination and the destruction of those who would not submit to them.

---

[32] Hymn numbers are given as follows: in the example 7.(72)[23ab], the first number 7 indicates the number of the hymn as it appears in the third chapter: If this number is not given, it means that the hymn is not translated in this volume. The second number in parentheses (72) indicates the sequence of the hymn according to Table 6, which corresponds to the place of that hymn in the manuscripts used in this work. The number and letters in square brackets [23ab…] indicates the stanza number (here 23) and the verses (here ab). Additionally, the first verse of each hymn functions as the title of the hymn and is underlined. In cases where the first verse is similar to another hymn, then the second verse is given also, in order to prevent confusion. The part where the liturgical occasion, melody and other information given about the hymns is considered the heading of the hymn.
[33] The first verse of each hymn cited in this work is underlined in order to indicate which hymn it is, since hymn numbers are not identical in all editions of the Wardā.
[34] The synod records of Patriarch Timothy II (1318-1332) mention a situation similar to what is mentioned here by our poet. See: H. Teule, "The Synod of Timothy II, 1318," (forthcoming). My thanks to Professor Herman Teule for sharing with me some forthcoming essays of his.
[35] See the full edition and translation of this hymn in Chapter 3. Unless otherwise noted in the footnotes, all translations from Syriac and Arabic in this work are mine.
[36] ʿA. ʿA. Al-Muḥāmī, *تاريخ العراق بين احتلالين* [The History of Iraq between Two Invasions], pp. 108-122.

At first, the Caliphs did not pay much attention to the spread of the Mongol Empire, but the great Abbasid dynasty came to an end because of the negligence of the Caliphs. The Mongols were not intimidated by the history of the Abbasids, and they easily conquered them. The fact that the Mongols were pagans generated a great deal of tension and anxiety among both Muslims and Christians.[37] The Mongols started their campaign in Iraq in 1219[38] during the reign of Caliph an-Nāṣir (1179-1225) assaulting Erbil from Marāġā in 1221, in the same year and after the fall of the Persian Capital of Nishapur the Mongols reached Georgia.[39]

2.4 Fourth Period: Catholicos Sabrīšōʿ IV (1222-1225)

After Yahḇālāhā II, Sabrīšōʿ IV (1222-1225), the bishop of Erbil and nephew of Yahḇālāhā, became Catholicos. He also obtained his position through bribery. He was an educated and competent leader of the community, taking good care of the education of his people,[40] but during the time of Caliph an-Nāṣir (1179-1225), many Christians were forced to convert to Islam if they wanted to keep their jobs. Only Christian doctors were allowed to keep both their faith and their profession.[41]

2.5 Fifth Period: Catholicos Sabrīšōʿ V bar Mšīḥāyā (1226-1256)

Sabrīšōʿ V was Catholicos in 1226-1256. Bar ʿEbrāyā alleges that he, like his predecessors, purchased his position.[42] Caliph aẓ-Ẓāhir (1225-1226) confirmed his ordination. During the time of this Catholicos, the whole country endured many crises, especially the Mongol attacks on Erbil, Karamlīs and Dāqūq in 1220 and 1223, mentioned in a hymn attributed to Gīwargīs, (Hymn (153), Table 6). When the Mongols reached Erbil,[43] they demolished everything.[44] They destroyed the general economy, causing a series of famines that killed multitudes and left the land destitute.[45]

After aẓ-Ẓāhir (1225-1226), al-Mustanṣir (1226-1242) became Caliph. These Caliphs were subject to the corrupting influences of Persian and Turkish cultures. They asserted the idea that they alone had the unquestionable right to rule, given to them by God. This attitude caused them to become even more oppressive and cruel blinding them to the thought that one day, their great Caliphate could come to an end.[46]

---

37 Ḥ. ʾAmīn, تاريخ العراق في العصر السلجوقي [The History of Iraq in the Seljuk Era], pp. 266-270.
38 Ḥ. ʾAmīn, تاريخ العراق في العصر السلجوقي [The History of Iraq in the Seljuk Era], p. 323.
39 S.H. Moffett, *A History of Christianity in Asia*, vol. I, p. 404. A hymn on the Mongol invasion of Georgia is found in the *Book of Wardā*. See: A. Pritula, "A hymn on Tiflis," pp. 217-237. Cf. (Hymn (142), Table 6).
40 P. Naṣrī, ذخيرة الأذهان في تواريخ المشارقة والمغاربة السريان, *Histoire des églises chaldéenne et syrienne*, p. 499.
41 J.M. Fiey, *Chrétiens syriaques sous les Abbassides*, p. 252.
42 B. ʿEbrāyā, ܡܟܬܒܢܘܬܐ ܕܐܩܠܣܝܣܛܝܩܝ [The Ecclesiastical Chronicle], p. 442.
43 Ḥ.D.Ḫ. Al-Arbalī, اربل تحت الأنظار [Erbil under the Spotlight], pp. 101-121.
44 W. Baum and D.W. Winkler, *The Church of the East*, p. 237.
45 A. Abouna, تاريخ الكنيسة السريانية [The History of the Syriac Church], pp. 7-12.
46 ʿA.T. Al-ʿAbūd, الشعر العربي في العراق [Arabic Poetry in Iraq], p. 74.

2.6 Sixth Period: Catholicos Makkīẖā II (1257-1265)

When Makkīẖā II became Catholicos (1257-65), the Caliph also required a bribe from him, according to Bar ʿEbrāyā.[47] Makkīẖā was the first among the candidates who complied. Requiring a Catholicos to pay for his office shows how the power of the Caliph affected the Church.[48] Makkīẖā was known for his strict personality.[49]

Caliph al-Mustaʿṣim reigned from 1242 to 1258 and was infamous for neglecting his Caliphal duties. His love for entertainment and dissolution put the whole Abbasid dynasty in jeopardy. He failed to appreciate the need to mount a stout military defense against the Mongols, which sealed the fate of the dynasty, although he won a short-lived victory against them in 1245.[50] During his time, Erbil was attacked again by the Mongols, in 1235, 1236, 1237 and 1238; the city could not withstand the siege for long because of a lack of food and water, especially for those who remained in the castle of Erbil; many people died and there were many corpses everywhere that had to be burned.[51] Many poets wrote about the painful situation of Erbil and the whole region such as ʾIbn al-Mustawfī al-Arbalī[52] and an-Nišābī.[53] Ḥ.D.Ḫ. Al-Arbalī mentions the castle of Erbil as the context in which the poetry of Gīwargīs was composed, perhaps suggesting our poet died with others in this castle.[54]

In 1251, Mōngki (1251-1259) became the fourth great Ḫān of the Mongols. Mōngki chose his brother Il-Ḫān Hūlāgū (1256-1265) to continue the conquest of the Abbasid Caliphate. Hūlāgū did so, becoming the founder of the Mongol Il-Ḫānate in

---

[47] B. ʿEbrāyā, ܡܟܬܒܢܘܬ ܕܐܩܠܝܣܝܣܛܝܩܝ [The Ecclesiastical Chronicle], p. 452.

[48] D. Wilmshurst, *The Martyred Church*, p. 240; P. Naṣrī, كتاب ذخيرة الأذهان في تواريخ المشارقة والمغاربة السريان, *Histoire des églises chaldéenne et syrienne*, p. 8.

[49] P. Naṣrī, ذخيرة الأذهان في تواريخ المشارقة والمغاربة السريان, *Histoire des églises chaldéenne et syrienne*, p. 8.

[50] Ğ.Ḥ. Ḫaṣbāk, العراق في عهد المغول الأليخانيين [Iraq in the time of the Il-Ḫānate Mongols], p. 11.

[51] Ḥ.D.Ḫ. Al-Arbalī, اربل تحت الأنظار [Erbil under the Spotlight], pp. 101-121; Ḥ.D.Ḫ. Al-Arbalī, المفصّل في تاريخ إربل [The History of Erbil in Detail], pp. 210-214.

[52] ʾIbn al-Mustawfī al-Arbalī's full name was ʾAbū al-Barakāt al-Mubārak bin ʾAbī al-Fatiḥ ʾAḥmad; also known as Šaraf ad-Dīn, he was born in 1169 in the castle of Erbil. He was a wazir and historian in Erbil during the time of Gukbūrī. A very important literary figure, he wrote works on literature, language, grammar and poetry; he is particularly famous of his four-volume work entitled 'The History of Erbil'. He died in 1239 in the castle of Erbil. Cf. ʾIbn Ḫalakān, وفيات الأعيان [The Deaths of Notables], vol. IV, p. 147.

[53] Known as ʾAsʿad bin ʾIbrahīm bin Ḥassan al-Ağal Mağd ad-Dīn an-Nišābī al-Arbīlī, He was born in Erbil, became a poet and writer during the time of Caliph Al-Mustanṣir and was later imprisoned by the ruler of Erbil, Muẓaffar ad-Dīn Gukbūrī, because of his satirical poetry. After the death of the ruler and Caliphs's capture of Erbil, he was released and rose to prominence in the Caliphal court. He died in 1258. ʿA.A. Ṣāliḥ, أربيل مدينة الأدب والعلم والحضارة [Erbil the City of Literature, Science and Civilization], p. 194; Ḫair ad-Dīn al-Zarkalī, الأعلام [Celebrities], vol. I, p. 299; Ḥ.D.Ḫ. Al-Arbalī, القال والقيل في سلطان أربيل [Tittle-tattle about the Sultan of Erbil], p. 100. Many poets were imprisoned during the rule of Gukbūrī to punish them for poems criticizing rulers or discussing the hard nature of life. See ʾA.ʿA.ʾI. Al-Fallāḥī, "أثر الحياة الاجتماعية في وجهة الشعر في إربل" [The influence of social life on the tendency of poetry in Erbil].

[54] Ḥ.D.Ḫ. Al-Arbalī, المفصّل في تاريخ اربل [The History of Erbil in Detail], pp. 272.

Persia. Hūlāgū prepared to invade Baghdad, which was weakened by internal problems. The caliphate was in disarray because of a civil war between Sunnis and Shīʿis, and was poorly defended due to the Caliph not paying his soldiers.[55]

In 1257 the Mongols prepared to attack Baghdad; a poem from this period criticizes al-Mustaʿṣim for not being prepared to defend Baghdad from their attacks:

’قل للخليفة مهلاً أتاك ما لا تحبُّ
ها قد دهتكَ فنونٌ من المصائب غربُ
فانهض بعزمٍ وإلا غشاك ويلٌ وحربُ
كسرٌ وهتكٌ وأسرٌ ضربٌ ونهبٌ وسلبُ‘[56]

‘Tell the Caliph: take your time, what you dislike is approaching you.
Here have come types of sinister misfortunes.
Hence raise resolutely, otherwise woe and war will overwhelm you,
Breaking, looting, capturing,
Beating, disgracing, plundering.’[57]

In one of his hymns, written for the Rogation of Nineveh (Hymn (25), Table 6) our poet mentions the destruction of Nineveh if it does not repent. Here Martin Tamcke sees Gīwargīs indirectly referring to the fall of Baghdad, which is described through the fall of Nineveh.[58]

Hūlāgū reached Baghdad 1258, hoping the city would surrender without a battle. He promised Caliph al-Mustaʿṣim that doing so would save his life and the lives of his family and people. Catholicos Makkīẖā II acted as a negotiator between the Mongols and the Caliph, encouraging al-Mustaʿṣim to surrender, but the offer was rejected, so Hūlāgū ordered that the Caliph be killed ruthlessly.[59] With the death of the Caliph, the Abbasid dynasty came to an end, a huge shock for Muslims. The intervention of the Catholicos kept the Christian community safe. Many Christians were also protected by the Christian wife of Hūlāgū, Duquz Ḫātūn. When the army of Hūlāgū entered Baghdad, many people were terrified and tried to hide from them. Since the Mongol soldiers did not attack the homes of Christians, many Christians saved Muslims by hiding them in their houses. Possibly the Mongols could not see a visible difference between Muslims and Christians, so they could not discriminate

[55] Ğ.Ḥ. Ḥaṣbāk, العراق في عهد المغول الأليخانيين [Iraq in the Time of the Il-Ḫānate Mongols], pp. 22-23.
[56] ʿA.T. Al-ʿAbūd, الشعر العربي في العراق [Arabic Poetry in Iraq], p. 174.
[57] A number of Arabic poems have been translated into English by Yaʿqūb ʾAfrām Manṣūr, an Iraqi author born in Baṣra in 1926. His many journal articles and books deal with subjects such as poetry, Sufism, literary criticism, and translation. He passed away in Erbil in 2020. I am so grateful for his help.
[58] M. Tamcke, “How Giwargis Warda Retells Biblical Texts”, pp. 265-266; A. Pritula, *The Wardā*, p. 275.
[59] B. ʿEbrāyā, ܡܟܬܒܢܘܬ ܙܒܢܐ [The Chronography], vol. I, pp. 430-431.

between them.[60] Bar ʿEbrāyā faced the same situation when he was negotiating with the Mongols for the Syriac Orthodox Christians in Aleppo in 1260. Thus, both East and West Syriac churches played significant roles as intermediaries during the Mongol conquest.[61]

When the army of Hūlāgū invaded Baghdad, so many people were killed that the city was filled with the stench of death.[62] This unhealthy atmosphere resulted in plague in the city; even Hūlāgū could not stay.[63] By contrast, Mosul in 1260 was spared the fate of Baghdad and was not destroyed. Ṣaliḥ Ismāʿīl bin Lūʾlūʾ the Muslim ruler of Mosul, ordered the execution of the Christian leaders. Many Christians escaped to Erbil, while some priests, deacons, and faithful converted to Islam because of fear.[64] A hymn in the *Book of Wardā* describes a deacon who converted to Islam.[65]

Under Hūlāgū, the *jizyah*[66] tax was removed, and Christians were allowed to build new churches and live freely without discrimination.[67] Although the influence of the wives of the Mongols was significant, credit must also be given to the tradition of Mongols. They respected weak people and minorities, punishing those who injured them. They also granted freedom of religion to their subjects and employed those of different religions to help them administer the Mongol empire.[68] At the same time, when Christians acted against Muslims, Hūlāgū punished them.[69] When Hūlāgū discovered that Christians in Tagrit, north of Baghdad, were becoming wealthy and rioting against Muslims, he killed many of them.[70] Muslims also enjoyed the freedom to practice their traditions and beliefs, as long as they submitted to the Mongol ruler.[71]

Under the Mongols, both the East and West Syriac churches were in a precarious position, with the support of Mongols changing often, depending on their own political aims. The church alternated between peaceful times, when it was able to grow

---

[60] M.Ṭ. Badr, مغول إيران بين المسيحية والإسلام [The Mongols of Iran between Christianity and Islam], p. 54. I mean here discrimination against Christians in terms of clothing. This idea is suggested by Maroš Nicák also. See M. Nicák, "Der Mongoleneinfall in Karmeliš," p. 210.

[61] B. ʿEbrāyā, ܡܟܬܒܢܘܬ ܙܒܢܐ [The Chronography], vol. I, p. 436.

[62] M. Nicák, "Symbolický obraz ako artikulačný," pp. 79-80.

[63] ʿA.ʿA. Al-Muḥāmī, تاريخ العراق بين احتلالين [The History of Iraq between Two Invasions], pp. 1, 46, 195-199.

[64] A. Abouna, تاريخ الكنيسة السريانية [The History of the Syriac Church], pp. 3, 23; Ḥ.D.Ḫ. Al-Arbalī, المفصّل في تاريخ إربل [The History of Erbil in Detail], p. 236.

[65] According to the hymn's title, it was written by someone from a church in Erbil. It is a lament on the topic of a deacon who converted to Islam. This hymn is found in manuscripts M2, C1, M3, D3, but manuscripts M2 and M3 have a longer version, with other information about this deacon (Hymn (137), Table 6). It seems the deacon's name was Abraham, according to the acrostic letters used in the hymn. He was the son of Ṣlībā, and had four brothers and many sisters; he was married and had daughters. See M. Nicák, *"Konversion" im Buch Wardā*, p. 153.

[66] We use here the standard transcription of this Arabic word.

[67] J.M. Fiey, *Chretiens syriaques sous les Mongols*, pp. 18-20.

[68] ʿA.ʿA. Al-Muḥāmī, تاريخ العراق بين احتلالين [The History of Iraq between Two Invasions], p. 142.

[69] S.H. Moffett, *A History of Christianity in Asia*, vol. I, p. 426; B. ʿEbrāyā, ܡܟܬܒܢܘܬ ܙܒܢܐ [The Chronography], vol. I, p. 433; S. Rassi, "*Justifying Christianity*," pp. 57-63.

[70] Ğ.Ḥ. Ḫaṣbāk, العراق في عهد المغول الأليخانيين [Iraq in the Time of the Il-Ḫānate Mongols], p. 189; S.H. Moffett, *A History of Christianity in Asia*, vol. I, p. 426.

[71] ʿA.ʿA. Al-Muḥāmī, تاريخ العراق بين احتلالين [The History of Iraq between Two Invasions], p. 279.

stronger, and times of weakness and persecution. The support of the Mongols was sometimes due to the influence of the Christian wives of some of their rulers.[72]

In 1260, after losing a battle with the Egyptian Mamluks at ʿAyn-Ǧālūt, the influence of the Mongols diminished. Those who had taken their side, especially Christians, were punished severely, especially those who had fought beside the Mongols. The situation worsened when Mongols began to convert to Islam.[73] In 1261, Hūlāgū attacked Mosul and many West Syriac Christians fled to Erbil. They needed to have a church of their own to celebrate the liturgy, but Catholicos Makkīḇā II refused their request. The metropolitan of Erbil, Denḥā, opposed his Catholicos and favored building a church for the refugees.[74]

A certain way of thinking spread among people after seeing the destruction of the country by the Mongols. The Abbasid Caliphate fell not only because of the power of the Mongols but also because of internal problems and corruption in the Caliphate. The golden age of the Abbasid Caliphate had declined rapidly because the last four Caliphs ignored justice and the will of God, while the Muslim believers squabbled among themselves. The people saw the victory of the Mongols over the Caliphate as punishment from God for the wrongdoing of the Caliphs and the people. The Caliphs had become tyrants who enslaved others and puffed themselves up, which was inconsistent with the message of Islam.[75]

The same thinking patterns were also found among Christians, who thought that, because of their sins, whether collective or individual, God had allowed the destruction of their communities by the Mongols. The idea of both collective and individual sin can be found in one of the poet's hymn, where he confesses that he also has sinned and deserves punishment with other wrongdoers. Both Muslim and Christian authors interpreted the event as divine punishment.[76] The concept of personal sin is found many times in the hymns of Gīwargīs, such as the following:

'ܫܢܬ ܐܠܦ ܘܚܡܫ ܡܐܐ[77]

[74] ܚܛܝܬ ܘܐܣܟܠܬ ܐܝܟ ܚܛܝܐ. ܘܐܝܟ ܚܛܝܐ ܡܡܠܠ ܐܢܐ
ܡܡܠܠ ܐܢܐ ܐܘ ܪܘܚܢܐ. ܪܚܡ ܥܠܝ ܘܥܠ ܡܪܟܒܢܐ܀'

'The year one thousand five hundred[78]

[74] I've sinned and behaved stupidly as a sinner, as a sinner I speak.
I speak, O spiritual one; have mercy on me, and on the composer.'[79]

---

[72] Le Coz, R., *Histoire de l'Eglise d'Orient*, vol. II, p. 404.

[73] W. Baum and D.W. Winkler, *The Church of the East*, p. 85.

[74] A. Abouna, *تاريخ الكنيسة السريانية* [History of the Syriac Church], p. 25.

[75] ʿA.ʿA. Al-Muḥāmī, *تاريخ العراق بين احتلالين* [The History of Iraq between Two Invasions], pp. 50, 116, 202.

[76] D. Bundy, "The Syriac and Armenian Christian Responses," pp. 41-42, 48; A. Pritula, *The Wardā*, p. 342. M. Nicák, "Der Mongoleneinfall in Karmeliš," p. 208.

[77] This hymn has no number, as it is not included in the collection of manuscripts used in this volume.

[78] The hymn refers to the year 1547 AG, which corresponds to 1236 CE. For other translations of this hymn, see Table 8.

[79] For other translations of this hymn, see Table 8.

In another hymn, Gīwargīs comments on the collective sin of the community and asks mercy on behalf of innocent children (Hymn (54), Table 6):

'ܥܘܢܝܬܐ (54). <u>ܡܢܘ ܕܒܥܐ ܥܠ ܚܛܗܝܢ</u>
[21] ܘܐܢ ܣܓܝ ܒܝܫܢ ܠܗ ܩܕܡܝܟ. ܘܣܓܝܐܝܢ ܚܛܗܝܢ ܩܕܡ ܥܝܢܝܟ
ܪܚܡ ܐܢܬ ܡܛܠ ܪܚܡܝܟ. ܘܠܐ ܬܒܣܐ ܠܨܠܘܬܐ ܕܥܒܕܝܟ܀
[22] ܘܐܢ ܐܪܓܙܘܟ ܟܗܢܐ ܘܩܫܝܫܐ. ܘܦܠܚܐ ܥܡ ܐܟܪܐ.
ܚܘܣ ܡܪܢ ܘܪܚܡ ܥܠ ܝܠܕܐ. ܕܠܐ ܠܡܡܪܪܘ ܗܘܘ ܥܕܟܝܠ܀'

'Hymn (54). <u>Who intercedes for our sins?</u>
[21] Even if our evil is great before you
And our sins are many before your eyes,
you have mercy because of your mercy,
and do not neglect the prayers of your servants.
[22] And if the priests and presbyters have made you angry,
the workers and the farmers,
forgive, O Lord, and have mercy on the children
who are not yet bitter.'[80]

2.7 Seventh Period: Catholicos Denḥā I (1265-1281)

Hūlāgū died in 1265 and his death was a big frustration for Christians.[81] That same year, the Catholicos Makkīḫā II died. Denḥā (1265-81) became Catholicos as Denḥā I. He was famous for his education, and he had the support of Hūlāgū's son and successor Abāqā Ḫān (1265-1282), along with the approval of Duquz Ḫātūn.[82] During the time of Denḥā I, tension increased between Christians and Muslims. When a Christian converted to Islam in 1264, the Muslims wanted to protect him against Catholicos Denḥā, who tried to drown him in the river and refused to release him.[83] In 1273, a Christian monk fell in love with a Muslim woman, became Muslim, and was saved by Muslims from execution by Christians.[84]

2.8 Eighth Period: Catholicos Yahḇālāhā III (1281-1317)

After the death of Catholicos Denḥā I the bishops elected a new Catholicos, Yahḇālāhā III (1281-1317), who was confirmed by a royal proclamation of Abāqā Ḫān (1265-1282). Yahḇālāhā preferred to refuse the office and remain in his monastery, but he had to yield to the bishops.[85] He was probably chosen because his Mongol lineage

---

[80] For other translations of this hymn, see Table 8.
[81] B. ʿEbrāyā, ܡܟܬܒܢܘܬ ܙܒܢܐ [The Chronography], vol. I, p. 444; A. Abouna, أدب اللغة الآرامية [*Literature of the Aramaic Language*], pp. 3, 26.
[82] B. ʿEbrāyā, ܡܟܬܒܢܐ ܕܐܩܠܣܝܣܛܝܩܝ [The Ecclesiastical Chronicle], p. 456.
[83] A. Abouna, تاريخ الكنيسة السريانية [History of the Syriac Church], p. 27.
[84] B. ʿEbrāyā, ܡܟܬܒܢܘܬ ܙܒܢܐ [The Chronography], vol. I, p. 451; Ğ.Ḥ. Ḫaṣbāk, العراق في عهد المغول الأليخانيين [Iraq in the Time of the Il-Ḫānate Mongols], p. 191.
[85] C. Baumer, *The Church of the East*, p. 229; A. Abouna, تاريخ الكنيسة السريانية [History of the Syriac Church], pp. 30-32.

would improve the standing of the church among the Mongols.[86] Since he was from China, he knew the Mongols and their language, but he was less familiar with Syriac and Arabic.[87] Bar ʿEbrāyā also spoke of him as a man who had a fear of God and loved all Christians from different denominations.[88] Yahḇālāhā had to comply with the Mongol leaders in order to protect his church, but many times they were cruel to him. In 1282-1284, Hūlāgū's son and successor, Taqūdār, was baptised under the name Nicholas, but then converted to Islam, taking the name ʾAḥmad. He attacked churches and Buddhist temples, turning them into mosques. He also put Yahḇālāhā in prison after several bishops accused him of inciting rebellion. He was forced to move the See from Baghdad to Marāġā and there he started rebuilding the churches. Yahḇālāhā III was a significant figure, and no previous Catholicos had the same kind of power and influence as he did.[89] He had to move the patriarchal residence again after its destruction in Marāġā, this time to Erbil.[90]

The status of the church declined in all aspects; in particular, it ceased to produce its own literature (see further in Part II, section 3 below). According to S.H. Moffett, despite the violence, the years of Mongols rule, from Hūlāgū in 1258 to Gāzān in 1295,[91] were the last fruitful years of the Church of the East. The subsequent history of the church is often referred to as the *Dark Period* or the *Black Clouds*.[92]

2.9 Ninth Period: Catholicos Timothy II (1318-1328)

This Catholicos was famous for his knowledge of languages and his theological writings. He made the canons of ʿAbdīšōʿ bar Brīḵā official for the East Syriac Church and issued his own canons dealing with the decline in his church.[93] The situation of Christians did not improve during his time.

With this, we end our review of the period during which our poet probably lived. We now consider how poets of the time described this period.

---

[86] W. Baum and D.W. Winkler, *The Church of the East*, p. 96.
[87] S. Rassam, *Christianity in Iraq*, p. 95.
[88] B. ʿEbrāyā, ܡܟܬܒܢܘܬ ܙܒܢܐ ܕܥܕܬܐ [The Ecclesiastical Chronicle], p. 462.
[89] C. Baumer, *The Church of the East*, pp. 225-226.
[90] C. Baumer, *The Church of the East*, p. 97.
[91] Ḥ.D.Ḥ. Al-Arbalī, *اربل تحت الأنظار* [Erbil under the Spotlight], pp. 118-121.
[92] S.H. Moffett, *A History of Christianity in Asia*, vol. I, p. 427.
[93] The canons from Timothy's synod discuss many issues that were affecting the situation of the church at the time. The following canons provide important examples. Canon 1: The importance of education of clerics and believers in general. Canon 4: Against selling or misusing the properties of the church. Canon 5: Ordination according to the canons to prevent scandals that happened in the past. Canon 6: Clerics must not exceed in drinking wine and monks are not allowed to. Canon 9: Against taking bribes, and the marriage of bishops. Canon 13: Books of visitation that in previous times were written by unworthy people, because of whom rules were broken and corruption increased. See H. Teule, "The Synod of Timothy II, 1318," (forthcoming).

Part II:
Interpretation of the Historical Context

1. HOW GĪWARGĪS INTERPRETED HISTORICAL EVENTS

We cannot be certain how soon after the events in question Gīwargīs commented on them; the poet may have needed time to reflect on what had happened, trying to express and explain them in and through his poetry. David Bundy has even suggested that the 'historical context' of this poetry caused later historians such as Bar ʿEbrāyā to use Gīwargīs as a source of information, a possibility also noticed by Bachi.[94]

There are many passages where Gīwargīs shows not only the church but also the common people suffering at the hands of the Mongols.[95] As a poet and theologian, he perceived the grace of God in these events and asked God why they happened to His followers. Again, David Bundy finds in Gīwargīs a historian and a theologian who used his talent as a witness for his church and his people, those who were suffering right in front of his eyes.[96]

In contrast, rather than thinking that the hymns combine qualities of history and theology, Gerrit J. Reinink considers some of them to have rather philosophical content such as 'the explanation of man as a microcosm'.[97] However, our focus here will be on the theological and historiographical views of our author.

As a historian Gīwargīs was able to describe the catastrophes suffered by his people in detail. Sometimes he gives a description of the events as they unfold, as in the hymn on Karamlīs,[98] the hymn on Jerusalem conquered by Ṣalāḥ ad-Dīn al-Ayyūbī in 1187,[99] and the hymn on the capture of Tiflis (Hymn (142), Table 6),[100] as well as hymns on hunger, plague and suffering, such as Hymns (55), (56), (57), (58), Table 6.[101] These hymns describe the suffering of the people and raise the question of whether that suffering was caused by individual or collective sin. Gīwargīs confesses that he himself is a sinner. He reflects on the idea that Christ was not able to bear more than three days of suffering while, His followers, under the Mongols suffered for months from hunger, death, torture, and the devastation of churches, lamenting that the invaders have raped women in churches and taken others into captivity, that children have been either killed or sold, and that the holy places have been desecrated (Hymn (55), Table 6). According to Gīwargīs, human beings have to pass through a time of testing, but even during difficulties, God can 'mix grace

---

[94] D. Bundy, "Interpreter of the Acts of God," p. 11; P.H. Bachi, "Marie dans la doctrine de Ghiwarghis Warda," p. 76.
[95] M. Nicák, "Symbolický obraz ako artikulačný," pp. 77-78.
[96] D. Bundy, "George Warda as Historian," pp. 191-200.
[97] G.J. Reinink, "George Warda and Michael Badoqa," pp. 65-74; G.J. Reinink, "Man as Microcosm," pp. 123-152; P. Gignoux, "Un poéme inèdit sur l'homme-microcosme," pp. 95-189.
[98] H. Hilgenfeld, *Ausgewählte Gesänge des Giwargis Warda von Arbil*, p. 49.
[99] A. Mengozzi, "A Syriac Hymn on the Crusades," pp. 187-203.
[100] A. Pritula, "A Hymn on Tiflis," pp. 217-237.
[101] A. Pritula, *The Wardā*, pp. 376-415.

with thorns', a gift that Gīwargīs begs from God. He can see hope even during these events, because he is sure of the help of God that will come to put an end to all tribulations.[102] In this meditation and prayer he recognizes the spiritual dimension of historical events.

The hymns of Gīwargīs portray how this devastation affected the spiritual and intellectual life of the Church. The prayers and liturgical ceremonies were suspended because of the suffering inflicted on the community, which could easily lead to spiritual poverty and destruction.[103] Another consequence was intellectual impoverishment; in such conditions, the human mind may become incapable of the kind of thought and creativity that produces and nurtures culture. However, despite these difficulties, this period results in the creation of some interesting literature.

2. THE PERIOD OF DECLINE

This period has been variously called *the dark night*, *dark ages* or *the years of darkness*.[104] Here we will sketch some of the echoes of this transition as they are found in the hymns of Gīwargīs. It may be that the end of the epoch comes after Bar Brīẖā, but Gīwargīs' poetry marks the beginning of the end, which definitely occurred after Bar Brīẖā.

1. The persecutions that took place against Christians, sometimes for unknown reasons, are mentioned in Hymn (55), Table 6.[105]

2. Gīwargīs documents the conversion of a Christian in Hymn (137), Table 6, sometimes in order to avoid the *jizyah*. Hymn (56), Table 6 demonstrates that the people were taxed, even though the text does not use the term *jizyah*.[106]

3. The new generation of educated Muslims rendered the Caliphs less dependent on Christians, who were becoming less literate because of a lack of schools and teachers (Hymn (56), Table 6).[107]

4. The deteriorating financial situation of the Christians made it impossible for the Church leaders to support many activities (Hymn (56), Table 6).

5. The emigration of Christians from the capital to the north led to a decline in education in schools. The monasteries became the new centres of learning and scholarship[108] (Hymn (55), Table 6).[109]

---

[102] D. Bundy, "Interpreter of the Acts of God," p. 28.
[103] D. Bundy, "Interpreter of the Acts of God," p. 23.
[104] H. Teule, *Les Assyro-Chaldèens*, p. 30; D. Wilmshurst, *The Martyred Church*, pp. 277-315.
[105] A. Pritula, *The Wardā*, p. 388; A. Deutsch, *Edition dreier Syrischen*, pp. 15-22; H. Hilgenfeld, *Ausgewählte Gesänge des Giwargis Warda von Arbil*, pp. 49-59; R. Patrous, "سبي كرمليس" [The Capture of Karamlīs], pp. 102-114; P.G. Borbone, "Due Episodi delle Relazioni Mongoli e Siri," pp. 205-228.
[106] A. Pritula, *The Wardā*, p. 403; Ḥ.D.Ḫ. Al-Arbalī, *القال والقيل في سلطان أربيل* [Tittle-tattle about the Sultan of Erbil], p. 197.
[107] A. Pritula, *The Wardā*, p. 396.
[108] H. Teule, "Christian-Muslim Religious Interaction," p. 15.
[109] A. Pritula, *The Wardā*, p. 388.

6. Christians became more concerned about survival and safety than gaining knowledge.[110]

7. The growing use of the Arabic language that followed the translation movement[111] meant that there was less need for Syriac. Christianity became Arabicized, which made the process of Islamization easier.

8. The marriage laws resulted in a gradual decrease in the number of Christians, since a Christian woman who married a Muslim had to have her children brought up as Muslims.[112]

9. The laws against apostasy meant that nobody dared to change his mind about his faith. A Christian who converted to Islam for career reasons would not revert to Christianity at the end of his life because such reversion was punishable by death.[113]

10. Plagues and natural disasters weakened all the communities[114] (Hymns (55), (56), (57), (58), Table 6).[115]

11. Some Christians who cared only about their position in the government did nothing to help support the church.[116]

12. Churches suffered direct attacks from pagans[117] and the community was scattered (Hymn (55), Table 6).[118]

3. TESTIMONY OF THE POETS ON THE PERIOD OF DECLINE

During the Abbasid Caliphate, poetry was an essential part of everyday life giving us insight into the situation at that time. However, according to Carl Brockelmann, the art of poetry was past its prime and had entered a state of decay because of the tense political climate.[119] The judgment of Brockelmann is still valid for the period we are considering. As noted above, the decline of the Abbasid era was followed immediately by the downfall of Syriac literature. The oppressive regime of the last Abbasid Caliphs and the attacks of the Mongols left few resources for cultural development. Those who were able to reflect and write poetry, despite the crises around them, provide us with evidence of the sufferings of their community.

Muslims and Christians passed through the same cataclysms and endured the same hardships. Despite their religious differences, their poetry shows similar patterns.

---

[110] H. Teule, "Christian-Muslim Religious Interaction," p. 16.

[111] The translation movement occurred between the eighth and the tenth century in Baghdad, when scholars from both East and West Syriac Churches translated Greek works, first into Syriac then into Arabic. See D. Gutas, *Greek Thought, Arabic Culture*.

[112] This law is still in force in Iraq.

[113] S. Rassam, *Christianity in Iraq*, pp. 88-89.

[114] S.A. Missick, "The Assyrian Church in the Mongolian Empire," p. 98.

[115] A. Pritula, *The Wardā*, pp. 366, 376, 388, 402.

[116] S.A. Missick, "The Assyrian Church in the Mongolian Empire," p. 101.

[117] D. Wilmshurst, *The Martyred Church*, pp. 277-280.

[118] A. Pritula, *The Wardā*, p. 386.

[119] C. Brockelmann, تاريخ الأدب العربي [History of Arabic Literature], vol. V, pp. 1-2.

3.1 Erbil

The attacks on Erbil led local Muslim poets to reflect on its capture in the same way that Gīwargīs wrote of the destruction of some towns by the Mongols.[120] An example can be found in the poetry of ʾAsʿad bin ʾIbrāhīm an-Nišābī, a native of Erbil and a witness of the events there. Here we find him asking Caliph al-Mustanṣir to send help to Erbil and to save it when it was attacked in 1237.

ʻسقى أربل الغراءَ صوب غمامةٍ　　لعل ثراها بعد مـــا جفّ يرتمي
وجادت عليها رحمةٌ من خليفةٍ　　مكـــــــارمه مأمولـــة للترحمِ
أبي جعفر المستنصر بن محمدٍ الـ　　إمام الفتى المعصوم من كل مأثمِ
فيا أيها المولى الوزير تعطّفـــــاً　　بأربل واكشف ضرّها اليوم وارحمʼ[121]

'He sprinkled on the famous Erbil the rain of a cloud
Maybe its land will multiply after the drought
And enhance on it mercy from a Caliph
That his generosities were expected for Mercy
ʾAbū Ǧaʿfar al-Mustanṣir bin Muḥammad the Imām
The Infallible man from any sin[122]
O lord vizier, take pity
On Erbil and reveal its harm today and have mercy.'

3.2 Living Martyrs

In the same way, the invasion of Baghdad was anticipated by poetry that drew a picture of the future of the city, reminding the reader that the prophet Muḥammad had promised that the city would never fall. Confidence in this prophecy led many people from different parts of Iraq to take refuge in Baghdad. The city was not attacked directly at first. The Mongols concentrated on the villages in the frontiers and sidestepped the caliphs' army. The fall of Baghdad became inevitable as time passed by. When the Mongols attacked the outskirts of Baghdad, people began to doubt the dream of the eternal capital of the Abbasid Caliphate. The following poem expresses how difficult it was to see all the dead people everywhere. The poet here is sure that these victims were beatified because they were considered martyrs. Aṣ-Ṣarṣarī[123] wrote a poem about this:

---

[120] P.H. Bachi, "Marie dans la doctrine de Ghiwarghis Warda," pp. 69-71; P.G. Borbone, "Due Episodi delle Relazioni Mongoli e Siri," pp. 205-228; A. Pritula, *The Wardā*, p. 388; E. Delly, "كيوركيس الملقب وردا" [Gīwargīs, the so-called Wardā], pp. 515-522; Ḥ.D.Ḫ. Al-Arbalī, *اربل تحت الأنظار* [Erbil under the Spotlight], pp. 101-114; Ḥ.D.Ḫ. Al-Arbalī, *المفصّل في تاريخ اربل* [The History of Erbil in Detail], p. 214.

[121] ʿA.T. Al-ʿAbūd, *الشعر العربي في العراق* [Arabic Poetry in Iraq], p. 159.

[122] This concept of the infallibility of the Caliph may indicate the influence of European thinking about the Pope.

[123] ʾAbū Zakarīā Yaḥyā bin Yūsif al-Anṣārī aṣ-Ṣarṣarī was a poet from a village called Ṣarṣar near Baghdad who died in 1258. C. Brockelmann, *تاريخ الأدب العربي* [History of Arabic Literature], vol. V, pp. 18-19.

'وعهدتَ أن بيضة الإســـلام أن لا تستباح ووعدُ مثلك يصدق
ولقد وجدنا صدق وعدك إذ نحوا دار الســـلام فأدبروا وتفرقوا
لكنهم فتــــكوا بأطراف القرى فتكاً له أحشــــاؤنا تتمزق
طوبـى لمن قُتـــلوا منهم انـه أبداً مع الشـــهداء حي يرزقُ
وهم على التهديد لكنّـــا على ثقةٍ أليـــس بمثل وعدك يوثق؟'[124]

'You have promised that the community of Islam
Will not be violated, and a promise from you is reliable,
And we have found this promise of yours was true when
they [the Mongols] returned and separated near Dār as-Salām [Baghdad].
But they attacked the villages, such an attack that the intestines tear out for it.
Blessed be those who were killed by them because they are alive with the martyrs.
And they [the Mongols] are still threatening but is it not that your promise is trustworthy?'

Gīwargīs expresses a similar idea to what aṣ-Ṣarṣarī highlights here. In the sixth line of the English translation of Gīwargīs' poem, he says that those who are killed enjoy beatitude because they are alive in the company of their fellow martyrs. Again, Gīwargīs expresses a similar view when he asks for justice: Why have the sinners and those who have not sinned died in the same way? Then justice answered him that those who died without sin are alive (Hymn (57), Table 6):

'ܡܥܢܝܬܐ (57). ܐܘ ܝܘܡܬܢ ܡܐ ܒܨܝܪܝܢ

[37] ܗܠܝܢ ܕܚܙܐ ܐܢܬ ܕܡܝܬܝܢ. ܐܡܪ ܕܒܚܛܗܝܗܘܢ ܡܝܬܝܢ
ܘܐܝܠܝܢ ܕܡܝܬܘ ܠܐ ܚܛܗܐ ܡܝܬܝܢ. ܚܝܝܢ ܗܫܐ ܗܘܘ ܘܠܐ ܡܝܬܝܢ܀
[38] ܡܛܠܬܟܝ ܐܘ ܕܘܝܐ. ܡܬܩܛܠܝܢ ܗܠܝܢ ܓܒܝܐ.
ܕܢܣܓܐ ܐܓܪܗܘܢ ܒܫܡܝܐ. ܘܕܐܟܘܬܟܝ ܢܐܪܬܘܢ ܘܝܐ܀'

'Hymn (57). O, our days, how mean they are!
[37] Those whom you see dead,
it said, died in their sins,
and those who died without sin
are alive now and will not die.
[38] For you, o weak one,
are those chosen killed
so that their reward is increased in heaven.
And those like you inherit grief!'[125]

3.3 Asking for Intercession

Again we see the poet aṣ-Ṣarṣarī asking for the prayers of the prophet Muḥammad. The poet was critical of the backwardness and corruption in the Caliphate, which had allowed the Mongols to invade all of Iraq. The prayer here is for triumph over the Mongols:

[124] ʿA.T. Al-ʿAbūd, *الشعر العربي في العراق* [Arabic Poetry in Iraq], p. 168, fn. 68.
[125] A. Pritula, *The Wardā*, pp. 411-413.

'عليك أزكى سلام الله ما بقيت — دار النعيم بقـــاءً ليس ينتقلُ
أجب نداء شجٍ مستصرخٍ قلِقٍ — من فتنةٍ امعنت أنيابها العصـلُ
البرُّ من رعبهـــا والبحر منزعجٌ — والحرث والليل والأنعام والخـــول
من عصـبةٍ تترٍ لـــولا تخلفنـا — ما صدنا عنهم وهنٌ ولا وشـلُ
وكان كل قيـــام من مقـــانبهم — يلقاه منا ولا يخشى الردى رجلُ
فاســـأل لنا الله نصراً قاهراً لهم — مثبتاً لقلوب شـــقّها الوجلُ'[126]

'The purest peace of God be on you
For paradise is lasting and not moved.
Answer the broken appeal we make with shouts of anguish
From a tumult that sinks its fangs into the nerve.
The land and the sea are disturbed by it –
The plants, the night, the camels and the slaves.
For a gang of Tartars, aside from our backwardness,
weakness or fear would not stop us from meeting them
and each rise from their legion
receives the same from us, for no man fears death.
Therefore, ask God for a victory that conquers them for us
To mend the hearts that are ruptured because of fear.'

Similarly, we see references to intercession in the hymns of Gīwargīs. In most of his hymns, he asks for the mediation of the saints for his people as well as himself. He often asks Christ, Mary, the apostles, the prophets and the martyrs to intervene and protect or forgive him and his people, to help them to endure their trials.

One such hymn is dedicated to the fifth Sunday of Fast. In two different stanzas, Gīwargīs asks the apostles to act as intermediaries, praying that the faithful will overcome the hunger, death and cruelty of that century:

'ܡܥܢܝܬܐ 8.(75). ܘܝ ܠܙܒܢܢ ܕܒܝܫܐ ܛܒ

[33] ܒܥܘ ܕܢܥܒܪ ܡܢܢ ܟܦܢܐ. ܘܟܘܪܗܢܐ ܘܙܘܥܐ ܘܐܘܠܨܢܐ.
ܘܢܬܟܠܐ ܠܡܘܬܐ ܡܚܒܠܢܐ. ܡܢ ܥܢܐ ܕܒܫܡܗ ܡܗܝܡܢܐ܀
[38] ܩܘܡܘ ܛܘܒܢܐ ܒܥܘ ܪܚܡܐ. ܥܠ ܕܪܢ ܕܚܣܝܪ ܡܢ ܪܚܡܐ.
ܘܥܠ ܡܪܟܒܢܐ ܕܡܠܠܐ. ܛܢܦܐ ܡܢ ܫܐܕܐ ܛܢܦܐ܀'

'Hymn 8.(75). Woe to our time, how wicked it is!

[33] Ask that the famine will pass us by,
along with illness, turbulence, and distress,
and withhold destructive death
from the flock that believes in His name.
[38] Rise up, O blessed ones, and ask for mercy,
for our century that is lacking compassion,
and for the composer of these words,
impure more than the impure demons.'[127]

[126] ʿA.T. Al-ʿAbūd, الشعر العربي في العراق [Arabic Poetry in Iraq], p. 171, fn 83.
[127] See the full translation of this hymn in Chapter 3.

3.4 The Cruel Image of the Events

It is interesting to note that the Arab historian ʾIbn al-Aṯīr, who witnessed the attacks of the Mongols, said that he was not able to write about the calamities for years. He could not endure the destruction of his people and wished that he had died before witnessing these tragedies.[128] It may well be that Gīwargīs also wrote some time after the incidents mentioned in his hymns took place.

Gīwargīs wrote some of his hymns about famines and plagues. As seen in Table 3 and 4, these happened many times, which gave the poets many opportunities to reflect on what was happening, especially when the leaders were unjust and imposed burdens on simple people who did not have the resources to defend themselves. The poor suffered from the neglect and greed of governors, as well as from natural disasters like famine and flood. These people were confronted with the cruelty of life itself and the fear of their enemies, which contributed to anxiety of every day. They felt bitter and desperate. Al-Ablah al-Baġdādī[129] remembered how his children cried for bread because of hunger. The poem comes from the time of Caliph an-Naṣir, who was able to fill a pool with gold because of the heavy taxes that he collected from the people, as was also the case with Caliph al-Mustaʿṣim:

'ما لصغاري باكين شـــوقاً منهم إلى الخبز في الزوايا
وأنت بعـــــد الإله تُجري بأمـــره الرزق في البرايـــا
فاحنُ على صبيةٍ صـــغارِ عادوا من الجوع كالحنايا'[130]

'Why are my children crying, yearning for bread in the corners
And you, after God, you do his will in providing subsistence for creatures
Have mercy on little boys who became as thin as bows from hunger.'

Gīwargīs also spoke of a time when people were dying of hunger (Hymn (57), Table 6):

'ܠܡܕܪܫܐ (57). ܐܘ ܝܘ̈ܡܝܢ ܟܡܐ ܒܨܝܪܝܢ
[16] ܐܝܬ ܕܩܥܘ ܠܚܡܐ ܠܚܡܐ. ܘܢܦܩܝ ܢܦܫܬܗܘܢ ܡܢ ܥܠܡܐ.
ܘܐܝܬ ܕܛܥܡܘ ܩܛܡܐ ܐܝܟ ܠܚܡܐ. ܐܝܟ ܕܒܡܙܡܘܪܐ ܕܡܐܐ ܘܬܪܬܝܢ܀'

'Hymn (57). <u>O, our days, how mean they are!</u>
[16] Some shouted: "Bread! Bread!"
And their souls left the world.
And some tasted ashes like bread
as in the Psalm one hundred and two.'[131]

Another hymn tells how the fathers wished to die instead of seeing the suffering of their children (Hymn (56), Table 6):

---

[128] ʾIbn al-Aṯīr, *الكامل في التاريخ* [The Complete History], vol. XII, p. 358.
[129] The poetry of Muḥammad bin Baḫtyār bin ʿAbd Allah al-Baġdādī, also called al-Ablah al Baġdādī, was famous for its beauty. He died in Baghdad in 1200. C. Brockelmann, *تاريخ الأدب العربي* [History of Arabic Literature], vol. V, p. 15.
[130] ʿA.T. Al-ʿAbūd, *الشعر العربي في العراق* [Arabic Poetry in Iraq], p. 196, fn. 8.
[131] A. Pritula, *The Wardā*, p. 407.

'ܥܘܢܝܬܐ (56). ܐܘ ܡܚܘܬܢ ܟܡܐ ܝܩܝܪܢ
[30] ܐܒܗ̈ܬܐ ܕܚܙܝܢ ܗܘܘ ܠܗܘܢ. ܟܕ ܡܬܥܕܩܝܢ ܒܝܢܝܗܘܢ.
ܣܢܘ ܚܝ̈ܐ ܘܓܒܘ ܡܘܬܐ ܠܟܠܗܘܢ. ܕܠܐ ܢܚܙܘܢ ܒܢ̈ܝܗܘܢ ܒܫܢܩܐ܀'

'Hymn (56). O, our misfortunes, how grave they are!
[30] Their parents are seeing them.
drooped because of them.
They came to hate life and chose death
so as not to see their children suffering.'[132]

3.5 The Voice of the Oppressed

There was also a type of poetry that vividly criticized the greed and unworthy behavior of the rulers. We already have seen above how a poem was written to warn Caliph al-Mustaʿṣim about the Mongols. Another poem, written by Ṣibṭ ʾIbn at-Taʿāwīḏī,[133] powerfully expresses the poet's anger against those who oppress the poor. He criticises them and warns them that they will face justice:

'تَهتُم على المستضعفين تكبرا والله أكبر
وغدوتم ذا قـــدرةٍ ففتـــكتم والله أقدر
لكم صحائف ريبةٍ تجزون فيها يوم تُنشر
وقبيحُ أثـــارٍ على اعقابكم تُروى وتـــؤثر'[134]

'You struck down the miserable arrogantly, and God is greater
You become dominant, so you assaulted, and God is mighty
How such misgiving acts, for which you will be punished
When they are uncovered, on the day of Resurrection!
And the ugly effects of your successors will be narrated and mentioned.'[135]

Gīwargīs expresses similar concerns about unjust rulers oppressing the poor. Despite the famine and all the other disasters that the people were facing, the rulers took everything they had (Hymn (56), Table 6):

'ܥܘܢܝܬܐ (56). ܐܘ ܡܚܘܬܢ ܟܡܐ ܝܩܝܪܢ
[55] ܫܠ̈ܛܢܐ ܐܡܪܝܢ ܗܒ ܠܝ. ܡܠ̈ܟܐ ܐܡܪܝܢ ܐܘܫܛ ܠܝ.
ܘܟܕ ܫܩܠܘ ܠܟܣܦܗ ܕܐܝܬ ܠܝ. ܐܡܪܝܢ ܠܝ ܗܘ ܟܡܐ ܕܐܝܬ ܠܝ܀'

---

[132] A. Pritula, *The Wardā*, p. 397.
[133] ʾAbū al-Fatiḥ Muḥammad bin ʿBeid Allah Ṣibṭ ʾIbn at-Taʿāwīḏī was of Turkish origins. Born in 1123, he was known for his Sufism and worked in the provincial *dīwān*. He lost his sight in 1183 and died in 1187. C. Brockelmann, *تاريخ الأدب العربي* [History of Arabic Literature], vol. V, p. 15.
[134] ʿA.T. Al-ʿAbūd, *الشعر العربي في العراق* [Arabic Poetry in Iraq], p. 123, fn. 56.
[135] Translation by Yaʿqūb ʾAfrām Manṣūr.

'Hymn (56). <u>O, our misfortunes, how grave they are!</u>
[55] The rulers say: "Give us!"
The kings say, "Give us more!"
And having taken everything we have
they demand from us what we do not have.'[136]

3.6 The Destruction of Culture

In this time of crisis, the Mongols destroyed all the centers of culture and literature. A poet named Saʿdī aš-Šīrāzī,[137] who lived in Baghdad, witnessed the Mongol attacks on the schools, especially the school of al-Mustanṣirīah.[138] In his poem, the poet wishes he had died rather than see his school demolished by the pagans:

'بَكَتْ جُدُرُ المستنصريةِ نُدبةً   على العلماءِ الراسخين ذوي الحِجْرِ
نوائب دهرٍ ليتني متُّ قبلها   ولم أرَ عدوان السـفيه على الحِبَرِ
محابرُ تبكي بعدهم بسوادها   وبعضُ قلوبِ الناس أحلكُ من حبرِ'[139]

'The walls of Mustanṣirīah cried with pain
On the firm scholars who had mind
Disasters of an era – I wish I had died before it
In order not to see the attack of the foolish on ink.
The inkstand cries after them [the scholars] with its darkness
And some human hearts are darker than ink.'

Gīwargīs also lamented the devastation of education, writers, teachers, pupils, and libraries (Hymn (57), Table 6):

'ܠܥܘܢܝܬܐ (57). <u>ܐܘ ܝܘܡܝܢ ܟܡܐ ܒܨܝܪܝܢ</u>
[28] ܕܥܟܘ ܟܬܒܐ ܘܩܪܘܝܗܘܢ. ܘܬܠܡܝܕܐ ܘܪܒܢܝܗܘܢ.
ܥܒܪܘ ܣܦܪܐ ܥܡ ܣܘܪܛܝܗܘܢ. ܘܪܥܘܬܐ ܥܡ ܡܪܥܝܬܗܘܢ :·'

'Hymn (57). <u>O, our days, how mean they are!</u>
[28] Books have vanished with their readers.
And pupils and their teachers,
writers and their writings have become extinct,
and pastors and their flocks.'[140]

Another hymn mentioned in the first part mourns the decline of culture and education (Hymn (56), Table 6):

---

[136] A. Pritula, *The Wardā*, p. 403.
[137] Aš-Šīrāzī (1213-1291) was a Persian poet who studied in Baghdad. He had two famous works, the *Būstān* and the *Gulistān.* He is especially famous for a poem written after the fall of Baghdad in 1258. H.A.R. Gibb, *al.*, *The Encyclopedia of Islam*, vol. VIII, pp. 719-723.
[138] The school of al-Mustanṣirīah was a school established by al-Mustanṣir in 633 AH (1233 AD) to teach doctrines of different Islamic sects.
[139] ʿA.T. Al-ʿAbūd, *الشعر العربي في العراق* [Arabic Poetry in Iraq], p. 187.
[140] A. Pritula, *The Wardā*, p. 409.

'ܥܘܢܝܬܐ (56). ܐܘ ܡܚܘ̈ܬܢ ܟܡܐ ܝܩܝ̈ܪܢ

[35] ܟܡܫܐ ܕܫܒܝܚܐ ܕܝܠܗ ܗܘܐ. ܚܫܟ ܕܡܘܬܐ ܚܒܝܒ ܗܘܐ

ܫܘܦܪܐ ܪܟܝܟܐ ܥܒܪ ܗܘܐ. ܘܗܘܢܐ ܘܡܕܥܐ ܡܫܢܝܐ ܗܘܐ܀

[36] ܟܗ̈ܢܐ ܚܣܝܐ ܥܡ ܕܪ̈ܓܝܗܘܢ. ܘܡܫܡܫ̈ܢܐ ܘܛܟܣ̈ܝܗܘܢ

ܘܝܠܘܕ̈ܝܐ ܘܠܘܚ̈ܝܗܘܢ. ܘܬܠܡܝ̈ܕܐ ܘܪ̈ܒܢܝܗܘܢ܀'

'Hymn (56). O, our misfortunes, how grave they are!

[35] The fair blossom had faded
and the dear form darkened.
The tender fairness disappeared.
Reason and sense withdrew.

[36] Priests with their orders had vanished
and the deacons with their ranks
and the schoolchildren with their tablets
pupils and their teachers.'[141]

3.7 Preferring Death to a Hard Life

After living amidst all these difficulties, destruction and corruption, many wished for death (as noted above, with what ʾIbn al-Aṯīr said in his book).[142] Saʿdī aš-Šīrāzī also expressed his sadness because of what happened in Baghdad:

'حبستُ بجفني المدامع لا تجري فلما طغى الماء استطال على السِكرِ

نسـيم صبا بغداد بعد خرابها تمنيـتُ لو كـانت تمر على قبري'[143]

'I held my tears in my lids so as not to fall down,
but when the water flooded, it extended the drunkenness.
The breeze of Baghdad after its destruction –
I wished it would pass over my grave'.

Similarly, the sorrow of Gīwargīs can be felt in Hymn (46), Table 6:

'ܥܘܢܝܬܐ (46). ܒܟܝܐ ܡܠܐ ܐܘܠܨܢܐ

[11] ܝ ܝܐ ܡܘܬܐ ܠܡܢ ܠܐ ܚܛܦܬܢܝ. ܘܡܢ ܟܪܣܐ ܠܡܢ ܠܐ ܫܕܝܬܢܝ.

ܘܟܒܫܬ ܬܒܪܬܢܝ ܘܫܕܝܬܢܝ. ܘܬܡܢ ܛܒܥܬܢܝ ܘܝ ܘܝ ܠܝ܀'

'Hymn (46). Crying full of distress

[11] Yodh: O death, why did you not steal me away?
And why did you not cast me from the womb?
But you have crushed down and thrown me into the underworld,
and drowned me there: woe, woe is me.'[144]

---

[141] A. Pritula, *The Wardā*, p. 397.

[142] ʾIbn al-Aṯīr, *الكامل في التاريخ* [The Complete History], vol. XII, p. 358.

[143] ʿA.T. Al-ʿAbūd, *الشعر العربي في العراق* [Arabic Poetry in Iraq], p. 187.

[144] A. Pritula, *The Wardā*, p. 339.

3.8 Repentance and Confession of Sins

Like Christians, Muslims too felt that the destruction of Iraq and its capital happened as punishment for their sins; had they lived according to the standards of their religion, not indulging in immorality, oppression and injustice, the calamities of this period would never have happened. The poet Aṣ-Ṣarṣarī wrote a poem in the time of Caliph al-Mustaᶜṣim on this theme.

'فلو أننا تُبنا إلى الله توبةً   نصوحـــــاً لزال الهمّ وارتفع اللّبكُ
وإلا فمما نحن نهمل أمرَه   فما هو إلا الخوف والعيشة الضنك'[145]

'If we had shown God proper repentance
The sadness would have vanished, and the confusion would have cleared away.
Instead, we neglect this
because of fear and the cruelty of life.'

Gīwargīs wrote hymns for the Rogation of Nineveh where penance is central theme,[146] in order to encourage his community to turn away from sin (Hymn (25), Table 6).

'ܥܘܢܝܬܐ (25). ܟܕ ܢܦܩ ܝܘܢܢ ܡܢ ܢܘܢܐ
[26] ܚܕܝ ܒܩܠܐ ܕܬܝܒܘܬܢ. ܘܠܐ ܬܬܕܟܪ ܩܕܡܝܬܢ.
ܘܬܫܝܓ ܨܐܝܢ ܠܛܘܠܫܢ. ܘܒܣܝܡܐ ܬܗܘܐ ܚܪܬܢ ܀'

'Hymn (25). On coming out of the fish, Jonah.
[26] Rejoice in the expression of our repentance
and do not remember our past!
And wash away our dirtiness
let our end be happy!'[147]

[145] ᶜA.T. Al-ᶜAbūd, *الشعر العربي في العراق* [Arabic Poetry in Iraq], p. 176, fn. 98.
[146] M. Nicák, "Penitential Theology," pp. 329-340.
[147] A. Pritula, *The Wardā*, p. 279.

4. TABLES OF IMPORTANT EVENTS ALLUDED TO IN THE HYMNS OF GĪWARGĪS

Table (2): Important Events[148]

1015	Plague in Baṣra	
1083	Plague	
1085	Plague in Baghdad	
1099	Plague	
1124	Plague	
1133	Rule of the Atabegs in Mosul	
1136	Many different diseases resulting in deaths	
1146	Another deadly disease	
1157	Chicken pox and cold weather	
1159	A flood in Baghdad	
1173	A flood in Baghdad resulting in different diseases	
1178	Drought	probable period during which Gīwargīs might lived
1179	An epidemic	
1184	An attack on Erbil because of tensions between the Atabegs and the Seljuks	
1187	The capture of Jerusalem by Ṣalāḥ ad-Dīn al-Ayyūbī	
1204	The attack on Mosul by Atabeg Muẓaffar ad-Dīn Gukbūrī of Erbil	
1221	-The Collaboration between the Caliph and Gukbūrī to repel the Mongol attack on Erbil in Dāqūq - Mongol attacks on Tiflis	
1223	An attack of the locust on the harvests	
1224	No rain in the winter and a Mongol attack on Erbil	
1223/4-1227/8	Famine in Mosul, Diyarbakir and Ǧazīrah, due to severe climate change	
1228	Mongol attack on Erbil	
1230-1231	Mongol attack on Erbil, to which the Caliph sent aid	
1233	Attack of Caliph al-Mustanṣir on Erbil after the death of Muẓaffar ad-Dīn Gukbūrī, who had given the keys of the city to the Caliph	
1235-1236	Mongol attack on Erbil	
1237	Mongol attack on Erbil	
1242	A plague in Baghdad	
1243	Flood of the Tigris River	
1244	The capture of Jerusalem by aṣ-Ṣāliḥ Naǧm ad-Dīn Ayyūb	
1245	Attack on the Mongols near Baghdad by Caliph al-Mustaʿṣim	
1248	Disease that killed many people	
1248,1254, 1256	Floods in Baghdad, Erbil and Mosul, weakening the cities.	
1252, 1258	Mongol attack on Erbil and Baghdad, rotting corpses spread illness	
1259	Kurdish attack on Christians in Erbil	

[148] Ḥ. ʾAmīn, تاريخ العراق في العصر السلجوقي [The History of Iraq in the Seljuk Era], pp. 410-429; ʾIbn al-Aṯīr, الكامل في التاريخ [The Complete History], vol. XI-XII.

1260-1261	Mongol capture of Mosul
1268	Bishops of Erbil tortured
1269	Attacks on Christians in Erbil
1277	Flood in Baghdad
1284	Flood in Baghdad
1285-1286	Attacks of Kurds, Turks and Arabs on Erbil and Mosul
1286	Diseases and many deaths in Baghdad
1296,1297,1298	Mongol attacks on the churches in Erbil
1305-1306	Mongol attack on Erbil
1310	Massacres in Erbil
1317	Massacres in Erbil
1318	Famine in Erbil and Mosul
1324	The great flood in Baghdad
1347,1349	Plagues in Erbil

Table (3)[149]: Mongol attacks on Erbil and surrounding villages alluded to in Gīwargīs' poetry

1224 April – May	Mongol attack on Erbil
1225	Winter: no rain June: hailstones November: famine and plague
1226	winter: animal sickness, fire, wolves attack the city
1227	February: plague March: fire in the fields April: fire in the city May: drought, attack of locusts December and January: no rain
1228	February – March: cold, snow, death of the crops April: Mongol attack
1235-6	Mongol attacks on Erbil, Karamlīs, Bēṯ Qōqā and Tellesquf.
1297	Capture of Erbil.

CONCLUSION

This chapter has provided a brief overview of the historical background to the life and work of Gīwargīs that may help us to understand some of the themes expressed in his poetry. In examining his hymns within the context of history, we discover that many of them record historical events. His hymns deal with the period of decline, his courage in criticizing corruption in the church and his laments over the suffering of his people from war, plague, famine and natural disasters. These problems and others gave rise to poetry as a way of looking at reality from the perspective of a

149 This table is based in part on the following works: P.H. Bachi, "Marie dans la doctrine de Ghiwarghis Warda," pp. 69-71; P.G. Borbone, "Due Episodi delle Relazioni Mongoli e Siri," pp. 205-228; A. Pritula, *The Wardā*, p. 388; E. Delly, "كيوركيس الملقب وردا" [Gīwargīs, the so-called Wardā], pp. 515-522; Ḥ.D.Ḫ. Al-Arbalī, *اربل تحت الأنظار* [Erbil under the Spotlight], pp. 101-114; Ḥ.D.Ḫ. Al-Arbalī, *المفصّل في تاريخ اربل* [The History of Erbil in Detail], p. 214.

religious conviction. The same feelings of anguish and despair flow through the hymns of the Christian Gīwargīs and his fellow Muslim poets. Despite the similarity of themes, however, it is difficult to determine whether Gīwargīs was directly influenced by specific Muslim Arabic poems. His use of rhyme and the similarity of many themes suggest at least a general Arab or Persian influence, something which is not only true of Gīwargīs. A more detailed study, falling outside the scope of this work, is needed to determine whether there was such a direct influence. After looking at the feelings and ideas of our poet and comparing them with Muslim poets, it is clear that the life at this time was difficult for both Muslims and Christians. Poetry expressed their emotions and preserved the history of the events that affected the lives of ordinary people.

CHAPTER TWO: GĪWARGĪS WARDĀ'S LIFE AND POETRY

INTRODUCTION

In this chapter, we will take a closer look at the life and works of Gīwargīs, as well as the sources that he used in composing his hymns.[1] Gīwargīs was a historiographer and to a certain extent a theologian. In general, his poetry is a combination of biblical, theological and historical elements which enable him to reflect on the situation of his church and community during the calamities that he witnessed. In order to situate our poet in the ecclesiastical context of his time, this chapter includes a survey of the most influential authors of hymns before and during the lifetime of Gīwargīs.

1. GĪWARGĪS WARDĀ'S LIFE

1.1 Dates concerning Gīwargīs' Life and Death and the Problem of the Book of Wardā

Ambiguity and a general lack of sources surround the life of our poet. As mentioned in the first chapter, some scholars have even questioned the existence of an author called Gīwargīs Wardā, suggesting rather that one can only speak of a *Book of Wardā*,[2] as in manuscript B2, which speaks of Gīwargīs as the composer "of Wardā". Bachi mentions that some manuscripts have the title *The Collection of the Wardā of Gīwargīs*.[3] An argument in favour of this interpretation is the existence of ܡܪܓܢܝܬܐ *The Pearl,* written by ʿAbdīšōʿ bar Brīḫā. Titles such as 'Rose' or 'Pearl' given to works suggest a Persian influence, as noted by Pritula.[4] Manuscript Mardin 41, folio 244r mentions 'the most luminous teacher Gīwargīs known as Wardā'. Whereas the heading

[1] The central theme of the hymns concerns the liturgical year. The Ancient Church of the East, the Assyrian Church of the East and the Chaldean Church each continue to use these hymns up to this day.

[2] A. Pritula, *The Wardā*, pp. 109-111; A. Mengozzi, "Giwargis Warda (13th cent.?)," pp. 176-177; M. Nicák, *"Konversion" im Buch Wardā*, p. 30; M. Tamcke, "How Giwargis Warda Retells Biblical Texts," p. 258.

[3] P.H. Bachi, "Marie dans la doctrine de Ghiwarghis Warda," p. 47.

[4] A. Pritula, *The Wardā*, p. 111.

of the hymn on folio 96r says 'another of Wardā written on the spelling of his name', followed by the name, which is spelled Gīwargīs!

The ܡܟܬܒܢܘܬܐ ܕܦܬܬܘܬܐ *Book of Crumbs*, however, claims that the surname Wardā (Rose) was given to Gīwargīs because of the beauty of his writings.[5] This lends credence to the interpretation that Wardā refers to a personal name. It also explains why some manuscripts calls Wardā ܡܠܦܢܐ 'teacher', or ܡܠܦܢܐ ܡܓܒ ܢܘܗܪܐ 'most luminous teacher'. In the same vein, Mengozzi mentions that Wardā is still a personal name used to-day in the Church of the East; this also may have been the case in the time of our author.[6] It is likely that this problem can only be solved when we have at our disposal a critical edition of all of his hymns. Only then will it be possible to establish which hymns were composed by a sole author whose name has been transmitted as Gīwargīs and who may have been surnamed Wardā.[7]

To understand *the Book of Wardā*, following our look at the political context of the *Book of Wardā* in chapter 1, our goal here is to understand the ecclesiastical context of the book by examining its direct or indirect references. For convenience sake, we speak here of Gīwargīs Wardā, following the tradition of the Church of the East. In assuming the existence of a poet named Gīwargīs Wardā, we do not mean that the whole collection of hymns found in the *Book of Wardā* was entirely his work. Other hymns written in the same style may have been incorporated into the *Book of Wardā* (see Table 4) and even attributed to him. This situation is reflected in the fact that the number of hymns varies from one manuscript to another.[8]

Scholars have not reached agreement about when the presumed Gīwargīs flourished. The Chaldean bishop J.E. Manna (1867-1928) claims that he died in the year 1300.[9] Baumstark argues that he died before 1300.[10] Assemani, Wright and Duval all argue that some of Gīwargīs' works can be dated to 1224-1228 or 1236,[11] due to their reference Mongol attacks. Chabot also places Gīwargīs in the 13th century.[12]

---

[5] Y. Qelaytā, ed., ܡܟܬܒܢܘܬܐ ܕܦܬܬܘܬܐ [The Book of Crumbs], p. 266.

[6] A. Mengozzi, "A Syriac Hymn on the Crusades," p. 187; A. Pritula, *The Wardā*, p. 111.

[7] In September 2019, I had the privilege of discussing this issue with Prof. Tamcke, who favors the theory of a composite book, called the Wardā, the author of which would be difficult to establish.

[8] This is because Gīwargīs' writings were frequently copied over the centuries for liturgical rites. It is understandable that the individual copyists arranged the material according to the purpose for which they were transcribing his hymns. This makes it difficult to establish a definitive collection. The differences in transmitting the material are discussed by Pritula and Mengozzi. For this study, focused on the Christology of Gīwargīs Wardā, we leave this issue aside. See A. Pritula, *The Wardā*, pp. 109-113; A. Mengozzi, "A Syriac Hymn on the Crusades," p. 187.

[9] J.E. Manna, *Morceaux choisis de littérature Araméenne*, vol. I, p. 31.

[10] A. Baumstark, *Geschichte der Syrischen Literatur*, pp. 304-306.

[11] J.S. Assemani, *Bibliotheca Orientalis*, vol. III, p. 561; W. Wright, *A Short History of Syriac Literature*, p. 283; R. Duval, *Syriac Literature*, p. 353.

[12] J.-B. Chabot, *Lettératures syriaque*, pp. 137-138. Pritula does not speculate on the poet's date of birth.

Only Ḥ.D.Ḫ. Al-Arbalī mentions that our poet died after 1245.[13] Thus, we have three suggestions. First, if we accept Bachi's suggestion that Gīwargīs was born in 1175 and died around 1236,[14] then he would have died in his sixties. Second, if we accept the view that he witnessed the fall of Baghdad in 1258,[15] he would have died in his eighties. Third if J.E. Manna is right that Gīwargīs died in 1300 (and if he was born in 1175), then he would have reached the age of 125, which seems completely unreasonable. The *Book of Wardā* contains a hymn on the Catholicoi of the East, ending with Timothy II (1318-1332). If Gīwargīs were the author of this hymn it would move his death into the fourteenth century, but in fact, this hymn, which is only found in the supplement of the book, is most probably a later addition.[16] It seems the first and second suggestions are most likely.

1.2 Gīwargīs Wardā's Personality and Career

Cardahi[17] and Ḥ.D.Ḫ. Al-Arbalī[18] describe Gīwargīs as one who was known for his sense of humour, friendly and joyful personality, good looks, and love of singing. On the other hand, he is only described as an older man, without any information about whether he belonged to the clergy or the laity. According to Baumstark, Gīwargīs was not ordained. E. Joseph,[19] without giving further information, mentions that the poet studied in one of the monasteries in Erbil.[20] Bachi attempts to present evidence that the poet was a priest-monk, based on the style of his hymns, his way of presenting doctrine, his theological, historical, exegetic and spiritual knowledge, and his awareness of many different aspects of the ascetic life.[21] The book of *Testi Mariani* states that Gīwargīs was neither a bishop nor a layman because the title of ܡܠܦܢܐ*'teacher'* or ܡܠܦܢܐ ܡܝܬܪ ܢܘܗܪܐ *'Most luminous teacher'* attached to his name is appropriate for a priest or monk but was never bestowed on a lay person.[22] In the later tradition other titles were given to Gīwargīs such as ܣܦܪܐ *'the writer'* in hymn (4), which is confirmed by what we know from his own hymns. Manuscript B1, dated to the sixteenth century, even considers him as ܛܘܒܢܐ *'the blessed one'*, showing how much he was esteemed in the later tradition.

One of the hymns can be read in two different ways, as supporting either the theory that Gīwargīs was an ecclesiastic or the theory that he was just a teacher (Hymn 8.(75), Table 6):

---

13 Ḥ.D.Ḫ. Al-Arbalī, القال والقيل في سلطان أربيل [Tittle-tattle about the Sultan of Erbil], p. 100; Ḥ.D.Ḫ. Al-Arbalī, المفصّل في تاريخ إربل [The History of Erbil in Detail], p. 178.
14 P.H. Bachi, "Marie dans la doctrine de Ghiwarghis Warda, " p. 94.
15 M. Tamcke, "How Giwargis Warda Retells Biblical Texts," pp. 265-266.
16 A. Mengozzi, "Giwargis Warda (13th cent.?)," pp. 176-177; M. Tamcke, "Remarks Concerning Giwargis Warda's ʿOnita," p. 122.
17 G. Cardahi, الكنز الثمين, *liber thesauris*, p. 51.
18 Ḥ.D.Ḫ. Al-Arbalī, المفصّل في تاريخ إربل [The History of Erbil in Detail], p. 272.
19 Emmanuel Joseph is the Bishop of Canada, for the Assyrian Church of the East.
20 E. Joseph, "Mary as Portrayed in the Hymns of George Warda," p. 44.
21 P.H. Bachi, "Marie dans la doctrine de Ghiwarghis Warda," pp. 88-94.
22 G. Gharib, et al., *Testi Mariani*, p. 370.

'ܥܘܢܝܬܐ 8.(75) <u>ܘܝܠܗ ܠܙܒܢܢ ܕܒܝܫܐ ܟܡܐ</u>
[26] ܬܐܘ ܚܙܘ ܪ̈ܫܝ ܡܪ̈ܥܝܬܐ. ܕܗ̈ܘ ܐܟܠܝܢ ܫܡܝ̈ܢܬܐ
ܘܠܐ ܚܝܪܝܢ ܠܡܟܝ̈ܟܬܐ. ܘܠܐ ܒܥܝܢ ܠܐܒܝ̈ܕܬܐ܀
[27] ܐܢ ܪܥܝܐ ܗܘܐ ܡܘܒܕܢܐ. ܘܡܕܒܪܢܐ ܡܚܒܠܢܐ.
ܘܡܠܦܢܐ ܡܛܥܝܢܐ. ܐܢܐ ܗܘ ܗܘ ܐܢܐ ܐ̄ܢܐ܀'

'Hymn 8.(75) <u>Woe to our time, how wicked it is</u>
[26] Come and see the heads of the flocks,
who eat fat things,
and do not take care of the suffering ones
and do not seek the lost.
[27] If the shepherd brings destruction,
and the leader brings corruption,
the teacher leads astray,
I am that one.'[23]

These stanzas can be understood as Gīwargīs referring to himself as a shepherd, a leader and a teacher. However, it is more probable that he is only referring to himself as a teacher, since he is presented as a teacher in the titles of several of his hymns, as we will see in the next section. Another hymn suggests that he might have an ecclesiastical status when he mentions that the ranks of priests and deacons will weep for him (Hymn (46), Table 6):

'ܥܘܢܝܬܐ (46). <u>ܒܟܝ ܢܦܩܐ ܡܠܐ ܐܢܝ̈ܩܬܐ</u>
[16] ܣ ܣܕܪ̈ܐ ܕܟܗ̈ܢܐ ܢܒܟܘܢ ܠܝ. ܘܡܫܡ̈ܫܢܐ ܢܐܠܘܢ ܠܝ
ܕܡܢ ܟܠܗܘܢ ܥܠܝ ܢܦܩܬ ܠܝ. ܘܛܒ ܐܬܬܥܝܩܬ ܠܝ ܘܝܠܝ܀'

'Hymn (46). <u>Crying full of distress</u>
[16] Semkaṯ: The ranks of priests will cry for me
and deacons will weep for me
For higher than all I have risen
And I was strongly blamed: woe, woe is me!'[24]

In another stanza of the same hymn he declares that he participated in festival parties and meetings, suggesting that he saw himself as having certain level of importance, but it is not clear again what kind of ecclesiastical position he may have held:

'ܥܘܢܝܬܐ (46). <u>ܒܟܝ ܢܦܩܐ ܡܠܐ ܐܢܝ̈ܩܬܐ</u>
[6] ܗ ܗܘܝܬ ܒܓܒܝܐ ܒܚܕܘܬܐ. ܘܡܫܡܫܐ ܒܡܘܬ̈ܒܬܐ
ܘܡܫܠܡܐ ܒܫܘܠܡܐ. ܘܒܟܢܘܫܬܐ ܠܝ ܘܝ ܠܝ܀
[7] ܘ ܘܐܬܢܨܚܬ ܠܝ ܒܗܘܠܢܐ. ܐܝܟ ܕܘܡܝܐ ܕܫܒܝܚܘܬܐ
ܘܐܬܦܪܫܬ ܠܝ ܠܒܪܝܬܐ. ܕܠܐ ܬܬܒܥܐ ܠܝ ܘܝ ܠܝ܀
[8] ܙ ܙܒܢܐ ܗܘܝܬ ܒܡܫܘܚܬ ܦܘܪܝ. ܘܡܫܟܝܢܐ ܗܘܝܬ ܠܐܚ̈ܐ ܕܝܠܝ
ܘܐܢܐ ܐܝܟ ܡܝܬܐ ܕܩܒܪܝ. ܘܠܐ ܦܓܪܐ ܘܡܘܬܐ ܠܝ ܘܝ ܠܝ܀'

[23] See the translation of the whole hymn in Chapter 3.
[24] A. Pritula, *The Wardā*, p. 338.

'Hymn (46). <u>Crying full of distress</u>

[6] Hē: I have been known at feasts,
and celebrated at meetings
But disgusting in actions
and deeds: woe, woe is me

[7] Wāw: And I had been given gifts
akin to prophecy
But I imitated animals
the irrational ones: woe, woe is me

[8] Zain: I would have sung like David,
but I have turned to someone who has perished.
And I'm like a deceased person, who is dead
and neither realizes nor remembers: woe, woe is me!'[25]

In the same hymn, Gīwargīs tells us that he preached or taught the message delivered by the prophets and the apostles, but did not live up to their teachings (Hymn (46), Table 6):

'ܥܘܢܝܬܐ (46). <u>ܓܥܬ ܥܩܬܐ ܡܠܝܐ ܬܢܚܬܐ</u>
[15] ܢ ܢܒܝܐ ܘܝܐ ܢܬܠܘܢ ܠܝ. ܫܠܝܚܐ ܟܪܝܐ ܢܘܣܦܘܢ ܠܝ
ܕܡܦܩܢܗܘܢ ܡܢ ܦܘܡ ܗܘܝܬ ܠܝ. ܘܡܥܒܪܢܐ ܠܟܠܗܘܢ ܠܝ ܘܠܝ܀'

'Hymn (46). <u>Crying full of distress</u>

[15] Nun: The prophets will give me woe
and the apostles will add to me more sorrow,
For I was repeating their scriptures with my mouth,
and trespassing on them: woe, woe is me!'[26]

In addition to titles of the hymns, being a teacher is also mentioned in one of the hymns, where he says that he is teaching but not learning from what he teaches (Hymn (47), Table 6):

'ܥܘܢܝܬܐ (47). <u>ܚܛܝܬ ܘܐܚܛܝܬ ܘܬܘܒ ܚܛܐ ܐܢܐ</u>
[1] ܡܠܦ ܐܢܐ ܘܠܐ ܝܠܦ ܐܢܐ. ܘܠܐ ܝܠܦ ܐܢܐ ܟܕ ܡܠܦ ܐܢܐ'

'Hymn (47). <u>I sinned and instigated to sin and I am sinning again</u>

[1] I teach but I do not learn
Yet I do not learn while I teach.'[27]

In another hymn, Gīwargīs blames himself because he learned but did not teach (Hymn (60), Table 6):

'ܥܘܢܝܬܐ (60). <u>ܡܠܦܢܐ ܕܬܫܒܚܬܐ</u>
[42] ܠܝ ܗܘ ܠܝ ܠܡܬܪܓܡܢܐ. ܕܝܠܦܬ ܘܠܐ ܗܘܝܬ ܡܠܦܢܐ
ܠܐ ܫܩܠܬ ܡܢ ܢܗܪܐ. ܗܘ ܗܘܐ ܕܡܘܬܒܗ ܠܝ ܚܫܘܟܐ܀'

[25] A. Pritula, *The Wardā*, pp. 337-338.
[26] A. Pritula, *The Wardā*, p. 338.
[27] A. Pritula, *The Wardā*, p. 343. Translation slightly adapted.

'Hymn (60). Teacher of virtues
[42] Woe, woe unto me, the author!
I learned but I did not teach.
May you not take away
what you have granted me by your mercy, o Clement one!'[28]

Hymn (28) can be understood in two different ways; when the poet says that he is a stupid farmer, it is unclear whether it should be understood literally or metaphorically:

'ܥܘܢܝܬܐ (28). ܥܘܗܕܢ ܚܛܗܝ ܐܬܐ ܠܝ
[11] ܘܝ ܠܝ ܕܗܘܝܬ ܐܟܪܐ. ܣܟܠܐ ܘܫܛܝܐ ܘܠܐ ܡܗܝܪܐ.
ܘܚܨܕܬ ܚܠܦ ܚܛܐ ܟܘܒܐ. ܘܟܢܫܬ ܬܒܢܐ ܚܠܦ ܥܒܘܪܐ ⁘
[12] ܘܝ ܠܝ ܕܗܘܝܬ ܓܢܢܐ. ܥܘܝܪ ܒܝܕܥܬܐ ܣܡܝܐ ܒܪܥܝܢܐ.
ܚܠܦ ܦܐܪܐ ܡܚܝܢܐ. ܠܩܛܬ ܦܐܪܐ ܡܡܝܬܢܐ ⁘'

'Hymn (28). The remembrance of my sins came to me
[11] Woe unto me that I was a farmer,
Stupid, foolish and unskilled;
I harvested brushwood instead of wheat
and collected chaff instead of grain.
[12] Woe unto me that I was a gardener,
Blind in knowledge, sightless in mind;
Instead of life-giving fruit,
I collected death-bringing fruit.'[29]

Regarding the poet's age, some hymns – for example (43), (114) and (102) – mention that he is an old man, while in hymn (107) he mentions his weak sight, strongly suggesting that he kept writing into old age.

'ܥܘܢܝܬܐ (43). ܫܠܡܘ ܝܘܡܝ ܘܩܠܝܠ ܪܗܛܝ
[21] ܪ ܪܣܣ ܙܘܦܟ ܠܕܟܝܘ ܣܝܒܘܬܝ.'

'Hymn (43). My days are finished and my course passes swiftly
[21] Reš: Sprinkle your hyssop to cleanse my old age.'

'ܥܘܢܝܬܐ (114). ܡܠܟܐ ܪܚܡ ܥܘܬܪܐ
[32] ܕܟܝ ܒܢܦܫܐ ܘܒܦܓܪܐ. ܠܡܣܝܒ ܢܦܫܐ ܘܦܓܪܐ.'

'Hymn (114). The king loves virtues
[32] Purify in soul and body
the one old in soul and body.'

'ܥܘܢܝܬܐ (102). ܡܘܡܐ ܐܘ ܟܪܝܗܐ ܕܚܛܝܬܐ
[30] ܗܐ ܐܢܐ ܣܒܐ ܠܡܪܥܝܬܐ. ܕܟܠܒ ܟܠܗ ܘܚܙܐ ܗܠܟܬܐ.
ܘܠܝܬ ܟܝ ܦܐܪܐ ܕܛܘܒܬܐ. ܕܡܩܪܒܢ ܠܡܪܗ ܕܓܢܬܐ ⁘'

[28] A. Pritula, *The Wardā*, p. 444. Translation slightly adapted.
[29] J.K. Hood, "Songs of Supplication," pp. 107-108. Translation slightly adapted.

'Hymn (102). Rise, o you who sleep in iniquity
[30] I am a barren fig,
that three generations have passed by,
And I have no fruit of religion
to appease the Lord of the garden.'

'ܥܘܢܝܬܐ (107). ܐܣܝܐ ܕܠܝܬ ܐܝܟ ܐܣܝܘܬܗ
[40] ܡܪܚܡܢܐ ܘܡܠܝܐ ܪ̈ܚܡܐ. ܕܠܒܝ̈ܫܐ ܐܠܦ ܪ̈ܚܡܐ.
ܒܪ̈ܚܡܘܗܝ ܕܐܒܘܟ ܚܘܢ ܪ̈ܚܡܐ. ܥܠ ܡܪ̈ܟܒܢܐ ܕܦܬܓ̈ܡܐ܀
[41] ܘܠܣܝܒܘܬܗ. ܘܠܟܡܝܪܘܬܗ.
ܐܩܝܡ ܡܪܝ ܥܠ ܦܬܘܪܟ. ܘܐܦ ܠܢ ܫܘܬܦ ܡܪܢ ܒܣܝܡܬܟ.'

'Hymn (107). Healer, whose healing has no likeness
[40] merciful and full of mercy
who has taught mercy to the wicked,
have mercy with the mercy of your Father
on the composer of these verses
[41] and on his old age and on his weak sight.
appoint [him], my Lord, over your table
and make us partakers, our Lord, in your treasure.'

Heinrich Hilgenfeld sees a contradiction between the joyful personality of Gīwargīs and the hymns, which reflect sorrow and sadness.[30] It is important to remember that, even though the poet lived during this time of calamities does not necessarily mean that he must have been sorrowful person who was always depressed, because his hymns often start with prayers expressing hope that the distress of his community would come to an end through the grace of God. Additionally, depicting himself as a sinner, who is not adequate for the high position he occupies is a literary *topos*, found in many other religious poems and one that should not be taken literally. Rather, his optimistic perspective and his love of music and poetry enables him to interpret various liturgical and historical events.[31]

2. GĪWARGĪS WARDĀ'S POETRY

2.1 Gīwargīs in the Context of the Syriac Renaissance

Despite the physical calamities listed in the first chapter, the Syriac Renaissance was very fruitful from a culturally perspective. Analysis of his poems can reveal the extent to which Gīwargīs was indebted to the cultural patterns characteristic of this period.[32]

According to some authors like ʾIġnāṭios ʾAfrām and Rubens Duval, the fact that Syriac authors allowed themselves to be influenced by Arabic and Persian poetry reflected a loss of their literary tradition and resulted in weaker Syriac poetry.

[30] H. Hilgenfeld, *Ausgewählte Gesänge des Giwargis Warda von Arbil*, p. 270.
[31] D. Bundy, "Interpreter of the Acts of God," p. 19.
[32] H. Teule, "The Syriac Renaissance and inner-Christian Relations," (forthcoming).

ʾIġnāṭīūs ʾAfrām uses ʿAbdīšōʿ bar Brīḫā and Ḫamīs bar Qardāḥe to make this point.[33] Duval agrees, saying that talent played only a minor role in the Syriac poetry of that time. For Duval, *The Paradise of Eden* by ʿAbdīšōʿ, which imitates the Arabic poetry of al-Ḥarīrī, has the qualities of a dead language.[34]

Though it is true that Gīwargīs abandoned classical patterns of Syriac poetry, this does not mean that his poetry was weaker; rather, we see richness of imagery, metaphors, and synonyms that display his creative genius.

Gīwargīs has been criticized for using Greek words.[35] Hymn (66) has a large number of Greek loanwords, more than any other hymn in the Collection of Wardā. Writing during this period, it is highly improbable that he knew Greek. For example, even the great scholar Bar ʿEbrāyā did not know Greek; when referring to the Greek Fathers, he always gives a Syriac translation.[36] The same is true for ʿAbdīšōʿ bar Brīḫā, whose book *The Paradise of Eden* abounds in Greek words; in this case, they are a matter of style rather than an example of Greek influence.[37]

Mengozzi suggested that Persian poetry influenced the poetry of Gīwargīs[38] and that he was familiar with both the Arabic and Persian literature of his day. Gīwargīs also used Mongol, Latin and Turkish terms.[39] We have as yet found no evidence that he used Armenian.

Gīwargīs mixed present events in the life of his community with past events, so that his readers would recognize the deeper significance of the present by correlating it to the historical context. In Hymn (55), Table 6 on the Rogation of Nineveh, which deals with hunger and the plague, he asks the prophets and the faithful from the Old Testament to intercede for the church of his day, giving how much they are suffering. In this prayer, Gīwargīs expresses the resonance between the past and present, as do many other authors from the Syriac Renaissance.[40]

2.2 Poetic Contemporaries of Gīwargīs

The Syriac Renaissance is characterized by literature in both the East and West Syriac Churches. Here we focus on poets who were Gīwargīs' contemporaries. Syriac poetry became more distinctive during this period, on the one hand because of the influence of Arabic poetry and on the other because of the need to preserve a Syriac identity under pressure from other languages.

Ephrem, Balai, Jacob of Serugh and Narsai used 7 or 12 syllable lines in their hymns. The following table shows how Syriac poets who were contemporaries of continued to write poetry along the traditional lines but also opened themselves up to new styles of poetry, for example rhyme and other influences from the Islamicate world.

---

33 ʾI.ʾA. Barṣūm, *اللؤلؤ المنثور* [The Scattered Pearls], p. 29.
34 R. Duval, *Syriac Literature*, pp. 15-20.
35 G. Cardahi, *الكنز الثمين*, *liber thesauris*, p. 51.
36 H. Teule, "Christian Spiritual Sources," p. 335.
37 See Appendix I.
38 A. Mengozzi, "A Syriac Hymn on the Crusades," p. 190.
39 A. Mengozzi, "The Book of Khamis," p. 426, fn. 42.
40 M. Tamcke, "Leben aus den Ursprüngen," pp. 53-63.

Table (4):
East-Syriac authors who wrote poetry during the time of Gīwargīs[41]

	Author	Cent.	Poetry and hymns
1	Gīwargīs of Arbela[42]	10	Hymns using the 7 syllable form
2	Ṣalībā al-Manṣūrī (al-Qas)[43]	10	Hymns using the 7 syllable form[44]
3	ʿAbdīšōʿ bar Šahārē[45]	10	Hymn in *The book of Wardā* using the 7 syllable form
4	ʿAmānūʾēl bar Šahārē	10	Hymns using 7 and 12 syllable forms
5	Ēlīā of Anbār	10	Mēmrē
6	Ēlīā bar Šēnāyā 'of Nisibis'	11	Liturgical prayers in Syriac[46]
7	Yahḇālāhā II	11	A hymn using the 7 syllable form[47]
8	ʾAḇrāham d-Zābā	11	7 syllable hymns about Barʿītā and Abraham of Kškar
9	Mari bar Mšīḥāyā	12	Maqāmāt, called Maqāmāt Ibn al-Masīḥī, imitating Maqāmāt al-Harīrī[48]
10	Ēlīā III Abū Ḥalīm	12	Morning prayers, throughout the liturgical year; wrote in Syriac and Arabic
11	Īšōʿyāhb bar Malkōn	12	Hymns in Arabic and songs; composed a hymn in Syriac about grammar and used the 12 syllable form, following the style of Ēlīā of Nisibis
12	Šemʿūn Šanqalwāyā	12	A difficult hymn which was explained by ʿAbdīšōʿ bar Brīḫā
13	Sabrīšoʿ bar Pawlis	12	Hymns using the 7 syllable form[49]
14	Šlēmūn of Baṣra	12	Hymns using the 7 syllable form[50]

---

[41] This table contain information from the following sources: G. Cardahi, الكنز الثمين, *liber thesauris*; W. Wright, *A Short History of Syriac Literature*; J.-B. Chabot, *Littérature syriaque*; S.P. Brock, *A Brief Outline of Syriac Literature*; ʾI.ʾA. Barṣūm, اللؤلؤ المنثور[The Scattered Pearls]; R. Duval, *Syriac Literature;* S.P. Brock, et al, *Gorgias Encyclopedic Dictionary of the Syriac Heritage*; A. Baumstark, *Geschichte der Syrischen Literatur*; A. Abouna, أدب اللغة الآرامية[Literature of the Aramaic language].

[42] This name occurs in the sources as Gīwargīs of Arbela, a metropolitan bishop who wrote a treatise on hereditary law, as well as the pseudonym of the author of a commentary on liturgical rites. This latter pseudonym has been confused with the names of Gīwargīs Wardā and Gīwargīs of Adiabene. See: A. Mengozzi, "Giwargis Warda (13th cent.?)," pp. 176-177.

[43] Ṣalībā bin Dāwūd al-Manṣūrī was born on the Island of Euphrates (جزيرة الفرات) He was famous for his poetry, especially his writings against the followers of the Pope. G. Cardahi, الكنز الثمين, *liber thesauris*, p. 57. The events described in the hymn makes one think that al-Manṣūrī used the Syriac version of *The book of Heracleides* as a source or that he had other sources concerning the story of Nestorius.

[44] Hymn (21), Table 6.

[45] ʿAbdīšōʿ bar Šahārē the brother of ʿAmānūʾēl bar Šahārē. Hymn (132) in the collection of Wardā is attributed to him, see Table 6. G. Cardahi, الكنز الثمين, *liber thesauris*, p. 136; A. Abouna, أدب اللغة الآرامية[Literature of the Aramaic language], p. 409.

[46] Hymn (52), Table 6.

[47] Hymn (151), Table 6.

[48] Hymns (30), (89), (155), Table 6.

[49] Hymns (74), (158), Table 6.

[50] Hymn (58), (152), Table 6.

15	Yōḥannan bar Zōʿbī	13	Prose about grammar, philosophy and logic using a 7 syllable form
16	Gīwargīs Wardā	13	*Book of Wardā*, a collection of hymns used 7 and 8 syllable forms
17	Ḫāmīs bar Qardāḥē	13	ʿOnyāṯā collected in a book called *Ḫamīs* and a supplement to the hymn of Wisdom written by Bar ʿEbrāyā; some hymns are found in the *Book of Wardā*[51]
18	Yōḥannan of Mosul	13	Many hymns collected in a book named ܟܬܒܐ ܕܫܦܝܪ̈ܐ ܕܘܒܪ̈ܐ the *Book of Good Morals* and hymns on wisdom using the 12 syllable form
19	Masʿūd Ḥakīm d-bēṯ Qāšā[52]	13	A hymn found in the *Book of Wardā*[53]
20	Gabriel Qamṣā	13	A hymn in the *Book of Wardā* used many Greek words and alternated 12 and 8 meter syllable[54]
21	Brīḫīšōʿ bar Eškāpē	13	Mēmrē using the 12 syllable form and other hymns
23	ʿAbdīšōʿ bar Brīḫā	13	*Paradise of Eden*, a collection of 50 hymns
22	Esḥaq Šbadnāyā	15	A hymn found in the *Book of Wardā*[55]

2.3 The Type of Hymns and Meter Used by Gīwargīs

It is easy to find different forms of Syriac poetry in the writings of early fathers of the church, such as Ephrem, Narsai, and Jacob of Serugh. There are five general types: ܡܕܪܫܐ *Medrāšā*, a lyric poem with a refrain; ܡܐܡܪܐ *Mēmrā*, a verse or narrative homily; ܣܘܓܝܬܐ *Sōġīṯā*, a dialogue between two personalities;[56] ܥܘܢܝܬܐ ʿ*Onīṯā*, a strophic hymn; and ܡܡܠܐ *Mamlā*, a speech. These forms are used both in liturgy and for teaching purposes. We are most concerned here with the ʿ*Onīṯā* and *Sōġīṯā*, the two forms used most often by Gīwargīs.[57] His hymns always have an introduction and a conclusion, most often a petition for mercy and blessing.[58] Not all of his hymns are identified as ʿ*Onīṯā*, even though the style is the same. Some are categorized in the epilogue as *Mēmrā* (Hymns (104) and (117)), and some as *Mamlā* (Hymns (2), (6), (12)) or a combination of ʿ*Onīṯā* and *Mamlā* in the same hymn (Hymn (97)). Some of the hymns

---

[51] Hymns (93), (143), Table 6.

[52] He was a doctor of the Caliph al-Mustaʿṣim (1242-1258); after the fall of Baghdad, he lived in isolation until his death in 1280. See: A. Abouna, أدب اللغة الآرامية [Literature of the Aramaic language], p. 443.

[53] Hymn (14), Table 6.

[54] Hymn (138), Table 6. The hymn is about Sabrīšōʿ the founder of the monastery of Bēṯ Qōqā. There is also another hymn attributed to Sabrīšōʿ of Bēṯ Qōqā (Hymn (133), Table 6).

[55] Hymn (144), Table 6.

[56] S.P. Brock, "Syriac Poetry on Biblical Themes," p. 55.

[57] The following hymns of Gīwargīs can be considered to be in the *Sōġīṯā* genre (5, 15, 17, 18, 20); see Chapter 3.

[58] A. Pritula, *The Wardā*, p. 102; D. Bundy, "Interpreter of the Acts of God," p. 9.

are identified in the manuscripts as a story ܬܘܢܝܐ *Tūnāyā* or a *Mēmrā* and include a plea for mercy for the *translator*[59] or *commentator* of the story or the speech,[60] such as ܡܦܫܩܢܘܬܗ ܕܝܠܝ ܬܘܢܝܐ or ܡܦܫܩܢܘܬܗ ܕܝܠܝ ܡܡܠܠܐ (Hymns (59), (67), (123)).

Gīwargīs used the heptasyllabic (seven syllable) meter, found in the early tradition (see Table 4). However, the introduction and the conclusion of his hymns are written in in either the heptasyllabic or octosyllabic (eight syllable) meter.[61]

2.4 Sources Used by Gīwargīs

E. Joseph says Gīwargīs drew on the Holy Scriptures, *The book of the Cave of Treasures,* some apocryphal stories about the Virgin Mary, and the poetry of Ephrem and Narsai, without giving any further evidence.[62] Anton Pritula suggests that Gīwargīs was also influenced by *The book of the Bee* of Šlēmūn of Baṣra.[63]

In Hymn (28) Gīwargīs says that in spite all that he had studied, he was still as ignorant as the Magi. Stanzas [3] and [6] mention that he studied other authors, but do not specify what type of writings; perhaps an in-depth study of all his hymns will reveal his sources. Stanzas [5] and [8] make it clear that he was familiar with the Bible, something which is very obvious in his hymns:

'ܠܡܐܡܪܐ (28). ܠܡܘܕܝ ܚܛܝܐ ܐܢܐ ܠܝ

[2] ܗܐ ܠܝ ܕܡܝܢܐ ܡܠܝܠܘܬܐ. ܘܗܘܝܬ ܡܕܒܪܢܐ ܘܝܪܘܬܐ
ܘܟܘܢܝܐ ܥܡ ܬܪܥܝܬܐ. ܘܐܬܕܪܫܬ ܠܝ ܠܫܘܬܐ܀

[3] ܗܠܝ ܕܡܕܢܐ ܒܡܬܪܬܐ. ܘܐܬܚܟܡܬ ܒܚܟ̈ܡܬܐ
ܘܐܬܕܪܫܬ ܒܟܬܒܢܬܐ. ܘܐܬܚܟܡܬ ܒܟܬܒܘܬܐ܀

[4] ܗܠܝ ܕܡܠܠܝܬ ܟܬܒܢܬܐ. ܗܠܝ ܕܦܫܩܬ ܦܬܓܡܬܐ
ܗܠܝ ܕܬܢܝܬ ܡܬܠܢܝܬܐ. ܘܕܪܫܬ ܟܠ ܟܬܒܢܝܬܐ܀

[5] ܗܠܝ ܕܝܠܦܬ ܒܬܒܘܢܬܐ. ܗܠܝ ܕܡܕܢܐ ܒܣܦܪܐ
ܘܚܣܝܪܘܬܐ ܗܘܬ ܠܗ ܚܘܟܡܬܐ. ܘܡܠܝܘܬܐ ܗܘܬ ܠܗ ܓܠܘܡܬܐ܀

[6] ܘܗܠܝ ܕܩܪܝܬ ܒܣܘܦܪܐ. ܐܦ ܢܡܘܣܐ ܘܢܒܝܐ
ܘܝܕܥܬ ܐܣܘܪܐ ܘܚܘܩܐ. ܐܝܟ ܗܘܕܪܐ ܚܕܘܝܐ܀

[7] ܘܗܠܝ ܕܝܬܒܬ ܒܐܠܗܘܬܐ. ܘܗܘܝܬܐ ܕܡܠܝܠܘܬܐ
ܘܦܣܩܬܗ ܒܕܝܠܝܬܐ. ܘܐܘܕܥܬܗ ܒܡܬܒܝܢܘܬܐ܀

[8] ܘܗܠܝ ܕܡܕܢܐ ܠܟܬܒܐ. ܘܠܦܘܩܕܢܐ ܐܠܗܝܐ
ܘܠܡܠܟܝܐ ܡܫܝܚܝܐ. ܘܐܬܕܪܫܬ ܠܡܕܒܪܢܘܬܐ܀'

[59] Most likely, '*translator*' here does not mean one who translate from one language to another but rather a '*commentator*'.

[60] A. Pritula, *The Wardā*, pp. 108-109.

[61] See the table made by Anton Pritula that gives the meter of each hymn. A. Pritula, *The Wardā*, pp. 19-81.

[62] E. Joseph, "Mary as Portrayed in the Hymns of George Warda," p. 44.

[63] A. Pritula, "The Wardā Hymnological Collection and Šlemon of Ahlat," pp. 149-207.

'Hymn (28). The remembrance of sins came to me
[2] Woe unto me, that I gained eloquence,[64]
reason, knowledge, freedom,
intelligence and consciousness,
but I seem like the animals.
[3] Woe unto me, that I read the commandments
and received wisdom from writings,
and was instructed by glorious matters
but I acted inappropriately.
[4] Woe unto me, that I spoke glorious things.
Woe unto me, that I did contradictions.
Woe unto me, that I narrated the highest matters,
but thought about lowly things.
[5] Woe unto me, that I learned the Old Testament.
Woe unto me, that I studied the New Testament,
but I held it in contempt
and stupidly moved away from it.
[6] Woe unto me, that I stepped on the commandments,
the life-giving laws,
and neglected the boundaries and the canons
like the unfaithful Jews.
[7] Woe unto me, that I received by grace
the gift of eloquence,
but I muted it by desires
and demolished it with hatred.
[8] Woe unto me, that I read the prophets
and the divine books
and the rightful apostles,
but I am like the Magi.'[65]

Anton Pritula has demonstrated that Gīwargīs used apocryphal texts in his poetry. This is evident in a hymn that echoes '*The Book on the Childhood of Christ*', possibly a reference to the Infancy Gospel of Thomas,[66] an argument also made by Bachi.[67] Pritula also suggests that these apocryphal texts were widespread because the poet treats them as stories that were already well known in his community. No Syriac version of this apocryphal text has survived; there is only an Arabic version preserved by the Syriac Orthodox.[68] Pritula uses a table to show how one of the hymns of Gīwargīs is very similar to apocryphal accounts of the life of the Blessed Virgin Mary.

[64] This word could also be translated 'logical thinking' or 'philosophy'.
[65] J.K. Hood, "Songs of Supplication," pp. 106-107. Translation slightly adapted.
[66] A. Pritula, "A Hymn by Givargis Warda on the Childhood of Christ," pp. 116-118.
[67] P.H. Bachi, "Marie dans la doctrine de Ghiwarghis Warda," p. 459.
[68] The complete edition was published by M. Provera, *Il Vangelo arabo dell'Infanzia.*

He is convinced that the East-Syriac Church used such texts in the liturgy, although the only indirect evidence for that view is in the hymns of Gīwargīs.[69]

Looking at the catalogue of Bar Brīẖā might help provide information on the sources of Gīwargīs by indicating which sources were circulating at that time.[70]

2.5 Themes of Gīwargīs

According to Barṣūm,[71] Syriac poetry has eight themes or purposes. Barṣūm's division is helpful for understanding and categorizing Gīwargīs' poetry. For each theme, an example of one of his hymns is given.

1. Renunciation of worldly things: This kind of poetry calls for repentance. Many of Gīwargīs' hymns fit into this category; Hymn (37), Table 6.

2. Descriptive poetry: Many of Gīwargīs' theological writings fit into this category, although it is also used to describe material things such as famine and drought; see Hymn (56), Table 6.

3. Praise: The hymns of Gīwargīs are filled with praise, especially the hymns in honor of Mary and the saints; see Hymn (10), Table 6.

4. Lamentation: Gīwargīs grieves for his people and for the difficulties that they have to face, and he prays for God's mercy on them; see Hymn (76), Table 6.

5. Satire: Gīwargīs criticizes church leaders who paid bribes and rulers who oppressed the community with taxes; see Hymn (75), Table 6.

6. Wisdom and Philosophy: These themes are found less often in Gīwargīs' hymns, but we may mention the hymn that treats man as a microcosm; see Hymn (19), or the hymn on the inhabitance of the world; see Hymn (65), Table 6.

7. Fraternity and Longing: Non of Gīwargīs' hymns fit into this category which concerns poems written for a friend or a brother.

8. Admiration of heroes: The hymn written to the Catholicoi contains this theme, but this hymn may not have been written by Gīwargīs; see Hymn (136), or many of hymns dedicated to Mary or saints; see Hymn (6) and (84), Table 6.

Some of the hymns of Gīwargīs cannot be restricted to just one category because they express many of these themes. Other characteristics in the poetry of Gīwargīs are simplicity and repetition, both of which are also found among his contemporaries from Erbil.[72]

2.6 Use of Gīwargīs' Poetry in the Liturgy

The hymns in the *Book of Wardā* are organized according to the liturgical year. They were used for Sunday services, feasts, the Rogation of Nineveh, the commemorations of the saints and other occasions.[73] Many are dedicated to specific individuals or

[69] A. Pritula, "A Hymn by Givargis Warda on the Childhood of Christ," pp. 427, 431; A. Pritula, *The Wardā*, pp. 118-119.

[70] ʿAbdīšōʿ B. Brīẖā, ܡܐܡܪܐ ܕܟܬܒ̈ܐ ܕܡܟܬܒܢܘܬܐ ܕܨܘܒܐ, *Catalogus Auctorum Abdišoʿ Sob. (1318+).*

[71] ʾI.ʾA. Barṣūm, *اللؤلؤ المنثور* [The Scattered Pearls], pp. 31-34.

[72] ʿA.A. Ṣāliḥ, *أربيل مدينة الأدب والعلم والحضارة* [Erbil, the City of Literature, Science and Civilization], pp. 108-114.

[73] A. Pritula, *The Wardā*, p. 85.

groups, such as Mary, Jesus, the apostles, the martyrs, the patriarchs, and other biblical characters used as examples for the believers of his day. What makes his work interesting is that he mixes theology with the story of these saints in order to highlight God's action in their lives. Bundy makes no distinction between the historical and theological hymns of Gīwargīs, because they combine both elements.[74]

The purpose of retelling the stories of saints in poetry was to encourage the church to recognize the mercy of God during disasters so the believers would not fall into despair.[75]

2.7 The Bible in the Words of Gīwargīs

The reader of Gīwargīs' poetry can easily see how many biblical elements have been transformed into poetry. Martin Tamcke viewed Gīwargīs as a poet who helped his community to learn how to contemplate the stories of the Bible. The purpose of this poetry was not just for chanting in church but also as a tool to preserve the tradition and history of the church at a time when Christians had become a minority.[76]

Gīwargīs reconstructed the biblical stories and related them to the predicament of his people. When he tells the story of Jonah and Nineveh, he associates the prayer of repentance prayed by the people of Nineveh with the need of his own community to beg God to accept their repentance[77] and save them from distress. In reimagining the stories, Gīwargīs went beyond the limits of the original biblical texts. This point will be discussed more in the fourth chapter in the context of analyzing the Christological themes in his hymns.

2.8 Gīwargīs' Theology

According to David Bundy, the hymns of Gīwargīs are not apologetic in nature or concerned with theological argumentation, but rather are a representation of the beliefs of the East-Syriac Church, an exercise in narrative theology that explains the tradition without offering new interpretations. Nicák has suggested that analyzing the theological elements of the poetry of Gīwargīs might help to determine the authenticity of the hymns. The theology of Gīwargīs, with the focus on his Christology, is the subject of Chapter four below.

CONCLUSION

The focus in this chapter has been on understanding Gīwargīs through the studies of other scholars,[78] all of which were based on a limited number of hymns. Much of Gīwargīs' work is still unedited, so these studies cannot be considered as definitive. Gīwargīs was only one of many who participated in the Syriac Renaissance. We have seen how his work was in line with the tradition of Syriac poetry that he received.

---

[74] D. Bundy, "Interpreter of the Acts of God," p. 27.
[75] D. Bundy, "George Warda as Historian," p. 198.
[76] M. Tamcke, "How Giwargis Warda Retells Biblical Texts," p. 259.
[77] M. Tamcke, "How Giwargis Warda Retells Biblical Texts," pp. 266-267.
[78] See the bibliography.

His poetry, which is still used in the liturgy and performed in church settings, is an important element in reviving the past culture of the Church. Gīwargīs' retelling of stories from the Bible makes it easier for the community to remember and memorize those stories.

CHAPTER THREE: CRITICAL EDITION AND TRANSLATION

INTRODUCTION

The base manuscript used for the text is Mardin Chald. 41 (M2), the oldest complete copy, written in 1541 published here. The critical edition is limited to the oldest manuscripts of the *Book of Wardā*. Mingana Syr. 505 (G1, 14th-15th cent.) is incomplete and the hymns are arranged in a chaotic order, making a systematic comparison with other manuscripts difficult. As a result, it has only been used where there are important variants between the manuscripts. The critical edition depends on the list provided by Anton Pritula,[1] with the addition of Diyarbakir 85 (D3, 1400-1600 CE). The sigla used by Pritula is adopted below.

The biblical illusions, poetic language and metrical nature of these texts makes their translation difficult. The translation is generally as literal as possible, in order to do justice to the author's original intention. At the same time, every effort has been made to make it as understandable as possible to an English-speaking readership. As a result, the translation does not always fit the verses of the individual stanzas. Square brackets [ ] are used in the translation to clarify difficult terms or unclear terms. When Syriac abbreviations are used in the manuscripts, such as ܥܘ for ܥܘܢܝܬܐ and ܬܫܒܘ for ܬܫܒܘܚܬܐ, they are written out in full for the sake of the reader. Orthographic variants are not indicated.

Our selection of edited and translated hymns is based on their Christological relevance. Although other hyms contain Christological allusions they are less overt, and therefore not included here. However, some of these other hymns are discussed in Chapter 4, which is devoted to an analysis of the *Book of Wardā*'s Christological views.

As we will see in this chapter the *Book of Wardā* is basically in line with the traditional Christology of the Church of the East, including references to the classical Greek and Syriac Fathers such Theodore and Narsai. The use of terminology deemed to be 'Nestorian', apparently, did not appeal to some later readers (probably of Chaldean background), who erased certain themes, such as the view that the Incarnation involved the divine good pleasure and love rather than a change in nature. Other

[1] A. Pritula, *The Wardā*, pp. 9-10.

things deleted include themes taken from apocryphal texts (such as Joseph having children from a previous marriage or Mary giving birth to Jesus with pain) and the names of the magi.[2]

The following names have sometimes been erased: Ephrem, Theodore, Diodore, Arion,[3] Nestorius, John, Narsai, Addai, Āḇā, Fāfā, Bābāi; in some cases these names have been replaced with Cyril, John Chrysostom, Ambrosius, Gregorius or Jacob.

Noteworthy in this respect are the following manuscripts: Diyarbakir 78 (1565), Vat Sir. 567 (1568), Diyarbakir 85 (1400-1600), Baghdad Chaldean 492 (1581) and Mingana Syr. 505 (14th-15th cen.). In the case of Diyarbakir 84 (1575), together with the name of Nestorius, a reader has even erased the name of Christ ! For more precise information, see the description of the manuscripts.

Although this aspect of the text falls outside the scope of this study, it shows that the *Book of Wardā* was not only read by members of the Church of the East, but also by those in the later Chaldean tradition.

The inconsistency that is observed in deleting or retaining Christological themes or names of early fathers in a given manuscript suggests various roles in the formation of the *Book of Wardā*: first the original poet(s) who composed the hymns, then those who copied them, followed by those who collected and assembled them, those who eliminated unwanted expressions or names, sometimes even eliminating folios from the manuscript. It is possible that those who collected the hymns and those who eliminated material from the collection could be one and the same, meaning that some hymns could have been added later and remained untouched, which would explains why, in the same manuscript, some themes or names are erased and others are not.

Critical Edition Conventions:

+	Added
-	Omitted
Illeg	Illegible
Rep	A verse replaced with another verse, or a word with another word.
marg	Written in the margin
*c	Corrected by the copyist or by a later hand
+ +	Repeated words
a, b, c, d...	Verse number within a stanza
[1, 2, 3...]	Stanza number
X	Erased by the copyist or by a later hand
⌜ ⌝ » « § §	These signs are used when the variants affect more than one word and the reader needs to go back to the text where the signs are found. Using more than one type of symbol is intended to prevent confusion, especially when there are several variants in one line; this is found more frequently in the headings of the hymns.

[2] Some of the themes erased in the manuscripts are also found in the text of condemnation of Synod of Diamper, Cf. Chapter 4.

[3] Arion, it has been written this way in the manuscripts, and probably it refers to Arius.

	1. If a letter is added or omitted at the beginning of the word, it is designated as follow: + / - followed by the letter.
	2. If a letter is added or omitted in the middle or at the end of the word, then the whole word is given.
	3. If a word/verse/stanza is omitted, then it is indicated by (-), without giving the entire word/verse/stanza.
	4. If a note is placed after the sign (⁘) in the stanza e.g. [1]⁘, it means that the note relates to the whole stanza.
	5. If a note is placed before a word, e.g. ܡܫܒܚܐ[1], this means that there is a word added before this word.
	6. If a word is written in the margins as well as in the text, it is indicated as follows: + in marg. If the word is only in the margins, it is indicated as follows: marg.
	7. The symbols +X in the footnotes indicate that there is a word added in the text and then erased, either by the copyist or by a later hand. The symbols + +X indicate that the word is written twice and one of the repeated words is deleted.
	8. Vocalization is based on the base manuscript used for this work: Mardin Chald. 41 (M2).

Manuscripts consulted:

	Manuscript		Sigla
1	Mardin Chald. 43	1483 CE, Mardin Chaldean Cathedral	M1
2	Mardin Chald. 41	1541 CE, Mardin Chaldean Cathedral	M2
3	Cambr. Add. 1983	1550 CE, Cambridge University Library	B1
4	Diyarbakir 78	1565 CE, Diyarbakir, Mardin Chaldean Cathedral	D1
5	Vat. Sir. 567	1568 CE, Vatican Library	C1
6	Vat. Sir. 184	1568 CE, Vatican Library	C2
7	Diyarbakir 84	1575 CE, Diyarbakir, Mardin Chaldean Cathedral	D2
8	Baghdad Chaldean 492	1581 CE, currently in ʿAinkawā – Erbil, Monastery of St. Hōrmīzd.	B2
9	Mardin Chald. 42	1586 CE, Mardin Chaldean Cathedral	M3
10	Mingana Syr. 505	14th-15th cent., University of Birmingham Library	G1
11	Diyarbakir 85	1400-1500 CE, Mardin Chaldean Cathedral	D3

Description of Manuscripts Consulted

1	**Mardin Chald 43 (1483 AD, Mardin, Chaldean Cathedral)**[4]	
	Dimensions	18 x 13.5 x 4 cm
	Script	Eastern
	Characteristics	132 leaves, 14 quires of 10 folios, 18 lines to the page
	Copied by	
	Place of copying[5]	
	Year	f127v The book was completed on Friday 12 Nīsān, in the year 1794 AG [1483 CE].
	Hierarchy	f132r The Catholicos is Mar Šemʿūn, and the Metropolitan is Mar Elīā, Bishop of Nisibis,[6] Armenia, ܡܪܕܐ Mardin,[7] Amida, Seʿrat and ܚܨܢܐ ܕܟܐܦܐ Ḥesnā d-Kēpā.[8]
	Owner's notes	f1r, f131v Some liturgical books were given to the priest Gīwargīs of the Church of Mar Yaʿqōb of Nisibis. f130r This book belonged to the church of Mar Yaʿqōb of Nisibis.
	Comments	Marginal notes in Arabic and Serṭō script.
	Colophon locations	f1r, f44v, f127v-128r, f129v-132v
2	**Mardin Chald 41 (1541 AD, Mardin, Chaldean Cathedral)**[9]	
	Dimensions	28 x 18 x 6.5 cm
	Script	Eastern; the style changes on f167r
	Characteristics	268 leaves, 27 quires of 10 folios, 24 lines to the page
	Copied by	f267v The priest monk the son of ʿAbdū the son of Esḥaq the son of Mubārak the son of Denḥā, who is called Bēṯ Danūḥ from Bēṯ Zabday.

---

[4] A. Scher, "Notice sur les manuscrits syriaques et arabes conservés dans la bibliothèque de l'évéché chaldéen de Mardin," p. 78.

[5] The data given in this table (e.g. copied by, place of copying, year, hierarchy, owner's notes) are all taken from the colophons of the manuscripts consulted.

[6] D. Wilmshurst, *The Ecclesiastical Organisation*, pp 49-50.

[7] This name sometimes can be read in different ways in the MSS either Merdā or Mardē so we opted to write it as it is found in Syriac also.

[8] This is a town on the river Tigris between Amed and the Island of Omar جزيرة عمر. Cf. D. Wilmshurst, *The Ecclesiastical Organisation*, pp. 51, 56, 84-85; Yāqūt al-Ḥamawī, معجم البلدان [Dictionary of countries], vol. II, p. 265.

[9] A. Scher, "Notice sur les manuscrits syriaques et arabes conservés dans la bibliothèque de l'évéché chaldéen de Mardin," p. 77.

		f268r The priest Brāhīm, deacon Tāġdīn and deacon ʿAṭallah, from the Church of Mar Gīwargīs in ܡܪܕܝܢ Mardin in the village of ܛܒܝܬܐ Ṭabyāṯā .[10]
	Place of copying	f266v Church of Mar Aḥā the brother of Yōḥannan the Copt[11] in Ṭūrā d-ʿŪmrē ܛܘܪܐ ܕܥܘܡܪܐ [The Mountain of Monastries] which is located on the river Tigris. f267r Near the strong ܚܨܢܐ ܕܦܢܟ Ḥesnā d-Penek near Gāzartā of Bēṯ Zabday.
	Year	f266v 5 Nīsān 1852 AG [1541 CE], the Tuesday before Palm Sunday.
	Hierarchy	f267r The Catholicos is Mar Šemʿūn and the Metropolitan is Mar Gabriel, Bishop of Gāzartā of Zabday.
	Owner's notes	f267v This book was bought by deacon ܓܘܪܓܝ Gōrgī and he gave it to its owner Mar Gīwargīs in the village of Ṭabyāṯā. f268v In that time there were persecutions, wars and evils.
	Comments	Marginal notes in Arabic. f150r The names of Greek fathers (Diodore, Theodore and Nestorius) have been erased.
	Colophon locations	f266v-268v
3	**Cambr. Add. 1983 (1550 AD, Cambridge, University Library)**[12]	
	Dimensions	19 x 25 cm.
	Script	Eastern.
	Characteristics	183 leaves, 20 quires of 10 folios, 24 lines to the page.
	Copied by	f183v ʿĪsā the son of the priest ʾAḇrāham the son of Hōrmīzd from the village of Debbōrīṯā, who makes honey,[13] ܐܘܪ

[10] D. Wilmshurst, *The Ecclesiastical Organisation*, pp. 81-82.

[11] The names Mar Aḥā and Yōḥannan the Copt are found in the title of hymn (128). D. Wilmshurst, *The Ecclesiastical Organisation*, pp. 109, 115-116; A. Vööbus, *History of Asceticism*, 218; A. Palmer and A. Pritula, "From the Nile Delta to mount Izlā and the Tigris Gorge," pp. 506-508.

[12] W. Wright, *A Catalogue of the Syriac Manuscripts*, pp. 265-282.

[13] In Wright's catalogue, ܩܪܝܬܐ ܕܕܒܘܪܐ is translated as 'the village of honeybees'. See W. Wright, *A Catalogue of the Syriac Manuscripts*, pp. 281-282.

		Ōz [!].[14] In the neighborhood of the fortress of ...[!], and the writer resides in the village of Bas...[!], the church of Mar Gīwargīs.
	Place of copying	
	Year	f183r 1861 AG [1549 CE].
	Hierarchy	
	Owner's notes	
	Comments	f15v, f48v, f99v The names of Greek fathers have been erased, along with certain themes, such as Joseph having children from a previous marriage.
	Colophon locations	f183r-183v
4	**Diyarbakir 78 (1565 AD, Diyarbakir; now in Mardin, Chaldean Cathedral)[15]**	
	Dimensions	27.5 x 18.5 x 7 cm
	Script	Eastern
	Characteristics	270 leaves, 28 quires of 10 folios, 25 lines to the page
	Copied by	f117r ʾAḇrāham
	Place of copying	
	Year	f269v The book was completed on the second Friday of [the liturgical season of] Summer in commemoration of Mar Mari the apostle in the month of Āb [August], on the 10th[day], in the year 1876 AG, 971 AH [1565 CE].
	Hierarchy	
	Owner's notes	f270v The book was bought from deacon Īšōʿ Gzīrānāyā for the church of Mar Qūryāqōs of ʿAin Tannūr.[16] It was bought by ʿAbd al-Aḥad the son of the priest Maqṣūd .... ʾArzūn[17] in 1147[18] AG. f270r (in the margins) In the year 1942... Yōḥannan was buried in the church of Mar Awgen.
	Comments	Marginal notes in Arabic. f54r[19]-54v, f55r, f56v, f57r, f78v, f145v, f208v, f258v

[14] Or maybe Hoz. See D. Wilmshurst, *The Ecclesiastical Organisation*, p. 120.

[15] A. Scher, "Notice sur les manuscrits syriaques et arabes conservés dans la bibliothèque de l'évêché chaldéen de Diarbékir," p. 39.

[16] D. Wilmshurst, *The Ecclesiastical Organisation*, pp. 52, 59, 60-62.

[17] This is the name of a person.

[18] Under this year is written 1947 ܐܨܡܙ [1635 CE].

[19] The hymn found on this folio is number (21), written by the priest Ṣalībā al-Manṣūrī and dedicated to Nestorius and the events of the Council of Ephesus. This hymn is very long and the

		The names of early fathers like Diodore, Theodore, Nestorius and Narsai have been erased and replaced with Cyril, Yoānīs [!], Ambrosius, Gregorius and Jacob. The name of Arion [!] is replaced by Jacob. f3r-3v, f7r, f18r-18v, f20r, f141v Various themes have been erased, such as Joseph having children from a previous marriage, Mary giving birth to Jesus with pain, the names of the magi, and the Incarnation happening out of love rather than a change in nature.
	Colophon locations	f117r, f269v-270v
5	**Vat. Sir. 567 (1568 AD, Vatican Library)**[20]	
	Dimensions	27 x 17 cm
	Script	Eastern
	Characteristics	272 leaves, 30 quires of 10 folios, 25 lines to the page
	Copied by	f266v The copyist is the priest ʾAḇrāham the son of Šemʿūn the son of Ḥabīb from the village of Barbīṯā.[21] f267r-267v The priest Hōrmīzd the son of ʿĪsā and the priest Esḥaq the son of Šaylelā[22] and his son the priest ʿAbdāl from the village of ʿAin Tannūr which is located at the gate called the gate of Rome of the city of Amida, in the Church of Mar Qūryāqōs.
	Place of copying	f266r Village of Barbīṯā on a hill named ܡܓܕܠ ܕܕܐܒܐ Maġdal Dēḇā [The Castle of the Wolf],[23] in the country of Gāzartā of Bēṯ Zabday.
	Year	f266r On the 7th Wednesday of the Lord's fasting, on the evening of Holy Thursday on the 14th of Nīsān [April] 1879 AG, 975 AH, [1568 CE], in the 16th of the month of Šawwāl.
	Hierarchy	f267r The Catholicos is Mar Ēlīā and the Metropolitan is Mar Īšōʿyāhb, Metropolitan of Nisibis and Armenia, the son of the priest Ēlīā *malpānā*, the nephew of the Catholicos.
	Owner's notes	

complete text is found only in Mardin Chald 41 (M2). Diyarbakir 78 (D1) and Vat. Sir. 184 (C2) each only contain two or three folios from it and other manuscripts do not contain it at all.

[20] A. Van Lantschoot, *Inventaire des manuscrits*, pp. 94-96.

[21] D. Wilmshurst, *The Ecclesiastical Organisation*, pp. 118-120.

[22] D. Wilmshurst, *The Ecclesiastical Organisation*, p. 61.

[23] D. Wilmshurst, *The Ecclesiastical Organisation*, pp. 118-120.

	Comments	f33r, f34r, f35r, f59r, f131r, f199r, f251r The names of Diodore, Theodore and Nestorius have been erased and replaced with Cyril, Yōānīs [!] and Ambrosius. f127r Various themes have been erased, such as the Incarnation not being a transaction of nature but of goodwill. The folios from the beginning of this manuscript that contain the hymns (1, 2, 5, 6) are not extant.
	Colophon locations	f36r, f266r-268v, f270v
6	**Vat. Sir. 184 (1568 AD, Vatican Library)**[24]	
	Dimensions	28 x 18.5 cm
	Script	Eastern
	Characteristics	248 leaves, 26 quires of 10 folios, 18 lines to the page
	Copied by	f248r The priest ʿAbdallah in the year 1873 AG [1561 CE] for the Church of Mar Pethion. f248v This book was written by monk Rabban Īšōʿ for the Church of Mar Pethion. f248v Catholicos ʿAbdīšoʿ in the year 188[?], ܢܦܩܣܬܐ [sic].
	Place of copying	f248r Mar Pethion in ܡܪܕܐ Mardin.
	Year	f247v Finished in Tammūz [July], on Tuesday in 1871 AG [1560 CE].
	Hierarchy	f248r The Catholicos is Mar Ēlīā and the Metropolitan is Mar Īšōʿyāhb, Metropolitan of Nisibis, Armenia and ܡܪܕܐ Mardin.
	Owner's notes	
	Comments	f46r, f71r, f135r, f190r, f244r. The names of Greek fathers like Diodore, Theodore and Nestorius have been erased.
	Colophon locations	f247, f248r-248v

[24] J.S. Assemani and S.E. Assemani, *Bibliothecæ Apostolicæ Vaticanaæ*, pp. 388-396.

7	**Diyarbakir 84 (1575 AD, Diyarbakir; now in Mardin, Chaldean Cathedral)[25]**	
	Dimensions	26.5 x 19 x 7.5 cm
	Script	Eastern
	Characteristics	303 leaves, 31 quires of 10 folios, 24 lines to the page.
	Copied by	f300v Archdeacon Yōḥannan the son of the priest Bayram, the son of Brāhīmšāh from Erbil, who lives in Nisibis.[26]
	Place of copying	f300r The book was written in the city of Nisibis .... the river ܡܫܐ Māšā.
	Year	f299v Tuesday in the middle of Latter Tešrīn [November] in the year 1887 AG [1575 CE], and in 980 AH [1572 CE].
	Hierarchy	f300r The Catholicos is Mar Ēlīā and the Metropolitan is Mar Īšōʿyāhb, Metropolitan of Nisibis and Armenia.
	Owner's notes	
	Comments	Marginal notes in Arabic. f59r, f149r, f220r The names of early fathers like Theodore, Nestroius and Narsai have been erased. The name of Nestorius has been replaced with Gregorius. In f282r the name of Christ has been erased, along with the name of Nestorius. f19r-19v, f21r, f35r. Various themes have been erased, such as Joseph having children from a previous marriage, Mary giving birth to Jesus with pain, the doubts of the Jews about the conception of Mary.
	Colophon locations	f299v-300v
8	**Baghdad Chaldean 492 (1581 AD, currently in ʿAinkawā – Erbil, Monastery of St. Hōrmīzd)[27]**	
	Dimensions	29 x 18 cm
	Script	Eastern
	Characteristics	464 leaves, 24 quires of 10 folios, 25 lines to the page.

[25] A. Scher, "Notice sur les manuscrits syriaques et arabes conservés dans la bibliothèque de l'évêché chaldéen de Diarbékir," p. 40.

[26] The colophon about Nisibis mentions the following: 'ܡܕܝܢܬܐ ܐܡܐ ܕܗܝ ܗܝ ܡܩܕܘܢܝܐ ܕܐܢܛܝܘܟܝ' [The capital city which is the Macedonia of Antioch].

[27] P. Haddad and J. Isaac, المخطوطات السريانية والعربية, *Syriac and Arabic manuscripts*, pp. 211-212.

	Copied by	f189 Daniel
	Place of copying	f463 Village of ܟܐܪܒ ܐܘܠܡܐ Kāreb ʾŌlmā or [Ḥarab Olmā][28] near ܡܪܕܐ Mardin.
	Year	f462 1892 AG [1580 CE], in the month of Former Tešrīn [October], on Thursday the 12th.
	Hierarchy	f463 The Catholicos is Mar Ēlīā, and the Bishop is Mar Yaʿqōḇ.
	Owner's notes	f189 This book was for the church of Mar Šimʿūn Kēpā in the village of Kāreb ʾŌlmā.
	Comments	f80, f87, f124, f240, f458-459 The names of early fathers like Diodore, Theodore and Nestorius, Tedasis, Joanianos have been erased. f1, f8, f25, f28. Various themes have been erased, such as Joseph having children from a previous marriage, Mary giving birth to Jesus with pain, the names of the magi.
	Colophon location	f189, f462-463.
9	**Mardin Chald. 42 (1586 AD, Mardin Chaldean Cathedral)**[29]	
	Dimensions	27 x 18 x 8.5 cm
	Script	Eastern
	Characteristics	297 leaves, 29 quires of 10 folios, 21 lines to the page.
	Copied by	f122r Gīwargīs f295r, f296r Ḥnānīšōʿ the metropolitan of ܡܪܕܐ Mardin .
	Place of copying	f294v The book was written in the church of the village of Ṭabyāṯā[30] in ܡܪܕܐ Mardin.
	Year	f294v 1898 AG [1586 CE], in the month of former Kānūn [December] on the 10th, the Saturday before the third Sunday of Annunciation.
	Hierarchy	
	Owner's notes	f295v

[28] D. Wilmshurst, *The Ecclesiastical Organisation*, pp. 80-81.

[29] A. Scher, "Notice sur les manuscrits syriaques et arabes conservés dans la bibliothèque de l'évéché chaldéen de Mardin," p. 77.

[30] D. Wilmshurst, *The Ecclesiastical Organisation*, pp. 81-82.

		The book was kept by Maryam the daughter of Ēlešḇāʿ the Nisibian, the wife of Marōgē from the city of Nisibis. The book was kept for the church of Mar Gīwargīs and Rabban Hōrmīzd in ܡܪܕܐ Mardin. The priests who served in that church are: Hōrmīzd, Marḥā, and Yawsep.
	Comments	f80v, f223v The names of Greek fathers like Theodore and Nestorius have been erased. f2v Various themes have been erased, such as Joseph having children from a previous marriage, Mary giving birth to Jesus with pain.
	Colophon locations	f122r, f294v-297v.
10	**Mingana Syr. 505 (14th-15th centuries, Birmingham, University Library)**[31]	
	Dimensions	280 x 170 cm
	Script	Eastern
	Characteristics	167 leaves, 24 lines to the page.
	Copied by	
	Place of copying	
	Year	
	Hierarchy	
	Owner's notes	
	Comments	Many pages are numbered using Hebrew characters. f15v, f63r-63v, f134v The names of Diodore, Theodore and Nestorius have been erased, with Cyril written under them. The name of Narsai has been replaced by Jacob. f6v, f106r-106v. Various themes have been erased, such as Joseph having children from a previous marriage, Mary giving birth to Jesus with pain.
	Colophon locations	
11	**Diyarbakir 85 (1400-1600 AD, Diyarbakir; now in Mardin, Chaldean Cathedral)**[32]	
	Dimensions	28 x 18 x 6.5 cm
	Script	Eastern

[31] A. Mingana, *Catalogue of Mingana Collection of Manuscripts*, pp. 930-932.

[32] A. Scher, "Notice sur les manuscrits syriaques et arabes conservés dans la bibliothèque de l'évéché chaldéen de Mardin," p. 40.

	Characteristics	221 leaves, 13 quires of 10 folios, 22 lines to the page.
	Copied by	f85r The monk Ēlīā the son of Asmar Ḥabīb from Amida.[33] f220v A note written in Garšūnī as follows: [illegible] [I, Priest Ēnslamōs the boastful, wrote this book].
	Place of copying	f85r In the city of Jerusalem for the Church of Mar Pethion of Amida.
	Year	f85r 1881 AG [1569 CE].
	Hierarchy	
	Owner's note	
	Comments	f39r, f68r, f207v The names of early fathers like Diodore, Theodore, Nestorius and Narsai have been erased and replaced by Cyril, Yōānīs and Ambrosius. The names of Diodore and Narsai have been replaced with Ephrem and John, and the name of Nestorius with John. f5r, f60r Various themes have been erased, such as the doubts of the Jews about the conception of Mary, the names of the magi.
	Colophon locations	f41v, f85r, f220v

[33] D. Wilmshurst, *The Ecclesiastical Organisation*, p. 56.

TEXT AND TRANSLATION

1.(12)[1]

[f. 36r] ܕܡܪܝ ܓܝܘܪܓܝܣ ⸢ܡܕܝܢܝܐ[1] ܕܡܝܟܝܠ ܕܚܝܘܪܐ ܕܦܘܠܘܣ ܕܥܠ ܡܠܦܢܐ ܐܬܬܣܝܡ ܢܒܘܐ ܘܕܘܪܫܝܗ ܩܪܝ ܩܠܐ ܒܥܢܝܢܐ. ܟܠܝܘܡ⸣[4][5]

[1] ܒܪܝܟ ܫܠܝܚܐ ܦܘܠܘܣ
ܕܐܬܟܫܦܘܗܝ ܘܗܘܐ ܢܪܕܝܟ[6] ܥܡܗ
ܘܕܫܠܝܚܐ[7] ܠܬܪܝܢܘܬܐ. ܢܡܣܟܢܘܬܐ
ܟܠܗ ܗܘܐ ܒܪܒܝܬܘܬܐ ܕ [f. 36v]
ܡܢ ܡܠܝܠ ܒܪ ܢܫܐ
ܐܝܟ ܕܐܬܢܨܒ ܡܢܨܚܐ ܥܒܕܐ
ܕܟܠܐ ܢܦܩܠܗ ܒܝܬ ܡܕܒܪܐ
ܕܡܠܐ ܘܡܘܗܒ ܐܝܟ ܚܒܩܘܪܐ
ܕܢܝܚܘ[8] ܗܟܠܐ ܘܗܝܟܠܐ
ܘܢܨܝܚܘ ܠܗ ܐܘܪܚܐ ܠܩܘܪܝܐ ܀

[2] ܐܦܐ ܗܘܐ ܗܢܐ ܢܓܝܪܐ. ܡܢ ܗܘ ܡܕܒܪܐ ܘܢܦܩܐ.
ܘܢܓܕܘ ܒܚܘܪܒܐ[9] ܣܘܪܕܐ. ܟܕ ܐܝܟ ܗܘܐ ܗܘܝܐ ܀

[3] ܗܘܝܘ[10] ܢܛܪܝܢ ܡܠܟܘܬ ܥܡܐ. ܘܡܫܝܚ ܡܠܟܐ ܢܟܠܐ.
ܠܟܝܪ ܕܘܡܝܐ[11] ܪܒܝܬܐ. ܕܢܝܚܘܬ ܠܟܢܫܐ ܢܟܪܝܐ[12] ܀

[4] ܦܬܝܚܐ ܘܫܦܝܪܐ ܚܙܝܢ ܗܘܘ. ܠܘܬܗ ܘܡܫܠܡܝܢ ܫܡܥܝܢ ܗܘܘ.
ܦܬܓܡܐ ܠܗ ܡܢܨܚܝܢ ܗܘܘ. ܐܝܟ ܕܗܘܝܘ ܡܣܬܟܠܢܐ ܀

---

[1] This hymn is found in: M2, B1, D1, C1, C2, D2, B2, M3, G1, D3.
[2] B1 – ܡܕܝܢܝܐ.
[3] ⸣ D3 rep. ܕܡܪܝ ܡܕܝܢܝܐ.
[4] Abbreviation for ܡܢ ܟܠܗ ܘܡܕܡ ܠܟܠܗ ܟܠܝܘܡ ܢܥܢܐ
[5] ⸣ D3 – ܩܪܝ ܩܠܐ ܒܥܢܝܢܐ ܟܠܝܘܡ.
[6] B1, D3 ܢܪܕܝܐ.
[7] B1 ܕܫܠܝܚܐ.
[8] D3 ܕܢܝܚ.
[9] B1 ܒܚܘܪܒܐ.
[10] B1 ܗܘܝ.
[11] B1 ܕܘܡܝܐ.
[12] B1 ܢܟܪܝܐ. Notice in the text how the poet plays with words: ܕܘܡܝܐ ܪܒܝܬܐ. ܠܟܢܫܐ ܢܟܪܝܐ

1.(12)[13]

For the holy Feast of the Epiphany of our Lord. By the luminous, Gīwargīs Wardā. According to "O you womb".[14] Forever[15]

[1] In the year three hundred and thirty-four[16]
of Alexander,
and fifteen of the king Tiberius,[17]
Christ was baptized
by John, the son of Zechariah,
as was predicted by the great prophet:
I heard a voice in the wilderness,
crying out and shouting like a trumpet,
make ready the ignorant and lost ones
and prepare the way to the Lord.[18]

[2] The chosen one came
from the desert of Zipho
and preached in the wilderness of Judea,
saying thus:

[3] 'Repent, for the kingdom of heaven has come near,
and the high king has arrived,
putting on an earthly likeness,
to give life to the race of dust.'

[4] The Pharisees and scribes gathered
near him and listened to his words,
they praised him with fear
as if he was the expected one.[19]

---

[13] For another English translation of this hymn, see: F.C. Conybeare and A.J. Maclean, *Rituale Armenorum*, p. 325.
[14] This means that the hymn should be sung to the tune of 'O you womb'.
[15] To be said by the priest: Forever and ever, Amen.
[16] According to the Greek (Seleucid) era, which corresponds to the time of the baptism of Christ in the Christian era.
[17] See Luke 3:1.
[18] See Matt 3:3; Mark 1:3; Luke 3:4; John 1:23.
[19] See F.C. Conybeare and A.J. Maclean, *Rituale Armenorum*, p. 325, where this verse is translated as follows: This is he that is waited for.

[5] ⸢ܥܡ ܚܘܒܐ⸣[20] ܕܐܬܒܪܘܣ ܡܬܓܢܝܢ. ܦܢܝܐ ܕܦܓܪܗ ܒܠܘܣ[21] ܩܘܡܝܢ.
ܢܦܫܐ ܒܝܫܐ ܒܡ ܕܘܟܝܢ. ܘܐܡܠܝܢ[22] ܡܢܗ[23] ܬܘܒܒܬܐ ⁘

[6] ܚܝܐ ܘܐܡܪ ܠܫܦܝܪܐ ܘܦܪܩܐ. ܢܠܒܐ ܒܝܫܐ ܕܐܦܝܐܝܐ.
ܢܝܪܬܐ ܒܬܪ ܢܝܪܬܐ. ܘܢܠܗ ܕܗܘܐ ܡܢܐ ܠܗ ⸢ܓܘܪܐ ܕܚܝܐ⸣[24] ⁘

[7] ܐܦܝܢ ܡܠܠܝܢ[25] ܒܗܘܢ. ܒܫܡ ܘܦܬܓܡܘܗܝ[26] ܠܐܒܘܗܝ.
ܘܦܪܥܝܢ[27] ܠܗ ܘܢܦܫܢ ܗܝܢ. ܘܗܒܝܐ ܗܘ ܓܝܣܐ ܗܘܐ ⁘

[8] ܐܬܪܥܠܡ ܕܐܝܟܢܐ ܢܗܘܘܢ. ܡܠܠܝܢ ܦܓܪܝܢ[28] ܥܝܢܝܗܘܢ.[29]
ܘܡܢܪܬܐ ܘܚܝܠܗ[30] ܗܘܘ ܠܦܪܘܩܝܢ. ܘܗܝܢ ܘܗܘܢ ܗܘܘ ܠܐܓܪܐ ⁘

[9] ܒܐܝܕܗ ܕܡܠܬܗ ܕܦܪܘܩܢܐ. ܐܘܦܝ ܠܝܫܘܥ ܘܡܫܝܚܐ.
ܦܗܘܘ ܠܟܠܗ ܡܫܝܚܐ. ܦܬܚܝܢܐ ܠܗܘܢ ܓܗܢܐ ⁘

[10] ܗܘܐ ܦܬܚ ܕܘܟܬܐ ܠܝܫܘܥ. ܒܟܠ ܒܝܫܐ ، ܡܠܐ ܗܝܟܠܗ.[f. 37ʳ]
ܕܐܬܓܪܬ[31] ܡܠܐ ܗܝܟܠܗ. ܗܒܝܠ ܕܗܘܐ ܠܗ[32] ܦܘܪܩܢܐ ⁘

[11] ܒܐܓܪܬܗ ܡܬܚܒܫܢܝܢ. ܦܬܝܚ ܒܬܪܐ ܣܒܪܬܗܝܢ.
ܠܫܪܐ ܦܬܪܐ ܡܫܝܚܝܢ. ܗܪܝܡ ܗܘ ܗܘܓܠܝܬܐ ܗܘܐ ⁘

[20] ⸣ B1 ܘܒܚܘܒܐ.
[21] D3 ܠܗ.
[22] B1 + ܠܗ ܗܘܘ.
[23] B1 –.
[24] ⸣ B1 ܦܘܪܩܢܐ.
[25] B1 ܡܠܠ.
[26] B1 ܘܦܬܓܡܐ.
[27] B1 – ܘ.
[28] B1 ܥܝܢ.
[29] B1 ܠܥܝܢܝܗܘܢ.
[30] B1 ܘܚܝܠ.
[31] B1 ܕܐܓܪܬܐ; D3 ܕܐܬܓܪܬܗ.
[32] B1 ܠܗܘܢ.

[5] When he saw [them] gathering towards him,
calling him by the name of his master,
wicked people running [to him],
asking forgiveness from him,

[6] He replied and said to the scribes and the priests:
'Wicked brood of vipers,
serpents, sons of serpents.
Tremble, for doomsday is close.

[7] Snakes kill their mothers
on the day of their mating with their fathers.
They tear her and go out;
so it is with this generation.[33]

[8] Jerusalem, which is their mother,
killed and stoned their prophets.
In the end, they crucified their Lord;
both they and her [Jerusalem] came to destruction.

[9] By the hand of Titus the Roman,[34]
he exterminated the mother and the sons.
They became odious to the world,
and Gehenna is preserved for them.

[10] The wrath has reached
a nation full of foolishness,
trusting that in Abram, full of faith,
it [the nation] will have salvation.[35]

[11] In Abraham[36] you take refuge
and you are proud of the name of a servant.
You deny the Lord and the Son;
your reliance is vain.[37]

---

[33] F.C. Conybeare and A.J. Maclean, *Rituale Armenorum*, p. 325, where this verse is translated as follows: Vipers kill their mother, and in the day of paring their father, and they rend her (?) and go forth, and so is this race. Maclean indicates that the genders in this stanza are confusing but the general meaning is clear, namly a type of the Jewish nation.

[34] Titus was the commander who destroyed the temple of Jerusalem in the year 70, and then became the Roman emperor in the year 79.

[35] F.C. Conybeare and A.J. Maclean, *Rituale Armenorum*, p. 325. Verses c and d are translated as follows: Who in faithful Abram, trusted that it had salvation.

[36] Notice in stanzas [10, 11] the change in the name of Abram to Abraham for the sake of the meter.

[37] F.C. Conybeare and A.J. Maclean, *Rituale Armenorum*, p. 325, where this verse is translated as follows: vain is this your trust.

[12] ܠܐ ܬܫܟܪܘܢ ܘܬܬܥܝܩܘܢ ܒܢܦܫܟܘܢ. ܕܐܒܐ ܐܒܪܗܡ ܐܝܬ ܠܟܘܢ.
ܕܠܗܐ ܡܫܒܚ ܢܦܫܟܘܢ.[38] ܡܢ ܪܘܚܗ ܕܡܠܟܐ ܗܘܐ ܀

[13] ܘܐܢ ܚܒܪܬܟܘܢ ܒܝܬ ܓܒܐ. ܚܠܦ ܕܐܝܬܝܟܘܢ ܠܗ ܒܢܝܐ.
ܗܘ ܒܥܕܬܐ ܡܫܒܚܬܐ. ܘܢܘܗܪܐ ܗܘܝܬܘܢ ܠܥܡܐ ܀

[14] ܡܢܐ ܕܝܠܗ ܠܗ ܕܪܘܫܐ. ܠܐܒܪܗܡ ܗܘܝܬܐ ܒܢܝܐ.
ܡܢ ⌈ܒܢܝܐ ܗܠܝܢ⌉[39] ܫܡܥܐ. ܕܫܡܥܐ ܝܠܕܘܢ ܠܡܫܝܚܐ ܀

[15] ܗܐ ܡܢܟ ܐܬܪܐ ܕܫܠܝܚܘܬܐ. ܠܡܫܒܚܘ ܕܒܝܬ ܦܘܠܘܣ.
ܡܢ ܐܬܠܝܬ ܘܐܬܓܠܝܬ. ܕܠܟܐ ܒܗܘܢ ܫܪܪܐ ܕܡܫܝܚܐ ܀

[16] ܚܠܦ ܐܬܠܝܬ[40] ܕܫܠܝܚܐ. ܫܪܫܗ ܘܫܘܪܗ ܠܐ ܫܟܝܚ.
ܘܠܡܫܒܚ ܗܘ ܠܐ ܫܟܝܚ. ܡܬܦܫܩ ܘܢܦܩ ܒܡܫܝܚܐ ܀[41]

[17] ܫܪܐ ܒܩܕܡ ܡܫܝܚ ܐܢܐ. ܗܘ ܡܫܒܚ ܐܚܪܝܢ ܠܐ ܗܘܐ ܐܢܐ.
ܗܐ ܐܘܐ ܫܡܥܝ ܐܚܪܢܐ. ܘܦܫܝܛ ܠܟܠ ܡܬܦܪܫܢܐ ܀

[18] ܦܘܠܘܣ ܐܢܫܝ ܕܦܬܐ ܐܢܐ.[42] ܠܫܠܝܚܘܬܐ ܠܐ ܫܘܐ ܐܢܐ.
⌈ܘܡܫܝܚܐ ܫܪܪܗ ܠܐ ܗܘܐ ܐܢܐ⌉.[43] ܦܘܠܘܣ ܕܡܫܠܡܢܐ ܕܗܘܐ ܀

[38] B1 ܡܦܝܣ ܠܟܘܢ.
[39] ⌈ B1 rep. ܗܠܝܢ ܫܡܥܐ.
[40] B1, B2 ܐܬܠܝܬ.
[41] B1 – [16].
[42] B1 ܕܡܫܝܚ ܐܢܐ.
[43] ⌈ B1 ܘܐܦܠܐ ܫܪܪܗ ܚܕܐ.

[12] Do not think and tell yourselves
that you have Abraham as a father.[44]
How can he save you
from the anger of this king?

[13] If you are proud of the name of the chosen [Abraham]
because you are his sons,
whereas with your deeds you deny him,
and you became strangers to this one [Christ],

[14] The creator can raise up
many sons for Abraham
from these tough people[45]
whose heart is like stone.

[15] Behold, the Axe of justice is near[46]
to give judgment [and take] vengeance
on the trees and arbors
that do not have tasty fruits.

[16] Any tree that has many
unworthy leaves and fruits
and is not useful for anything
will be cut and fall into the fire[47]

[17] I am baptizing with water,
whereas I do not possess anything else.
Look, another one comes after me,
and He existed before anything that was created.

[18] You think that I am great;
I am not worthy of slavery
and I am not able to untie the straps
of the shoes of this one's feet.[48]

---

[44] See Matt 3:9; Luke 3:8.
[45] See Matt 3:9; F.C. Conybeare and A.J. Maclean, *Rituale Armenorum*, p. 325, where this verse is translated as follows: from these nations children.
[46] See Matt 3:10; Luke 3:9.
[47] See Matt 3:10; Luke 3:9.
[48] See Matt 3:11; Mark 1:7; Luke 3:16; John 1:27.

[19] ܟܐܦܐ ܒܢܘܝܐ ܡܫܝܚܐ ܠܟܘܢ. ܘܫܘܝܬ ܒܗ ܥܕܬܐ ܕܚܘܒܟܘܢ.
ܦܛܪܘܣ ܡܘܕܐ ܡܫܝܚ ܠܟܘܢ. ܕܐܠܗܐ ܗܘ ܡܫܝܚܘܬܐ ܀

[20] ܘܒܡܘܕܝܢܘܬܐ[49] ܡܕܝܢܬ ܢܕܪܘܗܝ. ܘܠܝܫܘܥ ܒܪܐ / ܠܐܠܗܘܬܗ.[f. 37v]
ܦܠܚܬܐ ܫܘܝܬ ܒܟܘܡܪܘܬܗ. ܕܗܝ[50] ܐܝܟ ܠܗ ܫܘܠܛܢܐ ܀

[21] ܐܘܪܚܐ[51] ܫܪܐ ܠܫܘܠܛܢܗ. ܘܝܗܒܐ ܠܟܗܢܝ ܒܢܝܗ.
ܘܢܬܪܐ ܠܫܠܝܚܐ ܒܝܫܘܥ. ܘܠܗܘܢ ܫܘܝܬ ܒܟܢܘܫܝܐ ܀

[22] ܟܕ ܓܝܪ ܗܠܝܢ[52] ܐܡܪ ܗܘܐ. ⌈ܡܫܝܚܐ ܡܪܢ⌉[53] ܢܣܒܘܗܝ ܗܘܐ.
ܘܒܠܒܗ ܢܥܘ ܕܢܬܒܪ ܗܘܐ. ܫܪܐ ܕܘܪܫܐ ܡܢ ܫܘܪܐ ܀

[23] ܟܕ ܐܚܝ ܒܫܠܡܐ. ܟܕ ܫܘܒܚܐ ܒܪܘܚܘܬܐ.
ܘܡܫܒܠܠ ܗܘܐ ܒܪܚܡܬܐ. ܘܐܡܪ ܠܡܪܝ ܫܡܥܘܢ ܀

[24] ܐܝܟ ܒܪ ܫܠܚܐ ܫܡܝܢܐ. ܘܝܗܒ ܠܒܢܝܐ ܡܫܡܫܐ.
ܐܝܟ ܢܘܗܪܗ ܒܥܒܕܐ. ܘܐܝܟ ܡܘܕܝܐ ܕܡܠܟܐ ܀

[25] ܢܐܐ ܓܝܪ ܫܪܪܐ ܒܝܬܐ.[54] ܗܒܘ ܟܠ ܫܪܪܐ ܘܟܠ ܒܘܪܐ.
ܘܐܝܟܢ ܫܒܩܐ ܦܫܝܩܐ. ܠܟܘܢ ܠܝ ܠܐ ܚܢܢ ܐܢܐ ܀

[49] B1 + ܗܘ.
[50] B2 –.
[51] D1, D2, M3, D3 ܐܘܪܚܐ.
[52] D1 ܗܘܐ, added by later hand; D3 ܠܗܘܢ.
[53] ⌉ B1 rep. ܡܪܝ ܡܢ ܫܠܚ.
[54] B1 ܒܒܬܐ.

[19] This one will baptize you with fire[55]
and burn with it the thorn of your wickedness
and will sanctify you with the Holy Spirit,
He, whom God manifested.[56]

[20] With truth, He will purify His threshing floor,
He will collect the wheat in the stores,
He will burn the chaff with His coal;[57]
thus He has the authority.

[21] He will call the winnowing fork His authority,
Wheat for those who do His will,
Chaff for those who despise His kindness,
those He will burn in Gehenna.'

[22] Indeed, when he was saying these [things],
our Lord appeared [to him];
He bowed His head to be baptized
by a priest, the Lord of the high priests.

[23] John answered with fear,
as he cried with dread.
He talked with trembling,
and said this to our Lord:

[24] 'You are the Son of the heavenly king,
I am a poor servant.
You are a mighty ocean,
I am clay and mud.

[25] I am a little lamp,
that needs oil and light.
You are the Sun of truth,[58]
I am not at all useful to You in anything.[59]

---

[55] See Matt 3:11; Mark 1:8; Luke 3:16; John 1:33.
[56] F.C. Conybeare and A.J. Maclean, *Rituale Armenorum*, p. 325, where this verse is translated as follows: for he is God incarnate.
[57] See Matt 3:12; Luke 3:17.
[58] F.C. Conybeare and A.J. Maclean, *Rituale Armenorum*, p. 326, where this verse is translated as follows: and thou art the true Sun.
[59] F.C. Conybeare and A.J. Maclean, *Rituale Armenorum*, p. 326, where this verse is translated as follows: In nothing am I equal to thee.

[26] ܐܢܬܘܢ ܢܘܪܐ ܐܠܗܝܐ. ܘܢܘܗܪܐ[60] ܩܘܕܫܝܬܐ.
ܘܢܪܐ ܐܝܟ ܓܠܠܐ ܘܡܬܚܙܝܐ. ܠܐ ܗܘܝܐ ܠܟ ܡܫܒܩܢܐ ܀

[27] ܚܒܐ ܡܪܝ ܕܟܬܒܘܢ ܩܫܐ. ܘܠܐ ܗܦܟܬ ܐܝܟ ܒܪܢܫܐ.
ܕܟܠ ܗܕܐ ܗܘܝܬ ܒܪܢܫܐ. ܕܟܝ ܢܗܘܐ ܠܟܠ[61] ܦܘܪܩܢܐ ܀

[28] ܡܪܘܒ ܐܬܓܠܝܬ ܐܝܟ ܥܘܠܐ. ܕܢܬܐ ܐܬܐ ܡܘܪܩܢܐ.
ܡܘܪܩܢܐ ܘܡܩܪܒܢܐ. ܡܦܪܩܢܐ[62] ܘܡܦܪܟܢܐ ܀[63]

[29] ܩܡ[64] ܥܠܡܐ ܩܘܢܘܗ ܐܘܪܘܢ. ܕܗܟܢ[65] ܠܡܫܡܠܝܬ ܩܘܡܝܗܘܢ.
ܘܟܕ ܡܫܬܟܚܠܐ ܠܗܘ ܡܫܠܠܘܢ. ܚܕܘܢܐ ܠܡܘܠܕܗ ܕܘܒܪܐ ܀

[30] ܐܘܪܚ ܕܝܘ ܦܕܝܬܐ. ܘܚܘܒܐ ܗܘܐ ܡܢ ܒܪܢܫܐ.
ܒܪ ܦܫܐ ܐܝܟ ܒܪܢܫܐ. ܕܢܗܘܐ ܠܐܢܫܐ ܡܚܝܢܢܐ ܀

[31] ܚܕ ܗܘܝܘ ܡܪܝ ܡܢ ܡܬܐ. ܢܬܩܛܝܠ / ܗܕܐ ܕܡܫܐ.[f. 38r]
ܘܢܝܚ ܚܠܘܡ ܪܘܚܐ ܚܝܐ. ܒܡܘܗܒܬܐ ܕܠܘܫܡܐ ܕܢܘܪܐ ܀

[32] ܠܐ ܓܝܪ ܢܝܚ ܚܠܐ ܦܣܢܬܝ.[66] ܪܘܚܐ ܚܕ ܗܘ ܒܟܠܗ ܡܘܪܕܝܢ.
ܕܠܐ ܢܫܬܪܐ ܕܟܠ ܡܢܬܐ. ܢܝܚ ܘܗܘ ܗܘܐ ˹ܠܗ ܦܣܢܬܐ˺[67] ܀

[60] B1 – ܘ.
[61] B1 ܠܟܠܝ.
[62] C1 illeg.
[63] All the stanzas that come after this word are missing in G1.
[64] D2 ܚܕ.
[65] B1 ܕܗܟܢܐ.
[66] M3 marg.
[67] ˹ M3 written in the sequence ܦܣܢܬܐ ܠܗ but corrected by placing ܒ on ܠܗ and ܐ on ܦܣܢܬܐ.

[26] You are a consuming fire,
and a burning flame.
I am like grass and chaff.
Do not be harmful to me.'

[27] Our Lord answered: 'leave [this] now,[68]
and do not talk like a man.
For this, I became a man,
that through me salvation will be for all.

[28] Come near and baptize me as a priest,
because I am the sacrifice.
The sacrifice and the sacrificer,
The sacrificer and the one who accepts [the sacrifice].

[29] Through you,[69] the priesthood of Aaron is accomplished,
who tried to kill their[70] priests.
Through me, it will be brought to Simon,
till the end of time.'

[30] He bowed His holy head,[71]
and was baptized by a man,
the Son of the Invisible, like a man,
to be the forgiver of humankind.

[31] As our Lord ascended from the water,
the doors of heaven opened
and the living Spirit descended on him
in the likeness of the body of a dove.[72]

[32] The Spirit did not descend on our savior
when He was in the middle of Jordan
in order not to think that He [the Spirit] had descended on John
and that he had been the one who made Him descend.

---

[68] F.C. Conybeare and A.J. Maclean, *Rituale Armenorum*, p. 326, where this verse is translated as follows: Our Lord answered, Suffer (it to be so) now.
[69] John the Baptist.
[70] The Jewish people.
[71] F.C. Conybeare and A.J. Maclean, *Rituale Armenorum*, p. 326, where this verse is translated as follows: The Holy one bowed his head.
[72] See Matt 3:16; Mark 1:10; Luke 3:22; John 1:32.

[33] ܐܝܟ ܢܘܪܐ ܕܠܐ ܦܓܪ ܥܒܕ̈ܝ. ܕܗܘܐ ܦܠܚܝܢ ܒܓܕ̈ܝ.[73]

ܕܣܓܝܐܐ ܘܠܘܚܡܐ ܒܓܒܪ̈ܐ.[74] ܘܫܘܬܐ ܒܥܕܬܐ ܘܫܒܚ ܫܠܝ̈ܚܐ ∴

[34] ܘܩܠܐ ܕܝܢ[75] ܥܡܡܐ ܕܐܡܪܐ. ܕܦܘܡܗ ܓܒܪܐ ܘܓܒܘܗܝ ܠܡܪܐ.

ܢܒܝ̈ܐ[76] ܫܡܘܥܬܐ[77] ܘܒܗ ܡܬܬܡܪܐ. ܒܠܗ ܒܢܝ̈ܐ ܠܒܠܒܝ̈ܐ ∴

[35] ܒܬܓܠܝܬ ܕܠܒܘܫܬܐ. ܐܝܟ ܒܩܠ ܩܕܘܫܬܐ.

ܦܬܚܐ ܒܝܬ ܦܠܚܘܬܝܬܐ. ܘܕܘܚܐ ܕܗܘܝܐ ܡܕܢܚܬܐ ∴

[36] ܠܗܝܢ ܩܕܘܫ ܒܝܬ ܡܪܢܐ. ܕܒܫܘܝܐ ܚܠܘ ܒܗܢܐ.

ܕܒܥܕܢܗܘܢ ܒܪܬܐ ܘܪܥܝܐ. ܒܗܝܐ ܠܥܡܢ ܡܒܢܝܢܐ ∴

[37] ܘܒܫܘܝܐ ܒܪ ܩܪܝܒܐ. ܕܐܝܟ ܐܠܗܐ ܗܘ ܩܪܝܒܐ.

ܕܝܬܒܐ ܒܪܝܟܐ ܡܢ[78] ܫܡܝܐ. ܒܢܝܐ ܢܒܝܬܐ ܘܪܘܚܢܐ ∴

[38] ܦܕܡܩܒܪܐ ܗܘܐ ܡܪܢܐ. ܠܐܢܫܐ ܒܘܝܢܐ ܒܫܝܢܐ.

ܩܪܝܒܐ ܦܬܚܐ ܫܪܝܐ. ܒܗܘܢ ܗܘ ܗܘܝܐ ܠܗ ܦܢܝܢܐ ∴

[39] ܒܩܢܐ ܚܝܐ ܦܬܓܡܐ. ܡܬܦܫܩܝܢ ܒܠ ܠܒܒ̈ܐ.

ܗܘ ܩܪܝܒܐ ܕܟܠ ܒܢ̈ܝܐ. ܒܗܘܢ ܗܘܝܐ ܠܓܝܣ ܡܢܒܓܝܐ ∴

---

[73] B1, D1, C1, D2 ܦܓܪܐ.
[74] C2 ܒܓܒܪ̈ܐ has been added later.
[75] B1, C1 – ܕ.
[76] D1 ܚܡܝܐ; C1 ܚܡܝ; D3 corrected by a later hand to ܚܡܝܐ.
[77] D1, D3 + ܕ.
[78] B1 + ܕ.

[33] Like a dove, the Spirit came on[79] our Lord,
and liberated our race.
Sin and the curse passed away,
death was made idle and Satan was vanquished.

[34] A voice from heaven said:
'This is my Son,[80] and in Him dwells
the will of my Lordship and in Him will be perfected
the whole earthly nature.'[81]

[35] Trinity was revealed,
the Father by the voice of preaching,
the Son by baptism,
and the Spirit hovering over.

[36] Our Savior was baptized in the water
to show His hidden power
which, by its[82] free and unstable nature,
would be the fortifier of our nature.

[37] And to show the Son of the creator,
to be a creator like His Father,
and that He would create creation again,
a new spiritual nature.

[38] Water that brought destruction
to man in the time of Noah,[83]
the Savior and the Lord Son
through [water] became the giver of life for us.

[39] By the living perceptible water
earthly beings were established
and the creator of all natures
through [water] became the renovator of our race.

---

[79] Notice the poet referring to the Holy Spirit in the feminine gender in the Syriac text.

[80] See Matt 3:17; Mark 1:11; Luke 3:22.

[81] F.C. Conybeare and A.J. Maclean, *Rituale Armenorum*, p. 326, where this verse is translated as follows: The whole nature of them of dust.

[82] The water.

[83] See Gen 7.

[40] ܒܩܛܐ ܚܘܪ ܕܡܣܬܥܪܘܢ. ܒܠܗܘܢ ܐܝܟܢ ܕܫܩܠܝܢ ܒܗܘܢ.
ܘܩܕܘܡ ܚܘܒ ܠܝ ܒܗܘܢ. ܢܟܠܬܐ ܚܕܐ ܘܬܘܫܬܐ ܀

[41] ܒܩܛܐ ܩܠܝܠܐ ܡܬܢܠܠܝܢ. ܒܡܝܐ ܥܣܩܐ ܡܬܦܠܚܝܢ.
ܘܗܘ ܐܦܝܢ ܥܠ ܣܘܥܪܢܝ.[84] ܒܗܘܢ ܗܘ ܚܒܝܒ ܠܝ ܥܘܒܕܢܐ ܀

[42] ܡܛܐ ܦܪܨܘܦܐ / ܡܬܦܪܦܪܝܢ. ܘܚܕܘܬܐ ܒܗܘܢ ܡܬܦܬܚܝܢ. [f. 38v]
ܦܬܝܚܐ ܪܘܚܐ ܡܬܦܪܦܪܝܢ. ܘܡܬܢܠܝܢ[85] ܒܢܝ ܐܢܫܐ[86] ܀

[43] ܘܡܠܒܒ ܩܠܝ ܒܠܗ ܡܫܪܝܢ. ܕܐܬܚܙܘܢ ܡܢ ܗܕܡܝ ܦܓܪܝ.
⌈ܐܪܘ ܚܠܡܐ ܡܫܪ ܘܡܠܡܠܐ[87] ܕܝܠܝ⌉.[88] ܢܦܪ ܚܘܒ ܠܝ ܚܝܝܐ ܀

[44] ܡܕܝܢܬܐ ܘܡܫܒܚܬܐ. ܕܠܝܛܝܢ ܗܘܐ ܡܕܪܫܬܐ.
ܦܬܚ ܠܐܘܪܚܬܐ ܘܡܫܡܠܝܬܐ. ܡܕܪܫܬܗ[89] ܕܡܫܠܠܐ ܩܘܬܐ ܀

[45] ܦܠܚܘ ܐܚܝܢܝ
ܘܥܠ ܢܚܬܝܢ
ܕܡܘܚܝܢ ܠܒܝܬܐ ܩܕܫܐ
ܒܢܝ ܐܠܗܘܬܐ ܗܘܝ ܡܫܬܢܝܬܐ[90]
ܘܐܝܟ ܕܠܒܫܝܢ ܒܡܫܡܫܢܘܬܐ
ܦܬܚܝܢ ܬܪܥ ܒܝܬ ܡܠܟܘܬܐ ܀

---

84 B1 ܢܫܬܟܚܝܢ.
85 D3 ܘܡܬܢܠܝܢ.
86 B1 ܕܒܢܝܢܐ.
87 D1, C2, B2 ܒܩܛܐ.
88 ⌉ B1 ܕܝܠܝ ܥܩܪܗ ܕܐܬܚܙܝܬ ܡܫܪ ܐܪܘ.
89 M3 ܡܕܪܫܬܗ.
90 B1, D2 ܡܫܬܢܝܬܐ.

[40] In the water, their [the spectators'] likeness is seen
by all who look into it.
Our Savior showed to us
a living and spiritual image in them.

[41] In the water, the vessels are cleaned,
in the water, the deeds [of guilt] are torn.
He takes vengeance for all the reckonings,
but through [water] He brings salvation.

[42] Water will be made a womb
and the baptized ones are carried in it.
By the power of the Spirit, they will receive limbs
and be born at the same time.

[43] And our Lord was baptized in the Jordan
which comes from two springs,
the symbol of the Nation of Jor and the nations of Dnan,[91]
the merciful one depicted it to us and showed it.

[44] O Holy One and sanctifier,
who for our humankind became the purifier,
sanctify the impure and the ignorant,
the composer of this saying.

[45] For all nations,
and all tongues,
that celebrate this feast,
by Your grace be helpful,
and as we were clothed in You at baptism,
make us rejoice in You in Your kingdom.

[91] The word 'ܥܰܡܳܐ nation' indicates Israel, while ' ܥܰܡ̈ܡܶܐnations' indicates the Gentiles. See: R. Murray, *Symbols of Church and Kingdom*, p. 41. Jor and Dnan are the two springs from the sea of Tiberias. Cf. *Cause of all Causes*: Book 7 -ܡܐܡܪܐ ܕܫܒܥܐ ܕܟܠ ܡܘܕܥܢܘܬܐ ܕܫܪܪܐ, based upon C. Kayser ed., *Das Buch von der Erkenntniss der Wahrheit oder der Ursache aller Ursachen*, Leipzig: J.C. Hinrichs'sche Buchhandlung, 1889. https://syriaccorpus.org/512. [30 September 2021]. The same verse is found in hymn (14)[41], written by Masʿūd Ḥakīm d-bēṯ Qāšā.

(13).2[1]

[f. 38ᵛ] ܐܚܪܬܐ ܕܥܕܬܐ[2] ܕܒܝܫܐ ܀ ܕܒܠܗ ܕܦܬܟܪܐ ܠܚܘܪܒܗ[3] ܀ ܢܐܡܪ[4]

[1] ܒܥܘܬܗ ܕܥܕܬܐ ܩܕܝܫܬܐ
ܬܥܘ ܗܘܘ ܥܡܡܐ ܕܒܪܘܚܐ ܘܥܘܪܐ
ܕܣܓܕܘ ܠܦܬܟܪ̈ܐ ܕܠܐ ܪܓܫܝܢ ܗܘܘ
ܢܡܘܣܐ ܕܣܛܢܐ[5] ܘܒܗ ܬܠܝܢ ܗܘܘ
ܘܡܫܬܥܒܕܝܢ ܗܘܘ ܠܥܒܕܘܬܐ
ܘܦܠܚܝܢ ܦܘܠܚܢ ܛܥܝܘܬܐ ܀

[2] ܫܘܒܚܐ ܠܒܪܐ ܝܚܝܕܝܐ. ܕܠܥܡܡܐ ܩܪܒܐ ܐܝܬܝ.
ܘܐܦ ܠܒܥܘܬܐ ܕܡܟܝܟܐ. ܡܢ ܟܠ ܫܒܩ ܩܪܒܗ ܕܥܡܐ ܀

[3] ܡܢܘ ܕܢܚܙܝܢ ܡܢ ܫܡܝܐ. ܡܢ ܕܢܚܙܝܢ ܕܥܡܐ ܠܓܠܝܐ.
ܘܡܠܟܐ ܠܥܕܬܐ ܕܥܡܡܐ. ܘܡܫܝܚܐ ܒܗ ܝܬܒܐ ܀

[4] ܚܕܘ ܕܡܫܪܝܢ ܒܢܝܗ ܒܠܗܘܢ. ܘܒܥܘܕܪܢܘܬܐ ܦܪܩ ܒܠܗܘܢ.
ܘܠܥܕܬܐ ܚܕܬܐ ܫܘܒܚܐ ܒܠܗܘܢ. ܕܡܠܟܐ ܘܐܦܪܐ ܡܪܝܡ ܒܠܗܘܢ ܀

[5] ܩܠܗ ܠܒܘܣܡܘܬܐ. ܕܗܘܐ ܢܘܪܐ ܕܠܗܒ ܘܐܦܐ.
ܕܢܦܫܗ ܐܢܘܢ ܒܚܐܢܘܬܐ. ܕܠܟܐ ܒܗܘܢ / ܦܐܝܐ ܕܠܚܝܘܬܐ ܀ [f. 39ʳ]

[6] ܡܢ ܕܝܢ[6] ܐܬܐ ܗܘܐ ܠܦܬܗ. ܠܡܫܠܡܘ ܡܢܗ ܒܟܠ ܐܘܡܬܗ.[7]
ܗܕܐ ܗܘܬ ܠܦܬܗܘܢ ܡܠܟܗ.[8] ܘܐܝܕܐ ܩܠܐ ܕܒܪܘܙܘܬܗ ܀

[1] This hymn is found in: M2, D1, C1, C2, D2, B2, M3, D3.
[2] D3 + ܦܪܝܫܬܐ.
[3] M3 + ܦܪܕܝܣܐ; D1 ܠܚܘܪܒܐ.
[4] Abbreviation for ܢܐܡܪ ܒܠܗ ܚܡܫܐ ܐܡܝܢ ܘܐܡܝܢ
[5] M3 marg.
[6] C1 ܗܕܝܢ *c ܡܢ ܕܝܢ.
[7] M3 + +X b.
[8] M3 + +X c.

2.(13)

Another one for the Feast of Epiphany. By the teacher Gīwargīs. Say[9]

[1] By the baptism of the Son, the firstborn,
the ranks of spirit and fire were astonished
that they saw their Lord putting on
a garment of flesh and inhabiting it.
They were full of wonder
and started bestowing praise:

[2] 'Glory to the only begotten Son
that put on a human body
and came for the baptism of water
that His pure body does not need.

[3] Who has made You descend from heaven?
Who brought You, O Invisible, to the visible?
For what is Your baptism of water,
O holy one, the Son of the most high?'

[4] Around Jordan, they[10] all gathered
with wonder, all stood
and to the son of the barren ones, they all listened,
who was screaming and saying in front of all:

[5] 'Woe on Judaism,
the ax has drawn near and come
to cut them with justice,
because they do not have good fruits.'[11]

[6] Then they came towards him,
people from his nation to be baptized by him.
This was his word to them,
and the voice of his calling [preaching]:

[9] To be said by the priest: Let all the people say amen and amen.
[10] The Jewish people.
[11] See Matt 3:10; Luke 3:9.

[7] ܕܘܢܐ ܠܫܡ ܐܝܣܛܘܗܝ. ܠܥܠܡ ܘܫܒܚ ܠܥܒܕܐ ܠܡܫܝܚ ܐܠܗܘܗܝ.
ܐܘ ܟܕ ܠܥܒܕܐ ܚܒܝܒܘܗܝ. ܘܐܝܟ ܕܝܡܝܢ ܐܢܬ ܡܫܒܚܘܗܝ ܀

[8] ܗܐ ܐܢܬ ܐܢܬ ܚܠܘܝ ܟܢܫܐ. ܕܝܘ[12] ܐܝܟܘܢ ܟܠ ܟܠ ܥܒܕܐ.
ܘܝܘ ܡܠܝܟܝܢ ܒܕܘܚܐ ܘܢܘܪܐ. ܘܡܟܠܡܘܕܝܬܐ ܠܗ ܫܕܐ ܀

[9] ܘܟܕ ܡܘܣܝ ܡܫܠܠ ܗܘܐ. ܡܢ ܝܠܕ ܥܕܝ ܐܬܐ ܗܘܐ.
ܠܥܠܡܗ ܕܝܡܝܢ ܝܟܡܕ ܗܘܐ. ܘܝܘ ܗܟܝܢ ܘܥܕܝ ܕܝܐܡܪ ܗܘܐ ܀

[10] ܝܗܒ[13] ܗܝܡܢܐ ܘܫܡܥܢܐ. ܕܝܟܡܕ ܡܢܝ ܟܝܢܐ.
ܐܝܟ ܝܗܘܝܐ ܡܟܠܡܘܕܝܬܐ. ܠܡܕܝܢܬܐ ܘܡܫܡܫܢܐ ܀

[11] ܝܗܒ ܠܗܢܐ ܐܝܟܢ ܠܝܒܐ. ܡܢ ܕܝܘܡ ܐܕܡ ܟܠܟܕܢܐ.
ܠܢܡܘܣܐ ܠܐ ܡܬܠܟܕܢܐ. ܐܝܟܢܐ ܠܗ ܡܠܝܟܝܢ ܐܢܬ ܀

[12] ܘܦܬܚ ܡܕܝ ܟܠܘܡܕܢܐ. ܟܝܡܘܣ ܗܢܐ ܟܗܝ ܝܕܥܢܐ.
ܗܦܟ ܐܝܟ ܠܒ ܝܚܢܢܐ. ܕܝܦܩܪܘܗ[14] ܠܝܠܕܐ ܚܦܪܢܐ ܀

[13] ܐܝ ܝܗܒ ܠܝ[15] ܠܥܡܟ ܐܢܐ. ܠܐ ܗܘܐ ܠܟܘܢ ܡܫܡܫܢܐ.
ܘܐܝ ܟܡܢܐ ܠܐ ܗܘܝܐ ܐܢܐ. ܠܐ ܡܬܡܫܡܫܢܐ ܥܠ ܡܕܝܢܬܐ ܀

[14] ܘܡܕܝܢ ܟܘܢܐ ܒܪ ܚܡܪܐ. ܝܗܒ ܥܕܐ ܕܡܠܟܘܬܐ ܘܟܘܡܪܐ.
ܘܢܟܡܕܘ ܘܝܬܡܫܪܘ ܝܘܡܐ. ܘܝܟܢܐ ܟܡ ܠܥܡܕܐ ܕܟܝܢܐ ܀

---

[12] D1 ܘܝܘ.
[13] D3 marg.
[14] B2 ܕܝܦܩܪܘܗ.
[15] D3 + ܐܝܠ.

[7] 'O miserable ones why do you come towards me?
Why do you want to be baptized by me?
Or why do you look at me,
As if expecting something from me?

[8] There will come after me a man,
Who is the Lord of all.
He will baptize with spirit and fire,[16]
and baptism will gaze at Him.'

[9] While John was talking,
suddenly our Lord came
towards him, to be baptized by him,
he [John] kneeled and started saying:

[10] 'I am in need and poor,
I want to be baptized by You.
How can I become the baptizer
of the Holy and the sanctifier?

[11] I am indeed mud,
from the earthly Adam.
How can I baptize
the untouchable sea?'

[12] Our Lord answered with an order:
'Leave this for now,
because I have the will
to save the earthly race.

[13] If I am not baptized,
there will be no sanctifier for you,
and if in the water I am not immersed,
no fount will be sanctified.'

[14] The priest of the barren ones came
towards the Lord of the kings and high priests,
and he [John] baptized Him, and the ranks were astonished,
the multitudes and the choirs of watchers.

---

[16] See Matt 3:11; Mark 1:8; Luke 3:16; John 1:33.

[15] ܡܢ ܕܫܠܝܛ ܡܢ ܟܠ ܡܬܐ. ܢܝܚ ܪܘܚܐ ܠܟܠܗܘܢ ܒܡܘܬܢܐ.
ܘܫܪܝ ܐܒܐ ܡܬܦܝܣܢܐ. ܕܗܘܐ ܗܘ[17] ܟܕ ܚܝܒܐ ܀

[16] ܠܒܢܐ ܫܠܡ ܗܘܐ ܒܝܪܘܫܠܡ. ܘܒܚܘܒܐ ܘܒܪܚܡܬܐ [f. 39v]
ܘܡܪܝܢ ܦܪܥܝܢ ܐܘܪܚܬܐ. ܠܗܘ ܕܠܐܪܥܐ ܠܒܢ ܚܘܝܬܐ ܀

[17] ܐܘ ܢܘܗܪܐ ܕܟܢܝܫܘܬܐ. ܠܚܝܠܐ ܕܐܠܗܘܬܐ.
ܕܐܝܬܘܗܝ ܕܡܫܡܫܐ ܗܠܟܐ. ܐܝܟ ܕܢܝܫܢ ܕܫܡܫܬܐ ܀

[18] ܐܢܐ ܕܐܝܬܘܗܝ ܢܠܘܕܐ. ܘܒܪܐ ܕܐܝܬܘܗܝ ܝܠܝܕܐ.
ܘܪܘܚܐ ܕܐܝܬܘܗܝ ܠܐ ܡܥܒܕܐ. ܠܥܒܕܐ ܘܠܐ ܗܘܐ ܠܥܒܝܕܐ ܀

[19] ܒܪܐ ܕܡܕܝܢ ܒܡܫܡܫܢܘܬܗ. ܢܥܒܕܝܘܗܝ ܡܢ ܚܛܗ̈ܝܗ.
ܠܪܘܚܐ ܕܗܠܝܢ[18] ܐܘܪܚܬܗ. ܐܦ ܗܘܐ ܦܪܘܩܘܬܗ ܀

[20] ܦܓܠܗ[19] ܚܘܦܐ ܫܘܒܚܬܐ. ܘܟܝܢܐ ܠܗ ܡܢܬܐ ܬܫܒܘܚܬܐ.
ܠܗܡ[20] ܥܡܪܐ ܘܠܗܡ ܢܛܝܪܐ. ܘܠܢܗܪܐ ܕܒܝܬܘܠܬܐ ܀

[21] ܘܚܘܒܐ ܒܪܚܡܝܢ
ܘܠܟܠ ܫܒܝܢ
ܕܫܘܒܚ ܒܐܒܘܟ ܘܒܪܘܚܐ
ܘܐܢܬܐ ܠܟܠܢ ܕܒܫܠܡܘܬܟ
ܢܫܡ ܥܘܕܪܢܐ ܠܐܠܗܘܬܟ ܀

[17] C2, B2 – ܗܘ.
[18] D1, C1, D2 ܕܗܕܐ.
[19] M3 ܦܓܠܝ.
[20] C1 + ܘ.

[15] When He rose up from the water,
the Spirit descended on Him perfectly,
and the eternal Father witnessed,
'This is my only-begotten Son.'[21]

[16] The watchers rose with fear,
love and mercy,
and they started bestowing praise
for the one who made renewal for Adam.

[17] Come, let us confess in the assembly,
the nature of divinity
that is three *qnōmē*,[22]
as we have learned in the Gospel.

[18] The Father who is the begetter,
the Son who is the begotten,
the Spirit who is not begotten,
the maker who was not made.

[19] O Son who sanctified us by His baptism,
wash away the sins of the miserable one;[23]
this is[24] his confession,
and this is his belief.

[20] Give him forgiveness of sins,
and make for him a good portion
with the tax collector and the sinner woman,
and the thief of Golgotha.

[21] With Your mercy, have mercy on me,
and on all Your servants
to confess Your Father and Your Spirit,
and make us all worthy
that in Your kingdom we offer praise to Your divinity.

---

[21] See Matt 3:17; Mark 1:11; Luke 3:22.

[22] I have chosen not to translate the word *qnōmā* so as not to confuse it with the word *parṣōpā*, which the poet uses in other verses. In this I follow S.P. Brock, "The Christology of the Church of the East," p. 131.

[23] Here the poet is referring to himself.

[24] I have translated the word ܕܗܘܐ based on the manuscripts D1, C1, D2. See fn. 18.

(38).3[1]

[f. 91r] ܐܚܪܬܐ ܕܝܠܗ[2] ܕܫܡܥܘܢ ܩܘܩܝܐ ܥܠ ܗܕܐ ܥܢܝ̈ܬܐ: ܘܩܠܗ̇ ܦܩܬܐ[3]

[1] ܒܪ ܐ̈ܢܫܐ ܕܫܒܩܬ ܠܟܐ ܠܗ
ܬܘܩܢܐ ܕܥܘܠܡܐ ܕܟܠܐ ܡܬܕܒܪ ܠܗ
ܘܟܠ ܡܝܢܐ ܡܕܡ ܡܫܬܠܛ ܠܗ
ܒܗ̇ ܕܡܥܒܕܢܐ ܐܝܬܘܗܝ ܟܠܗ
ܘܡܕܡ ܠܐ ܩܢܐ ܕܠܟܐ ܗܘܐ ܠܗ
ܕܟܠ ܡܢܗ ܐܦ ܟܠ ܕܝܠܗ
ܚܘܝ ܠܒܢܝ ܕܫܒܩܬܐ ܠܟܐ ܠܗ
ܠܟܪ ܡܢܢ ܘܬܪܝܢ ܦܓܥ ܠܗ ܀

[2] ܐ ܐܘ ܟܐܢܐ ܘܡܪܚܡܢܐ. ܚܘܣ ܥܠ ܒܢܝܐ ܘܒܪܝܬܐ.
ܕܐܠܗܐ ܒܪܐ ܐܢܘܢ. ܘܝܢܐ ܟܦܪܐ ܘܡܫܠܛܐ ܥܠܝܐ ܀

[3] ܒ ܒܗ / ܗܘ ܒܠܗ ܒܥܘܬܐ. ܘܒܘܝܐܐ ܘܡܫܒܚܘܬܐ. [f. 91v]
ܘܚܢܢܐ ܘܡܬܝܒܘܬܐ. ܘܚܘܒܐ ܘܡܪܚܡܢܘܬܐ ܀

[4] ܓ ܓܥܒܕܐ ܐܝܬܝܟ ܒܐܝܬܘܬܐ. ܘܟܠ ܡܫܟܚܐ ܒܐܠܗܘܬܐ.
ܘܗܘܐ ܬܘܒ ܒܝܫܘܬܐ. ܘܒܫܒܝܚܘܬ ܝܕܥܬܐ ܀

[5] ܕ ܕܘܢܐ ܐܝܬܝ ܒܪ ܐ̈ܢܫܐ. ܘܡܢ ܓܠܝܘܬܝ ܢܛܪܐ ܒܥܒܕܐ.
ܡܢܐ ܐ̈ܢܫܐ ܒܥܘܩܝ ܢܓܝܪܐ. ܘܠܟܐ ܠܝ ܡܫܝܢ ܪܢܝ ܕܘܟܐ ܀

[6] ܗ ܗܘ ܕܕܘܡܝܐ ܒܐܪܥܐ ܠܟܐ[4] ܠܗ. ܘܟܠ ܒܥܡܝܐ ܕܦܢܝܢ ܠܗ.
ܘܗܘ ܓܠܝܘܬܗ ܪܡܐ ܠܗ. ܚܙܐ ܠܗ ܕܢܫܬܟܚ ܚܙܐ ܠܗ ܀

[1] This hymn is found in: M2, D1, C1, C2, D2, B2, M3.
[2] D1 ܕܘܪܕܬܐ.
[3] D2 + ܠܒܪܘܟܝܗ.
[4] C1 marg.

3.(38)[5]
Another one by him who is luminous.
On the Repentance of the Soul: And no limits[6]

[1] O sea of mercy that has no limit,
O ocean of love that is incomprehensible,
nothing can change Him,
because He is perfect, all of Him.
He does not possess what He does not have,
because all is from Him, and all is His own.
Have mercy on Your servant who has no hope,
except You, and open Your door for him.

[2] Ālap[7] O good and merciful one,
forgive the wicked and the cursed,
because You are the merciful God;
I am dust and I am ash.

[3] Bēṯ In You is all grace,
quietness and goodness,
tenderness and peace,
love and mercy.

[4] Gāmal You are perfect in essence
and unlimited in divinity,
like this also in wisdom
and in foreknowledge.

[5] Dālaṯ O miserable man am I,
since my childhood, evil desire
I have in my weak *qnōmā*,[8]
I cannot raise my head in front of You.

[6] Hē He, who has no likeness on earth,
no match for Him in heaven,
He, this one resembles Him,[9]
forbid that He changes, forbid!

[5] For another English translation, See J.K. Hood, "Songs of Supplication," pp. 147-150.
[6] See Ps 145:3; 147:5.
[7] Many hymns in the collection of Wardā are written in alphabetical order. See Table 5.
[8] Hood translates the term *qnōmā* as person. See J.K. Hood, "Songs of Supplication," p. 148.
[9] Christ.

[7] ܘ ܘܝܗܘܕ ܕܒܝܬܐ ܚܙܐ ܠܟ. ܠܐ ܡܫܬܘܕܐ ܚܙܐ ܠܟ.[10]
ܘܠܗ ܒܡܠܟܬܐ[11] ܚܙܝ ܠܟ. ܘܐܢܐ ܡ̄ܠܟܐ[12] ܠܟ ܣܓܕܝܢ ܠܟ ܀

[8] ܙ ܙܕܩ ܐܢܐ ܠܝ[13] ܕܝܢ[14] ܐܢܐ. ܕܒܨܐܢܘܬܐ[15] ܐܬܒܠ ܐܢܐ.
ܘܒܬܪ ܐ̄ܢܐ ܠܝ ܚܠܝ[16] ܐܢܐ. ܕܒܣܒܠܢܘܬܐ ܗܘ ܣܒܠ ܐ̄ܢܐ ܀

[9] ܚ ܚܙܐ ܝܫܥܝܐ ܘܩܪܐ ܐܡܪ ܐ̄ܢܐ. ܘܠܗ ܥܡ ܠܗ ܐܘܕܝ ܗܢܐ ܐ̄ܢܐ.
ܕܠܐ ܡܘܪܕܝܢ ܠܡܪܕܐ. ܐܠܐ ܒܩܝܣܐ ܘܒܚܫܐ ܀

[10] ܛ ܛܥܢܘܗܝ ܠܐ ܡܬܛܠܠܐ. ܘܛܥܢܘܗܝ ܠܐ ܡܬܬܥܒܠܐ.
ܘܐܠܗܘܬܗ ܠܐ ܡܬܚܠܠܐ. ܝܨܪܬܐ ܘܠܟܐ ܠܗ ܕܠܡܘܥܠܐ ܀

[11] ܝ ܝܕܥ ܐܢܐ ܕܠܟܐ ܥܒ ܛܥܢܬܐ. ܘܠܐ ܫܘܝܐ ܠܛܥܢܘܬܐ.
ܛܥܢܐ ܕܠܟܐ ܥܡ ܥܒܕܘܬܐ. ܢܛܝܪ ܠܒ ܥܡܝ ܛܥܢܘܬܐ ܀

[12] ܟ ܟܢܫܝ ܐ̄ܢܘܢ ܡܢ ܥܡ̈ܐ. ܘܥܠܝܢܫܝ ܡܢ ܕܫܥܒ̈ܕܐ.
ܘܠܟܐ ܐܥܒܕܝ ܒܡܥܒܕܐ. ܫܟ ܠܟ ܕܡܫܘܐ ܐܝܟ ܒܢ̈ܝܐ ܀

[13] ܠ ܠܐ ܚܢܢ ܡܠܟ ܐܢܐ ܠܟ. ܘܐܦܠܐ ܚܢܢ ܡܘܬܪ ܐܢܐ ܠܟ.
ܦܠܛܐ ܗ̄ܝ ܡܬܒܪܟܐ ܠܟ. ܥܡ ܡܘܒܠܐ ܠܡܠܘܟ ܠܟܐ ܠܟ ܀

[14] ܡ ܡܢ ܠܐ ܢܥܒܕ ܠܗܘܢ. ܢܬܒܢܐ ܣܘܥܪܝ[17] ܡܬܦܪܩܢܐ.[18]
ܠܐ ܐܬܚܙܝܬ ܠܡܣܦܩ ܪܘܚܐ. ܒܠܘܩܒܠܗ ܪܚܡܐ ܘܡܛܝܒܘܬܐ ܀ [f. 92^r]

---

[10] C2 rep. bc.
[11] D1, C1, D2 ܒܡܠܟܘ.
[12] In M2 a deletion marker has been placed slanted on the letter ܟ instead of ܡ and in stanza [8] it has been placed on the letter ܐ.
[13] D1 + ܕ.
[14] M3 ܕܡ.
[15] D2 + ܗܘ.
[16] B2 marg.
[17] C2, B2 ܟܣܝܘ.
[18] B2 +X ܡܬܩܝܡܢܘܬܐ *C ܡܬܦܪܩܢܐ.

[7] Wāw — And if I have sinned against You,
it is not only me who has sinned against You,
all creation has sinned against You,
You have reconciled, to Yourself, glory to You.

[8] Zēn — You are Just if You give judgment,
because You pursue Justice,
and You are merciful if You have mercy,
because by grace You forgive.

[9] Ḥēṯ — Once I said it, and I will say it,
and the same I will repeat again,
that the earthly one will not be justified
except by mercy and tenderness.

[10] Ṭēṯ — Your goodness is indescribable,
Your grace is immense,
Your divinity does not accept
effects and has no opposite.

[11] Yōḏ — You know that there is no good in me,
and I am not worthy of grace.
O good one who has no evil,
do good to me by Your grace.

[12] Kāp — Your nature is above passions,
and Your thinking above affections.
There is no one like You among the saints;
forbid that You are like the evil ones.

[13] Lāmaḏ — I will not teach You Your nature,
and I will not define my nature to You.
I am presenting to You a supplication,
although You do not need such a thing.

[14] Mīm — From nothing into existence
Your eternal love has brought me.
Do not destroy my miserable *qnōmā*,
because of its great and abundant wickedness.

[15] ܣ ܣܒܪܬ ܠܟ ܥܡܡܐ ܚܛܝܐ. ܒܪܐ ܕܢܘܟܪܝܘܬܗܘܢ ܠܥܡܡܐ ܚܛܝܐ.[19]
ܘܢܘܗܪܐ ܕܐܬܝܢ ܡܢ ܟܠ ܐܬܪ. ܕܠܘܬܟ ܥܒ̈ܕܝܢ ܐܬܪ܀

[16] ܥ ܥܝܢܐ ܕܒܝܫ ܒܥܡܡܐ. ܕܐܢܐ ܥܝܢܐ ܐܢܐ ܒܥܡܡܐ.[20]
ܐܝܟ ܠܟ ܩܪܐ ܣܒܪ ܥܡܡܐ.[21] ܕܡܫܒܚܝܢ ܠܟ ܦܘܡܐ ܥܡܡܐ܀

[17] ܦ ܦܬܟܠ ܡܦܪܫܢ ܒܪܚܡܬܟ. ܡܪܝܐ ܕܐܣܬܟܠ ܐܢܬܘܢ ܒܪܚܡܬܟ.
ܘܡܢ ܣܓܝܐܬܐ ܐܝܟ ܟܠ ܣܓܝܐܬܐ. ܕܫܘܒܚܐ ܘܐܝܟ ܠܟ ܫܘܒܚܬܟ܀

[18] ܨ ܥܡܡܐ ܡܢܗ ܣܒܪܬ ܠܟ. ܡܢ ܩܘܫܬܐ ܠܝܬ ܗܘܐ ܠܟ.
ܘܐܢܘܢ ܕܣܒܪܘ ܣܒܪܬ ܠܟ. ܐܝܟ ܕܡܫܒܚܐ ܐܦܝܗ[22] ܠܟ܀

[19] ܩ ܩܪܝܬܟ ܡܢ ܐܘܪܫܠܡ. ܘܩܕܫܬ ܒܗ ܒܢܝܢܐ ܚܕܬܐ.
ܘܢܘܗܪܐ ܠܒܢܝ ܚܛܝܐ ܠܥܡܡܐ. ܘܒܪܝܘ ܚܟܡܬܐ ܠܒ[23] ܒܗ ܡܥܡܘܕܝܬܐ܀

[20] ܪ ܪܚܡܬܐ ܕܟܠ ܐܢܫܝܢ ܠܗ. ܡܢ ܒܪܘܚܐ ܒܐܠܗܘܬܐ ܐܒܘܗ.
ܠܐ ܕܝܢ ܗܘܐ ܡܬܚܝܒ ܠܗ. ܡܢ ܚܛܗܐ[24] ܕܡܫܒܩ[25] ܠܗ܀

[21] ܫ ܫܘܒܚܐ ܠܚܟܡܬܐ ܒܗ ܘܒܪܘܚܬܟ. ܘܒܐܝܕܝ ܢܒܝܐ ܠܟܠܬܟ.
ܘܢܛܪܐ ܕܫܘܒܚܗ ܡܪܝܐ. ܘܒܫܘܒܚܗ ܕܒܪܝ[26] ܦܪܘܩܢ܀

---

[19] D2, M3 marg. b.
[20] B2 +X b.
[21] B2 ܠܥܡܡܐ.
[22] C1 ܐܦܝܗ.
[23] M3 ܠܗ.
[24] M3 ܚ̈ܛܗܐ.
[25] M3 ܘܡܫܒܩ.
[26] B2 –.

[15] Nūn Let him offer supplication for me,
Your Son that You gave to death for the sake of me.
Lighten Your face on my face,[27]
for my face desires Your promise.

[16] Semkaṯ You do not need supplication,
but I need supplication,
to You, O Lord, I offer supplication,
because my word has no supplication.

[17] ʿĒ You knew me before You created me,[28]
before I sinned, You knew me,
when You saw me as if You did not see me,
I lost You, but You did not lose me.[29]

[18] Pē Who offers You supplication
since You have no partner,[30]
unless Your love is offered to You,
and treated You as You are used to?

[19] Ṣādē You formed me from the earth,
You breathed in me a living soul,
You offered Your Son to death for me,
through Him, You mysteriously provided resurrection for me.

[20] Qōp O Holy one who did not despise
that He made my *qnōmā* by His hands.[31]
Now, He does not despise
the impure who is beseeching Him.

[21] Rēš You had mercy on me and created me,
and with the hands of Your will, You formed me,
You called me the image of Your Lordship,
and by the death of Your Son, You redeemed me.

---

[27] The same verse is found in hymn (115)[52], which belongs to Wardā.
[28] See Jer 1:5.
[29] J.K. Hood, "Songs of Supplication," p. 149, where this verse is translated as follows: and [though] I forgot you, you have not forgotten me.
[30] This might be an illusion to the Islamic idea that God has no partner.
[31] J.K. Hood, "Songs of Supplication," p. 150, where this verse is translated as follows: when he fashioned me with his hands.

[22] ܟ ܫܘܒܚܐ ܠܟ ܡܪܢ ܕܢܚܬܬܟ. ܫܘܒܚܐ ܠܟ ܡܪܢ ܐܘܪܚܬܟ.

ܘܡܢ ܟܠ ܒܡܪܐ ܐܢܐ ܠܐ ܒܥܪܬܟ. ܘܡܢ ܟܠ ܡܪܐ ܐܢܐ ܠܐ ܡܢܝܬܟ⁘

[23] ܗ ܗܦܟܬ ܠܚܘܒܬܗ ܚܝܐ. ܠܚܝܘܬܗ ܒܥܠ ܕܒܒܐ.[32]

ܚܠܦ ܗܘ ܕܥܒܕܐ ܡܫܝܚܐ. ܕܠܐ ܢܬܦܪܥ ܠܟܘܠ ܕܚܘܒܐ⁘

[24] ܐܒܐ ܢܘܚܐ

ܒܪܐ ܚܒܝܒܐ

ܪܘܚܐ ܕܩܘܕܫܐ ܡܬܘܕܝܢܐ

ܒܢܝܐ ܥܡܐ ܚܕ ܬܫܒܘܚܬܐ

ܫܘܒܚܐ ܒܩܝܡܐ ܠܟ ܢܣܩܐ

ܕܢܦܩܝܢ ܠܟ ܚܡܪܐ ܐܦ ܠܟ ܡܫܒܚܢ⁘

[32] D2 marg. b.

[22] Šīn Glory to You; how much You loved me,
Glory to You; how much You exalted me,
and although I am blameful, You did not blame me,
and although I am hateful, You did not hate me.

[23] Tāw O merciful one, let Your grace
at all-time, supplicate Your Justice,
on behalf of this poor servant,[33]
so that I will not be recompensed according to what I deserve

[24] The living Father,
the only-begotten Son,
the eternal Holy Spirit,
hidden Tri-une nature,
have mercy by Your grace on me, a sinner.
My soul is looking to You and putting its hope in You.

[33] J.K. Hood, "Songs of Supplication," p. 150, where this verse is translated as follows: on behalf of your poor servant.

4.(59)[1]

[f. 122v] [2]ܬܘܒ ܒܥܢܝܢܐ ܕܕܘܟܪܢܐ ⌈ܕܩܕܝܫ ܩܘܪܝܩܘܣ⌉[3] ⁘ ܕܩܠܗ ⌈ܐܘ ܕܩܠܗ⌉[4] ⌈ܕܡܠܟܐ ܠܡܘܪܠܝܬ ܦܪܕܐ⌉[5].

ܩܠܠܡ

[1] ܡܪܐ ܕܟܠ ܡܪܘܬܐ
ܐܦ ܢܘܗܪܐ ܕܟܠ ܡܘܗܒܬܐ
ܦܪܘܩ ܢܦܫܬܐ[6]
ܘܡܫܘܪ ܦܓܪܐ[7] ܕܡܫܡܫܢܘܬܐ
ܡܢ ܒܢܝܐ ܕܥܠܝܡܘܬܐ
ܢܨܪ ܗܘܐ ܘܦܪܩ ܗܘ ܩܠܝܬܐ
ܟܕ ܐܝܬ ܒܗ ܡܠܟܘܬܐ
ܠܗܘ ܢܦܫܐ ܕܒܛܝܢܬܐ
ܦܥܒܕܘܬܐ ܕܡܫܝܚܘܬܐ
ܟܕ[8] ܢܗܒܘܢ ܠܥܝܢܐ[9] ܢܝܚܬܐ
ܒܫܒܝܚܘܬܐ ܢܫܒܚܬܐ
ܡܢܗܘܢ ܢܥܡ ܠܗ ܠܫܒܚܬܐ ⁘

[2] ܐܘ ܡܫܒܚܐ ܒܟܠ ܫܘܒܚܬܐ. ܘܫܢܝܐ ܦܓܪܐ ܕܢܘܗܪܘܬܐ.
ܡܫܬܠܡ ܦܪܘܩܘܬܐ ܡܢܝܬܐ. ܘܡܫܬܡܠܝܘܬܐ ܦܬܓܡܐ ⁘

[3] ܗܘ ܕܟܠ ܝܕܥ ܢܟܝܠ ܗܘܐ. ܐܝܟ ܡܫܬܐܠܢܐ ܡܫܐܠ ܗܘܐ. [f. 123r]
ܘܢܦܠܬܗ ܫܪܝ ܗܘܐ. ܕܢܬܩܠ ܘܩܡ ܐܡܪ ܗܘܐ ⁘

[4] ܕܡܢܗ ܓܝ ܫܒܩܐ ܡܫܝܚܢܐ. ܐܡܪ ܢܟܝܠ ܟܠ ܗܢܐ.
ܕܢܘܟܠ ⌈ܕܫܒܩܐ ܗܘ⌉[10] ܒܟܠ ܙܒܢܐ. ܕܢܫܬܒܩ ܚܛܗܐ ܘܡܘܡܐ[11] ⁘

[5] ܡܫܝܚܢܐ ܠܦܪܘܫܘܬܐ. ܕܒܐܠܗܐ ܡܢܘܚܐ ܫܠܡܐ.[12]
ܡܫܝܚ ܘܡܘܕܐ ܒܛܘܒܬܐ. ܕܫܠܡ ܒܢܝܢ ܚܕܐ ܒܪܘܚܐ ⁘

---

1 This hymn is found in: M2, B1, D1, C1, C2, D2, B2, M3, G1, D3.
2 B1 ܐܚܪܬܐ.
3 ⌉ B1 + in marg.
4 ⌉ B1 –.
5 ⌉ M3 ܕܠܡܘܪܠܝܬ ܡܠܟܐ ܦܪܕܐ.
6 D2 ܢܫܝܡܬܐ.
7 M3 –.
8 B1 ܟܕ.
9 M3 –.
10 ⌉ B1 ܕܗܘܐ.
11 B1, D1, C1, D2, G1 ܘܡܘܡܢܐ.
12 D2 marg. b.

4.(59)
Again, hymns for the Commemoration of a Person. By the same teacher Gīwargīs Wardā. Forever

[1] Lord of all lords,
and the giver of all gifts,
and the head of all headships,
the donor of the ranks of the ministers.
In front of the company of the apostles,
He [Christ] depicted and composed this imagery,
which has a teaching in it,
for the heads of the churches,
that by the vigilance of the service[13] -
visiting the sons of the church
with continuous exertion -
He makes their portion perfect.

[2] O those who disgraced the ministry,
and disfavored the rank of priesthood,
they will receive severe hardship,
rebuke and punishment.

[3] He who knew everything,
He questioned like a questioner,
and with His imagery, He started
to tell a parable, and He said this:

[4] 'Who is this faithful servant?'[14]
said this all-knowing one,
to teach how difficult it is at anytime
to find the steadfast and the intelligent one

[5] The believer who firmly believes,
that in God there are three *qnōmē*.
Believing and confessing the doctrine,
that one sonship is in two natures.

---

[13] By respecting their priestly rank. See stanza [2].
[14] See Matt 24:45-51; Luke 12:41-48.

[6] ܚܒܝܫܐ ܠܦܪܢܣܘܬܐ. ܡܕܒܪܐ[15] ܠܒܘܫܐ ܕܡܕܒܪܢܘܬܐ.

ܘܢܘܪ ܙܕܩܐ ܒܟܠܝܬܐ. ܘܡܦܪܢܣ ܕܠܐ ܒܝܫܘܬܐ ܀

[7] ܘܐܦ[16] ܡܠܟ ܚܠܝܐ. ܘܐܦ ܗܘܐ ܡܟܝܟܐ.

ܘܐܦ ܗܘܐ ܕܝܢܐ. ܘܐܦ ܗܘܐ ܡܪܚܡܢܐ ܀

[8] ܒܗܝ[17] ܕܐܚܝܕܗ ܟܠ ܒܐܝܕܗ. ܗܘܝܘ ܕܝܢ ܟܠ ܟܠܗ ܢܝܚܬܗ.

ܦܩܕܬܐ ܠܡܠܟܘܬܗ. ܡܪܐ ܘܪܒܐ ܠܒܪܝܬܗ ܀

[9] ܛܘܒܐ ܠܗ ܠܥܒܕܐ ܗܢܐ. ܐܝܟ ܦܘܩܕܢܐ ܡܪܢܐ.

ܠܐ ܢܛܪ ܡܪܗ ܡܠܬܐ. ܘܢܫܬܡܥܘܢ ܕܥܒܕ ܗܘܢܐ ܀

[10] ܒܐܪܥ ܢܦܩ ܘܢܛܪ ܠܗ. ܕܢܫܬܡܥܘܢ ܟܠ ܟܠ ܕܐܝܬ ܠܗ.

ܗܘܝܘ ܕܝܢ ܕܡܫܬܘܕܥ ܠܗ. ܒܒܘܫܡܗܘܢ[18] ܘܡܢܝܚܐ ܠܗ ܀

[11] ܘܠܐ ܐܝܟ ܒܝܫܘܬ[19] ܬܪܥܝܬܗ. ܘܐܝܟ ܦܠܓܘܬܐ ܕܡܫܝܚܘܬܗ.

ܢܪܕܐ ܕܘܒܪܐ ܕܡܠܬܝܬܗ. ܕܡܪܗ ܕܢܨܝܒܐ[20] ܗܘ[21] ܫܠܡܗ ܀

[12] ܘܝܗܒܐ ܐܘܪܚܬܝܬܐ. ܘܐܬܚܙܝ ܘܝܗܒܐ ܬܫܒܘܚܬܐ.

ܘܢܪܘܐ ܒܡܫܪܐ ܕܠܝܠܝܐ. ܘܬܫܠܡܘܬܐ ܒܫܠܝܐ ܀

---

[15] B1, D2, G1 ܡܕܒܪܢ.
[16] B1 – ܘ.
[17] G1 ܘܒܗܝ.
[18] B1 ܢܛܪ ܒܫܡܗܘܢ.
[19] B1 ܡܫܝܚܘܬ.
[20] B1, C1, D3 – ܕ.
[21] C2 – ܗܘ.

[6] The wise who with wisdom,
educates the herds of the parishes,
and gives prescriptions as is due,
and manages without wickedness.

[7] Sometimes he teaches a discipline,
and sometimes he is a tithe collector,
sometimes he becomes a judge,
and sometimes a forgiver.

[8] Because He [Christ] appointed him over His house,
that is, over the sons of His church,
He calls His teaching food,
and its moment his days.[22]

[9] 'Blessed is this servant.'
the living mouth has said,
if his Just master comes[23]
and finds that he is doing this.

[10] With Amen, He sealed it and swore,[24]
that He will appoint him over all that He has,
that is, He will make him partake
in His enjoyments and will make him rejoice.

[11] But if according to his wicked mind
and the duplicity of his thinking,
he thinks that the hour of the time of the coming
of his master is far,[25]

[12] and he starts in greed,
eating and drinking diligently,
becoming drunk with wine publicly,
and secretly with dishonesty,

---

[22] Translation uncertain.
[23] See Luke 12:37.
[24] See Luke 12:44.
[25] See Luke 12:45.

[13] ܘܢܘܣܦ ܢܒܥܝܢ[26] ܡܢܗܘܬܗ. ܡܥܢܝܬܐ ܟܠܠ[27] ܚܢܢܘܬܗ.
ܘܢܡܕܘܪ ܘܢܛܠܐ ܡܠܟܘܬܗ. ܕܡܪܗ ܗܘ ܢܒܥܐ ܕܝܢܬܗ ܀

[14] ܢܐܦܐ ܡܪܗ[28] ܡܢ ܢܠܝܐ. ܒܢܘܗܪܐ ܕܠܐ ܡܥܒܕ ܪܘܚܐ.
ܘܢܦܠܓܝܘܗܝ ܒܢܐܡܪܗ ܡܥܢܐ. ܘܢܟܠܒܝܘܗܝ ܥܒܕܐ ܘܡܫܠܚܐ ܀

[15] ܢܒܒܐ ܕܡܢ ܒܝܬ ܢܒܝܐ. ܡܪܐ ܠܒܘܝܐ ܡܒܣܪܐ. [f. 123v]
ܕܡܥܒܪ ܕܪܫܝܡ ܗܘܐ ܕܝܢܐ. ܘܕܠܝܐ ܡܢܡܬܐ ܘܒܘܣܪܐ ܀

[16] ܡܢܘܬܐ ܕܢܢܘܬܗ. ܡܪܐ ܠܒܝܬܗ ܢܟܠܬܗ.
ܕܢܦܩܝ[29] ܕܚܘܪ ܠܒܢܝܬܗ.[30] ܗܘܠܐܐ ܢܡܪܩܝܢ ܒܝܠܬܗ[31] ܀

[17] ܒܘܠܝܢ ܗܕܝܠ[32] ܡܢܐ ܠܗܘܢ.[33] ܠܒܢܘܬܗ ܘܡܒܝܥ ܠܗܘܢ.
ܕܒܗ ܗܘ ܚܝܠܐ ܘܡܒܪܟ ܠܗܘܢ.[34] ܠܕܝܢܐ ܕܢܪܐܬܐ[35] ܡܥܠܡ ܠܗܘܢ ܀

[18] ܘܡܠܘܟ ܦܘܠܘܣ ܡܦܩܕ ܠܗܘܢ. ܠܡܦܩܢܘܬܐ ܘܐܡܪ ܠܗܘܢ.
ܕܐܢ ܒܐܢܫܘܢ ܡܫܡܠܝܢܘܢ. ܡܥܒܕܢܐ ܗܘ ܢܝܪܐ ܡܫܡܠܝܢܘܢ ܀

[19] ܗܢ[36] ܕܐܡܪ ܠܟܘܠܗܘܢ ܕܢܦܠܓܝܘܗܝ. ܘܟܠ ܢܟܣܐ ܒܐܦܐ ܢܣܝܡܝܘܗܝ.
ܕܡܢ ܘܕܝܢܐ ܢܦܪܥܝܘܗܝ. ܘܡܢ ܒܒܝ ܡܠܟܘܬܐ ܢܪܚܩܝܘܗܝ ܀

[20] ܗܕܐ ܐܝܬܝܗ ܦܠܝܓܘܬܐ. ܦܘܪܫܢܐ ܘܡܕܝܢܘܬܐ.
ܕܡܢ ܢܛܘܪܬܐ ܕܡܠܟܘܬܐ. ܒܗ ܡܬܦܠܓ ܡܢ ܓܗܢܘܬܐ ܀

---

26 G1 + ܘ.
27 B1 ܟܠܡ.
28 C1 + + ܡܪܗ.
29 B1 ܘܢܦܩܝ.
30 B1 ܠܒܢܝܬܗ.
31 B1 ܒܝܠܬܗ.
32 B1 ܗܕܡ.
33 B1 ܡܢܘܐ ܠܗܘܢ.
34 B1 ܘܡܒܪܟ ܠܗܘܢ.
35 B1 ܕܝܢܐ ܘܢܪܐܬܐ.
36 M3 ܘܗ.

[13] increasingly dealing blows,
in a strong way, on his companions,
the kingdom of his master will draw near,
while he is immersed in sleep.

[14] His master will come suddenly
in a day that this miserable one did not imagine.[37]
He will put him aside with harsh words
and make him despised and denied.

[15] Then the servant with ill will,
will call the bodily priest,
to hope that the day of judgment will be far,
and that there is no resurrection and examination.

[16] The wounds of his fellows,
he designates them as his evil deeds,
when they see his deeds,
many will fail because of him.

[17] With these, he hits them, his fellows,
and harms them,
because he sinned and seduced them,
and handed them over for the final judgment.

[18] And about this, Paul ordered
the Corinthians, and told them:
'If you offend your brothers,
then you offend Christ.'[38]

[19] He [Christ] told them that He will separate them,
and will place them with the hypocrites;
they will be segregated from the righteous ones,
and will be kept away from the sons of the kingdom.

[20] This is the separation,
segregation and division,
from the inheritors of the kingdom,
while he is deprived of grace.

---

[37] See Luke 12:46.
[38] See 1 Cor 8:12.

[21] ܢܒܝܐ ܫܡܘܐܝܠ ܢܒܝܐ. ܥܕܬܐ ܟܠܗ ܗܘ ܝܗܒܐ.
ܕܐܠܗܐ ܒܠܒܐ ܡܫܝܚܐ. ܕܡܕܒܪܘ ܡܬܩܢܐ ܘܡܠܐܟܐ܀

[22] ܗܢܘ ܡܫܡܫܢܐ ܥܒܕܐ. ܕܐܝܟ ܫܡܥܘܢ ܐܬܬܘܗ ܠܡܥܒܕܐ.
ܘܗܝܡܢܘܬܗ ܐܝܟ ܢܘܗܪܐ. ܠܟܠܗ ܥܠܡܐ ܢܗܘܪܐ܀

[23] ܗܢܘ ܢܒܝܐ ܠܡܥܒܕܐ. ܘܡܕܒܪܢܐ ܥܒܕܐ.
ܕܝܗܒ ܠܢܦܫܐ ܚܝܝܐ. ܘܡܫܡܫ ܠܢܦܫܐ ܕܫܡܝܐ܀

[24] ܗܢܘ[39] ܕܒܗ ܒܚܕܝܬܐ.[40] ܠܡܥܒܕܐ ܘܠܐ ܠܡܥܒܕܐ.
ܗܝܡܢܘܬܐ[41] ܥܒܕܬܐ. ܘܚܘܒܐ ܘܫܒܪܐ ܕܟܠ ܡܢܬܐ܀

[25] ܗܢܘ ܢܒܝܐ ܫܡܘܐܝܠ. ܕܐܡܪ ܥܕܬܐ[42] ܢܒܝܐ.
ܠܗ ܫܡܘܐܝܠ ܒܗܢ ܕܡܠܐܟܐ. ܘܠܗ ܥܕܬܐ ܗܘ ܒܢܘܗܪܐ܀

[26] ܠܢܒܝܐ ܢܒܝܗ[43] ܕܐܚܝܢܐ. ܡܫܡܫܢܘ ܕܗܘ ܒܢܘܗܪܐ.
ܐܘ ܕܢܒܝܗ ܠܟܠܗܘܢ ܥܡܡܐ. ܒܫܒܝܚܘ ܫܡܝܐ ܐܚܝܢܐ܀

[27] ܘܐܝܟ ܫܡܘܐܝܠ
، ܘܐܝܟ ܫܡܘܐܝܠ [f. 124r]
ܢܒܝܐ ܝܗܒܐ ܕܡܫܡܫܗ
ܘܥܕ ܚܘܒܐ ܠܡܫܡܫܢܘܬܗ
ܘܠܗ ܒܥܒܘܕܘܬܐ
ܡܢ ܟܠ ܦܘܩܕܢ
ܡܥܕܢܐ ܫܒܚܐ
ܠܟܠܗ ܥܠܡܝܢ܀

[39] B1 + ܘܗ.
[40] B1 ܡܥܒܕܬܐ.
[41] B1 + ܘ.
[42] B1 ܥܕܬܐ.
[43] B1 ܢܒܝܗ.

[21] But the first servant,
Mar, so and so,[44] the chosen,
who is exalted in the Christian people,
his glorious and fruitful commemoration.

[22] This is the true believer,
perfect like Simon,
and his faith is like light,
which enlightens all his people.

[23] This is the ideal wise
and diligent guardian,
who heals the broken hand
and slaps the hand that strikes.

[24] Here is he who gave us hope,[45]
perfect and not ephemeral,
true faith,
love and hope in the resurrection.

[25] Here is the good servant,
mentioned by the merciful Lord.
For him, the beatitude and commemoration
and for us, our Lord, give salvation.

[26] For the servant, the companion of the last one,
the translator of this story,
who made Saul a chosen one,
make him the last repentant one.

[27] According to Your grace,
and according to Your goodness,
change the punishment of his wounds,
and give forgiveness to his sins.
To You glory,
from all our mouths,
Christ, our hope,
forever and ever.

---

[44] 'So and so', it can be replaced with the name of any saint.
[45] I depend on B1 for translating this word.

[1](67).5

[f. 138r] [2]ܒܥܘܢܝܬܐ[3] ܕܡܕܒܚܢܘܬܐ[4] ⌜ܕܦܬܓܡܐ ܨܘܡܐ ܡܩܕܫܐ܀ ܕܝܠܗ ܥܡ ܕܝܠܗ ܕܟܘܠܗܘܢ ܦܪܨܘܦܐ܀ ܥܠܡܐ⌝[5]

[1] ܒܪܝܟ ܕܨܘܡܗ ܡܫܝܚܐ
ܦܪܩ ܚܘܒܘܗܝ ܕܓܢܣܐ ܕܐܢܫܐ[6]
ܘܢܛܪܗ ܘܐܣܩܗ ܠܫܡܝܐ
ܕܗܘܐ ܠܒܢܝܢ ܡܫܡܠܝܢܐ
ܘܦܫܛܗ ܘܫܠܡܗ ܠܡܘܠܕܝܗ
ܘܫܒܩܗ ܐܦ ܠܟܠܗ ܥܡܗ܀

[2] ܐܦ ܕܨܡܢ ܒܗܝܡܢܘܬܐ. ܨܘܡܐ ܕܢܟܦܢ ܒܘܚܕܬܐ.
ܫܡܥܘ ܒܝܘܡܐ[7] ܕܦܘܪܩܢܐ.[8] ܥܠ ܕܟܠ ܨܘܡܐ ܩܕܝܫܐ܀

[3] ܕܟܝܢܐ ܐܝܟ ܦܘܪܩܢܐ. ܘܐܝܟ ܗܘܐ[9] ܡܢ ܐܒܗܬܐ.
ܢܦܫ ܗܘܐ ܡܢ ܗܘ ܓܝܪ ܠܥܘܠܐ. ܠܐܪܥܐ ܕܫܒܝܚܬܐ ܡܠܟܐ܀

[4] ܘܦܠܚ ܒܥܒܘܕܘܬܐ ܠܨܘܡܐ. ܘܠܒܢܝܐ[10] ܥܡܡܐ ܢܟܦܐ ܫܒܚܐ.
ܘܗܢܘܢ ܒܩܢܘܢܐ ܕܡܢ ܒܬܘܠܘܬܐ. ܘܚܝܐ ܠܒܝܫܐ ܐܠܗܝܐ܀

[5] ܥܡ ܒܢܝܢ ܦܓܪܗ ܡܫܝܚܐ. ܗܘ ܠܗ[11] ܟܢܫܐ ܡܢ ܟܠ ܐܢܫܐ.
ܘܢܬܠ ܠܟܠܗܘܢ ܚܘܒܐ ܕܩܘܫܬܐ. ܕܗܘ ܐܒܐ ܡܚܣܢܐ ܘܡܪܚܡܢܐ܀

[6] ܦܬܚ ܬܪܥܐ ܡܢ ܫܡܝܐ. ܘܢܬܠ ܠܟܠܗܘܢ / ܚܘܒܐ ܒܝܠܕܐ. [f. 138v]
ܘܐܬܚܕ ܠܟܠܗܘܢ ܐܒܐ ܚܢܢܐ. ܕܗܘܝܘ ܝܗܒ ܚܝܐ܀

---

[1] This hymn is found in: M2, B1, D1, C1, C2, D2, B2, M3, G1, D3.
[2] B1, D3 + ܐܚܪܬܐ.
[3] B1 – ܒܥܘܢܝܬܐ.
[4] B1 + ܕܐܪܒܥܐ ܕܨܘܡܐ ܥܠ ܦܪܝܐ ܫܠܬܐ ܕܡܫܡܫ ܡܪܝ ܥܡ ܫܡܝܐ.
[5] ⌝ B1 –.
[6] C2 marg.
[7] B1 ܒܝܘܡܗ.
[8] M2 + + ܕܦܘܪܩܢܐ.
[9] D3 ܗܘܐ has been added later by the copyist.
[10] D3 ܘܠܒܢܝܐ.
[11] D3 ܕܠܗ.

5.(67)

A hymn on the Sunday of the Beginning of the Lord's Fasting. By the same Gīwargīs Wardā. Forever

[1] Blessed is the One who, by His holy fasting,
paid for the sins of the human race.
He suppressed and shamed the devil,
who was the misleader of our race.
He brought down and abolished his authority
and also broke all his weaponry.

[2] O you who fast with faith
the fifty days fasting,
listen with ears of sagacity;
words about pure fasting.

[3] Adam neglected the command
and ate from the tree,[12]
then he went out from that bridal room
to the earth full of curses.

[4] He worked slavery for death
and evil for six thousand years,
and our Lord with a body from the Virgin,
purified the human race.

[5] His holy body was baptized,
which is not made from human seed,
and the Holy Spirit descended on him,[13]
on that majestic and pure head.

[6] After He ascended from the water,
the Spirit descended on Him publicly,
and the Invisible Father witnessed about Him:
'This is my only-begotten Son.'[14]

---

[12] See Gen 3:6.
[13] See Matt 3:16; Mark 1:10; Luke 3:22; John 1:32.
[14] See Matt 3:17; Mark 1:11; Luke 3:22.

[7] ܒܝܫܐ ܕܝܢ ܦܬܠܐ ܥܩܡ ܗܘܐ. ܐܬܦܬܠ ܘܐܬܗܦܟܦܟ ܗܘܐ.

ܘܦܫܛܗ ܥܩܡܐ[15] ܘܝܫܪܗ ܡܫܚ ܗܘܐ. ܕܢܬܪܝܫ ܒܗܘܢ ܠܟܪ ܢܟܠܐ ✣

[8] ܘܚܙܐ ܕܐܦ ܒܝܠܕܘܬܐ. ܕܡܢܗ ܗܘܐ ܠܟܝܢܐ ܦܓܪܐ.

ܕܢܦܩܘܗ ܠܠܡܘܬ ܡܢܐ[16] ܕܢܘܪܐ. ܕܠܐ ܡܬܚܙܐ ܢܬܚܙܐ[17] ܒܝܕ ܥܩܡܐ ✣

[9] ܚܝܘܗܝ ܕܒܪܢܫܐ ܗܘ ܗܢܐ. ܐܝܟ ܐܕܡ ܒܗ ܠܟܠܗ ܐ̈ܢܫܐ.

ܘܐܢ ܐܠܗܐ ܗܘ[18] ܡܬܚܙܝܢܐ. ܕܢܬܚܙܐ ܠܟܝܢܐ ܦܓܪܐ ܡܠܟܐ[19] ✣

[10] ܢܚܬ ܒܐܝܕܗ ܢܦܫܗ ܡܫܝܚܐ. ܘܢܚܬ[20] ܠܟܝܢܗ[21] ܢܦܪܐ ܕܝܡܝܢܬܐ.

ܘܢܚܡܝ ܒܗ ܓܒܠܐ ܕܦܓܪܐ.[22] ܕܢܬܩܢ ܒܦܪܨܘܦܗ ܕܥܠܡܐ ✣

[11] ܦܪܝ ܢܦܫܗ ܠܡܫܬܡܠܝܘ. ܢܦܠܐ ܦܓܥܬ ܒܦܘܪܩܢܗ.

ܘܦܬܝܬ ܠܡܫܬܡܠܝܐ ܕܝܬܝܪܐ. ܢܦܫܐ ܢܦܠܬ[23] ܡܢ ܥܠܡܐ ✣

[12] ܘܟܠ ܗܕܐ ܢܦܫ ܗܘܐ ܠܡܫܡܠܝܐ. ܕܗܘ ܢܬܚܝܒ[24] ܦܓܪܐ.

ܒܗܘ[25] ܦܓܪܝܢ ܠܟܠ ܒܢܝ ܢܫܐ. ܕܠܝܬ ܒܗ ܩܘܫܬܐ ܐܢܫܐ ✣

[13] ܐܦ ܗܘ ܦܪܝ ܓܒܐ ܒܢܝܐ. ܕܢܬܒܢܐ ܠܗܘ ܗܝܟܠܐ.

ܕܡܢ ܠܐ ܦܪܝܫ ܒܪܢܫܐ. ܢܬܪܘܡ[26] ܦܓܪܢܐ ✣

---

[15] M2 illeg; in C1 this word has been added later by the copyist.
[16] B1 ܡܠܐ.
[17] B1 ܢܬܚܙܐ.
[18] D3 ܗܘ has been added later by the copyist.
[19] B2 ܡܠܟ; M3 marg.
[20] D2 ܕܢܚܬ.
[21] G1 ܠܗ.
[22] B1 ܕܢܚܬܐ.
[23] D1 +X ܟܝ.
[24] B1 ܢܬܚܝܒ ܗܘܐ.
[25] B2 ܒܗ.
[26] B2 + ܕ.

[7] When the evil one heard this voice,
he was agitated and embittered;
he took his sword and tightened his bow,
to hit the Son of the Most High.

[8] Then the enemy started to think:
'Who is this one clothed in a body
About whom I heard voices of wonder,
Which had not been heard before under heaven?

[9] If this is a man,
I will do to Him like [I did to] Adam,
and if He is God, I know,
He will destroy me, the one clothed in a manifested body.'

[10] He took the rough bow in his hand,
and put on it high heat,
and placed in it the arrow of enmity,
to fire it on His pure limbs.

[11] Our Lord knew his thought,
before it was fashioned in his mind,
He preceded him to the desert to expose his cunning deeds,
[and] destroy [them] immediately.

[12] For this, He went out to the desert,[27]
so that the dwelling place would be made there,
because it was dreadful for human beings,
with no human voice in it.

[13] And also there, the evil one was willing
to have a fight with Him,
so that because no human being could draw near,
the bodily one would be frightened.

[27] See Matt 4:1; Mark 1:12; Luke 4:1.

[14] ܩܪܐ ܐܪܥܝܢ[28] ܢܘܗܪܐ. ܕܢܚܡ[29] ܡܪܝ ܒܟܠܠܘܬܐ.[30]
ܘܡܢ ܒܝܠܕܪܐ ܐܬܐ. ܕܢܣܒܪ[31] ܓܒܠܐ ܠܗ ܐܪܥܐ ܀

[15] ܡܪܝ ܕܡܢ ܒܗܢ ܝܒܢܘ.[32] ܝܗܡܝܠ ܘܢܒܒܝܗ ܠܚܒܝܗ.
ܕܝܗܒ ܠܗ ܠܡܫܢܝܗ. ܐܬܪܐ ܒܡܕܒܚܗ ܡܢܗ ܀

[16] ܠܟܝܢ[33] ܕܡܫܝܚܐ ܘܚܝܐ. ܘܕܦܐ[34] ܗܘܐ ܠܗܘ ܕܦܓܪܐ.
ܘܓܒܪܐ ܠܢܦܫܗ ܢܚܫܒܐ. ܘܢܣܒܗ ܘܓܦܝܐ ܘܢܘܪܐ ܀

[17] ܘܢܣܒ ܘܐܬܐ ܡܪܘܡܐ. ܘܡܩܠܠ ܥܡ ܒܪ[35] ܐܢܫܘܬܐ.
ܕܠܘܬ ܕܡܢܗ ܠܐܒܘܬܐ. ܒܟܠ ܡܕܒܚܐ ܗܘܐ ܒܗܢܐ[36] ܀

[18] ܐܝ ܐܢܫܘ[37] ܒܕܝܗ ܕܐܠܗܘܬܐ. ⸍ ܐܬܚܙܝܗ ܐܢܫ ܕܐܠܗܘܬܐ. [f. 139r]
ܦܘܡܐ ܡܠܐ ܐܝܟ ܐܠܗܐ. ܘܚܝܠܐ ܕܐܠܗܐ ܠܗܘܪܝܐ ܀

[19] ܘܟܠܐ ܢܣܒܗ ܚܘܒܐ. ܘܡܢܗ ܕܫܡܝܐ ܘܣܢܝܐ.
ܠܗ ܢܦܫܝ ܘܐܦ ܥܡ ܡܪܐ. ܕܘܟܐ ܕܢܦܫܗ ܗܘ ܡܫܒܚܐ ܀

[20] ܘܚܙܝܗ ܡܪܝ ܒܢܝܢܗ. ܘܦܬܚ ܠܗ ܒܡܫܟܢܗ.
ܕܠܗ ܒܢܣܒܐ ܠܡܘܪ ܣܓܝ ܐܝܬ. ܠܐܢܫܐ ܐܠܐ ܒܝܠܕ ܡܪܝܐ ܀

---

[28] B1 + ܕ.
[29] B1 – ܕ.
[30] B1 ܘܒܟܠܠܘܬܐ.
[31] D3 marg. only the letter ܒ.
[32] B2 +X ܝܒܢܘܗ.
[33] B1 ܠܒܝܬ.
[34] B1, D1, C1, D2, G1 ܕܕܦܐ.
[35] B1 ܒܪܐ.
[36] M3 ܡܫܢܐ + in marg. ܒܗܢܐ.
[37] D1 ܐܢܫ ܗܘ.

[14] After forty days,[38]
when our Lord fasted during the nights,
then the enemy came
so that the fox would fight with the Lion.[39]

[15] Then our Lord, by His will,
became weak and strengthened His hunger,
to give to the tempter,
a place for His severe fighting.

[16] The spiritual one put on weaponry,
and looked like the bodily one;
He made himself like the poor
the foreigner, the hungry and the thirsty.

[17] The rebellious one came close
and talked to the Son of the Creator:
'Why do You look like a mortal being
in this desolate desert?

[18] If You are the Son of God,
like Him, You are God,
give an order now, like God,
and change the stones to bread.[40]

[19] Show Your mighty power,
and have mercy and compassion,
on Yourself and this,
the miserable one, whose soul is dying.'

[20] Our Lord responded to him softly,
and answered him humbly,
'that it is not only in bread that there is life
for man, but rather in the power of the Lord.'[41]

---

[38] See Matt 4:2; Mark 1:13; Luke 4:2.
[39] Here the poet uses the imagery of the lion for Christ and the fox for the evil one.
[40] See Matt 4:3; Luke 4:3.
[41] See Matt 4:4; Luke 4:4.

[21] ܗܡ ܚܘܪܐ ܕܐܬܬܒܪܬ ܡܟܐܢ. ܘܐܬܕܘܫܬ ܘܫܒܗ ܠܟܠܗ[42] ܒܡܕܝܢܬܗ.
ܐܘܣܦ ܒܝܫܬܐ ܥܠ ܒܝܫܬܗ.[43] ܘܦܫܐ ܝܬܝܪ ܚܛܗ ܡܕܝܢܬܐ ܀

[22] ܣܓܠ ܠܗ ܙܢܝܐ ܒܗܪܐ. ܕܥܘܠܐ ܗܕܝܡܐ ܒܡܟܪܝܬܐ.
ܘܫܒܩܗ ܙܟܝܬܗ ܠܒܣܝܪܐ. ܠܝܗܘܕܝ ܡܕܝܢܬܐ ܕܠܗ ܐܬܒܢܝܬ ܀

[23] ܥܠ ܐܝܟ ܗܝܟܠܐ[44] ܕܫܒܩܗ. ܘܫܒܩܬܗ ܦܬܚܗ ܠܩܘܡܗ.
ܘܐܬܚ ܡܗܪܐ ܡܠܝܟ ܥܡܗ. ܡܢ ܥܡܡܐ ܕܘܝܩܐ ܀

[24] ܐܝ ܐܝܟܢ ܬܪܥܐ ܦܬܚܐ. ܘܡܠܟܐ ܕܟܠ ܘܕܢܐ ܘܡܪܐ.
ܥܕܝ ܢܦܫܝ ܡܢ ܝܬܪܐ. ܘܒܝܫܬܐ ܠܚܛܝܐ[45] ܠܐ ܡܛܠܬܐ ܀

[25] ܥܡܠ ܦܓܪܐ ܕܐܡܝܪܝܢ. ܒܡܘܡܬܐ[46] ܕܟܬܒ ܢܥܠܝܢ.
ܕܡܠܟܐ ܥܠܡܐ ܗܘ ܩܡܝܢ. ܕܠܐ ܢܬܚܪܘܢ ܒܝܫܐ ܘܚܛܝܐ ܀

[26] ܠܥܕܬܐ ܩܡܝ[47] ܕܢܬܡܠܟܘܢ. ܘܟܠ ܕܒܪܢܗܘܢ[48] ܢܬܡܠܟܘܢ.
ܘܡܢ ܟܠ ܗܘܠܐ ܢܦܪܘܩܘܢ. ܫܒܐ ܠܝ ܚܝܠܐ ܒܝܬܐ ܀[49]

[27] ܒܗ[50] ܡܪܝ ܡܪܝ ܒܡܕܒܪܐ. ܕܐܘܪܚܬܐ ܐܦ ܚܝܬܐ.
ܦܘܩ ܠܡܠܟܐ ܕܡܕܝܢܬܐ. ܕܠܐ ܢܦܘܩ ܡܢܗܐ ܠܥܕܬܐ ܀

---

[42] B1 + ܘ.
[43] D3 ܒܝܫܬܐ.
[44] B1 ܗܝܟܠܐ.
[45] D2 ܠܚܛܝܐ.
[46] C2, M3 ܒܡܘܡܬܐ.
[47] B1 ܩܡܘ.
[48] B1 ܐܝܬܝܗܘܢ.
[49] B2 – [26].
[50] M3 ܒܗܝ.

[21] When he saw that his bow was broken,
and his arrows had returned and entered into his venom,
he added wickedness to his wickedness
and set another trap in place of the first one.

[22] He forged for Him the second weapon,
that of distinctive vain glory,
and he drove the one who gives life and made Him enter
the city of Zion that chose Him.[51]

[23] He made Him stand at the edge of the temple,
and then he slowly opened his mouth,
and like a priest, he spoke to Him,
from the book of David:

[24] 'If You are the inheritor and the Son,[52]
the king of all, the head and the Lord,
throw Yourself from the roof,
and no harm will reach Your body.

[25] Listen to the verses which were said
in the psalm [which comes] after ninety:
angels will be ordered for You
to protect You visibly and invisibly.[53]

[26] Order the angels to serve You
and carry You on their arms,
from each stumbling stone, they will protect You,
show me Your power in public.'

[27] Our Lord answered: 'Read in the book
of the Torah, O you sinner,
and look at the word that is written
and do not be a tempter to the Lord.'[54]

---

[51] See Matt 4:5; Luke 4:9.
[52] See Matt 4:6; Luke 4:9.
[53] See Ps 91:11; Matt 4:6; Luke 4:10-11.
[54] See Deut 6:16; Matt 4:7; Luke 4:7.

[28] ܘܡܢ ܢܛܥܡ ܕܡܢܐ ܗܢܐ. ܘܩܕܡ ܩܕܡܝ ܕܡܢܐ ܠܣܘܕܪܐ.
ܕܐܡܘܬܐ ܕܡܘܬܢܝܬܐ. ܘܗܘ ܗܕܐ ܕܢܝܘܬܐ ܕܟܝܐ ܀

[29] ܕܢܐ ܕܗܝܘ ܠܡܘܬܐ ܕܡܢܐ. ܘܫܘܝܘ ܡܠܟܘܬܐ ܕܫܠܡܐ.
ܡܘܪܒܐ[55] ܕܕܘܒܪܐ ܕܕܝܢܐ. ܒܚܫܒܐ ܘܦܢܛܝܣܝܐ ܀

[30] ܗܢܐ ܦܪܝܫܐ ܘܡܕܒܪܢܬܐ. ܘܣܓܝܐ ܒܗ ܡܥܕܪܢܘܬܐ. [f. 139ᵛ]
ܘܢܛܪܗ ܠܟܠܐ ܘܗܝܡܢܘܬܐ.[56] ܕܠܥܕܢ ܠܢܝܚܐ ܐܝܟܢܐ ܀

[31] ܘܢܬܐ ܒܢܝܢ ܢܟܪܝܢ ܠܢܦܫܐ. ܘܐܝܢܐ ܠܥܠܡܘ ܕܟܠ ܝܘܡܐ.
ܗܘܝ ܠܝ ܥܘܡܪܐ ܣܓܝܐܐ. ܕܐܘܪܚܝ ܒܠܘ ܗܝܟܐ ܥܡܝܐ ܀

[32] ܗܘܐ ܒܠܘ ܥܘܠܢܝܐ. ܕܫܘܐ ܢܦܫ ܢܝܐ ܡܝܐ ܐܝܐ.
ܘܢܗܠܟܘܢ ܠܢܦܫܐ ܕܢܝܚܐ. ܗܟܢܐ ܠܝ ܘܡܠܟܘܬܐ ܠܝ ܗܘܝܐ ܀

[33] ܘܦܩܕ ܡܢܝ ܠܡܠܟܐ. ܕܝܢ ܟܠ ܐܘ ܡܠܟܢܝܐ.
ܠܗܘ ܠܝ ܝܗܒ ܥܘܠܢܝܐ. ܒܟܠ ܝܘܡܐ ܐܪܥܐ ܀

[34] ܫܒ ܣܠܝ ܒܝܕ ܥܘܠܢܝܢ. ܘܢܥܒܕ ܒܠܘ ܒܘܥܝܢ.
⌈ܘܢܗܡܝܟ ܘܢܗܡܢܘ⌉[57] ܠܗ ܘܫܢܝ. ܡܢ ܒܢܝܐ ܢܟܪܝܐ ܀

---

[55] D3 ܡܘܪܒܗ.
[56] G1 ܘܢܝܚܬܐ.
[57] ⌈ M3 ܘܢܗܡܢܘ ܘܢܗܡܝܟ.

[28] When this weapon was broken,
he took and fashioned another weapon,
that of pride and power,
and he hoped that with this he would triumph.

[29] He [the evil one] took Him up to a high mountain,[58]
and showed Him the kingdoms of the world,
and the beauty of gold and silver,
by fiction and fantasy.

[30] He exhibited the knights and the carriages,
the armies with the camps,
he ordered troops and armies,
surpassing human power.

[31] The cursed slave of slaves answered
and told his Lord without fear:
'Be a good listener to me,
and I will make You inherit all that is under heaven.

[32] All this power
that You see, I possess it,
and I give it to whom I want.
worship me, and my kingdom will be for You.'[59]

[33] And our Lord answered Satan:
'Go away, you deceitful one,[60]
you do not have power
on Adam's race.

[34] Your power was vanquished, and your authority repealed,
all your strength was disabled,
your weaponry was cast down and pillaged
by the earthly nature.'[61]

---

[58] See Matt 4:8; Luke 4:5.
[59] See Matt 4:9; Luke 4:7.
[60] See Matt 4:10.
[61] The humanity of Christ.

[35] ܒܬܪ ܫܠܝܐ ܒܗ ܒܫܒܬܐ. ܗܘ ܒܗ ܣܕܘܡ ܒܕܚܠܬܐ.

ܒܗ ܡܫܬܒܩܝܢ ܚܛܗܐ ܘܚܘܒܐ. ܘܦܪܘܩܘܬܐ ܘܣܒܪܐ ܘܝܠܕܬܐ ܀

[36] ܒܝܬܗ ܠܡܐܬܐ ܕܩܘܫܬܐ. ܒܗ ܣܕܘܡ[62] ܕܥܘܕܪܢܐ.

ܕܠܐ ܠܡܦܪܫ ܗܘܐ ܝܕܥܐ. ܠܚܠܘ ܠܩܕܡ ܒܠܒܐ ܕܟܐܢܐ ܀

[37] ܡܫܬܪܪܐ ܡܦܪܢܣ ܗܘܐ ܠܗ. [63]ܡܫܬܥܢܝܢܘܬܐ ܡܬܥܩܒ ܗܘܐ ܠܗ.

ܡܕܒܪܐ ܡܢܗ ܗܘܐ ܠܗ.[64] ܠܡܦܪܩܗ ܕܡܠܟܐ ܐܡܝܢܐ ܀

[38] ܐܘ ܦܓܪܐ ܕܡܝܐ ܕܓܠܝܐ. ܘܢܘܪܐ ܠܥܒܕܐ ܚܛܝܐ.

ܕܢܫܒܘ ܡܕܡ ܠܐ[65] ܚܛܗܐ. ܦܪܝܣ[66] ܗܘ[67] ܐܝܟ ܙܟܝܐ ܀

[39] ܐܘ ܡܕܒܪܢܐ ܦܓܪܢܐ. ܕܕܝܢܐ ܠܠܘܩܒܠ ܚܛܝܬܐ.

ܕܢܫܒ[68] ܡܢܗ ܡܣܝܒܪܢܐ. ܠܥܕܐ ܠܐ ܠܡܬܒܥܢܐ ܀

[40] ܐܘ ܪܘܪܐ[69] ܡܦܩܓܢܐ. ܕܢܚܬܐ ܠܠܗܘܢ ܕܚܢܢܐ.

ܕܪܝܗ ܠܝܚܠܗ ܕܫܟܢܐ. ܘܡܚܒܪܗ ܐܝܟ ܗܢܢܐ ܦܪܥܐ ܀

[41] ܠܒܘܕܝ ܠܒܘܕܝ ܡܢܝܢ ܗܘܘ. ܒܦܘܠܝ ܦܠܝܐ ܕܚܕܝܢ ܗܘܘ.

ܢܗܘܐ ܢܗܘܐ ܙܟܝܢ ܗܘܘ.[70] ܒܠܠ[71] ܢܒܝܐ ܫܠܝܚܐ ܀

---

[62] B1 ܠܡܐܬܐ.
[63] B2 +X ܘܗ ܡܫܬܘܬܐ.
[64] M3 +X ܡܫܬܥܢܘܬܐ.
[65] C1 ܠܠܐ.
[66] C1, D3 ܦܪܝܣܘ.
[67] D3 ܐܝܟ.
[68] C2, M3 ܕܢܫܒܘ.
[69] B2 ܐܘ ܕܪܪ.
[70] M2 ܗܘܘ has been added by a later hand; C1 marg. ܗܘܘ.
[71] G1 ܢܡ.

[35] In that hour Satan ran away,[72]
he and his ranks with fear,
putting on sadness and pain
grief, crying and lamentation.

[36] The groups of the spiritual ones gathered
with the ranks of the fiery ones.
They saw this battle
and made for the Lord glorious crowns.

[37] They offered worship to Him,[73]
and raised praise to Him,
they cried out Holy to Him,
the hope of the human race.

[38] O body possessing senses,
and limbs wearing passions,
the impassionate ones fell short of Him,
and He triumphed like a victorious one.

[39] O You, corporeal warrior,
that looks like Adam by nature,
the fighter fell short of him,
the incorporeal watcher.

[40] O You, fighter who accepted,
all the passions of nature,
who smashed the power of Satan,
and made him like dirty mud.

[41] The various groups were crying out,
with loud voices,
Heh heh, they shouted
at the Satanic party.

[72] See Matt 4:11; Luke 4:13.
[73] See Matt 4:11.

[42] ܦܬܚܘ ܒܝܬܐ ܡܢ ܫܢܬܐ ܪܚܡܘ. ܘܥܡܝܠ ܚܝܐ ܒܪܚܡܘܗܝ.
ܦܫܛܘ ܫܢܬܐ ܥܠܡ ܬܘܒܠܗ. ܘܢܦܩ ܠܡܦܪܥܗ ܐܢܐ ÷ [f. 140r]

[43] ܐܝܟ ܕܡܠ[74] ܐܪܥܝܐ. ܐܘܪܚܐ ܘܫܒܝܠܐ ܕܒܢܝܢܫܐ.
ܓܒܝܬܐ ܥܠܡ ܢܘܚܡܐ. ܚܕܝܢ ܐܢܘܢ[75] ܒܥܒܕܝ[76] ܡܢܐ ÷

[44] ܢܦܫܐ ܡܢ ܐܬܪܝ ܡܬܬܠܝܢ. ܓܘܫܡܐ ܡܢ ܦܘܠܚܢܐ ܕܒܝܫܝܢ.
ܘܡܬܦܢܝܢ ܠܡܕܝܢܬܐ ܦܠܚܝܢ.[77] ܟܠܗ ܚܝܐ ܐܚܪܢܐ ÷

[45] ܗܘܐ ܐܒܕܢ ܠܟܘܠܗܘܢ. ܘܐܒܕܘ ܦܓܪܝ ܚܠܩܗܘܢ.
ܝܗܒܘ ܕܝܢܐ ܝܬܝܪܐ ܒܗܘܢ. ܗܘ ܥܡܐ ܐܠܗܝܐ ܕܥܡܡܐ ÷

[46] ܚܠܦ ܡܫܝܚܐ ܠܐ ܦܪܩ ܠܝ. ܘܕܘܟܪܢܐ ܠܡܫܡܫܐ ܒܗ ܠܟܠ ܠܝ.
ܕܡܠ ܒܥܒܕܐ ܝܕܥܬ ܠܝ.[78] ܕܐܬܕܟܪ ܠܝ[79] ܒܝܘܡ ܕܝܢܐ ÷

[47] ܒܪ ܐܠܗܐ ܕܝܗܒܗ ܠܥܒܕܐ. ܘܦܪܩܗ ܠܝܠܕܐ[80] ܚܛܝܬܐ.
ܚܘܝ ܠܡܪܚܡܢܐ ܕܥܒܕܐ. ܕܐܬܪܚܡܬ ܠܗܘܐ ܗܘܢܐ ÷

[48] ܘܚܘܝ[81] ܠܪܘܚܘܬܗ
ܘܠܐܒܗܘܬܗ
ܘܫܘܒܚܐ ܘܬܘܕܝܬܐ ܘܐܝܩܪܐ
ܘܢܦܫܐ ܒܘܝܐܐ ܠܫܢܬܘܬܗ
ܘܠܝ ܕܡܠܟ ܥܠܡܐ ܢܫܝܢ
ܘܐܬܪܐ ܕܒܚܝܢ ܗܘ ܢܫܝܢ
ܡܢ ܦܩܝܕܢ ܐܬܦܬܚ
ܐܢܫ ܕܝܬܒ ܒܗ ܠܡܠܟܘܬܐ
ܘܢܫܡ ܬܘܕܝܬܐ ܠܐܠܗܘܬܟ ÷

[74] C1 ܕܡܠܘܗܝ.
[75] B1 ܗܢܘܢ.
[76] B1 ܒܥܒܕܐ.
[77] C1 ܦܠܚܝܢ has been added later by the copyist.
[78] G1 – ܠܝ.
[79] D1 ܠܝ has been added by a later hand.
[80] B1 ܠܝܠܕܝܢ.
[81] B2 – ܘ.

[42] The evil one perished, for his weapon broke
and he received pain in his mind.
He lost his hope and confidence,
and lamented his *qnōmā*:

[43] 'Woe to me, I subdued all the people of Adam
priests, kings, and prophets,
members of the house and foreigners
with my harsh yoke.

[44] My hands killed the prophets,
my orders persecuted the righteous,
I hoped that they were working towards my dominion,
all of human nature.

[45] This one took revenge for their sins,
and thousands of times He punished me for them,
the thing that I did to them,
six thousand years [ago].

[46] I have no power or strength anymore,
I have no place to dwell;
I know that all people
will expel me in the name of the Nazarene.'

[47] Son of the Good One who destroyed the evil one,
and triumphed over the human race,
have mercy on the unfortunate composer,
who translated this story.

[48] Have mercy on his misery,
and his perdition.
Forgive and cleanse his sins.
Purify by Your hyssop his iniquity.
As for us, we fast for Your hope,
and knock at Your door of mercy,
because we are hungry and thirsty.
Give to us, that we might be satisfied in Your kingdom,
and offer up glory to Your divinity.

[1](71).6

[f. 145v] ܐܚܪܬܐ܀ ܕܝܚܝܕ̈ܝܐ ܕܐܪ̈ܒܥܐ ܕܢ̈ܘܩܐ܀ ܘܐܝܬܝܗ ܥܠ ܗܝܡܢܘܬܐ܀ ܕܝܠܗ[2] ܕܦܪܕܐ܀ ܬܐܦܪ܀

[1] ܐ[3] ܐܘ ܡܠܟܐ ܡܢ ܥܠ ܕܠܗ ܠܝܬ ܥܠ. ܟܠ ܡܬܚܙܐ ܠܥܠ ܘܚܙܐ ܠܥܠ.
ܗܘ ܕܒܟܠ ܥܠ ܘܗܘ ܠܒܪ ܡܢ ܥܠ. ܐܝܟܢܐ ܡܬܕܪܟ ܡܢ ܥܠ܀

[2] ܠ ܠܟ ܡܫܒܚ ܕܟܠܗ ܒܐܝܬܘܬܗ. [4]ܣܓܝܕ ܘܡܫܒܚ ܘܒܝܕܥܬܗ.
ܥܡ̈ܡܐ ܣܓܝܕܝܢ ܒܐܝܬܘܬܗ. ܘܡܕܝܢ̈ܬܐ ܟܠܗܘܢ ܒܝܕܥܬܗ܀

[3] ܗ ܗܘܢܐ ܠܐ ܡܕܪܟ ܠܗ. ܥܠ ܡܕܥܐ ܠܐ ܡܛܝܐ ܠܗ.
ܪ̈ܥܝܢܐ ܠܐ ܚܙܝܢ ܠܗ. ܚܘܫ̈ܒܐ ܠܐ ܡܩܦܝܢ ܠܗ܀

[4] ܐ ܐܝܬܘܬܗ ܟܣܝܐ ܡܢܟ ܠܟ. ܝܕܥܬܗ ܛܒܐ ܡܢܟ ܠܟ.
ܪܚܘܬܗ ܦܫܝܛܐ ܡܢܟ ܠܟ. ܛܝܒܘܬܗ[5] ܕܘܟܝܐ ܡܢܟ ܠܟ܀ [f. 146r]

[5] ܒ ܒܪܝܐ ܗܘ ܕܟܠܗܘܢ ܒܪ̈ܝܬܐ. ܘܗܘ ܒܢܝܗ ܠܟܠܗܘܢ ܒܪ̈ܝܬܐ.
ܡܬܩܪܝܐ[6] ܕܟܠ ܥܘܒܕܐ. ܐܡܝܢܐ ܕܟܠ ܥܘܒܕ̈ܐ܀

[6] ܓ ܓܡܝܪ ܒܐܝܬܘܬܐ ܘܝܨܝܦܘܬܐ.[7] ܘܡܫܟܠ ܘܡܕܒܪܢܘܬܐ.
ܘܚܘܒܐ ܘܬܫܒܘܚܬܐ.[8] ܘܚܟܝܡܐ[9] ܘܚܟܝܡܘܬܐ܀

[7] ܕ ܕܝܠܗ ܠܚܘܕ ܡܬܩܪܝܘܬܐ. ܕܝܠܗ ܠܚܘܕ ܐܡܝܢܘܬܐ.
ܘܠܐ ܡܬܚܫܚܢܘܬܐ. ܘܠܐ ܡܬܒܣܝܡܘܬܐ܀

[1] This hymn is found in: M2, D1, C1, C2, D2, B2, M3, G1, D3.
[2] D1 + ܕܝܠܗ ܕܡ.
[3] The first three stanzas begin with the letters in the name ܐܠܗ, after which it continues in alphabetical order.
[4] B2 + X ܘܡܕܝܢ̈ܬܐ.
[5] B2 illeg.
[6] B2 illeg.
[7] B2 illeg.
[8] D1 ܘܒܫܒܘܚܬܐ.
[9] B2 illeg.

6.(71)

Another one. For the fourth Sunday of the Fast, and it is on faith. By Wardā. Say.

[1] Ālap
O the one hidden from all, to whom all is revealed,
He who is unseen to all but sees all,
He who is within all and outside of all,
How can He be perceived by all?

[2] Lāmad̲
There is nothing is apart from His essence,
confined, bound, and in His knowledge.
Natures are contained in His essence,
And all knowledge in His intellect.

[3] Hē
Minds cannot grasp Him,
all knowledge cannot measure Him,
intellects cannot examine Him,
all thoughts are not enough for Him.

[4] Ālap
His essence has no boundary,
His knowledge has no limit,
His greatness has no equal,
His goodness has no likeness.

[5] Bēt̲
The creator of all creatures
and a created thing is not in His essence.
Eternal without beginning,
perpetual without changing.

[6] Gāmal
Perfect in essence and wisdom,
in power and greatness,
in love and goodness,
in tenderness and sweetness [clemency].

[7] Dālat̲
His only is eternity,
His only is perpetuity,
and no changing,
and no transformation.

[8] ܗ ܗܘ ܠܟܠܗ ܡܢ ܟܠ ܕܠܐ ܫܘܪܝܐ. ܘܗܘ ܠܒܪ ܡܢ ܟܠ ܕܠܐ ܫܘܪܝܐ.
ܠܟܠ ܕܥܒܕ ܐܝܬ ܫܘܪܝܐ. ܘܗܘ ܠܐ ܢܦܠ[10] ܬܚܝܬ ܫܘܪܝܐ ❖

[9] ܘ ܘܩܢܐ[11] ܫܘܠܛܢܐ ܘܡܕܒܪܢܘܬܐ. ܘܠܗ ܡܕܒܪܢܐ ܘܦܘܪܢܣܬܐ.
ܥܒܕܐ ܠܟܠܗ ܡܢ ܟܠ[12] ܒܡܠܬܐ. ⌈ܕܠܐ ܣܘܢܩܢܐ ܕܡܕܒܪܢܘܬܐ⌉[13] ❖

[10] ܙ ܙܒܢ[14] ܘܥܠܡܐ ܒܪܝܬܐ ܒܡܠܬܐ. ܘܗܘ ܒܟܠܗ[15] ܡܢܗ ܒܟܠܗ ܙܒܢܐ.
ܘܩܕܡ ܠܟܠܗ ܡܢܗ ܗܘ ܕܙܒܢܐ. ܠܐ ܡܬܚܫܒ ܒܗ ܙܒܢܐ ❖

[11] ܚ ܚܣܝܢ ܘܡܫܬܡܥܢ ܘܗܘܐ ܚܣܝܢ ܘܡܫܬܡܥܢ.
ܚܣܝܢ ܘܡܫܬܡܥܢ[16] ܒܡܠܟܐ ܕܡܠܟܐ.
ܟܠ ܡܠܟܐ ܠܐ ܡܫܬܡܥܢ. ܠܐ[17] ܡܫܬܡܥܢ ܟܠ ܡܠܟܐ[18] ❖

[12] ܛ ܛܝܒܘܬܐ ܕܠܐ ܒܕܡܘܬܐ. ܛܒܝܒ ܕܡܫܬܒܗ ܒܬܫܒܘܚܬܐ.
ܠܗܘ ܕܠܐ ܡܫܬܡܥ[19] ܒܩܠܬܐ. ܕܗܘܝܐ ܒܟܠܗ ܡܫܬܘܕܥܢܘܬܐ ❖

[13] ܝ ܝܕܥ ܘܡܫܬܪܐ[20] ܒܗ ܣܓܝܐܝܢ. ܥܡܡܐ ܘܐܪܥܬܐ ܒܗ ܣܓܝܐܝܢ.
ܡܕܝܢ ܡܢܗ ܘܒܗ ܠܐ ܕܥܝܢ. ܒܗ ܩܝܡܝܢ ܘܒܗ ܡܬܕܒܪܝܢ ❖

[14] ܟ ܟܠ ܕܡܬܒܠܝܢ ܘܕܡܬܕܥܝܢ. ܐܦ ܡܬܚܙܝܢ[21] ܕܡܠܟܘܬܗ ܡܫܬܠܛܝܢ.
ܠܐ[22] ܕܫܘܠܛܢܘܬܗ ܫܠܡܝܢ. ܘܠܐ ܕܡܫܬܠܛܢܘܬܗ ܡܬܚܫܒܝܢ ❖

[15] ܠ ܠܐ ܡܬܚܫܒ ܒܦܘܫܩܐ.[23] ܠܐ ܦܝܫ ܡܬܬܦܝܣ ܒܡܠܝܠܘܬܐ.
ܠܐ ܡܬܬܚܡ ܒܕܘܟܬܐ. ܠܐ ܡܬܬܚܡ ܠܝܩܝܢܬܐ ❖

[10] D2 ܢܦܫ.
[11] G1 ܕܩܢܐ.
[12] D1 –.
[13] ⌉ D1 marg.
[14] D1 marg.
[15] D1, C1, D2, G1 ܠܟܠܗ.
[16] G1 ܘܡܫܬܡܥܢ.
[17] D2 + ܘ.
[18] C1 ܟܠ ܡܠܟܐ has been added later by the copyist.
[19] D2 illeg.
[20] D2 illeg.
[21] D3 illeg.
[22] D2 + ܕ.
[23] C1 illeg.

[8] Hē

He, within all, is without limit.
He, beyond all, is without limit.
He holds the limit of everything in everything,
and He does not fall under the limit.

[9] Wāw

With minds and senses,
with knowledge and intelligence,
He abides within all souls,
without the mingling of joining together.

[10] Zēn

He who made and knitted the light in the eye,
and He who is inside the eye,
even though He is inside the eye,
the eye cannot see Him.

[11] Ḥēṯ

I sinned and stumbled, and again I sinned and stumbled.
I sinned and stumbled in what I said,
I did not understand what I said,
what I said, I did not understand.

[12] Ṭēṯ

I went astray in wandering without knowledge,
I wanted to speak about with letters,
the one about whom creatures are not able
to make utterance.

[13] Yōḏ

Sea and land are encompassed in Him,
heaven and earth are borne in Him.[24]
They are filled with Him but do not feel Him,
by Him, they exist, and by Him, they are preserved.

[14] Kāp

All who speak or are silent,
if they want to talk about Him,
they will not be able to speak,
and will not be capable of understanding Him.

[15] Lāmaḏ

He cannot be uttered by lips,
He cannot be understood by thoughts,
He cannot be compared to forms,
He cannot be subjected to wise things.

---

[24] See Gen 1:6-10.

[16] ܦ ܦܠܐܬܐ ܕܡܢܝܢ / ܠܝܬ ܠܗܝܢ. ܡܫܟܚܝܢ ܕܒܟܠܗܘܢ ܢܬܒܩܘܢ. [f. 146ᵛ]
ܘܐܦ[25] ܗܘ ܕܟܠܗܘܢ ܦܠܝܓ ܠܗܘܢ. ܠܐ ܡܫܟܚܝܢ ܕܟܠܗܘܢ ܢܚܘܘܢ ܀

[17] ܫܘܒܚܐ ܕܝܢ ܠܐܠܗܐ. ܘܠܐܠܗܐ ܚܕܐ ܐܝܬܘܬܐ.
ܬܠܬܐ ܘܒܠܕܗ ܡܠܟܐ. ܘܩܢܘܡܝܐ ܚܕܐ ܟܝܢܘܬܐ ܀

[18] ܡܘܕܝܢܢ ܐܦ ܕܝܠܗ ܡܠܟܐ. ܘܐܦܐ ܠܡܫܬܥܒܕܘܬܐ.
⌜ܚܘܒܐ ܘܟܠ⌝[26] ܗܘܐ ܒܐܝܬܘܬܐ. ܐܠܐ ܒܝܕ ܡܬܒܪܢܫܢܘܬܐ ܀[27]

[19] ܫܘܒܚܐ ܐܦ ܕܫܒܚܘܗ[28] ܠܒܪܐ. ܘܟܕ ܣܘܒܪܗ ܡܠܟܐ ܓܒܪܐ.
ܒܬܘܠܬܐ[29] ܝܠܕܬ ܓܒܪܐ. ܘܠܒܬܘܠܘܬܗ ܠܐ ܚܒܠܗ ܗܘ ܒܪܐ ܀

[20] ܡܘܕܝܢܢ ܐܦ ܕܒܟܪܣ ܝܠܕܬܗ. ܘܒܟܠܗܘܢ ܕܡܟܝܪܗ[30] ܝܘܣܦ.
ܘܐܟܪ[31] ܐܝܟ ܕܐܬܚܙܝ ܘܝܠܕܗ. ܘܫܡܗ ܘܩܪܝܗ ܠܒܪܗ ܀

[21] ܫܘܒܚܐ[32] ܕܩܕܡܝܬ ܗܘܐ. ܠܟܠ ܫܘܒܚܐ ܕܒܪܝܬ ܚܕ ܗܘܐ.
ܘܟܕ ܗܘ ܒܠܚܘܕܘܗܝ ܘܒܗ ܗܘܐ. ܚܟܝܡ ܗܘ ܕܐܬܚܙܝ ܗܘܐ ܀

[22] ܡܘܕܝܢܢ ܐܦ ܕܝܬܒܐ ܘܡܫܡܫܝܢ. ܘܚܟܝܡ ܚܙܘܗܝ ܘܣܓܕܘܗܝ.
ܘܐܦ ܚܟܝܡ ܢܒܝܐ ܘܡܠܟܘܗܝ. ܘܩܒܪܐ ܕܡܠܟܐ ܫܡܥܘܗܝ ܀

[23] ܫܘܒܚܐ ܐܦ ܕܩܡ ܡܢ ܩܒܪܐ. ܘܠܫܡܝܐ ܣܠܩ ܒܫܘܒܚܐ.
ܘܗܘ ܢܐܬܐ ܗܘ ܒܫܘܒܚܐ. ܘܠܟܠ ܕܝܢ ܒܫܘܒܚܐ ܀

[25] G1 ܘܐܝܟ.
[26] ⌝ B2 illeg.
[27] In D1, only the first word of verses a and b remains; the rest has been erased. In C1, only the words ܡܘܕܝܢܢ ܐܦ remain from verse a; the rest has been erased.
[28] D2, B2 ܕܫܒܚܘܗܝ
[29] B2 illeg.
[30] G1 ܕܡܟܝܪܐ.
[31] B2 illeg.
[32] D1 + ܐܦ has been added later by the copyist.

[16] Mīm[33] The angels who are without number
are too weak to tell about Him;
even if He teaches them about Himself,
they cannot relate about Him.

[17] I confess the one in three,
and the three have one essence.
The Begetter and His Begotten the Word,
and the Holy Spirit, one equality.

[18] I believe that the Word descended
and came for the incarnation,
in love and not in essence,
but in good pleasure.

[19] I confess that the watcher announced Him [the Word],
and with his announcement, the Word inhabited
the Virgin [and] was made flesh,
and forever and ever is one Son.

[20] I believe that He was baptized and purified us,
and with the baptism of His body, He forgave us.
He fasted and was tempted and justified us.
He vanquished and exterminated our captivity.

[21] I confess that He took revenge,
for all the sins that our humankind committed,
and that He alone triumphed;
He was condemned instead of us.

[22] I believe that He wished [so] and they took Him,
for us they condemned Him and judged Him,
for us they stretched out and crucified Him,
and put Him in the grave of the dead.

[23] I confess that He rose from the grave,
and truly ascended into heaven,
and He is truly on the right,[34]
and will truly judge all.

[33] The alphabetical order stops here.
[34] See Ps 110:1; Matt 24:64; Mark 16:19; Acts 7:56; Heb 1:3, 13.

[24] ܡܫܝܚܐ ܐܢܬ ܕܢܘܗܪܐ ܒܐܝܕܗ. ܫܘܒܚܐ ܕܥܘܡܪܐ ܒܐܝܕܗ.
ܘܠܗ ܫܡܝܢ ܠܟܝܢܐ ܡܢ ܐܝܕܗ. ܘܟܠ ܒܗ ܘܫܡܗ ܘܟܠ ܒܐܝܕܗ ܀

[25] ܫܘܒܚܐ ܕܥܘܒܕܐ ܘܫܦܝܪܘܬܐ. ܡܫܒܚ ܡܢ ܟܠ ܒܪܝܬܐ.
ܗܘ ܫܠܡܐ ܕܢܚܬ ܫܠܝܛܐ. ܐܚܘܝܗ ܒܬܫܒܘܚܬܐ ܀

[26] ܡܫܝܚܐ ܐܢܬ[35] ܗܘܝܬ ܕܗܘ ܦܓܪܐ. ܢܟܗ ܡܠܟܐ ܗܘ ܒܥܒܕܐ.
ܘܠܐ ܫܘܒܚܐ ܒܪܐ ܘܒܪܐ. ܐܠܐ ܐܝܟ ܒܪܐ[36] ܥܒܕܐ ܀

[27] ܒܗܝܢ ܡܠܟܐ ܫܘܒܚܐ. ܒܗܝܢ ܡܠܟܐ ܡܫܝܚܐ ܐܢܬ.
ܐܢܬ / ܪܘܚܐ ܡܬܪܚܡܢܐ. ܫܪܝ[37] ܗܘܝ ܠܝ[38] ܡܚܝܢܢܐ ܀ [f. 147r]

[28] ܘܢܫܒܚ ܒܕܚܝܠܝܢ
ܘܡܪܢܝܢ ܒܕܚܝܠܝܢ
ܘܡܒܢܝܢ ܒܪܚܡܝܢ ܒܗ ܕܚܝܠܝܢ
ܘܠܝ ܘܠܓܠܘܗܝ ܢܦܫܐ ܐܢܫܝܢ
ܘܓܠ ܕܝܠܝܕܝܢ[39] ܟܠܗ ܡܠܟܘܬܗ
ܘܐܘܪܐ ܠܥܡܝܢ ܟܠ ܫܒܝܬܗ ܀

35 D1 marg.
36 M3 ܒܥܒܕܐ.
37 C1 ܐܝܬ ܫܪܝ.
38 G1 ܠܗ.
39 G1 ܕܝܠܝܕܘܗܝ.

[24] I believe that the height is in His hand,
I believe that the depth is in His hand,
and there is nothing outside of His hand;
everything is in Him, from Him, and all in His hand.

[25] I confess that glory and worship
He accepts from all creatures;
that image which the Word took
is truly like Him.

[26] I also believe that this body,
is truly God of all,
and I do not confess a Son and a Son
but [only] one true Son.

[27] I confess in these words.
I believe in these words.
I am the miserable composer.
O our Lord, be my forgiver.

[28] Forgive me with Your mercy,
call me with Your mercy,
count me by Your mercy with Your beloved ones,
for me and all who have taken Your mysteries,
grant that we see You in Your kingdom,
and confess Your name for Your gifts.

(72).7[1]

[f. 147r] ܐܚܪܬܐ[2] ܠܗ ܠܡܕܒܚܢܐ ܀ ܕܒܝܬܗ[3] ܕܡܠܟܐ ܠܡܘܕܝܢ.[4]

[1] ܒܒܝ ܢܓܕܘܬܟ ܕܡܫܝܚܐ
ܕܗܘܐ ܒܒܢܐ ܠܡܕܝܢ ܡܢܝܢܐ
ܡܢܘ ܢܫܦܬܐ[5] ܡܗܝܡܢܐ
ܐܝܟ ܐܒܘܒܟ ܢܪܝ ܡܗܝܡܢܐ
ܘܢܪܝܫܘ[6] ܒܪܚܡܬܐ ܠܡܕܢܚܐ
ܢܕܒܢ ܢܦܫܟ ܠܡܠܟܐ ܠܡܕܢܚܐ
ܘܢܩܫܘ ܬܘܕܝܬܐ ܬܕܝܪܬܐ
ܘܗܡܝܢܘܬܐ ܫܪܝܪܬܐ ܀

[2] ܐ ܐܠܗܐ ܠܟ ܐܒܘܟܘܢ. ܘܡܢ ܟܠ ܠܡܕܢܚܐ ܠܡܕܢܚܘܬܗ.
ܢܝ[7] ܒܠܘܩܒܗ ܘܢܝ ܒܢܝܗ. ܘܐܝ ܒܟܠܗܘܢ ܕܒܢܝܢܗ ܀

[3] ܒ ܒܟܠ ܢܫܠܡܘܢ[8] ܢܬܒܢܝܢ ܠܗ. ܠܟ ܕܘܡܝܢܐ ܕܡܬܦܢܝܢ ܠܗ.
ܒܢܝܢܗ[9] ܕܡܬܬܕܝܢ ܠܗ. ܠܟ ܦܣܩܐ ܕܡܬܦܢܝܢ ܠܗ ܀

[4] ܓ ܠܡܕܢ ܟܠܗ ܒܟܠ ܗܘ ܕܐܬܓܠܗ. ܘܡܬܠܟܢ ܒܟܠܗܘܢ ܕܕܝܠܗ.[10]
ܘܠܐ ܡܢܐ ܦܓܪܡ[11] ܡܬܝܣܟ ܠܗ. ܘܠܐ[12] ܢܟܣ[13] ܐܘ ܥܩܝܡ ܠܗ ܀

[5] ܕ ܕܠܝܚܘܬܐ ܢܦܫܗ ܕܡܘܬܐ.[14] ܡܢ ܢܠܗܘܒܠܐ ܦܬܝܚܘܬܐ.
ܐܝܟ ܕܡܫܐ ܕܢܟܣܬ ܠܒܢܝܐ. ܘܢܬܐ ܠܚܘܒܒܐ ܥܩܒܬܐ ܀

[1] This hymn is found in: M2, D1, C1, C2, D2, B2, M3, G1, D3.
[2] G1 + ܥܠ ܦܬܓܡܐ ܬܕܡܘܪܬܐ.
[3] D2 –, G1 + ܒܡ ܕܒܝܬܗ.
[4] C1 ܦܪܙܐ.
[5] B2 illeg.
[6] B2 ܫ has been added by a later hand.
[7] D2 + ܘ.
[8] M2 + marg. ܐܘ ܢܬܠܡܕܘܢ; D1, C1, D2, M3, G1, D3 ܢܬܠܡܕܘܢ.
[9] D2 ܒܢܝܢܬܐ.
[10] G1 – ܕ.
[11] B2 ܦܓܪܡ has been added by a later hand.
[12] D1 ܐܘ.
[13] B2 ܢܟܣ.
[14] D1 ܕ has been added later by the copyist.

7.(72)

Another one for Sunday. By the same teacher Gīwargīs.

[1] Spiritual children of Abraham
who have become children of the Lord of natures.
Obtain hearts, O believers,
like your father, the head of the believers,
and incline with complete love,
the ears of your souls to the perfect word,
and learn the right religion,
and the true faith.

[2] Ālap God: there is no one like Him.
His perfection is above any perfect one,
whether in His essence or His being,[15]
or in all of His properties.

[3] Bēṯ In all His works that He has made
there is nothing like Him;
among the creatures that He has created
there is no equal that is compared to Him.

[4] Gāmal He is perfect in all that He has.
He is complete in all that He owns.
Nothing can change Him,
nothing defiles or confuses Him.

[5] Dālaṯ When there is confusion,
it can be seen in the opposite,
like the wind that confuses the water,
and passions [confusing] pure thoughts.

[15] For more explanation about the using of the words 'essence' and 'nature' by our poet, see Chapter 4.

[6] ܗ ܗܐ ܕܠܡܘܒܠܐ ܠܝܬ ܠܗ. ܘܠܐ ܫܘܒܠܐ ܗܘܐ ܠܗ.
ܘܠܐ ܚܘܫܒܐ[16] ܕܠܚ ܠܗ. ܘܐܦܠܐ[17] ܚܙܐ ܥܝܢ ܠܗ܀

[7] ܘ ܘܟܠ ܕܗܘܐ ܘܗܘܐ ܒܙܒܢܐ. ܕܝܠܗܘܢ[18] ܬܚܝܬ ܙܒܢܐ.
ܢܦܩ ܠܗ ܡܢ ܡܕܡ ܙܒܢܐ. ܥܘܒܕܐ ܠܗ[19] ܥܡ ܟܠ ܙܒܢܐ܀

[8] ܙ ܙܕܩ ܕܝܬܝܪܘܬܐ[20] ܒܝܠܕܐ. ܙܩܝܦܐ ܕܝܬܝܪܘܬܗ ܒܒܣܪܐ.
ܒܐܘܣܝܐ ܡܫܬܪܪܐ ܘܦܫܝܛܐ. ܐܬܚܙܝܐ ܕܐܝܬܘܗܝ ܘܝܠܕܐ܀

[9] ܚ ܚܙܐ ܠܐ ܡܬܚܙܝܢܐ. ܓܫܐ ܠܐ ܡܬܓܫܫܢܐ. [f. 147ᵛ]
ܡܕܪܟܐ ܠܐ ܡܬܕܪܟܢܐ. ܕܚܝܩܐ ܠܐ ܡܬܚܝܩܢܐ܀

[10] ܛ ܛܘܒܢܐ ܠܐܘܣܝܐ ܕܐܒܘܗ ܒܗ. [21]ܕܐܦ ܦܪܨܘܦܐ[22] ܚܙܐ ܠܗ.[23]
ܘܠܝܠܕܐ ܕܡܬܝܠܕ ܒܗ. ܕܐܦ ܚܝܠܐ[24] ܡܬܕܪܟ ܒܗ܀

[11] ܝ ܝܚܝܕܝܐ ܒܪܐ ܡܠܬܐ. ܚܕ ܡܢ ܩܢܘܡܐ ܕܐܠܗܘܬܐ.
ܐܝܟ ܠܡ ܚܕ ܒܬܠܬܐ. ܬܠܬܐ ܚܕܐ ܐܠܗܘܬܐ܀

[12] ܟ ܟܣܝܐ ܡܠܬܐ ܠܟܪܘܒܐ. ܒܦܓܪܐ ܕܠܒܫ ܝܠܕܗ.
ܘܒܗ ܥܒܕ ܠܚܝܘܗܝ ܟܠ ܚܝܘܗܝ. ܘܟܠ ܐܣܝܘܬܐ ܘܟܠ ܚܘܒܝܗ܀

[13] ܠ ܠܐ ܐܬܚܠܦ ܟܕ ܐܬܐ. ܡܠܬܐ ܠܡܬܒܣܪܢܘܬܐ.
ܘܠܐ ܐܝܟ ܕܝܠܝܕܘܬܐ. ܟܠ ܩܢܘܡܐ ܒܠܚܘܕܘܬܐ܀

[16] C1 + ܘܗ.
[17] M3 illeg.
[18] D1 ܘܕܗܘܐ.
[19] D3 +X ܡܢ.
[20] G1 ܕܝܬܝܪܘܬܐ.
[21] D3 +X ܕܡܢ.
[22] G1 ܕܦܪܨܘܦܐ.
[23] D3 ܒܗ.
[24] C2 illeg.

[6] Hē This one who has no opposite,
and no one who contradicts Him;
no thought confuses Him,
and no passion defiles Him.

[7] Wāw And all that was and is in the ages,
and that which will be after the ages,
He knew before all the ages,
glory to Him throughout all ages.

[8] Zēn It is right that we confess openly,
and glorious to believe in secret,
in the concealed and hidden essence,
through His bright and shining work.

[9] Ḥēṯ Power which is invisible,
knowledge[25] which is unknowable,
nearness which is imperceptible,
remoteness which is unreachable.

[10] Ṭēṯ Blessed be the mouth that confesses Him;
even if he dies, he will live.
And the heart that believes in Him;
even if it sins, it will be justified by Him.

[11] Yōḏ The only-begotten Son, the Word,
one of the *qnōmē* of the essence,
He taught us one in three,
three, one divinity.

[12] Kāp The Word hid His nature,
in a body which His will had put on,
and by it He revealed His tenderness,
His mercy and His forgiveness for our race.

[13] Lāmaḏ He did not change when He came,
the Word to the incarnation,
and He did not introduce quaternity
to the *qnōmē* of the Trinity.

[25] Here the word 'knowledge' refers to God; it can be translated as 'intellect'.

[14] ܡ ܡܛܠ ܗܘܐ ܢܡܘܣܐ. ܢܚܕܪܐ ܡܠܟܐ[26] ܟܗܢܐ.
ܕܐܢ ܡܠܟܐ ܢܬܡܣܒ ܟܗܢܐ. ܒܡܢܐ ܟܗܢܐ ܢܬܩܘܡ ܒܪܐ ⁘

[15] ܢ ܢܝܚ ܡܠܟܐ ܠܡܫܒܚܬܐ. ܘܠܥܕܬܗ[27] ܘܡܫܚܬܐ.
ܕܢܬܦܫܛ ܠܗ ܡܫܝܚܘܬܐ. ܕܗܘܐ ܠܟܗܢܐ[28] ܘܡܠܟܘܬܐ ⁘

[16] ܣ ܣܒܪܐ ܐܝܬ ܕܝܗܒ ܠܗ. ܘܕܒܠܗ ܥܡܠܐ[29] ܘܕܒܠܗ ܢܘܚ ܠܗ.
ܒܣܘܦܗ ܫܘܒܩܢܐ ܗܘܐ ܠܗ. ܘܦܪܘܩ[30] ܚܛܗ ܫܘܒܩ ܠܗ ⁘

[17] ܥ ܥܒܕ ܠܗ ܕܝܢܐ[31] ܐܝܟ ܕܝܢܐ. ܘܠܗܢ[32] ܠܡܫܪܐ ܕܟܠ ܩܢܐ ܕܝܢܐ.
ܠܗ[33] ܕܝܢܐ ܚܕܬܐ ܕܝܢܐ. ܕܒܗ ܡܕܡ ܠܠܩܢܐ ܗܘܐ ܕܝܢܐ[34] ⁘

[18] ܦ ܦܪܩܐ ܕܝܠܗܘܢ ܚܘܝܘ ܕܝܢܐ. ܘܕܝܢܝܗ ܢܝܚܐ[35] ܠܟܠ ܕܝܢܐ.
ܘܠܐ[36] ܡܢܐ ܕܢܫܠܚܝܘܗܝ ܒܕܝܢܐ. ܘܠܐ ܗܘܐ ܠܒܪܐ ܡܢ ܩܢܐ ܕܝܢܐ ⁘

[19] ܨ ܨܒܝܢܗ ܣܓܝ ܠܗܘܢ ܒܢܝܗ.[37] [38]ܘܒܢܝܗ ܠܗܘܢ ܨܒܝܢܗ.
ܘܐܢܫ[39] ܕܠܐ ܡܬܦܫܠܚ ܒܢܝܗ. ܩܒܠ ܘܠܐ ܨܒܝܢܗ ⁘

[20] ܩ ܩܪܒ ܠܟܠܗܘܢ ܕܢܬܡܪܐ ܐܢܫܐ.[40] ܒܪܐ ܐܠܗܐ ܒܪܗ ܕܐܢܫܐ.[41]
/ ܕܢܦܩܘܢ ܠܒܪܐ[42] ܘܐܢܫܐ.[43] ܒܡܫܬܘܕܥܢܘܬܗ[44] ܒܪܢܫܐ[45] ⁘ [f. 148r]

---

[26] D2, G1 + ܘ.
[27] G1 illeg.
[28] G1 –.
[29] G1 –.
[30] D1, C1, C2 ܘܦܪܘ ; D3 ܦܪܘ.
[31] G1 illeg.
[32] B2 + + ܘܠܟܢ.
[33] G1 illeg.
[34] G1 –.
[35] G1 illeg.
[36] B2 – ܘ.
[37] G1 illeg.
[38] M3 +X ܘܐܢܫ.
[39] G1 – ܘ.
[40] G1 ܐܢ̈ܫܐ.
[41] G1 ܐܢ̈ܫܐ.
[42] G1 illeg.
[43] G1 ܐܢ̈ܫܐ.
[44] C2 illeg.
[45] G1 ܒܪܢ̈ܫܐ.

[14] Mīm
Therefore in the Scripture,
the Word is called flesh;[46]
if the Word is called flesh,
how much more will the flesh be acknowledged as Son?

[15] Nūn
The Word descended on what is weak,
on what is despised and lowly,
so that we can believe in the glories,
and the sublime things that He gave to the flesh.

[16] Semkaṯ
He came to give us hope,
He took what is ours and gave us what is His.
He became a companion for us by His love,
And with it, He associated us with Him.

[17] ʿĒ
He did all that He desired, as He desired,
and no one says why He desired it,
it was not a new will that He desired,
because before the worlds He desired this.

[18] Pē
His love desired that He would put on a body;
through it He would give life to all.
He could not change it because He desired it,
because it is not outside of what He desired.

[19] Ṣādē
His will is equal to His nature,
and His nature to His will,
since His nature did not change,
His will also did not.

[20] Qōp
He accepted that he would be called man,
the Son of God, the Son of man,
so that watchers and human beings would believe
in the divinization of man.

---

[46] See John 1:14.

[21] ܪ ܪ̈ܚܡܐ ܕܐܠܗܘܬܐ.[47] ܘܡܚܝܠܘܬܐ ܕܐܢܫܘܬܐ.
ܒܪܡ ܠܟܝ ܬܒܥ ܚܐܪܘܬܐ.[48] ܠܐ ܥܒܕܐ ܘܠܐ ܡܫܥܒܕܘܬܐ[49] ܀

[22] ܫ ܫܪܐ ܢܡܘܣܐ ܕܥܘܒܕܐ ܘܢܒܝܘܬܐ. ܒܗ ܡܫܠܡܐ ܒܫܪܝܪܘܬܐ.
ܘܠܟܝ ܣܒܪܗ ܠܐܠܗܘܬܐ. ܕܠܐ ܢܬܒܝܥ ܠܐܢܫܘܬܐ ܀

[23] ܬ ܬܘܕܝܬܐ ܕܠܐ[50] ܦܠܓܘܬܐ. ܐܠܗܐ ܡܣܩܝܢ ܒܠܗܝܢ.
ܬܪܝܨܘܬ ܗܝܡܢܘܬܐ. ܗܪܟ ܒܢ̈ܝܗ ܕܚܐܪܬܐ ܒܪܘܚܐ ܀

[24] ܒܪܐ ܕܐܡܬܐ ܚܠܨ ܠܥܒܕܐ. ܚܙܝ ܘܠܐ ܗܘܝ ܠܡܫܥܒܕܢܐ.
ܕܐܘܕܝ ܦܘܡ ܒܐܠܠܗܐ[51] ܗܢܐ. ܐܘܪܚܐ ܒܗ ܒܕܝܢܐ ܓܠܝܐ ܀

[25] ܘܢܝܫܐ ܘܡܫܒܚܘ
ܘܒܪܟܘ ܘܡܘܕܘ
ܒܬܘܕܝܬܐ ܘܫܒܘܚܬܐ
ܠܗ[52] ܚܘܒܒܐ[53] ܘܡܚܝܠܘܬܐ
ܕܥܘܗܕܢ ܒܗ ܘܡܗܝܡܢܘܬܐ
ܘܠܟ ܢܦܩܘܣܬܐ[54] ܠܗ ܬܘܕܝܬܐ ܀

[47] G1 illeg.
[48] G1 illeg.
[49] M3 ܗܝܡܢܘܬܐ.
[50] G1 illeg.
[51] G1 illeg.
[52] D2 + ܘ.
[53] G1 illeg.
[54] G1 illeg.

[21] Rēš
The height of divinity,
and the weakness of humanity,
but after unity,
there is no dissolving or split.

[22] Šīn
The flesh is worthy of greatness and worship,
with the Word, in truth,
and there is nothing of divinity
which is not given to humanity.

[23] Tāw
Undivided praise,
God, three *qnōmē*,
the truth of the faith,
two natures in one Sonship.

[24]
The Son who came for judgment in our place,
have mercy and do not judge the composer,
who confessed You in this world;
confess him in Your Just judgment.

[25]
Forgive and remit,
blot out and cleanse,
the spots and bruises,
sins and mistakes,
of those who confess this faith,
and to You be glory and praise.

[1](75).8

[f. 151r] ⌐ܕܡܥܕܥܕܢܐ ܕܥܢܝܢܐ ܕܨܘܡܐ ܕܒܥܘܬܐ ܕܢܝܢܘܝܐ. ܗܐܡܢܐ ܒܟܠܕܘܬܐ ܕܟܗܢܐ :·[2]⌐ ܐܣܛܪܐ ܠܗ[3] ܠܥܕܥܕܢܐ :· ܘܠܣܘܕܥܕܢܐ ܕܠܥܢܝܢܘܬ ܡܥܢܘܬܗ: ܕܝܠܗ ܕܡܪܝ. ܢܐܡܪ[4]

[1] ܗܐ ܠܗ ܠܐܘܪܚܐ ܕܪܡܫܐ ܕܢܚ
ܗܢܐ ܪܒܐ ܠܕܪܝ ܒܣܦܐ ܥܒܝܕ[5]
ܘܪܠܦܐ ܗܘܝܘ[6] ܘܒܥܐ[7] ܗܘܐ
ܕܢܠܟܘܢ ܐܡܪ[8] ܗܘ ܡܣܟܢܐ
ܟܕ ܡܫܘܐ ܗܘܐ ܠܫܠܡܝܢܘܬ
ܘܦܠܓ ܗܘܐ ܠܗܘܢ ܟܕ ܦܬܓܡܘܗܝ
ܕܡܪܝܡ ܢܘܡܐ ܕܐܬܐ ܒܗ
ܡܟܐܝܟ ܠܗ ܫܠܡܐ ܘܡܠ ܕܒܗ :·

[2] ܟܕ ܫܠܡܝܢܐ ܟܕܝܢܝܢ ܗܘܘ. ܘܡܪܝܡ ܥܢܝ ܢܦܫܝܢ ܗܘܘ.
ܘܟܠ ܡܢܬܝܗ[9] ܠܗ[10] ܡܫܬܠܝܢ ܗܘܘ. ܘܗܠܝܢ ܡܟܠ ܐܡܪܝܢ ܗܘܘ :·

[3] ܥܢܝ ܥܢܝ ܦܝܫ ܠܝ. ܪܒܝ[11] ܪܒܝ ܪܥܝܟ ܠܝ.
ܢܘܗܪܝ ܢܘܗܪܝ ܢܦܫ ܠܝ. ܘܚܝܐ ܠܥܠܡ ܝܗܒ ܠܝ :·

[4] ܠܡܣܒܪ ܡܢܡܪܢ ܦܩܕܝܢ. ܠܥܠܡ ܚܝܐ ܗܘ ܡܘܬܢ.
ܘܠܫܠܡܐ ܡܫܬܡܠܝܢ. ܗܒ ܠܝ [12]ܡܢܝܢ ܕܫܠܝܢ :·

[5] ܕܐܠܗܐ ܪܒܐ ܡܗܝܡܢܝܢ. ܕܒܪܐ ܐܠܗܐ ܐܒܐ ܡܘܕܝܢ.
ܕܢܦܠ ܐܒܐ ܡܠ ܢܦܫܢ.[13] ܦܝܫ ܒܦܩܕܢܝ ܠܪܚܡܝܢ :·

---

[1] This hymn is found in: M2, B1, D1, C1, C2, D2, B2, M3, G1, D3.
[2] ⌐ This part of the heading is missing in D1, C1, D2, G1.
[3] D3 ܠܗ has been added later by the copyist.
[4] The heading in B1 is written as follows: ܐܣܛܪܐ :· ܠܗ ܕܦܘܠܚܢܐ ܘܥܢܝܢܐ :· ܕܝܠܗ ܕܡܠܦܢܐ ܡܪܝ + in marg. ܕܦܘܠܚܢܐ ܘܥܢܝܢܐ.
[5] B1 ܡܝܬܐ.
[6] B1 ܗܘ ܗܘ ܗܘܐ.
[7] D1 ܒܥܐ, has been added later by the copyist.
[8] G1 ܦܠܠ.
[9] B1 ܡܢܬܝܗ.
[10] B1 –; in D3 has been added later by the copyist.
[11] B2 +X ܪܒܝ.
[12] D3 + ܡܠܡܝ.
[13] D1 ܢܦܫܢ ܚܝܐ.

8.(75)

For the fifth Sunday of the Fast, with spiritual verses.[14] Written on Friday of the Deceased. Another for Sunday. And for the Sunday of the wickedness of its hardship. By Wardā. Say

[1] Woe to our time, how wicked it is.
Great misery to our century, how disordered it is.
Can it be this is the time,
that the life-giver spoke about,
making it clear to His disciples,
and teaching them
by His words,
that before the day when He comes,
the whole world and all that is in it will be disordered?

[2] When the disciples were gathered,
and sat in front of our Lord,
they then asked Him about His coming,
and said these words:

[3] 'Our Lord, interpret for us,
our master, teach us,
our light, our light, show us,
and by Your words comfort us.

[4] We are hungry to hear Your saying,
we are thirsty for Your living voice,
we are longing for Your word,
give us what we ask for.

[5] We believe that You are God,
we confess that You are the Son of God,
that You know all that we know;
sweeten our mind with Your knowledge.

[14] 'Spiritual verses' refers to the first verse of hymn (64) of Gīwargīs, on which see Table 6.

[6] ܢܦܩܝ ܗܘܢܐ ܒܐܬܪܟܝ. ܘܢܦܩܝ ܕܝܢܐ ܕܟܘܬܟܝ.[15]

⌈ܘܢܦܩܝ ܐܬܝܢ ܠܡܠܟܘܬܟܝ. ܘܡܬܢܝܚܢ ܠܟܠ ܥܡܘܪܟܝ⌉[16] ܀

[7] ܦܩܝ ܩܘܡܐ ܦܫܝܛܐ. ܝܘܡ ܐܬܡܢܝܢܘܢ ܗܘܢܐ.

ܕܡܢܐ ܢܘܡܐ ܕܐܬܬܐ ܐܝܬ. ܕܢܣܒܝܢ ܠܫܠܡܐ[17] ܗܝܐ ܀

[8] ܫܩܝܐ[18] ܒܘܠܝܢ ܒܚܕܝܬܐ.، ܘܐܚܕܐ ܠܗ ܘܒܝܡܘܬܐ.[f. 151v]

ܘܡܬܢܣܒܐ ܕܫܠܡܘܬܐ. ܘܡܬܐܕܒܩܐ ܒܡܫܝܚܘܬܐ ܀

[9] ܐܝܟܐ ܒܢܝܐ ܢܗܘܘܢ.[19] ܘܡܫܘܬܦܐ ܢܗܘܘܢ ܒܢܝܗܘܢ.

ܐܝܟܐ ܢܦܠܛܝܢ ܠܦܪܨܘܦܗܘܢ. ܘܐܬܡܢܝܢ ܠܩܕܝܫܗܘܢ ܀

[10] ⌈ܘܦܩܝܐ ܐܘܡܢܐ ܒܟܠ ܐܘܡܬܐ⌉.[20] ܘܦܠܚܘܬܐ ܒܟܠ ܡܠܟܘܬܐ.

ܘܫܪܟ ܡܢ ܡܢܐ ܕܣܠܩܬ. ܡܕܝܢܬܐ ܒܡܕܝܢܬܐ ܀

[11] ܘܫܩܝܢ ܙܡܪܐ ܘܐܘܠܝܬܐ. ܘܐܡܪܝܢ ܡܠܟܐ ܘܡܫܒܚܝܢ.[21]

ܘܦܠܚܐ ܡܢܢܐ ܘܡܫܡܫܢܐ. ܘܦܐܪܐ ܐܘܟ ܒܟܡ ܚܘܒܗܐ ܀

[12] ܘܢܗܘܘܢ ܒܚܒܪܐ ܦܩܝܢܐ.ܘܡܬܡܕܝܢ ܠܦܬܓܡܗܘܢ ܩܢܝܐ.

ܘܗܘܝܢ ܐܝܟܐ ܝܘܡ ܐܝܟܐ. ܒܕܡܘܬ ܕܐܝܟܐ ܫܬܘܚܐ ܀

[13] ܘܗܘܝܢ ܒܝܬܐ ܡܕܝܢܬܐ. ܘܐܡܪܝܢ[22] ܠܝܘܡܐ[23] ܕܒܫܒܬܐ.

ܘܡܬܐܕܘܢ ܒܝܩܕܐ ܕܡܝܬܐ. ܗܘܝܐ ܘܦܪܘܩܐ ܕܦܪܝܬܐ ܀

[15] D3 marg. b.
[16] ⌉ B1 rep. cd.
[17] B1, C1 ܠܢܦܫܐ.
[18] B1 + ܘ.
[19] D3 ܢܗܘܘܢ has been added later by the copyist.
[20] ⌉ B1 ܘܦܩܝܢ ܠܟܠܗܝܢ ܐܘܡܬܐ.
[21] D1 +X a.
[22] B1 ܘܐܡܪܝܢ.
[23] M2 ܠܝܘܡܐ has been added by a later hand.

[6] When will Your coming be?[24]
When will Your greatness shine?
When will Your kingdom come?
And Your Lordship be seen by all?'

[7] The life-giving mouth replied
thus, to His disciples:[25]
'Before the day that I come,
in order to terrify this world,

[8] error will increase,
righteousness will diminish,
dishonesty will be honored,
and faith will be persecuted.

[9] Fathers will be wicked,
their sons will be disobedient,
brothers will cheat their brothers,
and students their teachers.

[10] A nation will rise up against another nation,
a kingdom against another kingdom.
Out of fear,
cities will invade [other] cities.[26]

[11] Terror and hardship will increase,
wars and plagues will wax strong,
severe and destructive famines,
sickness and diseases.

[12] Servants will become audacious,
they will prepare traps for their masters.
Brothers will be against brothers,
like ferocious wolves.

[13] There will be bitter news,
that breaks the hearts of strong men;
they will be terrified by wondrous news,
the minds and knowledge of the righteous ones.

---

[24] See Matt 24:3; Mark 13:4.
[25] See Matt 24:1-31; Mark 13:3-27; Luke 21:5-28.
[26] See Matt 24:3-14; Mark 13:3-13; Luke 21:7-19.

[14] ܘܡܛܠ ܕܥܕܬܐ ܐܒܝܠܘܬܐ. ܘܩܪܝܢܐ ܠܗ ܐܒܝܠܘܬܐ.
ܬܦܘܩ ܚܕܘܬܐ ܘܒܣܝܡܘܬܐ.[27] ܡܢ ܡܠܘܗܝ ܕܟܬܒܐ ܀

[15] ܐܘ ܡܠܟܝܢܐ ܕܫܪܪܐ. ܚܙܘ ܘܚܙܘ[28] ܠܒܪܐ ܡܫܒܚܐ.
ܕܠܥܠ ܗܘܐ ܒܫܪܪܐ. ܗܘ ܕܡܫܡܠܝܢ ܡܢ ܢܒܝܐ ܀

[16] ܗܐ ܚܙܘ ܡܠܟܘܬܐ ܫܡܝܢܝܬܐ. ܪܒܐ[29] ܕܢܒܥ ܡܢ ܟܠ ܪܘܚܐ.
ܗܘܝܘ ܠܡܪܢ ܡܫܝܚܐ. ܕܢܦܪܘܩ ܒܚܘܣܢܗ ܠܒܢܝܢܫܐ ܀

[17] ܚܙܘ ܢܒܝܘܬܐ ܕܐܬܓܠܝܬ. ܘܡܦܩܬܐ ܕܗܘܬ ܡܬܬܟܣܝܐ.
ܘܩܪܒܐ ܕܗܘܐ[30] ܡܬܬܕܝܢ. ܐܬܚܙܝܬ ܕܗܘܐ ܡܬܟܣܝܐ ܀

[18] ܗܐ ܐܬܚܙܝ[31] ܫܒܝܠܐ. ܕܐܬܟܣܝ ܗܘܐ ܠܡܫܟܢܐ.
ܘܐܬܓܠܝ ܗܝܟܠ ܩܘܕܫܐ. ܥܡܗ ܢܒܝܐ ܕܫܘܒܚܐ ܀

[19] ܗܐ ܚܙܘ[32] ܐܬܘܬܐ[33] ܘܓܢܒܐ.[34] ܘܡܘܡܬܐ ܕܗܘܐ ܡܢܦܩܐ.
ܕܠܟܝ[35] ܗܘܐ ܠܗ ܡܬܚܙܝܐ. ܒܡܫܠܡܢܘܬܐ / ܐܝܟ ܕܟܬܝܒܐ ܀ [f. 152r]

[20] ܗܐ ܚܙܘ ܥܒܕܐ ܕܪܒܘܬܐ. ܘܩܪܒ ܥܒܕܐ ܕܫܒܝܚܝܢ.
ܕܒܟܠ ܕܘܟܘܬܗܘܢ ܡܬܚܙܝܢ.[36] ܡܢ[37] ܢܒܝܐ ܕܡܠܟܐ ܕܫܒܝܚ ܀

---

27 C1 marg. Contains only the two letters ܬܐ.
28 D1 ܘܚܙܘ has been added later by the copyist.
29 B1 ܪܒܬܐ.
30 D1 + +X ܗܘܐ.
31 B1 – ܘ.
32 G1 illeg.
33 B1 ܐܬܘܗ.
34 B1 + ܕ.
35 B1, D1 ܘܠܟܝ.
36 D1 + ܡܢܗܝܢ.
37 B1 + ܕ.

[14] Because deception will grow stronger
and iniquity will increase.
Love and faith will vanish
from all hearts.'

[15] O disciples of truth,
look and see the bitter century.
Was it truly this
that you heard from the firstborn?

[16] Come and see, O holy apostles,
our time which is worse than all times;
be intercessors to your Lord,
that He may save the believers by His mercy.

[17] Look at the unjust laws,
the commands that are ignored,
the laws that are smashed,
the boundaries that are crossed.

[18] Come and see the shepherds,
who oppressed the communities,
and ignored these duties,[38]
so the sheep and ewes were deluded.

[19] Come and see the priesthood purchased,
the pontificate sold,
woe to that one who sold it,
a Christian who bought it.[39]

[20] Come and see the priests persecuted,
the heads of the priests in custody,
they are seated and guided in their places
by the servants of servants.

---

[38] Patriarch Timothy II (1318-1332) mentioned in his Synod the same situation that is mentioned by our poet. See H. Teule, "The Synod of Timothy II, 1318".
[39] This suggests that the one who sold it was not a Christian; see Chapter 1.

[21] ܗܐ ܚܙܘ ܠܒܢܝ ܕܗܐ ܓܠܝܐ. ܘܠܥܒܕܘܗܝ ܗܘ ܐܬܐ.
ܘܣܘܡ ܠܠܒܗ ܕܟܐܢܐ ܘܐܒܝܠܐ. ܘܐܝܟ ܢܓܝܪܐ ܠܥܒܕܗ[40] ܡܪܢܐ ܀

[22] ܗܐ ܚܙܘ ܫܘܒܚܗܘܢ ܕܡܫܝܚܐ. ܕܐܫܬܠܛܘ ܒܗܘܢ[41] ܥܠ ܥܡܡܐ.
ܕܗܐ ܒܬܘܪܐ ܗܘܘ ܫܒܝܚܐ. ܐܝܟ ܫܡܫܐ ܒܝܢܬ ܟܘܟܒܐ ܀

[23] ܘܠܗܘܢ ܡܢ ܕܚܙܐ ܫܘܒܚܗܘܢ. ܘܠܐ ܕܫܡܥ ܫܘܥܝܬܗܘܢ.
ܕܢܗܘܐ ܐܟܘܬܗܘܢ ܒܡܫܝܚܘܬܗܘܢ. ܘܐܬܡܠܟ ܐܟܘܬܗܘܢ ܢܬܬܢܚܘܢ ܀

[24] ܗܐ ܐܦ ܫܡܝܐ ܢܬܚܕܬܘܢ. [42]ܚܙܘ ܠܥܠܡܐ ܕܟܠ ܢܬܚܕܬ.
ܕܠܢܦܫܬܗܘܢ[43] ܫܡܫܐ ܢܬܚܕܬ. ܘܫܡܫܐ ܒܢܘܗܪܗܘܢ ܕܟܠ ܢܬܚܕܬ[44] ܀

[25] ܗܐ ܡܠܟܘܬܐ ܠܥܡܡܐ. ܕܥܡܡܐ ܗܘܘ ܕܟܠܗܘܢ ܥܡܡܐ.
ܚܙܘ ܢܩܘܡ ܒܢܝܐ ܕܥܡܡܐ. ܕܐܬܒܚܪܘ[45] ܥܡܡܐ ܠܥܡܡܐ ܀

[26] ܗܐ ܚܙܘ ܟܠܗ ܡܠܟܘܬܐ. ܕܗܐ ܐܡܠܟ ܒܫܡܝܐ.
ܘܠܐ ܫܠܝܛ ܠܡܠܟܘܬܐ. ܘܠܐ ܟܠܗ ܠܐܪܥܝܬܐ ܀

[27] ܠܝ ܡܠܟܐ ܗܘܐ ܡܫܒܚܬܐ. ⌈ܘܡܫܒܚܬܐ⌉[46] ܡܫܠܡܬܐ.
ܘܡܠܟܘܬܐ ܡܫܠܡܬܐ. ܐܝܬ ܗܘ ܫܠܐ ܐܝܬ ܐܡܝܢ ܀

[28] ܢܫܬܒܚ ܠܟ ܡܠܟܐ ܫܠܝܛ ܐܝܬ. ܡܢ ܟܠ ܥܠܡܝܢ ܐܝܬ ܐܡܝܢ.
ܕܫܠܝܛ ܠܟ ܐܢܬ ܐܝܬ. ܘܠܟ ܡܠܟܘܬܐ ܕܠܥܠܡܝܢ ܀

40 G1 ܐܘܗ.
41 B1 ܠܗܘܢ.
42 B2 +X ܘܫܡܥܘ.
43 B1 ܕܠܢܦܫܗܘܢ.
44 D3 marg. d.
45 G1 illeg.
46 ⌈ B1 + ܘܠܐ ܡܫܒܚܬܐ.

[21] Come and see the flock that calls out,
and seeks a Savior,
which the wolf and the lion roar at,
and from which the shepherd fled like a hireling.

[22] Come and see your beloved scriptures,
by which all nations were made disciples,
but they were stored in rooms,
like mute ones with their mouths shut.

[23] No one recites your scriptures,
or listens to your words,
your disciples have trampled them,
and then your heirs have denied them.

[24] Come, O you who make laws,
look at the nations without laws,
who made laws for themselves,
and your sons remained without laws.

[25] Come O perfect shepherds,
who made the wolves sheep,
look at the shocking wonders of today,
that the sheep have become wolves.

[26] Come and see the heads of the flocks,
who eat fat things,
and do not take care of the suffering ones
and do not seek the lost.

[27] If the shepherd brings destruction,
and the leader brings corruption,
the teacher leads astray;
I am that one.

[28] I will keep silent; how can I accuse,
since I am the chief of all
sinners, for I speak,
but not of those remembered in time?

[29] ܣܘܡܐ ܐܦ ܠܐܠܝܫܒܥ ܕܡܘܫܐ. ܕܗܘܐ ܩܫܝܫܐ ܒܟܗܢܘܬܐ.

ܐܝ ܗܕܐ ܐܝܟܢܐ ܚܒܪܬܐ. ܒܟܠܗ ܕܠܐ[47] ܡܫܒܚ ܡܪܕܘܬܐ ܀

[30] ܣܘܡܐ ܠܐܠܝܫܒܥ ܚܙܐ ܗܫܐ. ܠܗܝ ܕܟܕ ܦܫܬ ܥܩܪܬܐ.

⌜ܕܐܬܐ ܦܘܡܐ ܥܩܪܬܐ. ܕܒܗ ܗܦܟܐ ܠܝܠܕܐ ܕܟܪܐ⌝[48] ܀

[31] ܣܘܡܐ ܐܫܬܡܠܝܘܗܝ ܐܦ ܥܩܪܬܐ. ܘܕܝܠܕ ܒܘܟܪܐ ܗܘܐ ܡܠܝܬܐ.[f. 152v]

ܠܘܩܒܠ ܕܘܝܬܐ ܚܝܠܐ. ܗܘܐ ܒܗ ܘܫܡܥܐ ܗܝܡܢܘܬܐ ܀

[32] ܘܐܢ ܠܥܩܪܐ ܠܐ ܫܘܝܢ. ܐܠܝܫܒܥ ܢܬܒܪܟܝܢ.

ܘܕܐܬܐ ܗܘ ܩܘܪܝܢ. ܗܘ ܕܝܠܕܬܝ ܒܟܠܗܘܢ ܢܒܝܐ ܀

[33] ܒܟܠ ܕܢܦܩܐ ܡܢ ܦܘܡܐ. ܘܫܒܚܐ ܘܬܘܕܝܬܐ ܘܩܘܠܣܐ.

ܘܝܗܒܐ ܠܣܘܟܠܐ ܡܢܗܝܪܢܐ. ܡܢ ܟܬܒܐ ܕܒܪܘܚܐ ܡܬܩܢܝܢ ܀

[34] ܒܟܠ ܥܕܢ ܩܕܡܝܬܐ.[49] ܘܥܠܡܐ ܗܘܐ ܠܡܫܒܚܢܘܬܐ.

ܘܢܥܒܕܝܢ ܠܗ ܦܘܠܚܢܐ. ܠܒܪܝܬܐ ܘܠܡܬܝܒܘܬܐ ܀

[35] ܣܘܡܐ ܢܠܗ ܟܠ ܗܝ ܕܐܬܐ. ܒܝܬܐ ܘܦܬܐ ܘܡܫܪܝܬܐ.

ܕܟܘܠܐ[50] ܕܒܪܝܬܐ ܢܣܒܐ. ܠܐ[51] ܚܒܝܒ[52] ܒܗ ܚܕ ܡܢ ܢܣܒܐ ܀

[36] ܗܘܝܢ ܠܐ ܗܘܬ ܐܦܝܬܐ. ܘܐܦܠܐ ܒܥܒܕܐ ܦܫܝܛܬܐ.

ܩܫܐ ܕܒܝܬܐ ܢܚܝܬܐ.[53] ܦܫܝܛܬܐ ܗܘܬ ܡܫܠܡܬܐ ܀

---

47 D3 ܘܠܐ.
48 ⌝ B1 rep. cd.
49 B1, C1 ܠܩܕܡܘܬܐ.
50 M3 ܕܟܘܠܐ
51 G1 illeg.
52 B1 + ܗܘ.
53 B1 ܐܦܝܬܐ.

[29] Stand up, O disciples of truth,
be merciful with grace;
if this is the end,
ask that the harm will not increase.

[30] Stand up, O disciples and see now,
this severe and wicked time,
of which the holy mouth said,
that in it is the beginning of birth pains.[54]

[31] Stand up, O you simple ones,
who by the power of the Spirit were attentive
to the times when wheat became weeds,
and authors became stupid.

[32] And though we are not worthy of mercy,
we are called your disciples;
we declare that He is our God,
from you [the disciples], we learned about Him.

[33] Ask that the famine will pass us by,
along with illness, turbulence, and distress,
and withhold destructive death
from the flock that believes in His name.

[34] Ask for tranquility, O you shepherds,
and peace also for the communities,
that hardship will change
to grace and calmness.

[35] Stand up and pray for this century,
wicked, hateful, and bitter.
The evil of ten centuries
is not considered as one tenth [of this century].

[36] Then there was no Torah,
nor the New Testament,
now what is Old is smashed,
and what is New has become denied.

---

[54] See Matt 24:7.

[37] ܗܐ ܚܙܘ ܕܐܫܥܝܐ[55] ܘܢܘܪܐ. «⸢ܡܫܡܫܝܢ[56] ܘܡܘܕܝܢ ܠܒܪܘܝܐ⸣.[57]
ܘܩܘܕܫܐ ܡܫܬܡܠܝܢ ܦܐܝܐ».[58] ܚܘܩܒܐ ܦܪܚ ܢܘܪܐ ∴

[38] ܩܘܡܘ ܠܒܘܫܐ ܒܠܗ ܕܫܡܝܐ. ܟܠ ܕܪܝ ܠܟܠܗܘܢ ܡܢ ܕܫܡܝܐ.
ܘܟܠ ܡܕܒܪܢܐ ܕܡܠܟܘܬܐ. ܕܠܒܫܐ ܡܢ ܢܘܪܐ ܠܒܘܫܐ ∴

[39] ܐܘ ܐܒܘܢ
ܐܘ ܡܠܟܘܬܢ
ܐܘ ܥܡܪܐ ܡܟܦܝܢ
ܐܦܝܘ ܠܥܡܪܘܗܝ
ܕܝܘܣ[59] ܒܠܝܢ
ܕܝܬܒܘܢ[60] ⸢ܒܠܚܘܕܘܗܝ ܫܒܝܚ⸣[61]
ܘܚܢ ܕܚܙܘܗܝ ܫܠܝܚܐ ܚܠܘܬܗ
ܘܐܝܟ ܕܟܠ ܫܢܬܐ ܡܕܒܪܐ[62]
ܫܠܝܡ ܕܫܡܝܐ ܟܠ ܗܝ ܕܪܐ
ܘܢܦܠ ܕܫܡܝܐ ܘܡܪܒܐ ܘܡܪܝܐ
ܘܠܗ ܡܫܒܚܝܢ ܒܟܠ ܥܕܢܐ ∴

---

55 B1 – ܕ.
56 M3 ܡܫܡܫܐ.
57 ⸢ B1 ܘܡܘܕܝܢ ܡܫܡܫܝܢ ܠܒܪܘܝܐ.
58 » The same verse is found in hymn (100)[38], which belongs to Wardā.
59 B1 ܕܢܛܪܝܢ.
60 B1, D2 ܘܝܬܒܘܢ.
61 ⸢ D1 written in the sequence ܫܒܝܚ ܒܠܚܘܕܘܗܝ after which it is corrected by placing ܐ on ܒܠܚܘܕܘܗܝ and ܒ on ܫܒܝܚ.
62 D2 ܡܕܒܪܢܐ.

[37] Come and see that wheat is called weeds,
vines [are called] thorns,
thistles are known as figs,
serpents are called doves.

[38] Rise up, O blessed ones, and ask for mercy,
for our century that is lacking compassion,
and for the composer of these words,
impure more than the impure demons.

[39] O our fathers,
O our doctors,
O true teachers,
beseech your Lord
to have mercy on us,
to forgive our sins by His grace,
and to eliminate our sins by His mercy
and that, like on the crowd in the desert,[63]
He may have mercy in this century,
and give [us] compassion, hope, and tranquility.
And to Him be glory at all times.

[63] See Matt 14:14; Mark 6:23; Luke 9:12.

[1](78).9

[f. 157r] ܠܣܘܬܐ ܕܓܠܝܢܐ ܕܦܨܚܐ ܥܢܝܢܐ[2]÷ ܕܒܠܗ ˹ܗܘ ܕܒܠܗ˺[3] [4]ܕܠܒܘܫܝܗ[5] ܦܪܝܐ[6]÷ ܘܡܬܦܪܫܐ ܩܠܐ
ܠܦܢܝܬܐ ܕܐܪܥܐ÷ ܐܘ ܒܡܫܡܫܢܐ ܕܐܪܥܐ÷ [7]˹ܠܠܡ. ܐܘ˺[8] ܒܪܬ ܡܠܟܐ ܒܡܘܬܢܐ[9]

[1] ܦܠܓܗ ܕܝܘܡܐ ܘܦܢܝܬܐ
ܕܠܥܕܪܐ ܡܠ ܗܘܬ ܠܗ̇[10] ܡܥܒܕܢܝܬܐ
ܘܢܣܒܐ ܠܗ ܕܠܐ ܡܙܘܓܘܬܐ
ܘܡܪܟܒܐ ܠܗ ܒܢܝܢ ܒܬܘܠܘܬܐ
ܒܒܢܝܐ ܡܥܘܕܝܢ ܒܬܠܬܐ
ܡܥܘܒܐ ܦܒܢܝܢ ܚܕܐ ܐܝܬܘܬܐ
ܚܕܐ ܒܦܪܨܘܦܐ ܡܠܟܐ ܦܪܝܫܘܬܐ
ܕܡܪܝܢ ܐܘܓܠܝܢ ܒܠܒܘܫܬܐ÷

[2] ܗܢܘ ܦܪܨܘܦܐ ܕܡܪܐ. ܕܐܬܓܠܝ ܠܥܠܡܐ ܒܒܣܪܐ.
ܠܡܪܢܐ ܡܬܚܙܐ ܘܠܡܠܐܟܐ. ܕܡܪܢܐ[11] ܡܠܐ ܠܥܠܡܐ÷

[3] ܒܗܘܢܐ / ܕܡܠܟܐ ܥܠܝܡܘ ܐܪܥܐ. ܒܗ̇ ܝܠܕܐ ܓܒܪܘ ܐܪܥܐ. [f. 157v]
˹ܕܐܝܟܐ ܠܗ ܡܠܟܐ ܐܪܥܐ[12]˺[13] ܡܟܪܐ ܒܐܪܥܘܬܗ ܠܟܠ ܐܪܥܐ÷

[4] ܒܗܘܢܐ[14] ܕܡܠܟܐ ܕܝܢ ܝܚܝܕܐ.[15] ܒܥܘܗܕܢܗ ܕܓܢܒܐ ܝܬܝܪܐ.
ܘܪܡܙܐ ܘܡܠܟܐ ܚܠܝܐ. ܒܬܘܠܡܕܗ ܕܒܡܪܐ[16] ܝܬܝܪܐ÷

---

[1] This hymn is found in: M2, B1, D1, C1, C2, D2, B2, M3, G1, D3.
[2] C1 – ܥܢܝܢܐ.
[3] ˺ C1 –, G1 + ܕܡܠܟܘܬܐ.
[4] G1 + ܕܦܠܟܘܬܐ.
[5] C1 ܕܠܒܘܫܗ. G1 – ܕ.
[6] G1 –.
[7] D2 + ܐܘ.
[8] ˺ G1 –.
[9] D1, C1, D2 – ܒܡܘܬܢܐ. G1 illeg.
[10] M2 We would expect ܒܗ here instead of ܠܗ̇; B1 ܗܘܬ.
[11] G1 + ܘ.
[12] B1 + ܕ.
[13] C2 c marg.
[14] B2 ܒܗ.
[15] G1 illeg.
[16] D3 marg.

9.(78)

Another one for the Easter Feast of the Lord, which is by the same Gīwargīs Wardā.
It is said after the responsorial of the mysteries,[17] or while taking the mysteries.[18]
Forever or The daughter of the king with glory.[19]

[1] The holy and pure bride,
who became betrothed to the Lord of all,
and without marriage gave birth to Him,
and raised Him with grace.
Children confessing three
qnōmē that have one essence.
Rejoice in Easter full of joy,
that Your Lord gave you with grace.

[2] This is the Easter of truth
that the firstborn made
perfect, great and complete,
perpetual and not temporal.

[3] In this evening, the mysteries are completed.
On this night, the mysteries are revealed.
Because the Lord of the mysteries came
and with His mysteries revealed all mysteries.

[4] In this evening, the crying was loud,
in the market of the Egyptian people,[20]
and songs with sweet voices,
in the congregation of the Hebrew people.[21]

---

[17] This is a prayer said before bringing out the body and blood of Christ and putting them on the altar during the mass.

[18] This refers to people taking holy communion.

[19] See Ps 45:9. This is a verse from the psalm that the priest says before starting a prayer.

[20] See Exod 12:29-32.

[21] See Exod 15:1-21.

[5] ܒܗܿܝ ܫܥܬܐ[22] ܢܦܩ ܗܘܐ. ܡܚܕܪ ܦܩܘܕܬܐ ܘܦܠܚ ܗܘܐ.
ܕܢܩܘܡ[23] ܠܦܘܠܚܢ ܢܦܠܝܢ ܗܘܘ. ܘܢܦܩܘ ܡܘܕܝܢ ܫܦܝܪ ܗܘܘ[24] ⁘

[6] ܒܗܿܝ ܫܥܬܐ ܕܐܬܒܨܪ ܗܘܐ. ܢܦܩܐ ܕܠܟܡܐ ܦܪܨ ܗܘܐ.
ܘܒܗܿܘ ܫܥܬܐ ܕܐܬܩܝܡ ܗܘܐ. ܦܬܚܐ ܕܠܒܒ ܐܢܫ ܗܘܐ ⁘

[7] ܗܢܘ ܠܫܥܬܐ ܕܬܠܬ ܫܥܝܢ. ܐܝܟ ܕܐܡܪ ܦܘܡܐ ܚܝܐ.
ܗܘ ܕܒܐܕܢܐ ܠܝܚܝܕܐ. ܢܘܪ ܫܡܥܐ ܒܥܝܢ ܚܘܫܒܐ ⁘

[8] ܗܢܘ ܠܫܥܬܐ ܕܫܬܐ. ܕܠܐ ܕܦܠܐ ܠܦܠܚܐ ܕܦܪܕܝܣܐ.[25]
ܗܘ ܕܦܠܐ ܗܘܐ ܠܥܘܕܪܢܐ. ܘܗܘܐ ܠܒܘܗܪܐ ܥܕܝܪܐ ⁘

[9] ܗܘ ܦܠܚܐ ܡܩܪܒܘ[26] ܐܬܦܠܓܘܗܝ. ܕܠܦܪܥܘ[27] ܗܘܘ ܐܬܦܠܓܘܗܝ.
ܗܢܐ ܦܠܚܐ ܠܐܬܦܠܓܘܗܝ. ܐܝܟ ܕܐܡܪ ܡܪܢܐ ܒܣܘܠܓܘܗܝ ⁘

[10] ܗܿܝ[28] ܠܫܥܬܐ ܚܕ ܥܣܪܐ. ܐܝܟ ܕܐܡܪ ܕܘܝܕ ܢܒܝܐ.
ܘܢܒܝܐ[29] ܕܐܡܪ ܠܗ ܒܫܘܒܚܐ. ܢܘܕܐ ܠܦܠܚܘ ܟܠ ܫܥܬܐ ⁘

[11] ܗܢܘ ܠܫܥܬܐ ܡܫܝܚܐ. ܕܗܘܐ ܠܦܠܚܐ ܡܬܚܣܢܢܐ.
ܘܠܢܦܫܐ ܦܝܘܣܐ. ܘܠܦܓܪܝܗܘܢ ܡܬܚܪܪܢܐ ⁘

[22] B1 ܝܠܠܐ.
[23] B1, D1, C1, G1 ܘܗܒܘ.
[24] M3 illeg. In D2 has been added later by the copyist.
[25] D2 ܒܦܪܕܝܣܐ.
[26] B2 written ܡܩܪܒܘ ܦܠܚܐ and then corrected by placing ܐ on ܦܠܚܐ and ܒ on ܡܩܪܒܘ.
[27] G1 ܦܠܡܪܗ.
[28] B1 + ܒ.
[29] B1 ܕܢܒܝܐ.

[5] In this evening Egypt was vanquished,
and the Synagogue[30] triumphed,
for in that [night] error fell down,
and the Holy church stood up.

[6] In this evening was sacrificed
the lamb which saved the people.[31]
In this evening was broken
the body that made life for all.

[7] This is the bread from heaven,[32]
as the living mouth said,
that to Isaiah in mystery,
the Seraphs gave in the house of atonement.[33]

[8] This is the bread of truth
that does not look like the Manna of the desert.
That one looked like a ray
and this one like the true light.

[9] Those who ate that Manna died,[34]
since they were deceivers of its master,
but this one gives life to those who eat it,
as the Lord said in His words.[35]

[10] This bread supports the heart,[36]
as the great David said,
and the one who eats it with love,
fire will not come close to his body.

[11] This is the living bread,
that nourishes the body,
illuminates the soul,
and exalts both.

---

[30] This word could also be translated as 'church' since the poet uses the image of the church in the same stanza in verse d. However, since he mentions Egypt, referring to the Old Testament, it is better to translate it as 'synagogue', referring to the Jews.
[31] See Exod 12:3.
[32] See Neh 9:15; Ps 105:40; John 6:33-35, 51.
[33] See Isa 6:5-7.
[34] See John 6:49, 58.
[35] See John 6:53-58.
[36] See Ps 104:15.

[12] ܗܘ ܢܣܡܐ ܕܠܐ ܡܣܒܝܢ. ܐܚܘܟܘܢ ܘܠܐ ܡܬܢܟܠܝܢ.
ܘܫܦܝܪ ܒܗ ܠܟܠܒܐ ܢܠܡܝܢ. ܘܗܘܝ[37] ܩܘܡܐ ܚܕ ܢܠܡܝܢ[38] ܀

[13] ܗܘ ܦܓܕܐ ܥܡܢܥܐ. ܥܡܢܥܐ ܘܠܐ ܐܕܠܢܐ.
ܠܐ[39] ܐܕܠܢܐ ܘܕܫܢܐ.[40] ܕܫܢܐ ܘܠܐ ܦܓܕܢܐ ܀

[14] ܢܓܘܠܘ ܡܢܗ ܐܘ ܕܓܦܝܢ. ܕܦܓܕܥܘܗܝ ܒܗ ܡܬܢܣܒܝܢ. [f. 158r]
ܘܢܥܬܪܘܢ ܒܗ ܡܬܦܠܠܝܢ.[41] ⌝ܘܢܣܬܪܘܢ ܒܗ⌜[42] ܡܬܦܪܠܝܢ ܀

[15] ܦܓܘ ܐܘܓܠܘܗܝ ܒܗܘܢܬܐ. ܕܦܠܘܠܘ ܗܘ ܕܣܠܝܬܐ.
ܘܢܥܠܘ ܕܝܗ ܦܟܝܣܘܬܐ. ܕܦܣܢܥܘ ܗܘ ܕܐܢܥܘܬܐ[43] ܀

[16] ܒܗܘܢ ܕܡܐ ܡܦܩܡܐ ܡܬܦܪܢܝܢ. ܒܗܘܢ ܕܡܐ ܫܘܩܐ ܡܥܒܕܝܢ.[44]
ܘܢܩܐ ܘܦܥܝܢܬܐ ܦܠܡܝܢ. ܘܦܪܘܢܘܗܝ ܠܐܘܡܐ ܦܠܡܝܢ ܀

[17] ܗܘ ܢܥܡܕܐ ܡܢܕܢܥܐ. ܕܐܡܪ ܦܪ ܐܢܝܢ ܓܐܥܐ.
ܕܝܘ[45] ܡܢܕܐ ܠܗ ܠܦܠܢܥܐ. ܘܒܗ ܕܘܝܢ ܦܕܠܐ ܘܗܘܥܐ ܀

[18] ܗܘ ܕܡܐ ܐܠܗܢܐ. ܘܡܘܓܐ ܠܐ ܐܢܥܣܐ.
ܕܡܝܬܘܬܐ ܒܫܢܘܗܝ ܫܢܐ. ܘܒܦܠܝܗ ܠܢܝܬܘ[46] ܦܠܥܐ[47] ܀

---

37 B1 – ܘ.
38 B1, G1 + ܠ.
39 G1 + ܘ.
40 B1 – ܘ.
41 C2 marg.
42 ⌝ C2 marg.
43 D1 ܕܡܟܘܬܐ.
44 D3 ܡܥܒܕܝܢ the letter ܥ has been added later by the copyist.
45 C2 ܗܘ.
46 B1 ܠܥܥܐ.
47 B2 marg.

[12] This is the bread; those who eat it
will not die and will not suffer corruption.
They will live by it forever and ever;[48]
the living mouth testifies to it.

[13] This is the heavenly body,[49]
heavenly and not earthly.
It is not earthly but spiritual,
spiritual and not corporeal.

[14] Eat from it, O you hungry,
that by it your bodies will be raised,
and your passions will be abolished,
and your life will be mixed with it.

[15] Take and eat with faith,
because it kills iniquity,
and drink His blood with joy,
because it gives life to humanity.

[16] With this blood, the stains will be cleansed.[50]
With this blood, sins will be forgiven.
Passions and anguishes will be lost,
and those who drink it will ascend on high.

[17] This is the joy-bringing wine,[51]
of which the righteous son of Jesse said,
that it pleases the intellect,
and knowledge and intelligence rejoice in it.

[18] This is the divine blood,
and not a human mixture,
by which mortality comes to life,
and by tasting, which passions are abolished.

---

48 See John 6:57.
49 See 1 Cor 15:40.
50 See Heb 9:14.
51 See Ps 104:15.

[19] ܗܘܐ ܢܘܗܪܐ ܡܢܗܪܢܐ. ܡܢܗܪܢܐ ܘܡܕܒܪܢܐ.
ܡܕܒܪܢܐ ܘܡܦܪܢܣܢܐ. ܡܦܪܢܣܢܐ ܘܡܙܘܢܢܐ ܀

[20] ܗܘܐ ܢܘܗܪܐ ܕܡܢ ܟܝܢܐ. ܠܐ ܕܒܪܝܬܐ ܘܐܦܠܐ[52] ܥܒܝܕܬܐ.
ܕܡܢܝܢܐ ܐܠܗܘܬܐ. ܡܙܠܓ ܠܒܪܝܬܐ ܥܠܝܫܬܐ ܀

[21] ܗܘܐ[53] ܕܝܢܐ ܕܡܬܝܠܕ ܡܢܗ. ܦܪܝܫܐ[54] ܠܟܝܢܝܘܬܗ.
ܦܪܝܫ ܒܪܘܚܐ ܡܬܝܠܕܘܬܗ. ܘܦܪܝܫ ܥܠܬܐ ܟܝܢܘܬܗ ܀

[22] ܗܘܐ ܫܡܫܐ ܕܦܘܪܩܢܐ. ܡܦܝܣܢܐ ܘܡܣܒܪܢܐ.
ܡܢ ܢܘܪܐ ܕܒܝܬܐ. ܕܠܝܬ ܠܢܡܘܣܗ[55] ܡܦܝܣܢܐ ܀

[23] ܗܘܐ ܢܘܗܪܐ ܕܦܪܘܩܐ ܠܗܘܢ. ܠܡܬܟܣܝܘܬܗ ܘܡܢܝܪܐ ܠܗܘܢ.
ܘܦܬܚܐ ܠܗܘܢ ܐܘܪܚܬܗܘܢ. ܘܦܬܝܚܐ ܠܗܘܢ ܥܠ ܢܗܝܪܘܗܝ ܀

[24] ܗܘܐ ܫܡܫܐ ܕܟܝܢܐ. ܕܠܐ ܕܡܐ ܠܗ ܕܡܢܗܪܐ.
ܗܘ ܒܟܐ ܘܐܦ ܠܗ ܕܒܝܐ. ܘܠܟܠܗܝܢ ܦܢܝܢ ܗܘܐ ܀

[25] ܗܘܐ ܕܡܐ ܕܟܝܠܝܬܐ. ܢܬܥܝܪ ܠܡܠܟܘܬܐ.
ܘܗܘܐ ܥܠܝܗ ܠܗ ܒܟܝܢܘܬܐ. ܠܟܝܢܐ ܕܠܐ ܡܬܚܘܝܢܘܬܐ ܀ [f. 158v]

[26] ܡܘܕܥܐ[56] ܒܕܘܡܝܐ ܕܝܠܗܘܢ. ܘܐܬܚܙܝܬ ܒܚܘܒܐ ܦܬܝܚܘܬܗ.
ܘܠܡܬܚܙܝܢܘܬܗܘܢ ܢܘܟܪܝܐ. ܘܠܗܘܢ ܢܒܝܐ ܢܚܝܠܘܗܝ ܀

---

[52] B1, G1 – ܘ.
[53] C1 ܗܘ ܗܘܐ.
[54] D3 ܦܪܝܫܬܐ.
[55] C2 marg; D2 ܠܢܡܘܣܗ.
[56] C2 ܡܘܕܥܐ the letter ܘ has been added by a later hand.

[19] This is the wine that gives forgiveness,
forgiveness and purification,
purification and sanctification,
sanctification and exaltation.

[20] This is the wine out of the vine,
that is not cultivated or planted,
that the divine right hand
mixed for the apostolic congregation.

[21] This is the blood of which the mixture
proceeded its pressing.
On Friday its mixing took place,
and on Saturday evening its pressing.

[22] This is the chalice of redemption,
saving and protecting
from the fire of Gehenna
for the burning of which there is no one to cool it.

[23] This wine that gives inebriation,
and gives joy to those who taste it,
abolishes their difficulties
and make them forget their passions.

[24] This is the spiritual drink
that does not look like that of stone.[57]
Passing by and disappearing with time,
but this one remains forever.

[25] This is the blood that was mixed
in the upper room[58] for the community of the apostles,
and behold, they drink it in the churches,
for life without mortality.

[26] The Jews pressed it with a spear,
the disciples accepted it with love,
and gave it to their disciples,
and they transmitted it till the last times.

[57] Referring to Moses. See Exod 17:1-7; Num 20:2-9.
[58] See Mark 14:15; Luke 22:12; Acts 1:13.

[27] ܒܗܘܐ ܚܡܕܐ ܕܘܝܢ ܫܠܝ̈ܚܐ. ܘܬܠܡܝܕܘܗܝ[59] ܢܝ̈ܚܐ.
ܘܗܘ ܫܠܛܗ ܠܚܒܪ̈ܘܗܝ ܕܠܒܫܐ. ܘܫܪܘ ܥܠ ܟܘܪ̈ܣܝܐ ܕܬܠܡܝ̈ܕܐ ܀

[28] ܡܫܒܚ ܕܗܘܝܐ ܫܠܝܐ.[60] ܕܝܢܐ ⌉ܟܠ ܕܝܘܡܬܐ⌈[61] ܗܘ ܟܠܢܐ.
ܗܘܝܐ[62] ܐܝܟ ܕܐܡܪ[63] ⌉ܟܕ ܘܟܕܝܐ⌈.[64] ⌉ܘܡܗܘܝܗ ܥܡܠ ܕܡܫܠܡܐ ܟܠܢܐ⌈[65] ܀

[29] ܒܦܓܪܗ ܢܦܠ ܒܩܒܘܪܬܗ. ܟܕܡܝ ܚܢܢܐ ܫܘܒܚܗ.
ܡܢ ܡܬܢܚܡ ܡܢܬܘܬܗ. ܕܢܘܚܐ ܕܗܘܐ ܠܦܢܝܬܗ ܀

[30] ܐܬܢܟܦܬ[66] ܡܢ ܢܦܫܘܬܗ. ܘܐܬܚܝܠ ܡܢ ܚܝܠܘܬܗ.
ܘܐܬܥܒܪ[67] ܡܢ ܝܬܝܪܘܬܗ. ܘܐܬܦܪܫ[68] ܡܢ ܚܒܝܒܘܬܗ ܀

[31] ܘܐܦ ܠܝ ܢܦܪܘܩ
ܡܢ ܕܟܠ ܡܬܦܪܩ
ܒܗܝ ܦܪܝܩܘܬܐ ܡܕܒܪܢܘܬܐ
ܕܒܗ ܦܪܩܢ ܐܢܫ[69] ܠܟܠܢ ܡܘܬܐ
ܘܢܬܦܨܐ ܡܢ ܠܘܚܡܐ ܕܚܝܐ
ܡܚܝܐ ܕܡܝܬܐ ܘܡܪܐ ܕܚܝܐ ܀

59 B1 – ܘ.
60 B1 ܫܠܝܐ.
61 ⌉ C2 illeg.
62 B1 –.
63 B1 + ܗܘ.
64 ⌉ D3 written in the sequence ܟܕ ܘܟܕܝܐ, and then corrected by placing ܒ on ܟܕ and ܐ on ܘܟܕܝܐ.
65 ⌉ B1 ܘܡܗܘܝܗ ܥܡܠ ܕܡܫܠܡܐ ܟܠܢܐ.
66 G1 + ܐܬܢܟܦܬ.
67 B1 – ܘ.
68 B1 – ܘ.
69 G1 has been added by a later hand.

[27] With this wine, the apostles became intoxicated,
as well as their victorious disciples;
with it, they forgot their passions,
and stepped on the torments of the instigators.

[28] The Lord of all, who is the shepherd,
the shepherd of all the sheep, the pure one.
As the son of Zechariah said,
and He takes away the sin of the worn-out world.

[29] By Your body, heal his [the poet's] demerits,
by Your blood, forgive his sins;
by You his mortality will be raised,
the miserable one who composed this hymn.

[30] His lowly state will be pleased in You,
his guilt will receive mercy in You,
his darkness will be enlightened in You,
his oppression will rejoice in You.

[31] Make us rejoice,
when all rejoice
in that exalted joy
in which You make the children of truth rejoice,
and let us find delight in You, O bread of life,
the hope of the dead and the Lord of the living.

10.(86)[1]

[f. 172v] «ܐܚܪܬܐ[2] ܕܝܠܕܒܫܒܐ ܝܠܕܐ[3] ⁘ ܕܒܠܗ[4] ܕܒܪ̈ܕܐ[5] ⁘ ⌜[6]ܠܟܠܟܡ⌝[7].»[8]

[1] ܥ̈ܘܢܝܬܐ ؍ ܕܥܠ ܝܠܕܘܬܐ
ܘܡܝܠܕܢܐ ܕܐܠܗܝܘܬܐ [f. 173r]
ܡܫܒܚܢܐ[9] ܕܡܫܝܚܘܬܐ
ܘܡܫܠܡܢܐ ܕܩܕܝܫܘܬܐ
ܘܫܘܒܚܐ ܕܪܒܘܬܐ
ܘܡܝܠܕܢܐ ܕܡܫܠܡܢܘܬܐ
ܘܡܚܣܢܢܐ ܕܡܝܬܘܬܐ[10]
ܘܦܪܘܩܐ ܕܟܠܗ ܐܢܫܘܬܐ ⁘

[2] ܒܝܠܕܢܐ ܕܒܗ ܦܪܐ ܒܪܝܬܐ. ܦܪܘ ܝܠܕܗ ܠܒܪܝܬܐ.
ܒܡܢܥܗ ܡܫܝܚܝܬܐ. ܕܟܠܗ ܗܘܬ ܡܝܠܕܢܝܬܐ ⁘

[3] ܗܘ ܕܡܢ ܠܝܬܐ ܐܬܚܙܝ ܗܘܐ. ܘܠܦܓܪܐ ܐܬܓܠܝ ܗܘܐ.
ܘܠܥܡܡܐ ܐܬܒܣܡ ܗܘܐ. ܘܡܢ ܕܝܢܐ ܠܗܘܢ ܦܠܝܓ ܗܘܐ ⁘

[4] ܒܡܫܝܚܐ[11] ܕܝܠܕܢܐ ܥܠܡ ܗܘܐ. ܘܐܡܢܥܢܐ[12] ܥܒܕ ܗܘܐ.
ܒܗ ܒܗܘ ܕܡܫܝܚܐ ܐܬܚܙܝ ܗܘܐ. ܠܥܡܡܐ ܕܟܠܗܘܢ ܝܠܝܕ ܗܘܐ[13] ⁘

[5] ܘܗܘ[14] ܒܝܠܝܬܐ ܡܢܝܢ ܗܘܘ. ܥܠܝܢܐ ⌜ܥܡܪܐ ܘܫܡܝܢ ܗܘܘ⌝.[15]
ܘܐܪܥܐ ܒܐܦܝܗܘܢ ܫܠܝܢ ܗܘܘ. ܕܡܢ ܫܡܝܐ ܢܚܠܝܢ ܗܘܘ ⁘

---

[1] This hymn is found in: M1, M2, B1, D1, C1, C2, D2, B2, M3, G1, D3.
[2] M1 [illegible], D1, C1, D2, G1 – [illegible].
[3] M1 + [illegible].
[4] G1 + [illegible].
[5] G1 [illegible].
[6] M3 – [illegible].
[7] ⌝ M1 –.
[8] The heading in B1 is written as follows: [illegible]
[9] M1 + ܘ.
[10] M1, G1 [illegible].
[11] M1, G1 [illegible].
[12] B1 [illegible].
[13] G1 illeg.
[14] G1 – ܘ.
[15] ⌝ G1 illeg.

10.(86)

Another one for the New Sunday.[16] By the same Wardā. Forever

[1] Creator of all new things,
renovator of old things,
fulfiller of what was written,
perfecter of what is mysteriously announced,[17]
rescuer of the captives,
liberator of slavery,
reviver of mortality,
the hope of all humanity.

[2] On the first day that He created the creation,
in it, He renewed the creation,
by His life-giving resurrection,
which became a renewal for all.

[3] When He appeared to the women,
and was revealed to [Mary] Magdalena,[18]
and was announced to Simon,
and He walked with those to the house of Luke.[19]

[4] On the evening of the first day, when
the second day had started, it was completed;
on that evening, He appeared
to the community that was mourning Him.

[5] While in the upper room,
the ten apostles gathered and hid,[20]
and the doors were closed
because they were scared of the people.

---

[16] 'New Sunday' is the Sunday which follows the Sunday of resurrection.
[17] Alternative translation: perfecter of the symbols.
[18] See Matt 28:1; Mark 16:9; Luke 24:10; John 20:11.
[19] See Mark 16:12; Luke 24:18. The biblical text mentions only Cleopas, not Luke. Luke is also mentioned in hymn (82)[1k] of Wardā and the book of ܬܘܪܓܡܐ Tūrgāmē, used during mass, in the hymn ܙܕܝܩܘ ܢܦܩܬܐ used for the Sunday of resurrection. See *Ktāḇā d-Tūrgāmē* ܟܬܒܐ ܕܬܘܪܓܡܐ [The Book of Interpretations], p. ܩܣܙ [167].
[20] See John 20:19.

[6] ܡܢܝ ܡܬܝܠܕ ܐܬܚܙܝ ܗܘܐ. ܘܒܝܢܬܗܘܢ ܥܐܠ ܗܘܐ[21] ܘܢܦܩ ܗܘܐ.
ܘܡܫܬܘܕܥ ܠܗܘܢ ⌈ܐܝܟ ܐܚܐ ܗܘܐ⌉.[22] ܘܡܡܠܠ ܠܗܘܢ ܐܝܟ ܐܚܘܗ ܗܘܐ ⁘

[7] ܒܟܠܗܝ ⌈ܕܘܟܝ ܐܬܚܠܛ ܠܗܘܢ⌉.[23] ܒܪܘܚܝ ܪܘܚܝ ܐܬܚܙܝ ܠܗܘܢ.
ܘܐܬܚܘܝ ܒܝܘܡܗ ܕܡܘܠܕܗܘܢ. ܘܐܬܚܘܝ ܒܗ ܒܥܠܝܡܘܬܗܘܢ ⁘

[8] ܗܘ ܕܝܢ ܡܢ[24] ܕܐܬܚܫܒ ܠܗܘܢ. ܒܫܒܝܠ ܫܠܡܐ ܚܙܐ ܗܘܐ ܠܗܘܢ.
ܕܒܗ ܢܫܬܟܚ ܫܘܝܘܬܗܘܢ. ܘܒܗ ܢܫܬܪܪ ܦܘܠܓܘܬܗܘܢ ⁘

[9] ܐܝܟܐ ܗܘ ܕܢܝܚܬ[25] ܡܢ ܫܡܝܐ. ܕܠܐ ܫܘܚܠܦܐ ܘܫܘܢܝܐ.
ܘܐܬܓܠܝ ܠܒܢܝ ܒܐܘܠܕܐ. ܕܠܐ ܫܘܚܠܦܐ[26] ܘܫܪܝܐ ⁘

[10] ܐܝܟܐ ܗܘ ܕܢܦܩ ܡܢ ܒܬܘܠܐ. ܒܗ ܚܬܝܡ ܘܚܬܝܡ ܒܬܘܠܘܬܐ.
ܠܐ ܫܪܝܘܗܝ ܕܡܒܪܐ.[27] ܕܟܠ ܗܘܐ ܡܟܠܐ ܠܡܒܪܐ ⁘

[11] ⌈ܐܝܟܐ ܐܢܐ ܗܘ⌉[28] ܕܐܬܝܠܕ ܠܟܘܢ. ܕܫܠܡܐ ܫܡܥ ܐܢܐ ܠܟܘܢ.
ܘܫܠܡܐ[29] ܚܙܐ ܐܢܐ ܠܟܘܢ. ܠܗܘܢ ܕܫܡܥܘ ܘܗܐ ܚܙܝܢ ܠܟܘܢ[30] ⁘

[12] ܒܗ ܡܫܬܒܚܝܢ ܐܘܪܚܐ. ܕܐܬܥܒܕܝ ܚܕܐ ܦܓܪܐ.
ܘܒܡܠܘܗܝ ܐܘܪܚ / ܐܪܥܢܐ. ܚܕܐ ܓܘܫܡܐ ܥܡ ܫܡܝܢܐ ⁘ [f. 173v]

21 D2 marg.
22 ⌉ G1 illeg.
23 ⌉ G1 illeg.
24 D3 +X ܕܝܢ.
25 D2 *c in marg. ܕܢܚܬ.
26 M3 ܫܘܚܠܦܐ.
27 G1 illeg.
28 G1 illeg.
29 G1 illeg.
30 G1 illeg.

[6] Then suddenly our Lord appeared,[31]
He entered and stood among them,
they were surprised by seeing Him,[32]
and were astonished by His entering.

[7] In our very likeness, he was revealed to them.
In our very image, he appeared to them.
Their knowledge was amazed by seeing Him.
Their intellect marveled at Him.

[8] But when He appeared to them,
He immediately greeted them,[33]
that in Him their commotion would calm down,
and in Him their doubt would become solid:[34]

[9] 'I am he who descended from heaven,
without changing or transition.
I was born from the virginal womb
without being defiled and dissolved.

[10] I am he who rose from the tomb,
which was truly closed and sealed.
Let stupor not confuse you
with this marvelous entering.

[11] I am the one who has told you
that I leave you peace,
and I give you peace.[35]
Remember that I have left [it] and given [it] to you.

[12] In me the spiritual ones are calm,
who feel angry towards the earthly ones.
And in my hands the earthly ones will become
one church with the heavenly ones.

---

[31] See Luke 24:36; John 20:19.
[32] See Luke 24:37.
[33] See Luke 24:36; John 20:19.
[34] The poet perhaps means here the doubts of some about the resurrection, such as Thomas, who did not initially believe that Christ had risen. See Luke 24:36-38.
[35] See Luke 36:24; John 20:21.

[13] ܦܬܟܪ̈ܐ ܐܒܕܬܘܢ ܘܦܘܠܚܢ̈ܝܗܘܢ. ܡܓܘܫܐ ܟܠܕ̈ܝܐ ܘܡܘܡܘܢ̈ܝܢ.
ܕܦܠܚܐ ܡܢ ܚܘܠ ܦܘܠܚܢ̈ܝܗܘܢ. ܕܗܠܡ ܐܢܐ ܠܟܝܠ ܢܦܘܠܚܢ̈ܝܗܘܢ܀

[14] ܡܪܐ ܕܥܠܡܐ ܢܣܓܕܘܢܝܗܝ. ܘܡܫܒܚܬܐ ܕܒܗ ܚܘܒ ܠܗܘܢ.
⌈ܦܬܚ ܦܘܡܗ ܢܦܫ ܒܐܦ̈ܝܗܘܢ. ܘܫܒܚܗ[36] ܪܘܚܐ[37] ܐܡܪ ܠܗܘܢ⌉[38]܀

[15] ܐܝܟܢܐ ܕܐܒܘܗܝ ܢܦܫ ܗܘܐ. ܒܐܕܡ[39] ⌈ܘܡܫܝܚܐ ܚܕܐ⌉[40] ܗܘܐ.[41]
ܗܘ ܒܥܠܝܬܗ ܢܦܫ ܗܘܐ. ܘܡܘܠܕܢܐ ܠܗܘܢ ܢܛܘܪ ܗܘܐ܀

[16] ܐܝܟ ܕܐܒܐ ܡܕܒܪ ܠܥܠ̈ܡܐ. [42]ܕܥܠܡܗ ܒܟ ܢܐܠܦ ܥܠ̈ܡܐ.[43]
ܗܘ ܡܕܒܪ ܐܢܐ ܠܟܘܢ[44] ܠܥܠ̈ܡܐ. ܕܒܟܘܢ ܟܠܗ ܢܐܠܦ ܥܠ̈ܡܐ܀

[17] ܐܝ ܦܐܪܘܗܝ ⌈ܠܐܢܫܐ ܚܕܘܬܐ. ܒܬܘܠܬܐ⌉[45] ܢܗܘܘܢ ܢܚܝܕܝܢ.
ܘܐܝ ܫܘܒܚܐ ⌈ܕܗܘܘܢ ܩܕܝܫܝܢ⌉.[46] ܒܬܘܠܬܐ ܢܗܘܘܢ ܡܚܝܕܝܢ܀

[18] ܢܗܘܘ ܕܝܢ ܩܕ̈ܝܫܘܬܐ. ܡܘܬ[47] ܡܘܠܕܬܐ ܐܠܗܘܬܐ.
ܡܛܠ ܢܛܪ ܒܬܘܠܘܬܐ. ܕܠܐ ܡܝܬܐ[48] ܕܝܠܕ ܐܠܗܘܬܐ܀

[19] ܐܦ ܚܘܒ ܡܘܩܕܬܐ.[49] ⌈ܒܦܓܪܗ ܕܐܕܡ ܡܢ ܟܠ ܢܫ̈ܐ.
ܠܐ ܚܘܒ ܢܡܣܒܠܘܬܐ. ܐܦܠܐ ܒܝܕ ܦܫܠܘܬܐ⌉[50]܀

---

[36] B1 – ܘ.
[37] G1 illeg.
[38] ⌉ C2 cd have been added later by the copyist.
[39] D3 + X ܡܘܠܕܢܐ ܠܗܘܢ.
[40] G1 illeg.
[41] C2 marg. bc.
[42] B2 + X ܕܒܗܘܢ.
[43] G1 ܥܠܡܐ.
[44] G1 has been added later by the copyist.
[45] ⌉ G1 illeg.
[46] ⌉ G1 illeg.
[47] G1 illeg.
[48] G1 illeg.
[49] D3 ܡܘܩܕܬܐ has been added later by the copyist.
[50] ⌉ D3 marg. bcd.

[13] Stretch out your hands and touch me;
stretch out your fingers and feel me.[51]
I rose from Sheol;
believe me that I will ascend on high, trust me.'

[14] After He had given them peace,
and showed His wounds to them,
He opened His mouth and breathed on their faces,[52]
and said to them: 'Receive the Spirit.'

[15] As His Father had breathed into Adam,
and all of a sudden, he became alive
thus He [Christ] breathed in the apostles,
and He gave them power.

[16] 'As the Father sent me into the world,[53]
that the world would learn about Him through me.
Behold, I am sending you into the world,
that through you, the world will learn about me.

[17] If you retain the sins of man,
they will be retained in heaven.[54]
And if [you] forgive their faults,
they will be forgiven in heaven.'

[18] If then to humanity,
the authority of divinity is given.
Who can say in insanity,
that He did not obtain the rank of divinity?[55]

[19] Even if He showed the wounds
in His body, which is above any touching,
He did not show [them] in weakness
or falsehood.

---

[51] See Luke 24:39; John 20:27.
[52] See John 20:22.
[53] See John 20:21.
[54] See John 20:23.
[55] See John 10:33-36.

[20] ܥܘܬܪܐ ܕܚܘܒ ܒܦܓܪܗ.[56] ܠܐ ܕܐܬܦܚܘܣ ܗܘܐ ܒܦܓܪܗ.
ܒܗ ܥܠܡܐ ܚܘܒ ܒܦܓܪܗ. ܥܒܕ ܕܢܘܟܪܝ ܗܘܐ ܠܦܓܪܗ ܀

[21] ܢܕܥܘ ܕܥܡ ܠܥܠ[57] ܡܢ ܚܢܢܐ. ⌈ܡܢ ܐܡܪܐ ܒܗ⌉[58] ܕܚܢܢܐ.
ܡܬܝܕܥ ܐܢܐ ܕܥܡ[59] ܕܚܢܢܐ. ⌈ܘܐܬܚܫܒ ܐܝܟ⌉[60] ܦܓܪܢܐ ܀

[22] ܕܥܡ ܦܓܪܗ ܒܬܪܒܪܘܬܐ. ܡܬܚܡܣܢ[61] ܒܟܠ ܦܠܚܘܬܐ.
ܘܢܬܦܢܐ[62] ܠܪܘܚܢܘܬܐ. ܡܘܕܝܢ[63] ܕܟܠ ܕܣܠܩܬܐ ܀

[23] ܘܠܢܘܡܐ ܗܘ ܕܡܫܢܐ. ܕܘܟ ܚܘܒ ܢܦܫܗ ܒܕܢܐ.
ܠܗܘ ܢܝܫܐ ܣܓܝܐܬܐ. ܘܗܘ ܒܢܝܚܘܬܐ ܥܕܡܐ ܒܫܘܠܡܐ ܀

[24] ܐܦܐ ܒܝ ܕܒܝܬܐ ܦܠܚܝܢ ܗܘܘ. [64]ܘܕܠܟܝܢܐ ܥܡܗ[65] ܒܥܝܢܝܢ ܗܘܘ.
ܒܝ ܟܕ ܐܢܫܐ ܡܦܝܣܝܢ ܗܘܘ. / ܕܢܫܡ ܠܥܡܝ ܚܙܘ ܘܡܠܝܢ ܗܘܘ ܀ [f. 174r]

[25] ܘܟܠ ܟܕ ܐܢܫܐ ܐܡܪ ܗܘܐ. ܕܟܠ ܡܬܝܕܥ ܠܥܡܐ[66] ܕܥܡܕ ܗܘܐ.
⌈ܒܕܘܟܐ[67] ܕܒܐܬܪܘܗܝ⌉[68] ⌈ܢܛܦܪ ܗܘܐ⌉[69]. ܦܓܪܐ ܗܘ ܕܢܬܚܙܐ[70] ܗܘܐ ܀

[26] ܗܘ ܢܛܪ ܒܠ ܒܫܬܝܬܐ.[71] ܡܢ ܕܒܠܒ ܗܘܐ ܠܟܘ ܢܝܠܬܐ.
ܘܗܘܐ ܥܠܡܐ ܠܥܠܝܢܘܬܐ.[72] ܠܗܘ ܕܐܢܫܐ ܕܦܪܝ[73] ܢܒܥ ܢܠܬܐ ܀

---

[56] D3 marg. a.
[57] D3 ܠܥܠ has been added later by the copyist.
[58] ⌉ G1 illeg.
[59] D3 ܕܥܡ has been added later by the copyist.
[60] ⌉ G1 illeg.
[61] C1, G1 ܡܬܚܡܣܢ ܣܢ.
[62] M1 ܘܢܬܦܢܐ.
[63] G1 illeg.
[64] D2 +X ܒܝ ܟܕ ܐܢܫܐ.
[65] G1 ܥܡܗ.
[66] G1 ܐܢܐ.
[67] B1 ܒܪܐ.
[68] ⌉ C1 is written in the sequence ܕܒܐܬܪܘܗܝ ܒܕܘܟܐ, after which it is corrected by putting ܐ on ܒܕܘܟܐ and ܒ on ܕܒܐܬܪܘܗܝ. Then the word ܕܒܐܬܪܘܗܝ is written in the marg.
[69] ⌉ G1 illeg.
[70] M1 ܕܢܬܚܙܐ.
[71] G1 illeg.
[72] G1 illeg.
[73] G1 illeg.

[20] The wounds He showed in His body
were not in His body.
In that hour He showed in His body,
something foreign to His body[74].

[21] If He rose beyond nature,
from where was His nature?
I believe that He rose as a spiritual being,
and He showed himself as a corporeal being.

[22] That His body truly rose,
we believe without division,
and that it was changed to the spiritual state,
we confess without fear.

[23] And on the eighth day,
again the Lord manifested himself,
to the gathering of the eleven,
that was staying in the upper room secretly.[75]

[24] He came, and the doors were closed,
and the disciples were gathered at the same moment.
They were telling Thomas[76]
how they had seen the Lord and touched Him.

[25] Thomas entered and said
that he would not believe what he had heard,
until he would touch by his hands,
that body that had been nailed.[77]

[26] When the one who knows all hidden things
entered the upper room
and gave peace to the group of apostles,
He directed towards Thomas the argument of [His] word:

---

[74] Bābāi dedicated a chapter in his ܟܬܒܐ ܕܚܕܝܘܬܐ *The Book of the Union* to explaining how Christ appeared to His disciples; it is quite similar to what Gīwargīs says in this hymn. See Bābāi, ܟܬܒܐ ܕܚܕܝܘܬܐ [The book of the Union], pp. 181-199.
[75] See John 20:19.
[76] See John 20:26.
[77] See John 20:25.

[27] ܝܗܒܬ ܐܝܕܝ ܠܐ ܡܬܚܫܚܢܐ. ܘܫܠܛ ⌈ܐܝܕܝ ܦܘܠܝ⌉[78] ܡܬܚܫܚܢܐ.
⌈ܘܐܘܫܛ ܐܝܕܐ ܕܡܚܝܢܐ. ܥܠ ܨܠܝܒܐ ܕܗܘܬ ܡܚܝܢܐ⌉.[79]
⌈ܕܚܝܐ ܠܟܝܢܐ ܢܦܩܬܐ⌉[80] ⁘

[28] ܫܐܘܠܐ ܕܚܙܝܬ ܡܢ ܥܠܝ ܗܘܐ. ܘܫܘܟܢܐ[81] ܦܩܚܝܢ ܠܐ ܐܝܬ ܗܘܐ.
ܘܡܘܩܕܬܐ ܕܢܘܪܐ ܐܝܬ ܗܘܐ. ܒܫܟܢܐ[82] ⌈ܕܠܥܠ ܢܛܘܪ ܗܘܐ⌉[83] ⁘

[29] ܢܘܚܡ[84] ܘܐܡܪ ܕܩܘܡܝܐ. ⌈ܩܘܡܝܐ ܦܘܡܗ ܐܝܬ⌉.[85]
ܩܕܝ[86] ܘܐܠܗܝ ܡܚܐ ܠܡܘܬܐ. ܡܢ ܐܝܟ ⌈ܐܝܕܝܐ ܘܕܡܢܐ⌉[87] ⁘

[30] ܦܬܚܐ ܩܕܝ ܘܐܡܪ ܠܗ. ܕܢܘܚܡܝ ܩܕܡܝ ܒܪ ܠܗ.
ܠܡܘܬܗ ܠܟܡ ܕܠܐ ܣܘܦ ܐܝܬ ܠܗ. ܘܡܬܘܡ ܕܡܚܝܐ ܐܝܬ ܠܗ ⁘[88]

[31] ܝܬܝ ܒܝܩܠܬܐ ܩܘܡܝܐ ܐܝܬ. ܘܒܝܕܥܬܐ ܡܬܘܡ ܐܝܬ.[89]
ܕܩܕܝ ܘܐܠܗܐ ܐܝܬܘܗܝ ܗܘܐ.[90] ܘܗܘ ܦܪܘܩܢ ܡܢܗ ܢܬܦܪܩܘܢ ܐܝܬ ⁘

[78] ⌉ G1 illeg.
[79] ⌉ M1, B1, G1 ܘܐܘܫܛ ܒܨܠܝܒܐ ܕܢܡܚܝܢܐ. ܘܡܢܡܪ ܦܩܢܐ ܕܗܘܐ ܡܚܝܢܐ.
[80] ⌉ G1 –.
[81] G1 ܒܫܘܟܢܐ.
[82] M1, B1, G1 ܒܫܟܢܗ.
[83] ⌉ G1 illeg.
[84] G1 illeg.
[85] ⌉ G1 illeg.
[86] G1 illeg.
[87] ⌉ G1 illeg.
[88] G1 abd illeg.
[89] M3 ܡܬܘܡܝܢܐ, G1 b illeg.
[90] G1 d illeg.

[27] 'Bring your hand, O unbeliever,
touch my hand and be a believer,[91]
and stretch the right hand,
on the side, that was the fount
of life for the earthly race.'

[28] Thomas, when he saw that He entered,
[even though] the door was not open,
touched the wounds made by nails,
in the body that astonished everyone.

[29] He cried and said: 'I confess,
I confess and believe.'
The blessed one cried: 'My Lord and my God'[92]
when he touched the hands and the side.

[30] Our Lord answered and told him:
'You saw me, and your intellect confirmed it,
blessed be the one who, [even though] I am not seen by him,[93]
still believes that I will revive him'.

[31] I confess by word,
and with intellect, I believe.
That this was my Lord and my God,
He saved me, and through Him, I will be saved.

---

[91] See John 20:27.
[92] See John 20:28.
[93] See John 20:29.

[32] ܫܒܚܐ ܕܥܠܡ
ܘܫܘܒܚܐ ܕܥܠܡ[94]
ܢܒܒܥ[95] ܒܡܫܝܚܘܬܐ
ܟܠ ܡܢܝܢܐ ⸢ܘܟܠ ܚܘܫܒܐ⸣[96]
⸢ܒܬܠܡܝܕܐ ܚܒܝܒܐ⸣[97] ܕܠܗ[98] ܦܠܚܘܬܐ
ܢܓܡܪ ⸢ܕܫܒܒܬܐ ܠܟܠ ܒܐܢܫܘܬܐ⸣[99]
ܘܐܬܐ ܕܝܫܘܥ ܒܗܝ ܡܠܟܘܬܐ[100]
⸢ܕܠܗ ܠܗ ܫܒܚܐ ܘܐܝܩܪܐ[101] ܚܕܬܐ⸣[102] ܀

[94] G1 illeg.
[95] G1 illeg.
[96] ⸢⸣ G1 illeg.
[97] ⸢⸣ G1 illeg.
[98] G1 ܕܠܗ ܒܗ.
[99] ⸢⸣ G1 illeg.
[100] G1 illeg.
[101] M1 – ܘ.
[102] ⸢⸣ G1 illeg.

[32] O hope of all,
Lord of all,
confirm us in faith,
in the resurrection and the renewal,
in the new world without division,
as You confirmed to Thomas;[103]
make us worthy to see You in that kingdom
that has no limits and no end.

---

[103] Written in Syriac as ܒܪ ܬܐܘܡܐ 'the son of the twin'; see the Syriac text stanza [32f]. See also John 11:16, 20:24, 21:2.

11.(91)[1]

[f. 180v] ܐܚܪܬܐ[2] ܕܒܝܬܐ[3] ⌜ܕܣܘܓܝܬܐ[4] ܕܡܪܝ⌝[5] ÷ ⌜ܕܥܝܠܗ[6] / ܕܦܪܕܐ[7] ÷ «ܘܥܒܝܕܐ ܕܣܘܡܟܐ[8] ÷ ⌜ܩܠܝܐ[9]⌝[10]»
[f. 181r] [11]

[1] ܐܘܪܚܗ ܕܒܪܐ ܚܒܝܒܐ
ܠܐ ܡܬܦܪܫܐ ܠܥܠܡܝܢ ܒܢ̈ܝܐ
ܘܩܘܪܒܐ ܡܠܟܗ ܕܢܚܒܫܐ
ܕܝܗܒܐ ܒܫܢ̈ܝܐ ܘܝܠܦܐ ܒܢܫܐ
ܘܝܡܝܢܐ ܕܪܫܝܦ ܒܟܠ ܥܘܠܐ
ܐܘܪܚܐ ܕܦܬܝܚ ܠܐ ܡܬܢܟܠܐ
ܘܝܬܝܪܘ ܕܦܬܝܚ ܩܒܪܐ
ܠܐ ܡܬܦܪܫܝܢ ܡܢ ܦܘܠܚܢܐ
ܒܫܡܐ ܓܝܪ ܐܘܪܚܗ ܕܡܫܪ̈ܝܬܐ
ܓܒܫܐ ܘܓܫܡܐ ܠܒܝܬܐ ܘܫܪܝܐ ÷

[2] ܡܠܟܗ ܕܐܒܐ ܚܒܝܒܐ. ܗܘ ܕܒܟܠܗ ܥܡܐ ܒܐܘܪܚܐ.
ܢܛܠܒ ܒܚܘܒܗ ܡܬܦܫܛܐ. ܘܝܬܠܠܒ ܒܡܠܟܐ ܐܢ̈ܫܐ ÷

[3] ܦܘܪܐ ܫܒܒܘ ܠܡܐܬܝܬܗ. ܕܡܢ[12] ܦܠܚܐ ܡܢܗ ܒܕܒܬܗ.
ܘܡܢ ܩܒܐ ܠܗ ܠܐܬܝܘܬܗ. ܗܝܟ ܫܪܐܢ̈ܐ ܒܫܠܡܘܬܗ ÷

[4] ܡܢܦܩܗ ܒܥܡܗ ܡܢ ܟܠ ܚܘܒܐ. ܘܠܐ ܡܬܪܕܐ ܡܢ[13] ܢܦܠ̈ܬܐ.
ܘܠܝܬ ܠܗ ܩܢܐ ܘܠܐ ܡܬܘܚܒܐ.[14] ܘܠܐ ܢܦܩܝܢ ܦܫܝܩܘܬܐ ÷

[5] ܗܢܐ ܕܗܘܐ ܦܪܘܩܬܐ. ܡܢܐ ܠܟܡ[15] ܐܚܘܗܝ ܒܐܝܬܘܬܐ.
ܝܒܐ ܒܚܘܒܗ ܥܒܪܐ ܫܒܝܘܠܬܐ. ܦܠܓܝܢ ܦܬܓܡܐ ܕܐܢ̈ܫܘܬܐ ÷

---

[1] This hymn is found in: M1, M2, B1, D1, C1, C2, D2, B2, M3, G1, D3.
[2] M1 + ܕܕܝܠܗ. The first letter ܕ is erased.
[3] B1, G1 – ܕܒܝܬܐ.
[4] G1 ܕܣܘܓܝܬܐ.
[5] ⌝ B1 ܕܣܘܠܝܬܐ.
[6] D1 + ܡܢ ܕܝܠܗ ܕܠܡܦܪܫܘ; C1, D2, G1 + ܡܢ ܕܝܠܗ.
[7] D3 ܦܪܕܐ.
[8] D2 + ܐܚܪܬܐ.
[9] Notice the vocalization. In C1 ܩܠܝܐ.
[10] ⌝ M1, G1 –.
[11] » B1 –.
[12] M1, B1 ܕܡܢ, G1 ܡܢ.
[13] M1, B1, G1 ܒܟܠ.
[14] C1 + X ܡܬܡܨܝܢܐ.
[15] M1, B1, G1 ܐܝܟ.

11.(91)

Another one for the Feast of the Ascension of our Lord. By the same Wardā. It is of the Mawtḇā.[16] Forever

[1] The way of the only-begotten Son
is incomprehensible to all creatures.
The word of the sage testifies
that the eagle in the sky and the ship in the sea,
and the serpent that creeps on the rock,
that the way of these is incomprehensible,[17]
and if these cannot be grasped by the intellect,
then how much more the way of the Most High,
which is hard and hidden, concealed and high.

[2] The only-begotten Word of the Father,
who is equal with Him in essence.
He consented by His eternal love
and revealed himself in a physical body.

[3] He made His coming a wonder;
His creation is full of Him.
Though there is no limit to His essence,
He became a man by His grace.

[4] His *qnōmā* was hidden from all sight,
and was incomprehensible by knowledge,
He has no limit and no measure,
no 'when'[18] nor quantity.

[5] This one of such greatness,
together with His Father in essence,
consented with His love and dwelt in the Virgin,
and put on a human body.

---

[16] This is a type of prayer that is chanted while siting.
[17] See Prov 30:19.
[18] By the word ܐܡܬܝ the poet means 'time'.

[6] ܠܐ ܫܒܩܗ ܗܘܐ ܡܢ ܐܒܐ. ܐܦܠܐ ܫܠܚܗ ܒܡܩܠܐ ܒܪܐ.
ܘܟܠ ܗܘܐ ܡܕ̈ܝܘܗܝ ܕܘܟܪܐ. ܒܟܝܢܐ ܘܝܠܕܗ ܒܬܘܠܬܐ ܀

[7] ܒܫܠܡܗ ܬܪܝܨ ܠܦܠܓܘܬܐ.[19] ܒܥܘܡܪܗ[20] ܥܡܢ ܫܘܬܦܘܬܐ.
ܦܪܨܘܦܗ ܚܙܝܢ ܙܗܘܬܐ. ܠܟܠܗ ܒܢ̈ܝܐ ܕܐܢܫܘܬܐ[21] ܀

[8] ⌜ܗܝܕܝܢ ܘܫܒܩ ܠܗ ܒܥܘܡܪܗ ܠܥܘܡܪܬܐ⌝.[22] ܘܫܪܝܗ ܒܝܥܩܘܒ ܠܫܠܝܚܘܬܐ.
ܘܥܡ ܦܠܓܝ ܠܓܝܣ ܡܢܘܬܐ. ܘܠܬܘܡܐ ܗܠܝܢ ܒܡܫܡܫܢܘܬܐ ܀

[9] ܗܢ ܫܪܝ ܒܗ[23] ܫܠܝܚܐ. ܕܢܥܒܪ ܠܟܬܒܗ[24] ܫܠܝܚܐ.
ܕܒܪܐ ܗܘܐ ܠܥܝܢܐ[25] ܥܠܝܡܐ. ܘܐܬܐ ܚܕܡܐ ܠܥܡܗ ܫܡܝܐ ܀

[10] ܘܗܢ ܫܪܝ ܠܡܫܡܫܘ ܥܡܗܘܢ. ܕܫܠܝܚܘܗܝ ܦܩܕ ܐܢܘܢ.
ܘܗܘܝܢ ܐܝܟ ܗܘܐ[26] ܠܗܘܢ. ܘܦܘܩܕܐ ܠܝܘܚܢܢ ܘܠܐ ܡܝܐ ܠܗܘܢ ܀

[11] ܟܕ ܡܫܠܚܘܗܝ ܕܐܙܠ ܐܢܐ. ܘܡܥܢܘܗܝ ܒܥܒܕܐ[27] ܡܟܝܠ ܐܢܐ.
ܕܐܝ ܢܝܚܐ / ܟܠ ܐܙܠ ܐܢܐ. ܕܫܡܥܘܢܝ ܟܠ ܡܟܝܪ ܐܢܐ ܀ [f. 181v]

[12] ܦܩܘ ܒܐܘܪܫܠܡ ܡܗܝܡܢܬܐ. ܠܚܡܐ ܕܡܐܟܠܐ ܦܬܘܪܬܐ.
ܘܡܬܚܫܚܝܢ ܒܥܒܕܘܬܐ. ܘܒܐܝܩܪܬܐ ܦܪܝܫܘܬܐ ܀

[13] ܒܗ ܟܠܗ ܐܢܐ ܫܒܩ[28] ܕܪܘܚܐ. ܘܥܫܘܢܐ ܐܢܐ ܒܬܪܘܕܘܗܝ.
ܘܦܘܠܚܢ ܐܢܐ ܥܘܠܢܝܢ ܘܦܪܘܩܝ.[29] ܘܡܬܒܪܘܢ[30] ܒܢܠܐ[31] ܐܠܗܘܬܝ ܀

---

[19] G1 −ܠ.
[20] D2 + ܘ.
[21] D3 illeg.
[22] ⌝ The same verse is found in hymn 12.(92)[4].
[23] D3 ܒܗ has been added later by the copyist.
[24] G1 ܠܟܬܒܐ.
[25] M1 +X ܗܘܐ.
[26] M1 −.
[27] G1 ܒܥܒܕܐ.
[28] G1 illeg.
[29] G1 − ܘ.
[30] M1, B1 ܘܡܬܒܪܘܢ, G1 ܕܡܬܒܪܘܢ.
[31] M1, B1, G1 + ܒܢ.

[6] His conception was not from a man
and His birth did not dispel the virginity,
and for this, He was called wonderful[32]
by the prophet, and his word is true.

[7] By His birth, He uprooted kingdoms,
by His baptism, He forgave sins,
by His fasting, He performed a victory
for all human nature.

[8] He died, and with His death, He killed death,
and with His flesh, He destroyed iniquity.
He rose and worked resurrection for our race,
and He ascended to heaven with glory.

[9] When the Son of the Most High began
to fly to His heavenly homeland,[33]
He assembled the apostolic gathering
and came to Bethany.

[10] And when He began to be separated from them,
He ordered His apostles
and thus He said to them:
'Go back to Zion and do not be sad,

[11] do not be sad that I am leaving
and departing from you in body,
for if I do not leave,
I will not send the Holy Spirit.[34]

[12] Wait in the city of Jerusalem,
until the gift arrives[35]
and you will triumph with great deeds,
miracles and marvels.

[13] By this, I will reveal the power of my greatness,
and show my mightiness,
and teach my authority and my greatness,
and my divinity will be preached to all.'

---

[32] See Isa 9:6.
[33] See Mark 16:19; Luke 24:50.
[34] See John 14:25-28.
[35] See Luke 24:49.

[14] ܘܟܕ ܚܙܐ ܠܡܫܬܪܝܘ ܚܝܠܗ̈ܝ. ܒܝܘܡܬܐ ܕܦܣܩ ܐܢܝ.
ܐܬܐ ܠܐܪܥܐ ܠܟܢܘܫܘܗ̈ܝ. ܘܐܬܬܟܫ ܗܘܐ ܡܢ ܚܘܒܘܗ̈ܝ ܀

[15] ܕܢܚܘܬ ܠܐܘܪܚܗ ܕܬܝܒܘܬܐ. ܘܐܬܦܢܝܗ[36] ܡܢ ܛܥܝܘܬܐ.
ܘܡܠܟ ܘܐܡܪ ܒܦܪܝܫܘܬܐ. ܒܠܗܘܢ[37] ܦܠܚܐ ܕܡܠܟܘܬܐ ܀

[16] ܡܢ ܛܠܝܐ ܕܥܒܕܘܬܐ. ܣܓܝ ܛܒܬܐ ܕܚܘܣܝܢܘܬܐ.[38]
ܒܥܒܕܐ ܝܩܝܪܐ. ܢܬܬܪܚܡ ܠܗ[39] ܡܪܝܡܘܬܐ ܀

[17] ܕܢܚܘܬ ܠܐܘܪܚܗ ܡܠܟܝܬܐ. ܕܘܢܚܐ ܢܟܦܝܢܬܐ.
ܦܬܚ ܕܪܥܘܗ̈ܝ ܒܩܢܝܢܗ. ܘܐܚܕܗ ܠܗ ܣܘܟܠܐ ܀

[18] ⌈ܡܠܝܐ ܠܗ ܡܬܚܫܒ ܗܘܐ⌉.[40] ܕܐܢ ܫܠܡܬ ܡܬܚܫܒ[41] ܗܘܐ.
ܘܠܒܐ ܠܡܗܘܐ ܡܘܕܐ ܗܘܐ. ܘܕܝܢܐ ܐܬܦܪܫ ܕܡܥܕܐ ܗܘܐ ܀

[19] ܥܠܝܡܘܬܐ ܡܬܚܫܒ ܗܘܐ.[42] ܘܡܪܕܘܬܐ[43] ܘܡܕܒܪ ܗܘܐ.[44]
⌈ܘܡܘܬܒܐ ܕܝܢ ܡܬܡܪܕܒ ܗܘܐ⌉.[45] ⌈ܗܕܟܐ ܡܘܕܝܢ[46] ܗܢܝ ܗܘܐ⌉[47] ܀

[20] ܒܕܘܟܐ ܗܘܐ ܠܗ ܬܟܠܘܬܐ. ܠܗܘ ܒܪ ܓܢܣܐ ܕܢܦܫܬܐ.
ܘܡܠܟ ܫܒܪܐ ܕܝܘܪܬܐ. ܘܢܬܠܘܬܐ ܕܪܘܚܐ ܀

[21] ܡܢܗ ܗܝ ܕܐܬܬ[48] ܒܥܘܒܝܐ. ܒܠ ܒܢܝܐ ܕܝܘܪܬܐ ܘܕܘܚܐ.
ܘܐܙܠ ܦܪܐ ܠܗ ܒܪܘܚܐ.[49] ⌈ܕܬܬܐ ܩܡ⌉[50] ܒܠ ܒܘܪܟܐ ܡܬܒܝܢܐ ܀

---

[36] B1 – ܘ.
[37] G1 –.
[38] B1 ܕܚܘܣܝܢܬܐ, G1 illeg.
[39] B1 ܠܗ, M1, D2, M3 ܠܗ.
[40] ⌉ D3 written in the sequence ܡܬܚܫܒ ܗܘܐ ܡܠܝܐ ܠܗ and then corrected by putting ܐ on ܡܠܝܐ ܠܗ and ܒ on ܡܬܚܫܒ ܗܘܐ.
[41] D3 illeg.
[42] D3 marg.
[43] G1 – ܘ.
[44] M1, B1 ܡܬܡܪܕܒ ܗܘܐ, G1 ܡܬܡܪܕܒ ܗܘܐ.
[45] ⌉ G1 ܗܕܟܐ ܡܘܕܝܢ ܗܢܝ ܗܘܐ.
[46] M1 ܡܘܕܝܢܐ.
[47] ⌉ G1 ܘܡܘܬܒܗ ܕܡܘܕܝܢ ܩܢܝ ܗܘܐ.
[48] G1 illeg.
[49] G1 ܒܪܘܚܢܐ.
[50] ⌉ G1 ܕܬܬܐ ܩܡ.

[14] When He started to separate himself from them,
He stirred them in wonder;
He embodied the air to their eyes[51]
and then He disappeared from their sight.

[15] The powers ran towards Him,
and the armies were gathered,
they cried out and called with trumpets
all the workers of the kingdom.

[16] Suddenly and quickly,
instead of scarlet vessels
in white clouds,
the chariot was adorned.

[17] They ran towards Him hastily,
the spiritual ones quickly,
they bowed their heads equally,
and worshipped Him with love.

[18] The angels were serving Him,
the commanders of the armies were glorifying Him,
the watchers were praising [Him] together with them,
and those of the house of the angels were hurrying [to Him].

[19] The Authorities were chanting,
the Dominions were singing,
the Thrones were exalting,
the Seraphim were singing 'He is holy'.

[20] The Cherubim carried Him,
He, the Son of the earthly race.
The fiery ranks cried out
with the spiritual powers.

[21] Who is this one who comes with glory
on the clouds of fire and wind?
And the Father calls Him with celebration:
'Come and sit on the glorious throne.'

[51] See Acts 1:9.

[22] ܡܢܘ ܗܘ ܕܐܝܟ ܒܪ ܐܢܫܝܢ. ܡܫܝܚܐ ܘܡܢ ܡܕܡܘܬܗ ܙܘܥܝܢ.
ܚܝܠܐ ܘܥܝܪ̈ܐ ܘܠܗ[52] ܡܫܒܚܝܢ. ܘܚܝܠܘܗܝ[53] ܟܕ ܠܐ ܡܬܡܫܚܝܢ[54] ܀

[23] ܡܢܘ ܗܘ ܕܐܬܐ ܒܥܢܢܐ. ܘܫܠܛ ܥܠܗ ܕܘܟܬܐ.
ܘܠܡܠܟܘܬܗ ܡܣܝܟ ܒܫܘܪܐ. ܒܗܘ ܕܢܐܪܘܗ ܡܬܚܙܝܢܐ ܀

[24] ܡܢܘ ܕܡܢ ܓܘܗ[55] ܢܣܒܗ. ܗܟܢ ܠܥܠܡܐ[56] ܕܝܠܗ.
ܘܗܘܐ ܩܪܝܒ ܠܪܘܚܢܐ. / ܘܡܬܚܠܛܐ ܠܚܘܒܐ ܀ [f. 182^{r}]

[25] ܡܢܘ ܕܣܝܡܗ ܢܗܝܪܐ. ܒܫܡܝܐ ܕܢܗܪܘܗ ܫܒܝܚܐ.
ܘܩܒܝܥ ܠܡܘܬܒܗ ܢܗܝܪܐ. ܘܠܗ ܡܢܗܪܝܢ ܒܟܠ ܐܢܫ̈ܐ ܀

[26] ܡܢܘ ܗܘ ܥܒܕܐ ܕܒܪܝܬܐ. ܘܥܒܕ ܘܫܠܡ ܡܢ ܐܪܥܐ.
ܘܐܬܐ ܘܡܠܟ ܒܪܘܡܝܬܐ. ܒܪ ܕܠܝܬ ܣܘܦܐ ܘܠܐ ܫܘܪܝܐ[57] ܀

[27] ܡܢܘ[58] ܗܢܐ ܕܐܬܘܟܠܬܐ. ܘܡܠܟܘܬܗ ܢܨܝܚܬܐ.
ܗܘܐ ܠܗ ܢܨܚܢ ܡܫܝܚܘܬܐ.[59] ⌈ܘܡܠܟܘܬܗ ܒܝܕ ܒܡܫܡܫܢܘܬܐ⌉[60] ܀

[28] ܡܢܘ ܗܢܐ ܕܫܡܫܐ ܠܗ. ܒܫܡܗ ܘܟܠ ܡܫܬܥܒܕܐ ܠܗ.[61]
ܘܐܝܟ ܒܪ ܐܢܫܝܢ ܡܫܝܚܐ[62] ܠܗ. ܘܐܝܟ ܥܒܕܐ ܠܐ ܡܫܬܘܕܐ ܠܗ[63] ܀

[29] ܐܝ ܫܡܫܐ ܗܘ ܡܢ ܢܘܗܪܐ ܠܗ. ܫܠܝܚܘܬܐ ܕܡܫܡܫܢܘܬܐ ܠܗ.
ܘܐܝ ܫܠܝܚܐ ܗܘ ܡܢܘ ܚܘܒ ܠܗ. ܕܡܫܬܒܚܐ ܡܫܬܥܒܕܐ ܠܗ ܀

[30] ܦܠܓܐ ܡܢܗ ܕܡܠܟܝܢ. ܦܠܓܐ ܡܢܗ ܕܥܒܕܝܢ.
ܘܟܠܗܘܢ[64] ܠܦܘܩܕܢܗ ܫܡܥܝܢ. ܘܠܝܩܪܗ[65] ܡܫܬܥܒܕܝܢ ܀

---

[52] D2, M3 – ܘ.
[53] G1 – ܘ.
[54] G1 ܡܬܡܫܚܝܢ.
[55] D3 + ܡܢܬܐ.
[56] G1 illeg.
[57] G1 illeg.
[58] G1 illeg.
[59] G1 c illeg.
[60] ⌈⌉ M1, B1 ܟܠ ܕܘܝܐ ܒܫܡܘܬܐ, G1 ܕܘܫܬܐ ܒܫܡܐ ܐܡܘܬܐ.
[61] B1 marg. ܠܗ.
[62] G1 illeg.
[63] M1 marg.
[64] M1, B1, G1 – ܘ.
[65] M1, B1, D1, C1, D2 ܘܠܝܩܪܗ.

[22] Who is this one who was seen as a human being?
They were trembling before Him;
the armies and the ranks glorified Him,
and they could not look at Him.

[23] Who is this one who comes in body,
and is full of all wonder?
He made the spiritual ones astonished
about that which was done to Him.

[24] Who is this one who ascends from below
to the home of those on high?
See, He made the spiritual ones afraid
and He terrified the fiery ones.

[25] Who is this one by whom the lights were darkened
compared to His beautiful garments?
And the watchers rejoiced in front of Him
and gave respect to Him with all honor.

[26] Who is this fruit that sprang up,
grew and ascended from the earth?
He came and passed through the firmament,
which has no crack or door.

[27] Who is this one for whom the flame
and burning blaze
became a bed today
and He sat on it in glory?

[28] Who is this one who is difficult for us to implore
and who cannot be explained by us?
We saw Him as a human being,
but we did not comprehend Him as the Lord.

[29] If He is hidden, from whence comes the revelation
by which he can be seen?
And if He is revealed, who gave Him
that the chariot would be subject to Him?

[30] The ranks are afraid of Him,
the assemblies are trembling from Him,
all of them expecting His commands,
and submitting to His will.

[31] ܡܢ ܡܠܟ ܠܝ ܟܠ ܗܕܐ. ܕܠܐ ܡܢܝܢܐ ܕܫܘܚܠܦܗ ܒܢܝܐ.[66]
ܘܠܐ ܡܕܝܢ ܠܗ ܕܝܢܐ. ܘܠܐ ܡܕܝܢܐ ܘܐܠܦܐ[67] ܗܘܐ ܀

[32] ܐܝܟ ܡܠܟܐ ܕܒܥܒܕܘܬܐ. ܐܠܦܢ ܐܢܘܢ ܒܫܘܒܚܐ.
ܕܗܘܐ ܗܘ ܢܠܦܐ ܕܐܝܠܘܬܐ. ܐܠܦܢ ܡܠܦܢܐ ܕܐܢܫܘܬܐ ܀

[33] ܗܢܘ ܡܪܝܐ ܒܡܪܐ. ܘܟܠ ܡܕܡ ܗܘ ܟܠܝ ܒܪܐ.
ܘܡܬܠܒܫܗ ܠܝܫ ܦܓܪܐ. ܕܢܣܐ ܠܟܠ ܠܒܢܝ ܢܫܐ ܀

[34] ܡܢ ܒܪ ܐܠܗܐ[68] ܠܥܡܐ. ܥܠܝܗ ܠܗܘܢ ܗܠܡܬܢܘܬܗ ܠܒܢܝܐ.
ܗܕܢ ܟܒܪܐ ܒܥܝܢܬܐ ܦܢܝܬܐ. ܘܐܡܪܘ[69] ܠܗܘܢ ܒܩܠܐ ܢܗܝܪܐ ܀

[35] ܠܠܒܠܠܐ ܠܗܘܢ ܦܘܩܕܢܗ. ܘܒܥܡܗܐ ܡܢܗ ܫܪܒܬܗ.
ܠܒܥܘܬ ܐܠܗܐ ܫܝܢܬܗ. ܘܦܩܕܘ ܠܐܝܟܐ ܕܢܬܦܩܕܘܢ ܀

[36] ܐܒܗܬܐ ܐܠܗܐ ܒܐܝܡܢܘܬܐ. ܗܘܝܐ ܐܬܐ ܒܡܕܪܐ.
ܘܡܢܝܢ ܒܠܗܝܐ ܒܪܐ. ܘܡܬܬܘܕܐ ܡܪܐ ܒܪܐ ܀

[37] ܐܦ ܕܐܬܚܘܝ ܘܦܢ ܐܬܬܐܝܬ. ܘܗܘܐ ܡܬܚܘܐ ܐܠܗܐܝܬ.
ܚܘܝ ܘܐܝܬܝܗ ܢܗܝܪܝܬ. ܠܕܐܡܪ ܗܠܝܢ ܡܫܝܚܐܝܬ ܀

[38] ܒܪܝܟ ܗܘ ܟܠܗܝ
/ ܥܒܝܕ ܕܘܡܪܗܝ [f. 182v]
ܒܪܐ ܕܦܪܩܢ ܒܝܕ ܡܢܗܬܗ
ܘܡܕܡ ܠܟܝܢܢ ܒܝܕ ܡܢܗܬܗ
ܘܐܬܚܘܝ ܠܝ ܒܥܒܕܘܬܐ
ܕܠܒܝܫ ܕܐܬܐ ⌈ܐܒܗܬܐ ܕܐܬܐ⌉[70]
ܘܦܪܩܢ[71] ܡܢ ܒܝܬ ܡܘܬܐ
ܘܢܛܠܩ ⌈ܒܗܘ ܒܗ ܡܠܟܘܬܐ⌉[72]
ܘܢܬܟܫ ܠܗ ܟܠ ܢܩܘܫܬܐ ܀

---

66 G1 ܠܒܢܝܐ.
67 B1 – ܘ.
68 D2 ܕ has been added later by the copyist.
69 M1 – ܘ.
70 ⌉ G1 illeg.
71 M1 marg. only the letter ܕ.
72 G1 illeg.

[31] Who taught us about this,
that the eye cannot see,
and the intellect cannot comprehend,
no knowledge nor mind?

[32] As the word in the prophecy
taught them [about] the invisibility,
that this is the Son of the essence,
who put on a human body.

[33] This is truly the Lord;
He made and created everything,
and with His grace He put on a body
to give life to all those clothed in flesh.

[34] When He ascended to heaven,
He sent to His chosen disciples
two watchers with glorious clothes
and they told them with sweet voices:

[35] 'O Galileans, why are you standing?[73]
And why are you looking at the sky?
Do you want Jesus who ascended?
Go back to where you were ordered.'[74]

[36] In the [same] way that He ascended with honor,
so will He come with sublimity,
and will renew everything that He made;
the Lord and the Son will be thanked.

[37] O the one who was seen in time as man
will again be seen as God.
Show pity and compassion mercifully
to he who has said these [things] in weakness.

[38] Blessed is Your ascension,
glorified is Your exaltation,
the Son who saved us by His descent,
and exalted our race by His ascension.
And it was confessed to us in truth,
that He would come as He came,
He would save us from death,
and we would rule with Him in the kingdom
and glorify Him every day.

[73] See Acts 1:11.
[74] See Mark 16:7.

[1]12.(92)

[f. 182v] [2]ܐܣܝܪܬܐ ܕܐܦܪܝܡ⸣ ܕܥܘܢܝܬܐ[3] ܀ §ܕܒܝܬܗ[4] «ܕܡܦܫܩܢܘܬܐ[5] ܩܕܝܫܐ»[6] ܀ ܘܡܚܝܐ ܕܪܘܚܢܝܬܐ ܀ §[7] ⸢ܠܠܝܐ[8]

[1] ܫܘܒܚܐ ܕܐܢܫ̈ܐ[9] ܠܫܘܒܚ[10] ܫܡܝܐ
ܠܫܘܒܚ ܡܢ ܫܡܝܐ ܘܦܩ ܠܫܡܝܐ
ܐܝܟ ܢܦܫܐ ܗܟܢ ܕܫܡܝܐ
ܢܦܫ[11] ܗܕܐ ܒܥܠܡܐ ܕܫܡܝܐ
ܬܫܒܘܚ ܕܗܘܐ ܠܗ ܒܪܐ
ܘܐܬܝܠܕ ܡܠܟܐ ܫܡܝܐ ܦܪܘܩܢܐ
ܡܠܟܐ ܒܚܘܒܗ ܗܘܐ ܓܒܪܐ
ܘܦܓܪܐ ܠܒܫ ܒܪܐ ܘܥܒܕܐ ܀

[2] ܡܢ ܠܐ ܫܒܩ ܒܝܬ ܡܠܟܐ. ܕܠܐ ܥܡܐ[12] ܢܦܩ ܒܢܦܫܗ.
ܕܠܐ ܘܥܠ ܦܘܠܐ ܥܒܕܐ. ܐܬܓܠܝ ܡܢ ܒܬܘܠܬܐ ܀

[3] ܢܚܬܘ[13] ܕܝܢ ܡܢ ܫܡܝܐ. ܘܢܛܪܗ ܐܝܟ[14] ܡܢ ܡܠܐܟܐ.
ܘܢܛܪܘܗ[15] ܥܒܕܝܢ ܠܟܠ ܢܛܪܐ. ܘܫܒܚܘ ܘܪܘܚܐ ܕܡܠܐܟܐ[16] ܀

---

[1] This hymn is found in: M1, M2, B1, D1, C1, C2, D2, B2, M3, G1, D3.
[2] In M1, before this hymn there is a heading that indicates the beginning of the second part of this manuscript, starting with the following phrase:
ܬܘܒ ܥܠ ܚܝܠܗ ܕܡܪܢ ܡܫܝܚܐ ܡܫܪܝܢܢ ܠܡܟܬܒ ܒܡܥܢܝܬܐ ܕܡܦܫܩܢܐ ܠܡܦܫܩܢܘܬܐ ܩܕܝܫܐ ܕܡܢܗܝܢ ܀ ܕܫܘܠܡܗ ܕܡܪܝ ܘܠܡܫܡܫ ܘܡܫܬܡܫܝܢ ܒܗܝܢ ܠܡܡܠܠܘ ܕܪܘܚܢܝܬܐ ܀ ܐܡܝܢ.
[3] G1 ܕܥܘܢܝܬܗ.
[4] B2 + ܡܢ ܕܒܝܬܗ.
[5] D1 ܕܡܦܫܩ; C1 – ܕܡܦܫܩܢܘܬܐ.
[6] » D3 ܕܡܦܫܩܢ ܩܕܝܫܐ.
[7] § ܕܒܝܬ ܕܠܥܕܢܐ.
[8] ⸢ B1 + ܘܫܘܠܡܗ ܕܒܝܬ ܕܠܥܕܢܐ.
[9] G1 ܕܐܢܫܐ.
[10] + ܡܢ.
[11] G1 ܢܦܫܘ.
[12] B2 ܥܡܐ has been added later by the copyist.
[13] M1 ܢܚܬ.
[14] G1 ܡܢܟܐ.
[15] G1 – ܘ.
[16] G1 ܘܫܒܚ ܪܘܚܐ ܕܥܠ ܡܠܐܟܐ.

12.(92)

Another one for the Feast of the Ascension. By the same Gīwargīs Wardā. Of the Gospel.[17] Forever.

[1] O race of humans, made [of] dust,[18]
made of dust and returning to dust,[19]
listen and hear the words of hope,
and obtain hope from the Lord of hope,
the Lord of all who became for you a Son.
In the image of your image, He made for Himself a dwelling place;
the Word became flesh by His love,[20]
and Your body with Him a Son and Lord.

[2] The Word descended without changing,
overshadowed[21] the woman without limit,
without seed and desire,
He became incarnate from the virginity.

[3] His conception is beyond understanding,
His birth is higher than rational beings,
His powers are exceeding all powers,
the knowledge and minds of those who speak.

[17] Referring to the chanting of the hymn after reading the Gospel.
[18] See Gen 2:7.
[19] See Job 34:15.
[20] See John 1:14.
[21] This word is usually used to indicate the action of the Holy Spirit.

[4] «⌈ܐܡܪ ܘܫܩܠܗ ܒܐܘܪܚܗ ܠܐܘܪܚܐ⌉.[22] ܘܠܓܝܓܠܬ̈ܐ ܕܢܘܗܪܐ».[23]
ܘܫܡܗ ܢܐܡܪ ܠܫܒܝܚܬܐ. ܘܫܡܗ[24] ܚܝܐ ܒܬܫܒܘܚܬܐ ܀

[5] ܟܕ ܩܪܐ ܗܘ ܡܒܕܪܐ ܗܘ ܗܘܐ. ܠܘܡܕܢ ܠܟܪ̈ܝܐ ܩܪܝܒ ܗܘܐ.
ܕܐܬܐ ܟܕ ܐܒܐ ܢܦܩ ܗܘܐ. ܟܠ ܡܢܗܘܢ ܗܘܘ ܥܡܗ ܗܘܐ ܀

[6] ܟܕ[25] ܩܪܐ ܥܠܝܡ̈ܐ ܡܫܡܫܝܢ ܗܘܘ. ܒܝܠܕܘܬܐ ܘܫܩܠܝܢ ܗܘܘ.
ܘܫܩܠ ܐܘܪܚܗ ܡܫܠܠܝܢ[26] ܗܘܘ. ܘܟܠ ܡܢܗܘܢ ܡܬܪܓܫܝܢ ܗܘܘ ܀

[7] ܡܢ[27] ܡܠܟܐ ܗܘ ܕܒܢܝܗܘܢ. ܟܕ[28] ܒܥܒܕܐ ܫܩܝܠ ܒܐܦ̈ܝܗܘܢ.
ܕܡܘܬܗ[29] ܢܦܫܗ ܐܒܘܢ. ܘܡܫܘܬܗ ܢܦܘܩ ܐܒܘܢ[30] ܀

[8] ܢܫܠܡ ܟܠܗܘܢ ܕܝܠܕܬܐ. ܘܢܚܕܐ ܐܒܘܢ ܕܝܠܕܬܐ.
ܡܢ ܕܚܝܠܘܬܐ ܕܬܘܕܝܬܐ. ܕܢܘܕܐ ܚܕܐ ܠܚܝܕܝܬܐ ܀

[9] ܗܘ ܡܢ ܕܩܡ ܗܘܐ ܕܒܢܝܗܘܢ. / ܥܠܡܐ ܠܥܕܡܐ ܐܡܪ ܠܗܘܢ. [f. 183r]
ܕܒܥܠܡܗ ܢܫܠܡ ܢܦܘܢ. ܡܬܚܘܬܐ ܠܬܒܥܝܬܗܘܢ ܀

[10] ܥܠܡܐ ܚܘܒ ܠܓܝܓܠܬܐ. ܗܘ ܥܠܡܐ ܕܒܘܚܪܢܐ.
ܕܢܘܕܐ ܕܟܠܗܘܢ[31] ܢܛܠܐ. ܡܬܦܢܝܢ ܟܗ ܒܫܡܝܐ ܀

---

22 ⌉ The same verse is found in an anonymous hymn 11.(91)[8].

23 » G1 ܕܢܘܗܪܐ ܠܫܒܝܚܬܐ. ܥܡܠ ܠܫܒܝܚܬܐ. ܢܐܡܪ ܡܠܟܐ ܒܫܡܗ.

24 G1 illeg.

25 G1 illeg.

26 D3 the first letter ܡ has been added later by the copyist.

27 M1 + ܘ.

28 G1 illeg.

29 G1 ܒܬܘܕܝܬܗ.

30 B2 – d.

31 B1 + ܚܝ̈ܠܐ.

[4] He died and by His death killed death,
the enemy of humanity.
With Him, He made inequity die
and with Him, mortality came to life.

[5] When He rose from the grave,
He was first seen by women.[32]
Adam, who lapsed because of a woman,[33]
from her, he heard about the resurrection.[34]

[6] When the apostles were gathered
in the upper room and were hiding,[35]
and they were speaking about His death,
and talking about His resurrection,

[7] suddenly He stood among them
while the doors were closed in front of them.[36]
He surprised them by His likeness,[37]
He astonished them by His appearance.

[8] Fear befell them,
and dread seized them,
because of the power of appearances,
which were foreign to one another.[38]

[9] He, when He stood among them,
said to them: 'Peace be with you'[39]
that by His peace, He might fill
their intellects with calmness.

[10] Peace He gave to the Galileans,
that peace of the spiritual beings,
in order to show that all those on high,
would have peace with those below.

---

[32] See Matt 28:9; Mark 16:9; John 20:14.
[33] See 1 Tim 2:14.
[34] See Matt 28:8; Mark 16:10; John 20:18.
[35] See John 20:19.
[36] See John 20:19.
[37] See Luke 24:37.
[38] The poet here probably means that the appearance of Christ this time was different from other times or that the two natures of Christ (divine and human) are different.
[39] See Luke 24:36; John 20:19.

[11] ܒܗ ܐܬܒܪܝ ܫܡܝܐ. ܘܒܗ ܐܬܟܠܠ ܒܟܠܓܘܢܝܘܬܐ.
ܘܗܘܐ ܠܥܕܬܐ ܘܐܢܫܘܬܐ. ܚܕܐ ܐܡܘܬܐ ܚܕܐ ܡܕܒܪܢܝܬܐ ܀

[12] ܗܘ ܐܘܪܚܐ ܕܚܝܘܬܐ. ⌈ܘܡܢܪ ܐܝܟܐ ܕܡܘܟܢܝܬܐ⌉.[40]
ܒܗܝܟܠܗ ܡܠܟܐ ܡܫܝܚܘܬܐ. ܡܫܝܚܐ ܗܘܐ ܠܗܝ[41] ܡܫܝܚܘܬܐ[42] ܀

[13] ܐܝܬ ܐܝܬ ܠܐ ܡܬܦܪܫܝܢ. ܠܐ ܡܬܦܪܫܝܢ ܘܠܐ ܡܬܚܫܠܝܢ.
ܠܐ ܡܬܚܫܠܝܢ ܘܠܐ ܡܬܡܫܚܝܢ. ܠܐ ܡܬܡܫܚܝܢ[43] ܘܠܐ ܡܬܦܫܩܝܢ[44] ܀

[14] ܗܘ ܚܘܒܪܐ ܒܝܫܝܬܐ. ܫܡܝܫܝ ܩܠܐ ܒܐܘܪܚܬܗ.
ܠܡܫܘܝܘ ܐܦ ܒܐܒܘܗܝ.[45] ܘܐܢܬ[46] ܒܚܘܫܒܝ ܚܘܫܒܝܗܘܢ ܀

[15] ܗܘ ܫܘܪܝܐ ܕܟܠܐ ܕܡܘܕܝܐ. ܘܫܠܝܐ ܫܪܝܐ.
ܕܐܬܢ ܠܟܠ ܡܬܩܪܝܐ ܠܗ[47] ܙܕܩܐ. ܘܣܡܟ ܠܗܘܢ ܫܪܝܪܐ ܘܬܘܕܝܐ ܀

[16] ܘܣܡܟ[48] ܐܢܘܢ ܕܢܩܢܘܢܬܐ. ܕܡܫܡܫܝܢ[49] ܡܢܝܫܬܐ.
ܘܡܘܬܐ ܠܗܘ[50] ܫܦܝܪܬܐ. ܐܟܠ ܠܡܣܒ ܒܗܝ ܥܡܠܬܐ ܀

[17] ܠܐ[51] ܡܬܚܫܒ ܐܦ ܒܝܬܝܬܐ. ܠܟܠ ܡܫܪܐ ܐܝܟ[52] ܕܠܟܠ[53] ܐܢܫܐ.[54]
ܕܢܬܠ ܡܢܐ ܦܘܪܥܢܐ ܕܐܢܫܐ. ܠܟܠܗܘܢ ܐܝܟ ܐܢܫܐ ܕܦܩܕܐ ܀

---

40 ⌈⌉ The same verse is found in hymn (107)[14] by Wardā.
41 B1 − ܠܗܝ.
42 B1 + ܠ.
43 M1 ܡܬܡܫܚܝܢ; D3 ܡܬܡܫܚܝܢ has been added later by the copyist.
44 M1 ܡܬܦܫܩܝܢ.
45 D3 the letter ܝ has been added later by the copyist.
46 G1 ܘܐܢܬ.
47 G1 illeg.
48 B1 − ܘ.
49 M1 ܘܡܫܡܫܝܢ; D2 +X ܡܫܡܫܝܢ; D3 ܕܡܫܡܫܝܢ.
50 M1 ܠܗ.
51 G1 illeg.
52 M1 ܕܐܝܟ.
53 G1 −.
54 G1 ܒܐܢܫܐ.

[11] In Him, hatred is abolished.
In Him, enmity is over.
The watchers and human beings
became one church and one flock.

[12] He who knows what is hidden,
and examines the heart and kidneys,[55]
with His words full of calmness,
its peace was for that commotion.

[13] 'It is me! Do not be afraid,[56]
do not be afraid and do not fear,
do not fear and do not be terrified,
do not be terrified and do not be fearful.

[14] Behold, you have seen me with your eyes,
listened to my words with your ears.
Touch me also with your hands,[57]
and heal your wounds by my wounds.'

[15] Behold, a miracle full of wonder,
a wonder that is full of miracle,
how He entered without opening the doors[58]
and showed them bones and flesh.[59]

[16] He showed them the places[60]
of the five wounds,
and He ate with them,
in that hour, fish and honey.[61]

[17] Do not think, O you human beings,
about the Lord in the same way as a man;
though He has a human body,
He is not like a man of the present.

---

[55] See Ps 7:10; Prov 17:3; Jer 11:20, 17:10; Rev 2:23.
[56] See Luke 24:36.
[57] See Luke 24:39; John 20:27.
[58] See John 20:19, 26.
[59] See Luke 24:39.
[60] See Luke 24:40.
[61] See Luke 24:42; although honey is not mentioned in the Greek text of the Bible, it is mentioned in the Peshiṭta.

[18] ܦܓܪܗ ܡܬܟܒܫܐ ܥܡ ܗܘܐ. ܓܫܡܗ[62] ܪܘܚܢܐ ܗܘܐ.
ܓܫܡܐ ܘܡܪܟܒܐ ܕܫܘܦ ܗܘܐ. ⌈ܡܬܡܪܐ ܕܗܘ ܕܡܢܝܢ ܥܡ[63] ܗܘܐ⌉[64] ܀

[19] ܘܐܢ[65] ܡܒܝܬܐ ܐܝܟ ܪܘܚܢܐ. ܩܕܝܫ ܒܡܘܟܠܐ ܕܘܟܝܐ.
ܦܓܪܐ ܡܬܝܕܥ ܥܠ ܒܢܝܐ. ܐܝܟ ܕܡܐ ܠܦܘܪܣܝܐ ܀

[20] ܘܐܦ ܐܝܟ ܗܘܝ ܒܗ ܕܘܟܝܬܐ. ܕܥܘܩܒܬܐ ܘܦܫܝܛܘܬܐ.[66]
ܠܗܘܢ ܩܢܝܢ ܡܫܠܡܝܢܐ. ܐܝܟ ܕܝܗܘܒ ܒܗ[67] ܡܫܬܠܡܐ ܀

[21] ܒܟܠܗܝܢ ܚܙܐ ܐܢܫ ܢܟܦܐ. ܕܬܘܠܡܐ[68] ܕܡܠܟܐ ܠܝܘܡܢܐ.
ܘܐܝܟ ܒܙܐ ܡܥܒܕܐ ܘܡܫܪܐ.[69] ܠܘܬܟܘܢ ܠܐ ܗܘܐ ܐܚܪܢܐ ܀

[22] ܢܠܒܫ ܠܒܪܢܫ ܥܒܕ ܗܘܐ. ܡܥܒܕ ܒܡܘܪܝܐ / ܢܗܝܪܐ ܗܘܐ. [f. 183v]
ܘܡܢ ܕܡܫܢܐ ܢܬܦܪܫ ܗܘܐ. ܘܦܓܪܗ ܕܝܢ ܡܢ ܡܠܐܟܐ ܗܘܐ ܀

[23] ܘܗܘ ܠܠܟܘܬ ܐܝܟ ܗܘܐ. ܡܢ ܬܚܘܬ ܕܦܓܪܗ ܡܛܠ ܗܘܐ.
ܢܦܩ ܡܒܝܬܐ ܕܡܬܒܬܠ ܗܘܐ. ܚܙܐ[70] ܘܡܠܟܐ ܘܫܘܒܚܐ ܒܗ ܠܒܗ ܗܘܐ ܀

[24] ܘܠܒܟܝܢ ܕܢܫܟܚܘܢ ܡܫܬܚܪ ܗܘܐ. ܘܢܕܝܗ[71] ܦܩܥܘ ܘܥܕܝܘ ܗܘܐ.
ܒܪܩܦ ܢܒܥܐ ܢܣܒܘ[72] ܗܘܐ. ܠܡܫܬܥܝܘ[73] ܐܝܟ ܠܐ ܠܒܝܒ ܗܘܐ ܀

[25] ܘܐܦ ܢܐܡܪ ܐܢܫ ܕܝܘܩܢܬܐ.[74] ܒܟܝܢܐ ܗܘܝ ܘܠܐ ܡܬܪܥܬܐ.
ܗܘ ܕܢܣܒ ܗܘܐ[75] ܠܡܘܬܒܬܐ.[76] ܠܟܠ ܥܒܕ ⌈ܕܝܘܡܬܐ ܕܥܘܩܒܬܐ⌉[77] ܀

---

62 G1 ܦܓܪܗ.
63 D3 ܥܡ has been added later by the copyist.
64 ⌈ G1 ܠܓܡܐ ܕܓܫܡܐ ܡܪܐ ܗܘܐ.
65 D2 – ܘ.
66 M3 ܘܦܫܝܛܘܬܐ.
67 M1, B1, C1 ܒܗ.
68 M1, B1, G1 ܒܬܘܠܡܐ; C1, D2 written as ܬܘܠܡܐ ܒ with the letter ܕ erased.
69 G1 – ܘ.
70 M1 ܚܙܐ.
71 G1 ܘܠܢܕܝܗ.
72 G1 ܢܣܒܘ.
73 G1 ܠܡܫܬܥܝܘ.
74 M1, B1 – ܕ.
75 M2 ܗܘܐ has been added later by the copyist.
76 G1 ܠܡܘܬܒܬܐ.
77 ⌈ G1 ܕܝܘܡܬܐ ܕܥܘܩܒܬܐ.

[18] His ethereal body rose up.
His flesh became spiritual.
The flesh and the bones that He showed,
were to confirm that the one who had died has risen.

[19] If dead ones like spiritual beings,
will rise at the end of times,
the body that will renew all natures,
how it resembles the earthly ones!

[20] And if there were places in it
of wounds and injuries,
the weakness was raised with Him,
God forbid that there are weaknesses in Him.[78]

[21] In one hour, the prophet healed
Hezekiah by a branch of figs.[79]
How can it be that the Son, Christ and Lord,
was not a healer for His own limbs?

[22] Elisha ordered Naʿaman[80]
to have a bath seven times in the Jordan,
when He bathed, He was purified,
and His body was better than silver.

[23] And He who raised Lazarus[81]
after his body had become decayed,
the dead one who had become corrupted
went out alive, sound and without any stain.

[24] And the servant that was struck by Simon,[82]
He cut his ear and threw it away;
in a twinkle of an eye, He healed him.
How can it be that He does not bind His own wounds?

[25] If someone says that the places
were colored [skin] and not holes,
He who healed the pains,
why did He leave the place of the wounds?

---

[78] I follow the reading of manuscripts M1, and C1 in translating ܒܗ because it refers to Christ.
[79] See Isa 38:21-22.
[80] See 2 Kgs 5:10.
[81] See John 11:39.
[82] See Matt 26:51; Mark 14:47; Luke 22:49; John 18:10.

[26] ܘܕܐܒܠ ܒܡܘܬܗ ܘܢܬܒܣܡ ܗܘܐ. ܟܠ ܕܒܟܠ ܡܐܟܘܠܬܐ ܚܫܝܫ ܗܘܐ.
ܐܝܟ ܕܒܥܐ ܐܒܪܗܡ[83] ܠܝܫܘܥ ܗܘܐ. ܗܘ ܒܗ ܒܐܝܩܪܐ ܐܒܠ ܗܘܐ ✤

[27] ܢܣܒܘ ܕܡܐ ܠܐܝܠ ܡܢ ܚܝܘܬܐ. ܒܗܝܠ ܚܝܘ ܡܠ ܕܚܝܘܬܐ.
ܘܟܠ[84] ܕܝܘ[85] ܕܠܒܝܫ ܒܟܠ ܚܝܘܬܐ. ܒܗ ܠܐ ܕܠܒܝܫ ܒܟܠܗܘܢ[86] ܚܝܘܬܐ ✤

[28] ܡܢ ܫܡܐ ܕܡܠܟܐ ܢܚܬܘܢ. ܘܟܠ ܫܘܚܠܦ ܢܦܫ ܐܒܘܢ.
ܘܟܠ ܡܢܗܘܢ ܐܘܕܥ ܝܬܗܘܢ. ܘܢܦܫܗ ܒܝܠܕܐ ܚܘܒ ܠܗܘܢ ✤

[29] ܠܒܫܗ ܢܒܝܐ ܢܦܫ ܐܬܘܢ. ܕܒܠܠܘܬܐ ܒܫܘܐ ܠܗܘܢ.
ܕܐܝܟ ܕܗܘ ܕܢܚܬܘ ܠܒܝܬܗܘܢ. ܐܣܬܪܬܐ[87] ܒܟܠܗܘܢ[88] ܠܐ ܝܕܥܘܢ ✤

[30] ܘܕܐܡܪ[89] ܕܡܫܬܡܠܝܢ ܠܗܘܢ. ܡܘܠܟܢܐ ܕܐܬܐ ܕܝܗܒܐ ܒܗܘܢ.
ܒܗܘܕܐ ܐܘܕܥ ܠܗ ܦܠܚܘܢ. ܕܐܠܗܐ ܗܘ ܕܒܠܗ ܘܕܒܠܗܘܢ[90] ✤

[31] ܘܦܩܕ ܠܗܘܢ[91] ܘܐܡܪ ܠܗܘܢ. ܕܗܐ ܐܘܠ ܐܢܐ ܡܢ ܠܘܬܟܘܢ.
ܠܐ ܬܕܚܠܘܢ ܕܒܚܝܠ ܐܢܐ ܠܟܘܢ. ܢܛܪܟܘܢ ܐܢܐ ܐܝܟ ܕܢܦܫܝ ܠܟܘܢ ✤

[32] ܒܐܘܪܫܠܡ ܒܝܬܗ[92] ܬܪܘܨܘܬܗ. ܘܒܗ ܢܘܪܗ[93] ܒܡܘܠܕܗ[94] ܘܬܪܘܨܗ.[95]
ܘܐܝܟ[96] ܕܣܡܐ ܫܘܒܚܗ ܘܡܫܒܚܘܬܗ. ܩܫܝܐ ܬܚܘܬܗ ܘܐܠܗܘܬܗ ✤

[33] ܗܘܐ ܚܘܒ ܐܢܐ ܠܟܘܢ ܫܠܡܐ. ܕܬܥܒܕܘܢ ܒܫܡܝܐ ܘܒܐܪܥܐ.
ܠܘܬܗ ܒܗܘܢ ܠܟܠ ܕܫܡܥܐ. ܘܐܬܚܫܒ ܕܡܫܡܫܐ[97] ܫܡܥܐ ✤

---

83 D3 illeg.
84 G1 –.
85 G1 ܕܝܘܗܝ.
86 M3 + +X ܒܟܠܗܘܢ.
87 D2 ܐܣܬܪܬܐ.
88 M3 + ܢܫܡܐ.
89 D2 ܘܐܡܪ.
90 G1 ܕܒܠܟܘܢ with ܗ written over the letter ܟ.
91 M1, B1, D2 + ܝܬܘܢ; D1 ܠܗܘܢ *c ܝܬܘܢ.
92 G1 ܒܝܬܗ.
93 G1 ܢܘܪܗ.
94 B1 ܒܡܘܠܕܗ.
95 G1 – ܘ.
96 B1, G1 ܕܐܝܟ.
97 G1 ܕܡܫܡܫܐ.

[26] When He ate and drank with them,
He did not need food.
As when He ate with Abraham,[98]
so He ate with His chosen ones.

[27] If He rose beyond nature,
then all that is of nature was abolished,
and he who dominates nature,
nature does not dominate Him.

[28] After He talked to them
and taught them about His death,
and informed them about His resurrection,
and manifested himself to them publicly,

[29] then He took them out to Bethany,[99]
and with Lazarus, He showed them,
that since He had raised him before their eyes,
they should not imagine other matters about Him.

[30] And He said: 'I will send to you
the promise[100] of my Father, that He may dwell in you.'
By this, He told them and us,
that He is our God and theirs.

[31] He ordered them and told them:
'Thus I will go away from you.
Do not think that I will leave you;
I am with you as I told you.

[32] In Jerusalem, preach about me,[101]
and there proclaim my authority and sovereignty.
As it saw my death and crucifixion,
so it will see my greatness and divinity.

[33] See, I am giving you swords
that cut stones and caves,
open the heart of the powerful with them,
the delusion of the idols and pagans.

---

[98] See Gen 18:1-8. The poet seems to mean here that one of the three angels who ate with Abraham was the Word, meaning the pre-existent Christ.
[99] See Luke 24:50.
[100] See John 14:15-16. The poet here means the Holy Spirit.
[101] See Acts 1:8.

[34] ܗܐ ܡܬܒܝܢܐ ܠܟܘܢ[102] / ܦܘܩܕܐ. ܘܠܝܬܝܐ ܕܓܠܝܘܗܝ ܟܬܒܐ.[103] [f. 184r]
ܕܡܫܚܠܦܝܢ[104] ܠܡܫܩܠܘ ܢܚܬܝܬܐ. ⌝ܘܡܬܥܬܕܐ ܠܐܘܪܚܐ ܢܩܝܡܬܐ⌜[105] ܀

[35] ܘܡܢ ܗܠܝܢ ܐܡܪ ܗܘܐ ܠܗܘܢ. ܟܕ ܡܠܟܗ ܢܬܦܬܚ ܥܝܢܝܗܘܢ.
ܡܢ[106] ܚܛܗܝ ܒܗ ܢܬܬܘܒܘܢ. ⌝ܘܢܬܡܘܛܝܢ[107] ܒܗ[108] ܕܚܢܢܗܘܢ⌜[109] ܀

[36] ܠܟܢܫܐ ܕܒܘܗܪܐ ܢܘܗܪܬܐ. ܐܝܟ ܕܡܫܝܚܐ ܡܕܡܕܡܬܐ.
ܢܬܦܪܫܘܢ[110] ܠܗ[111] ܒܕܡܘܬܐ. ܘܒܠܝܘ ܢܗܘܐ ܒܬܫܡܫܬܐ ܀

[37] ܐܪܥܐ ܠܟܗ ܙܘܥ ܗܘܬ. ܕܐܝܟ ܠܐܘܡܬܐ ܫܠܡ[112] ܗܘܬ.
ܥܡܡܐ ܢܝܚܘ[113] ܢܬܦܫܟ ܗܘܬ. ܕܟܠܗܘܢ ܦܠܚܐ[114] ܢܪܓܢ[115] ܗܘܬ ܀

[38] ܘܒܗ ܠܒܪܐ ܢܨܝܚܝܢ. ⌝ܘܢܬܡܬܪܡܘܢ ܗܘܘ ܡܒܪܟܝܢ ܡܒܪܟܝܢ.
ܘܡܫܒܚܝܢ ܠܡܪܝܐ ܠܡܪܝܐ⌜.[116] ܘܢܫܬܒܚܘܢ ܡܫܒܚܝܢ ܡܫܒܚܝܢ ܀

[39] ܐܪܥܐ ܠܡܠܟܐ ܕܥܠܡܐ. ܢܫܬܘܐ ܠܡܫܝܚܐ[117] ܕܢܦܪܩܝܘܗܝ.[118]
ܘܢܬܒܥܘܢ[119] ܗܘܘ ܒܬܫܒܘܚܬܗܘܢ. [120]ܢܬܬܒܥ ܦܠܚܐ ܡܢܗ ܒܪܗܘܢ ܀

[40] ܡܬܒܪܟܝܢ ܗܘܘ ܠܗ ܒܬܫܒܘܚܬܐ.[121] ܘܡܒܪܟܐ ܐܝܟ ܡܪܢܝܬܐ.
ܠܗ ܦܠܚܐ ܘܥܒܕܐ ܢܝܚܬܐ. ܕܒܪܟܐ ܢܦܫ ܕܐܠܗܘܬܐ ܀

---

102 C1 marg.
103 G1 ܟܬܒܐ.
104 M1 ܘܡܫܚܠܦܝܢ.
105 ⌝ G1 ܘܐܘܪܚܐ ܢܩܝܡܬܐ ܡܬܥܬܕܐ.
106 D2 + ܘ.
107 B1 ܘܡܬܡܘܛܝܢ; D1 ܝ has been added later by the copyist.
108 B1 – ܒܗ.
109 G1 ܘܡܬܡܘܛܝܢ ܒܗ ܚܢܢܗܘܢ.
110 C2 ܢܬܦܪܫܘܢ.
111 G1 ܠܗ
112 G1 ܫܠܡܐ.
113 G1 ܢܝܚܘ.
114 B1 ܦܠܚܝ.
115 B1 ܢܪܓܪܓ.
116 ⌝ C1 rep. bc, with the letter ܐ placed over verse c and the letter ܒ over verse b.
117 M3 +X ܒܡܠܟܘܬܗ.
118 G1 ܒܡܬܝܬܗܘܢ.
119 G1 – ܘ.
120 D2 + ܐܡܪ.
121 G1 ܬܫܒܘܚܬܐ.

[34] Behold, I am giving you mouths,
and the tongues of all nations,
to make the ignorant wise,
and the wrongful human beings perfect.'

[35] And when He said these things to them,
suddenly, He was separated from them;
While their eyes were looking at Him,[122]
their intellects were in wonder about Him.

[36] An illuminous cloud of light,
like a lifted bed,[123]
was spread miraculously,
and He sat on it gloriously.

[37] The heart of the earth was pleased,
that its head was ascending on high.
Heaven bowed its back
because the king was sitting on it.

[38] The watchers gathered in multitudes
and lined up in ranks.
They were arranged in choirs
and prepared themselves in orders.

[39] They frightened the world with their voices.
They disturbed the world with their trumpets.
They sang with their horns,
like workers in front of their master.

[40] They offered to Him hymns
and songs of 'holy' as a tribute
for that king and new Lord,
who had received the rank of divinity.

---

[122] See Acts 1:9.
[123] Or a chariot.

[41] ܚܙܘ ܕܡܠܟܐ ܒܢܫܐ ܕܢܘܪܐ. ܘܫܠܠܟ[124] ܗܘܐ[125] ܡܢܗ ܢܘܪܐ.
ܘܡܛܠ ܠܐܦܪܐ ⸢ܐܚܪ ܡܢܫܪܐ⸣.[126] ܕܠܐ ܐܢܫ ܥܠܝ ܠܗ ܘܠܐ[127] ܥܒܪܐ ܀

[42] ܐܦܐ ܡܦܐ[128] ܒܫܠܗ[129] ܚܝܐ. ܕܦܐ ܟܪܐ ܦܪ ܠܝ ܥܠ ܒܘܪܟܬܐ.
ܕܦܡ ܕܠܐܪܟܐ ܒܪܝܗ ܘܐܥܫܢܐ. ܠܝ ܩܪܥܝܗ ܦܪܩܐ ܥܫܢܐ ܀

[43] ܡܛܠܠܗ ܦܝܢܝܗ. ܘܡܛܠܠܗ ܦܝܓܪܗ.
ܘܠܝ[130] ܢܩܒܪܗ ܐܦ[131] ܠܝ ܚܒܪܗ. ܘܡܘܠܟܐ ܘܢܝܠܐ ܘܡܘܒܣ ܦܝ ܫܡܝܗ ܀

[44] ܦܝ ܐܘ ܐܠܗܐ ܢܒܪܬܐ. ܡܛܝܒܐ ܢܦܫܝ ܢܘܩܕܬܐ.
ܦܝ ܚܝܐ ܒܐܒܗܝ ܦܘܩܬܐ. ܦܝ ܕܢܝܐ ܒܐܢܒܝܝ ܡܢܥܬܐ ܀

[45] ܥܘܒܕܝܠܝ ܐܦܐ ܚܝܐ. ܥܒܝܕܐ ܒܪܐ ܦܫܝܐ ܘܟܠܝܐ.
ܗܒܝܒ ܐܢܐ ܪܘܚܐ ܡܦܘܩܬܐ. ܚܕ ܐܠܗܐ ܚܕ ܩܪܐ ܀

[46] ܢܥܩܪ ܕܒܐܢܝܗ ܡܠܟܘܬܐ. ܘܒܪܡܘܗ ܦܠܘܚܬܐ.
ܣܘܝ ܠܒܪܝܟ[132] ܠܩܢܝܬܐ.[133] ܥܠ ܥܘܒܕܝ ܦܘܠܩܢܝܬܐ[134] ܀ [f. 184v]

[47] ܕܠܝܐ ܕܗܦܟ ܠܝ
ܘܠܐ[135] ܕܫܘܦܐ ܠܝ
ܘܠܩܪܝ ܠܥܒܕܐ ܕܝܐܩܪܘܢܝ
ܘܠܗܘܢ[136] ܒܪܝܐ ܦܢܦܠܗܘܢܝ
ܦܘܫܟ ܡܘܫܟ ܡܘܫܟ[137] ܒܢܝܢ
[138]ܥܘܒܕܐ ܠܥܩܝ[139] ܦܠܠܢ ܚܢܝܢ ܀

---

[124] B1 ܘܫܠܠܟܐ; G1 ܘܫܠܠܟܐ.
[125] G1 ܗܘܝ.
[126] ⸢ D2 rep. ܡܢܫܪܐ ܘܐܚܪ.
[127] M3 +X ܒܥܕܘܢܐ + in marg. ܘܠܐ.
[128] M3 marg.
[129] G1 ܒܫܠܐ.
[130] M1, B1, D1, C1, D2, G1 – ܘ.
[131] M1, B1, D2 + ܘ.
[132] B1 ܠܒܪܝܟܗ.
[133] B1 ܠܟܘܢܬܐ.
[134] G1 + ܕ.
[135] G1 ܘܠܗ.
[136] G1 – ܘ.
[137] D2 marg. ܡܘܫܟ.
[138] C1 + X ܦܠܠܢ.
[139] C1 + ܦܠܠܢ.

[41] They saw that He was passing through the sea of fire,
and the fire was afraid of Him,
and entering the high and glorious place,
that no man nor watcher had entered.

[42] The Father cried out with His living voice:
'Come, my Son, and sit on the throne,
which, since I made earth and heaven,
I set apart for You in the heaven of heavens.

[43] I established it to You.
I prepared it for You.
I gave it to You and made it for You,
I place my power, strength, and glory on You.'

[44] In You, O new God
is seen the Ancient Days.[140]
In You is life, and in Your hands is death.
In You is the judgment, and in Your hands the resurrection.

[45] Glory to You living Father,
Glorious Son, hidden and revealed,
worshipped are You, O eternal Spirit,
one God and one Lord.

[46] Jesus, in whose hand is the kingdom,
and in whose mystery is the flame,
have mercy on he who wrote this hymn,
about Your glory with small things,

[47] There is no one who is adequate for You,
and no one who is sufficient for You.
Few are the creatures who can speak of You,
and [few] are all the created things that praise You.
Holy, holy, holy is Your nature,
Glory to Your name and upon us Your mercy.

---

[140] See Dan 7:10, 13, 22.

[1](95).13

[f. 187v] [2]ܥܘܢܝܬܐ ܕܟܠ ܚܕܫܐ ܩܕܡܝܐ܀ ܘܠܟܠ ܥܐܕܐ ܡܫܝܚܝܐ ܚܕܬܐ܀ ܘܫܘܒܚܐ ܠܩܘܪܒܐ ܕܦܢܛܩܘܣܛܐ:
ܕܝܠܗ[3] ܕܥܠܝܡܘܬܐ[4] ܦܪܘܫܐ܀ ܩܕܡܝܐ

[1] ܫܒܝܚ ܦܬܓܡܗ ܐ̄ܒ̈ܘܗܝ
ܬܪܥܐ ܬܪܥܝ ܘܪ̈ܘܪܒܢ ܠܟܠܗܘܢ
ܘܗܐ ܢܦܩܝܢ ܡܫܒ̈ܚܬܗ
ܘܠܐ ܡܬܦܩܕܝܢ ܐܦ[5] ܐܘܪ̈ܚܬܗ
ܘܠܐ ܗܦܟ ܠܟ ܕܘܟܐ[6] ܘܡܠܬܐ
ܘܠܐ ܐܬܪܐ ܘܐܦܠܐ ܕܘܟܬܐ܀

[2] ܡܠܟ ܥܠ ܠܥܠܡܝ ܥܠܡܝܢ. ܘܫܘܠܛܢܗ ܐܣܬܪܩܬ.[7]
ܘܡܢ ܦܘܡܗ ܡܦܩܝܢ. ܘܡܢ ܡܠܬܗ ܐܬܒܪܝܢ[8]܀

[3] ܐܬܐ ܒܥܝܢܐ ܒܫܘܠܛܢܗ. ܕܒܪܘܚܗ / ܒܣܘܓܐ ܕܚܝܠܗ. [f. 188r]
ܘܫܦܪ ܢܒܝܘܬܗ[9] ܠܗܘܢ ܥܡܗ. ܕܢܬܒܪܐ ܟܠ ܡܐܬܝܬܗ܀

[4] ⸢**ܐܘܪ̈ܚܬܐ ܕܫܘܒܚܐ**⸣[10]
ܟܝܢܐ ܕܐܬܝ ܡܢ ܥܠܡ ܗܘܐ. [11]ܫܡܝܐ ܕܠܐܝܬ ܠܗ ܣܟܐ[12] ܗܘܐ.[13]
ܘܠܟܠ ܥܠܡܐ ܡܚܝܐ ܗܘܐ. ܘܠܟܠ ܦܘܡܐ ܐܬܟܠܗ ܗܘܐ܀

[5] ܦܪܝ ܠܝܠܝܐ ܒܡܠܟܘܬܐ. ܘܐܬܐ[14] ܡܠܟܐ ܒܬܫܒܘܚܬܐ.
ܘܐܬܚܙܝ ܡܠܟܐ ܕܫܘܒܚܐ. ܠܩܕܡ ܡܪܢ ܫܒܝܚܬܐ܀

---

[1] This hymn is found in: M2, B1, D1, C1, C2, D2, B2, M3, D3.
[2] The heading in B1 is written as follows: ܐܚܪܬܐ ܕܥܐܕܐ܀ ܠܗ܀ ܕܝܠܗ ܕܡܪܕܘܬܐ.
[3] D1, C1, D2 + ܕܝܠܗ ܕܝ ܕܝܠܗ ܕܡܠܟܘܬܐ.
[4] D1 ܠܥܠܡܘܢ.
[5] B1 ܗܝ.
[6] B1 ܦܕܟܬܐ.
[7] B1 ܐܣܬܪܩܬ.
[8] D1, C1 ܐܬܒܪܝܢ.
[9] D3 ܢܒܝܘܬܗ has been added later by the copyist.
[10] ⸢ M2, D1, C1, C2, D2, B2, M3, D3 marg.
[11] B2 +X ܘܕܠܐ ܦܘܩܕܐ.
[12] B1 ܣܟܐ.
[13] B2 marg. ܗܘܐ.
[14] B1 ܘܐܬܬܐ.

13.(95)[15]

Hymn for the Eight Feasts. And for each feast, seven strophes. Required for the Mawtḇā of Pentecost. By Gīwargīs Wardā. Say

[1] Glorious and marvelous are Your mysteries,
and great are Your works, O Lord our Lord.
Exceedingly deep are Your thoughts,
and Your ways cannot be examined.
Mind and word are not enough for You,
no where and no place.

[2] King of all, make me enter Your land,
and in Your chamber make me walk,
and from Your table make me satisfied,
and from Your wines make me feel relieved.

[3] The Hidden One came with His grace
to save His creation with His love,
and sent His servant to His maid,
to announce His coming.

[4] **The strophes of Annunciation:**[16]
The spiritual one descended and was carrying
a letter not written by man.
He read it without the pupil of the eye,
He translated it without a mouth.

[5] The watcher flew hastily,
came and arrived quickly,
announced the words of joy,
to Mary, the Lady of women:

---

[15] This hymn follows the feasts of the liturgical year. For another English translation of this hymn, see F.C. Conybeare and A.J. Maclean, *Rituale Armenorum*, p. 327.
[16] In some manuscripts, the titles in bold are found in the margins to indicate the feasts.

[6] ܥܠܡܐ ܟܠܗ ܡܠܝܐ ܫܘܒܚܟ. ܡܪܝ ܟܢܫܐ ܗ̇ܘ ܢܫܒܚܟ.[17]
ܒܪܝܫܝܬ[18] ܒܝܘܡܐ ܠܬܚܝܬܟ. ܕܒܟ ܗܘ ܦܘܪܩܢ ܒܪܝܬܟ[19] ܀

[7] ܗ̇ ܡܠܟܝܢ ܫܡܝܐ ܘܐܪܥܢܝ ܒܪܐ. ܕܒܐܠܗܘܬܗ[20] ܠܟܠܟܢܐ ܒܪܐ.
ܘܒܗ ܗ̇ܘܐ ܡܒܪܐ ܠܡܒܪܐ. ܠܟܢܫܐ[21] ܠܟܒܝܪ ܡܢ ܦܬܓܡܐ ܀

[8] ܒܢܝ ܒܡܠܟܘܬܟ ܕܠܐ ܣܘܟܠܐ ܐܢܬ.[22] ܘܠܐ ܫܘܐ ܠܟ ܕܡܬܚܫܒܐ ܐܢܬ.[23]
ܒܡܠܟܝ ܦܓܪܐ ܘܢܦܫܐ ܐܢܬ. ܘܡܠܐܟܐ ܘܐܢܫܐ[24] ܣܘܟܠܐ ܐܢܬ[25] ܀

[9] ܒܟ ܢܒܪܐ ܕܪܘܚ ܩܘܕܫܐ. ܘܡܠܟܘܬܗ ܕܐܒܐ ܡܫܘܚܬܐ.
ܡܫܒܚ ܠܗ ܠܡܠܟܘܬܐ ܦܪܝܩܐ. ܘܫܘܒܚܐ ܝܗܒ ܠܟܢ ܡܪܢ ܀

[10] ܒܟ ܡܠܟܘܗ ܢܗܪܐ ܡܠܟܘܬܐ. ܘܠܦܓܪܐ ܗܘܐ ܠܒܝܬܘܬܐ.
ܘܠܢܦܫܐ ܗܘܐ ܢܦܝܫܘܬܐ. ܘܐܬܡܪܢܝ ܠܗ ܣܘܓܝܐܐ ܀

[11] **⌈ܣܒܪܬܐ ܕܡܠܟܘܬܐ⌉**[26]
ܡܢ ܐܒܐ ܠܐܒܪܗܡ. ܗܘ ܫܡܝܐ ܕܠܐ ܡܙܕܒܢܘܬܐ.
ܘܐܬܝܠܕ ܡܢ ܒܡܠܟܘܬܐ. ܠܟܠ ܡܢ ܒܢܝܐ ܕܐܢܫܘܬܐ ܀

---

[17] B2 written ܕܫܒܚܟ with ܢܫܒܚܟ written over it.
[18] D1 + +X ܒܪܝܫܝܬ.
[19] B1 ܒܘܪܟܬܟ.
[20] D2 ܕܒܐܠܗܘܬܗ the letter ܘ has been added later by the copyist.
[21] D3 ܠܟܢܫܐ has been added later by the copyist.
[22] B1 ܫܡܝܐ ܐܢܬ.
[23] B1 ܕܠܐ ܣܘܟܠܐ ܐܢܬ.
[24] M3 ܘܡܠܐܟܐ.
[25] B1, M3 marg.
[26] ⌉ M2, D1, C1, C2, D2, B2, M3, D3 marg.

[6] 'Peace be with you, full of grace,[27]
our Lord be with you, O virtuous one,
blessed are you among the cursed women,
who through you will be blessed.

[7] You will conceive and give birth to a son,[28]
who in His divinity created the worlds,[29]
and in Him hope will be completed
for the nature fashioned from dust.'

[8] The Virgin answered: 'I know not carnal union,[30]
God forbid that I will have a man,
I am a virgin in body and soul,
and I am sealed by my Lord and my God.'

[9] The watcher replied: 'The living Spirit
and the Word of the living Father
will sanctify your pure womb
and you will be a mother for the Son of the Lord.'[31]

[10] With his [the angel's] word, the Word overshadowed her
The body was formed,
The soul was given breath,
and unity was perfected.[32]

[11] **The strophes of Birth:**
Then He came to birth,
that conception without intercourse,
He was born from virginity
beyond human nature.

---

[27] See Luke 1:28.

[28] See Luke 1:31.

[29] F.C. Conybeare and A.J. Maclean, *Rituale Armenorum*, p. 327, where this verse is translated as follows: who in his God-head created the world.

[30] See Luke 1:34.

[31] See Luke 1:35.

[32] F.C. Conybeare and A.J. Maclean, *Rituale Armenorum*, p. 327, where this verse is translated as follows: and her joy was made full. Although Maclean chose 'joy' as a translation of the word ܚܕܝܘܬܐ, in the context it means 'unity'. According to Bar Bahlūl's *Lexicon*, this word can mean both 'joy' and 'unity'. See R. Duval, *Lexicon Syriacum Auctore Hassano Bar Bahlule*, p. 718.

[12] ܘܐܬܦܪܣܘ ܡܠܟܘܬܐ. ܕܥܡܡܐ ܚܕܪܝ ܡܕܝܢܬܐ.
ܠܘܩܒܠ ܟܠܗ ܡܢܝܢܘܬܐ. ܘܫܒܠܬܐ ܘܡܫܬܕܪܬܐ܀

[13] ܘܐܬܬܘܝܘ ܡܕܒܪܢܘܬܐ. ܕܢܦܩܝܢ ܠܗ ܫܠܝܚܘܬܐ.
ܘܡܘܕܥܝܢ ܟܠܗ ܥܘܬܪܬܐ. ܐܝܟ ܕܠܥܡܪܐ ܕܫܪܝܢܘܬܐ܀

[14] ܡܕܝܢܐ ܒܗܝ ܡܠܟܘܬܐ. ܡܬܕܪܟܐ ܒܢܝܢܘܬܐ.[33]
ܐܦ ܒܪܝܬܐ ܒܟܠܗܘܬܐ. ܒܫܡܝܐ ܘܐܪܥܐ ܒܫܠܝܛܘܬܐ܀

[15] ܡܠܐܟܐ ܡܫܡܫܝܢ ܗܘܘ. ܘܡܫܒܚܝܢ ܒܩܘܠܐ ܥܠܝܢ ܗܘܘ.
ܫܠܡܐ ܘܫܝܢܐ ܟܪܙܝܢ ܗܘܘ. ܠܐܢܫܐ ܕܫܦܪܬܗܘܢ ܩܕܡܘ ܗܘܘ܀

[16] ܡܢ ܩܕܡ ܡܠܟܐ ܙܥܘ ܗܘܘ. ܘܡܘܕܝܢܐ ܠܗ[34] ܢܦܠܘ ܗܘܘ.
ܕܒܫܬܩܐ ܩܘܡܢܐ[35] ܚܕܪܘ ܗܘܘ. ܘܡܫܒܚܝܢ ܒܩܠܐ[36] ܪܡܐ ܗܘܘ܀ / [f. 188ᵛ]

[17] ܘܡܠܟܘܬܐ ܢܦܪܘܩܟ. ܡܪܢܐ ܡܫܝܚܐ ܐܝܟ ܕܢܦܩܘܟ.
ܘܥܝܪܐ ܒܚܘܒܐ ܢܫܠܡܘܟ. ܢܦܫܐ ܕܝܢ ܒܟܠܐ[37] ܢܫܠܡܘܟ[38]܀

[18] **⸢ܩܠܐ ܕܡܘܫܐ⸣**[39]
ܘܡܢ ܐܦܐ ܠܡܬܡܠܟܘܬܐ. ܒܗ ܟܠ ܗܝܡܢ ܗܘܐ ܠܫܡܝܐ.
ܘܦܪܩܗ ܠܟܠܗ ܐܢܫܘܬܐ. ܒܨܠܝܒܗ ܡܢܗ ܦܪܝܩܘܬܐ܀

[19] ܘܢܫܒܗ ܒܟܠܗ ܠܐܢܫܘܬܐ. ܠܟܠܗ ܒܪܝܐ ܕܡܬܡܠܟܘܬܐ.
ܘܫܠܚܗ ܘܫܠܡܗ[40] ܠܫܠܝܚܘܬܐ. ܐܝܟ ܕܫܠܡܗ ܕܒܪܐ ܠܥܕܬܐ܀

[33] B1 ܦܢܝܢܘܬܐ.
[34] B1 ܠܗ.
[35] D1 ܩܘܡܐ.
[36] B1 ܒܩܠܐ.
[37] B1 ܒܟܠ.
[38] B1 ܢܫܠܡܘܢ.
[39] ⸢ M2, D1, C1, C2, D2, B2, M3, D3 marg.
[40] B1 – ܘ.

[12] The powers of heaven
gathered around the cave,
ranks and armies,
bands and companies.

[13] The four directions were moved
to offer worship to Him,
sacrifices and gifts,
as to the Lord of the creatures.

[14] The East with kingdoms,
the West with prophecies,
the North with shepherds,
the South, Egypt with adoration.

[15] The angels shouted
and sang 'glory' on high,
peace and hope they gave[41]
to human beings who had lost their hope.

[16] From Persia, the kings moved[42]
and brought sacrifices to Him.
They denied the worship of the stars
and, in front of Him, bowed their knee.

[17] And the shepherds announced Him,
the Lord Christ as they had learned,
and the Egyptians accepted Him with love,
like they had heard from the prophets.[43]

[18] **The strophes of Epiphany:**
Then He came for baptism,
though He was not in need of immersing.
He sanctified all humanity
with His body full of holiness.

[19] He brought down humanity with Him,
in the furnace of baptism
and He bore and abolished iniquity
according to the word of the son of the barren woman.[44]

---

[41] See Luke 2:14.
[42] See Matt 2:1.
[43] See Matt 2:15; Hos 11:1.
[44] John the Baptist.

[20] ܘܡܢ ܪ̈ܗܛܝܢ ܗܘܐ ܡܢ ܡܬܐ. ܐܬܟ̈ܢܫܘ ܟ̈ܗܢܐ ܕܥܡܐ.

ܘܐܝܟ ܐܘܡܐ ܢܣܒܘ ܡ̈ܢܝܢܐ. ܪܘܚܐ ܥܠܠ ܪ̈ܫܗ ܕܒܢܬܐ ܀

[21] ܠܐ ܡܕܡ̈ܝܢܐ ܠܠܘܬܗ ܢܝܚܐ ܗܘܐ. ܪܘܚܐ ܗܘ ܕܒܗ ܐܬܚܝܠ ܗܘܐ.

ܟܕ ܡܬܢܦܩܐ[45] ܐܘܪܚ ܗܘܐ. ܕܠܓܝܫ ܐܬܦܪܥ ܗܘܐ ܀

[22] ܘܦܓܥܗ ܪܘܚܐ ܐܝܟ ܢܘܪܐ. ܫܪܪܐ ܕܒܒܪܐ ܣܘܦ̈ܪܐ.

ܕܣܠܩܬܐ ܘܗܘܬ ܚܕܬܐ. ܒܥܕܬܗ ܦܓܪܗ ܕܢܘܚ ܟܐܢܐ ܀

[23] ܘܐܒܐ ܢܘܚܡ ܡܢ ܥܡܐ. ܕܗܘܘ ܒܝܬ ܚܣܕܐ.

ܠܘ ܝܗܒܘܗܝ ܡܠܘܗܝ ܒܪ̈ܟܐ. ܘܝܬܒܘܗܝ ܐܝܟ ܦܠܚ̈ܘܬܐ ܀

[24] ܕܐܡܪ[46] ܡܢܝܢ ܕܒܗ ܐܬܠܒܫ. ܠܘ ܕܒܗ ܐܬܠܒܫ ܡܕܡܝܬܐ.

ܐܠܐ ܕܒܗ ܚܘܫܒ̈ܢܝܬܐ. ܢܒܥܐ ܕܦܝܚܝܢ ܦܪ̈ܫܢܝܬܐ ܀

[25] ⸢ܬܫܥܝܬܐ ܕܫܡܥܘܢ⸣[47]

ܟܝܬܐ ܕܗܘ ܦܠܐ ܥܡܟ ܗܘܐ. ܐܬܦܠܓ ܘܡܬܦܪܦܪ ܗܘܐ.

ܘܪܝܫܗ ܦܬܝܐ ܢܦܝܠ ܗܘܐ. ܘܡܫܠܗ ܠܟܐܒ ܘܡܫܬܪܐ ܡܢܚܝ ܗܘܐ ܀

[26] ܗܘ ܐܘܪܚܐ ܕܦܩܝܕܬܐ. ܢܕܥܘ ܠܡܪܕܝܬܗ ܗܝܕܝܐ.

ܘܡܕܝܢܗ[48] ܢܦܩ ܠܦܪܕܝܣܐ.[49] ܠܡܕܒܪܐ ܕܠܝܬ ܒܗ ܦܠܓ ܨܘܒܐ ܀

---

45 D3 ܡܬܢܦܩܗ with the letter ܢ added later by the copyist.
46 B1 + ܘ; C1 with the letter ܘ added later by the copyist.
47 ⸢ M2, D1, C1, C2, D2, B2, M3, D3 marg.
48 D1 – ܘ.
49 C2 ܠܦܪܕܝܣܐ.

[20] When He ascended from the water,
the doors of heaven opened,
and the Spirit descended suddenly like a dove[50]
on His pure head.

[21] He did not descend on Him anew,
the Spirit by whom He had been formed;
by His going down, He made know
that He had taken care of our race.

[22] The Spirit descended like a dove,
announced that the flood of iniquity had passed,
and that peace was [there],
through the Lord and the Son of Noah the righteous one.[51]

[23] The Father called out from heaven:
'This is my only-begotten Son;[52]
all creatures give Him worship
and listen [to Him], as to the Lord.'

[24] He said: 'My beloved, I am pleased with Him.'[53]
It is not new that He was pleased with Him,
but through Him [Christ], with love,
He took pleasure in truly giving us life.

[25] **The strophes of Fasting:**
When the evil one heard this voice,
he spread terror and trembled,
and prepared his grievous weapon;
he sharpened his sword and stretched his bow.

[26] He who knows the hidden things,
knows his hated mentality,[54]
and He preceded him
to the fight in the desert where there is no sound.[55]

---

[50] See Matt 3:16; Mark 1:10; Luke 3:22; John 1:32.
[51] See Gen 7:1-23.
[52] See Matt 3:17; Mark 1:11; Luke 3:22.
[53] See Matt 3:17; Mark 1:11; Luke 3:22.
[54] F.C. Conybeare and A.J. Maclean, *Rituale Armenorum*, p. 328, where the verse is translated as follows: knew his hateful plan.
[55] See Matt 4:1; Mark 1:12; Luke 4:1.

[27] ܬܡܢ ܗܘܐ ܐܪܥܢܝ ܢܩܘܫܬܐ. ܣܠܩ ܠܫܡܝܐ ܐܬܩܫܬܐ.

ܕܒܗ ܦܘܝܐ ܠܗܘܢ[56] ܙܒܘܬܐ. ܕܢܬܐܢܝܢܘ ܒܗܕ ܡܬܒܘܠܬܐ ܀

[28] ܠܐ ܢܘܪܝܗ ܐܢܝ ܡܘܬܐ. ܕܡܫܘܚܐ ܕܒܢܬܐ ܦܡܩܒܪܬܐ.

ܕܠܐ ܢܣܘܦ ܣܬܠܐ ܕܡܢܬܐ. ܘܠܐ ܢܣܘܩܘܢ ܢܝܗ / ܗܕܐܘܪܬܐ ܀ [f. 189r]

[29] ܐܡܝܠ ⸢ܢܩܒܘ ܐܢܝ⸣[57] ܦܩܪܐ.[58] ܘܡܫܪ ܠܩܘܒܗ ܡܢܚܢܪܐ.[59]

ܘܐܦܐ ܦܩܪܐ ܠܡܥܩܪܐ. ܠܟܠ ܐܦܬܠܐ ܪܘܚܢܐ ܀

[30] ܘܡܫܚ ܠܐܪܐ ܗܪܢܪܐ. ܕܡܘܣܚܐ ܗܪܝܡܐ ܩܘܦܪܬܐ.

ܘܬܡܠܗ ܠܐܬܪܗ ܦܬܪܬܐ. ܘܡܫܚܐ ܒܠܒܗ ܕܪܘܚܢܐ[60] ܀

[31] ܒܠܗ ܘܢܗܘ ܦܝܫ ܗܘܐ. ܘܪܪܐ ܗܠܒܫܐ ܠܒܒ ܗܘܐ.

ܘܢܦܠ ܒܬܪܐ ܦܣܩܪ ܗܘܐ. ܘܒܠ ܢܒܠܗ ܠܘܬܗ ܢܝܚ ܗܘܐ ܀

[32] **⸢ܬܘܒܐ ܕܡܢܝܐ⸣**[61]

ܡܢ ܬܪܪ ܕܦܣܩܗ ܠܒܝܬܐ. ܘܦܒܗ ܐܢܝ ܦܬܪܐ ܕܒܝܬܐ.

ܗܘܢ ܡܪܒ ܘܠܗܐ ܠܢܝܬܐ. ܡܠܠ ܦܘܪܩܢ ܒܒܝܬܬܐ ܀

[33] ܣܝܢ ܝܡܬܐ ܘܠܡܠܠ ܗܘܪܐ. ܕܝܡܬܐ ܬܪܥܝܗ ܕܒܘܗܪܐ.

ܦܬܪܗ ܡܫܝܚܐ ܘܢܨܝܪܐ. ܕܦܬܝܗ ܗܘܐ ܦܬܚ ܠܚܝܪܐ ܀

[56] B1 ܠܟܘܢ.
[57] ⸢ B1 illeg.
[58] B1 ܕܡܢܢܬܐ.
[59] B1 ܕܡܢܢܬܐ.
[60] B1 – ܕ.
[61] ⸢ M2, D1, C1, C2, D2, B2, M3, D3 marg.

[27] He was fasting forty days[62]
instead of the Adamic creation,
that through Him they[63] would have the victory,
those who were guilty because of food.

[28] They were not bright like Moses,[64]
His pure and holy senses,
so that they would not see [His] mighty powers
and would not rise in the struggles.

[29] He made himself weak like a hungry person,
and the tempter came close to Him,
the hunger of the body triumphed,
over the non-eating spiritual one.

[30] The destroyer stretched the second arrow,
that of vain glory,
he took the corporeal arrow
and struck it in the heart of the spiritual one.

[31] He gathered all his weaponry,
and fighting, made the third;
then he fell in the well that he had dug,
and his wickedness came down upon his effort.

[32] **The strophes of Passion:**
After He destroyed the evil one,
and made him like trodden dust,
then He approached the passion
for the salvation of human beings.

[33] The sun darkened, and the moon grew dim,
the sun which brings forth light.
The shameful wood became the chariot of His[65]
glorious and honored body.

---

[62] See Matt 4:2; Luke 4:2.

[63] The word 'they' here refers to the Adamic creation.

[64] See Exod 34:33. Here the poet compares Moses with Christ.

[65] The same image is found in the writings of Ephrem. See R. Murray, *Symbols of Church and Kingdom*, p. 128.

[34] ܗܘ ܥܡܐ ܕܥܡ̈ܡܐ. ܕܐܪܡܝ ܡܢܗ ܢܘܟܪ̈ܝܐ.
ܢܥܒܕ ܢܦܫܗ ܠܓܢ̈ܒܐ. ܘܢܗܘܐ ܒܝܬܗ ܡܥܪܬܐ ܀

[35] ܪܒܘ ܚܝ̈ܠܐ ܕܕܘܫܢܐ.[66] ܕܚܙܘ ܒܗ ܐܕܝ̈ܢܐ.
ܠܡܪܐ ܕܡܝܬܐ ܘܚܝ̈ܐ. ܟܕ ܗܘܘ ܒܢ̈ܝܗ ܢܟܠܢ̈ܐ ܀

[36] ܢܩܦܘ ܒܗ ܬܠܡ̈ܝܕܐ. ܦܪܝܫܐ ܒܢ̈ܝܗ ܫܒ̈ܩܬܐ.
ܡܫܡܫܢܐ ܒܢ̈ܝܗ ܢܒ̈ܝܐ. ܓܡܝܪܐ ܒܗ[67] ܢܦ̈ܩܐ[68] ܀

[37] ܙܒܢ ܐܪ̈ܥܐ ܦܥܡ̈ܢܐ. ܘܐܬܒܪܟܘ ܥܡ̈ܡܐ ܡܕ̈ܝܢܬܐ.
ܘܐܬܦܬܚܘ ܡܟܐ ܬܪ̈ܥܐ. ܘܐܬܢܛܪܘ ܡܕ̈ܝܢܬܐ ܒܫܝܢܐ ܀

[38] ܦܠܚܘ ܠܡܪܘܬܐ ܘܠܫܘܒܚܐ. ܙܒܢܐ ܕܡܠܟܐ ܫܠܝܛ ܫܘܒܚܐ.
ܘܡܪܐ ܠܐܪ̈ܥܐ ܡܢ ܫܘܒܚܐ. ܐܝܟ ܡܠܟܐ[69] ܕܡܠܟܘܬܐ ܀

[39] ⌜ܒܩܠܐ ܕܡܕܪܫܐ⌝[70]
ܦܨ ܗܘܐ ܒܢܘܡܐ[71] ܕܐܠܗܐ. ܐܝܟ ܕܐܡܪ ܠܡܠܝܘܣܬܐ.
ܘܒܢܝܬܐ ܦܓܪܬܐ. ܘܐܡܪܐ[72] ܕܪܘܪܐ[73] ܡܠܝܘܬܐ ܀

[40] ܡܢ ܐܘܡܬܐ ܒܝܬܗ ܗܘܐ ܠܒܪܐ. ܡܢ ܥܡܐ ܢܦܫܗ ܡܠܬܐ ܡܠܟܐ.
ܦܪܦܘ ܠܗ ܠܡܠܟܐ ܗܕܝܐ. ܐܝܟ ܢܨܝܚܐ ܠܡܪܐ ܕܡܪܐ ܀

[41] ܘܠܒܢ̈ܝܐ ܫܘܪܗ ܡܫܝܚܐ. ܡܢܗ ܡܠܟܘܬܐ ܕܡܫܡܫܬܐ.
ܕܢܝܚ[74] ܕܒܐܝܬܘܬܐ ܒܟܠ ܥܠܡܐ. ܒܐܝܬܘܬܐ ܦܓܪ ܠܟܠ ܡܫܝܚܐ ܀

---

66 D2 – ܕ.
67 B1 ܒܢܝܗ.
68 B1 ܣܗܕ̈ܐ.
69 B1, C1, D2 ܡܠܟܐ.
70 ⌜ M2, D1, C1, C2, D2, B2, M3, D3 marg.
71 B1 ܠܢܘܡܐ.
72 B1 ܐܡܪܐ; D1 ܘܡܪܐ.
73 B1 ܕܪܘܪܐ.
74 B1 ܘܢܝܚ.

[34] That sun of the heavenly beings
of which the fiery ones are afraid,
surrendered Himself to the earthly beings,
and they judged Him like sinners.

[35] The powers of the spiritual beings were troubled
when they saw among the earthly ones,
the Lord of the dead and living,
suspended among the sinners.

[36] The merciful among the unjust ones,
the holy one among the impure,
the merciful one among the criminals,
the sweet one among the envious.

[37] Earth and heaven were shaken,
and the rugged rocks were broken.
The visible tombs were opened[75]
and the hidden dead were raised.

[38] He killed death and sin,
the righteous who died on behalf of sin,
and liberated human beings from sin,
according to the words of prophecy.

[39] **The strophes of Resurrection:**
He was raised on the third day,[76]
as He said to the apostolic community
many times,
and as prophecy had mysteriously alluded to.

[40] The watchers descended from on high,
the buried dead came out from Sheol.[77]
They made beautiful crowns for Him,
like servants for the Lord of lords.

[41] To the women, He showed His resurrection,[78]
before the company of the twelve,
because as through a woman death entered,
through a woman, we have hope of resurrection.

---

[75] F.C. Conybeare and A.J. Maclean, *Rituale Armenorum*, p. 329. This verse is not translated.
[76] See Matt 16:21, 17:23; Luke 24:7.
[77] See Matt 27:52.
[78] See Matt 28:9; Mark 16:9; John 20:11.

[42] ܚܕܪܘ ܠܟܢܘܫ ܢܠܠܒܐ. ܘܢܩܝܦܘ ܠܫܘܒܚܬܐ. [f. 189v]
ܘܫܠܡܘ ܠܗܘܕܝܘܬܐ. ܘܠܝܩܬܗ ܚܘܒ ܙܕܘܬܐ ܀

[43] ܓܘܪܐ ܕܪܚܡܐ ܠܗ ܟܘܡܪܐ. ܠܥܝܢ[79] ܕܢܠܓܐ ܕܥܘܫܢܐ.
ܒܥܘܠܓܐ ܠܘܟܐ ܣܓܝܐܐ. ܘܦܓܪܐ ܠܓܝܢܐ ܕܥܘܫܢܐ ܀

[44] ܓܠ ܒܬܘܠܬܐ ܡܢ ܢܣܝܢܝ. ܘܫܘܝ ܦܓܥܐ ܕܡܣܝܠܝ.
ܡܢ ܡܢ ܠܝܬܐ ܦܠܝܢܝ. ܘܡܢ ܡܠܘܗܝ ܚܫܐ ܪܡܝ ܀

[45] ܢܬܚܙܐ ܗܘܐ ܠܥܪܐ ܕܫܢܬܐ. ܒܬܪ ܡܢܡܬܗ ܦܓܝܥܬܐ.
ܘܓܒܪܐ ܐܪܥܠܝ ܢܘܩܬܐ. ܗܝܟ ܠܥܡܐ ܒܝܥܘܬܚܬܐ ܀

[46] **⌈ܬܘܒܐ ܕܥܘܠܡܐ⌉**[80]
ܡܠܐܟܐ ܠܗ ܦܓܥܝܢ ܗܘܘ. ܘܢܟܠܐ ܡܕܡܘܬ ⌈ܡܢܟܦܝܢ ܗܘܘ⌉.[81]
ܘܠܝܬܐ ܠܥܡܗ ܦܘܪܩܝܢ ܗܘܘ. ܘܒܢܝܠܐ ܠܗ ܡܬܡܟܝܢ ܗܘܘ ܀

[47] ܦܪܘܫܐ ܡܬܦܪܝܢ ܗܘܘ.[82] ܡܥܠܛܢܐ ܡܕܡܕܡܝܢ ܗܘܘ.[83]
ܘܐܬܪܘܬ ܠܒܢܐ ܡܫܘܚ ܗܘܘ. ܕܢܘܗܪܐ ܘܐܘܪܚܗ[84] ܦܪܫܝܢ ܗܘܘ[85] ܀

[48] ܦܘܪܩܢܐ[86] ܦܬܓܡܝܢ ܡܢܡܪܝܢ ܗܘܘ. ܗܕܘܪܐ ܡܘܕܥܗ ܐܝܟ ܗܘܘ.
ܒܪܥܝܐ ܐܣܦܪܐ ܢܬܚܝܒܗ ܗܘܘ. ܦܓܠܐ ܦܓܥܐ ܠܗ ܠܓܝܢܗ ܗܘܘ ܀

---

[79] B1 ܠܥܝܢ.
[80] ⌈ M2, D1, C1, C2, D2, B2, M3, D3 marg.
[81] ⌈ B1 ܦܪܩܝܢ ܗܘܘ.
[82] M3 ܗܘܘ has been added later by the copyist.
[83] M3 ܗܘܘ has been added later by the copyist.
[84] B2 ܘܐܘܪܚܗ.
[85] B1 ܡܫܘܚ ܗܘܘ.
[86] B2 ܡܦܩܢܐ.

[42] He destroyed the devouring Sheol,[87]
and raised mortality,
He overthrew Judaism,
and gave triumph to His church.

[43] A miracle that the mouth is too limited [to tell],
made by birth and resurrection!
the womb was sealed by giving birth,
and the grave was stamped by resurrection.

[44] He entered through the closed doors.
He showed the senses that were weak.
More subtle than the watchers,
but higher than all passions.

[45] [He] Was seen ten times[88]
after His holy resurrection,
and after forty days[89]
He ascended to heaven with glory.

[46] **The strophes of Ascension:**
The Angels worshipped Him
and the Powers sang in front of Him,
the watchers magnified His name,
and they served Him with strength.

[47] The Dominions honored [Him],
the Rulers exalted [Him],
the angelic powers furnished clouds of light[90]
and spread them on His way.

[48] The Thrones praised and honored [Him],
the Seraphim recited, 'Holy',
the Cherubim bowed down below Him,
and carried Him without sensation.

---

[87] See John 5:25; Eph 4:8; 1 Pet 3:19.
[88] For the ten poet-resurrection appearances of Christ, see Matt 28:9, 16; Mark 16:9, 12, 14; Luke 24:13, 36; John 20:14, 19, 26; John 21:1·;Act 1: 6-8; 1 Cor 15:6. The ten appearances are mentioned in hymn (90) also.
[89] See Acts 1:3.
[90] F.C. Conybeare and A.J. Maclean, *Rituale Armenorum*, p. 329, where the word ܢܘܗܪܐ is translated 'fire' instead of 'light', perhaps due to the author depending on another manuscript.

[49] ܐܒܐ ܒܘܪܫܐ ܝܗܒ ܠܗ. ܘܡܫܡܫܢܐ ܠܦܬܗ ܦܬܚ[91] ܠܗ.
ܘܟܠ ܝܘܡܐ ܫܡܫܗ ܠܗ. ܘܫܡܫܬܗ ܟܠ ܟܠ ܕܐܝܬ ܠܗ܀

[50] ⌈ܢܫܩ ܠܗ⌉[92] ܫܡܥܘܬܐ. ܘܫܩܠܗ ܦܬܓܡܐ ܕܡܠܟܘܬܐ.
ܐܦ ܗܕܐ ܕܐܠܗܘܬܐ. ܫܡ ܠܗ ܠܒܪ ܡܢܦܩܬܐ܀

[51] ܠܗ ܠܦܛܪܐ ܕܡܢ ܐܢܫܘܬܐ. ܕܢܗܘܐ[93] ܐܠܗܐ ܫܠܡܐ.
ܫܘܪ ܫܘܠܛܢܐ ܘܡܪܘܬܐ. ܐܦܩܗ ܦܪܨܘܦܘܬܐ܀

[52] ܗܘܐ ܫܠܝܚܐ ܠܥܠܡܐ ܟܠܗ. ܘܗܘܐ ܠܡܠܟܐ ܡܫܝܚܐ.
ܘܗܘܐ ܠܪܘܚܐ ܡܫܡܫܢܐ. ܕܟܠ ܫܘܒܚܐ ܡܫܘܚܬܐ܀

[53] ⌈ܬܘܕܝܬܐ ܕܦܛܪܘܣ ܟܐܦܐ⌉[94]
ܬܘܕܝ ܗܘܦܟܐ ܬܗܪܐ. ܡܢ ܡܘܗܒܬܐ ܕܟܘܪܐ.
ܟܠ ܫܠܝܚܐ ܕܢܗܪܐ ܒܘܕܐ.[95] ܐܬܠܒܫܘ ܗܘܘ ܚܝܠܐ ܡܢ ܪܘܚܐ܀

[54] ܒܕܡܘܬ ܡܪܥܝܬܐ ܕܐܒܘܗܝ. ܬܘܕܝ ܪܘܚܐ ܟܠ ܡܫܡܫܢܐ.
ܦܛܪܘܣ ܟܐܦܐ ܘܫܠܝܚܐ. ܢܗܘܐ ܕܟܠ ܢܬܚܘܝ ܠܫܡܝܐ܀

[55] / ܐܬܦܪܫ ܒܝܬܐ ܕܡܫܝܚܐ. ܦܬܚ ܠܫܡܝܐ ܦܬܓܡܐ. [f. 190r]
ܒܐܢܫܐ[96] ܡܫܝܚܐ ܘܫܠܝܚܐ. ܘܫܡܥ ܠܟܝܢܐ ܡܕܝܢܬܐ܀

91 B1 ܦܬܚ.
92 ⌈ B1 ܠܗ ܢܫܩ.
93 B1 ܗܘܐ ܢܗܘܐ.
94 ⌈ M2, D1, C1, C2, D2, B2, M3, D3 marg.
95 B1 ܒܘܕܐ.
96 B1 – ܒ.

[49] The Father prepared a throne for Him,[97]
and He placed a seat near Him,
He made all creatures subject to Him,
He gave Him dominion over all that is His.

[50] He granted Him to be the head,
the upright scepter of the kingdom,[98]
and the crown of divinity,
He placed on Him, the Son of mortality.[99]

[51] To the body from humanity,
that God the Word had taken,
He gave authority and Lordship,
like Him [God] in unity.

[52] He was the image of the living Father,[100]
and the temple of the only living Word,
the ark of the eternal Spirit,
without change and transformation.

[53] **The strophes of Pentecost:**
After ten days,
He sent the gift of fire,
on the uncultivated company of the apostles,
who were clothed in the darkest sadness.

[54] In the likeness of twelve tongues,[101]
the Spirit descended on the disciples,
nations and tongues were amazed,[102]
about the scene that eyes had not seen.

[55] The gathered assemblies were astonished,
To obtain different tongues,[103]
In the weak and pitiful people,
who looked like holy watchers.

---

[97] See Matt 25:31; Luke 1:32.
[98] See Ps 45:7-8; Heb 1:8.
[99] See Chapter 4 for more explanation.
[100] See 2 Cor 4:4; Col 1:15.
[101] See Acts 2:3. The biblical text does not mention the number of tongues.
[102] See Acts 2:7.
[103] See Acts 2:6.

[56] ܟܕ ܢܒܝܐܝܬ ܡܡܠܠܝܢ ܗܘܘ. ܐܠܗܝܬ ܐܝܟ ܕܡܟܪܙܝܢ ܗܘܘ.
ܠܡܫܝܚܐ ܕܠܗܘܢ[104] ܢܛܪܝܢ ܗܘܘ. ܒܝܠܕܝܗܘܢ[105] ܫܡܫܝܢ ܗܘܘ܀

[57] ܣܒܪܘ ܠܟܠܗܘܢ ܐܘ̈ܡܘܬܐ. ܘܩܕܫܘ ܠܟܠܗܝܢ ܡܠܟܘܬܐ.
ܘܐܘܕܥܘ ܠܟܠܗܝܢ ܥܡ̈ܡܐ.[106] ܒܥܒܕܐ ܕܐܠܗܘܬܐ܀

[58] ܟܕ ܦܘܩܕܐ ܠܐ ܢܛܪܝܢ ܗܘܘ. ܠܦܘܠܚܢܐ ܢܘܟܪܝܐ ܥܒܕܘ ܗܘܘ.
ܘܟܕ ܐܬܘܬܐ ܠܚܘܕ ܦܠܚܝܢ ܗܘܘ. ܠܟܠ ܚܘܠܩܐ ܦܠܚܘ ܗܘܘ܀

[59] ܟܕ ܝܗܒ ܠܗ ܗܘܐ ܡܫܗܘܢ. ܐܢܫܐ ܕܢܬܬܚܪܘ ܠܗܘܢ.
ܡܫܝܚܐ ܕܢܦܩ ܠܗ ܠܗܘܢ. ܟܕ ܦܠܓܐ ܕܢܫܬܠܡܘܢ ܠܗܘܢ܀

[60] ܕܐܬܡܠܝܬ[107]
ܦܪܩ[108] ܕܡܫܒܚܢܘܬܐ
ܚܙܝ ܠܡܫܝܚܐ ܒܟܢܝܫܬܐ[109]
ܘܠܥܠܡܐ ܗܘ ܠܗܘܢ ܡܢܬܐ
ܘܠܐܡܪܐ ܒܪܐ[110] ܝܠܝܕܘܬܐ
ܘܢܝܚ ܒܓܘܗ. ܘܐܪܐ ܪܘܚܗ
ܫܒܩ ܐܝܟ ܡܠܟܘܬܐ ܚܠܦܝܗܘܢ[111]
ܘܠܟܠ ܡܢܝܢ ܠܥܠܡܝܢ ܐܡܝܢ
ܘܫܡܥܬ ܠܝܠܝܐ ܙܒܢܐ
ܘܟܠ ܕܝܠܗ ܒܗ[112] ܡܠܟܘܬܐ
ܘܢܬܒܪܟ[113] ܠܗ ܒܫܘܒܚܐ܀

---

[104] B1 ܒܠܗܘܢ.
[105] B1 – ܒ.
[106] D3 +X ܡܠܟܘܬܐ.
[107] M2, D1, C1, C2, D2, B2, M3, D3 marg.
[108] B2 ܦܪܗ.
[109] B1 ܠܟܢܝܫܬܐ
[110] M3 + + ܒܪܗ.
[111] B1 ܚܠܦܝܗܘܢ.
[112] B1 ܒܗܝ.
[113] D2 ܘܢܒܪܟ.

[56] When the disciples spoke in Hebrew,
as they knew [it],
the nations who listened to them,
heard [them] in their own language.[114]

[57] They encompassed all the lands,
and dominated all the kingdoms,
they drew together all the souls,
into the yoke of the Trinity.

[58] Though they did not know the books,
they made the ignorant wise,
and teaching only Three,[115]
they demolished all the teachings.

[59] Not having a weapon,
the powerful came under their domination,
poor ones who did not have anything,
sons of kings were made disciples by them.

[60] Of the one who says:
O Lord of the dispensation,
have mercy on the one who assembled this in a hymn.
Make them[116] take part in the seven [feasts]
and in the eighth one, the mystery of crucifixion.
Renew his feelings,
and guard his movements,
forgive his sins by Your grace,
for all who remember Your eight feasts,
and worship Your living cross.
Grant us to see You in the kingdom
and to celebrate You always.

---

[114] See Acts 2:8.
[115] Although the Syriac text does not state this exactly, I suggest that it could also be translated 'and teaching Three as a unity' which would make it more theologically accurate.
[116] Here we see a change of pronoun from the previous verse.

14.(96)[1]

[f. 190r] [2]ܐܚܪܬܐ [3]⌈ܕܡܕܒܚܢܝܬܐ [4]ܕܦܢܛܝܩܘܣܛܐ⌉[5] ÷ ⌈ܕܝܠܗ [6]§ܕܡܥܠܬܗ ܠܗܝܟܠܐ⌉[7] ⌈ܦܐܪܐ. ܕܐܘܪܫܠܡ.. ܠܠܡ⌉[8]§[9]

[1] ܥܠ ܩܘܪܒܢ ܠܒܘܟܪܗ[10] ܕܡܪܝܐ
ܘܥܘܠ ܠܗܝܟܠ ܩܘܕܫ ܩܘܕܫܐ
ܘܫܡܥ ܫܡܥܘܢ ܦܘܩܕܢܗ
ܘܟܡܐ[11] ܛܥܢܗ ܠܥܘܠܡܐ ܒܕܪܥܘܗܝ
ܠܐ ܢܣܦܩ ܡܫܒܚܘܗ
ܘܐܢܐ ܕܠܛܠܘܡܐ ܚܙܝܬ ܒܕܡܘܬܗ
ܘܐܝܟ ܕܐܬܒܝܢ[12] ܒܠܚܘܕܘܗܝ
ܗܪܟܐ ܡܫܒܚܝܢ ܠܟܠ ܗܘܝܐ[13] ܫܒܚܘܗܝ
ܘܟܠ ܚܕܐ ܢܦܩ ܐܢܐ
ܘܩܠܡܘܬܗ ܫܡܥ ܐܢܐ ÷

[2] ܟܕ ܡܬܩܪܒܝܢܘܬܗ[14] ܠܟܢܫܐ ܗܘܐ. ܘܐܠܗܘܬܗ ܢܦܩܬ ܗܘܐ.
ܘܐܦ ܐܢܫܘܬܗ ܦܪܘܫ ܗܘܐ. ܘܣܓܝܐܬܗ ܥܘܡܩܐ ܗܘܐ ÷

[3] ܘܦܢ ܦܠܓܐ[15] ܟܠ ܐܢܫܘܬܐ. ܘܦܢ ܡܢܗ ܟܠ ܣܓܝܐܘܬܐ.[16]
⌈ܕܩܕܡܐ / ܡܢ ܟܠ ܡܕܡܢܝܬܐ⌉.[17] ⌈ܘܡܢܗ ܡܢܗ ܟܠ ܐܢܫܘܬܐ⌉[18] ÷ [f. 190v]

[4] ܟܕ ܡܦܩ ܦܓܪܐ ܕܝܠܗ ܗܘܐ. ܠܡܒܥܬܗ ܣܓܝܐܘܬܗ ܦܝܫ ܗܘܐ.
ܘܟܠ ܚܕܐ ܠܗܘܢ ܦܠܓܐ ܗܘܐ. ܘܟܠ ܡܢܗܘܢ ܦܓܪܐ ܗܘܐ ÷

[1] This hymn is found in: M1, M2, B1, D1, C1, C2, D2, B2, M3, G1, D3.

[2] The heading in M1 is written as follows: ܕܡܕܒܚܢܝܬܐ ܕܦܢܛܝܩܘܣܛܐ ܥܒܪ ܕܐܘܪܫܠܡ.

[3] B1 – ܐܚܪܬܐ.

[4] B2, G1 – ܕܡܕܒܚܢܝܬܐ; M3 ܕܡܕܒܚܐ.

[5] ⌉ M1 + in marg.

[6] C1, G1 + ܟܕ ܕܝܠܗ.

[7] B1 ܕܡܥܠܬܗ ܠܗܝܟܠܐ.

[8] ⌉ B1 –.

[9] § G1 ܕܦܐܪܐ.

[10] G1 ܠܒܘܟܪܗ.

[11] M1 ܕܟܡܐ.

[12] M1 marg.

[13] G1 ܥܡܗ.

[14] D3 ܡܬܩܪܒܝܢܘܬܗ with the letter ܗ written in the margins.

[15] M1, B1, D1, C1, D2, G1 ܦܠܓܐ.

[16] G1 ܐܢܫܘܬܐ.

[17] ⌉ G1 ܘܦܢ ܡܢܗ ܟܠ ܣܓܝܐܘܬܐ.

[18] ⌉ G1 ܕܩܕܡܐ ܡܢ ܟܠ ܡܕܡܢܝܬܐ.

14.(96)

Another one for the Sunday of Pentecost that is by Gīwargīs Wardā. Of the Gospel. Forever

[1] How great are the deeds of the Lord.[19]
The prophet David testifies to my words.[20]
How immensely deep are His thoughts;[21]
ignorant people, blind in their understanding,[22]
did not understand His glories,
and they thought of His miracles as if they were a delusion.
And from those who are righteous in their hearts,
He selected twelve and seventy.
He taught them about His passion
and showed His kingdom to them.

[2] When He had accomplished His dispensation
and had preached His divinity,
and also announced His humanity,
and made known His unity,

[3] at times He taught about the essence,
at other times about unity
which is beyond all thoughts,
at times about humanity.

[4] When the time that He would suffer had come near,
He gathered His group around Him.[23]
He taught them about His passion,
and He preached about His ascension.

---

[19] See Ps 92:5.
[20] See Ps 111:2.
[21] See Ps 92:5.
[22] See Ps 92:6.
[23] See Matt 26:17; Mark 14:12; Luke 22:7; John 13.

[5] ܦܬܚ ܦܘܡܗ ܘܐܡܪ ܗܘܐ ܠܗܘܢ. ܕܝܢ ܒܡܘܡܬܐ ܠܟ ܐܣܟܝܬܘܢ.
ܦܘܩܕܢܐ ܗܘܘ ܠܗܘܢ. ܒܟܝܢܗ ܐܢܘܢ ܘܐܬܠܝܘ ܐܢܘܢ ܀

[6] ܘܐܢܐ ܐܚܝܐ ܣܟܠܘܬܟܘܢ. ܡܢ ܐܝܢܐ ܕܫܪܝܪܐ[24] ܠܟܘܢ.
ܦܪܘܫܘܬܐ ܕܝܠܦܬܐ[25] ܒܟܘܢ. ܘܠܟܠܟܘܢ ܢܗܘܐ ܐܟܘܬܟܘܢ ܀

[7] ܗܘ ܫܠܚ ܠܟܘܢ ܢܒܝ ܩܘܕܫܐ. ܘܗܘ ܡܫܘܐ ܠܗܘܢ ܠܟܠ[26] ܩܪܝܬܐ.
ܘܗܘ ܡܟܪܙ ܠܗܘܢ ܠܟܠ ܥܡܡܘܬܐ. ⌈ܕܟܠ[27] ܐܢܫ ܕܢܥܒܕ ܗܝ ܒܩܘܫܬܐ⌉[28] ܀

[8] ܘܐܠܦܐ ܠܡܫܬܠܡܘܬܗ. ܠܐ ܡܢ ܕܢܚܒܠ[29] ܒܐܪܥܝܬܗ.
⌈ܘܚܘܒܐ ܕܡܫܝܚܘܬܗ⌉.[30] ܘܟܠ ܢܦܩ ܠܗ ܠܩܪܝܬܗ ܀

[9] ܫܡܥܬܘܢ ܕܝܢ ܢܒܝܝܬܘܢ ܠܗ. ܐܡܪܐ ܘܟܠ ܕܫܘܝܬܘܢ[31] ܠܗ.
ܕܒܢܝܗ ܠܟܘܢ ܕܫܘܐ[32] ܠܗ. ܗܘܝܐ ܗܘ ܒܟܠܗܘܢ ܢܒܝ ܠܗ ܀

[10] ܢܒܝܐ ܕܝܢ[33] ܕܐܡܪܗ ܠܟܘܢ. ܗܠܝܢ ܟܠܗ ܝܬܒܝܬܘܢ.
ܘܐܬܐ[34] ܡܪܘܬܐ ܒܟܠܟܘܢ. ܘܐܬܬܢܝܚܘ ܠܒܘܬܟܘܢ ܀

[11] ܒܪܗ[35] ܕܡܫܝܚܐ[36] ܘܟܠ ܥܒܕܐ ܠܟܘܢ. ܒܟܠ ܦܘܪܩܢܐ ܕܡܢ ܒܢܝܬܟܘܢ.[37]
ܕܝܢ ܠܐ ܢܙܠ ܡܢ ܠܟܘܢ.[38] ܡܫܬܢܝܢ ܠܐ ܐܢܬ ܠܟܘܢ[39] ܀

---

[24] G1 ܕܫܪܝܪܐ.
[25] M1 ܕܝܠܦܬ in marg. ܕܝܠܦܬܐ.
[26] B2 ܟܠ has been added later by the copyist.
[27] M1, B1, D1, D2 ܕܟܠ; C1 – ܕܟܠ.
[28] ⌉ C1 ܐܢܫ ܕܢܥܒܕܗ ܐܝܟ ܩܘܫܬܐ.
[29] B1, G1 + ܒ.
[30] G1 ܘܐܦ ܚܘܒܐ ܗܘ ܕܡܫܝܚܘܬܗ.
[31] G1 – ܕ.
[32] B2 marg.
[33] M1, B1 + ܕ.
[34] B1 ܘܐܬܐ.
[35] B1 illeg, G1 –.
[36] D3 ܬܫܡܫܬܢ with the letter ܘ added after ܫ by the copyist.
[37] G1 ܒܢܝܬܟܘܢ.
[38] B2 marg.
[39] B2 marg. d.

[5] He opened His mouth and told them:
'If you truly love me,
keep my commands,[40]
do them and teach them.

[6] I will ask for you,
from the Father to send to you,
the Paraclete to dwell in you
and forever to be with you.[41]

[7] He will teach you about my Lordship,[42]
He will show you my greatness,
He will announce to you my glory,
together[43] with the Father, from whom is my Sonship.'

[8] The world was unable to accept Him[44]
because of its weak thinking
and its little faith
that could not understand His greatness.

[9] But you know Him!
He said: 'It is not that you see Him,[45]
whose nature cannot be seen [by the eye];
only the mind can know Him.

[10] I know when I told you
these words, you were grieved[46]
and sadness came to you
and your hearts became suffocated.

[11] But listen to me and do not feel grief
about my separation from you.
If I do not leave you,
the Comforter will not come to you.[47]

---

[40] See John 14:15.
[41] See John 14:16.
[42] See John 14:26.
[43] For the translation of this verse, I depend on manuscripts M1, B1, D1 and D2, where the reading of the Syriac text makes more sense than in other manuscripts.
[44] See John 14:17.
[45] See John 14:17.
[46] See John 16:6.
[47] See John 16:7.

[12] ܘܐܝ[48] ܕܪܟ[49] ܡܬܥܕܪܝܢ[50] ܠܟܘܢ. ܘܢܘܗܪܐ ܒܫܡܝܐ ⌈ܡܬܚܙܐ ܠܟܘܢ⌉.[51]
ܘܡܬܒܪܟܐ ܐܘܪܚܟܘܢ.[52] ܘܡܠܟܘܬܐ ܕܫܡܝܐ[53] ܢܬܝܗܒ ܠܟܘܢ ܀

[13] ܥܠ ܕܐܬܐ ܪܘܚܐ ܕܩܘܕܫܐ. ⌈ܗܘ ܦܪܩܛ⌉[54] ܠܫܠܝܚܐ.
ܕܗܘܘ ܡܠܦܢܐ ܠܥܠܡܐ. ܘܢܚܬܘܢ ܐܝܟ ܦܠܓܘܬܐ ܀

[14] ܒܗܝ ܫܘܒܚܐ ܕܩܘܡܝܘܬܐ. ܦܠܘܛ ܠܝ ܕܐܒܢܐ[55] ܦܩܕܬܐ.
ܡܢ ܕܡܠܐܟܐ[56] ܘܡܢ ܕܢܦܫܐ.[57] ܘܡܢ ܗܢܝ[58] ܕܐܪܥܐ ܘܡܢ ܕܫܡܝܐ[59] ܀

[15] ܦܪܘܩ ܠܟܠܢܫ ܟܠܗ ܥܠܡܐ. ܟܠܗ ܕܐܬܦܪܩ[60] ܒܩܝܡܬܐ.
ܘܫܦܪ ܠܟܢܫܐ ܕܬܠܬܐ. ܘܠܐ ܢܫܟܚܘܢ / ܡܢ ܡܠܟܘܬܐ ܀ [f. 191r]

[16] ܦܪܘܩ ܟܠܗ ܘܕܝܢܘܬܐ. ܕܡܢ[61] ܕܝܠܗ ܐܝܟ ܡܠܟܘܬܐ.
ܡܠܟܐ ܦܘܪܩܢ ܐܢܫܘܬܐ. ܢܫܒܚ ܠܗ ܕܢܗܘܐ ܡܢܗ[62] ܀

[17] ܦܪܘܩ ܠܗܘܢ ܡܠܟܐ ܕܝܢܐ. ܕܡܢ[63] ܢܣܒܘܢ ܐܝܟ ܦܬܓܡܐ.
ܒܣܘܓܐ ܢܣܒܢ ܠܡܠܟܐ. ܘܒܕܝܢܐ ܥܒܕܗ[64] ܠܒܪܗ[65] ܕܝܢܐ ܀

[18] ܘܪܘܚܐ[66] ܕܡܬܒܪܟ ܐܢܐ ܠܟܘܢ. ܡܢ ܕܝܠܗ ܢܦܫ ܘܗܘ ܠܟܘܢ.[67]
ܠܐ ܬܫܬܪܘܢ ܘܬܐܡܪܘܢ ܒܢܦܫܟܘܢ. ܕܡܢ ܐܚܪܢ ܗܘܐ ܦܘܪܩܢܟܘܢ ܀

48 B2 ܕܝ.
49 B2 marg.
50 B1 illeg.
51 ⌈⌉ G1 ܐܘܪܚܟܘܢ.
52 G1 ܐܟܠ ܠܟܘܢ.
53 G1 + illeg word.
54 ⌈⌉ B1 illeg.
55 M1 ܕܐܒܢܘܗܝ.
56 G1 – ܕ.
57 G1 ܐܢܫܐ.
58 G1 –.
59 B2 – ܕ, G1 ܕܫܡܝܢܐ.
60 G1 ܕܐܬܦܪܩ.
61 C1, D2 – ܕ.
62 B1 marg.
63 G1 – ܕ.
64 M3 ܥܒܕ.
65 M1 illeg.
66 G1 – ܘ.
67 B2 ܠܗܘܢ.

[12] But if I go, I will send Him to you,
and He will reveal to you the hidden mysteries.
He will teach you future things,
He will remind you of all I have said.

[13] When the Spirit of Holiness comes
He will rebuke human beings,[68]
who have become disciples of the evil one
and considered me a magician.'

[14] With this appellation of Spirit of Holiness,
He taught us that He was distinct
from what is of angels and what is of soul,
from what is of air and what is of the evil one.

[15] 'He rebukes the world because of sin,[69]
because of those who lifted me up for crucifixion,
and I rose on the third day;
still, they did not return from their error.

[16] He rebukes them on account of justice:
Because the kingdom is mine;
for the redemption of humanity,
I deemed it good to die.

[17] He rebukes them because of judgment:
Because they accused me like a sinner;
through my condemnation, I destroyed Satan,
and by my judgment, Judgment is dissolved.

[18] The Spirit that I will send to you,
He takes from me and gives to you.
Do not think and say in your mind
that what is given to you is from another one.

[68] See John 16:8.
[69] See John 16:8.

[19] ܟܠ[70] ܕܐܝܬ ܠܐܒܐ ܕܒܢ̈ܝܐ. ܕܝܠܗ ܦܘܪܩܢܐ[71] ܗܘ ܠܒܢ̈ܝܐ.
ܘܟܠ ܗܕܐ ܗ̄ܝ[72] ܐܡܪ ܐ̄ܒܐ. ܕܢܚܙܘܢ ܒܢ̈ܝܢ ܐ̄ܒܗ̈ܝܢ ܥܘܠܒܢܐ ܀

[20] ܐܢ ܟܠ ܕܐܝܬ[73] ܠܐܒܐ ܕܝܠܗ. ܡܢܐ ܠܐ ܡܫܬܡܥܢܐ ܢܐܡܪ ܠܗ.
ܕܟܠ ܦܢ ܠܐ ܢܣܒ ܕܝܠܗ. ܦܘܪܩܢܐ[74] ܠܟܠ ܕܢܬܠ ܠܗ ܀

[21] ܟܠ ܬܠܝܬܝܘܬܐ ܐܝܬܝܗ ܗܘܬ. ܕܗܝ[75] ܐܪܙܐ ܕܝܢ ܟܠ ܟܝܢܐ ܗܘܬ.
ܘܐܒܐ ܒܦܘܩܕܢܐ ܠܟܠܗܘܢ ܐܡܪ ܗܘܐ. ܘܗܘ ܟܠ ܐܘܣܝܐ ܦܪܫ ܗܘܐ[76] ܀

[22] ܐܒܐ ܦܠܓ ܒܢ̈ܝܢܘܗܝ. ܟܠ ܚܠܩܗ ܕܐܝܬܘܗܝ ܢܐܪܬܘܗܝ.
ܦܠܓܐ ܦܠܓ[77] ܠܒܢ̈ܝܢܘܗܝ. ܟܠ ܐܘܣܝܐ ܟܝܢ ܥܘܬܪ̈ܢܘܗܝ ܀

[23] ܐܘ[78] ܟܡܐ ܬܡܝܗܐ ܚܟܡܬܐ. ܘܟܡܐ ܬܗܝܪܐ ܡܠܦܢܘܬܐ.
ܕܗܘ ܦܩܘܕ ܟܠ ܚܟܡܬܐ.[79] ܢܦܩܬ ܗܘܬ ܠܬܠܡܝܕܘܬܐ ܀

[24] ܐܝܟ[80] ܕܡܕܒܪܢܐ ܕܒܪܐ ܐܒܘܗܝ. ܘܠܬܘܡܗ[81] ܢܦܩ ܐܒܘܗܝ.
ܠܘܩܕܡ ܝܗܒܗ[82] ܫܘܒ ܠܗܘܢ. ܘܡܢ ܟܠ ܥܘܬܪܗ ܦܠܓ[83] ܠܗܘܢ ܀

[25] ܐܝܟ ܕܒܪܗ ܡܫܡܫܢܐ ܠܟܠ ܗܘܐ. ܘܦܪ̈ܫܐ ܒܦܘܩܕܢܐ ܠܗ ܥܒܕ ܗܘܐ.
ܘܡܢܝܢܐ ܠܟܠܗܘܢ ܢܦܩ ܗܘܐ.[84] ܘܟܠ ܢܟܣܘܗܝ ܠܗ ܦܪܫ ܗܘܐ ܀

[26] ܗܟܢܐ[85] ܗܘܐ ܠܟܠ ܗܘܐ. ܕܢܟܠܐ ܠܐܒܐ ܐܡܪ ܗܘܐ.
ܕܦܘܪܫܢܐ ܢܬܒܪ ܗܘܐ. ܘܡܢ ܐܡܪ ܕܗܘ ܢܬܒܪܝܘܗܝ ܗܘܐ ܀

---

70 D1 +X ܕܝܠܗ.
71 M3 ܦܘܪܩܢܐ with the letter ܘ added later by the copyist.
72 C2 ܗ̄ܝ has been added later by the copyist.
73 C1 ܕܐܝܬ with the letter ܕ added later by the copyist, G1 + +.
74 M1, B1 ܡܢܟ ܦܘܪܩܢܐ.
75 G1 ܕܗܝ.
76 D2 ܗܘܐ has been added by a later hand.
77 M1, B1, D2 ܦܠܓ.
78 D2 illeg.
79 G1 ܚܟܡ̈ܬܐ.
80 C1 + ܘ.
81 M1 illeg, G1 ܘܠܬܘܡܐ.
82 B2 + + ܝܗܒܗ, D3 ܝܗܒܗ has been added later by the copyist.
83 B1 ܦܠܓ.
84 M1 ܗܘܐ has been added later by the copyist.
85 G1 + ܘ.

[19] All that is of the Father by nature
is mine, and of the Spirit by nature,[86]
and for this I say,
'Behold! You will receive authority from me.'

[20] If all that the Father has is His,
perhaps a non-believer will say to Him
why did He not give what is His,
and also prepared to give the Spirit to Him?[87]

[21] He revealed the Trinity,
this mystery which was hidden from all,
and the Father indicated it beforehand,
as He had declared concerning the Spirit.

[22] The Father spoke through His prophets
about the infant who was with Him.
The Son told His apostles
about the Spirit through His promise.

[23] How astonishing is the wisdom!
How amazing is the teaching!
Which that font of all wisdom
taught to the company of the disciples.

[24] He arranged them according to ranks,
and lifted them up to His height;
first He showed them His passion,
and then He explained to them His glory.

[25] As He had done with the Samaritan woman;
in the beginning, He asked for water from her,[88]
and at the end, He taught her about himself,
He announced to her about himself.

[26] Thus He also did here,
that He would ask the Father[89]
to send the Paraclete
and then He said that He would send Him.

---

[86] See John 16:15.
[87] Translation uncertain.
[88] See John 4.
[89] See John 14:16.

[27] ܠܡܢ ܟܠ ܗܠܝܢ[90] ܦܠܝ̈ܓܘܬܐ. ܕܣܪܝܐ ܐܒܝܫܘ ܩܗܘܒܘܬܐ.
ܕܐܒܐ ܘܒܪܐ[91] ܒܩܢܘܡܘܬܐ. ܘܕܪܘܚܐ / ܒܒܪܝܘܬܐ ∻ [f. 191v]

[28] ܘܕܟܠ ܪܘܚܐ ܐܡܪ ܠܗܘܢ. ܕܟܠ ܕܝܬܡܪ ܗܘ ܢܦܠܓܘܢ.
ܒܗܝܢ ܕܝܢ ܒܠܒܗܘܢ ܐܡܪ ܗܘܐ ܠܗܘܢ. ܕܟܠ ܕܥܒܪܐ ܚܘܒ ܐܢܘܢ ∻

[29] ܘܟܠ ܕܡܕܡܕ ܣܘܪܐ[92] ܕܒܝܬܐ.[93] ܘܐܦܠܐ ܡܬܒܪܟܢ ܢܕܢܐ.
ܐܡܪ ܕܠܒܗܘܢ ܡܥܡܕ ܐܢܐ. ܥܠ ܕܣܘܢܗ ܘܡܦܠܓܢ[94] ܢܦܫܐ ∻

[30] ܟܠ ܕܐܘܚܘܕܝܐ[95] ܥܡܕ ܗܘܐ.[96] ܗܘ ܡܕܡ ܕܟܠܐ[97] ܢܒܥ ܗܘܐ
ܠܒܢܝ̈ ܐܢܫܐ ܡܥܡܕ ܗܘܐ. ܢܦܫܐ ܕܡܢܐ ܠܡܥܡܕ ܗܘܐ ∻

[31] ܠܐ[98] ܐܡܪ ܕܐܠܗܐ ܗܘܐ.[99] ܡܢ ܒܡܘܥܒܬܐ ܐܠܗܐ ܗܘܐ.
ܒܕܘܟܬܐ ܕܒܢ̈ܝܐ ܡܢܝܢ ܗܘܐ. ܘܦܠܓܗ ܠܟܠܗ ܗܘܐ ܕܝܗܒ ܗܘܐ[100] ∻

[32] ܡܢ ܟܠ ܚܕܐ ܢܦܩ ܠܗܘܢ. ܐܦ[101] ܟܠ ܡܢܗܘܢ ܒܝܬ ܠܗܘܢ.
ܟܠ[102] ܕܐܘܚܘܕܝܐ ܐܡܪ ܠܗܘܢ. ܕܝܢ ܡܥܡܕ ܠܗ[103] ܒܐܕܫܘܢ ∻

[33] ܢܥܒܕ ܕܐܒܐ ܒܗ ܠܥܡܐ. ܘܪܘܚܐ ܒܥܒܕܐ ܐܝܟ ܕܐܡܪ.
ܘܥܡ ܠܥܒܕܘܗ ܠܥܒܕܘܬܗ ܠܥܡܐ. ܠܥܠܝܬܗܘܢ ܐܝܟ ܡܐ ܕܐܡܪ ∻

[34] ܥܡ ܢܥܒܕ ܘܢܫܡܥ ܗܕܐ. ܕܒܠܚܘܕܘܗܝ ܡܪܐ ܕܒܟܬܒܐ.
ܘܡܢܣܒܢܐ ܕܒܟܬܒܐ. ܘܢܗܘܪܐ[104] ܕܚܝܐ ܠܟܠܝܬܐ ∻

[90] D1 ܗܕܐ.
[91] M1 marg; B1 ܘܒܪܐ.
[92] B1 ܣܘܪܗ.
[93] M1 – ܕ.
[94] B2 +X ܐܕܢܐ.
[95] B1 + ܕ.
[96] M1, B1, D2 ܥܡܕ ܗܘܐ
[97] M1, B1, D1, D2, C1 ܕܟܠܗ.
[98] M1 + ܘ.
[99] D3 written in the sequence ܗܘܐ ܕܐܠܗܐ and then corrected by putting ܐ on ܕܐܠܗܐ and ܒ on ܗܘܐ.
[100] D1 over verse d is written ܠܟܠܗ ܗܘܐ ܕܝܗܒ.
[101] M1, B1 + ܘ.
[102] G1 + ܘ.
[103] D3 ܠܗܘܢ.
[104] C2 ܘܢܗܘܪܐ with the letter ܘ has been added later by the copyist.

[27] There is no doubt about this,
that one is the gift
of the Father and the Son in agreement
and of the Spirit in truth.

[28] He told them about the Spirit
that He would teach you all that he would hear.[105]
Because He [Christ] told them about Him [the Spirit]
that He [the Spirit] would show them everything that He had seen.[106]

[29] And because what the eye saw was true,
and also the ear was not mistaken,
He said: 'I will make you hear
what I saw and heard.'

[30] He did not hear the Holy Spirit [saying]
something that He did not know,
He was making the human intellect hear
according to what it can hear.

[31] He did not say that He was God,
whereas indeed He was God,
because the time of the passion was drawing near,
and His body was ready to suffer.

[32] He taught them about His passion.
He also showed them His resurrection.
He told them about the Holy Spirit,
that He would send to be with them.

[33] If the Father inhabits Him
and He sends the Spirit as He said,
and He has perfected His apostles from the perfection of His perfection,
as He said,[107]

[34] who then dares to say this,
that He was not the Lord of creatures,
and the raiser of the dead
and the giver of the future life?

---

[105] See John 14:26.
[106] See John 16:13. Observe the pronoun transition from third person to second person to first person in this stanza.
[107] See John 17:23.

[35] ܩܪܐ ܢܩܘܫܬܐ ܫܡܝܐ. ܠܡܘܬܒܗ ܕܥܡܐ ܒܥܕܬܐ.
ܬܪܥܐ ܦܬܝܚܐ ܕܥܕܬܐ. ܥܠ ܗܝܟܠܐ ܗܘܝܢ ܘܫܡܫܐ܀

[36] ܡܫܠܠ ܕܒܫܡܝܐ ܢܩܫܝܢ. ܐܝܟ ܗܘܐ ܠܫܡܝܐ ܫܠܝܢ.
ܕܩܘܫܬܐ ܕܗܘܘ[108] ܒܡܝܬܝܢ.[109] ܐܟܠ ܒܒܢܝܢܐ ܕܦܢܝܢ܀

[37] ܬܠܬ ܫܡܝ̈ܐ ܐܝܬ ܗܘܐ. ܘܠܡܠܡܥܠܝܬܐ[110] ܐܝܟ ܗܘܐ.
ܘܐܢܝܢ ܢܘܪܐ ܒܠܚܘܕ ܥܕܐ ܗܘܐ. ܘܐܢܝܢ ܐܠܦܐ[111] [112]ܠܗܘܢ ܒܒܪ ܗܘܐ܀

[38] ܒܢܘܪܐ ܙܡܝܪܐ ܠܡܘܬܒܗ. ܕܠܝܬ ܠܗ ܕܘܡܝܐ[113] ܒܒܪܝܬܐ.
ܒܗ ܕܢܘܟܝܐ ܢܡܝܡܘܬܐ. ܘܡܟܝܟܐ ܢܘܚܪܘܬܐ܀

[39] ܒܗ ܫܠܡܘ ܦܪܝܫܘܬܐ. ܥܡ ܩܘܪܒܐ ܕܥܠܝܡܘܬܐ.
ܘܢܦܩܘ ܒܡܠܘܫ ܫܒܝܚܬܐ. ܒܟܠ ܫܒܝܢ ܕܟܠ ܫܥܬܐ܀

[40] ܘܐܝܟ ܕܡܫܒܚܢܐ ܢܘܪܐ. ܒܩܝܢܬܐ / ܘܟܠ ܙܡܪܐ. [f. 192r]
ܘܥܡ ܠܩܪܒܬܐ ܦܝܘܪܐ. ܕܠܩܘܕܫܐ[114] ܠܗ[115] ܡܫܒܚܪܐ܀

[41] ܝܗܒ ܠܗܘܢ ܢܘܚܪܘܬܐ. ܘܥܡܗ ܦܝܘܪܘܬܐ.
ܘܐܫܬܠܡܘ ܝܥܩܘܒܘܬܐ. ܒܡܠܐܟܘܗܝ[116] ܦܣܢܝܢܬܐ܀

[42] ܗܪܟܐ ܫܬܝܢ ܢܝܚܘ ܗܘܘ. ܒܠܚܘܕ ܘܠܟܠ ܢܬܦܪܩܘ ܗܘܘ.
ܕܥܡ ܒܢܝ ܫܪܐ ܡܬܠܠܝܢ ܗܘܘ. ܒܠ[117] ܫܪܐ ܡܫܬܡܠܝܢ[118] ܗܘܘ܀

---

108 G1 – ܕ.
109 G1 + ܕ.
110 G1 ܘܠܡܠܡܥܠܝܬܐ.
111 G1 ܡܠܝܬܐ.
112 D3 +X ܒܒܪ.
113 M1, G1 ܕܡܘܬܐ.
114 B1 ܒܩܘܕܫܐ.
115 D1 + ܘ.
116 G1 ܒܝܕܡܠܐܟܐ.
117 B1 ܒܟܠ.
118 M1, G1 ܡܫܬܡܠܝܢ ܗܘܘ.

[35] Ten days after
the ascension of the firstborn Son,
He sent the gift of fire[119]
on the disciples two and ten.

[36] Because during nine days,
He gave consolation to the nine ranks[120]
of the spiritual beings,
who were sad about human and mortal beings.

[37] After ten [days] He came
and gave consolation to the apostles
and stayed on them like fire,[121]
and made them like gods.

[38] He compared the gift to fire
that has no likeness in creation,
because it gives warmth
and bestows illumination.

[39] By it, the cold was abolished
from the mouths of the apostleship,
and they knocked, like fingers,
in all the ears of all the nations.

[40] When the fire is received in portions
And not diminished,
and when it illuminates the myriads
of lamps, it does not decrease.

[41] It gave them illumination
and they obtained enlightenment,
and darkness was abolished
by their life-giving words.

[42] Twelve tongues descended on them
and brought all in amazement;
while speaking with one language,
they were heard in all languages.

---

[119] See Acts 2:1.
[120] For the nine ranks of the angels, see Hymn 19.(127).
[121] See Acts 2:3.

[43] ܡܒܝܒܝܢ ܗܘܘ ܠܗܘܢ ܡܘܬܪܐ. ܘܦܘܪܢܣܐ ܘܡܫܩܠܝܬܐ.[122]
ܘܫܪܪܐ ܘܐܟܠܬܐ. ܘܡܫܪܝܐ ܘܦܠܘܚܝܬܐ ⁘

[44] ܘܠܚܡܐ ܘܡܘܬܒܐ. ܘܡܣܟܢܐ. ܘܟܪܝܐ.
ܘܥܘܗܕܢܐ ܠܗܘܢ ܢܗܝܐ. ܘܡܘܬܒܐ ܘܡܬܝܒܐ ⁘

[45] ܘܒܩܝܐ[123] ܘܦܩܝܘܬܐ. ܘܦܘܪܢܣܝܬܐ ܘܡܘܒܠܢܐ.
ܘܡܬܟܠܝܐ ܘܦܬܝܐ. ܘܥܕܪܐ ܕܠܡܣܟܢܐ ܢܘܚܡܐ ⁘

[46] ܠܗܘܢ ܓܝܪ ܡܒܝܒܝܢ ܗܘܘ. ܘܠܡܘܬܒܐ[124] ܚܘܝܢ[125] ܗܘܘ.
ܘܐܦ ܒܢܦܫܬܗܘܢ ܫܡܠܝܢ ܗܘܘ. ⌈ܢܦܫܬܗܘܢ[126] ܘܡܗܘܪܝܢ ܗܘܘ[127]⌉[128] ⁘

[47] ܡܢ ܗܠܝܢ ܕܒܢܦܫܗܘܢ. ܢܓܕܐܝܬ ܥܠܠܘ ܒܗܘܢ.
ܘܐܢܘܢ ܐܝܟ ܢܦܫܬܗܘܢ. ܢܘܗܪܐ ܥܡܗܘܢ ܗܘܐ ܠܗܘܢ ⁘

[48] ܐܘ ܒܢܝܢܐ ܩܕܝܫܐ. ܕܢܬܦܪܫܘܢ ܐܝܟ ܕܘܟܝܐ.
ܘܥܠܠܘ ܠܗ ܥܠ ܢܦܫܐ. ܒܝܕ ܢܦܫ ⌈ܕܠܐ ܡܬܦܪܫܝܢ⌉[129] ⁘

[49] ܡܫܝܚܐ ܡܪܐ ܕܟܠ[130] ܥܠܡܐ.[131] ܕܢܬܠܘ ܠܟܠ ܒܢܘܗܝ ܠܥܠ ܫܡܝܐ.
ܚܘܝ ܠܒܪܝܬ ܦܘܪܩܢܐ. ܘܥܠܘܗ ܗܠܝܢ ܕܢܝܚܐ ⁘

122 B2 marg.
123 D2 marg.
124 B1 ܘܠܡܘܬܒܐ.
125 D1 + ܘ which is then erased.
126 B1 + ܘ.
127 B1 ܡܗܘܪܝܢ ܗܘܘ.
128 ⌉ G1 ܘܠܢܦܫܬܗܘܢ ܡܗܘܪܝܢ ܗܘܘ.
129 ⌉ G1 ܘܡܬܦܪܫܝܢ.
130 M3 ܕܟܠ has been added later by the copyist, M1 ܠܟܠ.
131 M1, B1, G1 ܠܥܠܡܐ.

[43] The Jews were gathered,
Parthians and Cappadocians,
Medes and Alans,[132]
Egyptians and Phrygians,

[44] Libyans and the people from Cyrene,
Cretans and Arabs,
Romans and Greeks,
Phoenicians and Indians,

[45] Kushites and Pamphylians,
Pontians and the Syrians,[133]
Elamites and the Persians,
And other foreign nations.[134]

[46] All of them were gathered there
and saw the gift.
They also listened with their ears
to their languages and were amazed.[135]

[47] Though the disciples in their language
all spoke Hebrew,
they all heard them at the same time
as if [they were] their [own] languages.

[48] O corporeal human beings,
who looked like spiritual ones
and spoke with all tongues,
in one language without translators.

[49] Christ the Lord of all worlds,
who revealed His power in them [the apostles] to all nations,
have mercy on the one who composed the verses,
by the prayer of Your beloved disciples.

---

[132] This nation is found in the Peshiṭta text and probably it corresponds the 'Elamites' in other biblical texts, even though the poet mentions 'Elamites' later.

[133] I'm not sure if the poet by mentioning Syrians here he means Mesopotamia, because Mesopotamia is mentioned in the biblical text.

[134] See Acts 2:1-12. The names of the following nations are not mentioned literally in the biblical text: Greeks, Phoenicians, Indians, Kushites, Syrians and Persians.

[135] See Acts 2:12.

[50] ܘܢܬܒܣܡ ܒܪܚܡܝܟ
ܟܠ ܣܓܘܕܝܟ
ܕܡܘܕܝܢ ܠܛܝܒܘܬܟ[136] ܡܫܝܚܐ
ܕܢܦܩ ܡܢ ܟܪܣܗ ܕܩܕܝܫܬܐ ܕܟܝܬܐ
ܘܝܗܒ ܠܥܠܡ ܟܠܗ ܚܝܘܬܐ
ܕܢܚܐ ܠܗ ܒܗ ܡܠܟܘܬܐ ܀

136 B1 ܠܛܝܒܘܬܐ.

[50] And pour forth Your mercy
on Your worshippers
who are celebrating Your glorious feast
on the day of the descent of the Lord, the Spirit.
Make us all worthy by Your grace
to glorify You in Your kingdom.

15.(97)[1]

[f. 192r] ⌜ܐܚܪܬܐ ܕܬܘܢܓܠܝܘܢ[2] ܕܫܒܬܐ܀ ⌜ܥܠ[3] ܫܡܥܘܢܐ⌝[4]܀ ܕܒܝܬܗ[5] ܕܦܘܕܐ܀ ܥܠܡ⌝[6]

[1] ܡܢܘ ܗܦܟ ܕܥܡܠܬܐ
ܝܬܒܝܢ ܚܟܝܡ ܡܕܢܚ ܝܠܕܬܐ
ܕܡܢ ܒܝܬܠܚܡ ܡܬܟܪܙ ܐܢܐ
ܒܡܠ[7] ܗܘܒܢܬܐ ܠܐ ܡܬܕܪܫ[8] ܐܢܐ
ܘܐܢ ܗܘܢ ܒܗܢܐ / ܦܓܪܝ[9] ܐܢܐ
ܢܚܬܐ ܡܬܦܠܠ[10] ܐܢܐ[11]܀ [f. 192v]

[2] ܐܘ ܕܐܬܐ ܒܢܝ ܡܚܘܬܐ. ܘܡܬܟܢܫ ܕܠܐ ܡܘܫܒܬܐ.
ܘܐܬܝܠܕ ܡܢ ܒܬܘܠܬܐ. ܠܝܠܟ ܡܢ ܚܢܘܢ ܦܘܢܝܐ܀

[3] ܟܝ ܢܒܝܐ ܡܕܢ ܦܓܠܝ. ܗܘ ܕܫܦܪܐ ܠܝ ܘܡܘܕܐ ܠܝ.
ܕܝܠܠܢܝ[12] ܝܠܕܬܐ ܠܗ ܠܝ. ܐܢܐ ܡܕܢ[13] ܗܘܝ ܠܝ ܡܫܒܚܢܐ[14]܀

[4] ܐܘܪܘ ܚܫܘܟܐ[15] ܠܒܪ ܐܢܫܐ. ܕܐܬܓܠܝ ܒܫܦܪܐ ܐܠܗܐ.
ܘܡܕܢܚ[16] ܗܘܐ ܡܠܟܝܢ ܥܒܕܐ. ܒܗ ܡܠ ܚܫܘܟܗ ܕܒܢܝܐ܀

[5] ܒܥܕ ܒܡܘܕܝܢ ܘܢܘܗܪ ܫܘܒܚܝ. ܘܡܢ ܓܕܝ ܠܡܫܒܚ ܨܐܪܝ.
ܡܠ ܐܢܫܝܢ ܕܠܝܕܝ ܠܒܢܝܢ. ܥܘܒܕܗ ܒܓܠܝܢܘܬܐ܀

---

[1] This hymn is found in: M1, M2, B1, D1, C1, C2, D2, B2, M3, G1, D3.
[2] B2 illeg, G1 –.
[3] D1, C1, C2, B2, M3, D3 + ܘ.
[4] ⌝ G1 –.
[5] G1 + ܚܕ ܕܒܝܬܗ.
[6] ⌝ The heading in M1 is written as follows: ܘܫܒܬܐ ܕܒܝܬܗ ܕܦܘܕܐ, + in marg. ܘܫܒܬܐ; the heading in B1 is written as follows: ܐܚܪܬܐ ܕܫܒܬܐ ܕܒܥܘܬܐ ܢܫܘܢ.
[7] M1, G1 ܘܒܡܠ.
[8] C2 ܡܬܕܪܫ the letter ܕ has been added later by the copyist.
[9] B1 ܦܓܪܝܗ.
[10] M1, G1 ܡܬܦܠܠܗ.
[11] M1, G1 –.
[12] G1 + ܘ.
[13] D1 ܡܕܢ has been added later by the copyist.
[14] B1 ܫܒܚܢܐ.
[15] G1 ܚܫܘܟܐ.
[16] C2 ܘܡܕܢܚ.

15.(97)

Another one for the Gospel of Adoration.[17] On the Samaritan woman. By Wardā. Forever.

[1] Who is able, by word,
to speak about You, O Lord, the Word?
Though you are preached by all mouths,
you are incomprehensible by all intellects.
If You are thus hidden and invisible,
how can You be expressed in words?

[2] O He who came through grace
and was incarnated without marriage
and was born from virginity
beyond the habit of nature.

[3] Grant, O Lord, that I may loosen [a word]
that pleases You and helps me.
Without You, I do not have a word,
You, Lord, be a helper for me.

[4] The nations confessed the Son of essence
who was revealed in a human body.
And He struggled for thirty years
with all the passions belonging to nature.

[5] He was baptized in the Jordan and forgave our sins,
then He began to perform for us
all the things helpful to our lives.
Glory to Him at all the times!

---

[17] This is the name of a hymn that is chanted on the feast of Pentecost in the liturgy of Adoration ܐܘܢܓܠܝܘܢ ܕܣܓܕܬܐ, see T. Darmo, ed., *Ḥūḏrā* ܚܘܕܪܐ [The Cycle], vol. III, p. ܩܡܕ [144]. The hymn is chanted during the mass after reading the Gospel (which is from Jn 4:4-31), after the 'Glory, ܫܒܚ', see T. Darmo, ed., *Ḥūḏrā* ܚܘܕܪܐ [The Cycle], vol. III, p. ܩܢܕ [154]. The version of the latter hymn found in the Ḥūdrā is not the same as that of Gīwargīs which is translated here, but it has many similar words taken from the Peshiṭta text of the Bible, although some verses are in a different order from that of the Bible.

[6] ܟܕ ܢܫܬܠܛ ܡܢ ܚܘܒܪܐ. ܗܘ ܢܦܩܘܕ ܥܠ ܟܠܠܐ.
ܘܐܦܐ[18] ܠܗ[19] ܠܚܝܐ ܫܡܝܢܐ. ܘܢܬܚܘܐ ܒܢܨܚܢܐ ܗܢܐ ܀

[7] ܟܕ ܒܥܠܡܐ ܕܐܘܪܚܐ ܠܝܬ ܗܘܐ. ܥܠ ܫܡܝܐ ܓܕܐ ܢܦܩ ܗܘܐ.
ܘܡܢܐ ܠܡܥܡܪܐ ܒܟܪܐ ܗܘܐ. ܟܕ ܗܘ ܢܟܪ ܥܠ ܡܥܒܕܐ ܀

[8] ܐܦ ܠܗ ܠܝܘܚܢܢ ܕܟܠ ܝܘܡܐ. ܕܟܠ ܗܘܐ ܡܢ ܡܫܒܚܐ ܕܝܘܡܐ.
ܐܝܟ ܠܟܠ ܡܥܒܕܐ ܕܡܢܐ. ܐܟܠ ܛܘܒ ܒܚܕ ܛܒܢܐ ܀

[9] ܡܘܕܐ ܡܢ ܓܘܫܐ ܡܢܐ. ܢܘܕ ܗܘܐ ܠܟܠܡܐ ܝܓܕܠܐ.
ܘܢܦܩܐ ܒܕܐ ܚܒܪܐ. ⌈ܠܝܘܚܢܢ ܠܐ ܗܘܐ[20] ܡܫܒܚܢܐ⌉[21] ܀

[10] ܗܕܐ ܗܘ ܝܠܕܐ ܕܝܘܚܢܢ. ܢܒܥܕ ܥܠ ܐܢܫܘܬܗ.
ܘܕܢܘܢ ܚܝܠ ܡܫܒܘܚܬܗ.[22] ܒܐܢܫܘܬܐ ⌈ܕܝܘܡ ܡܢ⌉[23] ܢܓܕܐ ܀

[11] ܢܦܩܝ ܡܢ ܟܠ ܥܒܕ ܡܕܒܪܐ. ܗܘ ܕܡܫܠܠܬܗ ܐܝܟ.
ܘܢܦܩ ܗܘܐ ܒܕܘܒܪܘܬܐ. ܕܡܫܠܡ ܡܢܐ ܡܢ ܡܥܒܕܐ ܀

[12] ܗܘ ܕܡܢܐ[24] ܒܢܦܫܗ ܢܘܕ ܗܘܐ. ܥܠ ܡܥܒܕܐ ܘܟܦܪܬܐ ܠܝܬ ܗܘܐ.
ܘܠܢܦܫܗ ܡܢܐ ܫܐܠ ܗܘܐ. ܗܘܕ ܠܟ ܦܠܓܠ ܫܡܐ ܐܢܐ ܀

[18] B1 – ܘ.
[19] M3, D3 ܠܗ has been added later by the copyist.
[20] D1 –.
[21] ⌈ B1 ܠܐ ܗܘܐ ܠܝܘܚܢܢ ܡܫܒܚܢܐ.
[22] M1, C2, D2, B2 ܡܫܒܘܚܬܗ; B1, D1, C1, D3 ܡܫܒܘܚܬܗ; M3 ܡܫܒܚܬܗ.
[23] ⌈ G1 illeg.
[24] D2 – ܕ.

[6] Being rejected by the Jews,
He who is more honorable than those on high
came to the Samaritans
and was seen in this form.

[7] Being tired by the toil of the road,[25]
He sat on the side of the well[26]
and asked for water to drink,
He who is the source of each fount.

[8] O His thirst that is no thirst!
He who was not under the power of thirst,
He came to the fount of water,
but He was thirsty by will.

[9] Moses gave water from the rock[27]
to the Hebrew nation,
so how is it that the only-begotten Son
did not quench His thirst?

[10] This was the reason for His thirst,
to confirm for us His humanity,
and to make known the power of His grace
to a woman that [He] who liberated from perdition.

[11] She came out from the village of Sychar,
The one for whom He had come [Sychar],
and she came hastily
to fill water from the fount.[28]

[12] He who placed water in the seas,
was leaning on a small fount,
and was asking water from His handmaid:
'Give me a little to drink.'[29]

---

[25] See John 4:6.
[26] See John 4:6.
[27] See Exod 17:6; Num 20:11.
[28] See John 4:7.
[29] See John 4:7.

[13] ܫܡܫܐ ܡܢܗ ܡܬܢܗܪܐ ܗܘܐ. ܘܠܐ ܗܘܬ[30] ܚܫܟܐ ܫܠܝܛܐ ܗܘܐ.[31]
ܘܡܢܐ ܠܡܫܬܐܣ ܥܠܝܗ ܗܘܐ. ܢܗܝܪܘܬܐ ܠܟܠܐ ܡܢ ܦܘܪܩܢܐ܀

[14] / ⌈ܠܐ ܥܒܕ⌉[32] ܠܝ ܕܠܐ ܡܬܚܫܒܢ. ܗܘܦܟܐ ܘܠܐ ܡܫܬܚܠܦܢ. [f. 193r]
ܥܡ ܫܡܫܐ ܡܢ[33] ܠܥܘܠܡܝܢ. ܡܢܐ ܠܝ ܠܐ ܦܢܝܢܐ ܗܘܐ܀

[15] ܘܐ ܢܗܝܪܐ ܡܠܟܐ ܫܡܝܢܐ. ܘܡܢܐ ܡܬܠܒܟܐ[34] ܠܐ[35] ܢܘܗܪܐ.
ܘܡܠܟܐ[36] ܗܘܐ ⌈ܕܠܟ ܐܬܦܫܛ⌉.[37] ܝܚܝܕܘ[38] ܗܘ ܕܡܫܬܢܐ[39]܀

[16] ܢܠܘ ܒܘܠܚܝ ܡܢ ܠܥܘܠܡܝܢ. ܘܡܢܘ ܕܡܬܠܟ[40] ܢܡܠܟ.
ܘܢܦܝܫ ܠܝ ܡܢܐ ܐܡܪ[41] ܠܟܘܢ. ܟܠ ܕܠܝܠܗܘܢ ܢܫܠܡܘܢ ܢܘܗܪܐ܀

[17] ܟܠ ܕܡܫܐ ܗܠܝܢ ܡܢܐ. ܕܐܝܟܢ ܢܘܗܪܐ ܠܗ[42] ܢܥܘܠ[43] ܒܢܗܘܪܐ[44].
ܘܕܢܝܐ[45] ܢܣܒ ܠܗ ܡܢܐ. ܠܐ ܢܫܘܐ ܠܡܠܟܘܬ ܫܡܝܐ܀

[18] ܐܡܪܐ ܠܗ ܕܘܟܠܐ ܠܟܐ ܠܝ. ܘܒܪܐ ܠܐ ܡܬܚܫܒܐ ܠܝ.
ܦܬܝ ܚܝܐ ܡܢ ܢܗܪܐ ܠܝ. ܕܗܘܐ ܐܝܟ ܠܟ ܢܘܗܪܐ܀

[19] ܕܠܦܢܐ ܡܢ ܢܟܣܦܬ ܕܟ ܐܢܬ. ܐܘ ܡܢ ܐܒܪܗܡ ܝܠܕ ܐܢܬ.
ܕܡܢܐ ܚܝܐ[46] ⌈ܕܐܡܪ ܐܢܬ⌉.[47] ܠܐ ܡܚܝܡܘ ܗܝܝܢ[48] ܒܗܘ ܘܒܢܐ܀

30 M1, B1, G1 ܗܘܝܢ.
31 M1 marg.
32 ⌈ D2 illeg.
33 B1 + ܕ.
34 G1 ܡܬܠܒܟ ܐܢܬܝ.
35 G1 + ܘ.
36 M1, B1, G1 ܕܡܠܟܐ.
37 ⌈ M1, G1 ܕܐܬܦܫܛ ܐܢܬܝ.
38 C2 ܝܚܝܕܘ with the letter ܝ has been added later by the copyist.
39 C2 the letter ܕ has been added later by the copyist.
40 G1 ܕܡܬܠܟ with the second letter ܒ added later by the copyist.
41 M3 illeg. ܐܡܪ.
42 M2, G1 ܠܗ has been added later by the copyist.
43 M1 + ܠܗ.
44 B1 ܢܘܗܪܐ.
45 M3 ܘܕܢܝܐ with the letter ܕ added later by the copyist.
46 G1 + ܕ.
47 ⌈ G1 ܕܐܡܪܬ.
48 B1 ܗܘܝ.

[13] 'How is it that You, a Jew[49]
and not a Samaritan man,
ask for water to drink
from a woman, outside the command?

[14] Have You not heard that it is not allowed
for Jews to mix
with Samaritans?[50]
At the first, I will not give You water.'

[15] 'O woman, have you become foolish?
And do you not understand what you have said?[51]
This word that you said to me
is the will of Satan.

[16] If you had known who is in front of you,[52]
and who is speaking with you,
and saying to you, 'Give me water',
you would fall at His feet today.

[17] All who drink this water
to whom you have given will die of thirst,[53]
but if I give him water,
[he] will not be thirsty forever.'[54]

[18] She said to Him: 'Do You not have a water pot?[55]
Can You not reach the well?
From where do You have the living water[56]
that You give me today?

[19] Are You greater than Jacob[57]
or better than Abraham?
The living water that You mentioned,
they did not taste at that time.'

---

[49] See John 4:9.
[50] See John 4:9.
[51] See John 4:10.
[52] See John 4:10.
[53] See John 4:13.
[54] See John 4:14.
[55] See John 4:11.
[56] See John 4:11.
[57] See John 4:12.

[20] ⌈ܡܛܠ ܚܢܢܐ ܕܡܪܕܐ. ܠܐ ܐܬܚܫܘ ܡܢ ܥܕܬܐ⌉.[58]
ܡܢ ܐܒܐ ܕܢܚ ܥܡ ܥܕܬܐ. ܒܚܝܠܐ ܕܪܘܚܐ ܩܕܝܫܬܐ ܀

[21] ܘܟܠܗ ܡܢ ܕܘܟܬ ܡܛܐ. ܚܢܢ ܡܫܡܫܝܢ ܘܠܐ ܒܚܕ ܐܬܪܐ.
ܘܡܢ ⌈ܥܕܬܐ ܒܢܝܐ⌉[59] ܕܟܠܢܐ. ܕܡܠܟܘܬܗ[60] ܢܘܚ ܐܢܬ ܀

[22] ܘܟܠ ܠܟܢܫܐ ܡܕܡ ܠܝ[61] ܕܟܠܝܗ. ܘܕܒܪܝܗܘܢ[62] ܒܝܫܐ ܘܚܢ ܠܗܘܢ.
ܘܩܡܬ ܕܒܐܢܫ ܢܘܒܠܐ ܠܗܘܢ. ܐܘ ⌈ܢܚܫܒܬ ܕܟܠܢܐ⌉ ܀

[23] ܚܢܢ ܡܫܡܫܝܢ[63] ܕܟܠܟܠ ܠܗ ܠܝ. ܩܕܡ ܒܥܝܢ ܠܝ ܘܟܠܝ.
ܕܐܝ[64] ܒܟܠܟܠ ܩܕܝܫܐ ܒܬܪ ܠܝ. ܠܟܠܟܠ ܒܝܘܡܐ ܩܠܗܐ ܐܢܐ ܀

[24] ܟܦܪܐ ܐܫܬܪܝ ܕܡܪܕܐ. ⌈ܕܟܠܟܠ ܠܗ ܠܗܘܢ ܕܡܪܕܐ⌉.[65]
ܢܡܡܐ ܗܘܘ ܠܗܘܢ ܕܡܪܕܐ. ܘܩܡܐ ܠܟܪ ܡܢ ܦܘܩܕܢܐ ܀

[25] ܫܘܐ ܐܢܐ ܕܒܢܝܐ ܒܗܝ. ܘܢܘܦܠܐ ܕܓܒܘܢܬܐ ܐܢܝ.
ܕܟܠܢܐ ܕܡܫܘܚܐ ܐܢܗ. ܘܦܠܝܟ ܐܢܗ ܠܝ[66] ܢܘܩܒܐ ܀

[26] ܒܬܘܠ[67] ܥܢܢܐ ܐܠܗܐ. ܒܗܝ ܠܘܒܐ ܒܢܝܗ ܫܒܝܒܐ.
ܘܒܗܘ ܒܐܘܪܫܠܡ ܡܕܝܢܬܐ. ܐܡܪܝܗܘ ܕܫܡܥܬܝܢ[68] ܒܐܢܐ[69] ܀

---

[58] ⌉ rep. bc.
[59] ⌉ M1, B1, G1 ܐܒܐ ܥܕܬܐ.
[60] M1 ܡܡܠܟܘܬܗ; B1 ܘܡܠܟ ܥܡܗ.
[61] M1 –.
[62] M1 ܘܕܒܪܝܗܘܢ, G1 ܘܕܒܪܝܗܘܢ.
[63] B1 ܐܢܫܐ ܠܗ.
[64] D3 ܐܝ.
[65] ⌉ M1, B1, G1 ܘܠܗ ܠܗܘܢ ܟܠܟܠ ܕܡܪܕܐ.
[66] B1 ܠܝ.
[67] M3 ܒܬܘ.
[68] M1, G1 ܕܫܡܥܬܝܢ.
[69] C2 marg.

[20] 'The true living water,
does not come from the well,
[but] from the Father, flowing through the Son
by the power of the life-giving Spirit.'

[21] 'Give me from that water',
she answered and said: 'I have not come
and taken water from this well
by which I will be thirsty forever.'[70]

[22] 'Go to your house and call your husband[71]
and bring him with you and come;
when you come, I will give to you,
O you imperfect of mind.'

[23] She replied: 'I do not have a husband,[72]
what should I do? Woe to me!
If through a husband You give me water
I will die of thirst forever.'

[24] 'You said well, in truth,
that you do not have a husband, in truth[73]
you have five, in truth,
and this one is unlawful.'[74]

[25] 'I see that You are a prophet,[75]
and You know the hidden things,
I ask You to show
and to teach them[76] today.

[26] Our three righteous fathers,
offered worship on this mountain,
and You in the city of Jerusalem,[77]
You say that the Just One will be worshipped there.

---

[70] See John 4:15.
[71] See John 4:16.
[72] See John 4:17.
[73] See John 4:17.
[74] See John 4:18.
[75] See John 4:19.
[76] Since Jesus is only talking with the Samaritan woman in this scene, the wording of B1 is probably better: ܠܝ 'me' (see note 66).
[77] See John 4:20.

[27] ܗܟܐ / ܪܡܚ[78] ܫܒܝܚܝܢ. ܠܥܠܡܐ. ܘܪܡܚ ܢܣܒܝܢ. [f. 193v]
ܘܐܝܟ ܒܠܘܗܝ ܡܫܬܡܠܝܢ. ܐܢܐ ܥܒܕܐ ܗܘܝܬ ܠܟ ܡܠܟܘܬܐ ܀

[28] ܪܒܘܬܐ[79] ܦܫܝܛܝܢ ܕܗܘܐ ܥܠܡܐ. ܕܢܦܩܬ ܕܠܐ ܒܗܘܢ ܕܘܟܬܐ.
ܐܦܠܐ ܡܬܦܪܣܐ ܡܫܒܚܬܐ. ܒܝܘܡܝ ܠܚܘܕ ܠܗܘ ܡܫܝܚܐ ܀

[29] ܠܝ ܦܪܘܫܘܬܐ ܐܘܝ ܒܠܘܩܐ. ܐܘܝ[80] ܦܪܘܫܘܬܐ ⸢ܐܘܝ ܒܦܪܘܩܐ⸣.[81]
ܒܗ ܕܫܘܪܝ ܒܐܒܐ ܦܪܩܐ. ܘܫܒܝܚ ܠܪܘܚܐ ܡܫܝܚܐ ܀

[30] ܪܘܚܐ ܐܝܬܘܗܝ ܐܠܗܐ. ܦܢܝܐ ܒܗ ܡܢ ܐܠܗܐ.
ܘܙܘܥ ܕܢܫܬܒܚ ܐܠܗܐ. ܒܪܘܚܐ ܘܡܫܒܚܐ ܦܪܘܩܐ ܀

[31] ܗܠܝܢ ܐܢܘܢ ܦܫܝܪܬܐ. ܫܒܘܚܐ ܕܐܒܐ ܘܦܪܩܐ.[82]
ܘܒܗܘܢ ܢܥܒܕ ܦܫܝܪܬܐ.[83] ܪܘܚܐ ܚܝܐ ܘܡܫܝܚܐ ܀

[32] ܘܐܦ[84] ܐܒܐ ܗܠܝܢ ܒܪܐ. ܘܒܗܠܝܢ ܫܒܘܚܐ ܪܘܚܐ.
ܕܫܘܪܝ[85] ܦܫܝܩܘܬܐ[86] ܡܢܝܢܐ. ܗܠܝܢ ܦܪܘܩ ܦܫܝܛܐ ܀

[33] ܢܣܒܝܢ ܕܐܒܐ ܡܫܝܚܐ. ܐܝܟ ܕܐܡܪ ܫܠܝܚܐ ܒܪܘܚܐ.
ܘܦܠܓ ܠܢ ܫܪܪܐ ܕܚܝܐ. ܘܐܢܐ ܠܢ ܒܗ ܡܫܡܫܢܐ ܀

78 M3 ܪܡܚܐ.
79 C2 ܪܒܘܬܐ has been added later by the copyist.
80 B1 – ܘ.
81 ⸢ C2 marg.
82 M1 ܦܪܩܐ; C2 marg. b.
83 C2 marg. c.
84 M1, B1 – ܘ.
85 G1 ܘܫܘܪܝ.
86 B2 +X ܦܫܝܩܘܬܐ.

[27] 'Now, how do we worship God?
How do we know?
And how do we recognize him?
You, my Lord, be my teacher.'

[28] 'Woman, believe me; behold, there will be an hour
when neither at this place
nor only in Zion, will worship be offered,
to the one who gives life.[87]

[29] Whether in a city or on a mountain,
in a village or in the desert,
where they will confess the Father and the Son
and worship the life-giving Spirit.

[30] The Spirit is God,[88]
and is full of God;
it is right that God be worshipped
in spirit, intellect and mind.[89]

[31] These are truly,
the worshipers of the Father and the Son,
and truly inhabits in them
the living and life-giving Spirit.

[32] The Father also asks for those people,
and is pleased with those worshipers,
who confess the well-known *qnōmē*
three that are equal in nature.'

[33] 'I know that the Messiah will come,[90]
as the prophet said in the spirit,
and will teach us the shining truth,
and I liken You to him.

---

[87] See John 4:21-23.
[88] See John 4:24.
[89] See John 4:24 'in spirit and in truth'.
[90] See John 4:25.

[34] ܗܫܐ ܐܡܪ[91] ܠܝ ܒܫܪܪܐ. ܕܐܝܟܘ ܡܫܝܚܐ ܒܫܪܪܐ.
ܕܢܬܕܟܪܢ ܘܠܝ ܒܫܒܝܐ.[92] ܕܐܬܐ[93] ܡܫܝܚܐ ܦܪܘܩܐ ܀

[35] ܦܝܫ ܗܪܟܐ ܕܡܬܦܬܚܝܢ ܠܗܘܢ. ܦܘܪܩܢܗܘܢ ܘܗܐ ܗܘ ܠܡܬܦܠܚܘ.
ܗܘܝܘ ܕܡܬܦܠܚ ܒܢܝܢܐ. ܘܠܐ ܫܪܪܝ ܠܥܠܡܐ ܗܫܐ ܀

[36] ܗܝ ܕܝܢ ܡܘܠܕܗ ܢܒܝܐ ܗܘܬ. ܘܠܟܠܗ ܡܫܒܚܬܐ ܕܗܘܠܕܐ ܗܘܬ.[94]
ܦܩܕ ܡܠܟܐ ܗܟܢܐ ܗܘܬ.[95] ܕܠܡܫܝܚܐ ܣܘܓܐ ܢܘܟܪܝܐ ܀

[37] ܢܦܩ ܗܘܐ ܒܥܬܐ ܕܫܡܥܘܢ. ܠܫܒܝܬܗ ܕܚܙܐ ܕܝܠܗ.
ܗܝ[96] ܠܒܥܬܐ ܦܘܩܕܢܐ. ܦܩܕܘ ܒܗ ⌈ܠܟܠ ܢܘܟܪܝܐ⌉[97] ܀

[38] ܗܐ ܫܡܥܠ ܐܘ ܒܢܝ ܫܒܬܐ. ܝܗܒܘܢ ܠܗ ܒܥܪܒܪܘܬܐ.
ܠܗ ܐܒܘܗܝ ܒܚܙܝܘܬܐ. ܘܠܗ ܠܗ ܪܘܚܗ ܦܪܘܩܐ ܀

[39] ܗܐ ܐܘ ܒܢܝ ܦܠܓܘܬܐ.[98] ⌈ܠܗ ܥܠܝܬܐ ܒܢܝܗ ܫܠܝܛܐ.
ܝܗܒܘܢ ܠܗ ܒܫܘܝܘܬܐ⌉.[99] ܠܗܘ ܕܠܗܘܢ ܗܘܐ ܡܢܚܡܢܐ ܀

[40] ܪܘܚܐ ܢܝܚܐ ܐܠܗܝܬܐ. ܥܠ / ܡܠܡܕܢܐ ܠܡܫܪܝܬܐ. [f. 194r]
ܘܡܠܦܢܐ[100] ܕܐܬܬ ܗܘܐ ܥܒܕܐܝܬ. ܬܫܡܫܬ ܗܘܐ ܒܟܘܠܗܘܢ ܗܢܐ ܀

[41] ܫܠܝܚܐ ܦܠܠܗ ܢܒܝܐܝܬ. ܒܝܕ ܠܫܢܐ ܦܘܢܝܬ.
ܘܡܦܫܩܐ ܫܡܥܘ ܗܘܘ ܠܫܠܝܚܘܬܗ. ܘܠܟܠ ܚܕ ܒܝܕ ܠܫܢܐ ܀

91 B1 ܦܪ.
92 G1 ܒܫܪܪܐ.
93 B1, C2 ܕܐܬܐ.
94 D3 marg. b.
95 D3 marg. c.
96 M1, G1 ܦܘܩܕܗ.
97 ⌉ B1, G1 ܕܦܩܕܘ ܒܗ ܠܟܠܗܘܢ ܥܡܡܐ.
98 D3 +X ܒܢܝܗ.
99 ⌉ B1 rep. bc.
100 G1 ܘܡܦܫܩܢܐ.

[34] Now, tell me truly
that You are indeed the Messiah,
because I know, and for me, it is true
that the life-giving Messiah will come.'

[35] Our Lord replied: 'Blessed are you
because you saw Him and see He is in front of you,
He is who is speaking to you;
go and announce [it] to this nation.'

[36] She then left her pitcher,[101]
hurried to the village,
and cried out in front of all the people:
'Today I have seen the Messiah.'[102]

[37] The Samaritan people went out[103]
to worship the Lord of those on high.
Woe to the Jewish nation,
who have denied Him until this day!

[38] Come, O you children of the church,
let us worship Him in truth,
together with His Father in unity,
Him and His life-giving Spirit.

[39] Come, O you children of baptism,
with the apostles in the upper room,
let us worship Him with joy,
the one who was a teacher for them.

[40] The Spirit descended divinely
on the disciples perfectly,
and the nations who were gathered
were amazed at this thing.[104]

[41] The apostles spoke Hebrew
in one tongue equally,
and the nations heard differently,
each one in his language.[105]

---

[101] See John 4:28.
[102] See John 4:29.
[103] See John 4:30.
[104] See Acts 2:1-5.
[105] See Acts 2:8.

[42] ܡܥܒܕ ܐܠܗܐ ܕܟܠ ܟܠ. ܕܐܬܓܠܝܘܬܗ ܥܒܝܕܐ ܒܟܠ ܟܠ.
ܚܙܝ ܠܐܒܘܟ ܢܛܪ ܡܢ ܟܠ. ܡܪܚܡܢܘܬܗ ܕܡܫܠܠ ܗܘܐ ܀

[43] ܘܠܝ ܡܫܦܚܬܐ
ܘܠܐܒܘܟ ܫܝܢܬܐ
ܘܠܒܘܫ ܚܕܘܬܐ
ܘܐܝܟܢܐ ܕܢܬܠܘܢ ܠܗܝ[106] ܬܫܒܘܚܬܐ
ܚܙܝ ܠܒܢܝܟ ܠܗܘܢ[107] ܒܢܝܢܬܐ
ܘܠܝ ܦܠܚܠܗܘܢ ܢܠܒܫܘܢ ܕܝܢܬܐ[108]
ܕܢܗܘܢ ܫܝܢܝܢ ܒܟܠ ܦܢܝܬܐ
ܠܐܠܗܘܬܟ[109] ܡܫܒܚܬܐ
ܐܡܪܐ[110] ܠܟܠܢ ܠܗܝ ܡܠܟܘܬܐ
ܕܢܬܒܣܡ ܠܝ ܟܠ ܢܘܩܬܐ[111] ܀

[106] B2 ܠܗ.
[107] D2 – ܠ.
[108] B2 marg. ܕܝܢܬܐ.
[109] D2 + ܘ.
[110] B1 ܘܐܡܪܐ.
[111] B1 marg.

[42] Christ, God of all,
whose grace is effused on all,
have mercy on Your servant, the sinner, more than all,
the composer of this treatise.

[43] To You praise,
to Your Father adoration,
and to Your Spirit in unity.
Just as You had mercy on that Samaritan woman,
have mercy on the one who has composed this hymn.
On me and all the children of the church,
that today are everywhere worshipping
Your glorious divinity.
Make us all worthy of that kingdom
to glorify You all days.

(106).16[1]

[f. 208r] ܐܚܪܬܐ ܕܝܠܗ ܕܣܘܪܝܐ܀ ܘܐܡܝܪܐ ܠܩܢܘܢܐ[2] ܦܠܝܘܣܛܪܘܣ܀ ܘܠܡܠܘܗܝ ܕܡܠܦܢܐ ܕܥܠܝܬܐ܀
ܕܩܘܠܐ܀ ܒܐܡܐ[3]

[1] ܐܠܗܐ ܕܡܢ ܐܒܐ
ܒܪܗ / ܡܠܟ ܫܡܝܐ[4] ܠܦܘܪܩܢ ܐܢܫܐ [f. 208v]
ܐܬܐ ܕܢܠܒܫ ܐܢܫܘܬܐ
ܒܪܐ ܕܠܘܬ ܐܒܐ ܩܢܐ[5] ܡܬܦܠܐܝܬ
ܪܒܘܬܐ ܘܠܐ ܡܬܪܘܬܐ
ܐܦ ܫܘܝܘܬܐ ܕܠܐ ܡܫܢܝܘܬܐ
ܦܣܩܗ ܢܣܒܘܗ ܡܢ ܒܬܘܠܘܬܗ
ܕܢܘܕܥ ܚܘܒܗ ܠܒܢܝ ܐܒܗܘܗ
ܚܘܒܗ ܪܒܐ ܘܫܘܝܗ ܒܒܫܪܐ
ܘܐܝܟ ܕܢܦܩ ܠܗ ܠܒܐ ܠܗ ܒܣܒܪܐ
ܥܠܝܬܐ ܢܒܝܐ ܩܕܝܫܐ
ܘܫܠܝܚܐ ܦܬܓܡܐ ܐܡܪܝܢ ܢܒܝܐ
ܠܢܒܝܐ ܫܡܝܢ ܒܪܘܚܩܘܕܫܐ
ܘܗܘܐ ܒܟܠܗܘܢ ܚܕܐ ܢܦܫܐ܀

[2] ܐ ܐܢ ܟܠ ܚܕ ܚܕ ܐܡܪ ܐܒܐ. ܠܐ ܩܢܐ ܐܒܐ ܘܠܐ ܗܦܟ ܐܒܐ.
ܘܐܒܘܗ ܕܒܪ ܚܕ ܐܝܟ ܐܒܐ. ܠܟܠܗܘܢ ܦܪ ܐܒܐ ⌈ܘܦܪ ܡܫܝܚ ܐܒܐ⌉[6]܀

[3] ܒ ܒܪܒܘܬܗܘܢ[7] ܟܠ ܐܦܝܗ ܐܒܐ. ܐܦܝܗ ܐܒܐ ܘܟܠ ܐܦܝܗ ܐܒܐ.
ܐܦܝܗ ܐܒܐ ܘܡܬܬܪܡܐ ܐܒܐ. ܘܡܬܬܪܡܐ[8] ܐܒܐ ܘܐܡܪ ܐܒܐ܀

[4] ܓ ܓܠܐ ܠܟܢܫܐ ܘܩܕܡ ܠܒܪܐ. ܘܠܒܪܢܫܘܬܐ ܗܘܐ ܦܠܚܐ.
ܘܡܢ ܐܒܘܗܝ ܒܪܝ ܫܡܝܐ. ܚܒܪܗ ܠܫܪܒܐ ܕܒܪܢܫܐ ܘܢܘܪܐ܀

[5] ܕ ܕܢܒܥ ܒܐܠܗܘܬܐ ܟܠ ܡܢ ܫܡܝܐ. ܘܢܚܬ ܗܘ ܡܢܗܘܢ ܫܡܝܐ.
ܕܒܪܡܝܐ ܠܒܪ ܫܡܝܐ.[9] ܘܗܘܝ ܥܕܡܐ ܒܫܦܪܐ ܘܪܡܝܐ܀

---

[1] This hymn is found in: M2, D1, C1, C2, D2, B2, M3, G1, D3.
[2] C2 marg. ܗܦܟܐ.
[3] D1 ܐܡܐ ܘܐܡܐ; B2 marg.
[4] D3 ܫܡܝܐ has been added later by the copyist.
[5] D1 ܩܢܐ has been added later by the copyist.
[6] ⌈ ⌉ C2 + + X ܘܦܪ ܡܫܝܚ ܐܒܐ.
[7] D3 +X ܒܪܒܘܬܐ.
[8] B2 +X ܘܡܬܬܪܡܐ; D3 + ܘܡܬܬܪܡܐ ܐܒܐ.
[9] B2 +X ܘܢܚܬ ܗܘ ܡܢܗܘܢ ܫܡܝܐ.

16.(106)

Another one by the composer. It fits Pentecost and Nūsardēl[10] and all the commemorations of the apostles. Of Mawtḇā. Say

[1] God, have mercy on man;
He sent His Son to save man,
the essence which was begotten essentially,
the Son, who is with His Father, eternally possesses,
greatness and not smallness,
and equality without diminishment.
His mercy brought Him towards His servants,
to teach His love for the creation of His hands.
He willed His love and manifested it in the flesh,
and as [it] pleased Him, He chose the twelve apostles, a holy gathering,
and the seventy-two, another gathering.
He united [both] gatherings by the Holy Spirit,
and they all became one soul.

[2] Ālaph If I talk about each one
I cannot, and I will not be able!
And if I avoid one, [I have to avoid] all of them.
Who am I, and for whom am I counted?

[3] Bēṯ I am amazed a great deal by their stories,
astonished and immensely surprised,
surprised and in admiration,
in admiration, I say:

[4] Gāmal They were chosen by the Father and called by the Son
and they became a dwelling place for the Holy Spirit.
Though they are children of flesh,
they surpassed the rank of spirit and fire.

[5] Dālaṯ They shone in the world more than the sun;
the sun was smaller than them.
In the evening, the sun goes down,
but they are equal in the morning and evening.

---

[10] The word Nūsardēl means 'the feast of God'. According to the calendar of the Eastern Syriac Churches, this feast is celebrated at the end of the seventh week of the Apostles and the first week of Summer liturgical time. See T. Darmo, ed., *Ḥūḏrā* ܚܘܕܪܐ [The Cycle], vol. III, p. ܪܣܗ [265].

[6] ܗ ܗܘܘ ܒܒܪܝܬܐ ܐܝܟ ܡܠܟܐ. ܘܡܕܒܪܘ[11] ܠܦܠܚܝܗܘܢ ܪܘܚܐ.
ܘܒܚܘܒܗ[12] ܕܡܠܟܐ ܡܫܝܚܐ. ܪܘܝܘ ܒܒܪܟܬܐ ܘܣܒܥܐ ܪܘܚܐ ܀

[7] ܘ ܘܟܕ ܡܟܝܠ ܫܡ ܠܢܗ ܗܘܐ ܠܗܘܢ. ܟܠ ܡܟܝܠ ܕܐܬܝܗܒ ܠܗܘܢ.[13]
ܕܡܬܒܠ ܡܟܝܠ ܗܘܐ[14] ܠܗܘܢ.[15] ܘܠܡܟܝܠ ⌈ܚܘܒ ܒܐܝܕܝܗܘܢ⌉[16] ܀

[8] ܙ ܙܟܘ ܘܚܝܒܘ ܠܟܠ ܕܒܠܗܐ. ܒܡܬܘܡܝܘܬܐ ܘܚܣܝܘܬܐ.
ܘܦܫܘ ܒܫܘܠܡܘܬܐ. ܘܐܬܓܠܝܘܗܝ ܠܝܬ ܦܘܪܥܢܘܬܐ ܀

[9] ܚ ܚܢܝܢܐ ܒܒܢܝ ܐܠܗܝܗܘܢ. ܘܦܬܓܡܐ ܕܐܘܪܝܬܗܘܢ.
ܢܛܪܘ ܘܥܒܕܘ ܡܢ ܟܠ ܠܒܗܘܢ. ܕܐܠܗܐ ܐܝܬܘܗܝ ܒܪܝܬܗܘܢ ܀

[10] ܛ ܛܝܒܘܬܐ ܕܝܠܗ ܦܩܕܬܗܘܢ. ܛܘܪܐ ܕܓܒܝܐ ܕܟܠ ܒܘܡܘܗܝ.[17] [f. 209r]
ܘܫܪܪܐ ܕܡܢ ܡܫܪܝܬܐ ܕܦܘܠܚܢܗܘܢ. ܕܣܡܘ[18] ܘܐܚܕܘ[19] ܠܒܝܬܐ ܐܪܥܢܗܘܢ ܀

[11] ܝ ܝܩܝܪܐ[20] ܕܡܫܬܒܚܝܢ ܗܘܘ. ܕܐܘܪܚܐ ܘܬܘܕܝܬܐ ܢܛܪܝܢ ܗܘܘ.
ܟܕ ܚܙܐܠܗ ܕܝܠܗܘܢ ܚܙܘ ܗܘܘ. ܢܦܫܗܘܢ ܓܒܝܢܗܘܢ ܚܒܝܒܘ ܗܘܘ ܀

[12] ܟ ܟܢܫܘ ܟܠܗܘܢ ܒܐܠܗܘܬܗܘܢ. ܘܒܐܓܘܢܗܘܢ ܘܒܐܣܝܘܬܗܘܢ.
ܘܓܒܝܬܗܘܢ ܘܓܝܪܬܗܘܢ. ܘܐܦ ܒܢܦܫܗܘܢ ⌈ܘܦܘܠܚܢ ܒܦܘܪܗܘܢ⌉[21] ܀

---

[11] G1 ܘܡܕܒܪ.
[12] C1 illeg.
[13] C2 marg. b; D3 ܚܘܒ ܒܐܝܕܝܗܘܢ.
[14] D2 illeg.
[15] C2 marg. c.
[16] ⌉ D3 ܕܐܬܝܗܒ ܠܗܘܢ.
[17] Over the word ܒܘܡܘܗܝ in M2 and D3 is written ܡܠܟ or ܒܠܟ and over the same word in D3 is written ܢܟܠܐ. This word ܒܘܡܘܗܝ also means: ‘fluids in the body’. See J. Payne Smith, *A Compendious Syriac Dictionary*, p. 209.
[18] B2 ܕܣܡܘ, G1 illeg.
[19] G1 ܘܐܚܕܘ.
[20] This word could be plural: ܝܩܝܪ̈ܐ, ‘nobles’ as the next word indicates.
[21] ⌉ C2 ܘܒܐܢܫܝܗܘܢ ܘܒܢܫܝܗܘܢ.

[6] Hē They were in the created [world] as salt;
they seasoned those who are tasteless in spirit,
and by the love of Christ, the king,
they became ardent in body, soul, and spirit.

[7] Wāw Not having anything,
everything was given to them;
as the Lord of everything for them,
He gave everything into their hands.

[8] Zēn They triumphed and vanquished all fears,
the religion of magi and the pagans.
They confounded Judaism
and abolished the name of idolatry.

[9] Ḥēṯ Medical doctors, children of Galen,
and the philosophers of Athens
called and cried out from all sides.
that Christ is God.

[10] Ṭēṯ The shadow beside Peter[22]
healed sicknesses of all kinds;
straps of the shoes of Paul
smashed and crushed the evil angels.

[11] Yōḏ It is known that they were considered
to know the heights and depths;
when they saw their powers,
they made themselves their servants.

[12] Kāp All have denied their gods;
their fathers and their brothers,
their children and their women,
even themselves, and they believed in their Lord.

---

[22] See Acts 5:15.

[13] ܠ ܠܐ ܦܘܪܫܢܐ ܘܠܐ ܚܬܡܐ. ܘܠܐ ܕܝܢܐ ܘܠܐ ܦܘܠܓܐ.[23]
ܘܠܐ ܥܘܕܠܐ ܘܠܐ ܦܢܝܐ. ܐܝܠܐ ܒܢܫܐ ܘܡܬܦܠܓܐ[24] ܀

[14] ܡ ܡܛܠ ܠܐܪܥܐ ܡܢ ܫܘܒܚܗܘܢ. ܘܢܚܬܘܢ[25] ܠܗܘܢ ܡܢ ܡܪܝܡܘܬܗܘܢ.[26]
ܐܝܟܢܐ ܕܫܘܦܪܗܘܢ. ܐܠܗܐ ܥܒܕ ܐܢܘܢ ܀

[15] ܢ ܢܚܬܘ ܐܝܠܝܢ ܠܘܬ ܥܦܪܐ. ܘܐܬܚܠܛܘ ܒܒܢܬܐ ܦܓܪܢܝܬܐ.
ܘܐܘܠܕܘ ܓܢܒܪܐ[27] ܠܐܪܥܐ. ܘܐܝܠܝܢ ܗܘܘ ܢܦܝܠܐ ܀

[16] ܣ ܣܓܝܘ ܚܛܗܐ ܒܗ ܒܥܠܡܐ. ܘܐܬܡܠܝܬ ܒܗ ܐܪܥܐ ܥܘܠܐ.
ܘܚܙܐ ܐܠܗܐ ܘܐܬܬܘܝ. ܕܒܢܝܢܫܐ ܦܪܝܫܐ ܘܡܢܕܝܐ ܀

[17] ܥ ܥܒܕܘ ܢܦܫܗܘܢ ܡܫܝܚܐ. ܘܐܬܗܦܟܘ ܗܘܘ ܡܚܒܠܢܐ.
ܘܥܠ ܐܢܫܘܬܗܘܢ ܝܬܝܪܐ. ܕܚܛܝܬܐ ܗܘܘ ܡܬܚܪܢܐ[28] ܀

[18] ܦ ܦܩܕ ܠܢܘܚ ܒܝܘܡܬܗܘܢ. ܘܐܡܪ ܠܗ ܥܠ ܚܛܗܝܗܘܢ.
ܘܦܩܕܗ ܕܢܥܒܕ ܩܒܘܬܐ. ܘܢܟܢܫ ܡܢܗ ܒܢܝ ܒܝܬܗܘܢ[29] ܀

[19] ܨ ܨܒܐ ܠܡܥܒܕ ܩܒܘܬܗܘܢ. ܘܐܡܪܗ ܠܗܘܢ ܒܢܝ ܕܪܗܘܢ.
ܕܢܬܒܘܢ ܡܢ ܚܛܗܝܗܘܢ. ܠܐ ܫܡܥܘ ܠܗ ܒܢܝ ܕܪܗܘܢ ܀

[23] B2 ܦܠܓܐ.
[24] G1 illeg.
[25] G1 illeg.
[26] All the stanzas that come after this word are missing in G1.
[27] M3 ܗܘܘ.
[28] D2 illeg.
[29] M3 marg.

[13] Lāmaḏ No bags and no purses,
no dinars[30] and no small coins,
no flattery and no persuasion,
but only sackcloth and mantle.[31]

[14] Mīm They filled the earth with their treasures,
and confined it in their nets,
so that those who saw them,
called them gods.[32]

[15] Nūn They planted trees on rocks,
and made fountains spring up from stones,
they made ignorant ones intelligent,
who became listeners to their words.

[16] Semkaṯ They endured hunger and thirst,
tiredness and hard work,
extreme heat and cold,
but their soul was happy and joyful.

[17] ʿĒ They made themselves like seducers,
and became destroyers of error;
despite being poor,
they made the poor rich.

[18] Pē They labored for the world with their words,
and sowed their words[33] in it;
they flew in all their strength
and those who were dead received life by their death.

[19] Ṣādē They split the sky with their voices,
and raised the watchers with their anathemas,
so that if they transgressed their words,
they would not remain in their ranks.[34]

[30] From the Greek word Δηνάριον.
[31] See Luke 9:3.
[32] See Acts 14:11.
[33] Although the word ܦܣܘ̈ܩܐ usually means the verses of the Bible, it is translated here as 'words'.
[34] This is a tentative translation; the Syriac text is confusing.

[20] ܡ ܡܠܝܬܐ ܕܐܘܡܬܐ ܒܐܝܕܝܗܘܢ. ܘܐܬܕܟܝ ܫܡܥܐ ܒܦܘܩܕܗܘܢ.
ܕܐܝ ܐܣܝܐ ܠܟܠ ܕܦܫܝܚ ܠܗܘܢ. ܘܐܝ ܦܪܘܩ ܠܟܠ ܕܐܒܝܕ ܠܗܘܢ ܀

[21] ܢ ܢܘܕܘܢ ܐܢܘܢ ܕܬܫܒܘܚܬܗ. ܥܠ ܛܝܒܘܬܐ ܕܐܘܒܕܝܗܘܢ.
ܕܦܨܝ ܐܢܘܢ ܡܢ ܚܒܠܐ ܠܗܘܢ. ܘܐܦ / ܫܦܠܝܢ ܒܡܠܟܐ ܗܢܘܢ ܀ [f. 209v]

[22] ܣ ܣܓܝܐܐ ܐܢܫܐ ܐܝܬ ܒܥܠܡܐ. ܠܐ ܝܕܥܝ ܛܠܐ ܡܠܬܗ.
ܛܒܬܐ ܕܝܡܬܐ[35] ܡܠܬܗ.[36] ܕܐܦ ܒܥܒܕܐ ܡܕܡܪܬܐ ܠܗܘܢ ܀

[23] ܥ ܥܠܝܡܘܬܐ ܫܒܩܬ ܒܗܘܢ. ܐܒܐ ܫܡܝܐ ܦܠܚܝܗܘܢ.
ܒܪܐ ܠܫܡܐ ܦܘܠܚܢܗܘܢ. ܘܪܘܚ ܩܘܕܫܐ ܝܒܝܒܗܘܢ ܀

[24] ܠܥܠܡܝܢ ܘܥܠܡܐ ܕܥܠܡܐ ܐܡܝܢ. ܘܥܠܡܝܢ ܘܥܠܡܐ ܕܥܠܡܐ ܐܡܝܢ.
ܘܫܒܚܝܢ ܘܥܠܡܐ ܕܥܠܡܐ ܐܡܝܢ. ܕܐܦ ܡܫܒܚܝܢ ܘܥܢܝܢ ⌈ܠܥܠܡ ܐܡܝܢ⌉[37] ܀

[25] ܠܐܝܬ ܕܡܢ ܐܝܟ ܗܕܝܢܘܬܗ. ܡܪܢ ܡܫܝܚܐ ܒܦܠܚܢܘܬܗ.
ܠܡܪܕܝܬܐ ܕܥܕܬܗ. ܘܢܦܪܘܩ ܠܟܠܢ ܒܛܝܒܘܬܗ ܀

[26] ܒܪܢ ܡܫܒܚܢܘܬܗ
ܫܡܝܐ ܕܘܒܪܗ
ܘܥܡܡܐ ܢܣܓܕܘܢ ܠܗ
ܠܡܪܗ ܫܘܒܚܐ
ܠܗ ܕܘܒܪܐ
ܘܠܗ ܣܘܓܕܬܐ ܡܢ ܫܘܒܚܐ ܀

[35] D2 ܘܝܡܬܐ.
[36] B2 marg.
[37] ⌈ C1, M3 ܠܥܠܡ ܐܡܝܢ.

[20] Qōp
The keys on high are in their hands,
The doors of heaven are in their mouths;
whatever they close, no one can open
and whatever they open, no one can close.[38]

[21] Rēš
Their ranks are higher
than the spiritual ones in their orders,
because these [Apostles] bind and unbind
and they [angels] have no power over them.

[22] Šīn
Truly I say about them,
not [only] I but all
the tongues of the nations,
even the watchers, will exalt them.

[23] Tāw
The Trinity dwells in them,
the Father hears their words,
the Son completes their words,
and the Holy Spirit their will.

[24]
They are perfect, and I am in need,
they are honored, and I am worthless,
they are respected, and I am hateful,
they increase greatly, and I decrease immensely.

[25]
Their company is truly great,
O Lord of them, count him,
the composer of their hymn, as their disciple,
and help all of us by their prayer.

[26]
Blessed be their exaltation,
glorified be their commemoration,
their reward is kept in heaven.
Glory to their Lord,
remembrance to them,
and forgiveness and absolution to us.

[38] See Matt 16:19.

[1](109).17

[f. 213r] [2]ܕܡܬܟܬܒܢܐ ܕܗܠܟܬܐ[3] ܕܡܫܝܚܐ ⌈ܥܠ ܚܛܝܬܐ ܕܡܢ ܒܒܝܬ ܫܡܥܘܢ. ܕܥܒܕܗ[4] ܕܘܪܕܐ[5]. ܕܢܩܘܫܬܐ[6].
ܟܠܗ⌉[7]

[1] ܝܫܘܥ ܕܐܬܐ ܡܫܘܒܚܐ[8]
ܠܒܝܬ ܕܫܡܥܘܢ ܦܪܝܫܐ ܚܛܝܬܐ
ܕܩܪܘܗ ܠܒܝܬܗ ܐܢܬܬܐ
ܘܚܙܬ ܚܝܠܗ ܐܠܗܝܐ
ܘܐܬܬ ܩܒܠܬ ܠܡܫܝܚܐ
ܘܦܬܚ[9] ܒܬܪܐ ܕܫܡܝܐ ⁘

[2] ܐܠܗܐ ܠܒܝܬ ܦܪܝܫܐ. ܘܐܬܬܩܢ ܦܪܝܫܝܐ.
ܘܢܣܒ ܠܥܒܕܐ ܘܠܢܦܫܐ. ܡܢ ܟܠ ܡܘܡܐ ܘܟܠ ܚܛܐ ⁘

[3] ܦܪܝܫ ܒܫܡܝܐ ܕܠܐ ܢܟܦܬܐ. ܗܘ ܕܢܬܟܠܡ ܕܠܐ ܚܘܒܬܐ.
ܦܓܪܐ ܕܢܓܠܝ[10] ܠܐܢܫܘܬܐ. ܕܐܠܗܐ ܗܘ ܒܓܒܝܘܬܐ ⁘

[4] ܚܒܪܐ ܕܚܛܝܐ ܠܝܬ ܗܘܐ ܠܗ. ܘܐܦ ܡܠܟܐ ܕܢܘܚܐ ܗܘܐ ܠܗ.
ܕܘܟܪܢܐ ܐܝܟ ܗܘܐ ܠܗ. ܕܢܘܚܐ ܗܘܐ ܟܕ ܕܠܐ ܚܝܐ ܠܗ ⁘

[5] ܦܠܛ ܒܗ ܢܡܘܣܐ ܢܘܗܪܐ.[11] ܒܡܥܪܘܦܐ ܥܒܝܠ ܡܢ ܥܦܪܐ.
ܘܐܬܠܗ ܒܢܘܗܪܐ ܘܒܗ ܒܢܘܗܪܐ. ܠܡܘܬܒܐ ܥܠܝܘ ܡܢ ܒܢܘܗܪܐ ⁘

[6] ܡܬܝܠܕ ܗܘܐ ܘܡܫܬܒܩ ܗܘܐ. ܘܡܫܡܫ ܗܘܐ ܘܡܫܬܥܒܕ ܗܘܐ.
ܘܡܬܘܟܠ ܗܘܐ ܥܠ ܟܠܐ ܗܘܐ. ܘܡܢ ܒܟܐ ܗܘܐ ܐܟܪ ܗܘܐ ⁘

[7] ܒܥܘܠ ܡܚܝܠܐ ܦܪܘܩܐ. ܕܠܐ ܦܣܩ ⌈ܠܚܛܝܐ ܥܡܝܩܐ⌉.[12]
ܢܦܢܝܘܗܝ ܠܚܛܝܐ ܢܟܝܦܐ. ܕܠܝ ܗܐ ܚܛܐ ܡܢ ܪܘܚܐ ⁘

---

[1] This hymn is found in: M1, M2, B1, D1, C1, C2, D2, B2, M3, G1, D3.
[2] The heading in M1 is written as follows: ܕܡܬܟܬܒܢܐ ܠ ܕܡܫܝܚܐ ܥܒܕܗ ܕܘܪܕܐ.
[3] M1 ܠ.
[4] D1 ܕܥܒܕܗ ܗܘ ܕܥܠܗ.
[5] G1 ܕܢܘܪܕܝܬ.
[6] G1 –.
[7] ⌈ B1 ܕܟܘܠܗ ܗܟܢܐ ܕܝܘܠܦܢܐ ܕܥܠܗ ܕܘܪܕܐ.
[8] M1 Illeg.
[9] M1 – ܘ.
[10] G1 ܕܢܓܠܐ.
[11] C1 ܢܘܗܪܐ.
[12] ⌈ The same expression is found in hymn (49)[20], written by Wardā.

17.(109)

For the Third Sunday of Summer.[13] On the one who was blind from the womb of his mother. By Wardā. Of the Gospel. Forever.

[1] The ray of the eternal Father,[14]
by His grace, put on a revealed body
to save the human race.
He showed His divine power,
gave feet to the paralytics,
and opened the eyes of the blind.

[2] God put on a man,
and looked like human beings;
He healed body and soul
from all vice and all passion.

[3] He met the blind one without eyes,[15]
he who was born without sight,[16]
and wished to reveal to humanity
that He was truly God.

[4] A man who had no eyes,
and everyone who saw him
was amazed by him,
to see what was not seen by him.

[5] The bright sun [Christ] met with him,
with the person created from dust,
the light and the Son of light asked him,
the lump of earth deprived of light.

[6] He was walking and stumbling,
coming forward and prostrating himself;
he was crying out and not stopping,
and while he was crying, he said:

[7] 'Jesus Christ the Savior,
who does not deny a contrite heart,[17]
give joy to my grieved heart
that is calling from a far to you.

---

[13] According to the Church of the East, the liturgical season of Summer time consist of seven Sundays between July and September.

[14] See Heb 1:3.

[15] In Syriac, ܒܒ̈ܬܐ literary means the pupils (of the eyes).

[16] See John 9:1.

[17] See Ps 51:17.

[8] ܬܪܘܢܐ[18] ܘܒܪ ܬܪܘܢܐ. ܟܕ ܐܬܐ ܠܦܘܪܩܢ ܐܢܫܐ.
ܕܐܬܐܘ ܕܦܪܩܗ ܠܐܢܫܐ. ܘܦܪܩܗ ܐܪܥܐ ܟܠ ܡܢܐ ܀

[9] ܘܟܠܗ ܥܡܡܐ ܦܫܝܛܐ. ܕܐܢܐ ܢܘܒܠ ܠܐܠܗܐ ܫܠܡܐ.
ܘܒܗ ܢܘܪܐ ܢܫܦܝܘܬܐ. ܘܒܗ ܫܡܫܝܢ ܫܒܚܬܐ ܀

[10] ܠܐ ܫܒܩ ܐܢܫܐ ܠܦܘܪܩܢܗ. ܘܐܦܠܐ ܐܝܠܝܢ ܠܫܡܝܢ.
ܦܬܚܬ ܫܡܝ ܠܟܠܗ ܢܦܫܝܢ. ܘܫܒܩܬ / ܒܦܘܪܩܢ ܠܒܢܝܢܫܐ ܀ [f. 213v]

[11] ܚܙܝ ܕܐܬܝܬܘܢ ܠܦܘܪܩܢܗ. ܘܐܬܚܘܝ ܥܠܝ ܦܘܪܩܢܗ.
ܕܝܠܗ ܠܟܠܢ ܚܘܒ ܠܟܠܗ. ܒܚܘܒܗ ܐܢܘܢ ܦܪܩܢܗ ܀

[12] ܐܡܪܢ ܕܝܠܝܢ ܡܢ ܐܬܪܐ. ܫܡܥܬ ܘܐܬܝܬ ܘܐܬܒܪܐ.
ܡܢܐ ܬܘܒ ܟܠܗ ܠܥܠܡܐ. ܕܒܗ ܢܬܒܪܟ ܒܒܪܬܗ ܕܥܠܡܐ ܀

[13] ܘܐܠܗ ܢܘܪܐ ܟܠܗ ܚܝܘܬܐ. ܒܗܘ ܠܦܘܪܩܢܐ ܢܫܡܐ.
ܘܐܬܝܗ ܗܘ ܦܘܡܐ ܚܝܐ. ܠܦܘܪܩܢܐ ܡܫܝܚܐ ܕܚܝܐ ܀

[14] ܗܢ ܒܟܠ ܐܢܐ ܐܡܪܠܝ. ܚܝܐ ܕܢܚܘܬ ܗܢ ܡܫܝܚܐ ܠܝ.
⸢ܡܢܝ ܕܦܘܪܩܢ ܐܢܫ ܐܝܬ ܠܝ. ܡܢܝ ܕܡܫܝܚ ܚܝܐ ܐܝܬ ܠܝ⸣[19] ܀

[15] ܠܐ ܗܘܐ ܐܝܟ ܠܐ ܐܬܝܬ ܗܘܐ.[20] ܐܬܐܝܗ ܕܡܢܐ ܟܠܗ ܗܘܐ.
ܠܦܘܪܩܢܐ ܥܠܡܐ ܕܢܦܘܩ ܗܘܐ. ܘܠܗܘܢ ܚܝܠܗ ܢܦܫ ܗܘܐ ܀

[18] The word ܬܪܘܢܐ in M3 is written in two parts: ܬܪ and then ܘܢܐ (the latter added later by the copyist).
[19] ⸢ G1 rep. cd.
[20] M1, B1 ܠܗ.

[8] Creator and Son of the Creator,
create eyes for my blind *qnōmā*.
You who created the heaven
and spread the earth on the water.

[9] Give me open eyes,
You who gave the word to the donkey,[21]
in You, darkness becomes illuminous,
and in You, creatures will be resurrected.

[10] For it is not difficult for Your command
and not impossible for Your will!
Stretch Your right hand towards my eyes
and may Your help come to my *qnōmā*.

[11] See how many are his offences,
and how great are his mistakes.
He called out to You; look at him!
With Your sight give sight to his eyes.

[12] Your will,[22] that formed from dust
animals, human beings and beasts,
can create eyes for a man
who was formed in a womb of flesh.'

[13] The only-begotten Son called him towards Himself,
light for the blind person,
and that living mouth asked him,
the dead *qnōmā* that became alive:

[14] 'Tell me what do you want?'[23]
He answered: 'That I see! What are you asking me?'
'You knew me before I existed,
You understood me before I called [upon you].'

[15] It was not as if He did not know
when He asked him what he sought.
He wished to show His power to those who listen
and teach them about it.

[21] See Num 22:28.
[22] The word ܪܶܡܙܳܐ here refers to the divine will.
[23] See Mark 10:51; Luke 18:41.

[16] ܐܡ ܦܘܡܐ ܕܐܠܗܘܬܐ. ܥܠ ܕܒܪܐ ܕܘܩܐ ܕܡܢܐ.
ܘܐܒܕ ܒܗ ܠܒܝܬܐ ܕܡܢܐ. ܘܐܬܐ ܥܠ ܦܪܘܩܐ ܫܡܝܐ ܀

[17] ܢܡܘܣܐ ܕܦܠܚܝ ܥܡܢܐ. ܗܝ ܕܒܠܥܬ ܠܒܝܬܐ ܕܡܢܐ.
ܘܫܦܟ ܥܠ ܡܕܒܚܐ ܫܡܝܐ. ܘܡܢܚܬܐ ܗܘܬ ܚܕܬܐ ܀

[18] ܘܦܪܫ ܡܘܬܒܐ ܠܡܕܒܚܝܗ. ܘܚܕܬ ܗܘܬ ܥܘܒܕܝܗ.
ܘܡܫܟܢ ܗܘܐ ܠܟܠܝܬܗ. ܠܗܘ ܕܫܠܡܘ ܡܕܒܚܢܝܬܗ ܀

[19] ܚܙܘ ܡܘܒܕܢܐ ܠܥܒܕܬܐ. ܢܘܗܪܬܐ ܕܫܡܝܐ ܚܙܬܐ.
ܘܦܪܫܘ ܠܡܕܒܚ[24] ܕܫܠܝܚܘܬܐ. ܐܝܟ ܗܘ ܗܘܐ ܘܪܡܘܬܐ ܀

[20] ܡܪܐܘܗܝ ܠܥܒܕܐ ܕܡܢܝܚܬܐ. ܘܦܠܓܘܗܝ ܗܘܘ ܡܢܟܠ ܥܠܡܐ.
ܕܐܝܟ ܗܘܝ ܠܗ ܥܒܕܬܐ. ܘܟܕ ܚܙܐ ܠܗ ܢܘܗܪܗܬܐ ܀

[21] ܘܡܢܐ ܕܦܠܓܐ ܒܝ ܠܥܒܕܐ. ܘܦܬܐ ܗܘܬ ܠܥܠܡܝܢ ܥܡܪܐ.
ܘܐܒܕ ܡܢ ܕܘܟܬܗ[25] ܫܦܪܐ. ܘܐܬܐ ܥܠ ܡܕܒܚܐ ܘܚܙܝܗ ܟܘܗܢܐ ܀

[22] ܘܫܪܐ ܐܢܘܢ ܠܐܒܗܝܗܘܢ. ܕܫܡܫܐ ܘܦܠܚܘ[26] ܐܢܘܢ ܥܠܝܗܘܢ.
ܕܐܢ ܢܒܥܘܢ ܗܘ ܠܟܠܗ ܠܝ ܥܠܝܗܘܢ. ܕܫܡܘ / ܕܦܬܚ ܠܗ ܢܝܫܘܗܝ ܀ [f. 214r]

[24] D2 + ܘ.
[25] D1 +X ܕܦܫܐ.
[26] B1, C1, G1 ܘܦܠܚ.

[16] The divine mouth spat[27]
on earth some pure saliva,
and mixed with it delicate mud[28]
and put [it on] the blind person.

[17] The right hand that stretched out the sky,
formed the delicate mud
and put it on the blind *qnōmā*[29]
and he saw with [his] eyes.

[18] He began to walk with confidence,
and he saw brightly,
and he glorified openly Him
who had visited him mercifully.

[19] The Jews saw the pupils
new and full of sight.
They began saying:
'This is delusion and arrogance'.

[20] They called the man to the middle,
and asked about the cause.
How did he have pupils
and who gave him clarity?[30]

[21] He answered: 'A man met me;
He looked like someone clad in the flesh.
He formed dust with His saliva,
and put it on my *qnōmā*; then I saw the light.'

[22] They called the parents[31]
of that blind man and they asked them about him:
'If this is your son, make known to us about him;[32]
who opened his eyes for him?'

---

[27] See John 9:6.
[28] See John 9:6.
[29] The poet uses the words *parṣōpā* in stanza [16d] and *qnōmā* in stanza [17c] as synonyms, but this is not always the case. It seems he does not restrict himself to the classical meaning of these two technical terms. See the discussion in Chapter 4.
[30] See John 9:10.
[31] See John 9:18.
[32] See John 9:19.

[23] ܠܟܘܢ ܐܚܘܗܝ ܕܝܠܕܬܝ. ܕܗܘܐ ܒܪܝ ܗܘ ܕܝܠܕܬܢܝ.
ܕܐܝܟ ܚܕܪܐ ܟܠ ܝܠܕܬܝ. ܠܗ ܐܝܬܠܗ ܕܝܠܕܬܗ ܡܢܝ܀

[24] ܘܐܦ ܐܒܘܗܝ ܗܘ ܘܐܠܗܐ[33] ܠܗ ܐܒܘܗܝ. ܘܗܘ ܒܠܚܘܕ ܝܕܥ ܝܠܕܘܬܗ.
ܠܗ ܐܝܬܠܗ ܡܫܟܚܐ ܝܠܕܘܬܗ. ܘܗܘ ܗܘܐ ܡܠܟܐ ܠܟܠܗ܀

[25] ܘܡܕܡ ܕܐܬܚܙܝ ܘܫܡܥܬ. ܦܠܚܐ ܘܡܠܟܐ ܠܗ ܣܓܕܝܢ.
ܘܥܠ ܦܘܬܚ ܝܠܕܘܬܗ ܡܫܬܥܝܢ. ܘܫܡܝܐ ܠܟܘܢ[34] ܒܗ ܐܡܪܝܢ܀

[26] ܐܡܪ ܠܝ ܐܡܬܐ[35] ܡܢܘ ܝܠܕܟܝ. ܘܐܝܟ ܦܬܚ ܠܝ ܝܠܕܬܝ.
ܒܬܘܠܬܐ ܡܢܘ ܝܠܕܬ. ܐܘ ܝܠܕܬܐ ܟܕ[36] ܝܠܕܬ ܠܠܝܐ܀

[27] ܘܟܝܬ ܐܡܪܐ ܕܡܫܝܚܐ ܠܝ. ܠܡܐܡܪ ܘܠܐ ܫܡܥܬܘܢ ܠܝ.
ܢܫܡܥܘܢ ܠܟܘܢ ܕܗܕܐ[37] ܠܟܡܐ[38] ܠܝ. ܫܠܡܐ ܥܠ ܠܝ ܘܢܬܚܙܘܢ ܠܝ܀

[28] ܘܦܬܚܘ[39] ܐܬܪܐ[40] ܘܫܡܥܬܐ. ܕܫܡܥ ܠܝ ܒܝܠܕܘܬܐ.
ܐܝܟ ܠܟܘ ܠܝ ܒܬܘܠܬܐ. ܒܥܘܠܬܐ ܐܘ ܒܝܠܕܘܬܐ[41]܀

[29] ܘܐܡܪ[42] ܠܗܘܢ[43] ܕܢܫܡܥܘܢ ܠܟܘܢ. ܫܡܥܘ ܘܫܒܝ ܘܠܐ ܫܡܥܬܘܢ.
ܠܟܠܐ ܡܠܐ ܬܫܒܘܚܬܐ. ܠܟܠ ܠܗ ܠܡܫܒܚܘ ܫܘܒܚܗ܀

33 D2, G1 – ܘ.
34 C2 written in the sequence ܡܠܟܘܢ ܘܫܡܝܐ and then corrected by putting ܐ on ܘܫܡܝܐ and ܒ on ܡܠܟܘܢ
35 B1 ܐܡܬܝ.
36 B1 ܟܕ.
37 G1 – ܕ.
38 M1 illeg.
39 M1 illeg.
40 G1 ܐܬܪܐ.
41 G1 ܒܝܠܕܘܬܐ, M3 ܒܝܠܕܘܬܐ + in marg. ܒܥܘܠܬܐ.
42 M3 ܘܐܡܪܬ, G1 – ܘ.
43 B1 + ܗܘܐ.

[23] His parents answered: 'We know
that this is our son that we begot;[44]
how he sees, we do not know.
Ask him; he knows better than we do.[45]

[24] He is also [an adult man] in his years,[46]
and he alone knows his sadness.[47]
Ask him about his eyes;
he will tell you about them.'

[25] They called him a second time,[48]
the Pharisees, and they started asking him;
they were examining his opened eyes,
and thus they answered, saying:

[26] 'Tell us where He approached you
and how He opened your eyes.
Did He offer a supplication for you
Or say a prayer over you?'

[27] He answered and said: 'It is painful for me
to say, but you do not listen to me.[49]
I told you that this is what He did to me;
he put mud on me and was seen by me!'

[28] They answered a third time:
'Tell us truthfully,
how did He make for you pupils?
In truth or by magic?'

[29] He told them: 'I told you
two times, and you did not listen.[50]
Why do you make a long discourse?
Why, do you not want to worship Him?'

---

[44] See John 9:20.
[45] See John 9:21.
[46] See John 9:21.
[47] Although ܚܫܐ usually means 'passion', here it means 'sadness'.
[48] See John 9:24.
[49] See John 9:27.
[50] See John 9:27.

[30] ܚܠܦ ܘܐܬܥܒܕ ܥܡ ܡܢܝܢܐ ܠܗ. ܘܐܬܪܚܡ ܘܡܬܥܒܕ ܠܗ.
ܕܐܢܫ ܐܘ ܪܘܚܐ ܠܐ ܡܫܬܪܐ ܠܗ. ܘܐܘܪܚܐ ܠܗ ܘܢܬܬܠܦܢ ܠܗ ܀

[31] ܣܒܪ ܗܝܡܢܘܬܐ ܘܫܡܢܐ. ܕܫܡܫܐ ܫܒܝܐ ܫܘܒܚܐ.
ܗܘܝ[51] ܐܝܡܢܘܬܐ ܕܩܪ̈ܒܐ. ܕܠܫܡܫܐ ܗܘܐ ܫܪ̈ܒܐ ܀

[32] ܘܦܬܚ ܕܫܒܠܬܐ ܢܦܫܬܗܘܢ. ܕܠܫܪܟܐ ܗܘܐ ܫܡܫܬܗܘܢ.
ܘܠܫܡܫܐ ܗܘܐ ܡܢܫܪܬܗܘܢ. ܘܢܘܗܪܐ ܒܫܪܟܗ ܡܢܠܦܢܬܗܘܢ ܀

[33] ܡܢ ܪܘܡܐ ܢܚܬܬ ܠܫܡܫܐ. ܘܠܐ ܢܦܩܬ ܠܝ[52] ܚܕܘܬܐ.
ܘܗܘܐ[53] ܫܪܒܗ ܕܫܡܫܐ. ܡܢܗܘܢ ܠܡܥܡܕ ܢܘܗܪܘܬܐ ܀

[34] ܫܪܐ ܢܚܬܬ ܡܢ ܫܡܫܐ. ܝܠܕܐ ܠܝ ܡܢܝܢܐ ܕܙܕܝܩܘܬܐ.
ܢܬܦܫ ܡܚܕ ܠܗ ܫܒܝܠܐ. ܕܠܗ ܠܒܝܫ ܕܙܗܪܐ ܒܥܕܢܐ ܀ [f. 214v]

[35] ܪܡܢܐ ܫܡܫܐ ܐܝܟ ܓܠܝܐ. ܘܡܢܗܪܢܐ ܠܢܦܫܐ ܦܓܪܢܐ.
ܕܒܗ ܚܟܡܐ ܢܫܟܚ ܫܒܝܐ. ܘܒܗ ܪܥܝ ܢܘܗܪܐ ܠܒܢܝܢܐ ܀[54]

[36] ܪܡܢܐ ܫܡܫܐ ܐܝܟ ܐܪܥܐ. ܕܠܐ ܦܠܓܝܢ ܐܦܠܐ ܘܙܒܢܐ.
ܘܡܢܗܪܢܐ ܕܫܡܐ ܠܐܪܥܐ[55] ܪܡܝܢܐ ܠܠܝܠܐ ܘܫܪܒܐ ܀

[37] ܪܡܢܐ ܫܡܫܐ ܐܝܟ ܫܡܝܐ. ܘܡܢܗܪܢܐ ܒܫܪܘܪܐ ܡܫܡܥܬܐ.
ܒܪܝܢ ܕܢܗܘܐ ܠܝ ܢܘܗܪܐ[56] ܢܗܝܪܐ. ܘܢܠܦܘܢ ܒܡܢܗܪܢܘܬܐ ܠܫܡܫܐ ܀

---

[51] C1 + X ܢܘܗܪܐ.
[52] D2 ܠܝ has been added by a later hand.
[53] M1 the letter ܘ has been added by a later hand.
[54] G1 rep. [35][36].
[55] G1 ܠܐܪ̈ܥܐ.
[56] G1 illeg.

[30] They answered and said, insulting him,
shouting and reviling him:
'You, the miserable one, go and worship Him,
and confess Him and be His disciple![57]

[31] We are disciples and children
of the first prophet Moses;[58]
you have become a disciple of the Nazarene
who broke the Sabbath.'[59]

[32] He answered: 'You are truly going astray.
Behold, you have abandoned the Lord,
and you give honor to the Sabbath,
and you change the day for its master,

[33] From the beginning, I have kept the Sabbath,
and it did not give me happiness;
this man who broke the Sabbath
filled my *qnōmā* with light.

[34] What did I benefit from the Sabbath,
if not the morsels of charity?
Jesus gave me pupils
that have no likeness in creation.'

[35] The Sabbath looks like the night,
but Sunday like a glorious morning,
in which brutal darkness passes away
and great light shines.

[36] The Sabbath looks like land
that is neither cultivated nor planted,
but Sunday is like a plant
that pleases the heart and mind.

[37] The Sabbath looks like death,
but Sunday like resurrection;
blessed be He who gave me new light
and changed the Sabbath to Sunday.

---

[57] See John 9:28.
[58] See John 9:28.
[59] See John 9:16.

[38] ܢܘܗܪܐ ܢܕܢܚ ܒܒܪܝܬܐ. ܘܢܕܥܘܗ̇ ܠܟܠܗ̇ ܐܢܫܘܬܐ.
ܡܦܩܠ ܢܗܪܐ ܕܐܠܗܘܬܐ. ܡܢ ܡܕܢܚܗ ܕܡܫܝܚܘܬܐ ܀

[39] ܘܐܝܟ ܕܗܘ ܢܘܪ ܚܝ
ܘܢܘܗܪܐ ܚܘܪܐ ܗܝ
ܢܢܘܪܝܘ ܠܚܫܘܟܘܬܗ
ܕܦܓܪܗ ܠܗܘܢܐ ܗܟܢܐ ܒܓܪܥܝܬܗ
ܘܫܘܐ ܠܗ ܐܦܝܢ ܒܥܘܫܢܝܢ[60]
ܐܝܟ ܕܫܘܝܐ ܠܗܘ ܦܩܝܕ ܡܘܕܝܢ
ܘܐܬܦܬܘܚܐ ܚܝ ܐܒܘܬܗ
ܕܐܠܗܐ ܢܗܐ ܚܘܪ ܠܢܘܗܪܗ
ܘܢܫܘܐ ܠܓܠܝ ܠܥܘܒܕܢܗ ܦܐܝܐ
ܕܢܫܒܚܘܢ ܠܗ ܒܩܠܐ ܚܠܝܐ ܀

[60] G1 ܒܢܝܪܬܐ.

[38] O light that shines in creation,
and expels all delusion,
abolish the darkness of obscurity,
from the composer of the hymn.

[39] And as he received from You,
and saw light in You,
so give light to the darkness of him
whose body is blind, [and] whose thought is without vision,
Show him Your face in Your mercy,
as You showed [it] to that one and he worshiped You.
And for the one who confesses You like him,
that You are God, have mercy on his misery,
and make us worthy of Your great glory,
so that we may glorify You with sweet voices.

18.(121)[1]

[f. 231v] [2]ܕܡܕܒܚܢܐ ܕܡܫܝܚܐ ܕܐܠܗܐ[3] ܀[4] ܥܠ ܩܢܐ ܘܘܝ ܩܘܡܘ ܫܪܐ ܕܐܬܐܡܪܘ ܡܢ ܡܪܝ ܀ ܕܥܠܗ ܕܦܛܪܐ. ܕܐܫܬܠܛܘ ܀ ܥܠܡ[5]

[1] ܫܠܝܚܐ ܘܪܫܐ ܕܟܠ ܫܠܝ̈ܚܐ
ܕܓܒܝܘܗܝ ܐܒܘܗܝ ܟܠܗܘܢ ܫܠܝ̈ܚܐ
ܘܗܘ ܝܗܒ ܡܠܟܘܬܐ ܠܫܠܝ̈ܚܐ
ܘܫܕܪܗ ܫܠܝ̈ܚܐ ܘܫܡܥܘܢ ܫܠܝܚܐ
ܘܚܘܒ ܫܠܡ ܒܡܠܟܘܬܐ
ܐܝ ܡܠܟܘܬܐ ܘܐܝ ܫܪܘܬܐ
ܘܗܘܝܘ ܡܢܗܪ ܠܓܒܝܘܬܐ
ܘܠܗ ܡܫܒܚܝܢܢ ܒܚܕܘܬܐ ܀

[2] ܥܘܒܕܗ ܕܒܪܐ ܫܪܝܪ ܗܘܐ. ܒܐܝܕܗ ܓܠܝܐ ܓܠܐ ܗܘܐ.
ܒܦܓܪܐ ܕܝܢ ܒܥܘܠܡܐ ܠܒܝܫ ܗܘܐ.[6] ܘܚܕ ܒܪܐ ܥܡܗ ܫܘܬܦܘ ܗܘܐ ܀

[3] ܟܕ ܗܘ ܫܡܥܐ[7] ܐܒܘܗܝ ܗܘܐ. ܒܟܢܘܬܗ ܘܫܒܩܗ ܗܘܐ.
ܠܡܘܫܐ ܢܒܝܐ ܕܢܘܡܘܣ ܗܘܐ. ܘܟܠ ܗܘܐ ܕܐܫܬܡܥ ܗܘܐ ܀

[4] ܠܟܐܦܐ ܕܝܢ ܟܠ ܚܕ ܚܙܐ ܗܘܐ. ܟܕ ܡܠܟܘܬܐ[8] ܕܐܫܬܘܝ ܗܘܐ.[9]
ܘܒܡܕܝܢܬܐ ܚܕܐ ܗܘܐ. ܕܠܫܒܝܠܘܗܝ ܒܢܝܢܐ ܗܘܐ ܀

[5] ܠܓܒܪܢܘܬܗ ܐܝܟ ܗܘܐ. ܘܐܝܟ ܒܪܢܫܐ ܠܗ ܚܙܐ ܗܘܐ.
ܠܐ ܗܘܐ ܕܢܫܒܘܩ ܒܪܐ ܗܘܐ. ܐܠܐ ܕܢܦܠ ܥܠܝܗ ܗܘܐ ܀

[6] ܟܕ ܒܢܝܕ[10] ܡܢ ܬܪܝܢ ⌈ܥܝܢܐ ܗܘܐ⌉.[11] ܘܝܗܒܠܗ ܒܥܘܡܩܐ ܐܒܘܗܝ ܗܘܐ.
ܘܫܠܝܚܐ[12] ܕܫܪܪܐ ܕܐܬܐܡܪ ܗܘܐ. ܕܢܗܘܐ ܡܪܝ ܥܠ ܗܘܐ ܀

---

[1] This hymn is found in: M1, M2, B1, D1, C1, C2, D2, B2, M3, D3.
[2] The heading in M1 is written as follows: ܕܡܕܒܚܢܐ ܗ ܕܡܪܝ ܐܠܗܐ ܥܡܗ + in marg. ܕܡܕܒܚܢܐ ܗ ܕܡܪܝ ܐܠܗܐ.
[3] M2, C2, D2, B2 marg. ܕܡܕܒܚܢܐ ܕܟܠ ܡܪܐ ܦܘܡܐ.
[4] D1 + in marg. ܕܡܕܒܚܢܐ ܗ ܕܐܠܗܐ.
[5] The heading in B1 is written as follows: ܕܡܕܒܚܢܐ ܀ ܗ ܀ ܕܐܠܗܐ ܀ ܒ ܀ ܕܫܠܝܚܐ ܕܒܥܘܢ ܀ ܠܐ ܡܪܐ ܦܘܡܐ ܕܡܠܟܘܬܐ ܘܫܪܪܐ.
[6] B1 ܢܗܒ ܗܘܐ.
[7] D2 marg.
[8] M1 ܡܠܟܘܬܐ.
[9] B1 ܐܬܒܠܒ ܗܘܐ.
[10] M2 ܒܢܝܕ the letter ܒ has been added later by the copyist.
[11] ⌉ B2 marg.
[12] B1 – ܘ.

18.(121)

For the Fifth Sunday of Ēlīā.[13] On the double-coin[14] of the head tax which was asked from our Lord. By Wardā. Of the Gospel. Forever.

[1] King and Lord of all kings,
all kings are His servants,
He who gave the kingship to kings
makes kings depart and elevates kings.
He gives freely by grace,
either kingship or lordship.
He liberates from slavery,
and freedom is subjected to Him.

[2] He emptied His great glory,[15]
He hid His hidden nature,
in a body that He put on from a Virgin,
and one Son with Him became His associate.

[3] Being high
in His nature and elevated,
He wanted to exalt our humility,
and for this, He humbled himself,

[4] to a nation that was more evil than all,
He appeared by grace,
He walked around in the cities,
to make their foolishness wise.

[5] He came to Capernaum[16]
and entered into it like a man,
He did not seek to take something,
but He was anxious to give.

[6] While he was staying in one of the houses,
Simon was in the market,
and he was asked for the tax of the Lord
that he would give [it] instead of our Lord

---

[13] According to the Church of the East, the liturgical season of Ēlīā consists of seven Sundays between September and October.

[14] ܐܕܡܐ ܕܘܪܡܐ, 'double-coin' is the Syriac translation of the Greek δ-δραχμή.

[15] See Phil 2:7.

[16] See Matt 17:24.

[7] ܦܐܠܘܗܝ ܦܘܩܕܐ ܠܥܡܠܢܝ. ܩܢܐ ܐܦܪܐ ܐܢܐ ܥܡܠܢܝ.
ܡܘܢ ܠܝ ܥܡܘܡ ܪܒܝܢܝ. ܐܘ ܝܗܒܬ ܥܡܗ ܘܥܡܠܢܝ ܀

[8] ܚܕܐ ܥܡܠܗ̇ ܘܐܡܪ ܠܐܢܫ̈ܝܢ. ܗ̇ܢܘܢ ܕܢܥܒܕܘܢ ܒܟܪܡ ܘܩܘܡ.
ܕܘܟܐ ܠܓܒܝ ܠܐ ܥܒܕܬܘܢ. ܘܠܐ ܡܥܒܕܝܢ ܡܨܛܒܝܢ ܀

[9] ܥܡܠܢܝ ܕܒܗܘܢ ܦܬܝܟ ܗܘܐ. ܐܝܟ ܐܢܫܐ ܠܦܠܚܘ ܚܕܐ ܗܘܐ.
ܘܠܐ ܝܕܥ ܕܐܠܗܐ ܗܘܐ. ⸢ܘܡܫܝܚܐ ܦܠܚܐ⸣[17] ܒܒܝܬܗ ܗܘܐ ܀ [f. 232r]

[10] ܡܢ ܕܥܡܠܢܝ ܠܓܒܪܐ ܚܠܠ ܗܘܐ. ܡܢ ܡܕܡ ܕܝܡܠܠܐ ܦܝܠܠ ܗܘܐ.
ܩܪܝ ܒܒܬܝܠ ܦܬܝܚܗ ܗܘܐ. ܘܫܘܝܗ ܚܠܦܐ ܕܥܡܠܐ ܗܘܐ ܀

[11] ܥܡܠܢܝ ܡܢܐ ܥܡܠܢܐ ܕܐܦܪܝܢ. ܗܢܘܢ ܕܘܟܐ ܠܝ ܦܠܚܝܢ.
ܘܥܡܗ[18] ܘܥܡܝܢ ܕܢܗܘܘܢ ܗܢܘܢ. ܫܩܐ ܠܝ ܩܢܝܐ ܡܦܠܠܝܢ ܀

[12] ܥܡܟ ܠܝ ܩܠܗܘܢ ܓܘܒܠܐ. ܐܦ ܦܠܚܠܘܗܝ ܪܒܠܐ.
ܚܙܐ ܠܝ ܪܚܡܘܗܝ ܢܒܝܠܐ. ܕܦܬܚܐ ܕܠܗ ܒܗ[19] ܗܘܠܠܐ[20] ܀

[13] ܦܠܚ̈ܐ ܕܐܪܥܐ ܦܠܚܝܢ. ܘܟܠ ܐܘܪܚܬܐ ܡܦܠܚܝܢ.
ܒܗܘܢ ܪܒܐ ܡܢ ܦܢ ܐܚܪܢܝܢ. ܡܢ ܒܢܝܗܘܢ ܐܘ ܡܢ ܐܚܪܢܝܢ ܀

[17] ⸢ B1 rep. ܘܡܠܟܐ ܕܠܗ.
[18] M1, B1, C1– ܘ.
[19] B1 ܠܗ.
[20] B1 marg.

[7] The inspectors asked Simon,
what do you say, Simon?
Will Your Lord give us something[21]
or shall we pass over Him and you?

[8] Simon answered and told the men,
those who take the double-coin:[22]
'Our master has no coins,
but if they are found, they will be given.'

[9] Simon was simple in his mind,
He thought that His master was just a man,
He did not know that He was God,
and all the world was in His hand.

[10] When Simon entered the house,
before he spoke a word,
our Lord in a hurry came before him[23]
and showed to him all that he had heard:

[11] 'Simon, what did you hear them say,
those who ask you for my coins,[24]
and seek to take [them] from me and you?
Show me what they say.

[12] I heard their idle voice,
and their false speech,
I saw their weak mind,
of a nation that has no understanding.

[13] The kings of the earth rule,
and they dominate the countries.
From whom do they ask taxation,
from their children or from others?'[25]

[21] See Matt 17:24.
[22] In this hymn, ܙܘܙܐ is translated as 'coin' and ܐܣܛܝܪܐ as 'stater' even though the poet sometimes uses these two words interchangeably, depending on the meter of the verse.
[23] See Matt 17:25.
[24] See Matt 17:25.
[25] See Matt 17:25.

[14] ܦܠܚܐ ܘܐܡܪ ܠܗ ܫܡܥܘܢ. ⌈ܢܦܩܝܢ[26] ܡܢ ܦܠܚܘܬܗܘܢ.
ܘܗܘ[27] ܡܕܡ ܕܢܦܩܝܢ ܡܢܗܘܢ. ܡܬܒܝܢ ܘܫܩܠܝܢ ܠܒܝܬܗܘܢ⌉[28] ܀

[15] ܠܒܪ ܩܪܐ ܘܐܡܪ ܠܫܡܥܘܢ.[29] ܕܦܩܘܕܐ ܠܒܢܝ ܐܢܫܗܘܢ.
ܕܐܬܟܠܝܢ ܒܗܘܢ ܩܪܐ ܠܡܪܗܘܢ. ܘܡܫܒܚܐ ܡܢ ܦܪ ܢܓܪܗܘܢ ܀

[16] ܕܫܠܡܬܐ ܡܕܡ ܠܐ ܡܢܐ ܐܢܐ. ܠܐ ܗܘܐ ܘܠܐ ܫܡܥܬܐ.
ܡܢ ܕܝܠܝ ܗܘ ܫܠܡܬܐ ܗܢܐ ܘܗܘ ܐܚܪܢܐ ܀

[17] ܥܠ ܕܐܝܬ ܠܗ ܠܐܒܐ ܐܝܟ ܠܝ. ܘܠܝܬ ܠܗ ܡܕܡ ܕܠܐ ܚܘܒ ܠܝ.
ܒܪܡ ܠܐ ܦܠܚܐ ܕܝܠܗܘܢ ܠܝ. ܘܗܘܐ ܘܠܐ ܠܕܫܠܡܝܢ ܠܝ ܀

[18] ܟܡ ܕܝܠܝ ܐܝܬܝܗ ܡܠܟܘܬܐ. ܘܒܐܝܕܝ ܝܗܒ ܡܘܗܒܬܐ.
ܘܠܐ ܟܘܬܐ ܐܬܝܢ ܒܐܝܬܘܬܐ. ܘܠܗ ܡܫܘܚܬ ܐܢܐ[30] ܒܕܪܘܬܐ ܀

[19] ܡܢ ܒܪܐ ܐܝܟ ܕܐܠܗܐ. ܘܐܡܪܗ ܐܢܐ ܕܐܠܗܐ.
ܙܕܩ ܠܝ ܕܐܢܫ ܐܠܗܐ. ܝܗܒܘܢ ܝܘܡ ܕܟܠ ܐܠܗܐ ܀

[20] ܐܝ ܠܐ ܝܕܥܬ ܠܐ ܢܘܟܪܝ. ܘܝܠܕܬܐ ܚܠܦ ܚܟܝܡ ܫܡܥܢ.
ܠܐ ܩܒܠ ܕܟܝ ܡܫܬܡܠܝܢ. ܢܩܠܐ ܕܡܢ ܟܕܘ ܢܟܝܠܝܢ[31] ܀

[21] ܕܠܐ ܩܕܡ ܒܟܝܠ ܐܢܘܢ. ⌈ܘܝܠܕܬܐ ܕܝܥܠܐ⌉[32] ܝܗܒܐ ܠܗܘܢ.
ܕܐܝ ܚܢܢ ܟܠ[33] ܢܘܟܪܝܢ ܠܗܘܢ. ܡܬܒܪܝܢ ܠܗܘ ܒܡܬܒܪܝܢ ܠܗܘܢ ܀

---

[26] M1, C1 + ܕ.
[27] M1 – ܘ.
[28] ⌉ B1 marg. bcd.
[29] B1 marg. a.
[30] B2 –.
[31] M1, B1 ܢܟܝܠܝܢ.
[32] ⌉ D3 written as ܕܝܥܠܐ ܘܝܠܕܬܐ with the letter ܐ placed over the word ܘܝܠܕܬܐ.
[33] B2 ܟܠ has been added later by the copyist.

[14] Simon answered and told him:
'They take from those who work for them,
and anything they take from them
they hide it and keep it for their children.'

[15] Our Lord replied and said to Simon:
'They are wicked servants
that they ask the head tax from their Lord
and taxation from the Son of their God.

[16] Now I do not have anything,
no coin and no penny,
although this world is mine,
this world and the other one.

[17] All the Father has is mine,
and there is nothing that He has not given me,
but it is not good that I have
coins and those who listen to me do not.

[18] Whereas the kingdom is mine,
and the gifts are in my hands,
and I am equal in essence with the Father,
and partaking with Him in Lordship.

[19] As I am the Son of God,
And, like Him, God,
it is right for me as God
to visit him who is not God.

[20] If I do not give, they will not give,
and the entire fault will be placed on me.
It is not right that they stumble by me,
the stumblers who have fallen already.

[21] In order then not to scandalize them,
and become a pretext of scandal for them,
if we do not give to them,
they will scatter the one who collects them.

[22] ܙܠ ܠܒܢܝܐ ܡܠܝܠܐܝܬ. / ܘܡܠܘܟܐ ܥܡܝ ܪܘܚܢܐܝܬ. [f. 232v]
ܘܗܘܐ ܒܐܕ ܐܝܟ ܡܫܪܘܚܐܝܬ. ܥܘܬܐ ܒܥܝܠܐ ܒܣܘܓܐܝܬ ܀

[23] ܦܓܫ ܦܘܡܗ ܐܝܟܐ ܒܐܝܟܐ. ܘܗܘܐ[34] ܢܣܬܪܐ[35] ܒܡܟܬܒܬܐ.
ܕܠܐ ܢܫܬܥܠܐ ܠܟܬܒܐ. ܢܠܐ ܒܐܝܟܐ ܕܟܪܘܒܐ ܀

[24] ܡܢ ܒܐܝܟܐ ܠܗܘܢ ܢܣܬܪܐ. ܘܡܚܝܠܐ ܠܟܝܢܐ ܦܦܪܐ.
ܢܟܦ ܒܒܝܐ ܦܢܟܦ ܡܪܐ. ܢܬܒܘܥ ܗܘ ܢܣܬܪܐ ܀

[25] ܣܘܦ ܢܡܘܣܗ ܝܗܒ ܗܘ ܡܫܠܠܐ. ܘܢܪܕ ܥܘܬܐ ܒܚܝܠ ܗܘ ܚܝܠܐ.
ܘܢܣܬܪܐ ܒܦܘܡܗ ܚܒܝܠܐ. ܘܙܘܙܐ ܬܪܝܢ ܦܬܪܝܢ ܬܡܝܢܐ ܀

[26] ܐܦ ܚܝܠܐ ܕܪܒܐ[36] ܒܪ ܢܫܬܐ. ܕܠܐ[37] ܦܦܦܐ ܠܗ ܡܠܝܠܘܬܐ.
ܘܠܐ ܡܪܦܦܝܢ ܠܗ ܡܣܬܒܬܐ. ܟܘܐ ܠܥܘܒܕܐ ܘܠܘܒܝܬܐ ܀

[27] ܚܝܠܐ ܗܘ ܕܟܪܐ ܢܕܢܚܬܐ. ܕܢܬܚܝܢ ܒܗܘܢ ܐܢܫܘܬܐ.
ܟܪܐ ܘܢܬܒܝܢ ܘܙܘܐ ܚܝܒܬܐ. ܒܦܘܡܗ ܕܥܘܬܐ ܒܗܘܢ ܟܠܬܐ ܀

[28] ܐܦ ܚܝܠܐ ܕܕܘܡܝܐ ܠܝܬ ܠܗ. ܐܦ ܢܡܘܣܐ ܕܦܣܩܐ ܠܝܬ ܠܗ.
ܕܦܘܡ ܥܘܬܐ ܚܘܪܐ ܗܘܐ ܠܗ. ܘܢܣܬܪܐ ܒܦܘܡܗ ܚܝܠ ܠܗ ܀

[29] ܕܠܐ ܢܪܦܩܐ ܘܡܫܪܝܐ.[38] ܦܕܠܐ ܚܘܪܐ ܡܦܩܪܢܐ.
ܚܝܠ ܢܣܬܪܐ ܒܦܘܡ ܥܘܬܐ. ܘܢܬܪܚ ܠܢܡܘܣܗ ܒܪ ܚܘܝܐ ܀

[34] M1, B1 ܗܘܐ.
[35] M1 ܢܣܬܪܐ.
[36] M1, B1 ܕܪܒ.
[37] M1, B1 ܘܠܐ.
[38] B2 marg.

[22] Go quickly to the sea,
and throw in the fishhook hastily,[39]
Behold! You will rapidly catch
a fish immediately, at once.

[23] Open its mouth with your two hands,
and behold the stater that is ready,[40]
which was not melted by a created person,
but by the hand of the Creator.

[24] Take the stater with your hand,
and give it to the infidel nation,
instead of the servant and instead of the master,[41]
that stater will be given.'

[25] Upon that word, Simon went
and caught the fish with the strength of that power [of Christ];
the stater was melted in its mouth,
weighing two and two coins.

[26] O power that is greater than the word,
which reason does not grasp,
and thoughts do not destroy,
worthy of glory and praise.

[27] The power that created creatures,
that was united to that humanity,
created and made a new coin,
in the mouth of a fish in that hour.

[28] O power that has no likeness,
O incomparable mystery,
that the mouth of the fish was for Him a furnace,
and the stater was made in its mouth.

[29] Without hammer or anvil,
without a furnace for melting,
the stater was made in the mouth of the fish,
and was given to Simon, the son of Jonah.

---

[39] See Matt 17:27.
[40] See Matt 17:27.
[41] See Matt 17:27.

[30] ܘܗܘܐ ܐܝܟܢܐ ܐܝܬܘܗܝ ܗܘܐ. ܕܫܠܝܚܐ ܐܝܟܢܐ ܐܝܬܠܗ ܗܘܐ.
ܘܡܬܚܙܝܢܘܬܗ ܠܟܠܗܘܢ ܡܚܝܐ ܗܘܐ. ܒܪܒܗܘ[42] ܘܒܪܐ ܫܡܝܐ ܗܘܐ ܀

[31] ܘܐܝܬ ܗܘܐ ܠܟܠܗܘܢ ܠܡܦܩ ܒܚܘܪܐ. ܘܦܬܚ ܬܪܥܐ ܘܢܦܩܘ ܡܢ ܒܝܬܐ.
ܥܘܒܕܐ ܠܠܒܝܐ ܬܕܡܘܪܬܐ. ܕܠܝܬܝܗܘܢ ܗܘܘ ܫܡܥܘܬܐ ܀

[32] ܐܦ ܕܘܘܕ[43] ܣܒܠ ܒܟܘܠ ܢܦܫܐ. ܒܗ ܒܢܘܡܘܣܐ ܘܒܢܒܝ̈ܐ.[44]
ܣܒܪܗ ܘܐܝܟܢܐ ܠܡܫܡܫܢܘܬܐ. ܒܣܦܪܐ ܐܝܟܢܐ ܘܒܢܘܗܪܐ ܀

[33] ܘܠܝܬܐ ܐܝܟܢܐ
ܘܫܠܡܐ ܐܝܟܢܐ
ܢܗܘܐ ܠܗ ܒܗ ܫܘܒܚܐ
ܘܠܗ ܬܫܒܘܚܬܐ
ܘܥܠ ܕܝܠܗ ܒܟܠ ܕܪܐ ܘܟܠ[45] ܥܠܡܐ ܀

[42] M1, B1, D1, C1 ܒܪ ܗܘ; in B2 it is written ܒܪ ܗܘ and then corrected to ܒܪܒܗܘ.
[43] D2 the letter ܕ has been added later by the copyist.
[44] C1 ܘܢܒܝ̈ܐ.
[45] M1 ܘܟܠ.

[30] It was a new coin
that the new king had made,
and written on it was [the name of] Tiberius
because he ruled at that time.

[31] There was the image of Caesar on it,
and the name of the day, month, and year;
glory to the creating hand,
that made the stater.

[32] O He who made the coin in the mouth of the fish,
on that day and at that time,
make and renew for the composer,
a new and spiritual *qnōmā*.

[33] Establish by Your grace for him,
a new heart
and a new image;
give us to sing glory to You,
at all times and all hours.

(127).19[1]

[f. 242r] ܕܡܢܕܢܚܐ[2] ܕܡܘܪܢ ܡܫܝܚܐ ܀ ܥܠ ܡܓܘܫܐ ܡܠܟܐ ܘܡܕܢܚܝܐ[3] ܀ ܕܒܠܗ ܩܡ ܕܒܠܗ ܕܡܠܦܢܐ[1]
ܠܡܪܝ ܐܦܪܝܡ ܀[4] ܕܩܘܩܝܬܐ[5] ܀ ܥܠܡ

[1] ܫܘܒܚܐ ܠܗ ܠܗܘ ܡܫܝܚܐ
ܕܢܚ ܘܐܢܗܪ ܥܠ ܒܪܝܬܐ
ܡܓܘܫ ܡܢ ܡܕܢܚܝܐ
ܘܡܓܘܫ ܩܪܒܘ ܡܠܟܐ
ܘܐܬܘ ܠܗܝܢ ܡܠܝܠܬܐ
ܕܩܘܪܒܢܐ ܘܐܢܬܬܐ ܘܡܪܬܐ
ܘܐܘܪܚܐ ܕܝܢ ܒܡܕܢܚܐ
ܕܠܒܠܘܢ ܒܪܝܢ ܒܫܠܡܘܬܐ ܀

[2] ܐܒܐ ܐܝܬܘ ܡܫܘܕܥܢܐ. ܟܕ ܢܠܒܘ ܒܣܒܪܬܐ.
ܘܪܘܚܗ ܦܪܣܢܐ ܘܡܢܗ. ܟܒܐ ܘܐܬܚܙܝ ܥܠ ܟܘܟܒܐ ܀

[3] ܒܪܐ ܠܡܠܟܐ ܗܠܟ ܡܓܘܫܐ. ܘܥܠ ܡܓܘܫܐ ܡܛܝܘ ܗܠܟܘ.
ܘܦܠܚܝܢ ܠܟܠܗܘܢ ܡܘܕܥܢܐ. ܗܡܝܢܘܬܐ ܦܪܝܫܬܐ ܀

[4] ܟܘܟܒܐ ܡܛܝܐ ܡܠܟܐ. ܢܗܘܐ ܠܡܘܫܐ ܕܢܒܝܐ.
ܟܕ ܟܘܟܒܐ ܠܗ ܠܗܘ ܟܘܟܒܢܐ. ܕܠܝܬ ܠܗ ܕܘܡܝܐ ܗܝܟ ܫܡܫܐ ܀

[5] ܟܡܝܠܬܐ ܟܘܟܒܐ ܗܘܐ ܠܗ. ܒܪܗܝܬܐ ܡܠܟܝܢ ܗܘܐ ܠܗ.
ܘܟܪܒܠܠ[6] ܡܢܝܚܢ ܗܘܐ[7] ܠܗ.[8] ܠܡܠܟܐ ܕܟܠ ܥܠ ܫܘܒܚܗ ܀

[6] ܢܦܩܘ ܢܦܫܢ ܠܫܡ ܡܓܘܫܝ. ܘܢܦܫܗܘܢ ܟܡܠ ܐܒܗܘܢ.
ܘܗܢܐ ܐܦ ܡܠܟܘܗܝ. ܢܦܩܘܢ ܗܘܐ ܒܫܠܡ ܠܟܠܗܘܢ ܀

---

[1] This hymn is found in: M2, D1, C1, C2, D2, B2, M3, G1, D3.
[2] Before the main heading in M2, C2, D3 there is another heading as follows: ܕܡܢܕܢܚܐ ܕܡܕܝܢܬܐ ܕܡܘܨܠ: ܦܠܚܝܢ ܢܦܫܢ ܀ ܡܢ ܢܦܫ ܩܕܡ ܢܬܒܠܒܠܘܢ ܕܡܓܘܫܐ ܟܡ ܟܠܝܢܗ ܘܡܠܟܐ ܟܠ ܡܫܝܚܘܬܐ ܒܫܘܒܚܐ ܒܡܠܟܐ.
[3] D1 written ܡܕܢܚܝܐ ܡܠܟܐ after which the sequence is corrected by placing ܐ on ܡܠܟܐ and ܒ on ܡܕܢܚܝܐ.
[4] ⌐ C1 ܕܒܠܗ ܕܡܠܦܢܐ ܠܡܪܝ; B2 – ܕܒܠܗ ܩܡ ܕܒܠܗ ܕܡܠܦܢܐ.
[5] D1 + ܘܐܦܝܘܬܐ.
[6] D1, C1 ܘܟܪܒܠܐ.
[7] M3 ܗܘܐ has been added later by the copyist.
[8] D1 marg. c; C2 – c.

19.(127)

For the Sunday of the Consecration of the Church. On the angelic and ecclesiastical ranks. By the teacher Gīwargīs Wardā. Of the Mawtḇā. Forever

[1] Glory to that Wisdom
that created and established all creatures;
it made some of them silent,
then some of them endowed with speech.
It taught to those rational ones
its great and marvelous work;
it made them known through the dumb ones,
all of which it created in equality.

[2] The Father, the eternal essence,
with His only-begotten Son,
and His life-giving and living Spirit,
wanted to bring everything into existence.

[3] He created the watchers in three churches,
each church has three ranks,
and He distributed degrees to all of them,
marvelous and glorious!

[4] The highest rank, the Cherubim,[9]
was seen by the prophet Ezekiel,
when they surrounded that throne
that has no likeness under heaven.

[5] They surrounded Him with fear,
they carried Him with trembling,
they celebrated Him with dread,
the king of all, glory to Him.

[6] Each one has four faces,[10]
and their faces are on all sides;
and thus also their wings
were four, equally for all[11]

---

[9] See Ezek 10:1. The East Syriac Church traditionally counts the Cherubim as the first angelic rank, while many others, like Dionysius the Areopagite, count the Seraphim as the first rank. See Rosemary Arthur A., *Pseudo-Dionysius as Polemicist*, p. 43. The Angelic ranks are mentioned also in Hymn (77).
[10] See Ezek 10:21.
[11] See Ezek 10:21.

[7] ܢܒܝܝܗܘܢ ܕܠܐ ܡܢܝܢܐ. ܘܣܗܕܝܗܘܢ ܕܠܐ ܚܘܫܒܢܐ.
ܦܪܚܘ ܠܓܢܬܐ ܘܢܗܝܪܐ. ܟܠܗܘܢ ܐܝܟ ܘܟܘܟܒܐ ܀

[8] ܚܘܝ ܠܢ ܕܐܝܟ ܒܪܒܝܬܐ. ܒܓܢܬ⌈ܘ⌉ܗܘܢ[12] ܠܐ ܡܬܦܫܩܬܐ.
ܦܠܗܘܢ ܠܐ ܚܘܝܐ ܚܙܬ. ܥܝܢܐ ܒܥܘܬܐ ܘܡܫܪܒܝܬܐ ܀

[9] ܝܗܒܪܗܘܢ ܐܝܟ ܡܘܕܥܝܗܘܢ.. ܘܝܗܒܠܗܘܢ ܐܝܟ ܢܝܫܝܗܘܢ.
ܐܪܙܐ ܕܪܘܚܬܐ ܕܡܝܬ ܒܗܘܢ.. ܕܗܘ / ܕܪܚܝܡ ܠܟܠܗܘܢ ܕܝܢ ܠܟܠܗܘܢ ܀ [f. 242v]

[10] ܘܐܝܟ ܩܛܪܝܩܝܢ ܒܥܒܕܝܢ. ܘܝܠܝܕܬܐ ܡܢ ܠܝܠ ܡܬܚܠܒܢ.
ܠܦܠܛܝܢ[13] ܡܢܗܘܢ ܦܪܝܫܝܢ. ܒܢܝܢܐ ܡܬܪܒܐ ܡܠ ܢܦܠܝܢ܀

[11] ܗܕܐ ܡܬܚܡܐ[14] ܗܪܝܢܐ. ܠܐ ܢܗܘܘܢ ܘܫܘܡܪܐ.
ܦܘܝܬܐ ܘܡܦܘܪܫܬܐ. ܒܐܪܙ ܦܘܠܚܢܐ ܗܘ ܗܢܐ ܀

[12] ܠܗܠܝܢ ܠܟܠ ܚܝܐ ܢܥܒܢܢܐ. ܗܘ ܚܘܒܪܢ ܚܙܪ ܗܘ ܒܘܪܟܬܐ.
ܦܫܝܩ ܠܝܠ ܡܢ ܥܩܐ ܥܩܬܐ. ܘܠܐ ܢܚܝܘ ܠܒܒܝܘܬܐ ܘܚܪܒܐ ܀

[13] ܠܒܠ ܚܕ ܡܢܗܘܢ ܥܠܐ ܝܗܒ. ܗܠܗܐ ܗܠܗܐ ܦܬܓܡܝܢ.
ܐܪܙܐ ܕܗܠܗܐ ܡܢܘܩܝܢ. ܦܬܠܝܓܐܝܬ ܠܗܘܢ ܡܦܢܝܢ܀

[12] ܘ M3 marg.
[13] D3 ܠܦܠܛܝܢ the first letter ܠ has been added later by the copyist.
[14] C2 ܡܬܚܡܐ has been added later by the copyist.

[7] Their eyes are without enumeration,
their *qnōmē* are without counting,
their flying is frequent and continual,
their voice loud and strong.

[8] They see all that is in creation
with their incorporeal eyes,
but sight cannot see them
unless with mind and thought.

[9] Their back is like their front,
their left like their right,
the mystery of the cross was prefigured in them,
of Him mounted on it, mounted on them.

[10] They were made like Patriarchs,
they accept revelations from above,
they hand them over to those beneath them,
with the power that governs all powers.

[11] The second rank, the Seraphim,[15]
does not burn, but it consumes,
holy and making holy
mysteriously this one is the Catholicos.[16]

[12] For these then Isaiah saw
surrounding that throne,[17]
established above the heaven of heavens,
and not made by a worker or creature.

[13] Each of them has six wings,[18]
three by three which prefigured
the mystery of the three *qnōmē*
to whom they cry holy three times.

---

[15] See Isa 6:6.
[16] Although the two terms 'Patriarch' and 'Catholicos' usually indicate the same ecclesiastical rank in the East Syriac tradition, the poet seems to distinguish these two ranks from each other here and in stanza [10a].
[17] See Isa 6:2.
[18] See Isa 6:2.

[14] ܗܕܝܢ ܨܒܝܢ ܥܠ ܢܦܫܬܗܘܢ. ܚܕܝܘ ܘܗܕܝܢ ܥܠ ܕܝܠܗܘܢ.
ܗܕܝܢ ܐܚܪܢܝܢ ܦܪܚܝܢ ܗܘܘ ܒܗܘܢ. ܒܐܪܥ ܗܕܝܢ ܒܢܝܢ ܕܒܪ ܥܡܗܘܢ ܀

[15] ܕܐܝܟ ܡܘܕܥܐ ܗܟܢܐ. ܠܢܒܝܐ ܚܕܐ ܡܫܘܚܬܐ ܗܠܝܢ.
ܕܠܐ ܡܫܬܟܚܝܢ ܢܗܝܪܘܬܐ. ܘܠܐ ܫܠܝܛܐ ܒܗܘܢ ܒܢܗܝܪܘܬܐ ܀

[16] ܕܟܕ ܢܦܩ ܐܝܟ ܢܗܪܐ. ܦܬܚܘܗܝ ܠܥܝܢܐ ܥܠ ܒܘܪܟܬܐ.
ܐܪܘܐ ܗܘ ܕܝܠܡܐ[19] ܐܒܪܐ. ܕܢܬܒܝܢ ܠܥܠܡܐ ܐܢܫܐ ܀

[17] ܡܘܬܒܐ ܫܠܡܐ ܗܠܝܢܐ. ܠܡܫܠܡܘ ܡܠܟܝܢ ܕܡܫܝܚܐ.
ܘܡܫܬܡܥܝܢ ܠܗ ܠܡܪܘܬܐ. ܟܕ ܩܠܝܢ ܕܠܐ ܦܘܡ ܘܠܫܢܐ ܀

[18] ܩܠܝܢ ܫܪܪ[20] ܠܫܘܠܛܢ ܟܘܟܒܝܢ. ܘܡܘܬܒܐ ܕܫܡܝܐ ܡܬܦܪܣܝܢ.
ܒܗܘܢ ܕܐܦ ܐܝܟ[21] ܩܠܝܢ ܡܫܬܡܥܝܢ. ܘܠܐ ܙܥܝܪ ܘܠܐ ܡܬܦܠܓܝܢ[22] ܀

[19] ܫܠܡܐ ܗܘ ܕܒܗܪ ܗܟܢܐ. ܗܘ ܕܝܢ ܢܗܝܪܐ ܡܢ ܠܒܪ.
ܘܡܬܚܙܐ ܡܪܘܬܐ. ܘܫܘܠܛܢ ܟܕܡܐ ܒܝܠܕܬܐ ܀

[20] ܘܐܝܬ ܠܗ ܒܢܝܢܐ ܕܐܢܫܘܬܐ. ܢܨܝܚܘܬܐ ܒܟܠ ܕܡܘܬܐ.
ܘܗܝ ܫܠܡܐ ܡܢܐ ܡܫܬܠܡܘܬܐ. ܕܡܪܘܬܐ ܡܢ ܪܒܘܬܐ ܀

[19] D3 +X ܕܐܢܫܘܬܐ.
[20] C1 ܫܪܪ has been added later by the copyist.
[21] D2 marg + ܕ.
[22] D2 ܡܬܦܠܓܝܢ.

[14] Two wings encircled their faces,
and two their feet,
with two others they flew[23]
as a symbol of the two natures of the Son of their Lord.[24]

[15] They repeat the three times holy,[25]
to the one essence, three *qnōmē*,
that do not accept increase,
and with whom deficiency has no power.

[16] So that the prophet said,
when he saw the Lord sitting on the throne,[26]
it was the symbol of a human image
united with the Word, the essence.

[17] The Thrones, the third rank,[27]
they are like the metropolitans,
they glorify the Creator
with these who do not come to an end or cease.

[18] For these were mentioned by Paul,
and were called Thrones by name,
because like them, they were established;
they do not move, and are not disturbed.

[19] The rank after the third,
is the head of the middle church,
it has the name of Dominions,
and Paul announced it in the Letter,[28]

[20] and in the human church
the bishops correspond to it,
this rank that possesses the power
of Lordship from dominion,

---

[23] See Isa 6:2.

[24] Seeing Christ's natures in the symbol of the Seraphim can also be found in the writings of Origen. V. Van Vossel, مدرسة الإسكندرية [The school of Alexandria], p. 86.

[25] See Isa 6:3.

[26] See Isa 6:1.

[27] See Col 1:16.

[28] See Col. 1:16.

[21] ܦܘܩܕܢܝܢ ܦܫܝܩܝܬܐ. ܕܦܪܫܬܐ / ܒܡܫܝܚܘܬܐ. [f. 243r]

ܐܝܟ ܕܢܗܘܐ ܠܗ ܛܝܒܘܬܐ. ܕܠܐ ܣܥܘܪܐ ܘܠܐ ܒܝܫܘܬܐ ܀

[22] ܘܐܦ ܗܘ ܡܫܝܚܐ ܫܒܩ ܠܗܘܢ. ܠܪܫܐ ܘܡܫܡܠܝܐ ܠܝܕܥܬܗܘܢ.

ܘܡܢ ܒܝܬܝܬܐ ܙܒܢ ܠܗܘܢ. ܕܠܐ ܢܦܠܘܢ ܘܢܬܚܪܒܘܢ ܐܦܢ ܀

[23] ܡܫܝܚܐ ܗܘܝܠ ܣܡܝܟܬܐ. ܒܗܝܕܝܢ ܠܗ ܠܬܫܒܘܚܬܐ.

ܗܟܘܬ ܐܝܟ ܠܗ ܕܘܡܝܐ. ܒܛܘܒܬܐ ܢܦܫܝܬܐ ܀

[24] ܘܗܝ ܡܫܝܚܐ ܕܢܬܠܘܬܐ. ܡܢܐ ܢܣܒܐ ܡܢ ܕܒܘܬܐ.

ܕܝܠܝܕ ܒܡܫܩܐ[29] ܙܕܘܬܐ.[30] ܘܢܘܡܝܐ ܡܘܕܝܢܘܬܐ ܀

[25] ܡܫܝܚܐ ܗܘܝܠ ܥܒܕܬܐ. ܥܘܠܡܢܐ ܠܗ ܒܘܪܟܐ.

ܘܠܗ ܕܒܪܢ ܠܗܘܢ ܢܦܫܐ. ܘܡܥܒܪܢܐ ܐܝܟ ܠܗ ܕܘܡܝܐ ܀

[26] ܘܐܦ ܗܘ ܡܫܝܚܐ ܕܥܘܠܡܢܐ. ܡܦܪܢܣܐ ܗܘ ܕܡܥܘܕܢܐ.

ܐܦ ܦܠܚܝܢܐ ܘܐܘܡܢܐ. ܒܝܕܐ ܫܠܝܛ ܒܟܠ ܥܘܠܡܢܐ ܀

[27] ܡܫܝܚܐ ܕܐܬܒܘܣ ܕܫܒܥ ܥܕܬܐ. ܒܗܝܕܝܢ ܒܗܘܢ ܐܫܬܡܫܬ.

ܘܐܦ ܦܪܝܫ ܢܝܕܥܬܐ ܦܫܝܛܬܐ. ܘܡܩܒܠܐ ܕܘܡܝܐ ܒܠܝܕܬܐ ܀

[29] C1 ܒܢܦܫܗ; C2 marg. ܒܡܫܩܐ.
[30] M3 marg.

[21] to distribute the wages
of the earthly beings continuously,
according to the grace given to him,
without envy or wickedness.

[22] And this rank restrains
the demons and silences their vehemence,
and keeps them away from human beings
so that they will not harm or demolish them.

[23] This is the fifth rank;
they are mentioned by the man of Tarsus.
They are compared to the visitors[31]
in the ecclesiastical order.

[24] This rank of the Powers,[32]
possesses power from the Lordship
to work victory among the nations
and to put an end to defeat.

[25] The sixth rank
is called Rulers,[33]
they are remembered by this chosen one[34]
and priests are compared to it.

[26] And the rank of the Rulers,
is the leader of those who enlighten,
also of the climates and possessions,
by the power of He who has authority over all authorities.

[27] The rank of the Principalities, which is after the sixth,
are mentioned in this letter;[35]
it is the head of the church below,
and they are compared to deacons in the church.

---

[31] See H. Teule, "The Synod of Timothy II, 1318".
[32] See Eph 1:21.
[33] See Eph 3:10.
[34] See Gal 1:16.
[35] See Eph 3:10.

[28] ܘܗܝ ܡܙܡܪܝܢ ܠܫܒܚܐ. ܘܠܬܫܒܚܬܐ ܫܒܝܚܬܐ.
ܘܡܫܒܚܐ ܒܢܝܐ ܘܡܫܒܚܐ. ܒܐܝܕܗܘܢ ܗܘܝܢ ܒܟܠ ܙܒܢ ܀

[29] ⌜ܛܠܝܬܐ[36] ܗܘܬ ܚܛܝܬܐ⌝.[37] ܪܒܐ ܡܠܐܟܐ ܡܪܢܐ.
ܠܗܝܕܝܢ ܕܪܒܝܬܐ[38] ܒܣܡܐ. ܘܡܟܝܟܐ ܗܘܬ ܠܗܘܢ ܒܘܣܡܐ ܀[39]

[30] ܘܗܝ ܡܙܡܪܝܢ ܠܒܝܬܗ. ܘܠܛܒܪܐ ܘܠܦܪܨܘܦܐ.
ܘܠܬܒܪܐ ܕܦܫܝܛܐ. ܘܦܘܠܚܢܗܿ[40] ܠܗܘܢ ܕܡܘܬܐ ܀

[31] ܛܠܝܬܐ ܕܝܢ ܗܘ[41] ܚܛܝܬܐ. ܡܠܐܟܐ ܐܢܘܢ ܘܪܘܚܐ.
ܡܫܒܚܝܢ[42] ܠܟܝܢܐ ܐܢܫܐ. ܘܥܕܡܐ ܐܝܟ ܠܗܘܢ[43] ܕܡܘܬܐ ܀

[32] ܘܗܘܝܐ ܚܘܒ ܡܫܬܟܚܐ. ܕܗܘܐ[44] ܡܢܗ ܠܗ[45] ܛܠܝܬܐ.
ܐܝܟ ܡܢܗ ܠܗ ܒܝܬ ܫܠܡܐ. ܕܡܢ ܐܕܡ ܘܠܥܘܠܡܐ ܀

[33] ܡܢܘܬܐ ܗܘܬ[46] ܕܘܟܝܐ. ܪܘܚܐ[47] ܐܢܘܢ ܦܫܝܛܬܐ.
ܘܐܝܟܢܐ ܡܬܒܪܟܝܢ. ܘܐܝܟܢܐ ܡܬܒܪܟܝܢ ܀ [f. 243v]

[34] ܚܝܝܢ ܐܢܘܢ ܘܡܬܒܠܒܠܝܢ. ܘܟܠ ܡܫܬܒܚ ܘܠܐ ܡܬܒܠܒܠܝܢ.
ܒܪܘܚܗܘܢ ܡܬܢܨܚܝܢ. ܡܢܘܚܬܗܘܢ[48] ܠܐ ܡܬܢܨܚܝܢ ܀

[35] ܡܫܝܚܐ ܗܘ[49] ܫܠܡܐ ܝܗܒ ܠܗܘܢ. ܡܛܠ ܐܢܘܢ ܒܡܫܝܚܘܬܗܘܢ.[50]
ܡܢܘܬܐ ܠܗܘܢ ܘܠܐ ܡܬܡܚܝܐ ܠܗܘܢ. ܒܥܕܢܐ ܕܡܬܡܚܝܐ ܠܗ ܘܠܗܘܢ ܀

---

36 G1 illeg.

37 ⌜ C1 written ܚܛܝܬܐ ܛܠܝܬܐ ܗܘܬ with the sequence corrected by placing ܐ on ܛܠܝܬܐ and ܒ on ܗܘܬ and ܓ on ܚܛܝܬܐ.

38 G1 illeg.

39 All the stanzas that come before this are missing in G1.

40 G1 ܘܦܘܠܚܢܐ.

41 D3 – ܗܘ.

42 G1 ܡܫܒܚܝܢ.

43 D2 ܠܗ.

44 G1 ܗܘܐ.

45 G1 ܗܘ.

46 G1 illeg.

47 G1 ܡܢܘܬܐ.

48 B2 ܢܦܫܗܘܢ, G1 ܢܦܫܗܘܢ.

49 G1 –.

50 M3 ܗܘܢ has been added later by the copyist.

[28] They govern the clouds
and the intense storms;
the quiet and peaceful breezes
are in their hands at all times.

[29] Then the eighth rank
are called the Archangels;
they are mentioned by the prophet Daniel,[51]
and he gave them the name of watchers.

[30] They govern the animals,
the birds and all that flies,
and all kinds of swimming animals,
and sub deacons are compared with them.

[31] Then the ninth rank
are the honorable Angels,
the servants of the human race,
and readers are compared to them.

[32] And thus comes to an end
the enumeration of the ranks,
like the number of the children of the world
from Adam till the end.

[33] The spiritual *qnōmē*
are subtle movements,
they can be grasped by knowledge
but cannot be seen.

[34] They are alive and rational,
they neither die nor suffer corruption;
they think with their thoughts,
their *qnōmē* cannot be reckoned.

[35] Only Christ knows,
how many they are in number;
He sees them, but [He] was not seen by them,
until He was seen by us and them.

---

[51] See Dan 6:23; 1 Thess 4:16.

[36] ܒܬܪ ܚܘܝ ܠܗ ܒܝܘܬܐ. ܘܡܬܬܥܕܠܝܢ[52] ܠܗ ܒܫܠܝܐ.
ܕܡܦܩܝܢ ܡܕܝܢܬܐ ܘܟܘܪܐ. ܕܡܬܬܠܝܢ ܠܗܘܢ ܒܡܕܒܪܐ ܘܛܘܪܐ ܀

[37] ܕܘܫܐ ܕܡܠܟܐ ܕܡܬܩܢ. ܒܢܝ ܕܝܘܬܐ ܕܡܠܟܐ ܕܬܒܝܢ.
ܘܒܬܪܗܘܢ ܟܠܗ ܥܒܕܝܢ.[53] ܒܡܬܒܥܐ ܠܚܘܒ ܕܡܬܟܡܠܝܢ ܀

[38] ܗܘ ܕܥܐ ܕܦܟܪܘܬܐ. ܡܫܒܚܬܐ ܕܡܬܥܒܕܢܐ.
ܘܗܘ ܐܝܟ ܗܘܢܐ ܠܕܘܫܐ. ܡܬܟܢܫܐ[54] ܕܡܬܥܒܕܢܐ ܀

[39] ܐܝ ܒܥܒܕܐ ܘܐܝ ܥܒܕܐ. ܒܐܝܕܗ ܗܘ ܗܘܝ ܠܥܒܕܐ.
ܕܗܘܝܘ ܕܟܪ ܕܟܪܐ. ܘܡܬܬܕܟܪܐ ܕܟܠ[55] ܥܒܕܐ ܀

[40] ܗܘ ܡܬܐ ܕܟܠ ܡܬܝܢ. ܘܗܘܝܘ ܡܘܬܐ[56] ܕܟܠ[57] ܡܘܬܝܢ.
ܘܗܘܝܘ ܚܝܐ ܕܟܠ ܚܝܝܢ. ܐܦ ܢܘܗܪܐ[58] ܕܟܠ ܕܡܠܝܠܝܢ[59] ܀

[41] ܒܗ ܢܬܒܝܢ ܟܠ ܡܕܡ. ܘܒܗ ܢܬܚܙܐ ܒܠܝܡܕܡ.[60]
ܕܠܐܬܪܗ ܠܐ ܗܘܐ ܡܕܡ. ܘܠܐ ܡܫܝܢܐ ܕܢܗܘܐ ܡܕܡ ܀

[42] ܡܢܗ ܘܠܗ ܟܠ ܡܕܡ. ܘܡܢܗ[61] ܘܠܘܬܗ ܘܠܐ[62] ܡܕܡ.
⸢ܚܠܝܨ ܒܒܪܝܬܗ ܒܠܝܡܕܡ. ܘܗܘ ܠܐ ܡܬܚܝܨ ܡܢ ܡܕܡ[63]⸣[64] ܀

[43] ܒܗ ܚܒܝܫ ܟܠ ܒܪܝܬܐ. ܒܗ ܚܫܝܒܝܢ[65] ܟܠ ܢܦܫܬܐ.
ܠܗ ܢܛܪ ܟܠ ܒܪܝܬܐ. ܡܢ ܕܘܟܬܐ ܐܝܟ ܐܠܗܘܬܐ ܀

[44] ܗܘܝܘ ܒܪܘܝܐ ܒܪܝܬܐ. ܘܗܘܝܘ ܐܠܗܐ ܐܠܗܝܐ.
ܘܗܘ ܡܕܒܪ ܠܟܠܗܘܢ ܒܪܝܬܐ. ܘܕܡܬܕܒܪ ܗܘ ܟܠ ܡܫܝܢܐ ܀

52 B2 ܘܡܬܬܥܕܠܝܢ.
53 D3 ܥܒܕܬܐ.
54 C2 ܡܬܟܢܫܬܐ.
55 G1 illeg.
56 G1 illeg.
57 D2 marg.
58 G1 illeg.
59 D3 ܡܠܠܝܢ.
60 C2 marg. b.
61 G1 – ܘ.
62 G1 –.
63 M3 marg.
64 ⸣ B2 marg. cd.
65 D3 ܚܫܝܒܝܢ has been added later by the copyist.

[36] But they saw Him in visions,
and they recognized Him in revelations;
in the likeness of the saints and the righteous ones,
to whom He was revealed in intellects and minds.

[37] The spiritual ones are nine ranks;
the children of the church are nine degrees.
Both sides are defective;
they are complete in Christ alone.

[38] He is the head of the bodily ones,
who constitute those who can be seen,
and He is like the mind for the spiritual ones,
which sets in order that which is known.

[39] Whether humans or watchers,
they become perfect in His hand,
since He binds together the bonds,
and makes perfect all who are defective.

[40] He is the limit of all limits,
He is the boundary of all boundaries,
He is the life of all living beings,
and light for all those who are rational.

[41] Through Him, everything was made,
and in Him, everything was renewed,
without Him, nothing came into existence,
and it is impossible anything could exist!

[42] Everything here is from Him,
nothing is outside of Him,
everything is contained in His knowledge,
and He is not contained by anything.

[43] In Him, all creatures are encompassed,
in Him, all knowledge is enclosed,
all hidden things can be seen by Him,
from far as if they are manifest.

[44] He is the hidden creator,
and He is the revealed God,
He who grasps all created beings
but they cannot comprehend Him.

[45] ܝܗ ܢܣܒ ܚܠܗܘܢ ܠܦܓܪܐ. ܝܗ ܡܫܬܡܥܝܢ ܚܠ ܡܠܝܠܐ.
ܘܢܘܪܐ ܘܕܐܬܐ ܘܗܘܐ / ܠܗ ܐܟܝܠ. ܘܗܘ ܠܐ ܡܬܐܟܝܠ ܟܕ ܡܬܐܟܠ ⁘ [f. 244r]

[46] ܠܗ ܥܘܢܝܐ ܢܦܩ ܬܘܕܝܬܐ. ܠܗ ܕܝܢ[66] ܡܘܬܒܐ ܘܫܘܒܚܬܐ.
ܠܗ ܥܘܠܝܬܐ ܘܡܪܘܬܐ. ܘܪܒܘܬܐ ܘܐܠܗܘܬܐ ⁘

[47] ܡܪܐ ܕܒܝܬܐ ܦܩܐܢܝܐ.[67] ܦܪܘܩ ܐܢܝ ܡܢܗ ܐܢܝܐ.
ܚܠ ܡܦܪܩܢܐ ܢܟܝܐ.[68] ܕܦܪܩܢܗ ܠܗܘܢ ܝܠܕܐ ܡܦܪܩܐ ⁘

[48] ܢܪܐܬܐ ܦܪܝܐ
ܘܦܠܚܐ ܘܡܪܐ
ܢܟܠܗ ܦܪܢܣ ܒܪܐ ܠܡܪܝܐ
ܚܠܘܦܝܗ ܦܩܕܘܢ[69] ܕܟܝܢ ܟܘܗܪܐ
⌜ܠܡܦܪܩܢܐ ܕܗܿܝ⌝[70] ܝܠܕܬܐ
⌜ܘܝܘܢܗ ܘܝܘܡ⌝[71] ܠܗ ܬܫܒܘܚܬܐ
ܘܠܐܒܘܗܝ ܘܪܘܚܗ[72] ܩܕܝܫܘܬܐ ⁘

---

[66] D2 ܕܝܢ has been added later by the copyist.
[67] B2 ܦܩܐܢܝܐ with the first ܐ has been added later by the copyist.
[68] C1 ܢܟܝܐ has been added later by the copyist.
[69] D3 ܦܩܕܘܢ with the letter ܘ added by a later hand.
[70] ⌜ D3 ܠܡܦܪܩܢܐ ܕܗܿܝ.
[71] ⌜ G1 ܐܦ ܝܘܢܗ.
[72] G1 ܦܩܕܝ.

[45] In Him, all works come to rest,
in Him, all rational beings become joyful,
what was, what is and what will be, is revealed to Him
and He will not be revealed until He will be revealed.

[46] To Him glory and gratitude,
to Him honor and worship,
to Him power, sovereignty,
Lordship and divinity.

[47] The Lord of watchers and human being,
have mercy as a merciful person,
on the weak composer
who composed this homily of sanctification.

[48] Inheritor and Son,
King and Lord,
God-man, perfect Son,
unite with the children of light,
the composer of this homily,
glory to You from him and us,
and to Your Father and Your Spirit always.

(130).20[1]

[f. 247v] ⌜ܐܚܪܢܐ ܗܘ ܠܦܘܡܐ[2] ܕܢܦܫܬܐ⌝[3]: ܕܫܠܗ[4] ܕܦܪܦܪܐ[5] ܀ ܢܦܩܬ ܠܗ ܡܢ ܦܓܪܗ ܢܦܫܗ ܗܘ[6] ܩܘܠܐ ܕܪܕܝܡܘܬܐ.

[1] ܩܘܠܐ ܕܐܒܐ ܡܬܘܦܐ[7]
ܕܒܟ ܢܠܦܘܢ[8] ܥܡܐ ܒܐܘܣܝܐ
ܘܠܝܬ ܠܗ ܙܒܢܐ ܡܥܘܕܪܢܐ[9]
ܘܠܐ ܥܘܫܠܦܐ ܘܠܐ ܥܘܒܕܢܐ
ܘܡܢܗ ܗܘܐ ܟܠܗܘܢ ܐܘܪܚܬܐ
ܘܒܐܝܕܗ ܠܥܒܕܝܢ ܟܠܗܘܢ ܒܢܝܢܐ
ܒܚܘܒܗ ܠܝܬ ܦܓܪܐ ܢܦܠܢܐ
ܘܒܗ ܫܘܝܢ ܢܦܠܗ ܦܣܢܐ ܀

[2] ܠܢܦܫܐ ܕܚܛܬ ܡܢ ܟܠ ܢܦܫܢ. ܚܕܐ ܒܪܫܝܥܘܬܗ ܕܦܠܚ ܟܠ ܥܡܠܝܢ.
ܘܡܢܗ ܚܕܐ ܐܬܟܬܒܬ ܐܢܫܝܢ. ܘܐܚܪܢܐ ܐܬܪܝܡ ܟܠܗ ܢܦܫܬܢ ܀

[3] ܘܐܘܦ ܚܕܐ ܡܢ ܐܬܬܒܥܬ ܥܠܝܗܝܢ. ܠܝܫܘܥ ܘܐܦ ܠܐܦܝ ܢܦܫܝܢ.
ܢܟܪܘܬܗ ܢܗܘܘܢ ܡܫܝܚܝܢ. ܢܦܩܬ ܡܢ ܟܠ ܐܠܗܝܢ ܀

[4] ܠܡܘܬܐ ܕܐܬܒܪܬ ܕܚܛܐ ܝܬܗ. ܘܠܫܪܝܗ ܢܦܫ ܝܬܗ.[10]
ܘܡܠܟܘܬܗ ܫܡܝܢ ܝܬܗ. ܡܘܬܒܗ[11] ܚܕܐ ܡܢܗ ܢܚܬܘܗ ܀

[5] ܢܦܫܐ ܐܦܝܢ ܐܘܠܝܢ ܝܬܗ. ܗܢܘܢ[12] ܕܢܦܠܢ ܠܗ ܝܡܢܗ.
ܕܢܦܩܘܢ ܡܢ ܡܠܟܘܬܗ ܐܦܝܗ.[13] ܠܥܠ ܡܢ ܐܠܗܝܢ ܟܠܗܘܢ ܀

[6] ܡܢ ܢܦܫܗ ܠܦܪܗ ܕܡܘܬܐ. ܢܫܬܡܠܝܟ[14] ܥܘܕܝܗ ܐܬܝܬܐ.
ܘܟܠܗ ܗܘܐ ܒܘܝܐܐ ܒܒܘܝܐܐ. ܘܫܟܚ ܡܢܗ ܢܫܡܬܐ ܘܦܓܪܐ ܀

---

[1] This hymn is found in: M2, D1, C1, C2, D2, B2, M3, G1, D3.
[2] D1 + ܠ.
[3] ⌜ G1 ܕܦܘܡܐ ܕܢܦܫܬܗ ܕܦܪܝ ܚܕ ܦܘܡܐ ܐܚܪܢܐ.
[4] G1 + ܕܦܪܦܪܝܬܐ.
[5] G1 illeg.
[6] M3 – ܗܘ.
[7] C2 ܡܬܘܦܐ in marg. ܡܬܘܦܬܐ.
[8] G1 illeg.
[9] All the stanzas that come after this word are missing in G1.
[10] C2 ܝܬܗ has been added later by the copyist.
[11] D3 marg. the letter ܗ has been added later by the copyist.
[12] B2 ܗܢܘܢ has been added later by the copyist.
[13] D1 marg.
[14] C2 ܢܫܬܡܠܟܘܢ.

20.(130)

Another one for the Feast of the Transfiguration. By Wardā. That ray of justice shines on him from the house of David.

[1] The ray of the eternal Father,[15]
who with His begetter is equal in essence,
who has no time and no beginning,
no change and no transformation.
In Him, all beings came into existence
by His hand, all creatures were made,
by His love, He put on a revealed body
and in him [the Son], He showed His hidden power.

[2] A nation more wicked than all nations,
He chose, in His mercy that was spread on all
from it [the nation] He chose twelve men
and others, two and seventy,

[3] and again He chose from the twelve apostles,
Simon and the two brothers,[16]
that they might observe His mysteries
more than all the disciples.

[4] On the mountain of Tabor, He brought them,[17]
He brought them up to the top.
His kingship He showed to them,
His glory was revealed before their eyes.

[5] The two brothers were the ones
whose mother had asked Him,[18]
that they would sit on his sides, both of them
Higher than all the disciples.

[6] When He ascended to the top of the mountain
His marvelous glory changed,
all of Him became brilliant with light,[19]
the sun and moon were darker than Him.

---

[15] See Heb 1:3.
[16] See Matt 17:1-13; Mark 9:2-13; Luke 9:28-36.
[17] See Josh 19:22.
[18] See Matt 20:20-21; Mark 10:35.
[19] See Matt 17:2; Mark 9:3; Luke 9:29.

[7] ܚܠܝܟ ܝܘܡܐ ܦܨܝܚܐ. ܘܫܡܝܢ ܘܝܘܡܐ ܚܕܝܢܐ.
ܘܐܬܡܠܝ ܡܢ ܣܘܥܪܢܗ ܢܒܝܐ. ܘܫܪܝ[20] ܥܡܗ ܡܕܒܪܢܐ ܘܐܘܟܐ ⁘

[8] ܐܬܓܠܝ ܐܡܝܢܐ ܒܥܘܒܕܘܗܝ. ܘܐܬܓܠܝ ܢܘܗܪܗ ܒܥܘܗܕܢܗ.[21]
ܘܐܬܚܙܝ ܘܝܘܡܐ ܒܝܘܡܘܗܝ. ܘܢܦܩ ܙܥܘܪܐ ܠܐܬܩܛܢܘܗܝ ⁘

[9] ܠܥܘܬܪܘܗܝ[22] ܟܠ ܡܫܡܫܝܢ ܗܘܘ. ܐܦ ܒܢܝܐ ܕܗܘܢ ܡܬܠܡܕܝܢ ܗܘܘ.
ܘܬܪܥܘܬܗ ܡܬܚܙܝܢ ܗܘܘ. ܘܫܡܥܬܐ ܠܗ ܡܫܬܡܗܝܢ ܗܘܘ ⁘

[10] ܐܦ ܠܣܘܥܪܢܐ ܀ ܕܡܕܒܪܢܘܬܐ. ܕܟܠܗ ܥܠܘܗܝ ܡܕܒܪܢܘܬܐ.[23] [f. 248r]
ܘܠܐ ܡܬܚܙܝܢܐ ⌈ܒܚܒܝܒܘܬܐ. ܕܡܬܚܙܝܐ ܠܥܠܡܐ ܚܕܬܐ⌉[24] ⁘

[11] ܣܘܥܪܢܐ ܗܘܐ ܕܠܐ ܡܬܚܙܝܢܐ.[25] ܕܡܘܬܐ ܗܘܐ ܕܠܐ[26] ܡܬܒܪܝܢܐ.
ܘܠܗ ܠܗ ܦܨܝܚܐ ܘܠܐ ܕܘܡܝܐ. ܒܟܠܗ ܐܘܪܚܐ ܗܝܟܠ ܚܕܝܐ ⁘

[12] ܘܟܕ ܥܠܝܡܐ ܡܬܬܦܩܕܝܢ ܗܘܘ. ܘܒܣܘܥܪܢܐ ܡܬܬܥܝܪܝܢ ܗܘܘ.
ܘܦܪܥܝܢ ܗܘܘ[27] ܘܡܬܬܪܥܝܢ ܗܘܘ. ܘܢܦܩ ܥܒܕܝܢ ܠܗ ܢܨܚܝܢ ܗܘܘ ⁘

[13] ܐܬܐ[28] ܡܘܥܕܐ ܘܐܬܠܝܛ. ܚܕ ܡܘܬܐ ܘܐܣܝܪ[29] ܚܝܐ.
ܘܫܡܗ[30] ܒܢܝܗܘܢ ܡܢ ܥܠܡܐ. ܘܦܠܓܗ ܠܗܘܢ ܒܣܒܪܬܐ ⁘

[14] ܠܒܢܐ ܡܘܥܕܐ ܥܡ ܦܘܠܚܢ ܗܘܬ. ܘܥܒܕܐ ܗܘܬ ܥܡ ܐܒܐ ܗܘܬ.
ܘܡܥܡܘܕܐ ܢܟܪܝܐ ܠܟܠ ܗܘܬ. ܡܛܠ ܡܛܪܢ ܘܐܒܐ ܗܘܬ ⁘

[20] D3 ܘܫܪܝܗ.
[21] B2 marg. b.
[22] D3 ܠܥܘܬܪܘܗܝ followed by ܥܘܬܪܗ have been added later by the copyist.
[23] C1 b has been added later by the copyist.
[24] ⌈ C2 marg. ܒܚܒܝܒܘܬܐ. ܕܡܬܚܙܝܐ ܠܥܠܡܐ ܚܕܬܐ.
[25] C2 marg. a.
[26] D3 +X ܡܬܚܙܝܢܐ.
[27] C1, D2 ܟܕ.
[28] D2 ܘܐܬܐ.
[29] B2 ܘܐܣܝܪ.
[30] M3 ܘܫܡܗ.

[7] He changed His bodily looking,[31]
and He showed His heavenly splendor.
The eye turned blind because of seeing Him,
the knowledge and mind were afraid of Him.

[8] The sun was hidden by His beauty,
the light was abolished by His light,
His splendor was hidden by His magnificence,
His light covered His bodily appearance.

[9] His clothes became very white,[32]
His garments were like snow,
His limbs were shining,
and they could not be seen with the eye.

[10] O the sight of the miracle
that was full of miracles!
It cannot be seen with the pupils of the eye,
but it was seen by the company of the apostles.

[11] A vision that cannot be seen,
an image that has no likeness,
has no likeness and similarity,
in all that is under the sky.

[12] The apostles were amazed
and were astonished by the vision;
they were frightened and overwhelmed,
they did not know where they stayed.

[13] Moses and Elijah came,[33]
one is dead and the other alive;
they[34] stood among them suddenly
and they spoke with the only-begotten one.

[14] Moses answered, crying aloud,
he cried aloud and said,
He was revealed like a servant
before the Lord of all, and he said:

[31] See Matt 17:2; Mark 9:2; Luke 9:29.
[32] See Matt 17:2; Mark 9:3; Luke 9:29.
[33] See Matt 17:3; Mark 9:4; Luke 9:30.
[34] The text in M3 is to be preferred here, since it mentions Christ standing among them (Moses and Elijah). See note 30.

[15] ܐܦ ܡܢ ܟܠ ܡܕܡ ܡܚܣܢܝ. ܚܘܣܐ ܠܚܛܝܐ ܗܘ ܡܚܣܢܝ.
ܬܘܕܝܬܐ ܒܝܫܬܐ ܗܘ ܫܘܒܚܝ. ܐܡܪܬ ܕܠܟܐ ܕܢܩܒܐ ܠܚܣܘܟܝ ❖

[16] ܐܒܘܗ ܡܚܕܐܣ ܐܬܕܡܝܘ. ܘܡܢ ܚܝܕܐܝ ܐܟܣ ܐܢܘܢ.
ܘܒܝܡܐ ܐܚܟܪ ܐܢܘܢ. ܘܡܫܬܐ ܡܢ ܥܡܬܐ ܢܘܚ ܠܗܘܢ ❖

[17] ܘܡܬܐ ܡܢ ܓܘܦܐ ܗܦܟ ܠܗܘܢ. ܘܡܢ ܢܡܬܐ ܫܠܗܝ ܒܥܐ ܠܗܘܢ.
ܘܒܝܬܐ ܢܠܛܘܗܝ ܠܥܕܪܗܘܢ. ܘܢܘܚܘ[35] ܠܓܪܕܐ ܥܡܬܐ ܕܐܠܗܘܢ ❖

[18] ܒܐܒܘܗ ܚܟܡܐ ܐܬܚܬܢܘܢ. ܘܠܥܡܗܘܢ ܕܠܒܟܝ ܗܒܘ.
ܥܘܒܕܐ ܠܝ ܡܬܐ ܣܘܟܐ ܒܗܘܢ. ܕܢܓܠܐ ܠܡܚܟܡܐ ܒܢܝܗܘܢ ❖

[19] ܐܠܐ ܕܫܡܥܝ ܥܩܬܐ. ܕܢܫܡܥܘܢ ܠܥܘܕܪܝ ܐܕܝܐ.
ܘܠܡܒܝܫܘ ܠܚܫܘܟܬܐ. ܘܠܡܟܠܐܘ ܠܡܫܝܚܐ ❖

[20] ܙܕܩ ܠܝ ܥܕܪܐ ܙܕܩ ܠܝ. ܕܒܫܡܥܝ ܚܫܟܐ ܕܒܠܝ.
ܦܪܘܩ ܠܐܕܡ ܐܚܝ ܕܦܝܐ ܠܝ. ܕܙܒܢܐ ܠܗ ܕܡܫܝܚܐ ܠܝ ❖

[21] ܗܝܟܠ ܫܘܒܚ ܚܢܐ ܠܝ. ܒܦܚ ܙܕܝܩܐ ܒܟܐ ܠܝ.
ܫܠܟܒܘܕܡ ܚܘܡܪܐ ܕܠܒܟ ܠܝ. ܐܒܕܘܡ ܗܘ ܡܫܝܚ ܠܝ ❖ [f. 248v]

[35] D2 ܘܢܘܚܘ.

[15] 'O You who are higher than all, who made You low?
O hidden one, who made You visible?
O light, who showed You in the darkness,
where no one wishes to see You?

[16] Your Father sent me towards them,
He moved them out from Egypt,
He made them pass through the sea,
and He gave them manna from the sky.[36]

[17] He brought forth for them water from the rock,[37]
He gathered for them quails from the sea,[38]
they replaced their Lord with a calf,[39]
and gave to a bull the name of their God.

[18] Their fathers denied Your Father,
and they were longing for Your death.
Glory to You! What did You see in them,
that You came to live among them?

[19] Unless Your heavenly mercy
brought You to redeem the earthly beings,
to forgive the sinners
and to make the poor rich.[40]

[20] It is right for You, my Lord, it is right
that by Your mercy You visit what is Yours,
redeem Adam as it is fitting for You
because he is waiting for You for a long time.[41]

[21] Abel, Your witness, is looking at You,
Noah, the righteous, is seeking You,
Melchizedek, Your high priest, is longing for You,
Abraham is yearning for You.

---

[36] See Exod 16:35.
[37] See Exod 17:1-7; Num 20:2-9.
[38] See Num 11:13.
[39] See Exod 32:4.
[40] See Luke 1:53.
[41] See 1 Pet 3:19-20, 4:6. Here the poet is mixes imagery from the transfiguration and Christ's descent into the Hades.

[22] ܐܬܚܫܡ ܘܐܬܒܣܡ ܫܒܩ ܠܟ. ܐܘܪܗܝ ܘܣܘܕ ܕܐܬܝܬ ܠܟ.[42]
ܘܐܦ ܡܘܬܐ ܠܐ ܚܙܐ ܠܟ. ܠܐ ܫܡܥ ܠܗܘܢ ܕܚܙܝܢ ܠܟ܀

[23] ܗܐ ܣܓܝܐܐ ܥܠ ܥܘܩܒܝܗܘܢ. ܗܘܠܟܝܐ ܫܕܝܐ ܦܓܪܝܗܘܢ.
ܦܪܘܣ ܐܣܝܪܐ ܒܠܒܗܘܢ. ܘܡܘܬܐ ܢܓܕ ܘܡܛܐ ܠܗܘܢ܀

[24] ܗܐ ܓܦܬܐ ܒܗܝ ܣܦܘܬܗܘܢ. ܘܟܣܝܢܐ ܥܠ ܐܦܝܗܘܢ.
ܘܡܚܠܬܗܘܢ ܥܠ ܦܬܝܗܘܢ. ܘܡܪܪܐ ܒܠܗ ܝܬܝܪܬܗܘܢ܀

[25] ܣܦܩ ܠܦܬܗܘܢ ܦܪܘܩ ܐܢܝ. ܘܡܢ ܚܫܘܟܐ ܢܦܩ[43] ܐܢܝ.
ܕܦܪܩܗܘܢ ܐܢܐ ܘܡܬܟܢܫ ܐܢܘܢ. ܘܡܘܬܐ ܓܠܐ ܦܓܥ ܐܢܝ܀

[26] ܘܝܠܕܐ ܘܐܡܪ ܝܠܒܐ. ܟܕ ܡܟܐ ܕܫܒܥܬܐ ܘܡܣܟܢܐ.
ܡܢ ܐܚܪ ܗܘ ܢܗܪܐ. ܘܐܬܪܘܝ ܕܠܐ ܢܕܢܚ ܠܥܕܬܐ܀

[27] ܦܢ ܐܠܗܐܝܢ ܐܦ ܢܦܩܬܐ. ܝܗܒ ܓܡܪܐ ܕܠܗܘܢ ܒܗ ܚܣܝܪܐ.
ܘܡܢ ܟܘܪܗ ܝܬܪܗ ܝܬܐ. ܕܫܒܩܝܗ ܒܗ ܥܠ ܐܘܠܨܢܐ܀

[28] ܒܐܘܪܫܠܡ ܡܬܒܠܒܠܝܢ ܢܒܝ̈ܐ. ܒܝܘܡܝ ܪܒܩܝܢ ܦܪܘܩܢ.
ܥܘܒܕܐ ܠܟ ܒܦܪܐ ܫܒܝܗ ܕܣܡܝܢ. ܕܠܡܫܝܚܐ ܚܘܒܐ ܐܦܝܢ܀

[29] ܦܠܝܛܘ ܢܒܝ̈ܐ ܒܗ ܒܘܡܪܝܢ. ܘܫܝܩܘ ܡܕܝܢ̈ܬܐ ܒܗ ܐܬܘܫܢ.
ܘܬܢܝ ܠܫܘܦܪܗ ܠܒܢܝܢ. ܘܐܬܚܒܒ ܠܟ ܦܠܓܠܫܪܝܢ܀

[42] D3 +X ܗܐ ܣܓܝܐܐ ܥܠ ܥܘܩܒܝܗܘܢ. ܗܘܠܟܝܐ.
[43] M3 marg.

[22] Isaac and Jacob are looking for You,
Aaron and Hur[44] are longing for You,
and if death does not see You,
it [death] will not allow them to see You.

[23] Behold, the corruption of their beauty,
worms damaging their bodies,
Sheol holding them,
and death is sitting and guarding them.

[24] Behold, the dust on their lips,
and the ashes on their faces,
their tears on their cheeks,
and bitterness on their palate.

[25] Descend to them and release them,
and take them out from prison,
because You are their Lord and they are Your servants
and death humiliated them a great deal.'

[26] Elijah screamed and said,
screaming with tears and weeping
about Ahab, the sinner[45]
and Jezebel, who did not know the Lord:[46]

[27] 'What brought You, O You merciful one,
towards a nation that has no compassion,
I escaped from it
because I endured in it affliction.

[28] In Jerusalem, Your prophets were killed,[47]
in Zion, Your preachers were persecuted,
glory to You, how great is Your mercy,[48]
that You showed Your face to those who hate You.

[29] They murdered Your prophets and Your high priests,
they cast down Your altars and Your temples
and they want to destroy Your life
to stone You and Your disciples.

---

[44] See Exod 17:10.
[45] See 1 Kgs 16:30.
[46] See 1 Kgs 18:4.
[47] See Matt 23:37; Luke 13:34.
[48] See Ps 36:8, 119:156.

[30] ܐܝܟܢ ܫܒܩ ܡܪܡܪܘܬܝ. ܘܬܒܥܬܐ ܠܥܝܢܝ ܕܢܩܦܬܝ.
ܘܐܢ ܢܫܒܘܩ ܠܐ ܦܪܥܘܬܝ. ܢܬܒܥ ܕܝܢܐ ܐܢܬܬܝ:

[31] ܐܘܪܫܠܡ ܗܐ[49] ܠܚܝܡܐ ܠܝ. ܡܛܘܠ ܗܐ ܢܘܚܐ ܠܫܠܠܝ.
ܘܐܝܟ ܐܝܟܢ ܗܐ ܕܠܒܫܝܢ ܠܝ. ܗܐ ܢܫܒܚ ܐܢܐ ܡܘܕܝܐ ܠܝ:

[32] ܢܦܩܬ ܠܝ ܒܪܬ ܩܠܐ ܠܝ. ܕܡܦܪܣܐ ܠܢܦܫܝ ܒܗ ܣܘܦܝ.
ܕܡܒܗܘ ܒܟܠ ܦܪܕܝ / ܘܦܬܚܘ ܠܝ. ܘܢܦܩܬܗܘܢ ܫܠܡܘܬ ܠܝ: [f. 249r]

[33] ܗܠܝܢ ܫܠܐ ܡܫܬܠܠܝܢ ܗܘܘ. ܘܐܝܟ ܗܠܝܢ ܫܡܥܝܢ ܗܘܘ.
ܘܒܠܝܠܝܐ ܡܨܠܝܢ ܗܘܘ. ܒܫܡܐ ܕܫܘܝܢ ܗܘܘ ܘܡܫܟܢܝܢ ܗܘܘ:

[34] ܫܠܡ ܗܘܐ ܫܡܥܐ[50] ܒܟܠܗܘܢ. ܘܡܘܡܬܐ ܢܦܠܬ ܒܟܠܗܘܢ.
ܘܡܬܘܪܐ ܡܬܡܨܝܐ ܢܦܠ ܒܟܠܗܘܢ. ܒܥܘܗܕܐ ܕܟܠ ܫܠܡ ܒܠܒܐ ܒܟܠܗܘܢ:

[35] ܒܢܐ ܫܡܥܘܢ ܦܦܫܝܛܘܬܐ. ܘܐܡܪ ܗܘܐ ܦܩܝܕܘܬܐ.
ܡܫܬܡܥܝܢ ܩܪܝ ܒܗܕܐ ܕܘܟܬܐ. ܕܗܕܐ ܐܝܬܝܗ ܦܠܚܘܬܐ:

[36] ܠܝ ܐܡܪ ܐܢܬ[51] ܫܡܥܝܢ.[52] ܦܬܠܐ ܩܫܠܠܐ ܠܡܕܝܢ.
ܚܙܐ ܠܝ ܩܪܝ ܦܬܫܡܥܝܢ. ܘܬܩܬܢ ܠܪܘܚܗܘܢ ܕܩܢܝܢ:

[37] ܐܪ ܫܡܥܘܢ[53] ܩܪܐ ܦܫܝܛܐ. ܢܚܝܡܐ ܕܐܝܬܘܗܝ ܡܠܝܬܐ.
ܕܥܘܗܕܐ ܚܘܐ ܐܝܟ ܡܪܡܘܬܐ. ܘܫܘܠ ܡܫܬܠܠܐ ܕܠܐ ܫܠܝܐ:

[49] M3 ܗܐ has been added later by the copyist.
[50] D1, C1, C2, D2 ܫܡܥܐ.
[51] D3 marg.
[52] C1 + ܚܝܠ.
[53] C2 ܫܡܥܘܢ with the letter ܒ added later by the copyist.

[30] Jezebel saddened me greatly,
she persecuted me as far as Sinai;[54]
if Your right hand had not saved me,
the people of Naboth would have destroyed me.[55]

[31] Behold, Jerusalem is threatening You,
Behold, Zion is thirsty after Your death,
Behold, they will stone you like Jezebel;
how good You are! Glory to You.

[32] How beautiful, beautiful of You,
to redeem Your servants by Your love,
who died in the hope of You and believed in You,
and their souls took refuge in You.'

[33] These words they said,
similar ones, they repeated,
the apostles were astonished
about what they saw and heard.

[34] The sun fell on them,[56]
and sleep seized them,[57]
wonder and amazement fell on them
because of the light that suddenly prevailed over them.

[35] Simon answered simply
and said with joy:
'Leave us, Lord, in this place
because this is the kingdom.

[36] If you will, we will stand up,
and make three tents,[58]
one we will put for You, O Lord,
and two for the guests of Him who gives us life.'

[37] O Simon, simple older man,
wise and skillful,
who saw the light as a cloak of light,
and asked for tents without fear.

---

[54] See 1 Kgs 19:1-3.
[55] See 1 Kgs 21.
[56] See fn. 50, where some manuscripts read 'sleep' instead of 'sun', apparently adapting the text of the poet to the NT.
[57] See Luke 9:32.
[58] See Matt 17:4; Mark 9:5; Luke 9:33.

[38] ܒܗܘ ܝܘܡܐ ܢܬܚܙܐ ܗܘܢܗ. ܘܡܢ ܝܘܡܗ ܫܪܝ ܠܒܗ.
ܘܟܠ ܗܘ ܡܠܟ ܠܗܢܗ. ܢܦܩ ܕܠܐ ܢܥܒܕ ܢܥܒܕܗ ܀

[39] ܘܡܢ ܕܐܡܪ ܗܘܝܢ ܢܦܫܗܘܢ. ܗܐ ܚܙܝܐ ܐܠܗܐ ܚܠܦܝܗܘܢ.
ܦܪܘܫܘܬܗ[59] ܦܫܛ ܐܝܕܝ. ܘܒܪܘܟܬܗ ܐܬܒܗ ܦܪܝܫܘܬܗܘܢ ܀

[40] ܘܫܒܩ ܡܘܬܐ ܘܐܠܗܐ. ܘܫܠܡ ܢܬܦܬܚ ܡܢ ܥܡܢܐ.
ܕܗܘܐ ܦܪܝ ܚܝܒܐ. ܠܗ ܢܣܓܕܘܢ ܒܠܗܘܢ ܒܢܝܐ ܀

[41] ܒܠ ܐܠܗܘܬܗ ܚܒܝܒ ܗܘܐ. ܘܟܠ ܡܠܟܘܬܗ ܐܘܕܥ ܗܘܐ.
ܗܢܘܢ ܒܡܘܬܐ ܕܢܦܫܗ ܗܘܐ. ܘܐܠܗܐ ܕܦܓܪܗ ܫܒܩ ܗܘܐ ܀

[42] ܠܡܘܬܐ ܡܝܬܐ ܢܝܚ ܗܘܐ. ܕܢܘܕܥ ܕܝܠܗ ܐܡܝܬܗ ܗܘܐ.
ܘܐܠܗܐ ܡܢ ܚܕܝ ܕܒܪ ܗܘܐ. ܕܢܦܩ ܠܗܘܢ ܕܝܠܗ ܦܓܪܗ ܗܘܐ ܀

[43] ܢܣܒܘܢ ⌈ܡܝܬܐ ܚܕ ܚܝܐ⌉.[60] [61]ܕܦܓܪܐ ܗܘ ܕܡܝܬܐ ܦܪܝܫܐ.
ܠܗ ܢܦܫܗܘܢ ܡܝܬܐ ܘܚܝܐ. ܕܒܐܝܕܘܗܝ ܦܘܩܕܢܐ ܐܦ ܚܝܐ ܀

[44] ܢܘܗܪܐ ܠܐ ܡܬܚܙܝܢܐ. ܕܢܬܓܠܐ ܢܘܗܪ ܒܥܠܡܢܐ.
/ ܚܝܐ ܠܟܠܢ ܡܬܦܢܝܐ. ܢܘܦܪܘ ܒܥܠܡܐ ܕܪܚܡܐ ܀ [f. 249v]

[45] ܒܗܝ ܡܠܟܘܬܐ ܥܬܝܕܬܐ
ܕܠܟܢ ܠܗ ܒܗܝ ܢܦܠܛܐ ܕܡܘܬܐ[62]
ܦܫܛ ܠܟܠܢ ܦܪܝܫܘܬܐ
ܘܠܢ ܢܬܦܬܚ ܒܐܝܕܘܬܐ[63] ܀

---

[59] M3 ܦܪܘܫܘܬܗ.
[60] ⌉ D3 written ܚܝܐ ܚܕ ܡܝܬܐ with the sequence corrected by placing ܐ on ܡܝܬܐ ܚܕ.
[61] D1 +X ܚܕ.
[62] B2 marg.
[63] B2 – the letter ܒ.

[38] His mind was captivated by that vision,
his eye became blind because of seeing Him,
about this, his tongue said something
that his intellect did not grasp.

[39] When Simon said these things,
behold, the cloud overshadowed them,[64]
and covered them with its light,
and their minds were astonished by its beauty.

[40] He made Moses and Elijah go away,
and a voice was heard from the sky:[65]
'This is my only-begotten Son,
to Him all the creatures give worship.'

[41] He revealed His divinity,
and made known His kingship,
our Lord, with Moses, whom He had raised up,
and Elijah, who was present with Him.

[42] He raised the dead Moses,
to show that He had made him die,
and from Eden He brought Elijah,
to teach them that He brought him here.

[43] The dead and the living screamed,
that He is the Lord of dead and living,
the dead and the living glorify Him,
because in His hands are death and life.

[44] The invisible light
that was revealed today in the [feast of the] transfiguration,
show to the miserable composer,
Your beauty in the spiritual world.

[45] In that heavenly kingdom,
that has no likeness in this world,
cheer us all in this gathering,
glory to You always!

---

[64] See Matt 17:5; Mark 9:7; Luke 9:34.
[65] See Matt 17:5; Mark 9:7; Luke 9:35.

CHAPTER FOUR: COMMENTARY

INTRODUCTION

The outlook of Syriac writers (both East and West Syriac) before the Mongol conquest and after it was markedly different, especially in terms of Christology. Prior to the conquest, some East-Syriac writers condemned the Syriac Orthodox and Chalcedonians as heretics. Thus, in كتاب البرهان *The Book of Demonstration*, Ēlīā of Nisibis defended East-Syriac Christology while condemning the Syriac Orthodox and Chalcedonians, calling them enemies of truth. He seemed to be more concerned about maintaining a good relationship with Muslims about doing so with other Christians. The East-Syriac writer Bar Zōʿbay had the same outlook as Ēlīā.[1]

Some West-Syriac writers also bore animosity toward the East-Syriac Christians as well as Chalcedonians, Armenians, Copts and Latins. In ܟܬܒܐ ܕܣܝܡܬܐ *The Book of Treasures,* Severus Bar Šakkū gave a clear description of the different Christological heresies. He held the same opinion as Dionysius Bar Ṣalībī did in ܟܬܒܐ ܕܕܘܪܫܐ *The Book of Controversies*, arguing that only the Syriac Orthodox community was orthodox and that all others were heretics. Dionysius also condemned the Armenians but was more respectful of the Latins.[2]

However, this antagonistic approach to other Christians came to an end when later theologians realised that the divisions among Christians were more a terminological or political problem rather than evidence of genuine Christological differences.[3]

An example of this change is ʿAbdīšōʿ bar Brīḫā, who expresses some understanding for the council of Chalcedon in his ܡܪܓܢܝܬܐ *The Pearl.* Similarly, in the West Syriac tradition we have كتاب الحمامة *The Book of the Dove,* written by Bar ʿEbrāyā, which expresses the futility of discussions on natures.[4]

---

[1] H. Teule, "The Syriac Renaissance and inner-Christian Relations" (forthcoming).

[2] H. Teule, "The Syriac Renaissance and inner-Christian Relations" (forthcoming).

[3] H. Teule, "The Syriac Renaissance and inner-Christian Relations" (forthcoming).

[4] ʿAbdīšōʿ B. Brīḫā, ܡܪܓܢܝܬܐ [The Pearl], p. 24; B. ʿEbrāyā, كتاب الحمامة [The Book of the Dove], p. 148.

What was the underlying rationale for this new way of 'ecumenical' thinking (to use a modern term)? In part, the reality of persecution may have united Christians who faced a common fate. It may well be that the monotheism of the Turko-Mongolians also played a role. They believed in the sky God, Tengri. Ǧengīz Ḫān had decreed in 1206 that all religions were to be respected, without exalting one over another, because they all believe in one God, a view which might have been influenced by missionaries of the Church of the East.[5] Mōngki, the brother of Hūlāgū, advocated religious tolerance. He warned everyone about using quarrelsome or injurious words towards other religions, on pain of death.[6] Before the Mongol era, Christological discussions between the different Christian groups were very divisive, with each sect trying to defend its belief against the other. During the Mongol period, the West Syriac writer Bar ʿEbrāyā praised the East Syriac patriarch Yahḇālāhā III, for being open to all churches.[7]

Perhaps when Christians realized that the pagan Mongols believed in one God, it inspired them to proclaim religious tolerance and to respect the different religions in the empire themselves. This in turn may have helped Christians to think twice about the core of Christianity and the importance of tolerance.

Nevertheless, some authors continued to think along traditional lines. This is even true of the most 'ecumenical' authors, Bar ʿEbrāyā and Bar Brīḫā, who displayed more traditional views in some of their writings.[8]

This chapter examines the theological terminology found in the hymns of 'Gīwargīs Wardā', with a special focus on his Christology. The chapter aims at studying the poet's thinking, more specifically whether it is in line with the theological teaching of the East-Syriac Church, bearing in mind when reading the hymns that they were meant to be used as meditations on the liturgical year, with an intensive focus on the Bible, and were not composed as theological treatises. There are only two hymns (71, 72) that can be considered particularly theological. In order to determine our poet's theological views, it has been necessary to consider not only those hymns translated in chapter 3, but also some additional hymns. The poet's views will be compared with other important authors of the East-Syriac Church and other poets of the same period whose hymns are included in the *Book of Wardā*.[9]

Gīwargīs was condemned by the Synod of Diamper in 1599, along with the poet Ḫāmīs bar Qardāḥē.[10] This Synod was organized by the Portuguese in order to bring the local Syriac Thomas Christians, at that period living under the authority of the

---

[5] S.H. Moffett, *A History of Christianity in Asia*, p. 401.
[6] C. Baumer, *The Church of the East*, pp. 195-196.
[7] B. ʿEbrāyā, ܡܟܬܒ ܕܐܩܠܝܣܝܣܛܝܩܘܢ [The Ecclesiastical Chronicle], p. 462.
[8] H. Teule, "Gregory Bar ʿEbroyo and ʿAbdishoʿ Bar Brikha," pp. 543-551.
[9] In this chapter we shall analyze the Christological themes found in the hymns translated in the third chapter, as well as other hymns contained in the *Book of Wardā*. The stanzas that contain a Christological theme found in the hymns (either by Gīwargīs or by other authors) that are not translated in the third chapter will be translated in this chapter. Other hymns that are translated already by other authors, are referred to in the footnotes, which can also be found in Table 8.
[10] H. Hilgenfeld, *Ausgewählte Gesänge des Giwargis Warda von Arbil*, p. 7.

Church of the East, in line with Roman post-Tridentine teachings. The text of the condemnation mentions the following:

> 'Also the book entitled 'Uguarda', or 'the Rose'; wherein it is said, That there are two persons in Christ; that the union of the incarnation was accidental; that our lady brought forth with pain; and the sons of Joseph, which he had by his other wife, being in company, went for a midwife to her, with other blasphemies.
>
> Also the book entitled 'Camiz'; wherein it is said that the Divine Word, and the Son of the virgin are not the same, and that our lady brought forth with pain.'[11]

In contrast to the Synod of Diamper, Bachi argues that the hymns of Gīwargīs Wardā were written by order of an ecclesiastical authority to reform the liturgy as part of preparations for the East-Syriac Church to unite with Rome.[12] The unity mentioned by Bachi may perhaps be the one proposed by Catholicos Sabrīšōᶜ V bar Mšīḥāyā (1226-1256) in 1247, during the reign of Pope Innocent IV. The aim of this proposal was, however, more largely political, in order to obtain the support of the Mongols against the Muslims, since many Christians occupied important positions in the Mongol administration and army.[13]

In order to determine whether the Synod of Diamper, which accused the *Book of Wardā* of 'Nestorianism', or Bachi, who viewed Gīwargīs as a link between West and East, was correct, it is necessary to analyze the Christology in the *Book of Wardā*. This is still one of the lacunas in recent research on Wardā.[14] Our analysis will begin with some technical theological terms used by Gīwargīs.

1. TECHNICAL TERMS

1.1 Qnōmā ܩܢܘܡܐ

The poet uses the word *qnōmā* to indicate two things.[15] The first use is to indicate the three *qnōmē* of the Trinity. For example, in Hymn 7.(72)[11, 23ab], stanza [11], we find the poet referring to the Word as the second *qnōmā* of the Trinity. In Hymn 9.(78)[1ef], the three *qnōmē* of the Trinity are mentioned as having one essence. Finally, in Hymn 15.(97)[20, 32], Gīwargīs depicts the conversation between Jesus

---

[11] S. Zacharia, *The Acts and Decrees*, pp. 100-101. Note the different ways that the names of both Gīwargīs and Ḥāmīs are written in the text of condemnation.

[12] P.H. Bachi, "Marie dans la doctrine de Ghiwarghis Warda," pp. 276-281.

[13] C. Baumer, *The Church of the East*, pp. 216-220.

[14] I am very grateful to have had access to the critical edition of Anton Pritula, *The Wardā*, which has been extremely helpful to my work. Note that slight differences can be found in the translation of some verses, because of different interpretations I have adopted in order to address Christological theme.

[15] Only some hymns containing these themes and expressions are quoted here, in order to avoid excessive repetition.

and the Samaritan woman in poetical terms, freely paraphrasing the New Testament and mentioning the Trinity as well as the three *qnōmē*.[16]

The poet's second use of *qnōmā* is to indicate a person,[17] self or body, as in Hymn (23)[48a], which refers to the women of Sodom and Gomorrah when using their *qnōmē* (bodies) to seduce men:

'ܥܘܢܝܬܐ (23). <u>ܡܟܬܒܢܐ ܕܥܬܝܩܘܬܐ</u>
[48] ܦܚܐ ܥܒܕ ܗܘܝ ܩܢܘܡܝܗܝܢ.'

'Hymn (23). <u>The chronicler of antiquities</u>
[48] They [the women] made their *qnōmē* traps.'[18]

Many times the poet refers to himself in these hymns as *qnōmā,* such as in Hymn (35) [1ef]:

'ܥܘܢܝܬܐ (35). <u>ܒܓܘܡܨܐ ܕܥܘܠܐ ܢܦܠܬ ܐܢܐ</u>
[1] ܕܪܥܟ ܪܒܐ ܘܚܣܝܢܐ. ܐܘܫܛ ܠܩܢܘܡܝ ܡܚܝܠܐ܀'

'Hymn (35). <u>I fall in the pit of iniquity</u>
[1] Stretch out Your great and powerful arm to my weak *qnōmā*.'

The poet does not mention the two *qnōmē* formula when referring to the two natures of Christ; it seems enough for him to say that Christ has two natures. This reminds us of the professions of faith made before the Synod of 612, when the formula of 'two natures, two *qnōmē* in one person' became the official teaching of the East-Syriac Church.[19] Other East-Syriac writers and works that mention the two natures without emphasizing the two *qnōmē* include certain homilies of Narsai (5th cent.)[20]

---

[16] The use of dialogue in hymns is a very familiar characteristic of Syriac poetry. See S.P. Brock, "Syriac Dialogue Poems: Marginalia to a Recent Edition"; S.P. Brock, "A Dispute of the Months and Some Related Syriac Texts"; S.P. Brock, "Dramatic Dialogue Poems"; S.P. Brock, "The Sinful woman and Satan"; S.P. Brock, "Syriac Poetry on Biblical Theme. 1. The Prophet Elijah and the Widow of Sarepta"; S.P. Brock, "Syriac Dispute Poems: The Various Types"; S.P. Brock, "Two Syriac dialogue poems on Abel and Cain"; S.P. Brock, "The dispute poem: From Sumer to Syriac"; S.P. Brock, "The dialogue between the two thieves (Luke 23:39-41)"; S.P. Brock, *Mary and Joseph and other dialogue poems on Mary*.

[17] The dictionary of Bar Bahlūl (10th cent.), defines *qnōmā* as 'person', which goes well with what we find in this hymn. R. Duval, *Lexicon Syriacum Auctore Hassano Bar Bahlule*, pp. 1804-1805.

[18] A. Pritula, *The Wardā*, p. 263. Translation slightly adapted.

[19] S.P. Brock, "The Christology of the Church of the East," pp. 133, 135; B. Ebeid, "The Christology of the Church of the East," pp. 353-402. Ebeid states that the East-Syriac church adopted the Nestorian faith officially under Bābāi the Great in 612 while Winkler mentions that the Nestorian faith was recognized earlier in the synods of Bēṯ Lapat (484) and Seleucia-Ctesiphon (486), noting that this opinion is not accepted according to the sources. See: W. Baum and D.W. Winkler, *The Church of the East*, pp. 28, 39.

[20] For examples of the use of *qnōmā* in Narsai's homilies, see F.G. McLeod, *Narsai's Metrical Homilies*, a homily on Nativity, p. 64, verse 440-444; p. 68, verse 505; J. Frishman, "Narsai's Christology," p. 299, fn. 16; F. Martin, "Homélie de Narses sur les trois docteurs nestoriens," *JA* 9.14 (1899), pp. 453, 471.

Ēlīā of Nisibis (10th cent.)[21] and some of the writings of ʿAbdīšōʿ bar Brīḫā (14th cent.), although other writings by ʿAbdīšōʿ are more traditional and speak of two natures and two *qnōmē*.[22] In the case of the encyclopedia أسفار الأسرار *I libri dei misteri* by the priest Ṣalībā of Mosul (14th cent.), the approach of two *qnōmē* can be noticed clearly as a general accepted Christological definition.[23] This is also true for the writings of Ēlīā II (12th cent.).[24] In the collection of manuscripts used for the present work, a hymn by Gabriel, metropolitan of Mosul (14th cent.) which mentions the two *qnōmē* has been inserted into the *Book of Wardā*:[25]

'ܥܘܢܝܬܐ (138). ܣܓܕܝܢ ܠܚܕܐ ܐܘܣܝܐ
[91] ܕܚܕ ܗܘ ܡܫܝܚܐ ܒܬܪܝܢ ܟܝܢܝܢ ܘܒܩܢܘܡܝܢ ܬܪܝܢ.'

'Hymn (138). We worship the one essence
[91] That Christ is one in two natures and in two *qnōmē*.'

Interestingly, Ḫāmīs bar Qardāḥē (+1252) whose hymns are always classified or collected with the hymns of our poet and who is known as the student of Gīwargīs Wardā,[26] in some hymns he uses the word *qnōmā* in the same way as Gīwargīs Wardā, referring to the poet himself,[27] but in other hymns, the two *qnōmē* formula is found:

'ܡܛܠ ܕܗܘܝܘ ܨܡܚܐ ܕܫܘܒܚܗ
ܕܚܕ ܗܘ ܡܫܝܚܐ. ܒܬܪܝܢ ܟܝܢܝܢ ܘܩܢܘܡܐ ܬܪܝܢ' [28]

'Because He [Christ] is the ray of His [the Father's] glory
That Christ is one,
in two natures and two *qnōmē*.'

Hymn (21)[1d-i], written by the priest Ṣalībā al-Manṣūrī (10th cent.), is about the story of Nestorius and also does not mention the two *qnōmē*. Nevertheless, the writer uses the word *parṣōpā* to indicate the person of assumption:

---

21 Ēlīā of Nisibis, تفسير الأمانة [Elias of Nisibis. Commentary], p. 60.
22 ʿAbdīšōʿ B. Brīḫā, كتاب فرائد الفوائد, *Testi teologici di Ebedjesu*, p. 256; H. Teule, "The Syriac Renaissance and inner-Christian Relations" (forthcoming).
23 Ṣalībā B. Yoḥannā, كتاب أسفار الأسرار, *I libri dei misteri*, pp. 567-568.
24 Ēlīā II, كتاب أصول الدين [The Book of Foundations of Religion], vol. I, p. 62.
25 Another anonymous hymn found in manuscript CHE1, ff. 286-290 (Baghdad, Church of the East Archbishop's collection) located in the supplement of the *Book of Wardā*, mentions the two *qnōmē* formula in the first stanza. This manuscript is not part of the collection used in this work but for the sake of completeness, I mention it here. The hymn starts with ܫܘܒܚܐ ܠܗ ܠܒܪܐ ܝܚܝܕܝܐ.
26 Ḥ.D.Ḫ. Al-Arbalī, القال والقيل في سلطان أربيل [Tittle-tattle about the Sultan of Erbil], pp. 146, 162, 189. The year of death of Ḫāmīs bar Qardāḥē is mentioned by Ḥ.D.Ḫ. Al-Arbalī.
27 Š.Ī. Ḥadbšabbā, ܚܡܝܣ ܒܪ ܩܪܕܚܐ [Ḫāmīs bar Qardāḥē], pp. 6, 100, 161.
28 Š.Ī. Ḥadbšabbā, ܚܡܝܣ ܒܪ ܩܪܕܚܐ [Ḫāmīs bar Qardāḥē], p. 14.

‘ܥܘܢܝܬܐ (21). ܐܘ ܡܫܩܦܝ ܥܠ ܬܘܕܝܬܐ

[1] ܚܕ ܟܝܢܐ ܒܩܢܘܡܐ ܬܠܬܐ. ܐܒܐ ܥܠܬܐ ܐܝܬܘܗܝ ܥܠܬܐ.
ܘܥܠܠܬܐ ܕܝܢ ܪܘܚܐ ܘܡܠܬܐ. ܕܥܡܪܐ ܒܡܥܘܗ̇ ܕܒܬܘܠܬܐ.
ܘܐܬܓܫܡ ܒܗ̇ ܕܠܐ ܙܘܘܓܘܬܐ. ܘܐܬܝܠܕ ܕܠܐ ܡܙܘܓܘܬܐ.
ܒܬܪܝܢ ܟܝܢܝܢ ܕܠܐ ܚܠܝܛܘܬܐ. ܘܗܟܢܐ ܒܩܢܘܡܐ ܕܬܠܝܬܝܘܬܐ.
ܒܚܕ ܦܪܨܘܦܐ ܕܢܣܒܘܬܐ.’

‘Hymn (21). O you who pursue the confession

[1] One nature in three *qnōmē*,
the Father is the cause,
the Spirit and the Word are the effects,
that inhabited the womb of the Virgin,
and incarnated in her without marriage,
and was born without intercourse,
in two natures without mingling,
likewise, in the *qnōmā* of the Trinity,
in one person of assumption.’

The profession of faith written by Īšōʿyāhb bar Malkōn (12th cent.) also does not mention the two *qnōmē*.[29] However, not mentioning the two *qnōmē* does not deny the concept; Herman Teule shows that Īšōʿyāhb in his treatise inserted into the أسفار الأسرار *I libri dei misteri*, has in mind the presupposed existence of the word *qnōmā*.[30] Gīwargīs also does not reject the two *qnōmē* outright, but it seems he has the same approach as Īšōʿyāhb. Similarly, a hymn attributed to Bābāi mentions that the two natures preserve their *qnōmē* in only one stanza, but in other stanzas the author just refers to the one person with two natures, without indicating the two *qnōmē*. Thus, when it comes to poetry, the poet is free to use certain terms or leave them out, depending on the meter.[31]

Hymn 19.(127)[7] the poet indicates another aspect of the concept of *qnōmā* when he refers to the angels whose *qnōmē* and eyes are uncountable. In Hymn (77)[33-35], stanza [33], the word *qnōmā* can be understood in two ways, either referring to the humanity of Christ, or to His divinity (if we take in consideration other verses that speak about divinity), and this can be seen as a Chalcedonian perspective.

‘ܥܘܢܝܬܐ (77). ܥܕ ܥܠ ܚܕܝ ܠܐܘܪܫܠܡ

[30] ܐܘܪܫܠܡ ܠܒܪ ܥܡ̈ܡܐ. ܕܐܬܩܛܠܘ ܒܓܘܗ̇ ܢܒܝ̈ܐ.
ܘܐܬܒ ܒܬܘܩܦܗ ܡܫܝܚܐ. ܫܒܪܐ ܠܡܝܬܐ ܐܢܫܐ ܀
[31] ܐܘܪܫܠܡ ܠܗܘ ܒܠܚܘܕܐ. ܒܪܐ ܠܒܘܕܐ ܘܠܐ ܚܒܪܐ.
ܕܠܝܬ ܠܗ ܡܢ ܟܠ ܚܒܪܐ. ܘܐܦ ܒܩܢܘܡܗ ܗܘܐ ܒܠܚܘܕܐ ܀
[32] ܐܘܪܫܠܡ ܠܐܠܗܘܬܐ. ܐܝܬܘܬܐ ܡܫܘܕܥܐ ܬܠܬܐ.
ܕܐܬܦܪܫ ܒܦܪܨܘܦܝܘܬܐ. ܠܡܠܐܟܐ ܘܠܐܢܫܘܬܐ ܀

[29] J.S. Assemani, *Bibliotheca Orientalis clementino-Vaticana*, ‘Jesujabus Episcopus Nisibis’, vol. III/1, p. 295.

[30] H. Teule, “A theological treatise by Išoʿyahb bar Malkon,” p. 238.

[31] T. Darmo, ed. *Ḥūḏrā* ܚܘܕܪܐ [The Cycle], vol. I, pp. ܩܝܚ - ܩܝܛ [118-119]; *Ktāḇā d-Tūrgāmē* ܟܬܒܐ ܕܬܘܪܓܡܐ [The Book of Interpretations], pp. ܩܝܗ - ܩܝܘ [115-116].

[33] ܐܘܫܥܢܐ ܠܗܘ ܕܒܩܢܘܡܗ. ܦܪܥ ܚܘܒܝ̈ ܕܒܢܝ̈ ܥܡܗ.
ܘܙܟܝܗ ܠܟܝܢܢ ܒܨܘܡܗ. ܕܡܚܐ ܒܡܘܟܠܐ ܕܐܒܘܗܝ ܘܕܐܡܗ ܀
[34] ܐܘܫܥܢܐ ܠܡܪܐ ܟܝܢܐ. ܕܪܟܒ ܥܝܪܐ ܒܝܬ ܥܦܪܢܐ.
ܘܐܫܬܒܚ ܡܢ ܝܠܘܕܐ. ܫܒܪ̈ܐ ܐܝܟ ܪ̈ܘܚܢܐ ܀
[35] ܐܘܫܥܢܐ ܠܠܐ ܚܫܘܫܐ. ܕܠܒܫ ܦܓܪܐ ܚܫܘܫܐ.
ܘܡܛܠ ܦܘܪܩܢ ܒܢܝ̈ܢܫܐ. ܐܫܠܡܗ ܠܡܘܬܐ ܘܠܚܫ̈ܐ ܀’

‘Hymn (77). When our Lord entered Jerusalem

[30] Hosanna to the Son of the Highest
who was manifested in human flesh
and granted by His annunciation
hope to the humankind!

[31] Hosanna to this born
Son-Creator, and not created
who made for Himself a worshipped temple
and was born of a virgin!

[32] Hosanna to the Godhead
the essence in three *qnōmē*
who were proclaimed ‘holy’ at the Baptism
by the angels and humankind!

[33] Hosanna to Him who in His *qnōmā*
returned His people’s sons’ debts
and conquered their nature by fasting,
which had become weak from the food of father and mother.

[34] Hosanna to the Lord of Natures
who sat on the donkey in the abode of the earthly
and was glorified by the infants,
defenseless and like angels!

[35] Hosanna to the passionless
who put on passionate flesh
for the sake of saving people,
who gave it up to death and sufferings.’[32]

The use of the word *qnōmā* to refer to humanity is also found in ܟܬܒܐ ܕܚܝܕܘܬܐ *The Book of the Union* by Bābāi (6th cent.) when he states that through the *qnōmā* of humanity, the priesthood of Christ sacrificed/expiated the sins of humanity.[33] The same idea is found in Hymn (82)[21] by our poet:

[32] A. Pritula, *The Wardā*, pp. 471-473. Translation slightly adapted.

[33] Bābāi, ܟܬܒܐ ܕܚܝܕܘܬܐ [The Book of the Union], p. 123:5.

'ܥܘܢܝܬܐ (82). ܒܪܐ ܡܠܬܐ ܝܚܝܕܝܐ
[21] ܗܒܝܠ ܕܐܩܪܒ ܐܡܪܐ ܗܘܐ. ܘܡܛܠܬܗ ܐܬܕܒܚ ܗܘܐ.
ܪܐܙܐ ܕܡܪܟܘܢ ܪܡܙ ܗܘܐ. ܕܩܢܘܡܗ ܩܪܒܢܐ ܥܒܕ ܗܘܐ܀'

'Hymn (82). The only-begotten Son, the Word
[21] Abel, who offered a lamb,
and was sacrificed for it,
it indicates the mystery of your Lord,
that He made His *qnōmā* an offering.'

The only hymn where our poet uses the word *qnōmā* in a direct way to indicate the *qnōmā* of humanity of Christ, is Hymn (69)[29], where he relates the forty days of Christ's fasting to the forty days when a human body is formed in the womb:

'ܥܘܢܝܬܐ (69). ܨܝܡܐ ܨܠܘ ܠܝ ܗܘܢܐ
[29] ܟܠ ܕܩܢܘܡܐ ܕܐܢܫܘܬܐ. ܠܝܘܡܝܢ ܐܪܒܥܝܢ ܢܘܩܕܬܐ.
ܡܫܬܡܠܝܐ ܓܒܝܠܘܬܐ. ܒܓܘ ܡܪܒܥܐ ܙܒܢ ܒܛܢܘܬܐ܀'

'Hymn (69). Those who fast incline your mind to me
[29] For the *qnōmā* of humanity
in forty days
its formation is completed
in the womb, the time of conception.'

Conclusion: The poet uses the word *qnōmā* sometimes to refer to the *qnōmē* of the Trinity, (in accordance with traditional Trinitarian doctrines) and sometimes to refer to the self of a human person in a neutral way. In the field of Christology, he avoids speaking of two *qnōmē*.

1.2 Person – ܦܪܨܘܦܐ Parṣōpā

The word *parṣōpā* has a double meaning in the hymns of Gīwargīs; sometimes it indicates 'person' while at other times it has the original meaning of 'face'. Regarding Christology, it can refer to the human appearance of Jesus, as in Hymn (36)[23], or to Christ the person of unity:

'ܥܘܢܝܬܐ (36). ܡܪܢ ܡܫܝܚܐ ܕܐܬܬܚܝܬ
[23] ܒܦܪܨܘܦܟ ܚܕܝܐ ܟܡܝܪܘܬܝ܀'

'Hymn (36). Our Lord Jesus who descended
[23] In Your person [Christ], my sadness rejoices.'

Here, its meaning comes close to that of *qnōmā*. It is used to refer to the face in Hymn (23)[40], and to the person in Hymns (25)[14cd] and 17.(109)[5, 13]:

‘ܥܘܢܝܬܐ (23). ܡܟܬܒܢܘܬܐ ܕܥܬܝܩ̈ܬܐ
[40] ܐܢܬܬܗ ܕܪܥܝܢܗ ܚܣܝܪ ܗܘܐ. ܢܦܩܬ ܘܠܒܗ ܠܐ ܢܦܩ ܗܘܐ.
ܦܪܨܘܦܗ ܠܒܣܬܪܗ ܗܦܟ ܗܘܐ. ܕܬܪܥܝܬܗ ܬܡܢ ܩܡ ܗܘܐ܀’

‘Hymn (23). The chronicle of antiquities
[40] His wife, who had poor reason
left, but her heart had not.
Her face turned back,
for her thought remained there.’[34]

‘ܥܘܢܝܬܐ (25). ܟܕ ܢܦܩ ܝܘܢܢ ܡܢ ܢܘܢܐ
[14] ܘܐܘܟܡ ܓܘܢܐ ܕܙܝܘܝܗܘܢ. ܘܐܬܐܒܠܘ ܦܪܨܘܦܝܗܘܢ܀’

‘Hymn (25). On coming out of the fish, Jonah
[14] and their complexion blackened,
and their faces became mournful.’[35]

In Hymn 17.(109)[16, 17] it seems that Gīwargīs is using the words *qnōmā* and *parṣōpā* as synonyms; this is also clear when the poet says that Christ put mud on the blind *parṣōpā/qnōmā*; another instance is found in Hymn (47)[13], where the poet uses the words *qnōmā* and *parṣōpā* as synonyms referring to Christ:

‘ܥܘܢܝܬܐ (47). ܚܛܝܬ ܘܐܚܛܝܬ ܘܬܘܒ ܚܛܐ ܐܢܐ
[13] ܠ ܠܐ ܗܘܬ ܒܩܢܘܡܗ ܚܛܝܬܐ. ܐܦܠܐ ܦܪܨܘܦܗ ܠܘܛܬܐ.
ܫܡܗ̈ܐ ܩܒܠ ܕܨܥܪ̈ܐ. ܘܒܥܒ̈ܕܐ ܝܗܒ ܬܫܒ̈ܚܬܐ܀’

‘Hymn (47). I have sinned and instigated to sin and am sinning again
[13] Lāmaḏ: There was no sin in his *qnōmā*
nor any curse on his person
He received names of disgrace
and in deeds gave glories.’[36]

Using the words *qnōmā* and *parṣōpā* as synonyms developed after the fourth century[37], even though as early as the writings of Theodore of Mopsuestia (4th cent.) the word *parṣōpā* is used to indicate either *qnōmā* or honor, glory and sometimes face.[38] The same thing is found in the poetry of Ḫamīs when using *parṣōpā* to indicate honor:

[34] A. Pritula, *The Wardā*, p. 261.
[35] A. Pritula, *The Wardā*, p. 277.
[36] A. Pritula, *The Wardā*, p. 345. Translation slightly adapted.
[37] V. Van Vossel, مدرسة أنطاكيا [The School of Antioch], p. 65.
[38] V. Van Vossel, ثيودوروس المعلم الكبير [Theodore the Great Teacher], p.125, V. Van Vossel, مدرسة أنطاكيا [The School of Antioch], pp. 84-85; A. Grillmeier and T. Hainthaler, *Christ in Christian Tradition*, vol. I, p. 433.

'ܡܛܠ ܕܗܘܝܘ ܨܡܚܐ ܕܫܘܒܚܗ
ܘܚܝܕܗ ܦܓܪܗ ܥܡܗ ܒܐܝܩܪܐ ܦܪܨܘܦܝܐ
ܘܠܥܠܡܝܢ ܠܝܬ ܠܗ ܫܘܚܠܦܐ.' [39]

'Because He [Christ] is the ray of His [the Father's] glory
And it [His body] was united with Him in a prosopic honor,
and forever there will not be transference.'

In a hymn on the Resurrection, Ḫamīs uses the word *parṣōpā* to indicate the prosopic union. Does the *parṣōpā* here, according to Ḫamīs, means the same prosopon as in Theodore and Nestorius's writings? A similar idea is found in the writings of Ēlīā of Nisibis.[40]In the following hymn Ḫamīs mentions:

'ܐܡܪܐ ܕܩܒܠ ܕܒܚܗ
ܦܪܨܘܦܐ ܕܚܕܝܘܬܐ. ܕܐܠܗܘܬܐ ܘܐܢܫܘܬܐ.
ܠܬܪܬܝܗܝܢ ܚܕ ܒܙܒܢܐ. ܘܩܝܡܝܢ ܫܠܝܢ ܕܫܘܝܘܬܐ:·' [41]

'The lamb that accepted his sacrifice
The person of unity,
of humanity and divinity,
both set up at the same time,
and their reality is similar.'

In a hymn on the Annunciation, Ḫamīs shows that the person of the Word is united with the son of the Virgin. This means that sometimes the term *parṣōpā* is used to indicate the Word:

'ܡܛܠ ܕܗܘܝܘ ܨܡܚܐ ܕܫܘܒܚܗ
ܩ ܩܢܘܡ ܐܝܬܘܬܐ ܒܕܝܠܝܘܬܐ ܩܢܐ ܡܚܝܕܘܬܐ
ܒܦܪܨܘܦ ܡܠܬܐ ܗܘ ܕܒܪܘܬܐ ܒܒܪ ܒܬܘܠܘܬܐ:·' [42]

'Because He [Christ] is the ray of His [the Father's] glory
Qōp: The *qnōmā* of the essence possessed unity by attribution,
in the person of the Word, that is of sonship in the son of virginity.'

Conclusion: We can say that the use of *parṣōpā* fluctuates. In a neutral, non-Christological context, it indicates person or face, but in Christological passages, the *Book of Wardā* seems to relate *parṣōpā* to Christ's appearance, i.e. his humanity. However, Gīwargīs' contemporary Ḫamīs gives it a different meaning, indicating the union between humanity and divinity, with a meaning that is even more related to the Word or the divinity of Christ.

[39] Š.Ī. Ḥadbšabbā, ܚܡܝܣ ܒܪ ܩܪܕܚܐ [Ḫāmīs bar Qardāḥē], p. 24.
[40] Ēlīā of Nisibis, تفسير الأمانة [Elias of Nisibis. Commentary], p. 62.
[41] Š.Ī. Ḥadbšabbā, ܚܡܝܣ ܒܪ ܩܪܕܚܐ [Ḫāmīs bar Qardāḥē], p. 127.
[42] Š.Ī. Ḥadbšabbā, ܚܡܝܣ ܒܪ ܩܪܕܚܐ [Ḫāmīs bar Qardāḥē], p. 22.

1.3 Essence – ܐܝܬܘܬܐ ʾĪṯūṯā, ܐܝܬܝܐ ʾĪṯyā, ܝܬܐ Yāṯā, ܐܘܣܝܐ Ousia

Because of the close relationship in meaning between these terms, all denoting the idea of essence in Trinitarian passages, we discuss them together.[43] The term *ʾĪṯūṯā* sometimes refers to the Trinity, such as in Hymn 9.(78)[1ef]. In Hymns 11.(91)[32], 15.(97)[4ab] and 19.(127)[2ab], Gīwargīs mentions the Son as the Son of the essence. This means that the two terms *ʾĪṯūṯā* and *ʾĪṯyā* sometimes means the divinity of the Father. In Hymns 16.(106)[1] and 19.(127)[16], the poet attributes the incarnation to the *ʾĪṯyā* indicating the Word. In Hymns 6.(71)[3, 4], 11.(91)[3cd] and 18.(121)[18cd], *ʾĪṯūṯā* means the essence of God.

The terms Ousia, *Yāṯā* also denotes the divine essence. In Hymns 7.(72)[2], 11.(91)[2ab] and 20.(130)[1ab], the poet uses both words Ousia and *Yāṯā* as synonyms, like in Hymn 19.(127)[15ab], where *ʾĪṯyā* refers to the one essence of the Trinity.

In an anonymous Hymn (90)[32ab] the word Yāṯā seems to refer to Christ who appeared to His disciples. The same is true in Hymn (126)[2ab], when our poet says that Christ concealed His *Yāṯā* with a body:

’ܡܥܢܝܬܐ (90). <u>ܐܠܗܐ ܐܝܬܝܐ ܡܠܬܐ</u>
[32] ܥ ܥܣܪ ܙܒܢܝܢ ܚܘܝ ܝܬܗ. ܠܬܠܡܝܕܘܗܝ ܒܢܝ ܪܒܝܬܗ.‘

‘Hymn (90). <u>God, Essence, Word</u>
[32] ʿĒ: He showed His essence ten times,
to His disciples the sons of His education.’

’ܡܥܢܝܬܐ (126). <u>ܐܣܝܐ ܕܪ̈ܘܡܐ ܒܝܕ ܪ̈ܚܡܘܗܝ</u>
[2] ܐܬܐ ܠܐܪܥܐ ܒܛܝܒܘܬܗ. ܘܒܦܓܪܐ ܟܣܝ ܝܬܗ.‘

‘Hymn (126). <u>The doctor of the high by His mercy</u>
[2] He came to earth by His grace,
and hid His essence in a body.’

In Hymn (14), written by Ḥakīm d-bēṯ Qāšā (13th cent.), the author demonstrate that the essence *ʾĪṯyā* possesses natures, attributes and sovereignty. Ḥakīm gives the following interpretation:

’ܡܥܢܝܬܐ (14). <u>ܗܘ ܝܚܝܕܝܐ ܐܘܣܝܬܐ. ܢܦܩ ܥܘܗܕܢܐ ܠܐܝܬܝܬܐ</u>
[1] ܗܘ ܝܚܝܕܝܐ ܐܘܣܝܬܐ. ܢܦܩ ܥܘܗܕܢܐ ܠܐܝܬܝܬܐ.
ܠܪܥܝܢܐ ܡܬܘܣܦܝܬܐ ܟܝܢܝܬܐ. ܘܕܝܠܝܬܐ ܘܡܪ̈ܘܬܢܝܬܐ ܀
[2] ܟܝ̈ܢܐ ܡܬܘܬܒܘܬܐ ܘܦܪ̈ܨܘܦܘܬܐ. ܕܠܗ ܐܝܬ ܕܝܢ ܒܟܠ ܡܫܪܘܬܐ.
ܠܐܝܬܝܐ ܕܠܥܠ ܗܘܐ ܝܠܕܬܐ ܀
[3] ܘܕܝܠܝܬܐ ܕܝܠܗ ܐܢܝܢ ܒܡܪܒܪܘܬܐ. ܕܐܝܬܝܘܬ ܐܠܗܘܬܐ. ܘܪܒܘܬܐ ܘܢܨܝܚܘܬܐ ܀
[4] ܘܡܪ̈ܘܬܢܝܬܐ ܗܠܝܢ ܐܢܝܢ ܕܠܐ ܡܠܝܟܘܬܐ. ܠܐ ܡܫܬܘܚܠܦܘܬܐ. ܘܠܐ ܐܬܪܐ ܘܠܐ ܡܬܚܡܘܬܐ ܀‘

[43] Most dictionaries translate the words *ʾĪṯyā* or *ʾĪṯūṯā* as 'Essence' but Manna's dictionary also adds 'Nature' to the meaning of *ʾĪṯūṯā*.

'Hymn (14). Come, my beloved ones, with one accord
[1] Come, my beloved, with one accord
Let us lift up praise in a threefold song
to him who eternally possesseth
Natural attributes and properties and specific attributes.
[2] The natural attributes: eternity and creation
are His without change
the being who was the cause of all.
[3] and properties: are His in truth
which are Fatherhood and Sonship and procession.[44]
[4] and the specific attributes:
There are without doubt:
Immutability: not (being confined in) space, immensity.'[45]

Hymn (144), written by a priest named Esḥaq Šbadnāyā (15th cent.), also refers to the ʾĪṯyā as the divine essence. Here the poet plays with words to show beautifully the contrast of 'God, manifested invisibly':

'ܥܘܢܝܬܐ (144). ܬܘ ܚܒܝܒܝ ܫܘܝܐܝܬ
[46] ܬ ܢܘܕܐ ܢܚܢ. ܫܘܝܐܝܬ ܘܚܕܝܐܝܬ.
ܚܢܢ ܘܥܝܪܐ ܐܡܝܢܐܝܬ. ܠܐܝܬܝܐ ܕܐܬܓܠܝ ܟܣܝܐܝܬ ܀'

'Hymn (144). Come O beloved ones equally, with one accord
[46] Tāw: Let us give thanks,
equally and cheerfully,
we and the watchers always,
to the essence that was manifested invisibly.'

Gīwargīs sometimes uses the word *Yāṯā* to refer to his own nature, as in Hymn (40)[22]:

'ܥܘܢܝܬܐ (40). ܡܪܝܐ ܕܒܪܚܡܘܗܝ ܐܛܝܒܢ
[22] ܫ ܫܒܘܩ ܠܝ ܒܪܚܡܐ ܘܚܘܒܐ. ܕܚܛܝܬ ܒܝܬܐ ܘܨܒܝܢܐ.
ܘܠܝܬ ܠܝ ܓܘܣܐ ܘܬܘܟܠܢܐ. ܠܒܪ ܡܢܟ ܕܥܠܝܟ ܬܟܝܠ ܐܢܐ ܀'

'Hymn (40). Lord, who through His mercy, Has prepared us
[22] Šīn: Forgive with mercy and love,
because I have sinned with my own essence and will,
I have no refuge nor confidence
apart from You because I trust in You.'

Hymn (159)[135] was written by an otherwise unknown monk named Rabban Bāʿūṯ.[46] When describing the history of salvation and the resurrection of the body,

[44] The same explanation is found in: Ṣalībā B. Yōḥannā, كتاب أسفار الأسرار, *I libri dei misteri*, p. 121.
[45] F.C. Conybeare and A. J. Maclean, *Rituale Armenorum*, p. 350. Translation slightly adapted.
[46] There is no information about this person in the collection of Wardā but the same name is found in *The Book of Governors* written by Tōmā d-Margā (9th cent.) and he was known for his

he uses the word *Yāṯā* both as an indication of the divine essence and to denote human nature:

'ܥܘܢܝܬܐ (159). <u>ܫܘܐ ܠܫܘܒܚܐ ܒܪܘܝܐ ܐܝܬܘܬܐ</u>
[135] ܕܢܩܝܡܢ ܘܢܐܠܗܢ ܠܢ. ܠܡܠܟܘܬܐ ܪܡܬܐ ܘܢܥܠܢ ܠܢ.
ܠܐ ܗܘ ܩܛܝܪ ܚܐܪܘܬܢ. ܘܠܐ ܒܩܛܝܪܐ ܕܒܪ ܟܝܢܢ܀'

'Hymn (159). <u>Worthy of glory the creator, essence</u>
[135] He will raise us up and make us divine,
and make us enter the high kingdom.
He does not compel our freedom,
and will not by force lead our nature.'

Conclusion: From these passages taken from the hymns attributed to our poet and of various contemporary authors, it seems that the terms *ʾĪṯūṯā*, *ʾĪṯyā*, *Yāṯā* and Ousia are generally identical, denoting the divine essence, but the word *Yāṯā* is sometimes used also to indicate the human self.

1.4 Put on – ܠܒܫ Lḇeš

The use of this word is widespread in East-Syriac theological writings.[47] It is used as a standard expression for the Incarnation and is already found in the writings of Aphrahat and Ephrem.[48] In the poetry of Gīwargīs, *Lḇeš* has three meanings. The first meaning is that of the second *qnōmā* of the Trinity putting on or wearing a human body. Many examples can be given, such as Hymns 1.(12)[3c] and 2.(13)[1cd, 2cd]. In Hymn 7.(72)[12ab, 18a], the poet describes how the Word, by His will, put on a body. In Hymn (82)[1ab] says that the Word put on an Adamic body, while Hymn 17.(109)[1b, 2ab] shows the Word, the ray of the eternal Father, by His grace, putting on a body and states that God put on a human being. Only in Hymn 18.(121)[2] does the poet say that Christ put on a body from Mary:

'ܥܘܢܝܬܐ (82). <u>ܒܪܐ ܡܠܬܐ ܝܚܝܕܝܐ</u>
[1] ܒܪܐ ܡܠܬܐ ܝܚܝܕܝܐ. ܠܒܫܗ ܠܦܓܪܐ ܐܢܫܝܐ.'

'Hymn (82). <u>The only begotten Son Word</u>
[1] The only-begotten Son Word,
put on a human body.'

The second meaning indicates human beings, as in Hymn (40)[6], where the poet refers to himself as being impure and wearing or putting on a weak nature:

---

knowledge. However, it is unclear whether it is the same person to whom the hymn is attributed. Tōmā d-Margā, ܟܬܒܐ ܕܪܝܫܢܐ, *The Book of Governors*, vol. I, lviii, cxv. *Ibid.*, vol. II, p. 447.

[47] Bābāi, ܟܬܒܐ ܕܚܘܝܕܐ, [The Book of the Union], pp. 40:26, 48:5; S.P. Brock, *Bride of Light*, pp. 3-9; S.P. Brock, "The Robe of Glory," p. 251; T. Karukakalathil, *Christ's Humanity*, pp. 37-38; S.P. Brock, "The Christology of the Church of the East," pp. 133-142.

[48] R. Murray, *Symbols of Church and Kingdom*, pp. 69-82, 311-312.

'ܥܘܢܝܬܐ (40). <u>ܡܪܐ ܕܒܚܢܢܘܗܝ ܫܪܪܢ</u>
[6] ܗܐ ܐܡܪܬ ܘܐܡܪ ܐܢܐ. ܕܙܟܝܐ ܠܐ ܗܘܐ ܐܢܐ.
ܕܟܝܢܐ ܡܚܝܠܐ ܠܒܫ ܐܢܐ. ܘܢܦܫܐ ܡܪܝܪܬܐ ܩܢܐ ܐܢܐ܀'

'Hymn (40). <u>The Lord who made us firm in His mercy</u>
[6] Hē: This is what I said, and I am saying,
that I will not be pure,
because I put on a weak nature,
and I have a bitter desire [soul].'

The third meaning of this word indicates feelings, such as in Hymn (63)[39a], when our poet says that humans wear sadness:

'ܥܘܢܝܬܐ (63). <u>ܡܠܟܐ ܕܡܠܟܐ ܠܗ ܦܠܚܝܢ</u>
[39] ܒܢܝ ܐܪܥܐ ܚܫܐ ܠܒܫܝܢ.'

'Hymn (63). <u>King, for whom kings toil</u>
[39] The children of the earth will put on suffering.'[49]

Hymn 17.(109)[21ab], the poet sees Christ as someone who looks like those who wear flesh.[50] In Hymn (77)[10d], he describes Christ during temptation as wearing humility:

'ܥܘܢܝܬܐ (77). <u>ܟܕ ܥܠ ܡܪܢ ܠܐܘܪܫܠܡ</u>
[10] ܘܗܘ ܠܒܫ ܗܘܐ ܡܣܟܢܘܬܐ.'

'Hymn (77). <u>Our Lord entering Jerusalem</u>
[10] and [He] put on poverty.'[51]

Conclusion: The word *Lḇeš* has different meanings. Sometimes it refers to the Word putting on a body or flesh or to the humanity of Christ in line with the East Syriac tradition. Sometimes it has a more general, non-Christological meaning, indicating 'being subject' to passions or feelings.

---

[49] A. Pritula, *The Wardā*, p. 455. Translation slightly adapted.

[50] Interestingly the word *Lḇeš* is used in hymn (6)[10] to indicate the physical aspect of the angel Gabriel when speaking to Mary. This is the only hymn that describes the watcher as putting on a body:

ܥܘܢܝܬܐ (6). <u>ܥܠ ܫܡܝܐ ܬܢܝܢܐ</u>
[10] ܬܫܥ ܡܠܐ ܕܬܗܪܐ. ܘܥܣܪܐ ܕܡܠܝܢ ܕܬܕܡܘܪܬܐ.
ܡܠܠ ܗܘ ܕܕܡܐ ܠܠܒܫ ܦܓܪܐ. ܥܡ ܕܕܟܝܐ ܢܦܫܐ ܘܦܓܪܐ܀

Hymn (6). <u>On the second heaven</u>
[10] Nine words of astonishment,
and ten full of wonder,
spoke the one who looked like one clothed in a body,
with [the one] pure in soul and body.

The same idea is found also in the writings of Ēlīā Abū Ḥalīm (1176-1190) in his book التراجيم *The Interpretations,* on the feast of Annunciation, when he shows Mary meeting the angel who appeared to her putting on a body. See Ēlīā Abū Ḥalīm, *التراجيم السنيّة للأعياد المارانية*, *Discorus Religieux,* vol. I, p. 30.

[51] A. Pritula, *The Wardā*, p. 467. Translation slightly adapted.

1.5 Likeness, Image – ܕܡܘܬܐ Dmūṯā, ܕܘܡܝܐ Dūmyā, ܨܠܡܐ Ṣalmā

These terms are used frequently, such as in Hymn 1.(12)[3c, 31d] on the baptism of Christ, and in Hymn 5.(67)[16, 17cd, 39ab] on the temptation of Christ and in Hymn (47)[7a], presenting Christ being as equal with the Father:

'ܠܡܥܢܝܬܐ (47). ܚܛܝܬ ܘܐܚܛܝܬ ܘܬܘܒ ܚܛܐ ܐܢܐ
[7] ܘ ܘܐܦ ܒܪܐ ܕܕܡܐ ܠܝܠܘܕܗ.'

'Hymn (47). I have sinned and instigated to sin and am sinning again
[7] Waw: And also the Son who was like His parent [Father].'[52]

For Gīwargīs, ܨܠܡܐ *Ṣalmā* evokes the theme of man created in God's image, such as in Hymns 3.(38)[21] and 18.(121)[33]. Christologically, this word refers also to the man (the image) united with the Word, or to Christ who is the living image of God, such as in Hymns 1.(12)[40], 6.(71)[25], and 19.(127)[16]. In Hymn 13.(95)[52], there is a beautiful stanza where the poet gives three synonyms for the humanity of Christ – ܨܠܡܐ likeness, ܗܝܟܠܐ temple, ܢܘܣܐ shrine – each one indicating the dwelling of one of the respective three *qnōmē* of the Trinity. An almost similar imagery can be found in the *Book of the Union* by Bābāi.[53]

Conclusion: the words *Dmūṯā* ܕܡܘܬܐ and *Ṣalmā* ܨܠܡܐ are used to refer to Christ as the image of God, or to His humanity being united to the Word. Sometimes it refers to the appearance of Christ after the Resurrection or to His equality with the Father. In addition to its biblical origins, seeing Christ as the image of God can also be found in the writings of the Early Church Fathers, who consider Christ to be the true image of God as an example to be followed, in contrast to Adam's image, which was destroyed after the Fall.[54]

1.6 Garment, Form, Appearance – ܐܣܛܠܐ Esṭlā, ܐܣܟܡܐ Eskēmā

These two foreign loanwords reinforce the clothing imagery as expressed by the word *Lḇeš*. *Esṭlā* is also a classical term of the Antiochian School;[55] it is found in Hymn 2.(13)[1d], where it indicates the body that the Word assumed for inhabitation. The same meaning is found in Hymn (157)[2] written by Sabrīšōʿ the metropolitan of Barwar[56] (12th cent.), *Esṭlā* is used to refer to the Word taking a garment to inhabit:

[52] A. Pritula, *The Wardā*, p. 345.
[53] Bābāi, ܟܬܒܐ ܕܡܚܝܕܘܬܐ, [The Book of the Union] pp. 59:3,4,5.
[54] V. Van Vossel, مدرسة أنطاكيا [The School of Antioch], pp. 61-63.
[55] S.P. Brock, "Clothing metaphors," pp. 11-40; A. Grillmeier and T. Hainthaler, *Christ in Christian Tradition*, vol. II/3, p. 232
[56] A village situated in north Iraq.

‘ܒܥܘܬܐ (157). ܡܪܐ ܕܝܪ̈ܚܐ ܘܕܫܢ̈ܝܐ
[2] ܐܠܗܐ ܡܠܬܐ ܚܝܐ. ܠܐ ܡܢ ܡܠܐܟ̈ܐ ܓܒ̈ܝܐ.
ܢܣܒ ܠܗ ܠܒܘܫܐ ܠܥܡܘܪܘܬܐ. ܐܠܐ ܡܢ ܓܢܣ ܐܢ̈ܫܐ܀’

‘Hymn (157). <u>The Lord of months and years</u>

[2] God, The living Word,
did not take from the chosen angels,
a garment for the inhabitation,
but from the human race.’

In hymn (15)[30], *Esṭlā* refers to the clothes of John the Baptist:

‘ܒܥܘܬܐ (15). ܚܝܠܐ ܕܡܠܠ ܒܪܡܟܐ
[30] ܐܡܗ ܠܒܘܫܐ ܥܒܕܬ ܠܗ. ܣܥܪܐ ܕܓܡܠ̈ܐ ܘܐܠܒܫܬܗ ܠܗ.
ܘܥܡܗ ܪܒܐ ܗܘܐ ܠܒܘܫܗ. ܘܠܐ ܒܠܐ ܥܕܡܐ ܠܩܛܠܗ܀’

‘Hymn (15). <u>The power, which spoke in the jennet</u>

[30] His mother made him clothes-
camel hair- and dressed him in them.
And with him the clothes grew.
And did not wear out till his murder.’[57]

In the anonymous Hymn (68)[1], *Esṭlā* refers to ‘the robe of glory’ when fasting. This is a very famous expression found in Syriac writings;[58] in stanza [34], the robe of glory is used when describing the ascension of Christ:

‘ܒܥܘܬܐ (68). ܡܪܩܘ ܐܚܝ ܪܥܝܢܝܟܘܢ
[1] ܡܪܩܘ ܐܚܝ ܪܥܝܢܝܟܘܢ. ܒܗܝܡܢܘܬܐ ܘܕܟܝܘܬܐ.
ܘܐܬܥܛܦܘ ܠܒܘܫܐ ܕܫܘܒܚܐ. ܘܩܒܠܘ ܨܘܡܐ ܒܚܕܘܬܐ܀
[34] ܢܓܕܘܠ ܠܗ ܟܠܝܠܐ ܕܬܫܒܘܚܬܐ. ܘܢܙܩܘܪ ܠܒܘܫܐ ܕܫܘܒܚܐ.
ܘܢܦܪܘܥ ܛܝܒܘܬܐ. ܠܐܣܝܐ ܕܡܐܣܐ ܟܘܪ̈ܗܢܐ܀’

‘Hymn (68). <u>Clean your minds, O my brothers</u>

[1] Clean your minds, O my brothers,
with faith and purity,
and be covered by the robe of glory,
and accept fasting with joy.

[34] We will plait for Him the crown of praise,
and weave the robe of glory,
and repay gratitude,
to the doctor who heals sickness.’

In Hymn (108), stanza [18], *Esṭlā* refers to the robe that was given to the prodigal son by his father; in stanza [32] it refers to the robe of baptism:

---

[57] A. Pritula, *The Wardā*, p. 245.

[58] S.P. Brock, “The Robe of Glory,” p. 252.

'ܥܘܢܝܬܐ (108). <u>ܬܘ ܚܛܝܐ ܫܡܥܘ ܬܫܥܝܬܐ</u>
[18] ܐܒܘܗܝ ܩܒܠܗ ܒܚܘܒܐ. ܘܦܩܕ ܘܝܗܒ ܠܗ ܥܙܩܬܐ.
ܘܐܠܒܫܘܗܝ ܐܣܛܠܐ ܫܦܝܪܬܐ. ܘܐܥܠܗ ܒܐܝܩܪܐ ܠܗ ܒܒܝܬܐ܀
[32] ܐܣܛܠܐ ܕܡܢ ܡܥܡܘܕܝܬܐ. ܕܛܢܦܬܗ ܒܝܕ ܚܛܗܐ.
ܚܕܬܝܗ ܒܬܝܒܘܬܐ. ܘܥܬܝܩܬܐ ܗܘܝܐ ܚܕܬܐ܀'

'Hymn (108). <u>Come, sinners, hear the story,</u>
[18] The father lovingly accepted him
and ordered and gave him a ring.
And he was dressed in the best clothes,
and he led him with honour into his house.
[32] I have marred the robe of baptism
With filth!
Renew it with penance!
And make a new one of the old!'[59]

The word Eskēmā is found in Hymn 15.(97)[6cd], where it refers to the outward appearance of Christ. In an anonymous Hymn (131)[5], it indicates the monastic dress which was accepted by Kōdāhūi,[60] when he became a monk. The same idea is found in Hymn (132)[12].

'ܥܘܢܝܬܐ (131). <u>ܐܝܬܘܬܐ ܕܡܢ ܡܬܘܡ ܒܚܘܒܗ ܒܪܢ</u>
[5] ܒ ܒܚܒܪܘܬܐ ܕܡܪܝ ܐܘܓܝܢ ܢܨܝܚܐ. ܐܬܚܠܛ ܡܢ ܫܘܪܝܐ.
ܘܩܒܠ ܐܣܟܝܡܐ ܫܦܝܪܐ. ܘܗܘܐ ܡܙܡܢܐ ܠܫܡܝܐ.'

'Hymn (131). <u>The essence who created us by His love from the beginning</u>
[5] Bēṯ: In the company of Mar Awgen[61] the splendid,
[he] joined from the beginning,
and accepted the beautiful robe,
and was invited to heaven.'

In Hymn (100)[12] Gīwargīs uses the word *Eskēmā* to refer to the appearance of wicked people as righteous ones:

---

[59] A. Pritula, *The Wardā*, p. 525.

[60] According to the hymn, the name Kōdāhūi means Yahḇālāhā. This monk lived in the seventh century under Patriarch Gīwargīs I; he was from Mīšān and was the founder of a monastery in Bēṯ Ḥālī and the monastery of Mʿarrī. See A. Abouna, *ديارات العراق* [Monasteries of Iraq], pp. 241, 322, 435, 451, 455, 467-468. Other sources state that this monk was from Egypt, where he was a student of Mar Awgen. See A. Scher, *سيرة أشهر شهداء المشرق القديسين* [Biography of the Most Famous Holy Martyrs of the East], p. 105.

[61] He was from Egypt and is the one who established ascetic life in the fourth century on mount Īzlā in Southern Turkey. A. Abouna, *ديارات العراق* [Monasteries of Iraq], p. 16.

ܥܘܢܝܬܐ (100). ܗܘ ܡܠܟܐ ܕܫܡܝܢܐ'
[12] ܘܝ ܠܟܘܢ ܕܡ ܡܬܩܪܝܬܘܢ. ܟܐܢ̈ܐ ܘܢܟܠܝܢ ܒܝܫܝܢ ܐܢܬܘܢ.
ܕܒܐܣܟܡܐ ܕܟܐܢ̈ܐ ܡܗܠܟܝܢ ܐܢܬܘܢ. ܘܐܝܟ ܒ̈ܝܫܐ ܡܣܬܠܝܢ ܐܢܬܘܢ܀'

'Hymn (100). <u>That king of heavenly ones</u>
[12] Woe to you that you are called,
as virtuous ones but you are wicked.
You walk with the uniform of righteous ones,
but like evil ones you are rejected.'

Conclusion: The Greek word *Eskēmā/schema* appears already in Nestorius's writings, especially in the famous passage explaining the unchangeable nature of the Word after unity, by giving the example of a king who wears the garments of a soldier, showing that the king and the garments are one.[62] In another remarkable passage, Nestorius states that God appeared in the schema of fire, and the schema of the real flesh.[63] The word *Eskēmā* is also found in the writings of Theodore,[64] Narsai,[65] and the Catholicos Mar Gīwargīs I.[66] It seems that in the hymns of the *Book of Wardā, Eskēmā* and *Esṭlā* are also used to indicate clothes in the literal sense, which makes it all the more challenging to see it referring to the appearance of Christ. As noted above, it reinforces the clothing imagery used by Gīwargīs and other writers before him.

1.7 Dwelled, Inhabited – ܫܪܐ Šrā, ܥܡܪ ʿĀmar

The inhabitation of the Word is depicted in Hymn 2.(13)[1cd], which says that the Lord inhabited *Šrā* in the *Esṭlā* of flesh, or in Hymn 14.(96)[33] and 16.(106)[4], where the poet says that the Father inhabits the Son.

In Hymn 6.(71)[9c], we find the word *Šrā* ܫܪܐ referring to God inhabiting all souls without mingling. In Hymn 16.(106)[23], the word indicates the inhabitation of the Trinity in the apostles and in Hymns (151)[22] and (154)[25], both words are addressed to Mary:

ܥܘܢܝܬܐ (151). ܫܘܒܚܐ ܠܛܝܒܘܬܟ ܦܪܘܩܢ'
[22] ܫ ܫܘܒܚܐ ܠܐܒܐ ܕܩܢܐ ܒܟܝ. ܘܠܒܪܐ ܕܐܬܝܠܕ ܡܢܟܝ.
ܘܠܪܘܚܩܘܕܫܐ ܕܒܪܝܗ ܒܟܝ. ܘܫܘܝܐ ܠܡܫܪܝܗ ܥܒܕܟܝ܀'

'Hymn (151). <u>Glory to Your grace, our Saviour!</u>
[22] Shīn: Glory to the Father, who has claimed you,
and to the Son who was born by you,
and to the Holy Spirit, that has created Him in you
and made you the place of His dwelling.'[67]

---

[62] Nestorius, ܬܐܓܘܪܬܐ ܕܗܪܩܠܝܕܝܣ [The Treatise of Heracleides], pp. 30-31.
[63] Nestorius, ܬܐܓܘܪܬܐ ܕܗܪܩܠܝܕܝܣ [The Treatise of Heracleides], pp. 76-77.
[64] Theodore of Mopsuestia, *III. Fragmenta libri de incarnatione*, p. 73 [ܥܓ]; A. Grillmeier and T. Hainthaler, *Christ in Christian Tradition*, vol. I, p. 433.
[65] F.G. McLeod, *Narsai's Metrical Homilies*, p. 56:315.
[66] B. Ebeid, "La Cristologia del catholicos Mar Georgis," p. 214.
[67] A. Pritula, *The Wardā*, p. 237.

In Hymn (154), written by Gīwargīs of Adiabene[68] (10th cent.), both words are found in stanza [25]:

'ܠܥܘܢܝܬܐ (154). ܒܢܨܪܬ ܡܕܝܢܬܐ ܓܠܝܠܝܬܐ.
[25] ܩ ܩܥܘ ܠܗ ܫܘܒܚܐ ܘܬܫܒܘܚܬܐ. ܠܗܘ ܕܝܬܒ ܥܠ ܡܪܟܒܬܐ.
ܘܟܠܗ ܒܥܘܒܐ ܕܒܬܘܠܬܐ. ܥܡܪ ܘܫܪܐ ܒܚܕܝܘܬܐ܀'

'Hymn (154). In Nazareth, the Galilean city
[25] Qōp: They cried for Him glory and praise,
to the one who stands on the chariot.
All of Him, in the womb of the Virgin,
inhabited and dwelled in unity.'

Conclusion: 'Indwelling' is expressed by two different terms which seem to be synonyms reinforcing each other when they are used as a pair. Our poet is following here an earlier tradition, as can be seen in the work of Gīwargīs of Adiabene.

1.8 Overshadowed – ܐܓܢ ʾAggen

Usually, this word refers to the hovering of the Holy Spirit. In some hymns it is used to indicate the Spirit that overshadows the Virgin, as in Hymn (9)[31cd]. In Hymns 12.(92)[2] and 13.(95)[10], it refers to the Word overshadowing Mary to express the relationship between the divine and the human natures:

'ܠܥܘܢܝܬܐ (9). ܒܝܡܐ ܕܚܛܗܐ ܗܐ ܪܡܐ ܐܢܐ
[31] ܗܟܢ ܒܡܪܝܡ ܐܓܢ ܗܘܐ. ܪܘܚܐ ܘܩܕܫܗ ܟܠܗ ܗܘܐ܀'

'Hymn (9). Here in the sea of sins I am cast!
[31] So did the Spirit overshadowed Mary
and sanctified her entirely.'[69]

In Hymn (151), written by Mar Yahḇālāhā II (11th cent.), we find the word *ʾAggen* in two stanzas. Stanza [11] declares that the right hand of the Lord overshadowed the Virgin; the Holy Spirit is perhaps here understood as the right hand of the Father, an image that was used by Irenaeus (2nd cent.).[70] Stanza [17] refers to the power of the Lord that overshadowed the Virgin, asking that the right hand of the Lord would overshadow us also like the Virgin. Here Yahḇālāhā II uses the expression that Mary became the mother of the Only-begotten Son, while in stanza [11] he shows that Mary carries the humanity that became a temple for the Word.

---

[68] An author whose name is often confused with that of our poet. S.P. Brock, "Gewargis of Arbela," p. 176.
[69] A. Pritula, *The Wardā*, p. 225.
[70] Irenaeus, *The Five Books*, p. 310.

'ܥܘܢܝܬܐ (151). ܫܘܒܚܐ ܠܪܚܡܝܟ ܦܪܘܩܢ

[11] ܝ ܝܡܝܢܗ ܕܡܪܝܐ ܐܓܢܬ. ܥܠ ܒܪܝܟܬ ܒܢܫ̈ܐ ܕܫܘܝܬ.
ܕܬܛܥܘܢ ܠܐܢܫܘܬܐ ܕܗܘܬ. ܗܝܟܠܐ ܠܡܠܬܐ ܕܐܬܚܝܕܬ ܀
[17] ܥ ܥܠܝܐ ܕܐܓܢ ܚܝܠܗ. ܥܠ ܒܪܝܟܬ ܒܢܫ̈ܐ ܐܡܬܗ.
ܕܗܘܬ ܐܡܐ ܠܝܚܝܕܗ. ܐܓܢ[71] ܥܠܝܢ ܝܡܝܢܗ ܀'

'Hymn (151). Glory to Your mercy, our Savior!

[11]: Yōḏ: The right hand of the Lord overshadowed
the blessed among women, so that she was deemed worthy.
to bear the humanity that became
a temple for the Word, which it [the humanity] became united to.
[17] ʿĒ: the Most high, His power has overshadowed
His handmaiden, blessed among women,
So that she has become the mother of His [the Father's] Only-begotten,
Let His right-hand overshadow us.'[72]

In Hymn (157)[39], written by Sabrīšōʿ the metropolitan of Barwar, ܐܓܢ refers to the Holy Spirit overshadowing the gathering of the apostles:

'ܥܘܢܝܬܐ (157). ܡܪܐ ܕܝܪ̈ܚܐ ܘܕܫܢ̈ܐ

[39] ܪܘܚܐ ܗܝ ܦܪܩܠܝܛܐ. ܕܐܓܢ ܥܠ ܟܢܫܐ ܦܫܝܛܐ.
ܘܐܬܚܟܡܘ ܒܟܠ ܚܘܦܛܐ. ܕܢܟܪܙܘܢ ܣܒܪܬܐ ܕܠܐ ܕܚܠܬܐ ܀'

'Hymn (157). The Lord of months and years

[39] The Spirit, indeed the Paraclete,
that overshadowed the simple gathering,
and they became wise with all courage,
to preach the Gospel without fear.'

Conclusion: Although the word ʾAggen is primarily used to indicate the hovering of the Holy Spirit, it is also used to indicate the 'hovering' of the Word when referring to the unity between the divinity and humanity of Christ.

1.9 Temple – ܗܝܟܠܐ Hayklā

This word also has various meanings. In Hymn (26)[18cd], Gīwargīs uses 'temple' to refer to a human body:

---

[71] We expect here that the verb would be ܐܓܢܬ instead of ܐܓܢ since the word ܝܡܝܢܗ is feminine.

[72] A. Pritula, *The Wardā*, p. 235. Pritula translates as follows:

[11] Jod: She sat to the right of the Lord
for she was blessed among women, which she deserved.
For she bore mankind, for she was
a temple for the Word, which she united.
[17] ʿE: the Most high, His power has overshadowed
His slave blessed among women,
for she has become mother of His Only-begotten,
His right-hand rests upon us.

‘ܥܘܢܝܬܐ (26). <u>ܐܘ ܢܦܫܐ ܕܚܒܝܒܐ ܡܢ ܟܠ</u>
[18] ܘܗܘܝܐ ܠܣܣܐ ܚܕܘܬܐ. ܒܚܘܪܒܐ ܕܗܝܟܠܟ ܘܝܠܟ܀’

‘Hymn (26). <u>O soul, which is dearest of all</u>
[18] when there will be joy for the moth
of the devastation of your temple [the poet’s body]. Woe unto you!’[73]

In Hymn (31)[25], our poet shows how he is sanctified by the temple of the Lord in order to be the temple of the Lord:

‘ܥܘܢܝܬܐ (31). <u>ܡܪܐ ܕܢܒܝܘܬܐ</u>
[25] ܡܢ ܡܩܕܫܘܬܗ ܕܗܝܟܠܟ. ܐܬܩܕܫ ܘܐܗܘܐ ܗܝܟܠܟ.
ܐܫܘܐ ܕܐܚܙܝܟ ܓܘ ܗܝܟܠܟ. ܡܪܢ ܐܬܪܚܡ ܥܠܝ܀’

‘Hymn (31). <u>Lord of the prophecies</u>
[25] From the sanctuary of Your temple
consecrate me and let me be Your temple.
Favour me to see You inside Your temple.
Our Lord, have mercy on me!’[74]

Christologically, this word is used to indicate the body of Jesus that became a temple for the Word, as in Hymn 13.(95)[52], but in Hymn (2)[8], interestingly, it refers to the body of Christ as the temple of the Trinity, which is an unusual expression:

‘ܥܘܢܝܬܐ (2). <u>ܝܠܕܗ ܕܠܝܬ ܠܝܠܕܗ ܙܒܢܐ</u>
[8] ܗܐ ܨܠܡܐ ܕܐܠܗܘܬܐ. ܘܗܝܟܠܐ ܕܬܠܝܬܝܘܬܐ.
ܕܡܠܠܗ ܡܠܠܝ ܐܝܬܘܬܐ. ܟܕ ܒܪܐ ܠܐܕܡ ܥܦܪܢܐ܀’

‘Hymn (2) <u>The Nativity of Him, whose nativity is not time-ridden,</u>
[8] Here is the image of the Godhood
and the sanctuary of Trinity!
Of which the essence spoke
having created terrestrial Adam.’[75]

The word Hayklā is also used to designate Mary, who became a temple full of holiness for the indwelling of the Word, as in Hymn (7)[8]:

‘ܥܘܢܝܬܐ (7). <u>ܒܢܨܪܬ ܡܕܝܢܬܐ ܕܓܠܝܠܐ.</u>
[8] ܫܠܡ ܠܟܝ ܡܠܝܐ ܛܝܒܘܬܐ. ܘܗܝܟܠܐ ܡܠܝܐ ܡܩܕܫܘܬܐ.
ܘܡܫܪܝܐ ܕܐܠܗܘܬܐ. ܡܫܪܝܐ ܠܡܪܝܡܬܐ܀’

‘Hymn (7) <u>In Nazareth the Galilean town</u>
[8] ‘Peace to you, full of grace!
Temple, full of holiness!

[73] A. Pritula, *The Wardā*, p. 289. The poet here is lamenting himself.
[74] A. Pritula, *The Wardā*, p. 301.
[75] A. Pritula, *The Wardā*, p. 173.

Abode of Godhood
and second heaven.'[76]

Similar expressions as those used for Christ in Hymn 13.(95) are found in Hymn (10)[1ij] to refer to Mary:

'ܥܘܢܝܬܐ (10). ܡܢ ܡܨܐ ܕܒܡܕܥܗ ܢܬܪܥܐ
[1] ܕܬܗܘܐ ܒܝܬܐ ܘܡܥܡܪܐ. ܘܡܫܪܝܐ ܘܗܝܟܠܐ ܘܡܢܝܚܢܐ܀'

'Hymn (10). Who can mentally conceive?
[1] To be an abode, dwelling-place,
habitation, temple, resting-place.'[77]

Conclusion: The word ܗܝܟܠܐ Temple is used to refer either to the human body, especially when the poet talks about himself, Or to the body of Christ as the temple of the Word or the temple of Trinity. It is also used to refer to Mary as the temple of God. Calling Christ a temple is a classic expression of the Antiochian school.[78] It can also be found in various Synodical texts and other East Syriac writings.[79] The image of the temple used for both Mary and Christ is a beautiful poetic evocation of one temple dwelling inside the other for the indwelling of the Word. The imagery is already found in the writings of Aphrahat and Ephrem.[80]

2. THEOLOGICAL THEMES

The following themes were discussed by the East-Syriac Church in the context of the Christological controversies in order to clarify its position: the two natures of Christ and their own individual properties, the motherhood of Mary related to the humanity of Christ, the voluntary union of love, the immutability of the divine nature, the rejection of any form of theopaschism, and the refusal of a duality of sonship (and thus a rejection of any quaternity within the Trinity). This section will highlight these themes found in the hymns of our poet, as well as other additional ones that will be taken into consideration.

2.1 The Two Natures of Christ and Their Own Individual Properties

As noted above, there are no verses in our poet's hymns that contain the famous East-Syriac formula of 'two natures and two *qnōmē* in one person'; rather, we found that

[76] A. Pritula, *The Wardā*, p. 207.

[77] G.P. Badger, *The Nestorians and their Rituals*, vol. II, pp. 51-52.

[78] Nestorius, ܬܐܓܘܪܬܐ ܕܗܪܩܠܝܕܘܣ [The Treatise of Heracleides], p. 230; S.P. Brock, "The Christology of the Church of the East," p. 132. A. Grillmeier and T. Hainthaler, *Christ in Christian Tradition*, vol. I, p. 419; vol. II/3, p. 232; R. Murray, *Symbols of Church and Kingdom*, pp. 218-228, 261, 307-309.

[79] S.P. Brock, "The Christology of The Church of The East," pp. 125-142; B. Ebeid, 'The Christology of the Church of the East', pp. 353-402; Ēlīā of Nisibis, تفسير الأمانة [Elias of Nisibis. Commentary], p. 60.

[80] R. Murray, *Symbols of Church and Kingdom*, pp. 225-226. S.P. Brock, *Bride of Light*, p. 10.

the word *qnōmā* sometimes refers to the divine nature and other times to the human nature.

In Hymns 4.(59)[5] and (35)[16ab], the poet confesses the unity of the two natures in one Sonship, but without any reference to a duality of *qnōmē*:

'ܡܥܢܝܬܐ (35). ܒܓܘܡܨܐ ܕܚܘܒܐ ܢܦܠܬ ܐܢܐ

[16] ܢ ܢܦܫܝ ܡܘܕܝܐ ܒܐܠܗܘܬܗ. ܗܟܢܐ ܐܦ ܒܐܢܫܘܬܗ.'

'Hymn (35). I fall in the pit of sins
[16] Nūn: My soul confesses His divinity
Like this also His humanity.'

In Hymn 19.(127)[9], we see how the poet considers that the Cherubim represent the cross, whereas in stanza [14] he sees in the Seraphim the mystery of the two natures of Christ and in stanza [16] he refers to the unity between the Word and its human image. In Hymn 14.(96)[3], there seem to be some influences from the writings of Nestorius.[81] Our poet points out various New Testament passages that show, on the one hand the divinity of Christ and on the other His humanity, which leads to the distinction of natures. This thinking is found also in the declaration of faith made between the Antiochians and Alexandrians in 433 after the conflict of the Council of Ephesus (431).[82] Ēlīā of Nisibis and Ēlīā II take the same approach[83] as our poet.

In Hymns 6.(71)[7], 10.(86)[9ab], 12.(92)[2ab], (94)[1cd], 13.(95)[52] and 20.(130)[1cd], Gīwargīs shows that Incarnation does not affect the divinity, whose essence remains intact. That Christ's divine nature was not subject to change or alteration is a key element in the teaching of Nestorius,[84] Bābāi the Great[85] and other East-Syriac theologians, as well as conciliar statements.[86] In this way the distinction between Christ's divinity and humanity is preserved, the latter only being subject to accepting death and pain.

Hymn (47)[5cd] seems to echo the teaching of Nestorius, who in some instances explains that God can do whatever he wishes, apart from being subject to change. In other words, he cannot cease to be God:[87]

---

[81] Nestorius, ܬܐܓܘܪܬܐ ܕܗܪܩܠܝܕܘܣ [The Treatise of Heracleides], p. 442.

[82] Nestorius, ܬܐܓܘܪܬܐ ܕܗܪܩܠܝܕܘܣ [The Treatise of Heracleides], p. 442; T.P. Halton, al., *The Fathers of the Church*, pp. 148-149; V. Van Vossel, مدرسة الإسكندرية [The School of Alexandria], p. 284.

[83] Ēlīā of Nisibis, تفسير الأمانة [Elias of Nisibis. Commentary], pp. 61-62, 118, 120; Ēlīā II, كتاب أصول الدين [The Book of Foundations of Religion], vol. I, pp. 226-235.

[84] Nestorius, ܬܐܓܘܪܬܐ ܕܗܪܩܠܝܕܘܣ [The Treatise of Heracleides], pp. 28, 38.

[85] Bābāi, ܟܬܒܐ ܕܚܘܝܕܐ [The Book of the Union], p. 60:14.

[86] S.P. Brock, "The Christology of the Church of The East," pp. 125-142; B. Ebeid, "The Christology of the Church of the East," pp. 353-402.

[87] Nestorius, ܬܐܓܘܪܬܐ ܕܗܪܩܠܝܕܘܣ [The Treatise of Heracleides], p. 20.

‘ܥܘܢܝܬܐ (47). ܚܛܝܬ ܘܐܚܛܝܬ ܘܗܐ ܚܛܐ ܐܢܐ
[5] ܕܬܥܒܕ ܡܐ ܕܨܒܝܬ ܐܝܬ ܠܟ. ܕܬܫܚܠܦ ܕܝܠܟ ܠܝܬ ܠܟ܀’

‘Hymn (47). I have sinned and instigated to sin and am sinning again
[5] To do whatever You like is intrinsic of You.
To change Your qualities is not intrinsic of You.’[88]

In Hymn 7.(72)[21, 22, 23], the poet declares that after the union there was no dissolving or separation, but on the other hand that the body was equal with the Word in greatness and worship; what pertains to divinity was also given to humanity. This statement is then followed by the poet's confession of the two natures united in one Sonship, a clear example of Antiochian roots.

The poet distinguishes between the two natures and confirms the existence of each one by keeping its properties. Thus, concerning the humanity of Christ, the poet declares in hymn 5.(67)[4] that the body of Christ was taken from Mary. To demonstrate the humanity of Christ, Gīwargīs uses the story of temptation in the desert, when Christ had a body that put-on sorrow, as expressed in stanza [38ab]. Another indication of Christ's humanity can be found in passages where Jesus practices fasting feels thirsty, such as Hymns (69)[10] and 15.(97)[4ab, 10ab]:

‘ܥܘܢܝܬܐ (69). ܨܝܡܐ ܨܠܘ ܠܝ ܗܘܢܐ
[10] ܨܡ ܕܢܚܘܐ ܛܝܒܘܬܗ. ܕܠܐ ܢܣܒܪ ܕܒܐܠܗܘܬܗ.
ܠܚܘܕ ܓܡܪ ܡܕܒܪܢܘܬܗ. ܘܕܢܫܬܪܪ ܐܢܫܘܬܗ܀’

‘Hymn (69). O those who fast, incline [your] mind to me
[10] He fasted to show His grace,
so that one should not think that He completed
His dispensation only in His divinity,
and in order that His humanity would be confirmed.’

Hymn 5.(67)[17cd, 19cd] is cast in the so-called ܣܘܓܝܬܐ *Sōġīṯā* genre, typical of Syriac poetry. It concerns a conversation between biblical individuals as a way of meditating on the spirituality of the liturgical year.[89] Here the poet makes the Evil One know that Christ was the concealed God. The Evil One asks Christ to have mercy on the human being in which the Word is dwelling, because His humanity is suffering from hunger. In this passage, we see the distinction of the two natures confessed by the Evil One when speaking to Jesus. In Hymn 6.(71)[25c] and 19.(127)[16], the poet uses the word ܨܠܡܐ *Ṣalmā*/Image to indicate the human nature that the Word took upon himself. Only in Hymn 13.(95)[51] does the poet uses the verb ܢܣܒ Nsaḇ/assumed, referring to God the Word who took a body. Additionally, our poet refers in Hymns (88)[8cd] not to the second *qnōmā* putting on a body, but to the whole divinity doing so:

[88] A. Pritula, *The Wardā*, p. 345.

[89] M. Nicák, “Der Mongoleneinfall in Karmeliš,” pp. 214-215; M. Nicák, “The Direct Speech of John the Baptist,” p. 332.

'ܥܘܢܝܬܐ (88). ܠܩܪܒܐ ܕܣܗܕܐ ܢܦܩܬ
[8] ܘܡܘܕܐ ܐܢܐ ܠܐܠܗܘܬܐ. ܕܠܒܫܬ ܦܓܪܐ ܕܐܢܫܘܬܐ܀'

'Hymn (88). I have joined the battle of martyrs
[8] And I profess the Godhead [divinity]
that put on the body of humanity.'[90]

A similar expression is found in Hymn (154)[22] by Gīwargīs of Adiabene, who says that the divinity dwelled in the humanity:

'ܥܘܢܝܬܐ (154). ܒܢܨܪܬ ܡܕܝܢܬܐ ܓܠܝܠܝܬܐ. ܐܫܬܡܥ ܡ̈ܠܐ ܕܠܒܪ ܡܢ ܚܝܠܐ
[22] ܥ ܥܝܪ̈ܐ ܫܡܥܘ ܣܒܪܬܐ ܚܕܬܐ. ܕܐܡܪ ܪܫ ܚܝ̈ܠܘܬܐ.
ܕܗܐ ܥܡܪܬ ܠܗ ܐܠܗܘܬܐ. ܒܐܢܫܘܬܐ ܒܚܕܝܘܬܐ܀'

'Hymn (154). In Nazareth, the Galilean city words were heard beyond the power
[22] 'Ē: The watchers heard a new announcement,
that the head of the powers said:
See! That divinity dwelled
in humanity in unity.'

Our poet uses some specific titles to indicate the divinity of Christ, such as referring to Christ as the 'corporeal God' ܐܠܗܐ ܦܓܪܢܝܐ in Hymns (1)[36d] and (3)[11]:

'ܥܘܢܝܬܐ (1). ܒܫܢܬ ܐܪܒܥܝܢ ܘܬܪ̈ܬܝܢ ܫܢ̈ܝܐ
[36] ܕܗܐ ܝܠܝܕ ܡܫܝܚܐ ܡܪܝܐ. ܐܠܗܐ ܦܓܪܢܝܐ܀'

'Hymn (1). In the year forty-two
[36] Behold, Christ the Lord is born,
the corporeal God!'

'ܥܘܢܝܬܐ (3). ܡܢ ܗܦܟ ܠܗ ܠܪܒܘܬܟ
[11] ܐܠܦ ܐܢܘܢ ܐܪܡܝܐ. ܠܡܨܪ̈ܝܐ ܕܡܬܓܠܐ ܒܐܘܪܝܐ.
ܐܠܗܐ ܦܓܪܢܝܐ. ܘܠܦܬܟܪ̈ܐ ܚܪܒ ܠܡܒܘܥܐ܀'

'Hymn (3). Who would perceive Your greatness
[11] Jeremiah taught
the Egyptians that the corporeal God
would be revealed in the manger would be
and He would terminate the idols.'[91]

Hymn (8)[13] refers to Jesus as God putting on man:

'ܥܘܢܝܬܐ (8). ܒܪܐ ܕܦܩܕܢ ܒܗ ܫܒܩܬܐ
[13] ܗܘ ܕܐܝܬܘܗܝ ܒܗ ܡܢ ܪܘܚ ܩܘܕܫܐ. ܠܒܫܗ ܘܐܠܗܘܬܗ ܡܢ ܙܪܥ ܐܢܫܐ.
ܘܝܫܘܥ ܫܡܗ ܐܝܟ ܐܢܫܐ. ܘܐܠܗܐ ܗܘ ܠܒܝܫ ܒܪܢܫܐ܀'

---

[90] A. Pritula, *The Wardā*, p. 485. Translation slightly adapted.
[91] A. Pritula, *The Wardā*, p. 187. Translation slightly adapted.

'Hymn (8). <u>The Son in whom treasures are hidden</u>

[13] The one who is in her was made from the Holy Spirit,
and was not from a human seed.
Jesus will be called like man,
and He is God clothed with man.'[92]

Other titles are given to Christ, some of which can refer to both natures. Thus, in Hymn 17.(109)[3], the poet shows how Christ wanted to reveal to humanity that He was God. Hymn 16.(106)[9cd] refers to Christ as God. Another epithet of Christ is found in (2)[26d], where he is called ܐܠܗܐ ܡܬܚܘܝܢܐ the manifest God; in (2)[38d], ܐܠܗܐ ܡܬܓܫܡܢܐ the incarnate God; in (2)[52c], ܐܠܗܐ ܘܒܪ ܐܠܗܐ God and the Son of God; in (3)[22a], ܐܠܗܐ ܟܣܝܐ the concealed God; in (7)[28d], ܐܠܗܐ ܡܒܣܪܐ God made flesh; in (31)[14c], ܐܠܗܐ ܕܡܢ ܐܠܗܐ God from God; in 19.(127)[48 b], ܐܠܗܐ ܒܪܢܫ God-man, a title also frequently found in the hymns of Narsai.[93]

In Hymn (122)[7], our poet tells the story of the Canaanite woman whose daughter was possessed by a demon,[94] depicting her as someone asking mercy 'for His image', i.e. her daughter. There is a subtle and poetic 'confusion' between the 'image of God' and the 'image of Christ', thus indirectly suggesting that Christ is God:

'ܬܘܫܒܚܬܐ (122). <u>ܡܠܟܐ ܕܪܘܡܐ ܥܠܝܐ</u>
[7] ܝܫܘܥ ܡܫܝܚܐ ܒܪܗ ܕܕܘܝܕ. ܡܪܗ ܘܐܠܗܗ ܕܕܘܝܕ.
ܚܘܣ ܥܠ ܨܠܡܟ ܕܐܒܕ. ܘܒܟ ܓܘܣܐ ܒܪ̈ܚܡܝܟ ܢܣܒ܀'

'Hymn (122). <u>The king of lofty heights</u>

[7] Jesus Christ the Son of David,
the Lord and God of David,
have mercy on Your image because it will perish,
and in Your mercy, it will hold refuge.'

In Hymn 18.(121)[2], our poet paraphrases Philippians 2:7, the core of Christology.

By way of conclusion, we can say that there are many names and titles mentioned above that refer to the Incarnation of the Word-God. Sometimes, they are difficult to translate into English. This rich imagery and these many titles demonstrate the creativity of our poet.

2.2 Incarnation as an Expression of God's Grace and Good Will

In many hymns, Gīwargīs meditates on the fact that the Incarnation is to be ascribed to God's grace (ܛܝܒܘܬܐ Grace, ܨܒܝܢܐ will, ܚܘܒܐ love). Examples can be found in Hymns (35)[7ab], 6.(71)[18] and 11.(91)[2cd, 3cd, 5cd, 33cd].

This emphasis is to be seen against the background of Theodore who often refers to 'the union of good pleasure' or 'grace'.[95] Nestorius too repeats that the union was

---

[92] For other translations of this hymn, see Table 8.
[93] F.G. McLeod, *Narsai's Metrical Homilies*, p. 98:452.
[94] Matt 15:21.
[95] A. Grillmeier and T. Hainthaler, *Christ in Christian Tradition*, vol. I, pp. 421-439; V. Van Vossel, مدرسة أنطاكيا [The School of Antioch], p. 87.

a voluntary one, to keep the natures safe from confusion.[96] The same idea exists in other writings of Nestorius[97] as well as other early fathers like Narsai[98] Bābāi the Great,[99] Ēlīā of Nisibis,[100] Ēlīā II[101] and ʿAbdīšōʿ bar Brīẖā, who says that the unity was by will, power, pleasure, and volition.[102]

2.3 The Immutability of the Divine Nature and Theopaschism

Discussion on this point started in the early days of Christianity, especially when interpreting John 1:14, "The Word became flesh and made his dwelling among us". The main problem was how to explain 'became' and 'dwelling'; many times we find writers from the East-Syriac Church confirming that the word 'became' does not mean a change in the nature of God to a human nature, thus protecting God from the problem of Theopaschism. Our poet often confirms that God, or the divine nature, has not changed, a theme found often in the writings of East-Syriac authors, especially Bābāi in ܟܬܒܐ ܕܚܘܝܕܐ *The Book of the Union*. Gīwargīs uses the following words to indicate that the nature neither changed nor was transmitted: ܫܘܠܝܢܐ, ܫܘܚܠܦܐ, ܫܘܢܝܐ. This can be found in Hymns 6.(71)[5], 7.(72)[13], 10.(86)[9], 13.(95)[52] and 20.(130)[1].

From the conjunction of the two natures as described by Gīwargīs, it is evident that our poet rejects the idea that God can suffer or die as a result of the union between the natures. In Hymn 3.(38)[1c, 6d, 10cd], the poet clearly says that the divinity neither changes nor accepts effects and that the nature of God is beyond pain. In Hymns 3.(38)[12ab] and (77)[35ab], the poet affirms the same idea by saying that the one who does not suffer put on a body that suffers. Rejecting of the suffering of God is also found in the synodical texts[103] as well as in ܟܬܒܐ ܕܚܘܝܕܐ *The Book of the Union*,[104] and in the homilies of Narsai:[105]

---

96 Nestorius, ܬܫܥܝܬܐ ܕܗܪܩܠܝܕܘܣ [The Treatise of Heracleides], pp. 54-55; L. Scipioni, *Ricerche Sulla Cristologia del 'Libro di Eraclide'*, pp. 25-29.

97 Nestorius, ܬܫܥܝܬܐ ܕܗܪܩܠܝܕܘܣ [The Treatise of Heracleides], pp. 54-55.

98 F.G. McLeod, *Narsai's Metrical Homilies*, p. 36:5; p. 62:411.

99 Bābāi, ܟܬܒܐ ܕܚܘܝܕܐ [The Book of the Union], pp. 50:10, 131:11-14.

100 Ēlīā of Nisibis, تفسير الأمانة [Elias of Nisibis. Commentary], pp. 66, 126.

101 Ēlīā II, كتاب أصول الدين [The Book of Foundations of Religion], p. 240.

102 ʿAbdīšōʿ B. Brīẖā, كتاب فرائد الفوائد, *Testi teologici di Ebedjesu*, pp. 118-119, 256-257; ʿAbdīšōʿ B. Brīẖā, كتاب أصول الدين, *I fondamenti della religione*, pp. 228-229.

103 S.P. Brock, "The Christology of the Church of the East," pp. 133, 135.

104 Bābāi, ܟܬܒܐ ܕܚܘܝܕܐ [The Book of the Union], p. 60:7.

105 Narsai says: 'The natures I have distinguished because of the passion and the glories; one are the passible and the impassible, the Word and the Body'. F.G. McLeod, *Narsai's Metrical Homilies*, p. 64:448.

'ܬܫܒܘܚܬܐ (77). ܟܕ ܥܐܠ ܡܪܢ ܠܐܘܪܫܠܡ
[35] ܐܘܫܥܢܐ ܠܕܠܐ ܚܫܘܫܐ. ܕܠܒܫ ܦܓܪܐ ܚܫܘܫܐ܀'

'Hymn (77). Our Lord entering Jerusalem
[35] Hosanna to the one who is without passion
who put on a body subject to passion.'[106]

An anonymous hymn in the *Book of Wardā*, Hymn (22)[20], shows that it was not God who was crucified, but a human being 'from us, ܡܢܢ', the author of this hymn stating that this was the argument of Narsai against the heretics:

'ܬܫܒܘܚܬܐ (22). ܫܘܒܚܐ ܠܚܝܠܐ ܡܣܝܟܢܗܘܢ
[20] ܘܩܥܐ ܘܐܡܪ ܕܗܐ ܟܠܒܐ ܢܒܚܝܢ ܠܡܪܗܘܢ.
ܠܘ ܐܠܗܐ ܚܫ ܘܐܙܕܩܦ. ܐܠܐ ܒܪܢܫܐ ܕܡܢܢ. ܡܫܡܠܝ ܒܦܓܪܐ ܘܒܢܦܫܐ.'

'Hymn (22). Glory to the power, their supporter
[20] He [Narsai] cried and said:
'O dogs who bark at their master.
It was not God who suffered and crucified,
but a human being from us,
perfect in body and soul.'[107]

Rejecting the suffering of God can be traced back to the writings of the Antiochian fathers, such as Nestorius.[108] Narsai also adds that God the Word suffered in love but not in nature.[109] The same idea can also be found in some creedal formulas from the Synods of the Church[110] and in some other East-Syriac writings.[111] For the contemporary period, the same rejection is to be found in a letter written by Yahḇālāhā III when expressing the faith of his Church by confirming that the divinity does not accept suffering.[112]

2.4 Duality of the Sons and Quaternity

This theme is often treated by the East-Syriac Church, which rejects it outright. The accusation of quaternity was made because of the formula of the two *qnōmē* which, according to opponents of the East-Syriac Church,[113] meant that there must be two

---

[106] A. Pritula, *The Wardā*, p. 473. Translation slightly adapted.

[107] The homily mentioned in this hymn might be the one on the Greek fathers: Diodore, Theodore and Nestorius. Narsai also demonstrates that the one who was crucified was a human being and not God the Word. See F. Martin, "Homélie de Narses sur les trois docteurs nestoriens," *JA* 9.14 (1899), p. 453; F.G. McLeod, *Narsai's Metrical Homilies*, pp. 106, 136.

[108] Nestorius, ܬܐܓܘܪܬܐ ܕܗܪܩܠܝܕܣ [The Treatise of Heracleides], pp. 57-58.

[109] J. Frishman, "Narsai's Christology," pp. 293, 295-296. F.G. McLeod, *Narsai's Metrical Homilies*, p. 28.

[110] S.P. Brock, "The Christology of the Church of The East," pp. 133-142; B. Ebeid, "The Christology of the Church of the East," pp. 353-402.

[111] L. Abramowski and A.E. Goodman, *A Nestorian Collection*, pp. 98-100, 120.

[112] L. Bottini, "Due lettere," p. 246.

[113] S. Rassi, "Justifying Christianity," p. 137.

sons: one divine, and the other human. Gīwargīs clearly shows that he does not confess two sons,[114] such as in Hymn 6.(71)[19, 26]; for that reason the Trinity is not a quaternity, as expressed in Hymns 7.(72)[13] and 19.(127)[15], where he says that the Trinity does not accept addition or subtraction.

The refusal of quaternity is already found in Theodore's writings,[115]as well as in those of Nestorius,[116] Bābāi[117] and the Synodal texts.[118]

2.5 Mary's Motherhood

Gīwargīs has been called 'The poet of Mary' because of the many hymns dedicated to her. We will not discuss here all the titles of Mary, only those related to the humanity and divinity of Christ. In Hymns (5)[4], (6)[1] and (7)[8], he named her 'the second heaven'. This title is common in the general Syriac tradition and can be found in the works of many authors, including Ephrem,[119] Narsai,[120] Jacob of Serugh,[121] Ēlīā III,[122] and Ḫāmīs.[123] According to Bachi, this title and others refer to Mary as the 'Mother of God',[124] but Bachi's Chaldean background may have influenced him to interpret certain texts too eagerly as 'orthodox' according to a Catholic views, whereas this is not necessarily implied by Gīwargīs or by the other poets.

'ܡܕܪܫܐ (5). ܕܟܝܐ ܘܪܚܡ ܠܕܟܝܐ

[4] ܪ ܠܘܐ ܡܨ ܡܠܬܐ ܫܪܒܗ. ܘܣܦܘܬܐ ܠܗ ܚܣܝܪܢ.

ܕܡܥܬ ܠܗ ܠܡܦܫܩܘܬܗ. ܘܠܐ ܡܨܝܐ ܠܗ ܪܥܝܢܘܬܐ.:'

'Hymn (5). <u>The pure and the lover of the pure</u>

[4] Rēš: The word cannot explain her story,
the lips are inadequate for her,

[114] The same idea is found in Narsai when he says ܠܘ ܦܘܠܓܐ ܕܒܪܐ ܘܒܪܐ ܕܒܛܢܗ ܣܘܟܠܝ : [It is not a division of Son and Son (that) my thought has conceived]. See F.G. McLeod, *Narsai's Metrical Homilies*, p. 64:439. See also ʿAbdīšōʿ when he says that the essence of God does not accept addition. ʿAbdīšōʿ B. Brīḫā, كتاب فرائد الفوائد, *Testi teologici di Ebedjesu*, pp. 90-91, 108-109; ʿAbdīšōʿ B. Brīḫā, كتاب أصول الدين, *I fondamenti della religione*, pp. 228-229.

[115] V. Van Vossel, ثيودوروس المعلم الكبير [Theodore the Great Teacher], pp.84-90.

[116] Nestorius, ܬܫܥܝܬܐ ܕܗܪܩܠܝܕܝܣ [The Treatise of Heracleides], pp. 69-71.

[117] Bābāi, ܟܬܒܐ ܕܚܘܝܕܐ [The Book of the Union], p. 154:7.

[118] S.P. Brock, "The Christology of the Church of The East," pp. 125-142; B. Ebeid, "The Christology of the Church of the East," pp. 353-402.

[119] G. Ricciotti, *Inni alla Vergine*, p. 73, stanza [37].

[120] S.P. Brock, *Bride of Light*, p. 116, stanza [37]. According to Brock, this hymn is wrongly attributed to Narsai.

[121] Jacob of Serugh, *On the Mother of God*, p. 18.

[122] The hymn of Elia III is found in T. Darmo, ed. *Ḥūḏrā* ܚܘܕܪܐ [The Cycle], vol. I, p.ܬܪ [600], Also in Ēlīā Abū Ḥalīm, التراجيم السنيّة للأعياد المارانية, *Discorus Religieux*, p. 30. The expression 'second heaven' is also found in another anonymous hymn in the T. Darmo, ed. *Ḥūḏrā* ܚܘܕܪܐ [The Cycle], vol. I, p.ܬܪܗ [605].

[123] Š.Ī. Ḥadbšabbā, ܚܡܝܣ ܒܪ ܩܪܕܚܐ [Ḫāmīs bar Qardāḥē], p. 17.

[124] P.H. Bachi, "Marie dans la doctrine de Ghiwarghis Warda," pp. 514-520. Further study is needed to determine if the early fathers truly understood this title as 'Mother of God'.

because she is the second heaven,
and humanity does not reach her.'[125]

'ܥܘܢܝܬܐ (6). ܥܠ ܫܡܝܐ ܬܢܝܢܝܬܐ
[1] ܥܠ ܫܡܝܐ ܬܢܝܢܝܬܐ. ܨܒܝܬ ܗܘܝܬ ܕܐܪܫܘܡ ܒܟܬܒܝܬܐ.'

'Hymn (6). On the second heaven
[1] On the second heaven,
I was willing to inscribe in the books.'

'ܥܘܢܝܬܐ (7). ܒܢܨܪܬ ܡܕܝܢܬܐ ܕܓܠܝܠܐ.
[8] ܫܠܡ ܠܟܝ ܡܠܝܬ ܛܝܒܘܬܐ. ܘܗܝܟܠܐ ܡܠܝܐ ܩܕܝܫܘܬܐ.
ܘܡܫܪܝܐ ܕܐܠܗܘܬܐ. ܘܫܡܝܐ ܬܢܝܢܝܬܐ܀'

'Hymn (7). In Nazareth, the Galilean town
[8] 'Peace to you, full of grace!
Temple, full of holiness!
Abode of Godhood
and second heaven!''[126]

In Hymn (2)[12], the poet uses the burning bush as an example of Mary bearing the life-giver. This example is also found in the writings of Nestorius, Cyril and Bābāi:[127]

'ܥܘܢܝܬܐ (2). ܝܠܕܗ ܕܠܝܬ ܠܝܠܕܗ ܙܒܢܐ
[12] ܘܗܘ ܣܢܝܐ ܕܝܩܕܢܘܬ ܗܘܐ. ܒܢܘܪܐ ܘܠܐ ܝܩܕ ܗܘܐ.
ܐܪܙܗ ܕܡܪܝܡ ܨܘܪܐ ܗܘܐ. ܕܝܠܕܬ ܒܟܪܣܗ ܠܦܪܘܩܢܐ܀'

'Hymn (2). The Nativity of Him, whose nativity is not time-ridden
[12] And the bush, which burned
with fire and did not burn down
was an image of Mary's mystery,
who bore the Savior in her womb.'[128]

The image of the burning bush is used in other hymns of Gīwargīs, such as (9)[16], and (10)[130]:

'ܥܘܢܝܬܐ (9). ܒܢܝܫܐ ܕܫܘܒܚܐ ܗܘ ܕܡܢ ܐܒܐ
[16] ܗܕܐ ܗܝ ܣܢܝܐ ܕܒܛܘܪܣܝܢܝ. ܕܡܫܐ ܒܟܠܗ ܓܘܙܠܬܐ.
ܘܠܐ ܐܚܕܬ ܒܗ ܢܘܪܐ ܡܫܟܚܬܐ܀'

[125] For other translations of this hymn, see Table 8.
[126] A. Pritula, *The Wardā*, p. 207.
[127] Nestorius, ܬܐܓܘܪܬܐ ܕܗܪܩܠܝܕܘܣ [The Treatise of Heracleides], p. 229; V. Van Vossel, مدرسة الإسكندرية [The School of Alexandria], p. 300; Bābāi, ܟܬܒܐ ܕܚܘܝܕܐ [The Book of the Union], p. 85:14. It is interesting to note that Nestorius, Cyril, Bābāi and Gīwargīs all used the same example of the burning bush despite interpreting it in different ways. The image of the burning bush is also found in the writings of ʿAbdīšōʿ when referring to the unity between God and man. See ʿAbdīšōʿ B. Brīḫā, كتاب أصول الدين, *I fondamenti della religione*, pp. 232-233.
[128] A. Pritula, *The Wardā*, p. 173. Translation of Pritula slightly adapted for the sake of theological implications related to the word ܣܢܝܐ.

'Hymn (9). Here in the sea of sin I am cast!
[16] She is a wonderful bush,
inside which a flame was conceived.
And three and six months
a burning fire dwelled in her.'[129]

'ܥܘܢܝܬܐ (10). ܡܢ ܡܨܐ ܕܒܡܕܥܗ ܢܬܕܪܟ
[130] ܛܘܒܝܟܝ ܣܢܝܐ ܕܬܕܡܘܪܬܐ. ܕܠܐ ܐܬܚܪܟ ܡܢ ܫܘܠܗܒܝܬܐ.'

'Hymn (10). Who can mentally conceive
[130] Blessed art thou, O wonderful bush,
which was not burnt by the flame.'[130]

In Hymn (7)[28d], Mary is called the mother of the corporeal God. In Hymn (10)[57], the poet shows how she is like a closed-door; entering it and going out from it is only allowed of the Lord. In the same hymn, stanza [60], the poet does not specify the second *qnōmā* of the Trinity, merely stating that God dwelt in her and was born from her as the Son of God:

'ܥܘܢܝܬܐ (7). ܒܢܨܪܬ ܡܕܝܢܬܐ ܕܓܠܝܠܐ.
[28] ܘܐܠܗܐ ܡܒܣܪܐ ܒܪܟܝ.'

'Hymn (7). In Nazareth, the Galilean town
[28] And the incarnate God is your son!'[131]

'ܥܘܢܝܬܐ (10). ܡܢ ܡܨܐ ܕܒܡܕܥܗ ܢܬܕܪܟ
[30] ܕܐܚܝܕ ܘܐܢܫ ܠܐ ܥܐܠ ܠܗ. ܕܡܪܝܐ ܒܠܚܘܕ ܥܐܠ ܘܢܦܩ ܒܗ.
[31] ܗܕܐ ܗܝ ܕܒܗ ܫܪܐ ܐܠܗܐ. ܘܢܦܩ ܡܢܗ ܒܪܐ ܕܐܠܗܐ.'

'Hymn (10). Who can mentally conceive
[30] which is shut [the door i.e. Mary], which none can enter.[132]
But Lord only who enters and goes out by it.
[31] This is she in whom God dwelt
and from whom sprang the Son of God.'[133]

[129] A. Pritula, The *Wardā*, p. 221.
[130] G.P. Badger, *The Nestorians and their Rituals*, vol. II, p. 55.
[131] A. Pritula, *The Wardā*, p. 211. Translation slightly adapted.
[132] The same image is found in hymn (9)[34]:

ܥܘܢܝܬܐ (9). ܒܝܡܐ ܕܚܛܗ̈ܐ ܗܐ ܪܡܐ ܐܢܐ
[34] ܗܕܐ ܗܝ ܬܪܥܗ ܕܡܪܝܐ. ܕܐܡܝܪ ܠܚܙܩܝܐܝܠ ܢܒܝܐ.
ܕܠܐ ܢܕܘܫܝܘܗܝ ܦܓܪܢܝܐ. ܕܒܗ ܡܪܝܐ ܘܢܦܩ ܥܒܪܐ܀

Hymn (9). Here in the sea of sins I am cast!
[34] She is the gate of the Lord,
Of which it is said by the prophet Ezekiel,
That no bodily being would tread upon it,
For the Lord would come through them in and out.

See A. Pritula, *The Wardā*, p. 225. Translation slightly adapted.
[133] G.P. Badger, *The Nestorians and their Rituals*, vol. II, p. 53.

In Hymn (7)[20], Gīwargīs calls Mary 'mother of the humanity of Christ'; the same expression is found in Hymn (74)[2ab] which is written by Sabrīšōʿ bar Pawlis. In Hymns (9)[61a] and (10)[87a], our poet mentions Mary as the mother of the Lord, which accords with the teaching of the Church of the East:

‘ܥܘܢܝܬܐ (7). ܒܢܨܪܬ ܡܕܝܢܬܐ ܕܓܠܝܠܐ
[20] ܐܒܐ ܢܫܪܐ ܒܟܝ ܡܠܬܗ. ܒܪܐ ܢܥܡܪ ܒܟܝ ܒܛܝܒܘܬܗ.
ܘܟܕ ܐܢܬܝ ܒܪܝܬܗ ܘܐܡܬܗ. ܐܡܐ ܗܘܝܐ ܠܐܢܫܘܬܗ܀’

'Hymn (7). In Nazareth, the Galilean town
[20] The Father will settle His Word in you,
the Son will dwell in you by His grace.
And although you are His creature and servant,
you will become mother to His humanity.'[134]

‘ܥܘܢܝܬܐ (74). ܡܫܝܚܐ ܡܪܗ ܕܫܘܒܚܐ
[2] ܡܪܢ ܒܨܠܘܬ ܝܠܕܬܟ. ܡܪܝܡ ܐܡܐ ܕܐܢܫܘܬܟ.’

'Hymn (74). Christ the Lord of glory
[2] Our Lord, by the prayer of Your mother,
Mary, the mother of Your humanity.'

‘ܥܘܢܝܬܐ (9). ܒܝܡܐ ܕܚܘܒܐ ܗܐ ܪܡܐ ܐܢܐ
[61] ܡܪܬܝ ܘܐܡܗ ܕܡܪܝ ܒܨܠܘܬܐ.’

'Hymn (9). Here in the sea of sins I am cast!
[61] My lady and mother of my Lord! In the prayer.'[135]

‘ܥܘܢܝܬܐ (10). ܡܢ ܡܨܐ ܕܒܡܪܢܝܬܐ ܢܬܪܓܡ
[87] ܗܝ ܕܠܡܪܝܐ ܐܡܐ ܗܘܬ.’

'Hymn (10). Who can mentally conceive
[87] She who became the mother of the Lord.'[136]

In the same hymn, stanza [133b], Gīwargīs writes that her Son was called Ēl ܐܝܠ. Bachi sees again this verse as evidence that Gīwargīs is confessing that Mary is the 'Mother of God'.[137] For a poet like Gīwargīs playing with words is an art, and the evidence as seen by Bachi might be weak if we compare it with Hymn (7)[20], which says that she is the mother of the humanity of Christ. Notably, we also find the discussion on the title 'Mother of God' in the writings of early fathers like Theodore, Nestorius and Bābāi for whom the title Theotokos is by relation and Anthropotokos is by nature, but it is obvious that they preferred Christotokos:[138]

---

[134] A. Pritula, *The Wardā*, p. 211.
[135] A. Pritula, *The Wardā*, p. 231.
[136] G.P. Badger, *The Nestorians and their Rituals*, vol. II, p. 54.
[137] P.H. Bachi, "Marie dans la doctrine de Ghiwarghis Warda," p. 519.
[138] Theodore of Mopsuestia, *Theodori Mopsuesteni fragmenta exegetica et dogmatica*, PG 66, lib. xv, 992 BC; V. Van Vossel, مدرسة أنطاكيا [The School of Antioch], p. 165; V. Van Vossel, ثيودوروس المعلم الكبير [Theodore the Great Teacher], p. 123; Bābāi, ܟܬܒܐ ܕܚܘܝܕܐ, [The Book of the Union], p. 100: 2-11.

‘ܬܫܒܘܚܬܐ (10). ܡܢ ܡܨܐ ܕܒܡܕܥܗ ܢܬܕܪܟ
[133] ܛܘܒܝܟܝ ܕܐܫܥܝܐ ܫܒܚܟܝ.
ܘܒܬܘܠܬܐ ܩܪܟܝ ܘܐܝܠ ܠܒܪܟܝ.’

‘Hymn (10). Who can mentally conceive
[133] Blessed art you that Isaiah praised you,
calling you a Virgin, and your Son, God [Ēl].’[139]

In Hymn (42)[2] the term Ēl, is used even twice:

‘ܬܫܒܘܚܬܐ (42). ܐܒܕ ܓܒܪܐ ܒܪܓܝܓܬܐ
[2] ܐ ܐܠܗܝ ܘܡܪܝ ܥܡܢܘܐܝܠ. ܫܡܥܝܢܝ ܐܝܟ ܕܠܐܝܫܡܥܝܠ.
ܘܚܘܝ ܡܒܘܥܟ ܘܗܒ ܚܝܠ. ܘܐܪܘܐ ܡܢܟ ܐܝܠ ܒܪ ܐܝܠ܀’

‘Hymn (42). A man perishes by desires
[2] Ālap: My God and my Lord, Emmanuel,
listen to me as You listened to Ismael,
show me Your fount and strengthen me,
and I will be inebriate from You, God [Ēl], Son of God [Ēl].’[140]

In Hymn (152)[41], written by Šlēmūn the metropolitan of Baṣra (12th cent.), the author mentions that the angels celebrated the mother of the Lord Ēl:

‘ܬܫܒܘܚܬܐ (152). ܛܘܒܝܟܝ ܐܡܐ ܡܒܪܟܬܐ
[41] ܪ ܪܫ ܡܠܐܟܐ ܓܒܪܐܝܠ. ܥܡ ܒܪ ܬܓܡܗ ܡܝܟܐܝܠ.
ܙܡܪܘ ܠܐܡܗ ܕܡܪܐ ܐܝܠ. ܠܐܝܩܪܗ ܕܥܡܢܘܐܝܠ܀’

‘Hymn (152). Blessed are you, blessed mother
[41] Rēš: Gabriel, the head of the angels,
with Michael the one of his [Gabriel’s] rank,
celebrated the mother of the Lord God [Ēl],
for the honor of Emmanuel.’

An anonymous hymn, (153)[1ef], mentions Mary as the mother of Christ; in the same hymn, stanza [9], the author says that the watcher told the Virgin that Ēl would dwell in her and be called Emmanuel:

‘ܬܫܒܘܚܬܐ (153). ܬܘܕܝܬܐ ܢܩܪܒ ܟܠܢ
[1] ܘܛܘܒܐ ܐܡܪܝܢ ܥܡ̈ܡܐ. ܠܐܡܗ ܕܡܫܝܚܐ ܡܠܟܢ܀
[9] ܚ ܚܝܠ ܥܝܪܐ ܓܒܪܐܝܠ. ܠܒܬܘܠܬܐ ܒܪܬ ܐܝܣܪܝܠ.
ܘܐܡܪ ܠܗ ܕܒܟܝ ܫܪܐ ܐܝܠ. ܘܡܬܩܪܐ ܫܡܗ ܥܡܢܘܐܝܠ܀’

‘Hymn (153). We all offer praise
[1] Nations bless
the mother of Christ, our king.
[9] Ḥēṭ: The watcher Gabriel strengthened
the Virgin, the daughter of Israel,

[139] G.P. Badger, *The Nestorians and their Rituals*, vol. II, p. 56. Translation slightly adapted.
[140] J.K. Hood, “Songs of Supplication and Penitence,” p. 162. Translation slightly adapted.

and told her: 'In you will dwell God [Ēl],
and He will be called Emmanuel'.'

A final image of the Word dwelling in Mary occurs when the poet refers to her as a corporeal throne (10)[139]:

'ܥܘܢܝܬܐ (10). ܡܢ ܡܨܐ ܕܒܡܕܥܗ ܢܬܕܪܟ
[139] ܛܘܒܝܟܝ ܟܘܪܣܝܐ ܦܓܪܢܝܐ. ܕܒܟ ܚܣܡ ܟܘܪܣܝܐ ܗܘ ܢܘܪܢܝܐ.'

'Hymn (10). Who can mentally conceive
[139] Blessed art thou O bodily throne,
which was envied by the throne of fire.'[141]

In summary Mariology is important for Christology. The various titles given to Mary confirm the traditional picture of Mary giving birth to the man Jesus. But interestingly, a number of expressions used in the hymns almost suggest the appellation 'Mother of God',[142] though Bachi goes too far when he thinks that Gīwargīs accepts 'Mary, Mother of God'. Gīwargīs remains within the orbit of classical East-Syriac thinking, using terms already found in the early tradition.

2.6 The Sonship of Christ

The Sonship of Christ is expressed in various ways. In Hymns (6)[19] and 8.(75)[5], ܒܪܐ ܕܐܠܗܐ Son of God; in (8)[50a], 11.(91)[32c], (14)[52], 15.(97)[4a] and (159)[50, 78], ܒܪ ܐܝܬܘܬܐ, ܒܪܐ ܕܐܝܬܘܬܐ Son of the essence (this latter title is also used by Narsai[143] and Ḥakīm d-bēṯ Qāšā in his hymn (14)[52]); in Hymn (10)[46b] and 2.(13)[3d], ܒܪ ܥܠܝܐ Son of the Most High; in 1.(12)[37a] and 17.(109)[8a]; ܒܪ ܒܪܘܝܐ Son of the creator; in (42)[3c]; the interesting expression ܒܪܘܝܐ ܒܪ ܒܪܘܝܐ creator, Son of the creator, which highlights Christ's divinity; in (29)[3a], ܒܪܐ ܕܐܒܘܗܝ Son of His Father; in (7)[21d], 15.(97)[9c] and 19.(127)[2b]; ܒܪܐ ܝܚܝܕܝܐ, ܒܪܗ ܝܚܝܕܝܐ, ܒܪܐ ܝܚܝܕܝܐ only-begotten Son; in (7)[2a], (81)[7a], 13.(95)[51b] and (119)[23b], ܐܠܗܐ ܡܠܬܐ God the Word; in 15.(97)[1b]. ܡܪܝܐ ܡܠܬܐ Lord the Word; in (14)[70], ܒܪܐ ܝܚܝܕܝܐ ܡܠܬܐ the Only-begotten Son the Word.

In other hymns, the poet refers to the unity of the subject, such as in Hymn (2)[16], when he calls Christ a son born from Mary, who at the same time was also called God.[144] The same idea is found in Hymns 12.(92)[1gh] and 18.(121)[19a].

Speaking of 'the Son of God' and the 'Son of mortality' does not imply that our poet accepts a duality of sons. This becomes visible in Hymn 6.(71)[26]. Other titles given to Christ are, in Hymn (2)[8a, 21a], ܨܠܡܐ ܕܐܠܗܘܬܐ the image of the divinity; in

---

[141] G.P. Badger, *The Nestorians and their Rituals*, vol. II, p. 56. In the second verse Badger wrongly translates the word ܢܘܪܢܝܐ as 'light'.

[142] Maroš Nicák states that not using the term 'Mother of God' directly is also due to the Islamic context, since in the eyes of Muslims the term 'Mother of God' would affect God's transcendence. See M. Nicák, "Der Mongoleneinfall in Karmeliš," p. 202. This argument does not seem very convincing, since Muslims did not read Syriac books.

[143] F.G. McLeod, Narsai's *Metrical Homilies*, p. 64:434.

[144] A. Pritula, *The Wardā*, p. 175.

17.(109)[1a] and 20.(130)[1a], ܨܡܚܗ ܕܐܒܐ ܡܬܘܡܝܐ the ray of the eternal Father; in 13.(95)[52ab], ܗܝܟܠܐ ܠܡܠܬܐ the temple for the Word, a title used also by Sabrīšōᶜ bar Pawlis in Hymn (74)[1b] and by Yahḇālāhā II in Hymn (151)[11]. Finally, the poet uses the unusual titles, such as: in Hymn (2)[8b][145] ܗܝܟܠܐ ܕܬܠܝܬܝܘܬܐ the temple of the Trinity; in Hymn (76)[49] ܡܘܬܗ ܕܡܘܬܐ the death of the death; in Hymn (11)[1] ܒܪܐ ܐܒܝܬܘܬܢܐ the Consubstantial Son; in Hymn (6)[14] ܨܠܡ ܚܫܘܟܐ the image of obscurity; in hymn 12(92)[44] ܐܠܗܐ ܚܕܬܐ the new God; and in Hymn 13.(95)[50d] ܒܪ ܡܝܘܬܘܬܐ the Son of mortality.

When comparing these names given to Christ with those listed by Bābāi in one chapter of ܟܬܒܐ ܕܚܕܝܘܬܐ *The book of the Union*,[146] we find that Gīwargīs is more creative in his naming of Christ, especially when using unusual titles such as 'The Son of mortality' and 'The temple of the Trinity' and 'the death of the death'. Bābāi depends on Bible more than Gīwargīs, who does not hesitate to be creative.

2.7 The Equality With the Father

Hymn (99)[11] is the only hymn where the poet refutes the idea that Christians believe in two gods; we may assume that here he has Muslims in mind because the hymn is addressed to those who 'say that God is one', a common expression to designate Muslims:

'ܡܕܪܫܐ (99). ܫܘܒܚܐ ܠܗ ܠܗܘ ܚܢܢܐ
[11] ܗܘ ܕܐܡܪ ܕܚܕ ܐܠܗܐ. ܫܡܥ ܐܘ ܪܚܡ ܐܠܗܐ.
ܚܕ ܐܘܕܝܐ ܒܗ ܘܒܐܠܗܐ. ܕܚܕ ܐܢܘܢ ܘܠܐ ܗܘܘ ܬܪܝܢ ܗܘܘ܀'

'Hymn (99). Glory be to the merciful one
[11] The one who says that God is one.
Listen, O lover of God.
It is one acknowledgement in Him and God,
that they are one and not two.'

In other hymns, the poet confirms the equality between the Father and the Son in terms of Lordship, nature, power, majesty, and will, as well as the Son being the creator like His Father. For example, Hymns 1.(12)[37], (7)[3, 19cd], 6.(71)[25] and 18.(121)[18, 19]:

'ܡܕܪܫܐ (7). ܒܢܨܪܬ ܡܕܝܢܬܐ ܕܓܠܝܠܐ.
[3] ܕܠܐ ܫܘܪܝ ܩܢܐ ܐܝܬܘܬܐ. ܘܐܠܗܘܬܐ ܘܡܪܘܬܐ.
ܘܐܦ ܐܝܬ ܠܗ ܫܡ ܒܪܘܬܐ. ܫܘܐ ܥܡ ܐܒܘܗܝ ܒܡܪܘܬܐ܀
[19] ܘܡܠܬܐ ܕܠܗ ܫܘܐ ܒܐܘܣܝܐ. ܟܢܝܫ ܒܗ ܟܠܗܘܢ ܒܪܝܬܐ܀'

'Hymn (7). In Nazareth, the Galilean town
[3] [The Word][147] without beginning,
Possesses Essence, divinity and Lordship.
And although He has the name of Sonship,

[145] A. Pritula, *The Wardā*, p. 173.
[146] Bābāi, ܟܬܒܐ ܕܚܕܝܘܬܐ [The Book of the Union], pp. 199-227.
[147] I have added [The Word] based on the context of this hymn.

He is equal with His Father in majesty.
[19] and the consubstantial Word
will fashion His fair image in you!.'[148]

CONCLUSION

After listing and discussing the many Christological attributes and themes in the poetry of Gīwargīs, it is clear that his Christology conforms to that of other East- Syriac theologians, albeit with more liberty. Gīwargīs addresses the same themes that the East-Syriac Church has always discussed, whether in the Synods or in the writings of major theologians.

On the other hand, it is also clear that the *Book of Wardā* is not a theological treatise. Christological themes are evoked rather than discussed, meditated upon rather than explained in detail. Gīwargīs plays with words, sings the wonders of the divine economy and expresses amazement. This is what has to be conveyed to the listeners or readers of his poetry. Moreover, he writes hymns meant to be sung (and therefore needing to follow a strict meter) not texts meant to be studied.

One could say that his hymns are meditations on, or evocations of, the Gospel and the liturgical year. However, Gīwargīs as a poet, rooted in his own ecclesiastical tradition, uses the traditional themes and terms that are at the back of his mind, without caring too much about consistency or precise definitions. This becomes especially clear when he uses terms such as: ܡܕܥܐ intellect, ܝܕܥܬܐ knowledge and ܗܘܢܐ mind, such that it is unclear whether he considers these as synonyms or as different terms. By contrast, Īšōʿyāhb III of Adiabene clarifies in his letters that each of these terms has its own meaning.[149]

In this way, we should not see him as a systematic theologian, comparable for example to the authors of sections of كتاب أسفار الأسرار *I libri dei misteri.*

When stating that Gīwargīs is in line with the previous tradition, it must be emphasized that there is one important difference. It is striking that nowhere does he mention the duality of the *qnōmē* in Christ, a traditional emphasis of the Christology of the Church of the East, also found in contemporary writings such as the work of ʿAbdīšōʿ bar Brīḫā or the treatises in the كتاب أسفار الأسرار *I libri dei misteri.* How to interpret this absence? It is tempting to speculate that the fact that he wrote his poetry in the so-called period of the Syriac Renaissance - often seen as a period of ecumenical awareness where Christological differences were no longer seen as relevant issues - he may have down-played somewhat an outspoken 'Nestorian' Christology, often considered as a divisive issue between the Churches. But of course, this cannot be proven. Some previous authors did also not speak of a duality, and as said above, Gīwargīs is in the first place a poet, not a systematic theologian.

---

[148] A. Pritula, *The Wardā*, pp. 207-209. Translation slightly adapted.

[149] Īšōʿyāhb III, *رسائل البطريرك إيشوعياب الثالث الحديابي* [The Letters of Patriarch Īšōʿyāhb III of Adiabene], p. 160.

GENERAL CONCLUSION

The critical edition and translation of a substantial number of so far unstudied hymns that circulated under the name of Gīwargīs Wardā or as the *Book of Wardā* was the starting point of an investigation of the author's Christological views. The critical edition is based on a selection of the most ancient manuscripts. Interestingly, when looking at the manuscript tradition, it was clear that this work of/by Wardā was also read by those in the Chaldean tradition; likely some who possessed these manuscripts were not happy with some of the 'Nestorian' or 'Apocryphal' expressions or names of early East-Syriac fathers they discovered in the hymns, names and expressions which they tried to correct, albeit not in a consistent way. Concessions had to be made in translating the hymns, in order to find a balance between rendering a poetical text, doing justice to the technical terminology and presenting a text that is understandable to an English readership.

The Christological aspect has not yet received the attention it deserves, even though Christological issues continued to play an important role during the period in which the *Book of Wardā* can be situated. Examples include أصول الدين *I fondamenti della religione* by ʿAbdīšōʿ bar Brīḫā or the many texts inserted into أسفار الأسرار *I libri dei misteri*. Though these examples suggest that Christology was basically discussed in an Arabic-speaking milieu, in the Syriac field we could mention two works by ʿAbdīšōʿ ܡܪܓܢܝܬܐ *The Pearl* and his book ܦܪܕܝܣܐ ܕܥܕܝܢ *The Paradise of Eden.*

In order to understand the *Book of Wardā,* it has been necessary to address a few preliminary questions. The first issue is that of authorship. Though I believe that there are enough indications to accept the existence of an author called Gīwargīs, it seems better not to jump to conclusions, but rather to postpone a final judgment on this issue till the totality of the hymns attributed to him have been edited and/or translated. It is clear that assuming the existence of a poet called Gīwargīs does not imply that all hymns attributed to him are in fact his.

The author is of course a child of his times. Hence the importance attached to the discussion about the potential time frame in which he lived. Living in the middle of the 13th century, Gīwargīs was likely a witness to the beginning of Mongol rule in his region of origin (probably the surroundings of Erbil) as well as possibly the fall of Baghdad. Several historical events are alluded to in his hymns, making his work a veritable source of historical information.

The 13th century is a period which has been labelled the Syriac Renaissance. Among other things, this period is characterized by the acceptance of Islamicate influences. Well known examples here are Bar ʿEbrāyā and Bar Brīḫā. It seems that this also holds true for our author. Though it is difficult to pinpoint direct influences, it is likely that Muslim Arabic poetry composed during this period influenced Gīwargīs. In chapter 1, we discussed a number of parallels between Gīwargīs' hymns and those by certain Muslim contemporaries. If Wardā is to be seen as the title of a book rather than a personal name, it would confirm even more how our author was indebted to Persian-Arabic culture.

The main focus of this research, Wardā's Christology, needs to be discussed against the background of the Syriac Renaissance. During this period, various authors, both East and West Syriac, had expressed their dissatisfaction with the traditional Christological discussions and suggested new approaches. At the same time, we still find examples of more traditional modes of thinking from this period. Our reading of the hymns of Gīwargīs leads us to the conclusion that the author's Christological views are in line with the classical authoritative writings of his Church, works by authors such as Bābāi and Narsai, but he also exercises more freedom in using new terms to describe Christ, such as ܐܝܠ Ēl, ܒܪ ܡܝܘܬܘܬܐ the son of mortality, ܗܝܟܠܐ ܕܬܠܝܬܝܘܬܐ The temple of the Trinity, ܡܘܬܗ ܕܡܘܬܐ the death of the death.

The author nowhere emphasizes the idea of two of *qnōmē* in Christ, a key element of traditional 'Nestorian' Christology. Is this to be seen as an example that Gīwargīs is an adept of the Renaissance approach to Christology? To answer this question, we must take into account the fact that Gīwargīs was not a systematic theologian, comparable for example to Ēlīā of Nisibis or bar Brīḫā. He wrote poetry, liturgical and biblical hymns, which are meditations on passages from the gospel. His hymns were meant to be recited and sung, therefore his words are musical as if he has melodies in his mind while writing the verses, which explains some repetitions, perhaps at the cost of theological precision. On the other hand, he is not afraid of freely using technical Christological vocabulary.

TABLES

DESCRIPTION OF THE TABLES

1. Table (5): In this table, the hymns are organized in alphabetical order with the opening and closing lines of each hymn. The second column of the table indicates the number of the hymn in Table (6). The last column, indicated by the letter 'A', means that the hymn has an alphabetic acrostic structure.
2. Table (6): This table contains the hymns as they appear in the manuscripts used in this work, with the number of the folio in which they appear. This table has three parts, 6A, 6B, and 6C, each of which contains a number of manuscripts used in this work organized chronologically.
3. Table (7): This table contains the name of the author of each hymn as it appears in the title of the hymn. This shows the hymns in which the name of the author appears differently in other manuscripts. This table has three parts, 7A, 7B, and 7C, each of which contains a number of manuscripts used in this work organized chronologically. These three parts correspond to the three parts in Table (6). For example, if a hymn appears in Table (6), the author of that hymn can be found in Table (7). Hymn that is anonymous and no particular name is mentioned in its heading will be indicated by an asterisk (*). If the following indications ܕܝܠܗ, ܕܝܠܗ ܡܢ ܕܝܠܗ [by] is found in the headings without a specific name of an author, then they will be given in the table. If a hymn is not found in a manuscript it will not be indicated by any sign in those particular lists.
4. Table (8): This table contains a chronological list of the hymns from the book of Wardā that have been published or translated into different languages; the last column indicates the number of the hymn in Table (6).

TABLE 5: HYMNS IN ALPHABETICAL ORDER

	Table 6	Opening Lines	Closing Lines	
1.	83	ܐܦ ܗܘܝ ܠܝ ܡܥܕܪܢܐ. ܒܪܐ ܚܢܢܐ ܗܘܝ ܡܦܨܝܢܐ	ܫܘܒܚ ܠܫܡܗ܆ ܒܦܘܩܕܢܘܗܝ	
2.	119	ܐܘ ܒܪܝܐ ܕܒܝܬ ܡܠܟܘܬܐ. ܢܛܘܪ ܐܡܘܗܝ ܘܕܝܢܘܬܐ	ܒܪܝ ܘܢܛܪ ܕܝܠܟ ܡܠܟܘܬܟ	
3.	27	ܐܘ ܕܒܕܝܢܬܐ ܐܬܒܪܟܬ. ܘܐܝܟ ܕܒܝܬܐ ܕܦܘܪܫܢܐ ܒܟܠܗ	ܕܫܪܐ ܕܫܠܡܘܬܗ ܠܗ ܠܝܬ ܕܦܩܘܣ ܠܗ	A[1]
4.	37	ܐܘ ܕܒܪܟܢܐ ܒܬܠܡܝܕܘܬܐ. ܘܒܐܝܕ ܡܨܥܝܐ ܐܝܟ ܕܒܪܘܬܐ	ܐܬ ܗܘܐ ܠܒܢܝܐ ܘܫܬܠܝܐ ܠܟܘܪܢܫܐ	A
5.	143	ܐܘ ܪܘܚܢܐ ܕܫܠܝܚܘܬܐ. ܘܪܘܚܢܐ ܕܪܘܚܘܬܐ	ܚܘܒ ܟܠ ܫܠܝܚܐ ܘܪܘܚܢܐ ܥܘܬܪܗ ܘܢܛܘܪ ܠܫܪܪܗ	
6.	70	ܐܘ ܕܠܒܥܒܪܝܬܐ ܐܠܝܢ. ܘܠܡܫܝܚܝܬܐ ܡܬܪܢܝܢ	ܘܢܗܘܐ ܚܝܒܐ ܒܥܘܠܝܗ ܢܘܗܪܐ	
7.	111	ܐܘ ܕܐܬܥܠܝܬ ܥܠ ܟܠܗܘܢ. ܘܫܡܫܬܘܪܝ ܥܠ ܥܘܡܪܗܘܢ	ܡܫܝܚܐ ܡܪܢ ܘܦܪܘܩܢܐ ܕܟܠܢ	
8.	115	ܐܘ ܫܪܝܪܐ ܘܪܘܚܢܐ. ܗܘ ܕܩܕܡ ܦܬܟܪܗ ܕܝܚܝܕܝܐ	ܕܒܗ ܡܬܬܩܢ ܘܠܗ ܢܬܒܪܟ	
9.	57	ܐܘ ܢܘܗܪܗ ܕܐ ܒܥܒܕ. ܘܕܐ ܗܝܟ ܫܪܝܪ ܘܕܐ ܡܕܒܪ	ܘܢܬܟܠܘܢ ܘܢܫܬܒܚܘܢ ܘܡܘܕܝܢ ܢܫܡܗ	
10.	137	ܐܘ ܚܕܐ ܫܒܝܩ ܩܛܐ ܗܘܐ. ܐܘ ܚܕܐ ܩܕܝܫ ܩܕܝܫܐ ܗܘܐ	ܘܠܝ ܬܫܒܘܚܬܐ ܒܟܠ ܥܕܢ	A[2]
11.	71	ܐܘ ܚܝܐ ܡܢ ܟܠ ܕܠܗ ܐܝܬ ܟܠ. ܠܐ ܡܬܚܙܐ ܠܟܠ ܘܚܙܐ ܠܟܠ	ܘܢܘܕܐ ܠܫܡܟ ܒܟܠ ܥܕܢ	A[3]
12.	56	ܐܘ ܫܡܥܝܗ ܕܐ ܫܡܥܬ. ܐܘ ܡܕܒܪܢܐ ܕܐ ܫܪܝܪܐ	ܘܠܟ ܬܫܒܘܚܬܐ ܡܢ ܟܘܠ ܟܠ	
13.	21	ܐܘ ܡܫܩܠܢ ܥܠ ܐܘܪܚܬܐ. ܘܡܫܬܪܝܢ ܥܠ ܦܘܪܫܘܬܐ	ܢܬܘܕܐ ܠܡܫܝܚܐ ܒܟܠܗܘܢ	
14.	26	ܐܘ ܢܩܝܐ ܕܫܒܩ ܡܢ ܟܠ. ܡܢܘ ܢܫܟܚ ܕܢܬܒܥ ܡܢ ܟܠ	ܘܢܘܕܐ ܥܘܠܝܐ ܠܐܠܗܘܬܗ	
15.	58	ܐܘ ܫܡܥܬܐ ܕܫܠܡܘܬܐ. ܘܡܬܟܫܠܢܐ ܕܩܕܝܫܘܬܐ	ܠܟ ܥܡ ܐܒܘܟ ܘܪܘܚܟ ܩܘܕܫܐ	
16.	91	ܐܘܪܚܗ ܪܒܬܐ ܚܕܬܐ. ܠܐ ܡܬܕܪܟܐ ܠܟܠܗܘܢ ܒܢܝܢܐ	ܘܡܫܒܚ ܠܗ ܟܠ ܢܦܫܬܐ	
17.	55	ܐܝܟ ܕܐܝܬܠܗ ܪܚܡܐ. ܘܕܝܐ ܪܒܐ ܘܢܘܗܪܐ ܗܘܐ	ܚܘܒܢܐ ܒܫܡܝܐ ܐܘ ܡܫܝܚܢܐ	
18.	131	ܐܝܬܝܟ ܕܡܢ ܡܬܩܪܒ ܘܚܘܒܗ ܒܟ. ܘܐܝܬܝܟ ܒܥܠܡܐ ܢܗܝܪܐ	ܠܥܠܡ ܥܠܡܝܢ ܐܡܝܢ ܘܐܡܝܢ	A[4]
19.	11	ܐܝܬܝܟ ܚܕ ܘܥܡ ܚܕ. ܒܢܝܐ ܠܐܒܘܟ ܦܫܝܛܐ ܘܫܠܝܛܐ	ܐܒܐ ܘܒܪܐ ܘܪܘܚܐ ܕܩܘܕܫܐ	A

[1] In the critical edition of Anton Pritula there are hymns that are not considered acrostic but we checked them and they were acrostic. According to the order of this table, these hymns are 11, 28, 54, 55, 67. Other hymns were considered acrostic but actually they are not, such as hymn number 47, 112, 156. See A. Pritula, *The Wardā*, pp. 19-81.

[2] It starts acrostic with the name ܐܒܪܗܡ.

[3] It starts acrostic with ܐܠܗ then alphabetic acrostic until the letter ܡ.

[4] Acrostic with double letters.

	Table 6	Opening Lines	Closing Lines	
20.	90	ܐܠܗܐ ܐܝܬܝܟ ܡܠܟܐ. ܫܘܐ ܠܟ ܐܒܘܗܝ ܒܐܝܬܘܬܐ	ܕܓܒܠܗ ܒܢܝܢܐ ܠܥܠܡܐ ܫܡܝܐ	A[5]
21.	33	ܐܠܗܐ ܒܪܘܝܐ ܘܡܦܪܢܣܐ. ܡܪܝܐ ܡܕܒܪܢܐ ܘܡܫܠܛܢܐ	ܫܘܒܚܐ ܠܟ ܠܥܠܡ ܥܠܡܝܢ	
22.	106	ܐܠܗܐ ܟܣܝܐ ܐܢܬ. ܒܪܗ ܫܠܚ ܓܠܝܐ ܠܦܘܪܩܢ ܐܢܫܐ	ܘܠܟ ܣܘܓܕܐ ܥܡ ܫܘܒܚܬܐ	A
23.	103	ܐܝܢܐ ܕܐܝܬ ܠܗ ܦܘܩܕܢܐ. ܕܘܫܢܐ ܘܠܐ ܠܘܩܒܠܐ	ܕܐܠܗܝ ܐܝܬ ܒܬܕܡܘܪܬܐ	
24.	107	ܐܝܢܐ ܕܠܝܬ ܐܝܟ ܐܝܬܘܬܗ. ܠܐ ܘܐܦܠܐ ܐܝܬ ܐܝܟ ܝܚܝܕܘܬܗ	ܒܠܚܘܕܘܗܝ ܠܥܠܡ ܥܠܡܝܢ	
25.	126	ܐܝܢܐ ܕܐܘܡܢܐ ܟܠ ܕܣܘܥܪܢܘܗܝ. ܐܦܐ ܠܒܪܝܬܐ ܕܢܚܙܐ ܠܫܘܒܚܘܗܝ	ܠܒܝܬ ܐܒܘܬܐ ܡܫܒܚܐ ܦܐܝܐ	
26.	148	ܢܘܪܐ ܒܝܬܐ ܒܢܝܚܬܐ. ܕܡܠܐܟܐ ܕܢܘܪܐ ܢܝܚܬܐ	ܢܘܗܪܐ ܠܐܒܘܟ ܕܢܘܪܐ ܐܢܬ	A[6]
27.	141	ܒܐܘܪܚܐ ܕܒܢܝܐ ܪܕܘ ܣܘܥܪܢܐ. ܘܡܛܘ ܠܗ ܐܪܚܐ ܕܢܝܫܗܘܢ	ܠܐܒܐ ܘܒܪܐ ܘܪܘܚܐ ܕܩܘܕܫܐ	
28.	35	ܒܥܘܬܐ ܕܒܬܘܠܬܐ ܢܩܒܠ ܐܠܗܐ. ܒܨܘܡܐ ܕܫܩܠܐ ܗܘ ܐܬܝܠܕ ܐܠܗܐ	ܒܟܘ ܗܘ ܫܒܚܐ ܢܗܝܪܐ	A
29.	81	ܒܢܘܗܪܐ ܢܘܗܪܐ ܢܩܒܠ. ܒܪܐ ܕܐܠܗܐ ܘܒܪܐ ܕܐܢܫܐ	ܘܠܟ ܬܫܒܘܚܬܐ ܡܢ ܟܠ ܒܪܝܬܐ	
30.	52	ܒܐܝܡܡܐ ܠܘܬܟ ܐܠܗܢ. ܒܠܠܝܐ ܘܒܨܦܪܐ ܠܡܫܝܚܘܬܟ	ܡܢ ܥܝܪ̈ܐ ܘܩܕ̈ܝܫܐ ܠܥܠܡ	A[7]
31.	79	ܒܢܘܗܪܐ ܕܡܕܢܚ ܗܘܐ ܢܘܗܪܐ. ܘܐܢܗܪ ܐܘܪܚܐ ܠܟܝܢܐ ܘܐܢܫܐ	ܘܠܡܫܘܕܥܢܘܬܐ ܒܐܡܝܢܘܬܐ	
32.	9	ܒܢܝܐ ܕܫܩܠܐ ܗܘ ܕܝܠܗ ܐܠܗܐ. ܘܒܡܫܝܚܘܬܐ ܗܘ ܡܫܬܟܚ ܐܠܗܐ	ܘܒܪܟܘ ܫܘܒܚܐ ܒܟܠ ܝܘܡܐ	A[8]
33.	46	ܝܗܒ ܫܝܢܐ ܡܠܟܐ ܡܫܝܚܐ. ܘܝܗܒ ܦܪܘܩܘܬܐ ܡܠܟܐ ܦܪܘܩܢ	ܘܝܗܒ ܠܥܡܐ ܫܘܒܚܐ ܦܐܝܐ	A
34.	45	ܝܗܒ ܫܠܡܐ ܕܒܠܒܝܗܝܢ. ܘܝܗܒ ܦܪܘܩܢܐ ܕܡܫܝܚܘܬܐ	ܘܠܟ ܬܫܒܘܚܬܐ ܡܢ ܦܘܡ ܟܠ	A
35.	135	ܒܟܠ ܩܪܢܘܬ ܘܒܟܠ ܕܘܟܘܬ. ܠܟܐ ܘܠܟܐ ܠܟܘܢ ܡܫܝܚܐ ܡܪܢ	ܕܒܫܡܗ ܝܗܒܐ ܡܢ ܫܡܝܐ	
36.	112	ܚܒܝܒܐ ܡܪܝܐ ܚܒܝܒܬܐ. ܘܒܟܠܗ ܕܝܠܗܘܢ ܚܒܝܒܬܐ	ܘܠܟ ܬܫܒܘܚܬܐ ܡܢ ܦܘܡ ܟܠ	A[9]
37.	80	ܒܫܡܗ ܕܒܪܐ ܡܫܝܚܐ. ܘܒܫܡ ܐܒܘܗܝ ܘܪܘܚܗ ܩܕܝܫܐ	ܠܗܘܢ ܡܠܟܘܬܐ ܫܡܝܢܝܬܐ	
38.	72	ܒܟܢ ܢܩܕܫ ܕܘܫܢܐ. ܕܗܘܘ ܟܗܢܐ ܠܦܪܘܩܐ ܡܪܢܐ	ܘܠܟ ܬܫܒܘܚܬܐ ܥܡ ܐܒܘܟ	A
39.	7	ܒܢܝܢܗ ܡܕܝܢܬܐ ܕܫܠܝܚܐ. ܝܗܒܬ ܫܠܡܐ ܕܡܫܝܚܐ ܠܟܢܫܐ	ܘܝܗܒ ܕܝܢ ܫܘܒܚܐ ܡܢ ܟܠ ܢܦܫ	
40.	154	ܒܢܝܢܗ ܡܕܝܢܬܐ ܕܫܠܝܚܐ. ܝܗܒܬ ܫܠܡܐ ܕܡܫܝܚܐ ܠܟܢܫܐ	ܠܟ ܬܫܒܘܚܬܐ ܒܟܠܙܒܢ ܘܗܫܐ	A

[5] Acrostic with double letters.

[6] Alphabetic acrostic until the letter ܡ.

[7] Acrostic without the letter ܐ.

[8] Acrostic only with the names ܝܥܩܘܒ ܡܠܦܢܐ.

[9] Alphabetic Acrostic after the word ܫܒܚܝܢ in the first verse of each stanza.

	Table 6	Opening Lines	Closing Lines	
41.	18	ܒܫܦܝܪ̈ܝ ܪܘܚܐ ܕܦܪܩܠܝܛܘܬܗ ܕܩܘܠܗܘܢ ܦܬܝܐ. ܥܠܝܡܐ ܓܒܝܐ ܩܕܝܫܐ ܘܦܪܝܫܐ	ܘܠܝ ܒܝܠܕܗܘܢ ܚܛܝܐ ܘܕܫܡܐ ܐܪܝܡ ܘܐܪܝܡ	
42.	62	ܒܫܦܝܪ̈ܝ ܪܘܚܐ ܦܬܐ ܗܘܢܐ. ܘܒܫܠܝܛܗܘܢ ܡܫܬܪܝܐ ܗܘܢܐ	ܠܟܠ ܘܟܠ ܕܢܓܘܥ ܘܠܝ ܡܫܒܚܘܬܐ	
43.	65	ܒܟܠܥܕܢ ܡܪܝܐ ܫܪܪܐ ܗܘܝܐ. ܘܒܬܠܘܬܗ ܡܫܬܒܚܐ ܗܘܝܐ	ܘܠܝ ܡܫܒܚܘܬܐ ܡܢ ܟܠ ܦܘܡܐ	
44.	13	ܒܟܠܦܘܡ ܢܒܪܐ ܒܘܒܪܐ. ܬܦܝܗ ܗܘܐ ܗܘܐ ܡܝܬܐ ܕܪܘܚܐ ܘܡܘܪܐ	ܢܝܫ ܚܘܒܐ ܠܐܠܗܘܬܟ	
45.	64	ܒܝܬ ܓܒܪܐ ܪܘܚܢܝܐ. ܕܒܝܬ ܓܒܪܘܗ ܕܒܪ ܓܒܪܘܗܝ	ܘܟܦܝ ܝܕܘܥ ܒܝܬ ܡܠܟܘܬܐ	
46.	139	ܒܪܐ ܕܢܓܘܪܐ ܡܬܩܢܐ. ܕܒܪ ܒܪܝܬܐ ܡܢ ܚܘܪܢܐ	ܠܒܝܬܐ ܕܢܘܪܐ ܕܗܦܟܝܐ. ܕܚܘܒܗ (!)	
47.	8	ܒܪܐ ܕܦܩܝܢ ܒܗ ܗܢܝܐܬܐ. ܕܟܠ ܝܚܝܕܝܐ ܘܒܢܝܬܐ	ܘܟܠܗ ܕܫܡܝܐ ܒܗ ܠܚܘܒܬܐ	
48.	61	ܒܪܐ ܕܠܐܒܘܗܝ ܠܗ ܫܘܬܦܬܐ. ܘܢܬܗ ܒܗܘܠܬܐ ܘܟܠ ܡܪܘܬܐ	ܘܬܘܕܝܬܐ ܠܐܒܘܟ ܘܠܝ ܘܠܪܘܚܟ	
49.	82	ܒܪܐ ܡܠܬܐ ܚܣܝܢܐ. ܓܒܪܗ ܠܦܓܪܐ ܐܕܡܝܐ	ܢܗܪܐ ܠܟܠܢ ܘܟܠܝ ܡܫܒܚܘܬܐ	
50.	86	ܒܪܘܢܐ ܕܟܠ ܚܕܬܐ. ܘܡܚܕܬܢܐ ܕܒܪܝܬܐ	ܕܠܗ ܠܗ ܫܘܒܚܐ ܘܐܝܩܪܐ ܚܕܬܐ	
51.	67	ܒܪܝܟ ܕܒܝܘܡܗ ܡܕܒܪܐ. ܦܪܓ ܫܘܬܦܗ ܕܒܢܝܐ ܕܐܕܡ	ܘܢܝܫ ܚܘܒܐ ܠܐܠܗܘܬܟ	
52.	48	ܒܪܝܟ ܕܒܡ ܒܦܪܩܢܗ ܠܐ ܦܫܛ. ܐܠܐ ܐܘܦ ܘܠܝܬ ܦܫܛ	ܠܟ ܡܕܒܪܐ ܒܟܠ ܢܚܒܝܐ	A
53.	49	ܒܪܝܟ ܕܒܡ ܠܝܢ ܘܢܦܪ ܓܒܪܐ. ܦܣܝܠܗ ܐܪܟܒ ܓܒܪܐ	ܘܢܦܪܘܩ ܚܘܒܐ ܠܟܠܝ ܕܐܬܩܢ	A
54.	133	ܒܪܝܟ ܗܘ ܡܫܝܚܐ ܡܚܝܢܢ. ܐܒܘܗܝ ܘܗܝܐ ܕܦܪܘܩܝ ܘܦܪܩܝ	ܚܘܒܐ ܠܟܠܝ ܒܪ ܚܝܐ	A[10]
55.	134	ܒܪܝܟ ܡܫܝܚܐ ܡܓܠܓܠܢ. ܐܒܘܗܝ ܘܗܝܐ ܕܓܒܪܝ ܘܦܪܝܫܝ	ܚܘܪܐ ܕܡܐ ܘܒܝܬ ܓܘܫܐ ܐܪܝܡ	A[11]
56.	140	ܒܪܝܟ ܡܫܝܚܐ ܦܪܘܩܢ. ܕܒܢܝ ܚܘܒܗ ܐܘܪܒ ܘܢܦܪ	ܚܘܒܢܐ ܠܐܒܐ ܘܒܪܐ ܘܪܘܚܐ	
57.	1	ܒܪܝܟ ܢܦܩܝܢ ܘܩܝܡܝܢ ܚܝܝܢ. ܠܦܩܪ ܦܠܚܐ ܕܪܗܘܡܝܐ	ܘܠܪܘܚܘܬܐ ܡܠܟܐ ܬܘܕܝܬܐ	
58.	142	ܒܪܝܟ ܦܠܚܢܐ ܒܝܬܐ. ܕܚܘܠܛ ܗܠܝܢ ܚܝܝܢ ܒܥܝܬܐ	ܐܝܬܘ ܚܒܘܒܐ ܠܟܠܢ ܥܠܡܝܢ	
59.	85	ܒܪܝܟ ܚܒܪܘܬܐ ܘܗܠܟܝܢ. ܕܐܝܬܘܗܝ ܘܢܛܪ ܗܠܝܢ ܚܝܝܢ	ܘܠܝ ܬܫܒܘܚܬܐ ܠܟܠܢ ܥܠܡܝܢ	
60.	12	ܒܪܝܟ ܗܠܝܢ ܘܗܠܝܢ. ܕܐܝܬܘܗܝ ܘܗܘ ܢܦܩ ܚܝܝܢ	ܒܝܦܝܢ ܒܗ ܒܝܬ ܡܠܟܘܬܐ	
61.	66	ܒܪܗܘܢ ܒܪܐ ܦܩܕ ܗܘܝܐ. ܕܡܫܠܠ ܦܬܐ ܒܠܝܠ ܦܘܩܕܐ	ܠܐܒܐ ܘܒܪܐ ܘܪܘܚܐ ܕܩܘܕܫܐ	
62.	42	ܓܒܪܐ ܠܡܬܪ ܒܓܒܝܬܐ. ܝܕܝܥ ܕܐܝܬܝ ܒܦܪܝܫܘܬܐ	ܘܬܫܒܘܚܬܐ ܢܝܫ ܦܬܓܡ	A[12]

[10] Alphabetic Acrostic after the word ܒܫܡܐ in the first verse of each stanza.
[11] It starts acrostic but from the second word of the first verse in each stanza.
[12] It starts acrostic with the name ܓܒܪܐܝܠ then alphabetic acrostic.

	Table 6	Opening Lines	Closing Lines	
63.	44	ܠܥܐܕܐ ܕܫܠܝ̈ܚܐ ܘܣܗ̈ܕܐ. ܢܪܕܐ ܕܡܠܐ ܥܠ ܣܗ̈ܕܐ	ܘܠܝ ܗܟܢܫܬܐ ܘܫܠܡܬܐ ܘܬܘܕܝܬܐ	A[13]
64.	29	ܠܥܐܕܐ ܒܚܠܘܢ ܕܒܢܝܗ̈ܘ. ܒܥܘܕ ܕܢܚܝܢ ܥܡ ܡܠܐܟ̈ܘܗܝ	ܘܠܝ ܗܟܢܫܬܐ ܒܐܡܝܢܘܬܐ	A[14]
65.	43	ܠܥܐܕܐ ܢܩܘܫ ܘܢܫܠܘ ܪܘܚܢܐ. ܠܟܘܢ ܢܬܠܩܛܘܢ ܗܝܢ ܗܘܠܕܝܢ	ܒܗܘ ܕܒܥܘܬܐ ܡܢܝܢ ܠܟ ܩܕܝܫܝܢ	A[15]
66.	92	ܠܝܘܡܐ ܕܐܝܬܘܗܝ ܠܥܕܬܐ ܫܦܝܪܐ. ܠܥܕܬܐ ܡܢ ܫܦܝܪܐ ܘܗܘܝ ܠܫܦܝܪܐ	ܥܘܕܪܢܐ ܠܥܡܡ ܘܠܟܠܢ ܚܝܝܢ	
67.	5	ܪܒܐ ܘܪܫܝܡ ܠܒܢܝ̈ܐ. ܘܠܒܝ ܒܩܫܝܫܝܢ ܡܕܝܢܬܐ ܕܪܒܐ	ܘܐܦ ܠܡܘܕܝܢܐ ܠܝ ܢܚܒܐ	A[16]
68.	100	ܗܘ ܡܠܟܐ ܕܥܩܢ̈ܐ. ܘܡܪܐ ܕܒܢܝ̈ܐ ܘܕܩܠܝܕ̈ܐ	ܘܥܘܕܪܢܐ ܠܐܒܘܟ ܘܠܪܘܚܟ ܩܘܡ	
69.	75	ܗܘ ܠܗ ܠܡܪܝܡ ܕܫܒܚܐ ܒܟ. ܗܢܐ ܕܪܐ ܠܪܡܪܝ ܣܒܪܐ ܥܠܝܟ	ܘܠܗ ܫܘܒܚܐ ܒܟܠ ܥܕܢܝܢ	
70.	155	ܘܠܗܘܢ ܗܘ ܡܘܒܠܐ ܕܝܬܡܬܐ. ܐܦ ܥܠܝܡܬܐ ܕܝܬܡܬܐ	ܘܫܘܒܚܐ ܫܩܠܐ ܒܥܠܡܝ̈ܢ	A
71.	15	ܫܠܡܐ ܕܡܫܝܚܐ ܒܢܦܫܢ. ܘܢܦܩ ܡܢܢ ܡܢ ܫܡܝܐ	ܢܗܘܐ ܗܘ ܚܝܠܐ ܕܡܢ ܢܨܚܢܐ	
72.	47	ܫܡܝܢ ܘܦܫܝܛܝܢ ܘܡܬܘܒ ܫܡܝܐ ܐܢܐ. ܘܡܬܘܒ ܫܡܝܐ ܐܢܐ ܐܦ ܦܫܝܛܐ ܐܢܐ	ܕܐܢܬ ܙܟܝܬ ܘܪܘܚܟ ܪܒܐ	A[17]
73.	152	ܠܘܚܡܐ ܝܩܝܪܐ ܡܫܒܚܬܐ. ܒܡܠܟܘܬܐ ܕܫܡܝܐ ܘܡܫܝܚܘܬܐ	ܠܫܠܡܗ ܡܪܘܡܗ ܐܡܝܢ	A[18]
74.	2	ܢܠܕܐ ܕܠܝܬ ܠܢܠܕܗ ܪܒܐ. ܘܠܐ ܚܙܐ ܘܐܦܫܗ ܘܠܐ ܢܒܝܐ	ܘܠܝ ܗܟܢܫܬܐ ܡܠܟܐ ܝܗܒܬ	
75.	38	ܢܛܪ ܩܫܝܫܐ ܕܫܒܝܐ ܠܟܝ ܠܗ. ܗܘܘܕܐ ܕܫܘܒܚܐ ܕܠܐ ܡܬܘܕܝܐ ܠܗ	ܕܢܦܩܬ ܠܝ ܫܒܪܐ ܐܦ ܠܝ ܡܫܡܫܢܐ	A
76.	41	ܢܦܫܝ ܥܒܕܐ ܘܡܬܦܪܚ ܒܟ ܠܟ. ܡܠܟܐ ܡܥܝܢܐ ܕܡܫܠܛ ܥܠ ܟܠ	ܘܥܘܕܪܢܐ ܠܥܡܡ ܒܡܘܕܝܢܐ ܘܕܘܟܪܢܐ	A[19]
77.	120	ܒܝܕܥܬܐ ܕܠܒܠ ܒܕܐ. ܕܠܒܕ ܡܢܗ ܠܐܒܘܗܝ ܠܟ ܒܕܐ	ܘܥܘܕܪܢܐ ܠܥܡܡ ܒܕܘܟܪܢܐ ܘܡܘܕܝܢܐ	
78.	24	ܒܕ ܒܟܘܪܐ ܕܒܩܘܫܬܐ ܡܙܝܢܗ. ܘܡܬܚܢܢܬܐ ܕܒܢܝ̈ܐ ܒܝܬܗ	ܘܠܝ ܗܟܢܫܬܐ ܡܢ ܟܘܠ ܥܠܡ	
79.	25	ܒܕ ܢܦܫ ܢܘܚ ܡܢ ܬܘܒܐ. ܐܘܠ ܠܒܝܬܐ ܐܝܟ ܦܘܡܝܗ̈	ܘܠܕܘܟܪܢܐ ܒܐܡܝܢܘܬܐ	
80.	53	ܒܕ ܗܠܝܢ ܐܢܫܐ ܒܒܪܝܬܐ. ܘܝܬܦܪܥܘ ܠܗܘܢ ܡܢܝܬܐ	ܢܬܒܣ ܠܥܡܡ ܥܠ ܢܩܘܫܬܐ	
81.	147	ܒܕ ܗܠܝܢ ܡܢܝ ܠܪܒ ܦܫܗ. ܐܦܐ ܡܘܬܐ ܘܫܠܝܐ	ܘܠܚܠܘܢ ܢܠܕܬܗ ܕܚܕܬܐ	
82.	77	ܒܕ ܢܠܠ ܡܢܝ ܠܐܘܪܚܝܢ. ܕܩܠܠ ܢܒܝܐ ܪܒܐ ܕܢܒܠܢ	ܘܢܘܪܐ ܠܐܒܘܟ ܘܠܝ ܘܠܪܘܚܟ	

[13] It starts acrostic with the name ܥܒܕܝܫܘܥ then alphabetic acrostic.
[14] It starts acrostic with the name ܥܒܕܝܫܘܥ then alphabetic acrostic. In each stanza each verse begins and ends with the same letter except the end of the last verse it ends with ܥܡ.
[15] It starts acrostic with the name ܥܒܕܝܫܘܥ then alphabetic acrostic.
[16] It starts acrostic with the name ܥܒܕܐ then alphabetic acrostic.
[17] It starts acrostic with alphabetic then in the end with the name ܥܒܕܝܫܘܥ.
[18] Alphabetic acrostic with double letter.
[19] It starts acrostic with ܥܒܕܝܫܘܥ ܡܛܪܢܐ ܕܨܘܒܐ then it ends acrostic with the name ܥܒܕܝܫܘܥ.

	Table 6	Opening Lines	Closing Lines	
83.	78	ܦܠܓܗ̇ ܕܫܒܬܐ ܘܦܘܫܩܗ̇. ܕܠܦܘܪܐ ܡܢ ܗܘܬ ܠܗ̇ ܡܫܒܚܬܐ	ܗܕܐ ܕܫܒܬܐ ܘܦܘܪܐ ܕܣܬܘܐ	
84.	145	ܟܠ ܓܢܣܐ ܦܘܪܫܐ. ܐܦܟܐ ܕܫܡܘܟܐ ܦܘܪܫܢܐ	ܒܪܝܫܝܬ ܦܪܘܩܘܬܢ ܘܫܪܝܪ ܠܟܠ	
85.	88	ܠܐܓܘܢܐ ܕܩܘܕܫܐ ܫܠܡ. ܦܪܘܩܘܬܐ ܕܟܠ ܥܡܡܐ	ܘܟܠܢ ܩܘܫܢ ܠܐܠܗܐ ܠܥܠܡܝܢ	
86.	104	ܠܐܠܗܐ ܕܫܘܬܐ ܫܠܡ ܗܘܝܐ. ܘܐܪܥܐ ܫܡܝܐ ܫܬܝܩ ܚܝܠܗ ܗܘܬ	ܦܪܘܩܢ ܡܢ ܠܘܬܗܘܢ	
87.	105	ܠܡܫܝܚܐ ܐܠܗܢ. ܕܫܪܝܪ ܒܫܘܬܗ ܡܢ ܚܝܘܬܐ	ܘܠܟ ܬܫܒܘܚܬܐ ܫܠܡ ܘܫܘܒܚܐ	
88.	96	ܗܐ ܐܘܪܚܢ ܠܡܕܢܚܐ ܕܡܪܢܐ. ܘܗܘܐ ܠܟܠܢ ܐܘܪܚ ܢܘܗܪܐ	ܕܢܬܚܣܐ ܠܢ ܫܘܫܬܐ ܡܠܟܘܬܟ	
89.	110	ܦܪܘܩ ܥܠܡܐ ܫܠܡ ܠܟ. ܘܡܢܟ ܥܠܡܐ ܦܘܪܩܢܐ	ܘܠܟ ܬܫܒܘܚܬܐ ܥܠ ܦܪܘܩܘܬܟ	
90.	125	ܦܪܘܩܐ ܕܟܠ ܥܠܡܐ. ܢܘܪܐ ܕܒܪܐ ܡܪܝܐ ܢܘܗܪܐ	ܫܒܚܐ ܠܟ ܡܪܝܐ ܕܒܝܬܢܐ	
91.	23	ܦܪܘܩܢܐ ܕܦܪܘܩܘܬܐ. ܘܡܫܝܚܐ ܕܡܫܝܚܘܬܐ	ܘܠܟ ܬܫܒܘܚܬܐ ܡܢ ܟܠ ܦܘܡ	
92.	63	ܡܠܟܐ ܕܡܠܟܐ ܠܗ ܫܠܡ. ܘܫܘܒܚܐ ܠܫܡܗ ܡܫܒܚܐ	ܘܗܘ ܢܬܒܪܟ ܠܐܠܗܐ ܠܥܠܡܝܢ	
93.	122	ܡܠܟܐ ܕܫܘܒܚܐ ܫܠܡ. ܕܐܬܐ ܕܢܦܪܘܩ ܠܐܢܫܐ	ܘܠܟ ܬܫܒܘܚܬܐ ܒܟܠ ܕܪ ܘܐܬܪܐ	
94.	121	ܡܠܟܐ ܘܡܪܐ ܕܟܠ ܡܠܟܐ. ܕܫܘܒܚܗ ܐܢܘܢ ܡܠܐܟܐ ܡܠܟܐ	ܒܟܠ ܫܢܝܢ ܘܒܟܠ ܥܕܢ	
95.	114	ܡܠܟܐ ܪܒܐ ܫܠܝܛܐ. ܕܒܪܢܫܐ ܘܠܐ ܗܘܐ ܕܡܠܟܐ	ܫܪܪܐ ܒܫܘܬܟ ܘܡܠܟܘܬܟ	
96.	118	ܡܠܟܐ ܐܠܗܐ. ܡܢ ܫܡܝܐ ܐܠܗܐ	ܐܒܐ ܘܒܪܐ ܘܪܘܚܐ ܕܩܘܕܫܐ	
97.	60	ܡܠܟܐ ܕܫܠܝܛܘܬܐ. ܡܫܝܚܐ ܐܠܗܘܬܗ ܒܐܪܥܝܘܬܐ	ܠܗ ܘܠܝܘܚܢܢ ܕܥܡܗ ܐܢܬ ܠܟܠ	
98.	19	ܡܢ ܫܡܝܐ ܕܡܫܝܚܐ. ܫܠܡܐ ܠܘܬܢ ܐܘ ܗܘܐ	ܢܐܠܗ ܕܫܡܗ ܫܘܒܚܐ ܘܫܘܒܚܐ	
99.	10	ܡܢ ܫܡܝܐ ܕܫܡܝܐ ܫܠܝܛܐ. ܐܘ ܦܪܘܩܢܐ ܢܦܠ ܘܫܡܝܐ	ܘܟܠܢ ܠܐܠܗܐ ܘܠܡܫܝܚܐ ܕܫܘܒܚܐ	
100.	3	ܡܢ ܫܡܝܐ ܠܗ ܠܐܠܗܘܬܟ. ܒܪܐ ܕܐܠܗܐ ܘܐܠܗܘܬܟ	ܘܗܘܐ ܠܐܠܗܐ ܘܠܪܘܚܐ ܟܠ	A[20]
101.	39	ܡܢܐ ܐܝܬܝܟ ܕܡܫܒܚܝܢ. ܫܒܚܘ ܘܫܒܚܘ ܘܡܪܢ ܫܡܝܢ	ܕܐܢܐ ܗܘ ܫܡܗ ܟܠܗ ܘܡܫܒܚܐ ܠܟܠܢ ܗܘܐ ܠܢ	A
101.				
102.	54	ܡܢܘ ܕܢܦܩܘ ܥܠ ܫܘܒܚ. ܘܡܢܘ ܢܫܒܚ ܐܦ ܢܫܒܚ ܠܟܠ	ܢܫܡ ܠܫܡܗ ܡܢ ܫܡܝܐ	
103.	87	ܡܢܘ ܫܡܝܐ ܕܫܡܝܐ. ܫܒܚܐ ܠܡܫܝܚܐ ܘܫܒܚܐ ܠܡܫܝܚܐ	ܠܫܡܗ ܕܡܪܢ ܗܘܐ ܕܫܘܒܚܗ	
104.	97	ܡܢܘ ܗܦܟ ܕܫܡܝܐ. ܢܫܒܚ ܠܟܠ ܡܪܐ ܡܠܟܐ	ܕܢܬܚܣܐ ܠܢ ܡܢ ܢܘܗܪܐ	
105.	94	ܡܪܐ ܕܐܪܥܐ ܘܫܡܝܐ. ܪܡܐ ܡܫܒܚܐ ܡܫܒܚܐ ܡܫܒܚܐ	ܕܢܘܗܪܐ ܠܐܠܗܐ ܘܪܘܚܐ ܫܡܝܐ	
106.	40	ܡܪܐ ܦܪܘܩܘܬܢ ܢܦܫܢ. ܘܦܪܘܩܘܬܗ ܦܪܘܩ ܠܢ	ܘܠܟ ܬܫܒܘܚܬܐ ܒܟܠ ܫܢܝܢ	A
107.	157	ܡܪܐ ܕܫܡܝܐ ܘܕܐܪܥܐ. ܗܘܐ ܒܫܡܝܐ ܦܪܘܩܐ ܦܪܘܩܐ	ܘܫܘܒܚܐ ܠܫܡܗ ܠܫܡܗ ܡܠܟܘܬܐ	

[20] It starts acrostic with the name ܝܫܘܥ.

	Table 6	Opening Lines	Closing Lines	
108.	59	ܡܪܐ ܕܟܠ ܡܕ̈ܥܬܐ. ܐܦ ܝܗܘܒܐ ܕܟܠ ܡܘܗ̈ܒܬܐ	ܡܫܝܚܐ ܦܪܘܩܢ ܠܥܠܡ ܥܠܡܝܢ	
109.	124	ܡܪܐ ܕܦܓ̈ܪܐ ܘܕܪ̈ܘܚܐ. ܐܦ ܢܛܘܪܐ ܕܟܠ ܒܪ̈ܝܬܐ	ܢܣܩ ܣܘܓܕܐ ܠܐܠܗܘܬܟ	
110.	101	ܡܪܐ ܕܡܠ̈ܟܐ ܘܡܫܠܛܢ̈ܐ. ܕܒܪܐ ܐܢܘܢ ܐܝܟ ܡܨܒܝܢܘܬܗ	ܘܠܟ ܬܫܒܘܚܬܐ ܡܢ ܦܘܡ ܟܠ	
111.	31	ܡܪܐ ܕܒܪ̈ܝܬܐ. ܕܠܗ ܘܡܢ ܕܩܕܡ ܕܒܪܝܬܐ	ܐܒܐ ܘܒܪܐ ܘܪܘܚܐ ܕܩܘܕܫܐ	
112.	68	ܡܪܘܡܐ ܐܝܟ ܕܡܢܫܡܥ. ܒܡܫܒܘܚܬܐ ܘܒܪܘܚܬܐ	ܢܬܬܘܕܐ ܠܥܘܒܕܟ ܡܫܠܡܬܐ	
113.	34	ܡܪܐ ܕܒܪܝ ܒܚܟܡܬܗ. ܘܐܬܩܢ ܒܡܕܝܢܘܬܗ	ܕܢܣܩ ܣܘܓܕܐ ܠܐܠܗܘܬܟ	
114.	123	ܡܫܡܫܐ ܘܒܢܝܗ ܕܡܫܡܫܢܐ. ܗܘ ܕܐܬܝܠܕ ܡܢ ܟܠ ܕܡܐ	ܕܐܢܬ ܗܘ ܒܠܚܘܕ ܡܠܝܐ ܫܘܒܚܐ	
115.	117	ܡܫܡܫܐ ܘܒܢܝܗ ܕܡܫܡܫܢܐ. ܕܐܬܝܠܕ ܡܢ ܟܠ ܕܡܐ	ܘܠܟ ܬܫܒܘܚܬܐ ܡܢ ܦܘܡ ܟܠ	
116.	129	ܡܪܝ ܕܡܢ ܟܕ ܐܬܝܠܕ ܗܘܐ. ܕܢܘܕܥܗ ܠܬܫܒܘܚܬܗ ܕܐܒܘܗܝ	ܠܟ ܗܘ ܝܐܝܐ ܕܬܫܒܘܚܬܐ	
117.	158	ܡܪܝ ܕܗܝܟܠܐ ܠܒܫܬܐ. ܒܐܘܪܚܐ ܕܡܠܐܟܐ ܠܒܢܝܐ	ܘܠܪܘܚܩܘܕܫܐ ܠܥܠܡ ܥܠܡܝܢ	
118.	36	ܡܪܝ ܡܫܝܚܐ ܕܐܬܓܫܡ. ܘܐܬܚܙܝ ܒܦܓܪܐ ܐܢܫܝܐ	ܡܫܒܚܐ ܕܠܐ ܫܠܝܐ ܠܟ ܬܫܒܘܚܬܐ	A
119.	74	ܡܫܝܚܐ ܡܪܢ ܕܐܬܒܣܡܬ. ܒܡܠܬܗ ܕܐܠܗܐ ܡܠܟܐ	ܘܠܪܘܚܩܘܕܫܐ ܠܥܠܡ ܥܠܡܝܢ	
120.	128	ܢܘܪܐ ܘܡܫܝܚܐ ܠܐܠܗܘܬܟ. ܘܕܒܪܬ ܠܒܢܝܢ ܒܪܝܐ ܕܝܠܟ	ܠܥܠܡ ܥܠܡܝܢ ܐܡܝܢ ܘܐܡܝܢ	A
121.	116	ܢܘܗܪܐ ܕܢܚ ܥܠ ܢܘܗܪܝܢ. ܕܡܢܗ ܡܬܢܗܪܝܢ ܒܝܬܗ ܠܒܢܝܗ	ܘܠܟ ܬܫܒܘܚܬܐ ܡܢ ܦܘܡ ܟܠ	
122.	149	ܢܦܩ ܦܘܪܩܢܐ ܡܢ ܡܠܟܐ. ܘܐܬܬܚܕ ܠܝܬܗ ܒܐܬܘܬܐ	ܠܥܠܡ ܥܠܡܝܢ ܐܡܝܢ ܘܐܡܝܢ	A
123.	113	ܢܦܫܐ ܡܢܗ ܒܝܬܝܐ. ܒܢܒܠܐ ܝܗܒܐ ܫܘܡ ܠܢܘܗܪܐ	ܘܫܘܐ ܘܡܬܩܕܫ ܫܡܟ ܘܕܝܠܟ ܕܐܒܘܟ	A[21]
124.	138	ܣܝܒܪܢ ܠܚܘܒܐ ܐܦܝܢܐ. ܒܝܘܦܝܣܝܣ ܘܕܝܢܐ...	ܘܠܟ ܘܐܒܘܟ ܫܘܒܚܐ ܢܣܩܘܢ ܠܥܠܡ ܥܠܡܝܢ	
125.	20	ܫܡܥܐ ܫܡܝܢ ܘܐܪܥܐ ܒܗ ܚܙܝܢ. ܘܡܫܡܠܐ ܠܡܪܝ ܕܦܩܕ ܒܡܠܬܗ	ܢܗܘܐ ܠܥܒܕܐ ܕܝܠܦܘܬܗܘܢ ܘܡܫܡܠܝܢ	
126.	28	ܠܘܬܟ ܫܩܠ ܐܢܐ ܠܝ. ܘܡܘܕܐ ܕܝܗܒܬ ܡܢ ܕܝܠܟ ܐܝܟ ܠܝ	ܕܐܘܕܝ ܒܥܩܒܝ ܠܐ ܡܬܥܩܪ ܒܗ	
127.	6	ܟܠ ܥܡܐ ܐܬܢܒܝܬܐ. ܒܢܝܐ ܗܘܝܐ ܕܐܬܥܒܕ ܒܡܫܒܚܬܐ	ܠܥܠܡ ܥܠܡܝܢ ܐܡܝܢ ܘܐܡܝܢ	A[22]
128.	98	ܫܬܝܬܐ ܕܠܝܬ ܐܝܟܘܬܗ. ܒܗ ܐܬܬܕܝܢ ܦܫܝܛ ܗܘܢܗ	ܕܗܘ ܢܬܒܣܡ ܒܐܡܝܢܘܬܐ	
129.	76	ܦܐܪܐ ܕܪܚܡܐ ܠܢܠܗܘܢ. ܕܡܘܪܐ ܘܡܘܗܒܬܐ ܠܒܢܝ ܒܐܝܬܗ	ܕܢܒܠܟ ܐܝܟܢ ܒܢܒܝܪܘܬܐ	
130.	93	ܦܬܐ ܠܥܒܕܗ ܝܗܒ ܫܡܐ. ܘܫܠܡ ܘܐܬܬܚܕ ܠܥܠܡܐ ܥܡܗ	ܕܝܗܒ ܚܝܘܗ ܠܟܠ ܡܠܟܘܬܗ	A

[21] Reversed alphabetic acrostic.
[22] The second stanza starts acrostic with the name [illegible].

	Table 6	Opening Lines	Closing Lines	
131.	156	ܨܘܡܐ ܘܨܠܘܬܐ ܥܡܘܕ̈ܐ. ܢܬܬܚܝܕܘ ܘܢܬܦܨܘܢ ܒܗ ܟܠܒܪ̈ܝܬܐ	ܠܥܠܡ ܥܠܡܝܢ ܐܡܝܢ ܘܐܡܝܢ	A
132.	69	ܨܒܘܬܐ ܨܠܘ ܠܝ ܐܘܡܬܐ. ܘܢܨܝܚܘ ܟܢܫܐ ܘܢܬܒܣܡܘܢ ܝܠܕ̈ܐ	ܠܗܘ ܢܗܘܐ ܠܒܢܝ ܫܘܒܚܐ	
133.	130	ܨܠܘܬܗ ܕܒܪܐ ܡܬܩܒܠܐ. ܕܒܗ ܢܠܦܘܢ ܟܠ ܒܢܘܫܐ	ܘܟܠ ܬܫܡܫܬܐ ܕܐܡܝܢܘܬܐ	
134.	109	ܨܠܝܢܢ ܕܒܪܐ ܡܬܦܩܕܐ. ܠܟܠ ܕܡܬܚܘܝܢ ܩܕܡܘܗܝ	ܕܢܫܒܚܘܢ ܠܗ ܒܩܠܐ ܣܓܝܐܐ	
135.	102	ܩܘܡܘ ܐܘ ܟܢ̈ܫܐ ܕܡܫܝܚܝܐ. ܢܬܬܚܝܕܘ ܕܟܠܢ ܒܟܢܫܬܐ	ܘܠܗ ܬܫܒܘܚܬܐ ܡܢ ܦܘܡ ܟܠ	
136.	132	ܩܕܝܫ ܘܡܫܒܚܐ ܡܪܝܐ ܟܠ. ܕܥܒܕܐ ܒܚܘܒܗ ܘܢܛܪܗ ܠܓܢܣܢ	ܝܘܡܐ ܩܕܝܫܐ ܠܡܫܝܚܘܬܗ	
137.	95	ܩܕܝܫܝܢ ܘܡܫܒܚܝܢ ܐܒ̈ܗܝܢ. ܡܪܢܐ ܡܪܝ ܘܐܘܪܚܝܢ ܚܠܦܝܢ	ܘܢܣܒܪܘܢ ܠܗ ܒܐܡܝܢܘܬܐ	
138.	159	ܪܡܐ ܠܩܘܕܫܐ ܕܒܝܬܐ ܩܕܡܝܐ. ܡܢܝܢܐ ܕܡܫܐ ܘܐܡܪܐ ܘܡܫܒܚܐ	ܘܠܒܪܗ ܫܒܚܐ ܘܠܪܘܚܐ ܕܩܘܕܫܐ ܠܥܠܡ ܥܠܡܝܢ	
139.	136	ܪܘܚܐ ܩܕܝܫܐ ܡܫܝܚܐ. ܒܪܬܐ ܕܠܥܠܡ ܘܫܪܝܬܐ ܕܠܗܘܢ - ܗܘܝܐ ܕܒܘܝܢܐ ܕܒܪ̈ܝܬܐ	ܠܥܠܡ ܥܠܡܝܢ ܐܡܝܢ ܘܐܡܝܢ - ܕܢܛܪܢ ܠܟܠ ܐܢܫ ܩܠܝܠܐ	
140.	99	ܪܘܚܐ ܠܗ ܠܗܘ ܚܝܐ. ܗܒܝ ܩܕܡܐ ܘܦܬܚ ܣܓܝܐ	ܣܘܦ ܘܕܝܢܐ ܠܟܠܢ ܡܛܠ ܣܘܓܐ	
141.	127	ܪܘܚܐ ܠܗ ܠܗܘ ܝܚܝܕܝܐ. ܕܒܪܝ ܘܢܬܬܣܝܡ ܟܠ ܒܪ̈ܝܬܐ	ܘܠܐܒܘܗ ܘܪܘܚܗ ܒܐܡܝܢܘܬܐ	
142.	160	ܪܘܚܐ ܠܣܘܓܐ ܩܕܡܝ. ܟܠܗܝ ܗܒܝܠܐ ܡܪܚܡܢܘܬܐ	ܐܦ ܣܘܗܕܐ ܠܡܫܠܡܘܗܝ	
143.	22	ܪܘܚܐ ܠܣܓܝܐܐ ܡܢ ܝܫܘܥ. ܕܟܘܠܗ ܘܟܠܐ ܘܡܕܝܢܬܐ	ܘܢܗܘܐ ܠܟܘܠܗ ܘܕܝܢܐ ܠܟܠܗ	
144.	30	ܪܘܚܐ ܠܩܕܝܫܐ ܡܪܝܐ. ܕܦܪܩܢ ܠܓܢܣܢ ܢܦܫܬܐ	ܠܥܠܡ ܥܠܡܝܢ ܐܡܝܢ ܘܐܡܝܢ	A[23]
145.	151	ܪܘܚܐ ܠܩܕܝܫܐ ܩܕܡܝ. ܕܒܗ ܝܗܒܐ ܣܘܓܐ ܕܡܫܡܫܐ ܠܓܢܣܢ	ܠܥܠܡ ܥܠܡܝܢ ܐܡܝܢ ܘܐܡܝܢ	A
146.	32	ܪܚܡܗ ܗܘܐ ܡܠܟܢ ܠܟܠܐ. ܕܠܡܫܝܚܐ ܟܠ ܗܘܘ ܡܠܟܘܬܐ	ܘܠܗ ܬܫܒܘܚܬܐ ܡܢ ܦܘܡ ܟܠ	
147.	51	ܪܚܡܗ ܘܢܬܬܪܡܪܡܘܢ ܩܕܡܝܐ. ܘܟܠ ܡܘܬ ܡܫܝܚܐ ܘܟܠ ܐܢܫ	ܘܠܡܫܡܫܢܐ ܚܘܒܐ ܕܠܒܗܘܬܐ	A[24]
148.	146	ܫܒܚܐ ܕܡܠܟܐ ܕܫܘܒܚܐ. ܗܘ ܕܒܗ ܒܢܝܬܐ ܕܝܠܗ	ܕܢܗܘܐ ܡܠܟܐ ܘܟܠܗ ܢܦܫܬܐ	
149.	84	ܫܒܚܐ ܕܡܫܝܚܐ ܝܫܘܥ ܗܘܝܘ. ܘܡܫܝܚܐ ܘܙܟܝܐ ܘܢܬܦܩܕ ܗܘܝܘ	ܘܒܟܠ ܠܟܘܢ ܡܢܗ ܒܩܕܝܫܐ	
150.	73	ܬܘ ܐܚܝ ܢܬܟܢܫ ܒܗ. ܒܝܘܡܐ ܕܡܠܟܐ ܢܬܟܢܫ ܠܗ	ܢܩܘܡ ܩܘܕܫܐ ܠܡܪܘܬܗ	
151.	17	ܬܘ ܚܒܝܒܝ ܝܘܡܐ ܩܕܝܫܐ. ܒܥܘܗܕܢܗܘܢ ܕܩܕܝܫܐ ܩܕܝܫܘܗܝ ܕܡܫܝܚܐ	ܘܠܟܘܢ ܢܗܘܐ ܕܘܟܪܢܐ ܒܪܘܡܐ ܕܠܥܠܡ	
152.	16	ܬܘ ܚܒܝܒܝ ܢܬܟܢܫ ܒܥܘܗܕܢܗܘܢ. ܕܩܕܝܫܐ ܩܕܝܫܐ ܩܕܝܫܘܗܝ ܕܡܫܝܚܐ	ܘܟܠ ܠܟܘܢ ܢܗܘܐ ܚܝܐ ܕܠܐ ܡܘܬܐ	

[23] Alphabetic Acrostic and each verse begins and ends with the same letter.
[24] Alphabetic Acrostic with double letters.

	Table 6	Opening Lines	Closing Lines	
153.	150	ܗܘ ܚܒܝܒܢ ܝܗܒܗ. ܦܪܩܬܗ ܕܥܡܗ ܘܥܡܐ	ܠܐܒܐ ܘܠܒܪܐ ܘܠܪܘܚܩܘܕܫܐ	
154.	144	ܗܘ ܚܒܝܒܢ ܡܫܝܚܐ. ܝܗܒܐ ܕܚܝܐ ܘܡܠܟܘܬܐ	ܘܟܠ ܓܪܒܐ ܠܫܒܚܐ ܕܝܡܝܢ. ܘܣܓܝܕ ܠܟܠܢ	A[25]
155.	14	ܗܘ ܚܒܝܒܢ ܡܫܝܚܐ. ܢܗܘܐ ܥܘܕܪܢܐ ܠܟܢܘܫܬܗ	ܥܡܗܘܢ ܫܒܚܝܢ ܦܠܚܝܢ ܣܓܕܝܢ ܘܣܓܝܕ ܠܟܠܢ	
156.	50	ܗܘ ܚܒܝܒܢ ܥܒܕܗ ܘܝܬܪܘܬܗ. ܘܦܪܩܗ ܡܢ ܕܘܝܐ ܕܥܘܠܐ	ܠܥܠܡ ܥܠܡܝܢ ܐܡܝܢ ܘܐܡܝܢ	A
157.	108	ܗܘ ܚܫܟܐ ܢܘܗܪܐ ܐܬܚܙܝ. ܕܒܢܐ ܟܠܗ ܒܢܝ ܐܢܫܐ	ܘܠܟ ܬܫܒܘܚܬܐ ܡܢ ܟܠܢܫ	
158.	89	ܗܘ ܡܠܟ ܝܘܡܢܐ ܫܘܒܚܐ. ܠܫܡܗ ܡܠܟ ܡܠܟܘܬܗ ܫܡܝܐ	ܠܥܠܡ ܥܠܡܝܢ ܐܡܝܢ ܘܐܡܝܢ	A
159.	153	ܗܘܝܬܐ ܢܫܡ ܡܠܟ. ܡܠܟܘܬܐ ܢܫܡܗ ܕܦܪܘܩ	ܠܥܠܡ ܥܠܡܝܢ ܐܡܝܢ ܘܐܡܝܢ	A
160.	4	ܐܡܝܢ ܐܝܟ ܫܘܒܚܗ. ܕܫܡܝܐ ܡܠܐ ܕܟܠ ܡܢ ܦܘܡܗ	ܝܗܒܐ ܫܘܒܚܐ ܠܐܠܗܘܬܟ	

[25] Two Alphabetic Acrostic one normal and the other is inverted and they both are intertwined together.

TABLE 6: HYMNS IN MSS

Table 6A

		M1 1483	M2 1541	B1 1550	D1 1565
1.	ܫܡܥܘ ܐܪܥܢܐ ܘܫܡܝܢܐ ܥܡܡܐ. ܠܦܘܩܕ ܡܠܟܐ ܕܪܘܪܒܢܐ		1v, 4r-4v, 2r-2v, 3r-3v[26]	4r-7r	2v-5v
2.	ܫܠܡܐ ܕܫܠܚ ܠܫܠܝܚܘܗܝ ܙܟܝܐ. ܘܠܐ ܚܟܡܐ ܘܡܦܩܢ ܘܠܐ ܐܢܫܐ		3v, 5r-7v	1v-4r	5v-8r
3.	ܡܢ ܫܡܫ ܠܗ ܠܡܪܘܬܗ. ܒܪܐ ܕܐܠܗܐ ܘܠܘܬܘܪܘܬܗ		7v-12r	9v-10r	8r-12v
4.	ܐܡܝܢ ܐܚܝ ܚܒܪܝܗܘܢ. ܕܐܢܫܐ ܢܫܐ ܕܟܠ ܒܪ ܡܪܗܘܢ		12r-15v		12v-16r
5.	ܒܪܐ ܘܪܚܡ ܠܒܪܝܬܐ. ܘܓܠܐ ܒܬܫܡܫܬܗ ܡܕܒܪܢܐ ܕܒܪܐ		15v, 16r-16v, 21r-21v, 17r-17v	13v-16v	16r-19r
6.	ܟܠ ܥܡܐ ܐܕܢܝܬܐ. ܝܗܒ ܗܘܐ ܕܢܬܥܒܕ ܒܡܬܒܥܬܐ		17v-20r		19r-21v
7.	ܒܢܝܢܗ ܡܕܝܢܬܐ ܕܫܠܝܚܐ. ܝܘܒܠܐ ܡܠܟܐ ܕܡܕܒܪ ܠܢܝܚܐ		20v, 22r-23v	7r-9v	21v-24r
8.	ܒܪܐ ܕܒܩܢܐ ܓܘ ܗܝܡܢܘܬܐ. ܕܟܠ ܚܝܘܬܐ ܘܡܢܚܬܐ		23v-27v	10r-13v	24r-27v
9.	ܒܢܫܐ ܕܫܘܒܚܐ ܗܘ ܕܡܝܐ ܐܒܐ. ܘܒܡܫܝܚܘܬܐ ܗܘ ܡܢܝܢ ܐܒܐ		27v-30v	16v-19v	27v-30v
10.	ܡܢ ܡܥܡܕ ܕܒܡܕܒܪܐ ܝܘܚܢܢ. ܘܐ ܕܒܥܘܡܩܐ ܢܦܠܬ ܘܡܥܡܕܢܐ		30v-35r		30v-34v
11.	ܐܝܬܝܐ ܚܝܐ ܘܒܪ ܚܝܐ. ܚܢܢܐ ܠܟܝܢܐ ܦܫܐ ܘܡܠܟܐ		35r-36r		35r-36r
12.	ܫܡܥܘ ܐܠܗܝܐ ܘܐܠܗܝ. ܕܐܠܗܘܬܗ ܘܐܦ ܐܪܥܢ ܥܡܝ		36r-38v	19v-22r	36r-38r
13.	ܒܟܠܕܝܗ ܒܒܠܐ ܒܘܪܟܐ. ܐܬܗܘ ܗܘܘ ܗܕܝܐ ܕܪܘܚܐ ܡܢܘܪܐ		38v-39v		38v-39v
14.	ܐܘ ܚܒܝܒܐ ܒܘܢܝܐ. ܢܚܫ ܥܘܒܕܢܐ ܐܠܗܝܐ		39v-42v	25r-28r	39v-42v
15.	ܚܝܠܐ ܕܡܠܟܐ ܒܪܐܝܐ. ܘܪܒܝ ܡܢܐ ܡܢ ܒܪܝܐ		42v-45v	28r-31r	42v-45v
16.	ܐܘ ܚܒܝܒܐ ܝܬܒܗܬ ܒܟܘܗܪܘܗܝ. ܕܐܢܫܐ ܥܠܝܢܐ ܩܫܝܫܘܗܝ ܕܡܥܡܕܐ		45v-47v		45v-47r
17.	ܐܘ ܚܒܝܒܐ ܝܘܡܐ ܥܘܕܐ. ܒܕܘܟܪܢܘܗܝ ܕܥܠܝܢܐ ܩܫܝܫܘܗܝ ܕܡܥܡܕܐ		47v-48v		47r-48r
18.	ܒܗܦܟܬ ܐܘܚܐ ܕܡܠܟܘܬܗ ܕܦܘܠܘܣ ܐܕܐ. ܥܠܝܐ ܓܒܪܐ ܦܛܪܘܣ ܘܦܘܠܘܣ		48v-50v		48r-50r
19.	ܡܢ ܢܡܘܣܐ ܕܡܫܝܚܐ. ܢܛܝܪܘ ܛܘܒܝ ܐܘ ܗܘܕܐ		50v-52r		50r-51v
20.	ܗܦܟܐ ܦܛܪܘܣ ܘܦܘܠܘܣ ܓܒܪܐ ܚܘܒܐ. ܘܝܘܚܢܢ ܠܦܪܘ ܕܦܬܚ ܒܡܟܢܫܘܗܝ		52r-54v		51v-54r
21.	ܐܘ ܡܫܒܚܝܢ ܟܠ ܐܘܡܢܘܬܐ. ܘܡܬܬܢܝܢ ܟܠ ܦܠܚܘܬܐ		54v-64v		54r-55v

[26] The sequence of the pages of a hymn appears as it is mentioned in the table.

		M1 1483	M2 1541	B1 1550	D1 1565
22.	ܫܘܒܚܐ ܠܡܫܝܚܐ ܡܚܝܢܗܘܢ. ܕܟܗܢܐ ܘܥܡܐ ܘܡܕܝܢܬܐ		64v-67r		55v-58r
23.	ܦܬܓܡܐ ܕܦܬܓܡܬܐ. ܘܡܬܓܡܢܐ ܕܡܫܒܚܬܐ		67v-70r	54r-56v	58r-60v
24.	ܡܢ ܟܢܘܫܐ ܕܦܘܩܕܢܐ ܡܪܢܝܐ ܘܡܫܡܠܝܢܘܬܐ ܕܟܬܒܐ ܩܕܝܫܐ		70r-71v	56v-58v	61r-62v
25.	ܡܢ ܢܦܫ ܢܘܗܪ ܡܢ ܢܘܗܪܐ. ܐܘܠ ܠܥܒܕܐ ܐܝܟ ܦܘܩܕܢܐ		71v-74r	58v-60v	62v-64v
26.	ܐܘ ܢܩܦܐ ܕܢܚܬܬ ܡܢ ܥܠ. ܡܢܘ ܢܒܕܘܟ ܦܢܝܐ ܡܢ ܥܠ		74r-76r	60v-63r	64v-66v
27.	ܐܘ ܕܡܝܬܐ ܢܗܝܪܬܐ. ܘܐܝܟ ܕܡܢܗܪܐ ܕܘܢܐ ܕܡܕܢܚܐ		76r-77v	63r-64r	66v-68r
28.	ܠܘܬܟ ܫܡܥܢ ܐܒܐ ܠܟ. ܘܬܘܠܐ ܕܬܫܒܘܚܬܐ ܡܬܕܟܪ ܐܒܐ ܠܟ		77v-78v	64r-65v	68r-69r
29.	ܠܡܪܝ ܕܡܠܘܟ ܕܒܟܢܫܗ. ܢܬܦܠ ܕܢܝܚ ܕܡܢ ܡܬܠܬܝܬܗ		78v-80r	65v-67r	69r-70v
30.	ܫܘܒܚܐ ܠܩܕܝܫܝ ܡܪܘܡܐ. ܕܦܪܘܩ ܠܟܠܗܘܢ ܒܕܡܐ		80r-81v	67r-68v	70v-72r
31.	ܡܪܐ ܒܡܢܝܢܘܬܐ. ܕܠܗ ܘܡܪ ܪܘܚܐ ܒܡܢܝܢܘܬܐ		81v-83v	68v-71v	72r-74v
32.	ܫܡܥܘ ܗܕܐ ܡܠܟܐ ܢܟܣܐ. ܕܠܩܕܡܐ ܡܠ ܗܘܘ ܫܠܡܘܬܐ		84r-85v	96v-98v	74v-76v
33.	ܐܠܗܐ ܠܡܝܢܐ ܘܟܢܫܐ. ܟܢܫܐ ܡܪܢܝܐ ܘܡܫܠܡܐ		85v-86v	95r-96v	76v-77v
34.	ܡܪܝܐ ܒܪܟ ܕܠܒܘܬܗ. ܘܒܫܘܒܚ ܒܡܪܝܡܘܬܗ		86v-87v	98v-99v	77v-79r
35.	ܕܗܘܝܐ ܕܬܘܕܝܬܐ ܢܩܒܠ ܐܒܐ. ܕܠܘܩܒܠ ܕܫܡܥܐ ܗܘܐ ܫܡܝܐ ܐܒܐ		87v-89r		79r-80r
36.	ܡܪܝ ܡܫܝܚܐ ܕܐܬܬܓܠܝ. ܘܐܬܓܠܝ ܒܦܓܪܐ ܐܬܚܙܝ		89r-90r		80r-81v
37.	ܐܘ ܕܪܡܙܐ ܒܬܘܠܬܐ. ܦܪܘܩ ܠܓܒܝܐ ܐܝܟ ܕܒܗܘܬܐ		90r-91r		81v-82v
38.	ܒܗ ܩܝܡܐ ܕܗܒܐ ܠܡܐ ܠܗ. ܬܗܘܡܐ ܕܫܘܒܚܐ ܕܟܠ ܡܬܕܟܪ ܠܗ		91r-92r		82v-83v
39.	ܡܪܢ ܢܨܝܚ ܕܐܬܓܠܝ. ܫܠܚܘ ܘܫܡܥܘ ܘܫܒܚ ܢܦܫܝܢ		92v-93v		83v-85r
40.	ܡܪܐ ܒܪܩܝܡܘܬܗ ܒܫܡܝܐ. ܘܬܫܒܘܚܬܗ ܦܪܝܩ ܠܟܠܗܘܢ		93v-94v		85r-86r
41.	ܢܨܝܚ ܫܡܫܐ ܘܢܗܪ ܡܢ ܥܠ. ܦܠܚܐ ܡܫܝܚܐ ܕܦܬܚܠܝ ܟܠ ܥܠ		94v-96r		86r-87v
42.	ܒܪܟܐ ܠܡܪܝ ܒܩܠܝܠܬܐ. ܝܕܥܬ ܕܐܝܬܝ ܟܪܝܗܘܬܐ		96r-97r		87v-88v
43.	ܠܡܪܘ ܢܩܡܘ ܘܦܠܚܘ ܕܫܘܬܦ. ܠܟܝ ܢܩܠܦܢ ܗܝܟ ܗܘܟܕܢ		97r-98r		88v-90r
44.	ܠܡܪܝ ܒܫܠܘܬܐ ܘܬܫܒܚܬܐ. ܢܦܠ ܒܡܚܠܐ ܡܢ ܦܬܢܬܐ		98r-99v		90r-91v
45.	ܒܝܬ ܢܟܠܐ ܕܩܠܝܠܬܐ. ܘܒܝܬ ܦܫܝܩܘܬܐ ܒܪܝܬܐ		99v-100v	49r-50r	91v-92v

		M1 1483	M2 1541	B1 1550	D1 1565
46.	ܓܢܗ ܕܟܪܐ ܡܠܟܐ ܝܬܝܒܘܬܐ ܘܓܢܗ ܕܡܕܡܘܕܥܬܐ ܡܠܟܐ ܕܡܕܡܪܬܐ		100v-102r		93r-94r
47.	ܣܓܝܢ ܘܡܫܒܚܝܢ ܡܘܟ ܚܝܠܐ ܐܢܐ. ܡܘܟ ܚܝܠܐ ܐܢܐ ܐܦ ܡܫܝܚܐ ܐܢܐ		102r-103r		94r-95v
48.	ܒܪܝܟ ܕܡܕ ܒܡܪܢܝܬܗ ܠܐ ܡܫܟܚ. ܐܠܐ ܐܘܣܦ ܘܠܡܐ ܡܫܟܚ		103r-104v		95v-97r
49.	ܒܪܝܟ ܕܡܕ ܒܟܝ ܘܒܦܪ ܠܒܒܢ. ܒܫܢܝܗ ܢܦܠܝ ܠܒܒܢ		104v-105v		97r-98v
50.	ܐܘ ܡܒܪܒܟ ܥܡܟܘ ܘܝܬܢܡܪܘ. ܘܦܝܠܘ ܡܠܟܐ ܕܪܘܚܐ ܕܩܘܕܫܐ		105v-106v		98v-99v
51.	ܥܡܟܘ ܘܝܬܢܡܪܘ ܦܪܘܫܐ. ܘܠܐ ܗܘܝܬ ܡܠܟܘܬܐ ܡܠܟܐ ܪܘܚܐ		106v-108v		99v-101v
52.	ܒܝܬܠ ܟܘܕܪܢܝ ܠܟܦܘܬ. ܒܝܬܠ ܘܡܪܕ ܠܡܫܝܚܘܬ		108v-110r		101v-103r
53.	ܟܕ ܗܠܒܘ ܐܢܫܐ ܒܒܪܝܬܐ. ܘܝܬܦܪܫܘ ܠܗܕܡܝ ܦܬܓܡܐ		110r-112r		103r-105r
54.	ܡܒܘ ܕܢܦܒܗ ܟܠ ܫܘܒܚ. ܘܡܒܘ ܝܟܝܐ ܐܦ ܝܐܠܐ ܟܠܟܝ		112r-114r		105r-107v
55.	ܢܒܘ ܕܐܒܬܠܗ ܕܟܢܫܐ. ܘܕܝܐ ܡܕܠܟܐ ܘܢܘܒܕ ܦܘܫܐ		114r-116r		107v-110r
56.	ܐܘ ܡܫܘܬܗ ܡܐ ܡܫܒܚ. ܐܘ ܡܕܕܘܬܗ ܡܐ ܡܠܒܢ		116r-119r		110r-113r
57.	ܐܘ ܢܘܩܒܗ ܡܐ ܒܒܥܒ. ܘܡܐ ܗܝܡ ܡܢܬܢ ܘܡܐ ܡܕܒܕܒ		119r-121r	43r-45v	113r-115r
58.	ܐܘ ܥܡܘܒܐ ܕܝܠܘܬܐ. ܘܡܡܠܟܢܐ ܕܒܠܬܘܬܐ		121r-122v	84v-87r	115r-117r
59.	ܡܪܐ ܕܟܠ ܡܪܘܬܐ. ܐܦ ܢܘܪܐ ܕܟܠ ܡܘܬܒܬܐ		122v-124r	87r-88r	117r-118v
60.	ܡܠܦܢܐ ܕܡܦܒܪܬܐ. ܡܥܒܕܐ ܐܒܬܘܗܝ ܒܥܕܒܕܘܬܐ		124r-126r	88r-90v	118v-121r
61.	ܒܪܐ ܕܐܠܗܘܬܗ ܠܝܬ ܥܘܬܦܬܐ. ܘܝܡܗ ܒܬܘܠܬܐ ܘܠܐ ܡܘܢܒܬܐ		126r-127v	105r-107v	121r-123r
62.	ܒܗܦܪܝ ܪܘܚܐ ܦܪܐ ܗܘܢܗ. ܘܒܗܠܬܗܘ ܡܬܘܠܐ ܗܘܢܗ		127v-129v		123r-125r
63.	ܡܠܟܐ ܕܡܠܟܐ ܠܗ ܦܠܚܝܢ. ܘܕܘܫܢܐ ܠܪܡܘܗ ܡܩܪܒܝܢ		130r-131v	93r-95r	125r-127v
64.	ܒܝܬܓܡܐ ܕܘܫܢܐ. ܕܝܐܓܪܬܗ ܕܒܪ ܓܕܡܦܘܫܝܐ		132r-133v		146v-148r
65.	ܒܠܠܡܐ ܗܢܐ ܫܪܬ ܗܘܦܝ. ܘܒܠܘܦܫܘ ܡܬܒܝܐ ܗܘܦܝ		133v-135r		127v-129r
66.	ܒܦܘܪܐ ܦܪܐ ܡܦܬ ܗܘܦܝ. ܕܡܠܟܠ ܡܢܐ ܒܠܒܠ ܠܘܦܫܐ		135r-138r	81r-84v	129r-132v
67.	ܒܪܝܟ ܕܒܝܘܡܗ ܡܕܒܪܐ. ܦܪܒ ܫܘܦܬܗ ܕܠܝܫܐ ܕܐܢܫܐ		138r-140r	99v-102r	132v-134v
68.	ܡܪܘܡܘ ܐܢܬ ܕܟܢܝܬܟܘܢ. ܒܘܡܦܬܘܬܐ ܘܒܕܟܘܬܐ		140r-141v		135r-136v
69.	ܢܘܩܦܐ ܝܠܗ ܠܒ ܗܘܢܐ. ܘܢܡܠܘ ܠܒܢܐ ܘܢܪܡܘ ܝܕܢܐ		141v-143v		136v-138v

		M1 1483	M2 1541	B1 1550	D1 1565
70.	ܐܘ ܕܠܥܒܝܕܘܬܐ ܕܠܝܟ. ܘܠܡܫܟܢܘܬܐ ܡܬܕܒܪܝܢ		143v-145v		138v-141r
71.	ܐܘ ܡܫܝܚܐ ܡܢ ܟܠ ܕܠܗ ܚܝܠܐ ܟܠ. ܟܠ ܡܬܚܙܐ ܠܟܠ ܘܚܙܐ ܠܟܠ		145v-147r		141r-142r
72.	ܒܢܝ ܒܪܢܫܘܬܐ ܐܘܫܥܐ. ܕܗܘܘ ܒܢܝܢܐ ܠܩܕܡܐ ܡܢܝܢܐ		147r-148r		142r-143v
73.	ܐܘ ܐܚܝ ܢܬܟܬܒ ܒܗ. ܒܪܘܚܐ ܕܟܠܐ ܢܟܬܒ ܠܗ		148r-149v		143v-145r
74.	ܡܫܒܚܐ ܩܕܡܘ ܕܬܫܒܘܚܬܐ. ܘܡܟܠܗ ܕܐܠܗܐ ܡܠܟܐ		149v-151r		145r-146v
75.	ܩܢ ܠܗ ܠܡܪܝܢ ܕܒܩܕܐ ܒܝܬ. ܩܢܐ ܕܒܪܐ ܠܐܕܡ ܩܕܡ ܥܠܝܒ		151r-152v	31r-33r	148r-150r
76.	ܦܐܪܐ ܕܕܝܢܐ ܠܢܠܘܕܗ. ܕܐܘܡܐ ܘܟܘܡܡܐ ܟܚܒܘܒܝ ܒܐܒܘܗ		153r-155v	107v-110v	150v-153r
77.	ܡܢ ܟܠ ܩܕܡ ܠܐܘܪܫܠܡ. ܕܩܛܠ ܢܒܝܐ ܘܟܐ ܕܢܒܠܡ		155v-157r	110v-112v	153r-154v
78.	ܒܠܝܐ ܕܓܒܝܐ ܘܦܪܘܫܬܐ. ܕܠܩܕܡܐ ܡܢ ܗܘܐ ܠܗ ܡܚܒܪܬܐ		157r-158v	112v-114r	154v-156r
79.	ܒܢܥܗ ܕܩܕܡ ܗܘܐ ܢܥܐ. ܘܐܒܘ ܓܗܪܐ ܠܟܒܪܐ ܘܐܢܫܐ		158v-161r	114r-117r	156r-158v
80.	ܒܩܘܬܗ ܕܒܪܐ ܡܫܒܚܬܐ. ܙܟܝ ܐܪܟܐ ܘܕܟܠܝ ܥܡܡܐ		161v-162v	119v-121v	158v-160r
81.	ܒܢܒܘܒܝܬܐ ܢܘܡܐ ܦܘܩܐ. ܟܐ ܬܪܘܢܐ ܘܒܪܐ ܠܠܡܐ		162v-164v	121v-122v	160r-162r
82.	ܒܪܐ ܡܠܬܐ ܒܫܒܝܚܬܐ. ܠܒܝܬܗ ܠܦܝܪܐ ܐܪܡܫܐ		164v-167r		162r-164v
83.	ܐܬܐ ܗܘܝ ܠܟ ܡܫܒܚܬܐ. ܒܪܐ ܒܫܒܝܚܐ ܗܘܝ ܡܫܒܚܢܐ		167r-169r		164v-167r
84.	ܫܪܪܐ ܕܩܘܕܫܐ ܢܩܪܒ ܗܘܢܐ. ܘܕܫܠܡ ܘܪܚܡ ܘܐܬܕܒܪ ܗܘܢܐ.		169r-171r		167r-169r
85.	ܫܡܝܐ ܥܫܢܩܐ ܦܬܠܝܢ. ܕܐܠܗܘܬܗ ܘܫܡܝܢ ܗܟܘ ܥܡܝܢ		171r-172v		169r-171r
86.	ܬܪܘܢܐ ܕܟܠ ܢܒܝܐ. ܘܡܢܒܝܬܐ ܕܫܬܝܩܬܐ	41v-44r	172v-174r	123v-125v	171r-172v
87.	ܦܢܝܘ ܡܥܡܕ ܕܢܟܝܐ. ܫܪܪܐ ܠܢܒܝܐ ܘܡܠܟܐ ܒܠܝܠܐ		174r-175v		172v-174v
88.	ܠܬܓܘܪܐ ܕܩܘܕܫܐ ܫܠܡ. ܘܒܟܘܪܝܬܐ ܕܟܠܐ ܩܦܚ		175v-177v		174v-176v
89.	ܐܘ ܟܠܝ ܝܘܡܢ ܥܘܒܕܐ. ܠܟܠܗ ܟܠܐ ܒܕܘܟܬܐ ܩܗܝܕܐ		177v-178v		176v-177v
90.	ܐܠܗܐ ܐܒܐ ܡܠܬܐ. ܥܝܪܐ ܒܡ ܐܒܘܗܝ ܒܐܒܗܘܬܐ		178v-180v		177v-180v
91.	ܐܘܪܚܗ ܕܒܪܐ ܡܫܒܚܬܐ. ܠܐ ܡܬܐܪܟܐ ܠܟܠܗܘܢ ܒܢܝܢܐ	48v-51v	180v-182v	128r-130r	180v-182v
92.	ܫܝܬܐ ܕܐܢܬܐ ܟܒܝܠ ܫܘܪܝ. ܟܒܝܠ ܡܢ ܫܘܪܝܐ ܘܦܘܩ ܠܫܘܪܝܐ	44v-48v	182v-184v	125v-128r	182v-184v
93.	ܩܒܐ ܠܐܒܪܗ ܟܒܝܢ ܫܡܐ. ܘܡܠܟܐ ܘܐܬܐܪܡ ܠܥܩܒ ܥܡܢܐ	51v-54r	184v-185v	130r-131v	184v-186r

		M1 1483	M2 1541	B1 1550	D1 1565
94.	ܩܕܡ ܕܐܪܥܐ ܘܫܡܝܐ. ܐܡܐ ܡܫܡܫܢ ܡܫܒܚܢܐ ܡܫܒܠܢܐ		185v-187v		186r-188v
95.	ܫܒܝܚ ܦܬܓܡܘܗܝ ܕܩܘܪܝܣ. ܩܕܡܐ ܩܕܡ ܘܐܘܪܚܝ ܠܟܠܗܝ		187v-190r	22r-25r	188v-191r
96.	ܩܐ ܐܘܪܚܝ ܠܒܪܘܗܝ ܕܩܕܡܐ. ܘܗܘܐ ܠܩܠܠ ܐܘܕܝ ܫܒܢܐ	54r-58r	190r-192r	131v-134r	191v-193v
97.	ܡܢܘ ܗܟܢ ܕܢܚܠܬܐ. ܢܥܒܕ ܠܠܝܐ ܡܕܡܐ ܡܠܬܐ	58r-61r	192r-194r	134r-136r	193v-195v
98.	ܢܬܒܪܐ ܕܠܘܬ ܐܒܘܬܗ. ܒܝܬ ܐܩܕܝܫܐ ܦܓܪ ܗܢܦܫܗ	61r-64r	194r-195v	136v-138v	195v-197v
99.	ܫܘܒܚܐ ܠܗ ܠܗܘ ܚܢܢܐ. ܦܠܓ ܩܫܝܐ ܘܥܩܒܬ ܚܢܢܐ	64r-68v	195v-198r	138v-141r	197v-200r
100.	ܗܘ ܦܠܚܐ ܕܫܩܝܢܐ. ܘܩܕܡܐ ܕܟܒܪܐ ܘܕܟܒܪܢܐ	68v-72r	198r-200r	141r-143v	200v-202r
101.	ܩܕܡ ܕܦܟܪܐ ܘܡܘܠܚܬܐ. ܒܐܪܟܐ ܗܠܝ ܐܝܟ ܡܩܫܘܢܐ	72r-73v	200r-201r	143v-144v	202r-203r
102.	ܫܘܡܫ ܐܘ ܠܒܝܬ ܚܝܠܬܐ. ܢܬܬܠܒܪܘ ܕܩܒܠ ܒܬܠܒܬܐ	73v-76r	201r-202r	144v-146v	203r-204v
103.	ܐܡܢܐ ܕܐܝܬ ܠܗ ܫܩܝܩܐ. ܕܘܫܢܐ ܘܠܐ ܠܘܫܩܝܐ	76r-79r	202r-204r	146v-148v	204v-206r
104.	ܠܐܠܝܢ ܕܢܝܚܬܐ ܢܠܬ ܗܘܢܬ. ܘܐܪܐܢܝܬܐ ܢܬܬܐ ܚܘܢܬ ܗܘܝܬ		204r-206v	45v-49r	206v-209r
105.	ܠܩܪܝܫܐ ܐܟܘܢܐ. ܕܢܝܢ ܒܝܬܗ ܒܪܐ ܚܒܝܒܐ		206v-208r	33r-35r	209r-211r
106.	ܐܠܗܐ ܕܝܗܒ ܐܢܫܐ. ܒܪܗ ܫܠܚ ܢܒܝ ܠܦܘܪܩܢ ܐܢܫܐ		208r-209v		211r-212v
107.	ܐܡܢܐ ܕܠܘܬ ܐܝܟ ܐܡܘܬܗ. ܠܐ ܘܐܦܠܐ ܐܝܬ ܐܝܟ ܢܝܫܡܬܗ	79r-82r	209v-211r	148v-150v	212v-214v
108.	ܗܐ ܚܙܝܐ ܝܘܡܐ ܕܫܒܝܬܐ. ܕܐܡܪ ܩܕܡ ܒܢܝ ܦܠܐܬܐ	82r-85r	211v-213r	150v-152v	214v-216r
109.	ܝܡܝܢܗ ܕܐܒܐ ܡܬܘܩܢܐ ܐܚܕ ܒܚܠܒܘܬܗ ܦܠܓܐ ܐܠܐ	85r-88r	213r-214v	152v-154v	216r-218r
110.	ܦܢܘܢ ܟܠܗ ܕܢܘܬܐ. ܘܡܢܢ ܟܠܗ ܦܪܝܫܘܬܐ	88r-90v	214v-216r	154v-156r	218r-219v
111.	ܐܘ ܕܬܓܠܝܢ ܠܟܠ ܚܝܠܘܗܝ. ܘܡܫܬܒܗܪܝܢ ܠܟܠ ܠܘܬܐܪܗܘܢ	90v-93r	216r-217v	156r-158r	219v-221r
112.	ܒܓܒܐ ܡܪܢܐ ܕܒܪܝܬܐ. ܘܒܢܝܢܐ ܕܢܪܫܘܡ ܒܓܒܝܬܐ		217v-218v	90v-91v	221r-222v
113.	ܢܩܫܐ ܡܢܬܐ ܒܝܬܢܢܐ. ܒܪܠܐ ܢܐܬܐ ܚܘܡ ܠܘܫܪܢܐ		218v-219v	91v-93r	222v-223v
114.	ܦܠܚܐ ܕܢܗܪ ܫܩܝܐ. ܕܒܥܠܝܐ ܘܠܐ ܗܘܐ ܕܩܠܕܐ	93v-96r	219v-221r	158r-159v	223v-225r
115.	ܐܘ ܚܝܠܝܐ ܘܕܩܢܐ. ܗܐ ܝܘܡܐ ܦܬܠܗ ܕܝܚܝܕܝܐ	96r-100r	221r-223v	159v-162v	225r-227v
116.	ܫܘܒܚܐ ܒܪܐ ܠܟ ܫܘܒܚܝܢ. ܕܐܘܡܐ ܘܠܘܡܫܐ ܒܐܝܕܗ ܠܚܒܝܒܝܢ	100r-102v	223v-225r	162v-164r	228r-229r
117.	ܡܕܒܪܢܐ ܘܒܪܝܗ ܕܡܕܒܪܢܐ. ܕܢܠܝܕܘܬܗ ܡܢ ܟܠ ܐܡܐ	102v-105r	225r-226v	164r-165v	229r-231r

		M1 1483	M2 1541	B1 1550	D1 1565
118.	ܦܠܐܬܐ ܐܠܗܝܬܐ. ܡܢܐ ܕܒܢܝܢܐ ܐܠܗܝܬܐ	105r-108r	226v-228r	165v-167v	231r-233r
119.	ܐܘ ܕܒܪܐ ܒܢܝ ܡܠܟܘܬܐ. ܟܠܝܠܐ ܗܕܝܪܘܗܝ ܘܡܫܒܚܬܐ		228v-229v		233r-234v
120.	ܚܣܝܪܐ ܕܠܒܠ ܒܪܐ ܕܠܒܪ ܡܢܗ ܠܐܒܘܗܝ ܠܗ ܒܪܐ	108r-111r	229v-231v	168v-170v	234v-236v
121.	ܦܠܚܐ ܘܫܪܪܐ ܕܟܠ ܦܠܚܐ. ܕܒܬܪܘܗܝ ܐܢܬ ܒܗܘܢ ܦܠܚܐ	111r-113v	231v-232v	170v-172r	236v-238r
122.	ܦܠܚܐ ܕܪܘܡܐ ܢܟܝܐ. ܕܐܬܐ ܕܢܦܪܘܩ ܠܐܪܥܝܐ	113v-118r	232v-235r	172r-175r	238r-240v
123.	ܡܪܝܡܐ ܦܪܝܗ ܕܡܪܝܡܘܬܐ. ܗܘ ܕܐܬܓܠܝܗ ܡܢ ܟܠ ܪܡܐ		235r-236v	181r-183r	240v-242v
124.	ܫܪܐ ܕܒܪܝܬܐ ܘܕܢܚܬܐ. ܐܦ ܢܦܫܬܐ ܕܟܠ ܐܢܫܐ	118r-121r	236v-238r	175r-176v	242v-244r
125.	ܫܘܒܚܐ ܕܟܠ ܚܝܠܘܬܐ. ܢܡܐ ܪܒܐ ܡܠܟܐ ܢܨܚܬܐ	121r-125r	238r-240v	176v-177v	244r-246r
126.	ܐܝܟܢܐ ܕܪܘܡܐ ܒܢܝ ܩܕܫܘܗܝ ܐܬܐ ܠܐܪܥܐ ܕܢܩܝܦ ܠܒܢܝܢܘܗܝ	125r-127v	240v-241v		246r-247v
127.	ܫܘܒܚܐ ܠܟ ܠܟܘܢ ܡܫܝܚܬܐ. ܕܒܪܟ ܘܐܬܚܡܝ ܟܠ ܥܕܬܐ		241v-244r	180r-181r	248r-250r
128.	ܢܘܗܪܐ ܘܢܚܬܘ ܠܐܠܗܘܬܟ. ܪܦܪܦܬ ܠܟܝܢܢ ܒܒܪܐ ܕܝܠܟ		S[27] 244r-245v		S254v-255v
129.	ܡܪܝ ܕܝܢ ܡܢ ܐܝܟ ܒܪ ܗܘܐ. ܕܫܘܒܚܗ ܠܩܕܝܫܘܬܗ ܥܡܘܪܐ ܗܘܐ		S245v-247v		250r-252r
130.	ܓܡܝܪܘ ܕܐܬܐ ܡܫܘܕܥܐ ܕܟܠ ܢܟܦܘܬܗ ܥܘܡܐ ܒܐܘܪܚܐ		S247v-249v		252r-254r
131.	ܐܒܗܬܐ ܕܝܢ ܡܫܟܢ ܕܒܣܘܟܠܗ ܒܪܝ.. ܘܢܦܩܬܐ ܒܟܒܫܐ ܢܘܓܪܐ		S249v-251v		S255v-258r
132.	ܫܒܚ ܦܡܪܡܪܝܢ ܡܪܐ ܟܠ. ܕܥܒܕܐ ܒܣܘܟܠܗ ܘܢܦܩܗ ܠܟܝܢܢ		S251v-256r		S260r-265r
133.	ܒܪܝܟ ܗܘ ܡܫܒܚܐ ܡܢܝܚܢܐ. ܐܒܘܢ ܕܒܗ ܕܦܪܩܢܢ ܘܦܕܢܢ		S256r-257v		S265r-266r
134.	ܒܪܝܟܘ ܡܫܒܚܐ ܡܚܝܠܢܢ. ܐܒܘܢ ܕܒܗ ܕܚܝܝܢ ܘܢܝܚܢ		S257v-258v		S268r-269v
135.	ܒܟܠ ܫܢܝܢ ܘܒܟܠ ܕܪܝܢ.. ܠܟ ܘܠܐܒܘܟ ܡܫܒܚܐ ܡܪܝ		S258v-260v		S266v-268r
136.	- ܫܘܒܚܐ ܠܡܪܢ ܝܫܘܥ. ܠܒܪܐ ܕܠܐܠܗܐ ܘܠܡܠܟܐ ܕܡܠܟܘܬܐ..... - ܗܘܡܢܐ . ܘܡܬܘܒ ܗܠܝܢ ܡܪܝ ܕܒܢܝ		S260v-262v, S263r-264r		S258r-260r
137.	ܐܘ ܡܫܝܚܐ ܣܒܪܢ ܛܒܬܐ ܗܘܬ. ܐܘ ܡܫܝܚܐ ܦܪܘܩܢ ܚܕܬܐ ܗܘܬ		S262v, 265r-266v		
138.	ܗܓܝܢ ܠܫܡܐ ܐܢܫܝܐ. ܕܐܝܘܦܢܛܝܐ ...ܕ ܘܕܝܢܐ	1v-41r			
139.	ܒܪܐ ܕܒܬܘܠܬܐ ܡܫܘܒܚܐ. ܕܒܪܐ ܒܪܝܬܐ ܡܢ ܥܘܪܢܐ	127v-129r		167v-168v	
140.	ܒܪܝܟܘ ܡܫܒܚܐ ܦܪܘܩܢ. ܕܒܪܗ ܣܘܓܝܐ ܐܘܪܒ ܘܢܦܩ			35r-38v	

[27] The letter **S** means that the hymn is located in the Supplement of the *Book of Wardā*.

		M1 1483	M2 1541	B1 1550	D1 1565
141.	ܒܥܘܕܪܢܐ ܕܩܠܝܠܐ ܕܪܗ ܚܘܫܒܢ. ܘܡܛܠܗ ܕܕܒܪܐ ܕܝܢ ܫܒܩܢܘܗܝ			38v-43r	
142.	ܫܥܝܬܐ ܡܠܝܬ ܒܝܬܐ. ܕܥܘܠܡ ܗܠܡ ܥܡܝ ܫܥܝܬܐ			50v-54r	
143.	ܐܘ ܙܘܥܝܐ ܒܡܠܟܘܬܐ. ܘܙܘܥܝܐ ܒܩܝܡܬܐ			71v-73r	
144.	ܐܘ ܚܒܝܒܝ ܫܘܢܝܬ. ܥܒܕܐ ܒܛܥܝܐ ܘܐܠܗܝܬ			73r-75r	
145.	ܟܠ ܫܒܒܐ ܦܪܝܫܐ. ܐܦܠܐ ܒܦܓܪܐ ܦܪܝܫܐ			75r-81r	
146.	ܫܪܒܐ ܙܡܝܪܐ ܫܪܝܪܬܐ. ܦܠܓ ܒܝ ܒܙܒܢܐ ܕܒܪܝܬܐ			102r-105r	
147.	ܫܡ ܗܠܝܢ ܡܪܝ ܠܥܒܕ ܦܩܕܐ. ܐܬܐ ܥܡܬܐ ܘܫܠܝܐ			117r-119v	
148.	ܙܕܝܩ ܒܝܬܐ ܒܢܘܚܡܬܐ. ܕܟܠܢܐ ܕܗܘܢܐ ܐܢܫܝܬܐ			122v-123r	
149.	ܢܦܩ ܦܘܩܕܢܐ ܡܢ ܡܠܟܐ. ܘܐܬܦܫܛ ܠܟܠܗ ܒܐܬܪܘܬܐ				
150.	ܐܘ ܚܒܝܒܝ ܢܬܟܢܫ. ܫܠܡܬܗ ܕܐܒܘܢ ܘܗܝܐ				
151.	ܥܘܒܕܐ ܠܒܢܝܢܢ ܩܪܘܡ. ܕܫܡ ܡܪܐ ܚܘܒܐ ܕܐܬܓܠܝ ܠܡܬܚܫ				
152.	ܛܘܒܝܗ ܠܐܡܐ ܡܒܪܒܬܐ. ܒܬܘܠܬܐ ܕܡܝܬܐ ܘܡܦܝܬܬܐ				
153.	ܐܘܕܝܬܐ ܢܦܩ ܡܠܟ. ܒܕܘܒܪܝ ܢܦܫܗ ܕܩܕܘܫ				
154.	ܒܢܝܪܝ ܡܕܝܢܬܐ ܙܒܠܝܬܐ. ܢܬܦܫܛ ܩܠܐ ܕܫܒܚܝ ܠܡܠܟܐ				
155.	ܘܠܐܦ ܗܘ ܦܘܪܩܢܐ ܕܝܬܒܝܐ. ܐܦ ܠܚܛܝܐ ܕܝܬܒܝܐ				
156.	ܝܘܡܐ ܘܐܬܦܫܛܘ ܥܡܘܕܐ. ܐܬܬܠܝܡܘ ܘܐܬܦܢܝܘ ܐܘ ܠܚܝܒܐ				
157.	ܡܪܐ ܕܪܚܡܐ ܘܡܪܚܡܢܐ. ܘܥܠܝ ܒܪܚܡܝܗ ܦܘܪܩܢܐ ܕܒܢܝܐ				
158.	ܡܪܝ ܕܗܠܝܢ ܠܥܡܢܐ. ܒܝܘܡܐ ܕܡܠܟܘܬܐ ܚܕܬܐ				
159.	ܥܘܐ ܠܥܘܒܕܐ ܐܝܬܝܐ ܒܪܘܚܐ. ܒܢܝܐ ܫܡܝܐ ܘܪܡܐ ܘܡܫܠܡܐ				
160.	ܥܘܒܕܢܐ ܠܚܘܒܐ ܩܪܘܡ ܒܦܬܐ ܗܠܝܢܐ ܡܪܚܡܢܘܬܗ				

Table 6B

		C1 1568	C2 1568	D2 1575	B2 1581
1.	ܒܥܝܢܐ ܢܗܝܪܬܐ ܘܫܦܝܪ ܥܩܪܐ. ܠܡܫܐ ܡܠܟܐ ܕܐܬܘܪܝܐ		1v-4r	1v-4v	1[28]-5
2.	ܐܠܗܐ ܕܐܝܬܗ ܠܐܠܗܘ ܘܟܬܐ. ܘܠܐ ܡܫܐ ܘܢܦܩܬ ܘܠܐ ܐܢܫܐ		4r-6r	4v-7v	5-10
3.	ܡܢ ܦܘܡ ܠܗ ܠܐܬܘܪܝܐ. ܒܪܐ ܕܐܠܗܐ ܘܐܠܝܩܘܪܝܐ		6r-10v	7v-12v	10-15
4.	ܬܡܝܗܝܢ ܐܢܘܢ ܒܢܝܢܫܐ. ܕܐܝܬܝܗ ܒܢܝܐ ܕܟܠ ܒܪ ܐܕܡ		10v-13r	12v-16v	16-21
5.	ܕܝܢܐ ܘܐܢܫ ܠܕܡܝܢܐ. ܘܟܠܝ ܒܡܫܝܚ ܡܠܟܐ ܕܝܢܐ		13r-15v	16v-19v	21-26
6.	ܒܟܠ ܥܕܢܐ ܬܫܒܘܚܬܐ. ܝܗܒܬ ܗܘܢܐ ܕܢܐܡܪ ܒܬܫܒܘܚܬܐ		15v-18r	19v-22v	26-30
7.	ܒܝܘܡܐ ܡܕܝܢܬܐ ܕܫܠܝܛ. ܥܡܢܘܐܝܠ ܡܠܟܐ ܕܡܠܟܝܢ ܠܥܠܡ		18r-20r	22v-25r	30-34
8.	ܒܪܐ ܕܩܡܝܢ ܒܗ ܡܗܝܡܢܐ. ܕܟܠ ܚܝܘܬܐ ܘܒܪܝܬܐ	1r[29]-4v	20r-23v	25r-29r	34-40
9.	ܒܝܘܡܐ ܕܫܒܬܐ ܗܘ ܐܝܟ ܐܢܐ. ܘܒܥܒܕܘܗܝ ܗܘ ܡܫܒܚ ܐܢܐ	4v-8r	23v-26v	29r-32v	40-46
10.	ܡܢ ܡܥܒܕ ܕܒܥܒܕܐ ܢܬܒܪܟ. ܐܘ ܐܒܗܘܬܐ ܢܦܫܟ ܘܢܥܒܕܐ	8r-12v	26v-30v	38v-43r	46-53
11.	ܐܝܬܐ ܚܝܐ ܘܗܒ ܚܝܐ. ܡܪܝܐ ܠܥܠܡܐ ܒܚܝܐ ܘܫܠܡܐ	12v-13v	30v-31v	43r-44v	53-55
12.	ܒܥܝܢܐ ܬܠܬܝܘܬܐ ܘܬܠܬܝܢ. ܕܐܠܗܘܬܗ ܘܬܘܒ ܢܗܝܪ ܥܡܝܩ	14r-16r	31v-34r	44v-46v	55-59
13.	ܒܫܡܥܗ ܕܒܪܐ ܒܘܟܪܐ. ܬܫܒܘܚܬܐ ܗܘܘ ܦܓܪܐ ܕܐܘܚܕ ܘܒܘܪܐ	16r-17r	34r-35r	46v-48r	59-61
14.	ܐܘ ܚܒܝܒܐ ܓܘܢܝܬܐ. ܢܦܫ ܒܘܚܢܐ ܬܠܝܬܝܬܐ	17v-20v	35r-38r	48r-51r	61-66
15.	ܚܝܠܐ ܕܫܠܝܛ ܒܢܗܪܐ. ܘܢܗܪܝܢ ܡܢܐ ܡܢ ܝܠܕܐ	20v-23v	38r-40v	51r-53v	66-71
16.	ܐܘ ܚܒܝܒܐ ܢܬܦܫܛ ܒܠܘܗܕܢܗܘܢ. ܕܝܠܗܐ ܥܠܝܬܐ ܕܫܡܗܘܢ ܕܡܫܝܚܐ	23v-25v	41r-42v	53v-55v	71-74
17.	ܐܘ ܚܒܝܒܐ ܝܘܡܢܐ ܒܘܚܢܐ. ܒܕܘܓܡܐܗܘܢ ܕܥܠܝܬܐ ܕܫܡܗܘܢ ܕܡܫܝܚܐ	25v-26v	42v-43v	55v-56v	74-76
18.	ܒܗܦܟܐ ܐܘܚܐ ܕܡܠܟܘܬܗ ܕܦܘܠܘܣ ܒܪܐ. ܥܠܝܗ ܚܝܐ ܦܬܝܚܐ ܘܦܬܝܚܐ	26v-28v	43v-45v	56v-58v	76-79
19.	ܡܢ ܢܬܝܒܗ ܕܡܫܝܚܐ. ܬܫܒܘܚ ܠܒܘܒܐ ܐܘ ܦܘܪܐ	28v-30r	45v-47r	58v-59v	79-82
20.	ܦܩܕܐ ܦܬܝܚܐ ܘܦܬܝܚܐ ܒܗ ܚܘܒܐ. ܘܡܫܡܠܝܐ ܠܡܪܝ ܕܦܩܕ ܒܫܒܚܐ	30r-33r	47r-49v	59v-62r	82-89
21.	ܐܘ ܡܢܩܒܐ ܒܟܠ ܬܘܕܝܬܐ. ܘܡܫܒܚܐ ܒܟܠ ܬܫܒܘܚܬܐ		49v-50v		

[28] The beginning of this hymn is missing.

[29] The beginning of this manuscript is missing.

		C1 1568	C2 1568	D2 1575	B2 1581
22.	ܥܘܗܕܢܐ ܠܚܝܠܐ ܡܢܝܫܬܗܘܢ. ܕܒܘܬܐ ܙܗܐ ܘܡܙܝܥܐ	33r-36r			
23.	ܡܫܒܚܬܐ ܕܒܬܘܠܘܬܐ. ܘܡܫܒܚܬܐ ܕܩܕܝܫܘܬܐ	36r-39r	50v-53v	62v-65v	89-93
24.	ܡܢ ܒܥܒܕܐ ܕܦܘܩܕܢܐ ܡܢܗ ܘܡܫܠܡܢܘܬܐ ܕܡܢܬܐ ܒܝܫܬ	39r-41r	53v-55r	65v-67r	94-96
25.	ܡܢ ܢܦܫ ܐܢܫ ܡܢ ܢܘܪܐ. ܐܘܠ ܠܒܝܬܐ ܐܝܟ ܦܘܡܝܐ	41r-43v	55r-57r	67r-69r	96-100
26.	ܐܘ ܢܦܫܐ ܕܚܝܒܬ ܡܢ ܟܠ. ܡܢܘ ܢܦܩܘܢ ܩܝܡܬ ܡܢ ܟܠ	43v-45v	57v-59v	69r-71v	100-104
27.	ܐܘ ܕܒܥܝܬܐ ܡܫܒܚܬܐ. ܘܐܝܟ ܕܒܝܬܗܪܐ ܕܘܪܐ ܒܦܘܪܩܢܐ	45v-47r	59v-60v	71v-72v	104-106
28.	ܠܗܘܢ ܫܘܒܚܐ ܐܢܐ ܠܟ. ܘܠܘܬܐ ܕܡܠܟܘܬܐ ܡܬܕܟܪ ܐܢܐ ܠܟ	47r-48v	60v-62r	72v-74r	106-108
29.	ܠܡܪܢ ܒܬܠܘܬ ܕܐܠܗܘܬܗ. ܡܫܠܡ ܕܢܚܬ ܒܝܕ ܡܠܬܗ	48v-50r	62r-63v	74r-75v	108-111
30.	ܥܘܗܕܢܐ ܠܩܕܝܫܐ ܦܘܠܘܣ. ܕܦܫܛ ܠܢܦܫܗ ܢܘܡܘܣܐ	50r-51v	63v-65r	75v-77r	111-113
31.	ܡܪܝܐ ܢܒܝܘܬܐ. ܕܠܗ ܘܡܪܐ ܕܘܝܕ ܢܒܝܘܬܐ	52r-54v	65r-67v	77r-79v	113-118
32.	ܥܡܠܗ ܗܘܐ ܠܟܠܗܘܢ ܠܩܢܐ. ܕܠܡܪܝܐ ܟܠ ܗܘܐ ܢܠܘܩܐ	54v-56v	67v-69r	79v-81v	118-121
33.	ܐܠܗܐ ܠܒܝܬܐ ܘܡܫܐ. ܒܢܝܐ ܡܕܝܢܬܐ ܘܡܫܠܡܐ	56v-58r	69r-70v	81v-82v	121-123
34.	ܡܪܝܐ ܕܝܢܐ ܠܥܠܡܘܬܗ. ܘܢܘܡܘܣ ܢܡܪܐ ܣܦܪܘܬܗ	58r-59r	70v-71v	82v-84r	123-125
35.	ܒܩܘܬܐ ܕܡܠܟܐ ܢܦܫܟ ܐܢܐ. ܒܬܘܡܡܐ ܕܫܘܒܚܐ ܐܘ ܡܫܒܚ ܐܢܐ	59r-60v	71v-72v	84r-85r	125-127
36.	ܡܪܝ ܡܫܝܚܐ ܕܐܬܐܬܝܗ. ܘܡܠܟܘܬܝ ܒܦܩܕܐ ܐܬܐܬܟ	60v-62r	72v-74r	85r-86v	127-129
37.	ܐܘ ܕܡܪܝܐ ܢܟܠܬܐ. ܦܪܘܩ ܡܠܟܐ ܐܝܟ ܕܒܬܘܬܐ	62r-63r	74r-75r	86v-87v	129-132
38.	ܒܪ ܐܢܫܐ ܕܦܓܪܐ ܠܒܟ ܠܗ. ܬܘܩܢܐ ܕܢܘܪܐ ܕܠܐ ܡܬܕܒܪ ܠܗ	63v-64v	75r-76r	87v-89r	132-134
39.	ܡܪܝܐ ܐܠܗܢ ܕܡܫܒܚ. ܣܓܕܘ ܘܫܒܚܘ ܘܐܡܪ ܒܥܒܝܕ	64v-66r	76r-77v	89r-90r	134-136
40.	ܡܪܝܐ ܕܒܩܢܘܡܗ ܐܠܗܘܬܗ. ܘܒܠܥܘܬܗ ܦܪܘܩ ܠܟܝܢܐ	66r-67r	77v-78v	90r-91r	136-138
41.	ܢܡܪ ܥܒܕܐ ܘܢܥܒܕ ܡܢ ܟܠ. ܦܠܚܐ ܡܫܝܚܐ ܕܦܪܩܢ ܒܟܠ ܟܠ	67r-68v	78v-80r	91r-92v	138-141
42.	ܐܒܪܐ ܠܡܪܢ ܒܓܠܝܘܬܐ. ܝܕܝܥܐ ܕܐܝܟ ܒܥܒܝܕܘܬܐ	68v-70r	80r-81r	92v-94r	141-143
43.	ܠܡܪܐ ܢܘܗܪܐ ܘܩܠܐ ܕܘܝܕ. ܠܡܢ ܢܦܠܩܝ ܗܝܢ ܗܘܠܕܝ	70r-71v	81r-82v	94r-95r	143-145
44.	ܠܡܪܢ ܒܫܠܡܐ ܘܫܝܢܬܐ. ܢܦܠ ܕܡܠܟܐ ܟܠ ܫܝܢܬܐ	71v-73r	82v-83v	95r-96v	145-147
45.	ܒܗ ܐܟܠܠ ܕܐܠܝܬܐ. ܘܒܗ ܡܫܘܠܠ ܕܥܡܝܕܬܐ	73r-74v	83v-85r	96v-97v	147-149

		C1 1568	C2 1568	D2 1575	B2 1581
46.	ܒܝܬ ܢܦܩܐ ܡܠܟܐ ܢܫܒܚܝܟ ܘܒܝܬ ܡܕܒܪܢܘܬܐ ܡܠܟܐ ܡܕܒܪܢܐ	74v-76r	85r-86r	97v-99r	150-152
47.	ܣܓܕܢܢ ܘܡܫܒܚܝܢ ܘܡܘܕܝܢ ܚܝܠܐ ܐܒܐ. ܘܡܘܕܝܢ ܚܝܠܐ ܐܒܐ ܐܦ ܡܫܒܚܝܢ ܐܒܐ	76r-77v	86r-87v	99r-100v	152-154
48.	ܒܪܡܫ ܕܡܢ ܒܡܬܪܢܘܗܝ ܠܐ ܬܫܒܘܩ. ܐܠܐ ܐܘܣܦ ܘܠܒܝܫ ܬܫܒܘܩ	77v-79r	87v-88v	100v-102r	154-157
49.	ܒܪܡܫ ܕܡܢ ܠܟܝܢ ܘܢܦܪ ܬܠܬܝܢ. ܒܢܝܢܘ ܢܫܠܡ ܬܠܬܝܢ	79r-80v	88v-90r	102r-103r	157-159
50.	ܗܘ ܕܒܪܒܪ ܥܒܕܗ ܘܝܬܒܪܟܗ. ܘܦܝܠܗ ܡܟܠ ܕܪܘܚܐ ܕܩܘܕܫܐ	80v-81v	90r-91r	103r-104v	159-161
51.	ܥܒܕܗ ܘܝܬܒܪܟܗ ܦܪܘܩܐ. ܘܠܐ ܗܘܒ ܡܚܢܦ ܡܟܠ ܪܘܚܐ	81v-84r	91r-93r	104v-106v	161-165
52.	ܒܝܕܠ ܒܘܕܪܝܢ ܠܒܘܠܝ. ܚܝܠ ܘܢܕܪ ܠܡܚܝܠܘܬܝ	84r-85v	93r-94r	106v-108r	165-167
53.	ܒܢ ܗܒܝܘ ܐܒܐ ܒܒܪܝܬܐ. ܘܐܬܦܪܫܘ ܠܬܐܡ ܦܥܩܬܐ	85v-88r	94r-96r	108r-110v	167-171
54.	ܡܢܘ ܕܢܦܢܩ ܠܟܠ ܚܘܒܝܢ. ܘܡܢܘ ܢܦܩܐ ܐܦ ܢܬܠܐ ܠܟܠܝܢ	88r-90v	96r-98r	110v-112v	171-174
55.	ܢܚܘ ܕܐܢܬܬܗ ܢܒܝܐ. ܘܕܢܐ ܡܕܢܚܐ ܘܢܘܗܪ ܗܘܐ	90v-93r	98r-100v	112v-115r	174-178
56.	ܐܘ ܡܫܝܚܐ ܡܪܐ ܡܪܝܢ. ܐܘ ܡܥܕܪܢܐ ܡܪܐ ܡܚܝܢܐ	93r-96r	100v-103r	115r-118r	178-183
57.	ܐܘ ܢܘܗܪܢ ܡܪܐ ܒܪܝܟ. ܘܡܪܐ ܗܝܢ ܚܢܢ ܘܡܪܐ ܡܪܒܝܢ	96v-98v	103r-105v	118r-120v	183-187
58.	ܐܘ ܥܡܘܢܐ ܕܢܠܘܬܐ. ܘܡܥܡܕܢܐ ܕܢܚܬܘܬܐ	98v-100v	105v-107r	120v-122r	187-189
59.	ܡܪܐ ܕܟܠ ܡܪܘܬܐ. ܐܦ ܢܘܪܐ ܕܟܠ ܡܘܗܒܬܐ	100v-102r	107r-108v	122v-124r	190-192
60.	ܡܠܟܐ ܕܡܫܒܚܬܐ. ܡܥܒܕܐ ܐܒܗܘܗܝ ܒܥܒܕܘܬܐ	102r-104v	108v-110v	124r-126r	192-196
61.	ܒܪܐ ܕܐܠܗܘܗܝ ܠܟ ܥܘܬܦܬܐ. ܘܝܗܒ ܒܗܘܠܬܐ ܘܠܐ ܡܘܗܒܬܐ	104v-107r	110v-112v	126r-128r	196-199
62.	ܒܫܦܝܪ ܪܘܚܐ ܡܪܐ ܗܘܢܐ. ܘܒܫܠܝܗܘܢ ܡܬܗܦܟܐ ܗܘܢܐ	107r-109v	112v-115r	132r-134r	199-203
63.	ܡܠܟܐ ܕܡܠܟܐ ܠܗ ܦܠܚܝܢ. ܘܪܘܚܢܐ ܠܪܡܘܗ ܡܫܡܫܝܢ	109v-111v	115r-117r	134r-136r	203-207
64.	ܒܫܘܒܚܐ ܪܘܚܢܐ. ܕܒܐܒܪܗܘܗ ܕܢܒܪ ܐܣܛܪܛܝܘܛܐ	132r-134r	117r-118v	150v-152r	207-210
65.	ܒܫܠܡܐ ܗܘܐ ܫܪܝܬ ܗܘܢܐ. ܘܒܬܘܪܓܡܐ ܡܬܚܡܐ ܗܘܢܐ	112r-113v	119r-120v	244v-246v	210-213
66.	ܒܬܗܪܐ ܪܒܐ ܥܠܡܐ ܗܘܢܐ. ܕܡܛܠ ܡܪܐ ܒܠܒܟ ܬܘܟܠܐ	113v-117r	120v-123v	246v-249v	213-219
67.	ܒܪܡܫ ܕܒܥܘܡܗ ܡܕܒܪܐ. ܦܪܝܫ ܫܘܒܚܗ ܕܥܝܪܐ ܕܐܒܪܐ	117r-119v	123v-125v	136r-138v	219-222
68.	ܡܪܘܡܘ ܐܢܫ ܕܟܢܫܬܟ. ܒܗܝܡܢܘܬܐ ܘܒܕܒܘܬܐ	119v-121v	125v-127r	138v-140r	222-225
69.	ܢܬܩܪܐ ܪܝܫܗ ܠܟ ܗܘܢܐ. ܘܢܣܒܘ ܠܒܪܐ ܘܢܪܒܘ ܢܕܢܐ	121v-123v	127r-129r	140v-142v	225-229

		C1 1568	C2 1568	D2 1575	B2 1581
70.	ܐܘ ܕܠܡܥܡܪܢܘܬܐ ܫܒܝܚ. ܘܠܡܫܬܟܠܢܘܬܐ ܡܬܬܦܝܣ	123v-126r	129r-131r	142v-144v	229-232
71.	ܐܘ ܡܫܝܚܐ ܡܢ ܟܠ ܕܠܗ ܝܠܝܕܐ ܟܠ. ܟܠ ܡܬܚܣܝܐ ܠܟܠ ܘܚܘܝܐ ܠܟܠ	126r-127v	131r-132v	144v-146r	232-234
72.	ܒܢܝ ܐܒܪܗܡ ܕܐܘܪܚܐ. ܕܗܘܘ ܒܢܝܢܐ ܠܫܪܪܐ ܡܢܝܐ	127v-129r	132v-133v	146r-147r	235-237
73.	ܐܘ ܐܚܝ ܢܬܦܪܫ ܒܗ. ܒܝܘܡܐ ܕܒܠܐ ܢܟܢܫ ܠܗ	129r-130v	133v-135r	147r-148v	237-239
74.	ܡܥܒܕܐ ܡܪܢ ܕܐܡܥܡܘܕܝܬܐ. ܗܝܟܠܗ ܕܐܠܗܐ ܡܠܟܐ	130v-132r	135r-136r	148v-150r	239-241
75.	ܗܝ ܠܗ ܠܪܚܡ ܕܦܩܕܐ ܒܢܝ. ܗܢܐ ܕܒܢܐ ܠܕܪܝ ܚܩܐ ܥܠܝܡ	134r-136r	136r-138r	152r-154r	241-246
76.	ܦܠܐ ܕܪܘܚܐ ܠܫܠܝܚܘܗܝ. ܕܐܘܡܢܐ ܘܡܘܡܢܐ ܚܒܝܒܝ ܒܐܝܕܗ	136r-139r	138r-140v	154r-157r	246-250
77.	ܡܢ ܩܕܡ ܡܪܝ ܠܐܘܪܫܠܡ. ܕܩܛܠܬ ܢܒܝܐ ܪܓܡܬ ܫܠܝܚܐ	139r-141r	140v-142v	157r-158v	250-253
78.	ܫܠܡܐ ܕܒܝܬܐ ܘܫܝܢܬܐ. ܕܠܡܪܢ ܡܢ ܗܘܐ ܠܗ ܡܥܒܕܢܘܬܐ	141r-143r	142v-143v	158v-160v	253-256
79.	ܒܝܘܡܗ ܕܡܪܢ ܗܘܐ ܢܘܚܐ. ܘܐܝܟ ܫܘܪܐ ܠܒܝܬܐ ܘܐܢܫܐ	143r-145v	143v-146r	160v-163r	256-260
80.	ܒܩܝܡܬܗ ܕܒܪܐ ܚܒܝܒܐ. ܙܠܝܓ ܐܪܥܐ ܘܪܒܠܝܢ ܥܡܡܐ	146r-147v	146r-147v	163r-164v	260-263
81.	ܒܝܕܥܬܐ ܢܘܡܐ ܦܘܩܕܐ. ܡܢܐ ܬܪܘܢܐ ܦܪܕܐ ܚܠܡܐ	147v-149v	147v-149v	165r-167r	263-266
82.	ܒܪܐ ܡܠܟܐ ܝܚܝܕܝܐ. ܠܒܝܬܗ ܠܦܠܓܘܬܐ ܐܪܥܐ	149v-152v	149v-152r	167r-169v	266-271
83.	ܐܦܐ ܗܘܝ ܠܝ ܡܫܒܚܬܐ. ܒܪܐ ܝܚܝܕܝܐ ܗܘܝ ܡܫܡܠܝܬܐ	152v-155r	152r-154r	169v-172r	271-275
84.	ܫܪܪܐ ܕܩܘܕܫܐ ܝܫܘܥ ܗܘ. ܘܕܢܚܗ ܘܙܠܝܓܗ ܘܐܬܓܠܝܬܗ ܗܘܝܘ.	155r-157r	154r-156r	172r-174r	275-278
85.	ܫܡܥܢ ܫܠܝܚܐ ܦܬܓܡܝ. ܕܐܬܡܫܚܬܘܗܝ ܘܫܡܥܝ ܗܢܐ ܥܡܝ	157r-159v	156r-157v	174r-176v	278-282
86.	ܬܪܘܢܐ ܕܟܠ ܒܪܝܬܐ. ܦܡܢܝܬܐ ܕܫܡܝܢܐ	159v-161r	157v-159r	179v-181r	282-285
87.	ܦܘܩ ܡܫܝܚ ܕܢܚܬ. ܫܪܪܐ ܠܚܝܐ ܘܡܠܟܐ ܒܠܒܐ	161v-163v	159r-160v	181r-183r	285-288
88.	ܠܐܦܘܢܐ ܕܩܘܕܫܐ ܝܠܦܢ. ܦܠܘܓܬܐ ܕܪܐ ܩܦܝ	163v-165v	160v-162v	183r-185r	288-291
89.	ܐܘ ܟܠܢ ܢܘܕܐ ܥܘܒܕܐ. ܠܐܠܗܐ ܟܠܐ ܒܘܫܪܢ ܫܘܒܚܐ	165v-166v	162v-163v	185r-186v	291-294
90.	ܐܠܗܐ ܐܝܬܝܐ ܡܠܟܐ. ܥܡܐ ܚܕ ܐܒܘܗܝ ܒܐܝܬܘܬܐ	167r-169v	163v-165v	186v-189r	294-298
91.	ܐܘܪܚܐ ܕܒܪܐ ܚܒܝܒܐ. ܠܐ ܡܬܕܪܟܐ ܠܟܠܗܘܢ ܒܪܢܫܐ	169v-171v	165v-167v	189r-191r	298-302
92.	ܝܫܘܥ ܕܐܬܐ ܚܒܝܒ ܫܦܝܪܐ. ܚܒܝܒ ܡܢ ܫܦܝܪܐ ܘܗܦܟ ܠܫܦܝܪܐ	171v-174r	167v-169v	191r-193v	302-306
93.	ܦܬܐ ܠܠܒܪܗ ܝܠܕܬ ܫܡܫܐ. ܦܬܝܚ ܘܡܬܬܪܝܡ ܠܫܡܫ ܥܡܡܐ	174r-175v	169v-170v	193v-195r	306-308

		C1 1568	C2 1568	D2 1575	B2 1581
94.	ܫܪܐ ܕܐܪܥܐ ܘܕܫܡܝܐ. ܪܡܐ ܡܫܡܠܝܐ ܡܫܒܚܐ ܡܫܠܛܢܐ	175v-178r	170v-171v	195r-197v	308-312
95.	ܥܒܝܕܝܢ ܦܬܓܡܝܢ ܓ̄ܕܘܢܝ. ܫܪܝܐ ܫܪܝ، ܘܪܘܪܒܝܢ ܠܟܬܒܝ	178r-181r	171v-174r	197v-200v	312-317
96.	ܫܪܐ ܪܘܪܒܝܢ ܠܚܕܪܘܗܝ ܕܫܪܝܐ. ܘܫܘܪ ܠܫܠܝܚ ܪܘܝܚ ܚܒܝܒܐ	181r-183r	174r-176r	200v-203r	317-321
97.	ܡܢܘ ܗܦܟ ܕܒܝܠܬܐ. ܝܥܩܘܒܐ ܚܠܝܐ ܡܪܝܐ ܝܠܕܬܐ	183r-185v	176r-178r	203r-205r	321-325
98.	ܢܬܒܪܐ ܕܠܗ ܐܬܦܠܓܗ. ܒܗ ܐܬܚܙܝ ܦܬܚ ܗܝܟܠܗ	185v-187r	178r-179v	205v-207v	325-328
99.	ܥܘܒܕܢܐ ܠܗ ܠܗܘ ܚܝܠܐ. ܦܬܚ ܬܪܥܐ ܦܬܓܡ ܚܛܝܐ	187v-190r	179v-182r	207v-210v	328-332
100.	ܗܘ ܦܠܚܐ ܕܥܩܪܢܐ. ܘܫܪܐ ܕܒܝܬܐ ܘܕܦܓܪܐ	190r-192r	182r-184r	210v-212v	332-336
101.	ܫܪܐ ܕܦܠܓܘܬܐ ܘܡܘܠܕܬܐ. ܒܐܪܥܐ ܗܘܠܝ ܐܝܟ ܡܨܥܝܬܐ	192r-193r	184r-185r	212v-213v	336-338
102.	ܡܘܡܐ ܐܘ ܠܒܝܒܐ ܢܚܠܝܬܐ. ܐܬܬܚܒܪܘ ܪܫܝܢ ܒܪܚܡܬܐ	193r-195r	185r-186r	213v-215v	338-341
103.	ܐܘܢܐ ܕܐܝܬ ܠܗ ܫܡܫܐ. ܕܘܫܢܐ ܘܠܐ ܠܘܬܫܡܐ	195r-196v	186r-188r	215v-217v	341-344
104.	ܠܐܠܗܐ ܕܝܕܥܬܐ ܝܠܕܬ ܗܘܢܐ. ܘܬܪܬܝܢܝܬܐ ܢܬܬܠ ܚܘܢܐ ܗܘܝܐ	196v-199v	188r-190r	217v-220v	344-349
105.	ܠܦܪܘܩܐ ܐܠܗܢܐ. ܪܢܝܢ ܒܝܕܬܗ ܒܪܐ ܚܒܪܐ	199v-201v	190v-192r	220v-222v	349-352
106.	ܐܠܗܐ ܪܚܡ ܐܢܫܐ. ܒܪܗ ܫܠܚ ܢܒܪ ܠܦܘܪܩܢ ܐܢܫܐ	201v-203r	192r-193v	222v-224r	352-355
107.	ܐܘܢܐ ܕܠܗ ܐܝܟ ܐܘܢܗ. ܠܐ ܘܐܦܠܐ ܐܝܬ ܐܝܟ ܡܝܬܘܬܗ	203r-205r	193v-195r	224v-226v	355-358
108.	ܬܘ ܚܙܘܢ ܢܘܗܪܐ ܬܡܝܗܐ. ܕܐܡܪ ܫܪܝ، ܒܢܝ ܦܠܓܬܐ	205r-206v	195v-197r	226v-228r	358-361
109.	ܢܡܝܢ ܕܐܒܐ ܡܬܘܦܝܐ ܠܒܢܝ ܒܝܬܗܘܢ ܦܪܝܐ ܓܠܝܐ	206v-208v	197r-198v	228r-230r	361-365
110.	ܦܬܘܚ ܚܠܘ ܕܡܘܬܐ. ܘܡܚܝܢ ܚܠܘ ܦܕܝܢܘܬܐ	208v-210r	198v-200r	230r-232r	365-367
111.	ܐܘ ܕܫܒܝܚܝܢ ܚܠ ܚܝܠܘܗܝ. ܘܡܬܬܢܝܢ ܚܠ ܚܘܒܪܘܗܝ	210r-212r	200r-201v	232r-233v	367-370
112.	ܢܒܒܐ ܡܪܝܐ ܕܚܪܝܬܐ. ܘܚܢܢܐ ܕܐܪܥܐ ܢܒܝܬܐ	212r-213r	201v-202v	234r-235r	370-373
113.	ܢܦܫܐ ܡܒܟܝܐ ܒܝܒܢܝܐ. ܢܒܠܐ ܝܗܒܐ ܚܘܪ ܚܘܒܪܢܐ	213r-214v	202v-204r	235v-236v	373-375
114.	ܦܠܚܐ ܪܚܡ ܥܦܪܐ. ܕܒܕܚܢܐ ܘܠܐ ܗܘܐ ܕܦܓܪܐ	214v-216r	204r-205r	236v-238v	375-378
115.	ܐܘ ܚܝܝܐ ܘܕܦܢܐ. ܬܘ ܢܘܗܘ ܦܬܓܡܗ ܕܚܝܐ	216r-218v	205r-207v	238v-241v	378-383
116.	ܒܘܗܪܐ ܚܪܐ ܚܠ ܒܘܗܪܝܢ. ܕܪܘܡܐ ܘܚܘܡܨܐ ܒܐܝܕܗ ܠܚܝܕܝܢ	218v-220r	207v-209r	241v-242v	383-385
117.	ܡܕܡܟܐ ܘܚܕܗ ܕܡܕܡܟܐ. ܕܝܠܝܕܘܬܗ ܡܢ ܚܠ ܪܡܐ	220r-221v	209r-210v	243r-244v	385-388

		C1 1568	C2 1568	D2 1575	B2 1581
118.	ܦܠܓܘܬܐ ܐܠܗܝܬܐ. ܡܢܐ ܦܠܚܝܢܐ ܐܠܗܘܬܐ	222r-223v	210v-212r	249v-251v	388-391
119.	ܐܘ ܦܓܪܐ ܕܝܢ ܡܫܝܚܝܬܐ. ܛܠܠܬܐ ܕܒܪܝܫܘܗܝ ܘܒܝܫܝܡܬܐ	223v-225r	212r-213v	251v-253v	391-394
120.	ܚܣܝܢܐ ܕܠܒܟ ܒܪܐ ܦܠܓܐ ܡܢܗ ܠܐܒܘܗܝ ܠܝܬ ܒܪܐ	225r-227r	213v-215r	253v-255v	394-398
121.	ܦܠܚܐ ܘܦܪܐ ܕܟܠ ܦܠܚܐ. ܕܡܬܒܪܘܗܝ ܐܢܘܢ ܟܠܗܘܢ ܦܠܚܐ	227r-228v	215r-216v	255v-257r	398-401
122.	ܦܠܚܐ ܕܪܘܚܐ ܝܬܝܪܐ. ܕܐܬܐ ܕܝܗܒܘܗ ܠܐܪܡܝܐ	228v-231r	216v-219r	257r-260r	401-406
123.	ܡܕܝܢܬܐ ܦܬܓܡܗ ܪܡܕܝܢܬܐ. ܗܘ ܕܐܬܒܢܝܗ ܡܢ ܟܠ ܪܡܬܐ	231r-233r	219r-220v	260r-262r	406-409
124.	ܡܪܐ ܕܒܪܝܬܐ ܘܕܒܢܝܢܐ. ܐܦ ܢܝܪܘܬܐ ܕܟܠ ܐܢܫܝܐ	233r-234r	220v-222r	262r-264r	409-412
125.	ܦܪܘܩܐ ܕܟܠ ܡܚܫܒܬܐ. ܢܗܘܐ ܦܪܐ ܡܠܝܐ ܢܨܚܬܐ	234v-236v	222r-224r	264r-266v	412-416
126.	ܐܫܝܐ ܕܪܘܚܐ ܒܝܕ ܫܠܝܚܘܗܝ ܐܬܐ ܠܐܪܥܐ ܕܢܐܡܪ ܠܡܬܒܪܘܗܝ	236v-238r	224r-225v	266v-268v	416-419
127.	ܫܘܒܚܐ ܠܗ ܠܗܘ ܡܫܝܚܐ. ܕܒܪܗ ܘܐܬܡܢܝ ܟܠ ܒܪܝܬܐ	238r-240v	225v-227v	268v-271v	419-424
128.	ܢܘܪܐ ܘܫܠܗܒܝܬܐ ܠܐܠܗܘܬܗ. ܦܩܕܬܗ ܠܟܘܢ ܦܓܪܐ ܕܝܠܝ	S247r-248r	S227v-229r	S276v-278r	S424-427
129.	ܡܪܝ ܕܝܢ ܗܘ ܕܐܬܓܠܝ ܗܘܐ. ܕܫܘܒܚܗ ܠܫܠܝܚܘܗܝ ܫܘܝܐ ܗܘܐ	240v-242v	S229r-231r	271v-273v	S427-430
130.	ܝܫܘܥ ܕܐܬܐ ܡܫܘܦܪܐ ܕܒܗ ܢܬܠܘܗ ܫܘܬܐ ܒܐܘܪܚܐ	242v-244v	S231r-233r	273v-276v	S430-435
131.	ܐܢܫܐ ܕܝܢ ܡܢܗܘܢ ܦܪܘܩܗ ܒܪܝ.. ܘܐܬܦܪܐ ܠܟܝܦܐ ܢܘܓܠܐ	S248r-250v	S233r-235r	S278v-281r	S435-439
132.	ܫܒܝܚ ܘܡܪܡܪܡ ܡܪܝܐ ܟܠ. ܦܓܪܐ ܒܣܘܪܗ ܘܢܦܫܗ ܠܟܝܢܗ	S252v-257r	S235r-239v	S284r-289v	S439-448
133.	ܒܪܝܟ ܗܘ ܡܫܒܚܐ ܡܬܝܩܪ. ܐܒܘܗܝ ܘܗܘܐ ܕܦܪܩܢ ܘܡܕܝܢܝ	S260v-261v	S239v-240v	S289v-291r	S448-451
134.	ܒܪܝܟܘ ܡܫܒܚܐ ܡܬܠܠܟܝ. ܐܒܘܗܝ ܘܗܘܐ ܕܓܒܝ ܘܢܝܫܢ	S257v-258v	S240v-242r	S291r-293r	S451-453
135.	ܒܟܠ ܩܢܘܢ ܘܒܟܠ ܕܩܝܩ.. ܠܟܐ ܘܠܒܝܐ ܠܗܘܢ ܡܫܒܚܐ ܡܪܝ	S258v-260v	S242r-244r	S293r-295v	S453-455[30]
136.	- ܫܘܒܚܐ ܘܡܩܪ ܢܨܚܬܐ. ܠܒܬܐ ܕܠܝܠܝܐ ܘܝܘܡܬܐ ܦܠܓܢܝܐ..... - ܗܘܝܬܐ . ܘܒܬܪ ܗܠܝܢ ܡܪܝ ܕܝܢܐ	S250v-252v	S244r-246r	S281r-284r	S458[31]-461
137.	ܐܘ ܒܩܕܐ ܣܓܝܐ ܡܓܢܐ ܗܘܝܐ. ܐܘ ܒܩܕܐ ܦܪܝܕ ܦܪܕܝܐ ܗܘܝܐ	S245r, 246v	S246r-247v		S461[32]-462
138.	ܗܓܝܪܐ ܠܣܒܪܐ ܐܘܗܢܐ. ܒܝܢܘܦܗܠܗܝܢ ...ܕ ܘܕܢܢܐ				
139.	ܒܪܐ ܕܐܠܗܐ ܡܬܘܩܢܐ. ܕܒܪܐ ܒܪܝܬܐ ܡܢ ܫܘܪܝܐ				

[30] The end of the hymn is missing.
[31] The beginning of the hymn is missing.
[32] It has only some stanzas from the beginning and the end.

		C1 1568	C2 1568	D2 1575	B2 1581
140.	ܒܪܝܟܘ ܡܫܒܚܐ ܦܪܘܩܢ. ܕܓܢܐ ܚܘܒܗ ܠܘܬܢ ܘܦܪܩܢ				
141.	ܒܐܘܪܚܐ ܕܟܐܢܐ ܪܕܘ ܚܘܫܒܝܢ. ܘܢܬܘܒ ܠܒܪܐ ܕܐܝܬܝܗܘܢ				
142.	ܒܫܡܝܐ ܡܠܟܐ ܒܫܡܝܐ. ܕܫܘܒܚܐ ܗܠܗ ܫܡܥ ܒܥܒܕܬܐ				
143.	ܐܘ ܪܘܚܐ ܒܫܠܝܡܘܬܐ. ܘܪܘܚܐ ܒܪܘܚܘܬܐ				
144.	ܬܘ ܚܒܝܒܐ ܒܘܢܝܐ. ܢܚܝܐ ܒܚܘܢܐ ܘܠܟܢܝܐ				
145.	ܠܟ ܒܓܠܝܐ ܦܢܝܐ. ܐܦܠܟ ܒܦܓܠܟ ܦܢܝܬܐ				
146.	ܒܪܒܐ ܕܡܠܟ ܒܪܘܝܐ. ܦܠܚ ܒܢ ܒܪܚܐ ܕܒܥܢܝܐ				
147.	ܒܕ ܗܝܡ ܡܪܝ ܠܪܒ ܦܫܐ. ܐܒܐ ܦܘܫܐ ܘܫܠܚܐ				
148.	ܢܪܟܒ ܒܒܝܬܐ ܒܢܫܡܬܐ. ܕܟܠܢܐ ܕܦܘܢܐ ܒܢܒܬܐ				
149.	ܢܥܡ ܦܘܡܪܐ ܒܢ ܦܠܚܐ. ܘܐܥܒܕ ܠܒܘ ܒܐܬܪܘܬܐ	S261v-263r			
150.	ܬܘ ܢܒܒܒ ܢܬܟܢܫ. ܒܠܩܬܗ ܕܐܒܘܝ ܘܗܐ	S263r-265v		128r-131v	
151.	ܥܘܒܕܐ ܠܡܫܝܚ ܦܪܘܩܢ. ܕܒܕ ܝܒܐ ܚܘܒܐ ܕܐܫܬܘܕܝ ܠܒܝܬܢ			32v-33v	
152.	ܫܘܒܚܐ ܝܗܒ ܡܒܪܟܬܐ. ܒܬܘܠܬܐ ܕܚܒܬܐ ܘܦܒܝܫܬܐ			33v-36r	
153.	ܬܘܒܝܬܐ ܢܫܡ ܚܠܝ. ܒܕܘܒܪܝ ܝܕܗ ܕܦܪܘܩ			36r-37r	
154.	ܒܢܝܪܝ ܡܒܝܬܐ ܕܡܠܟܘܬܟ. ܝܥܬܒܕ ܩܠܟ ܕܚܒܪܝ ܠܢܝܟ			37r-38v	
155.	ܘܥܘܪ ܗܘ ܦܒܠܐ ܕܝܬܪܒܝܐ. ܐܦ ܠܥܐ ܕܝܥܬܒܝܐ			176v-178r	
156.	ܝܘܒܘ ܘܐܬܓܒܠܘ ܥܡܘܠܐ. ܐܬܬܚܒܪܘ ܘܐܬܒܦܝܘ ܐܘ ܫܒܝܬܐ			178r-179v	
157.	ܡܪܐ ܕܡܫܚܐ ܘܕܥܒܐ. ܗܒܠܒ ܒܡܫܝܚ ܦܒܠܐ ܕܒܢܐ			S295v-299v	
158.	ܡܪܝ ܕܗܝܡܢ ܠܥܡܢܐ. ܒܪܘܫܐ ܕܦܠܠܩܐ ܠܚܒܐ				
159.	ܥܘܐ ܠܥܘܒܕܐ ܐܒܗܐ ܒܪܘܚܐ. ܚܢܢܐ ܒܫܐ ܘܪܡܐ ܘܡܒܠܚܐ				
160.	ܥܘܒܕܐ ܠܚܘܒܐ ܦܪܘܩ ܚܢܢܐ ܗܒܝܐܐ ܡܪܚܡܢܘܬܗ				

Table 6C

		M3 1586	G1 1300-1400	D3 1400-1600
1.	ܒܥܝܢܐ ܦܬܟܝܪ ܘܡܫܬܡܠܝ ܥܒܝܕܐ. ܠܡܫܕܪ ܦܠܚܐ ܕܪܗܘܡܝܐ	1v-5r	1r	1v-3v
2.	ܢܠܦܐ ܕܢܚܐ ܠܢܠܦܘܗܝ ܪܒܬܐ. ܘܠܐ ܚܙܐ ܘܐܬܚܙܝ ܘܠܐ ܐܫܬܐ	5r-8r	1r-2v	3v-5v
3.	ܡܢ ܦܠܡ ܠܗ ܠܐܕܡܘܬܟ. ܚܕܐ ܕܐܠܗܐ ܘܐܬܘܚܕܘܬܟ	8r-13v		5v-9r
4.	ܐܬܝܗܝܒ ܐܝܟ ܥܒܕܘܗܝ. ܕܡܠܐ ܢܩܝܐ ܕܟܠ ܚܕ ܡܕܡܘ	13v-17r	5r-5v	9r-12r
5.	ܕܢܚܐ ܘܕܢܚ ܠܥܕܬܐ. ܘܚܠܦ ܒܕܫܡܫܝ ܡܕܝܢܬܐ ܕܢܚܐ	17r-20v	5v,105r-106v	12r-14r, 60r
6.	ܚܠܦ ܥܡܐ ܐܪܡܝܐ. ܡܥܢܐ ܗܘܢܐ ܕܐܪܥܘܬ ܒܡܠܝܘܬܐ	20v-23r	6r-6v	14r-15v 60r-60v
7.	ܒܢܝܪܐ ܡܕܝܢܬܐ ܕܚܠܝܠ. ܝܡܬܟ ܦܬܠ ܕܡܬܪܝܢ ܠܚܝܠܐ	23r-25v	169r	15v-17v
8.	ܚܕܐ ܕܦܠܘܫ ܒܗ ܚܝܡܬܐ. ܕܡܠ ܚܝܩܡܬܐ ܘܕܢܩܠܬܐ	25v-29v	107r-109r	17v-20v
9.	ܒܝܘܡܐ ܕܫܒܥܐ ܗܘܐ ܕܝܢܐ ܐܒܐ. ܘܒܦܣܩܘܠܐ ܗܘܐ ܡܫܬܒܚ ܐܒܐ	30r-33r	109r-111v	20v-22v
10.	ܡܢ ܡܥܡܕ ܕܒܡܕܒܪܐ ܝܗܒܝܢܐ. ܐܘ ܕܒܥܘܡܕܐ ܢܦܠܛ ܘܝܥܡܪܐ	33r-37v	111v-114v	22v-26r
11.	ܐܝܬܝܐ ܚܝܐ ܘܚܕ ܚܝܐ. ܒܢܝܐ ܠܚܝܘܬܐ ܦܫܛܐ ܘܚܠܝܐ	37v-38v	3r, 169r-169v	26r-27r
12.	ܒܥܝܢܐ ܐܠܗܝܐ ܘܐܠܗܝ. ܕܐܬܓܠܝܬܘܗ ܘܐܘܦ ܐܒܐ ܥܡܝ	38v-41r	3v-4v	27r-29r
13.	ܒܠܡܕܗ ܕܒܪܐ ܒܘܚܕܐ. ܐܦܪܘ ܗܘܘ ܡܪܕܐ ܕܪܘܚܐ ܘܡܘܕܐ	41r-42r		29r-29v
14.	ܐܘ ܚܒܝܒܐ ܦܘܢܝܬܐ. ܢܦܩ ܥܘܕܢܐ ܐܠܝܩܐܝܬ	42r-45v		29v-32r
15.	ܚܝܠܐ ܕܦܝܠܠ ܒܢܘܗܪܐ. ܘܐܪܕܝ ܡܢܐ ܡܢ ܓܢܒܪܐ	45v-48v	8r-10v	32r-34v
16.	ܐܘ ܚܒܝܒܐ ܝܬܒܬ ܒܠܘܗܪܘܗܝ. ܕܓܐܝܐ ܥܠܝܬܐ ܩܫܝܫܘܗܝ ܕܡܫܝܚܐ	48v-50v	10v-12r	34v-36r
17.	ܐܘ ܚܒܝܒܐ ܝܘܡܢܐ ܥܘܒܕܐ. ܒܕܘܒܪܘܗܝ ܕܥܠܝܬܐ ܩܫܝܫܘܗܝ ܕܡܫܝܚܐ	50v-51v	12r-13r	36r-37r
18.	ܒܝܘܡܝ ܪܘܚܐ ܕܦܠܛܝܘܬܗ ܕܦܘܠܘܣ ܪܒܐ. ܥܠܝܡܐ ܐܝܟܢܐ ܦܓܥܗ ܘܦܢܝܗ	51v-53v	13v-15r	37r-38v
19.	ܡܢ ܢܡܝܢܗ ܕܡܫܝܚܐ. ܬܠܝܕܘ ܚܘܒܝ ܐܘ ܗܘܕܐ	54r-55v	15v, 7v, 7r	38v-40r
20.	ܗܦܟܐ ܦܓܥܗ ܘܦܢܝܗ ܒܗ ܣܘܡܐ. ܘܝܦܟܗ ܠܦܪܝ ܕܦܩܕ ܒܡܚܕܗ	55v-58r	7r, 16r-17v	40r-41v
21.	ܐܘ ܡܢܩܒܢ ܚܠܦ ܐܘܪܚܬܐ. ܘܡܢܬܢܝ ܚܠܦ ܗܡܢܘܬܐ			
22.	ܥܘܒܕܐ ܠܚܝܠܐ ܡܢܝܫܝܗܘܢ. ܕܓܒܪܐ ܙܕܩܐ ܘܡܕܝܢܬܐ	58r-59r		
23.	ܡܓܠܬܐ ܕܓܠܝܬܐ. ܘܡܓܕܡܐ ܕܡܥܝܕܢܐ	59r-61v		

		M3 1586	G1 1300-1400	D3 1400-1600
24.	ܟܕ ܒܥܒܕܐ ܕܦܘܩܕܢܐ ܡܪܢܐ ܘܡܫܬܠܡܢܘܬܐ ܕܥܕܬܐ ܟܪܝܟܐ	61v-63r		
25.	ܟܕ ܢܦܩ ܢܘܚ ܡܢ ܩܒܘܬܐ. ܐܘܦ ܠܥܕܬܐ ܐܝܟ ܦܘܩܕܢܐ	63v-65v	18r	
26.	ܐܘ ܢܦܫܐ ܕܫܒܩܬ ܡܢ ܟܠ. ܡܢܘ ܢܦܪܘܩ ܢܦܫܟ ܡܢ ܟܠ	65v-67v	18r-20r	
27.	ܐܘ ܕܒܟܝܬܐ ܚܛܝܬܐ. ܘܐܝܟ ܕܒܢܝܬܐ ܕܘܢܐ ܒܦܪܩܝܐ	67v-69r		
28.	ܒܘܗܪܝ ܫܘܒܚܐ ܐܢܐ ܠܟ. ܘܬܘܕܝܬܐ ܕܫܦܝܪܬܐ ܡܩܪܒ ܐܢܐ ܠܟ	69r-70v	20r-21v	
29.	ܠܥܠܡ ܒܟܠܝܘܡ ܕܒܠܝܗ. ܢܥܒܕ ܕܢܚܝܢ ܒܗ ܡܢ ܕܡܫܝܚܘܬܗ	70v-72r	21v-22v	
30.	ܫܘܒܚܐ ܠܡܫܝܚܐ ܡܪܢ. ܕܦܪܩܢ ܠܟܠܢ ܒܨܠܝܒܗ	72r-73v		
31.	ܡܪܐ ܕܥܒܕܘܬܐ. ܕܠܗ ܘܡܪܐ ܕܘܝܕ ܒܥܒܘܬܐ	73v-76v	23r-25v	
32.	ܫܒܚܘ ܗܕܐ ܠܠܗܘܢ ܟܠܗܝ. ܕܠܡܪܐ ܟܠ ܗܘܘ ܫܠܘܡܐ	76v-78r		
33.	ܐܠܗܐ ܠܥܒܘܕܐ ܘܚܝܐ. ܟܢܝܐ ܡܪܝܡܐ ܘܡܫܠܠܐ	78r-79v		
34.	ܡܪܢ ܕܒܪܝ ܒܛܝܒܘܬܗ. ܘܪܘܚܝ ܒܡܪܚܡܢܘܬܗ	79v-81r	25v-26v	
35.	ܒܩܘܡܐ ܕܫܘܒܚܐ ܢܦܝܠ ܐܢܐ. ܒܬܘܕܝܬܐ ܕܫܘܒܚܐ ܗܘ ܐܢܐ ܡܫܒܚ ܐܢܐ	81r-82r		
36.	ܡܪܝ ܡܫܝܚܐ ܕܐܬܐ ܠܫܠܡܐ. ܘܡܠܠܗ ܒܦܘܡܐ ܐܬܐ ܠܟ	82r-83v		
37.	ܐܘ ܕܪܚܡܐ ܒܐܠܗܘܬܐ. ܦܪܘܩ ܠܡܚܝܠܐ ܐܝܟ ܕܒܛܝܒܘܬܐ	83v-85r		
38.	ܢܫ ܩܝܡܬܐ ܕܡܩܡܐ ܠܢ ܠܗ. ܬܫܘܡܫܬܐ ܕܫܘܒܚܐ ܕܟܠ ܡܬܕܪܝܢ ܠܗ	85r-86r		
39.	ܡܪܐ ܐܠܗܢ ܕܡܫܒܚ. ܚܝܠܐ ܘܫܘܒܚܐ ܘܐܝܩܪܐ ܢܥܒܕ	86r-87v		
40.	ܡܪܐ ܕܒܚܢܢܘܬܗ ܐܬܦܢܝ. ܘܒܛܝܒܘܬܗ ܦܪܩܗ ܠܟܠܢ	87v-88v		
41.	ܢܥܒܕ ܫܘܒܚܐ ܘܬܘܕܝܬܐ ܡܢ ܟܠ. ܡܠܟܐ ܡܫܝܚܐ ܕܡܫܠܡ ܒܟܠ ܟܠ	88v-90r	26v	
42.	ܒܪܐ ܠܥܕܬܐ ܒܫܠܝܚܘܬܐ. ܝܕܥܝܢ ܕܐܝܬܝ ܒܚܕܝܘܬܐ	90r-91v		
43.	ܠܥܠܡ ܢܘܗܪܐ ܘܩܠܗ ܕܡܪܢ. ܠܟܢ ܢܩܠܦܝܢ ܗܝܢ ܗܘܠܕܝܢ	91v-92v		
44.	ܠܥܒܕ ܒܫܠܝܚܐ ܘܫܡܝܢܬܐ. ܢܪܟ ܕܡܝܠ ܟܠ ܫܡܝܢܬܐ	92v-94r		
45.	ܝܘܡ ܢܟܠܠ ܕܥܕܬܐ. ܘܝܘܡ ܦܘܪܩܢܐ ܕܥܡܝܕܬܐ	94v-95v		
46.	ܝܘܡ ܢܟܝܐ ܡܠܟܐ ܫܡܝܢܬܐ ܘܝܘܡ ܦܪܘܩܘܬܐ ܡܠܟܐ ܦܪܩܢܐ	95v-97r	27r	
47.	ܫܠܝܡ ܘܡܫܠܡ ܘܡܘܕܐ ܫܠܡܐ ܐܢܐ. ܘܡܘܕܐ ܫܠܡܐ ܐܢܐ ܐܦ ܦܫܠܡܐ ܐܢܐ	97r-99r	27r-28v	

		M3 1586	G1 1300-1400	D3 1400-1600
48.	ܒܪܝܟ ܕܚܕ ܒܦܪܨܘܦܘ̈ܗܝ ܠܐ ܡܬܦܠܓ. ܐܠܐ ܐܘܣܝܐ ܘܟܝܢܐ ܡܬܦܠܓ	99r-100v	28v-30r	
49.	ܒܪܝܟ ܕܚܕ ܒܝܬ ܘܒܢܐ ܐܒܪܗܡ. ܓܢܣܗ ܐܬܒܚܪ ܐܒܪܗܡ	100v-102r	30r-31r	
50.	ܐܘ ܡܫܒܚܐ ܥܡܟܘ ܘܐܬܪܡܪܡܘ. ܘܦܝܠܘ ܡܠܟܐ ܕܪܘܚܐ ܕܩܘܕܫܐ	102r-103v	31r-32v	
51.	ܥܡܟܘ ܘܐܬܪܡܪܡܘ ܦܪܘܩܐ. ܘܠܐ ܬܘܒ ܬܬܠܠܘܢ ܡܠܟܐ ܪܘܚܐ	103v-106r		
52.	ܒܝܫܐ ܚܘܕܪܢܐ ܐܚܕܢܝ. ܫܝܠ ܘܡܛܪ ܠܡܣܟܠܘܬܝ	106r-107r		
53.	ܡܢ ܫܠܝܘ ܐܢܫܐ ܒܒܪܝܬܐ. ܘܐܬܦܪܥܘ ܠܬܩܘܢ ܦܫܩܬܐ	107r-109v	32r-34r	
54.	ܡܛܘ ܕܢܦܫܗ ܚܠܦ ܫܘܒܚܢ. ܘܡܛܘ ܢܣܒܐ ܐܦ ܢܬܠ ܚܠܦܝܢ	109v-111v	34v-35v	
55.	ܐܝܟܘ ܕܐܝܬܠܗ ܒܢܝܢܐ. ܘܒܢܝܐ ܡܕܒܪܐ ܘܢܘܗܪ ܗܘܝܐ	111v-114v	35v-38r	
56.	ܐܘ ܡܫܝܚܘܬܝ ܡܪܐ ܡܪܢ. ܐܘ ܡܩܪܒܘܬܝ ܡܪܐ ܡܠܟܢ	114v-117v	38r-41r	
57.	ܐܘ ܢܘܗܪܝ ܡܪܐ ܒܝܬܝ. ܘܡܪܐ ܫܡܝܐ ܐܢܫܝܢ ܘܡܪܐ ܡܕܒܪܢ	117v-120r	41r-43r	
58.	ܐܘ ܡܫܪܝܢܐ ܕܥܠܘܬܐ. ܘܡܫܟܠܠܢܐ ܕܒܪܝܬܐ	120r-122r	43r-44v	
59.	ܡܪܐ ܕܟܠ ܡܪܘܬܐ. ܐܦ ܢܘܪܐ ܕܟܠ ܡܘܗܒܬܐ	122r-123v	45r-46r	41v-43r
60.	ܡܠܦܢܐ ܕܬܫܒܘܚܬܐ. ܡܫܝܚܐ ܐܝܬܘܗܝ ܒܥܒܕܘܬܐ	123v-126r		43r-44v
61.	ܒܪܐ ܕܐܠܗܘܗܝ ܠܗ ܫܘܬܦܘܬܐ. ܘܐܡܪܗ ܒܬܘܠܬܐ ܘܠܐ ܡܙܘܓܬܐ	126r-128v		44v-46v
62.	ܒܫܦܪܐ ܪܘܚܐ ܡܪܐ ܗܘܢܐ. ܘܒܡܠܟܘܗܝ ܡܬܘܟܠܐ ܗܘܢܐ	128v-131r	46r-48v	46v-48v
63.	ܡܠܟܐ ܕܡܠܟܐ ܠܗ ܦܠܚܝܢ. ܘܩܘܫܬܐ ܠܪܡܘܗ ܡܫܡܫܝܢ	131r-133r	48v-50v	48v-50v
64.	ܒܫܘܒܚܐ ܩܘܫܬܐ. ܕܒܐܠܘܗ ܕܒܪ ܐܠܗܘܬܐ	133r-135r	64v, 66r-67r	50v-52r
65.	ܒܟܠܡܐ ܗܘܐ ܫܪܐ ܗܘܢܗ. ܘܒܠܘܚܬܗ ܡܬܒܝܢܐ ܗܘܢܗ	135r-137r	149v, 149r	52r-53v
66.	ܒܓܘܪܐ ܐܪܒܐ ܡܠܟܐ ܗܘܢܐ. ܕܡܠܠ ܡܪܐ ܒܠܒܐ ܠܘܚܡܐ	137r-140v	149r-152v	53v-56v
67.	ܒܪܝܟ ܐܬܝܘܡܗ ܡܕܝܢܬܐ. ܦܪܩ ܫܘܒܚܗ ܕܝܢܗܐ ܕܐܢܫܐ	140v-143v	50v-53r	56v-58v
68.	ܡܪܘܡܘ ܐܚܝ ܒܫܝܢܝܟܘܢ. ܒܗܝܡܢܘܬܐ ܘܒܕܚܠܬܐ	143v-145r	53r-54v	58v-60r
69.	ܢܩܫܐ ܥܠܗ ܠܒ ܗܘܢܐ. ܘܐܡܪܘ ܚܒܪܐ ܘܐܪܡܝܘ ܐܕܢܐ	145r-147v	54v-56v	61r-62r
70.	ܐܘ ܕܠܥܒܕܝܫܘܬܐ ܐܠܝܢ. ܘܠܡܬܢܟܢܬܐ ܡܬܪܒܪܒܝܢ	147v-150r	56v-58v	62r-64r
71.	ܐܘ ܒܢܝܐ ܡܢ ܟܠ ܕܠܗ ܚܕܝܐ ܟܠ. ܟܠ ܡܬܚܘܝܐ ܠܒܠ ܘܚܘܝܐ ܠܒܠ	150r-151v	58v-60r	64r-65r

		M3 1586	G1 1300-1400	D3 1400-1600
72.	ܒܢܝ ܐܒܪܗܡ ܪܘܚܢܐ. ܕܗܘܘ ܒܢܝܢܐ ܠܦܪܘܩܐ ܒܢܝܢܐ	151v-153r	60r-61r	65r-66v
73.	ܗܘ ܐܚܝ ܡܫܒܚܝܢ ܒܗ. ܒܝܘܡܐ ܢܓܠܐ ܡܫܒܚܝܢ ܠܗ	153r-154v	61v-63r	66v-67v
74.	ܡܫܝܚܐ ܡܠܟܐ ܕܡܠܟܘܬܐ. ܘܡܠܟܗ ܕܐܠܗܐ ܡܠܟܐ		63r-64r	67v-69r
75.	ܗܘ ܠܗ ܠܟܠܗܝܢ ܦܪܘܩܐ ܒܟܠ. ܗܢܐ ܦܪܐ ܠܦܪܝ ܡܢ ܥܠܡܐ	155v-157v	67r-68v	69r-71r
76.	ܦܐܪܐ ܕܦܪܝܫܐ ܠܫܠܝܚܘܗܝ. ܕܦܪܘܩܢ ܘܡܫܘܡܠܐ ܠܚܒܝܒܢ ܒܟܠܝܘܡ	157v-161r	70v-73r	71r-73v
77.	ܡܢ ܒܬܪ ܩܡܬܗ ܠܦܘܪܩܢܢ. ܕܩܛܠ ܢܟܪܝܐ ܒܐ ܦܪܩܢܢ	161r-163r	73r-74v	73v-75r
78.	ܦܠܚܐ ܕܒܝܬܐ ܘܦܪܝܫܘܬܐ. ܕܠܩܪܝܐ ܡܢ ܗܘܬ ܠܗ ܡܫܝܚܝܬܐ	163r-164v	74v, 65r-65v, 75r	75r-76v
79.	ܒܝܬܗ ܕܩܪܝ ܗܘܐ ܝܫܘܥ. ܘܐܝܟ ܐܘܪܐ ܠܟܝܢܐ ܘܐܢܫܐ	164v-168r	75r-77v	76v-79r
80.	ܒܩܘܠܗ ܦܪܝܐ ܡܫܝܚܐ. ܙܟܝ ܐܪܥܐ ܘܦܪܩܢ ܥܡܡܐ	168r-169v	77v-79r	79r-80v
81.	ܒܝܕܒܪܬܐ ܢܘܪܐ ܦܪܩܬܐ. ܒܪܐ ܬܪܘܢܐ ܦܪܐܐ ܢܛܠܡܐ	169v-172r	79r-81r	80v-82v
82.	ܒܪܐ ܝܠܕܬܐ ܡܫܝܚܐ. ܠܒܝܬܗ ܠܦܠܚܐ ܐܪܥܐ	172r-175r	81r-83r	82v-85r
83.	ܐܒܐ ܗܘܝ ܠܝ ܡܦܪܩܢܐ. ܒܪܐ ܡܫܝܚܐ ܗܘܝ ܡܚܝܢܐ	175r-177v	83v-85v	95v-98r
84.	ܦܪܩܐ ܕܩܘܕܫܐ ܝܩܪܬܐ ܗܘܝܐ. ܘܕܚܠܬܐ ܘܪܚܡܬܐ ܘܐܘܪܕܢܐ ܗܘܝܐ.	177v-179v	85v-87r	98r-100r
85.	ܦܪܝܫ ܡܫܡܫܢܐ ܦܬܠܡܝܢ. ܕܐܠܗܡܫܡܫܢܘܬܐ ܘܡܫܡܫܝܢ ܗܟܢ ܥܡܝ	179v-182r	87v-89v	100r-102v
86.	ܬܪܘܢܐ ܕܡܢ ܝܕܥܬܐ. ܘܡܝܕܥܢܐ ܕܦܪܝܫܘܬܐ	182r-184r	92r-93v	102v-104r
87.	ܦܪܘ ܡܫܒܚ ܦܪܝܩܐ. ܦܪܩܢܐ ܠܚܝܝܢ ܘܡܝܬܐ ܒܠܒܢܐ	184r-185v		104r-106r
88.	ܠܬܪܝܢܐ ܕܩܘܕܫܐ ܝܬܠܝ. ܦܬܟܘܪܬܐ ܦܪܐ ܩܕܝܫܐ	185v-187v	104r-104v	106r-108r
89.	ܗܘ ܡܠܟ ܝܘܩܪܐ ܥܘܒܕܐ. ܠܐܠܗܐ ܡܠܐ ܒܘܡܪܐ ܩܘܕܫܐ	188r-189r		108r-109v
90.	ܐܠܗܐ ܐܝܬܝ ܝܠܕܬܐ. ܥܡܐ ܟܠ ܐܒܘܗܝ ܒܐܝܬܘܬܐ	189v-192v		109v-112v
91.	ܐܘܪܚܗ ܦܪܝܐ ܡܫܝܚܐ. ܠܐ ܡܬܦܪܫܐ ܠܟܠܗܘܢ ܒܪܢܫܐ	192v-194v	99r-101r	112v-114r
92.	ܝܫܘܥ ܕܐܢܫܐ ܠܟܝܢܐ ܦܩܪܐ. ܠܟܝܢܐ ܡܢ ܦܩܪܐ ܘܗܘܝ ܠܦܩܪܐ	194v-197r	97r-99r	114r-117r
93.	ܩܒܠ ܠܐܝܪܗ ܝܒܠܢ ܦܥܠܐ. ܘܬܠܡ ܘܐܬܬܪܝܡ ܠܒܩܝ ܥܡܡܐ	197r-198v	101r-101v, 115r	117r-118r
94.	ܡܪܐ ܕܐܪܥܐ ܘܫܡܝܐ. ܪܡܐ ܡܬܩܠܣ ܡܫܒܚܐ ܡܦܠܛܢܐ	198v-201v		118r-121r
95.	ܥܒܝܕ ܦܬܡܝܬܝ ܐܬܘܪܝܐ. ܡܪܝܐ ܡܪܝ ܘܪܘܡܢ ܠܟܠܝܘܡ	201v-204v		121r-123v

		M3 1586	G1 1300-1400	D3 1400-1600
96.	ܡܐ ܪܘܪܒܝܢ ܥܒܕܘܗܝ ܕܡܪܝܐ. ܘܗܘܝ ܠܥܠܡ ܪܘܝܐ ܝܗܒܢ	204v-207r	115r-115v, 125r-125v, 122r-122v	123v-126r
97.	ܡܢܘ ܗܟܢ ܕܢܫܠܡܬܐ. ܝܥܩܘܒ ܒܟܝܢ ܡܪܝܐ ܝܠܡܬܐ	207r-209r	122v, 116r-117v	126r-128v
98.	ܫܡܝܪܐ ܕܠܝܬ ܐܟܘܬܗ. ܒܝܬ ܐܒܗܬܐ ܦܪܫ ܗܫܬܘܬܗ	209r-211r	117v-119v	128v-130v
99.	ܥܘܢܝܐ ܠܗ ܠܗܘ ܚܢܢܐ. ܩܠܝܒ ܩܫܝܐ ܘܥܩܝܒ ܚܢܢܐ	211r-214v	119v-121v, 123r	130v-133r
100.	ܗܘ ܡܠܟܐ ܕܥܠܡܝܢܐ. ܘܡܪܐ ܕܟܝܢܐ ܘܕܦܓܪܢܐ	214v-216v	123r-124v, 126r	133r-135v
101.	ܡܪܐ ܕܡܠܟܐ ܘܫܘܠܛܢܐ. ܒܪܐܬܐ ܗܘܠܝ ܐܝܟ ܡܫܡܫܢܐ	216v-217v	126r-127r	135v-136v
102.	ܡܘܫܐ ܐܘ ܠܒܢܝܐ ܒܣܠܝܩܬܐ. ܢܗܘܢܝܗܘ ܕܥܩܒ ܒܕܠܝܠܬܐ	217v-219v	127r-127v, 130r-130v	136v-138v
103.	ܐܚܝܐ ܕܐܝܬ ܠܗ ܫܥܒܕܢܐ. ܕܘܫܢܐ ܘܠܐ ܠܘܬܥܒܕܐ	219v-221r	130v-132r	138v-140r
104.	ܠܐܠܝܡ ܕܝܘܬܐ ܝܠܬ ܗܘܝܬ. ܘܡܪܡܝܢܘܬܐ ܝܬܝܪ ܣܘܢܬ ܗܘܝܬ	221r-224r	132r-135r	140r-143v
105.	ܠܦܪܘܩܐ ܐܠܗܢܐ. ܕܢܦܩ ܒܝܘܬܗ ܒܪܐ ܚܣܝܢܐ	224r-226r	135r-135v, 128r-129r	143v-145v
106.	ܐܠܗܐ ܪܚܡ ܐܢܫܐ. ܒܪܗ ܥܠܝܚ ܫܕܪ ܠܦܘܪܩܢ ܐܢܫܐ	226v-227v	129r-129v	145v-147r
107.	ܐܚܝܐ ܕܠܝܬ ܐܝܟ ܐܚܘܬܗ. ܠܐ ܘܐܦܠܐ ܐܝܬ ܐܝܟ ܝܘܩܪܗ	228r-230r	168r-168v, 136r	147r-149r
108.	ܐܘ ܚܢܢܐ ܝܬܘܬ ܡܥܕܒܬܐ. ܕܐܡܪ ܡܪܝ ܒܢܝ ܦܠܐܬܐ	230r-232r	136v, 139r-139v, 137r	149r-151r
109.	ܝܫܘܥ ܕܐܝܟܐ ܡܬܘܡܝܐ ܠܒܢܝ ܒܝܬܘܬܗ ܦܓܪܐ ܠܒܫ	232r-234r	137r-138v, 140r	151r-153r
110.	ܡܫܘܒܚ ܡܠܟ ܕܡܠܘܬܐ. ܘܡܒܪܟ ܡܠܟ ܕܡܫܝܚܘܬܐ	234r-235v	140r-141v	153r-154v
111.	ܐܘ ܕܡܬܓܠܝܬ ܒܟܠ ܚܝܠܘܗܝ. ܘܡܬܕܒܪܢ ܒܟܠ ܒܘܪܟܘܗܝ	235v-237v	141v-142r, 167r-167v	154v-156v
112.	ܒܝܬܐ ܡܪܢ ܕܡܪܝܬܐ. ܘܒܢܝܢ ܕܐܪܥܘܢ ܒܝܬܝܕܬܐ	237v-238v	142r-142v	156v-158r
113.	ܢܦܫܐ ܡܝܬܐ ܒܝܬܢܐ. ܒܕܠܐ ܢܐܬܐ ܚܘܡ ܒܘܢܝܐ	238v-240r		158r-159r
114.	ܡܠܟܐ ܪܚܡ ܥܒܕܐ. ܕܒܪܢܫܐ ܘܠܐ ܗܘܐ ܕܦܓܪܐ	240r-241v	147r-147v, 143r	159r-161r
115.	ܐܘ ܚܝܢܝܐ ܘܪܦܝܐ. ܐܘ ܝܘܬܘ ܡܬܠܝܗ ܕܚܣܝܕܐ	241v-244r	143r-145v	161r-164r
116.	ܢܘܗܪܐ ܒܪܐ ܒܟܠ ܢܘܗܪܝܢ. ܕܐܘܪܐ ܘܢܘܡܘܣܐ ܕܐܝܬܘܗ ܠܒܝܬܝܢ	244r-245v	146r-146v, 148r	164r-165v
117.	ܡܪܢܘܬܐ ܘܒܪܗ ܕܡܪܢܘܬܐ. ܕܝܠܝܕܘܬܗ ܡܢ ܟܠ ܐܘܡܐ	245v-247v	148r-148v	165v-167r
118.	ܡܠܟܘܬܐ ܐܠܗܝܬܐ. ܡܝܬܐ ܕܒܢܝܢܐ ܐܠܗܝܐ	247v-249v	152v-154v	167r-169r
119.	ܐܘ ܕܒܪܐ ܒܢܝ ܠܫܒܘܬܐ. ܟܠܩܘܡ ܟܪܘܗܝ ܘܒܝܬܝܬܐ	249v-251r	154v-156r	169r-171r

		M3 1586	G1 1300-1400	D3 1400-1600
120.	ܚܣܝܪܐ ܕܠܟܠ ܛܒܐ ܕܠܟܝܐ ܡܢܗ ܠܐܝܬܘܗܝ ܠܗ ܛܒܐ	251r-253r	156r-157v	171r-172v
121.	ܡܠܟܐ ܘܡܪܐ ܕܟܠ ܡܠܟܐ. ܕܡܬܬܪܘܗܝ ܐܝܟ ܟܠܗܘܢ ܡܠܟܐ	253r-255r	158r	172v-174v
122.	ܡܠܟܐ ܕܪܘܡܐ ܥܠܝܐ. ܕܐܬܐ ܕܢܦܪܘܩ ܠܐܪܥܝܐ	255r-258v	158r, 103v, 103r, 158v, 166r-166v, 159r	174v-177v
123.	ܡܫܝܚܐ ܦܪܘܩܗ ܕܡܫܝܚܝܐ. ܗܘ ܕܐܒܗܘܗܝ ܡܢ ܒܝܬ ܕܘܝܕ	258v-260v	159r-161r	177v-179v
124.	ܡܪܐ ܕܒܪܝܬܐ ܘܕܒܢܝܢܐ. ܐܦ ܢܘܗܪܐ ܕܟܠ ܐܢܫܐ	260v-262v	161r-162v	179v-181r
125.	ܡܫܒܚܐ ܕܟܠ ܝܚܝܕܝܬܐ. ܢܡܪܐ ܕܪܒܐ ܡܠܝܐ ܢܗܝܪܬܐ	262v-265v	162v-165r	181r-183v
126.	ܐܣܝܐ ܕܪܘܡܐ ܒܝܕ ܟܘܫܦܗܘܢ ܐܬܐ ܠܐܪܥܐ ܕܢܐܣܐ ܠܟܐܒܝܗܘܢ	265v-267r	165r-165v	183v-185r
127.	ܫܘܒܚܐ ܠܗ ܠܗܘ ܝܚܝܕܝܐ. ܕܒܪܝ ܘܐܬܩܢ ܟܠ ܒܪܝܬܐ	267v-270r	102r-102v	185r-188r
128.	ܢܘܗܪܐ ܘܡܚܝܢܐ ܠܐܢܫܘܬܢ. ܕܩܪܒܗ ܠܓܒܗ ܒܒܪܐ ܕܝܡܝܢ	S270v-272r		S188r-189v
129.	ܡܪܝ ܕܝܢ ܒܢ ܐܬܚܠܦ ܗܘܐ. ܕܫܘܒܚܗ ܠܐܒܘܗܝ ܢܬܠ ܗܘܐ	S272r-274r		S189v-191v
130.	ܢܘܚܡܗ ܕܐܒܐ ܡܬܦܪܣܐ ܕܒܗ ܢܠܒܫܘܢ ܫܘܒܐ ܒܐܘܪܚܐ	S274r-276v	102v	S191v-194r
131.	ܐܝܬܘܗܝ ܕܝܢ ܡܬܩܪܐ ܦܪܘܩܗ ܕܝܠܝ. ܘܐܝܟܢܐ ܒܫܒܩܐ ܢܘܗܪܐ	S276v-279v		S194r-196v
132.	ܫܒܝܚ ܘܡܪܘܡܡ ܡܪܐ ܟܠ. ܕܝܗܒ ܒܣܘܟܠܗ ܘܢܦܩ ܠܒܝܬܗ	S279v-286r		S196v-202r
133.	ܒܪܝܟ ܗܘ ܡܫܒܚܐ ܡܢ ܟܠ. ܐܒܘܢ ܘܗܘܐ ܕܦܪܩܢ ܘܦܪܘܩܢ	S286r-287v		S202r-203r
134.	ܒܪܝܟܘ ܡܫܒܚܐ ܡܫܠܛܢ. ܐܒܘܢ ܘܗܘܐ ܕܒܪܝܢ ܘܦܪܩܢ	S288r-289v	95v-97r	S203r-204v
135.	ܒܟܠ ܥܕܢܝܢ ܘܒܟܠ ܙܒܢܝܢ. ܠܒܪܐ ܘܐܒܐ ܠܗܘܢ ܡܫܒܚܐ ܡܪܝ	S289v-292r	94r-95v	S204v-207r
136.	- ܫܘܒܚܐ ܘܡܩܢܝ ܢܨܚܢܐ. ܒܝܬܐ ܕܠܟܝܠ ܘܢܗܝܪܬܐ ܕܠܚܝܡܐ..... - ܗܘܡܝܬܐ. ܘܒܬܪ ܗܠܝܢ ܡܪܝ ܕܢܫܐ			S207r-209r
137.	ܐܦ ܒܥܕܐ ܚܕܝܬ ܥܢܬܐ ܒܝܬܐ. ܐܦ ܒܥܕܐ ܡܪܝܡ ܒܪܬܐ ܒܝܬܐ	S292r-294r		S209r-219v
138.	ܗܠܝܢ ܠܚܕܐ ܐܦܢܝܐ. ܒܝܘܦܢܛܝܩܣܘܢ ...ܕ ܘܕܢܚܐ			
139.	ܒܪܐ ܕܐܠܗܐ ܡܬܦܪܢܐ. ܕܒܪܐ ܒܪܝܬܐ ܡܢ ܫܘܪܝܐ			
140.	ܒܪܝܟܗ ܡܫܒܚܐ ܦܪܘܩܢ. ܕܒܪܐ ܚܘܒܗ ܐܘܪܒ ܘܢܦܩ			
141.	ܒܐܘܪܚܐ ܕܩܢܝܐ ܪܒܐ ܚܘܫܒܢܐ. ܘܚܘܒܗ ܓܪܒܐ ܕܢܫܝܢܗܘܢ			
142.	ܒܛܝܒܘܬܐ ܡܠܝܐ ܒܟܠܗ. ܕܫܘܠܛܢ ܗܠܗ ܫܡܝܢ ܓܥܝܬܐ			

		M3 1586	G1 1300-1400	D3 1400-1600
143.	ܐܘ ܕܘܪܫܐ ܒܬܠܡܝܕܘܬܐ. ܘܕܘܪܫܐ ܒܪܒܘܬܐ			
144.	ܐܘ ܡܫܒܚܐ ܒܡܘܬܒܗ. ܝܚܝܕܐ ܒܟܝܢܐ ܘܒܐܠܗܘܬܗ			
145.	ܟܠ ܒܪܝܬܐ ܡܕܒܪܢܐ. ܐܝܟܢ ܒܡܫܟܠ ܡܕܒܪܢܐ			
146.	ܫܪܒܐ ܕܡܠܟܐ ܫܪܝܘܬܐ. ܦܟܝܪ ܒܗ ܒܪܥܐ ܕܒܪܝܬܐ			
147.	ܒܕ ܫܠܡ ܡܪܝ ܠܒܪ ܡܫܐ. ܐܒܐ ܡܘܬܐ ܘܣܒܠܢܐ			
148.	ܢܒܝܪ ܒܒܥܐ ܒܫܘܠܡܐ. ܕܒܠܢܐ ܕܡܘܢܐ ܠܫܒܬܐ			
149.	ܢܦܫ ܦܘܡܪܐ ܡܢ ܡܠܟܐ. ܘܐܬܬܦܝܪ ܠܟܘܢ ܒܠܬܘܬܐ			
150.	ܐܘ ܡܫܒܚ ܝܬܝܪܘܬ. ܒܠܒܬܗ ܕܐܒܘܗܝ ܘܗܘܐ			
151.	ܥܘܗܕܢܐ ܠܒܣܝܡܝܢ ܩܕܘܡ. ܕܒܕ ܦܪܝܐ ܣܘܟܠܝ ܕܡܫܡܠܝܢ ܠܓܝܢܐ			
152.	ܠܘܒܝܒܐ ܢܦܫܐ ܡܒܪܟܬܐ. ܒܬܘܠܬܐ ܕܚܝܬܐ ܘܡܕܝܢܬܐ			
153.	ܐܘܕܝܬܐ ܢܦܫ ܟܠ. ܒܕܘܒܪܝ ܢܦܫܗ ܕܩܕܘܫ			
154.	ܒܢܝܪܗ ܡܕܝܢܬܐ ܕܠܠܝܟܐ. ܢܥܬܕܪ ܩܠܐ ܕܡܠܟܐ ܠܝܫܘܥ			
155.	ܘܚܘܪ ܗܘ ܡܕܒܪܐ ܕܝܬܒܝܐ. ܐܦ ܠܒܢܐ ܕܝܥܩܘܒ		89v-91r	
156.	ܓܘܕܘ ܘܐܫܬܒܚܘ ܥܡܘܕܐ. ܢܬܬܠܒܪܘ ܘܐܬܒܢܝܘ ܐܘ ܡܫܒܚܐ		91r-92r	
157.	ܡܪܐ ܕܡܪܚܐ ܘܕܥܕܐ. ܘܒܠܒ ܒܪܚܡܝܢ ܡܕܒܪܐ ܕܒܢܐ			
158.	ܡܪܝ ܕܫܠܝܡ ܠܥܡܢܐ. ܒܪܘܚܐ ܕܡܠܐܟܐ ܠܚܝܐ	154v-155v		
159.	ܥܘܐ ܠܥܘܗܕܢܐ ܐܒܗܐ ܩܕܘܫܐ. ܡܢܥܐ ܒܫܘܐ ܘܪܡܐ ܘܡܟܬܒܐ			85v-95v
160.	ܥܘܗܕܢܐ ܠܣܘܟܠܝ ܩܕܘܡ ܡܥܐ ܫܒܝܬܐ ܡܪܕܝܬܘܬܗ		69r-70v	

TABLE 7: THE NAMES OF THE AUTHORS OF THE HYMNS

Table 7A

		M1 1483	M2 1541	B1 1550	D1 1565
1.	ܒܥܝܢܐ ܕܪܚܡܝܢ ܡܫܒܚܝܢ ܥܡ̈ܡܐ. ܠܝܫܘܥ ܡܠܟܐ ܕܢܘܗܪ̈ܝܢܐ		ܡܠܦܢܐ ܓܝܘܪܓܝܣ ܘܪܕܐ	ܘܪܕܐ	ܡܠܦܢܐ ܓܝܘܪܓܝܣ ܕܡܬܩܪܐ ܘܪܕܐ
2.	ܢܠܟܐ ܕܝܠܗ ܠܢܠܟܐ ܘܓܒ̈ܐ. ܘܠܐ ܚܛܐ ܡܫܬܒܩ ܘܠܐ ܥܘܠܐ		ܡܠܦܢܐ ܓܝܘܪܓܝܣ ܘܪܕܐ	ܡܠܦܢܐ ܘܪܕܐ	ܡܠܦܢܐ ܓܝܘܪܓܝܣ
3.	ܡܢ ܫܡܫܐ ܠܗ ܠܕܢܚܗ. ܒܪܐ ܕܐܠܗܐ ܡܫܬܒܚܢܘܬܗ		ܘܪܕܐ		ܘܪܕܐ
4.	ܫܡܥܘܢ ܐܢܬܘܢ ܥܡ̈ܡܝ. ܕܐܬܐ ܡܠܟܐ ܕܟܠ ܒܪ ܐܢܫܐ		ܓܝܘܪܓܝܣ ܘܪܕܐ		ܘܪܕܐ
5.	ܕܟܝܐ ܘܐܢܫ ܐܒܗ̈ܬܐ. ܘܟܠܝ ܒܩܘܫܛܐ ܦܓܪܐ ܕܟܝܐ		ܡܠܦܢܐ ܓܝܘܪܓܝܣ ܘܪܕܐ	ܓܡܝܪܐ ܘܪܕܐ	ܡܠܦܢܐ ܓܝܘܪܓܝܣ ܘܪܕܐ
6.	ܟܠ ܥܡܐ ܫܪܝܪܬܐ. ܡܫܝܚܐ ܗܘ ܕܐܬܐ ܒܫܪܝܪܬܐ		ܡܠܦܢܐ ܓܝܘܪܓܝܣ ܘܪܕܐ		ܡܠܦܢܐ ܓܝܘܪܓܝܣ ܘܪܕܐ
7.	ܒܢܝܢܐ ܡܕܝܢܬܐ ܕܝܠܝܕܬܐ. ܢܦܩܬ ܩܠܐ ܕܡܪܝܡ ܠܢܝܠܐ		ܓܝܘܪܓܝܣ ܘܪܕܐ	ܡܠܦܢܐ ܘܪܕܐ	ܓܝܘܪܓܝܣ ܘܪܕܐ
8.	ܒܪܐ ܕܒܪܝܢ ܒܗ ܫܡܝܐ. ܕܡܠ ܢܘܗܪܐ ܕܢܦܩܬܐ		ܘܪܕܐ	ܡܠܦܢܐ ܓܝܘܪܓܝܣ	ܡܠܦܢܐ ܓܝܘܪܓܝܣ ܘܪܕܐ
9.	ܒܢܝܐ ܕܫܡܝܐ ܗܘ ܕܝܠܗ ܐܒܐ. ܘܡܫܝܚܘܬܐ ܗܘ ܡܢܝܢ ܐܒܐ		ܓܝܘܪܓܝܣ ܘܪܕܐ	ܘܪܕܐ	ܓܝܘܪܓܝܣ ܘܪܕܐ
10.	ܡܢ ܫܡܝܐ ܕܡܢܗܘܢ ܫܡܝܢܐ. ܐܘ ܕܡܫܝܚܐ ܢܦܩܠ ܡܫܝܚܐ		ܘܪܕܐ		ܘܪܕܐ
11.	ܐܝܟܐ ܝܘܡܐ ܡܢܐ ܝܘܡܐ. ܚܢܢܐ ܠܥܠܡܐ ܒܝܬܐ ܘܐܠܗܐ		*		*
12.	ܒܥܝܢܐ ܫܠܡܘܬܐ ܦܫܠܡܢ. ܕܐܠܗܘܬܗ ܡܫܒܚ ܕܪܚܡܝܢ ܥܡ̈ܡܐ		ܚܟܝܡ ܬܘܕܪܐ ܓܝܘܪܓܝܣ ܘܪܕܐ	ܡܠܦܢܐ ܓܝܘܪܓܝܣ	ܚܟܝܡ ܬܘܕܪܐ ܓܝܘܪܓܝܣ ܘܪܕܐ
13.	ܒܠܫܢܗ ܕܒܪܐ ܒܡܕܝܢܬܐ. ܫܡܥܘ ܗܘܘ ܫܡܥ̈ܐ ܕܪܘܚܐ ܡܢܗܪܐ		ܡܠܦܢܐ ܓܝܘܪܓܝܣ		ܡܠܦܢܐ ܓܝܘܪ [sic]
14.	ܐܘ ܢܒܝܐ ܦܘܠܘܣ. ܢܦܫ ܡܫܝܚܐ ܫܠܝܚܐ		ܚܡܝܣ ܕܒܝܬ ܩܕܚ	ܘܪܕܐ	ܚܡܝܣ ܕܒܝܬ ܩܕܚ
15.	ܝܠܕܐ ܕܦܠܠ ܒܢܗܪܐ. ܡܢܕܝܢ ܡܪܝܐ ܡܢ ܝܠܕܬܐ		ܓܝܘܪܓܝܣ ܘܪܕܐ	ܘܪܕܐ	ܓܝܘܪܓܝܣ ܘܪܕܐ
16.	ܐܘ ܢܒܝܐ ܝܫܥܝܐ ܒܢܒܝܘܬܗ. ܕܐܬܐ ܡܠܝܟܐ ܫܡܥܘܢ ܕܡܫܝܚܐ		*		*
17.	ܐܘ ܢܒܝܐ ܝܘܚܢܢ ܡܥܡܕܢܐ. ܒܕܘܟܪܢܗ ܕܡܠܝܟܐ ܫܡܥܘܢ ܕܡܫܝܚܐ		*		*
18.	ܒܫܩܠܐ ܪܘܚܐ ܕܦܠܠܟܘܬܗ ܕܟܘܠܗܘܢ ܕܪ̈ܐ. ܡܠܝܚܐ ܟܢܫܐ ܦܓܪܐ ܘܦܪܩܐ		*		*
19.	ܡܢ ܢܒܝܘܬܗ ܕܡܫܝܚܐ. ܢܠܝܕܘ ܦܓܪܐ ܠܐ ܫܘܟܐ		*		*
20.	ܫܡܥܘ ܦܓܪܐ ܘܡܥܕܐ ܒܗ ܣܘܦܐ. ܡܢܦܩܠܐ ܠܡܪܝ ܕܩܝܡ ܒܡܫܝܚܘ		*		*

		M1 1483	M2 1541	B1 1550	D1 1565
21.	ܐܘ ܡܫܒܚܐ ܥܠ ܬܫܒܘܚܬܐ. ܦܪܘܩܢܐ ܥܠ ܦܘܪܩܢܐ		ܡܥܢܐ ܝܠܕܐ		ܡܥܢܐ ܝܠܕܐ ܕܐ ܡܥܢܐ ܕܘܝܕ ܕܐ ܡܢ ܡܥܢܐ ܡܢ ܡܪܢܐ ܕܐܝܬܘܗܝ ܦܬܓܡܐ ܕܒܝܬ ܕܠܘܪܐ
22.	ܬܘܒܐ ܠܚܝܠܐ ܡܢܝܫܗܘܢ. ܕܦܩܕ ܘܩܡ ܘܡܬܪܨ		*		*
23.	ܦܬܓܡܐ ܕܒܪܝܬܐ. ܦܪܘܩܢܐ ܕܗܝܡܢܘܬܐ		ܘܪܕܐ ܡܠܦܢܐ ܗܦܟ ܒܥܘܬܐ	*	ܡܠܦܢܐ ܗܦܟ ܒܥܘܬܐ
24.	ܡܢ ܒܥܘܬܐ ܕܦܘܩܕܐ ܡܪܢܐ ܡܬܥܢܝܐ ܕܒܢܝܐ ܒܪܢܫ		ܘܪܕܐ	ܘܪܕܐ	ܘܪܕܐ
25.	ܡܢ ܢܦܫ ܢܨܝ ܡܢ ܢܨܒܐ. ܐܘܠ ܠܚܝܘܬܐ ܚܝ ܦܘܡܟܐ		ܡܠܦܢܐ ܠܡܕܢܚܐ ܘܪܕܐ	ܘܪܕܐ	ܡܠܦܢܐ ܠܒܘ [sic] ܘܪܕܐ
26.	ܐܘ ܢܦܫܐ ܕܡܚܝܒ ܡܢ ܟܠ. ܡܢܘ ܢܦܩܘܢ ܦܢܝܢ ܡܢ ܟܠ		ܠܡܕܢܚܐ ܘܪܕܐ	ܕܝܠܗ ܗܝ ܕܝܠܗ	ܡܠܦܢܐ ܠܒܘ [sic] ܘܪܕܐ
27.	ܐܘ ܕܒܝܬܐ ܢܛܝܪܬܐ. ܡܛܠ ܕܒܝܫܬܐ ܦܪܫܬ ܒܥܘܬܐ		ܘܪܕܐ	ܕܝܠܗ ܗܝ ܕܝܠܗ	ܕܝܠܗ
28.	ܒܥܘܬܝ ܫܡܥ ܐܠܗܐ ܠܝ. ܡܛܠܬ ܕܚܛܗܝ ܡܬܚܪܐ ܐܢܐ ܠܝ		ܡܠܦܢܐ ܠܡܕܢܚܐ	ܡܠܦܢܐ ܠܡܕܢܚܐ	ܡܠܦܢܐ ܠܡܕܢܚܐ
29.	ܠܥܝܪܐ ܒܟܠܙܒܢ ܕܢܬܒܝܗ. ܢܥܒܕ ܕܢܚܢܢ ܒܗ ܡܬܚܝܠܝܢ		ܕܝܠܗ ܗܝ ܕܝܠܗ	ܡܕܢܚܝܐ ܠܡܕܢܚܐ	ܕܝܠܗ ܗܝ ܕܝܠܗ
30.	ܬܘܒܐ ܠܡܫܝܚܐ ܡܪܢ. ܕܦܪܩܢ ܠܟܠܢ ܒܨܠܝܒܗ		ܐܪܡܠܬܐ ܫܒܝܬܐ ܘܐܚܐ ܐܪܡܠܘܬܗܘܢ ܩܘܡ ܡܪܝܐ ܕܡܬܚܢܢ ܥܠ ܡܣܟܢܐ	ܩܘܡ ܡܪܝܐ ܕܡܬܚܢܢ ܥܠ ܡܣܟܢܐ	ܐܪܡܠܬܐ ܫܒܝܬܐ ܘܐܚܐ ܐܪܡܠܘܬܗܘܢ ܣܓܝܐܐ ܩܘܡ ܡܪܝܐ ܕܡܬܚܢܢ ܥܠ ܡܣܟܢܐ
31.	ܡܪܝܐ ܢܛܪܝܢܬܐ. ܕܠܗ ܘܡܪܐ ܕܡܢ ܢܛܝܪܘܬܐ		ܡܠܦܢܐ ܠܡܕܢܚܐ ܘܪܕܐ	ܡܠܦܢܐ ܠܡܕܢܚܐ ܘܪܕܐ	ܡܠܦܢܐ ܠܒܘܪ [sic] ܘܪܕܐ
32.	ܬܘܒܐ ܗܘܐ ܠܟܢܫܐ ܚܕܬܐ. ܕܠܥܠܡܐ ܟܠ ܗܘܘ ܫܠܝܚܐ		ܠܡܕܢܚܐ ܘܪܕܐ	ܕܝܠܗ ܗܝ ܕܝܠܗ	ܘܪ [sic]
33.	ܐܠܗܐ ܠܚܝܘܬܐ ܡܦܩܬ. ܚܝܐ ܡܕܡܝܐ ܘܡܫܬܠܡܐ		ܘܪܕܐ	ܘܪܕܐ	ܘܪܕܐ
34.	ܡܪܝܐ ܦܪܘܩܝ ܒܪܚܡܘܗܝ. ܡܬܚܢܢ ܦܪܘܩܢܘܬܗ		ܘܪܕܐ	ܕܝܠܗ ܗܝ ܕܝܠܗ	ܘܪܕܐ
35.	ܒܥܘܬܐ ܕܚܘܠܬܐ ܢܦܩܬ ܠܝ. ܒܚܘܫܒܐ ܕܫܡܥܐ ܗܘ ܢܛܝܪܬ ܠܝ		ܘܪܕܐ		ܘܪܕܐ
36.	ܡܪܝ ܡܫܝܚܐ ܕܐܬܓܠܝ. ܘܐܬܠܒܫ ܒܦܓܪܐ ܕܐܢܫ		ܕܝܠܗ ܗܝ ܕܝܠܗ		ܘܪܕܐ
37.	ܐܘ ܕܪܚܡܬܐ ܒܛܠܝܬܐ. ܦܬܘܚ ܬܪܥܐ ܚܝ ܕܒܥܘܬܐ		ܘܪܕܐ		ܘܪܕܐ
38.	ܒܗ ܩܝܡܐ ܕܦܩܕ ܠܢ ܠܗ. ܐܬܩܢܐ ܕܢܘܚܐ ܕܠܐ ܡܬܕܢܝ ܠܗ		ܗܦܟ ܒܥܘܬܐ		ܘܪܕܐ
39.	ܡܪܝܐ ܢܛܝܪ ܕܡܬܚܢܢ. ܚܢܢܐ ܘܫܡܥ ܘܥܢܝ ܒܥܝܢ		ܕܝܠܗ ܗܝ ܕܝܠܗ		ܕܝܠܗ ܗܝ ܕܝܠܗ
40.	ܡܪܝܐ ܕܒܚܢܢܘܗܝ ܢܬܪܚܡ. ܡܬܚܢܢ ܦܪܘܩܢ ܠܟܠܢ		ܗܦܟ ܒܥܘܬܐ		ܗܦܟ ܒܥܘܬܐ
41.	ܢܥܒܕ ܬܘܒܐ ܡܫܒܚ ܡܢ ܟܠ. ܡܠܟܐ ܡܫܝܚܐ ܕܡܫܠܛ ܥܠ ܟܠ		ܡܠܦܢܐ ܠܡܕܢܚܐ		ܡܠܦܢܐ ܠܡܕܢܚܐ ܘܪܕܐ

		M1 1483	M2 1541	B1 1550	D1 1565
42.	ܐܒܪܐ ܠܥܒܕ ܒܡܠܟܘܬܟ. ܢܕܢܚ ܒܢܘܗܪܐ ܒܫܘܒܚܘܬܐ		ܗܪܟܐ		ܗܪܟܐ
43.	ܠܥܕܪܐ ܢܩܘܡ ܘܢܠܗ ܕܗܘܐ. ܠܟܠ ܡܩܠܣܝܢ ܗܝܢ ܗܘܠܠܝܢ		ܡܠܦܢܐ ܠܚܘܕܝܗ		ܡܠܦܢܐ ܠܚܘܕܝܗ ܗܪܟܐ
44.	ܠܥܒܕ ܟܣܝܐ ܘܫܡܝܐ. ܢܦܪ ܕܡܠܟܐ ܗܠ ܫܡܝܐ		ܟܠܗ ܗܘ ܟܠܗ		ܟܠܗ ܗܘ ܟܠܗ
45.	ܟܝܡ ܐܟܠܠܐ ܕܡܠܟܘܬܐ. ܘܟܝܡ ܫܘܒܚܐ ܕܥܡܝܩܬܐ		ܗܪܟܐ	ܗܪܟܐ	ܟܠܗ ܗܘ ܟܠܗ
46.	ܟܝܡ ܒܢܝܐ ܗܝܠܐ ܝܬܝܪܬܐ ܘܟܝܡ ܦܪܘܫܘܬܐ ܗܝܠܐ ܦܪܘܫܬܐ		ܡܠܦܢܐ ܠܚܘܕܝܗ ܗܪܟܐ		ܡܠܦܢܐ ܠܚܘܕܝܗ ܗܪܟܐ
47.	ܣܓܝܐ ܡܢܣܓܝܐ ܡܩܒܠ ܚܛܝܐ ܐܢܐ. ܡܩܒܠ ܚܛܝܐ ܐܢܐ ܐܦ ܡܚܛܝܐ ܐܢܐ		ܟܠܗ ܗܘ ܟܠܗ		ܠܚܘܕܝܗ ܗܪܟܐ
48.	ܒܪܝܟ ܕܗܘ ܒܚܪܝܢܘܗܝ ܠܐ ܟܦܪ. ܐܠܐ ܐܘܕܝ ܘܠܟܝܢ ܒܗܝܢ		ܟܠܗ ܗܘ ܟܠܗ		ܟܠܗ ܗܘ ܟܠܗ
49.	ܒܪܝܟ ܕܗܘ ܒܟܝܢ ܡܫܝܚ ܐܠܗܢ. ܟܣܝܘ ܐܬܓܠܝ ܐܠܗܢ		ܗܪܟܐ		ܗܪܟܐ
50.	ܐܘ ܡܫܬܒܚ ܫܡܗܘ ܡܬܬܪܡܪܡܘ. ܘܡܫܬܠܡ ܗܠܐ ܕܪܘܚܐ ܕܩܘܕܫܐ		*		*
51.	ܫܡܗܘ ܡܬܬܪܡܪܡܘ ܩܕܡܝܐ. ܘܠܐ ܗܘܐ ܡܬܚܙܐ ܗܠܝܢ ܕܪܘܚܐ		ܐܦܪܝܡ ܡܠܦܢܐ		ܐܦܪܝܡ ܡܠܦܢܐ
52.	ܒܝܫܐ ܠܗܘܕܝܐ ܐܟܪܙܘ. ܫܝܢܐ ܡܢܘܪ ܐܠܡܫܝܚܘܬܗ		ܐܠܗܐ ܡܫܬܪܝܘܬܗ ܒܝܘܡܐ		ܐܠܗܐ ܡܫܬܪܝܘܬܗ ܒܝܘܡܐ
53.	ܗܘ ܗܝܡܢܘ ܐܢܫܐ ܒܒܪܝܬܐ. ܡܬܦܪܥܘ ܠܬܩܢܝܢ ܦܬܩܬܐ		ܠܚܘܕܝܗ ܗܪܟܐ		ܡܠܦܢܐ ܠܚܘܕܝܗ ܗܪܟܐ
54.	ܡܢܘ ܕܢܦܩܬ ܒܟܠ ܫܘܒܚܢ. ܘܡܢܘ ܝܒܒܐ ܐܦ ܝܠܕܐ ܒܟܠܢ		ܡܠܦܢܐ ܠܚܘܕܝܗ		ܗܪܟܐ
55.	ܐܝܬܘ ܕܢܬܠܗ ܕܠܝܬܐ. ܦܪܝܩܐ ܒܪܝܟܐ ܡܢܬܢܐ ܗܘܢܐ		ܗܪܟܐ		ܗܪܟܐ
56.	ܐܘ ܦܬܚܬܢ ܩܢܐ ܦܬܚܢ. ܐܘ ܡܩܕܫܬܢ ܩܢܐ ܦܠܚܬܢ		ܡܠܦܢܐ ܠܚܘܕܝܗ ܗܪܟܐ		ܗܪܟ [sic]
57.	ܐܘ ܢܘܩܡܢ ܩܢܐ ܒܒܥܝܢ. ܘܩܢܐ ܗܝܢ ܫܒܩܢ ܘܩܢܐ ܡܕܒܪܝܢ		ܗܪܟܐ	ܗܪܟܐ	ܗܪܟܐ
58.	ܐܘ ܥܘܗܕܢܐ ܕܠܝܠܘܬܐ. ܘܡܫܟܚܢܐ ܕܫܠܘܬܐ		*	*	*
59.	ܩܪܐ ܕܡܠܟ ܩܪܘܬܐ. ܐܦ ܢܘܚܪܐ ܕܡܠܟ ܩܪܘܒܬܐ		ܡܠܦܢܐ ܠܚܘܕܝܗ ܗܪܟܐ	ܟܠܗ	ܡܠܦܢܐ ܠܚܘܕ[sic] ܗܪܟܐ
60.	ܡܠܦܢܐ ܕܫܦܝܪܘܬܐ. ܡܥܒܕܐ ܐܝܬܘܗܝ ܒܥܒܝܕܘܬܐ		ܗܪܟܐ	ܗܪܟܐ	ܗܪܟܐ
61.	ܒܪܐ ܕܠܒܪܘܗܝ ܠܟܐ ܥܘܡܩܐ. ܘܢܗܘܐ ܒܗܘܠܟܐ ܗܠܐ ܗܘܦܟܐ		ܗܪܟܐ	ܟܠܗ	ܗܪܟܐ
62.	ܒܝܫܬܐ ܕܪܘܚܐ ܩܪܐ ܘܝܠܗ. ܘܒܝܫܬܗܘܢ ܢܛܘܪܐ ܘܝܠܗ		ܡܠܦܢܐ ܠܚܘܕܝܗ ܗܟܢ ܢܗܘܐ		ܡܠܦܢܐ ܠܚܘ [sic] ܗܪܟܐ
63.	ܡܠܟܐ ܕܡܠܟܐ ܠܗ ܩܠܝܢ. ܘܩܘܫܬܐ ܠܪܘܡܐ ܡܫܡܫܝܢ		ܡܠܦܢܐ ܠܚܘܕܝ [sic]	ܟܠܗ	ܠܚܘܕܝ [sic] ܗܪܟܐ
64.	ܒܝܬܐ ܟܠܗܐ ܕܩܘܫܬܐ. ܕܒܐ ܠܟܪܘ ܒܝܬ ܐܠܗܘܬܗ		ܗܪܟܐ		ܗܪܟܐ

		M1 1483	M2 1541	B1 1550	D1 1565
65.	ܒܟ̈ܠܡܬܐ ܗ̈ܘܐ ܚܘܒܐ ܗܦܝܟ. ܦܬܟܘܪ̈ܬܗ ܡܬܟܢܫܐ ܗܦܝܟ		ܘܪܕܐ		ܘܪܕܐ
66.	ܒܓܘܕܐ ܕܒܢ̈ܐ ܫܦܝܪ ܗܦܝܟ. ܕܡܬܠ ܫܒܐ ܒܠܒܝ ܠܡܘܩܕܐ		*	ܘܪܕܐ	ܘܪܕܐ
67.	ܒܕܝܢ ܕܒܝܘܡܗ ܡܕܝܢܬܐ. ܦܕܝܩ ܫܘܒ̈ܚܘ ܕܡܠܟܐ ܕܐܠܗܐ		ܠܚܘܕܝܗ ܘܪܕܐ	*	ܠܚܘܕܝܗ ܘܪܕܐ
68.	ܡܪܘܡܡ ܐܢܬ ܕܥܠܝ̈ܢܝܐ. ܒܡܫܒܚܘܬܐ ܦܪܘܫܘܬܐ		*		*
69.	ܢܬܩܢ ܝܠܗ ܠܝ ܗܘܢܐ. ܡܢܗܘ ܓܢܐ ܡܕܒܪܢܗ ܝܘܢܐ		ܘܪܕܐ		ܘܪܕܐ
70.	ܐܘ ܕܠܥܡܝܩܘܬܐ ܕܠܟܝ. ܘܠܡܬܒܟܝܢܘܬܐ ܡܬܕܠܓܝܢ		*		ܘܪܕܐ
71.	ܐܘ ܒܥܐ ܡܢ ܟܠ ܕܠܗ ܠܟܠܐ ܟܠ. ܠܐ ܡܬܡܨܝܐ ܠܟܠ ܡܫܘܐ ܠܟܠ		ܘܪܕܐ		ܘܪܕܐ
72.	ܒܢܝ ܝܒܪܘܬܗ ܩܕܝܫܬܐ. ܕܗܘܘ ܒܢ̈ܝܐ ܠܥܕܬܐ ܚܝ̈ܐ		ܡܠܦܢܐ ܠܚܘܕܝܗ		ܡܠܦܢܐ ܠܚܘܕܝܗ
73.	ܐܘ ܐܢܬ ܝܬܝܪܐ ܒܗ. ܒܝܬܐ ܢܛܪܬ ܝܬܝܪ ܠܗ		*		*
74.	ܡܥܒܪ ܬܪܬܝܢ ܕܡܫܡܫܢܘܬܐ. ܘܡܟܠܗ ܕܐܠܗܐ ܡܠܟܬܐ		ܡܪܝܫܘܥ ܒܪ ܩܠܝܛܐ ܡܝܛܪܢܐ		ܡܪܝܫܘܥ ܒܪ ܩܠܝܛܐ ܡܝܛܪܢܐ
75.	ܡܢ ܠܗ ܠܐܘܪܚ ܕܦܩܕܐ ܒܝܬ. ܡܪܐ ܕܒܢܐ ܠܐܘܪܝ ܦܩܕܐ ܥܒܝܕ		ܘܪܕܐ	ܡܠܦܢܐ ܘܪܕܐ	ܠܚܘܕ. ܘܪܕܐ
76.	ܦܓܪܐ ܕܐܘܪܚܐ ܠܐܠܗܘܬܗ. ܕܐܘܡܬܐ ܡܟܘܡܬܐ ܠܚܝܒܝܢ ܒܠܒܘܗ		ܠܚܘܕܝܗ ܘܪܕܐ	*	ܘܪܕܐ
77.	ܡܢ ܓܒܠ ܡܪܝ ܠܐܦܪܝܩܘܢ. ܕܝܗܠܒ ܢܦܫܐ ܝܕܥ ܕܝܫܠܟ		ܠܚܘܕܝܗ ܘܪܕܐ	ܕܝܠܗ ܗܘ ܕܝܠܗ	ܠܚܘܕܝܗ ܘܪܕܐ
78.	ܦܠܓܐ ܕܒܝܬܐ ܘܫܒܝܩܬܐ. ܕܠܩܕܡܐ ܟܠ ܗܘܐ ܠܗ ܡܫܒܚܬܐ		ܠܚܘܕܝܗ ܘܪܕܐ	ܕܝܠܗ ܗܘ ܕܝܠܗ	ܠܚܘܕܝܗ ܘܪܕܐ
79.	ܒܝܬܗ ܕܫܡܝ ܗܘܐ ܚܝܐ. ܡܠܝܐ ܓܘܕܐ ܠܟܝܢܐ ܡܠܝܐ		ܘܪܕܐ	ܡܠܦܢܐ ܘܪܕܐ	ܘܪܕܐ
80.	ܒܫܡܗ ܦܓܪܐ ܚܣܝܢܐ. ܙܟܝ ܐܪܟܐ ܘܡܬܟܠܠ ܥܡܗ		ܘܪܕܐ	*	ܠܚܘܕܝܗ ܘܪܕܐ
81.	ܒܝܘܒܒܝܗܐ ܢܘܡܐ ܦܘܩܕܐ. ܝܕܐ ܬܪܘܨܐ ܦܓܪܐ ܢܟܠܡܬܐ		ܘܪܕܐ	*	ܠܚܘ. [sic] ܘܪܕܐ
82.	ܒܪܐ ܡܠܟܐ ܚܣܝܢܐ. ܠܓܘܗ ܠܦܓܪܐ ܐܦܩܬܐ		ܘܪܕܐ		ܘܪܕܐ
83.	ܐܦܐ ܗܘܝ ܠܝ ܡܬܓܕܪܐ. ܒܪܐ ܚܣܝܢܐ ܗܘܝ ܡܬܚܫܟܢܐ		ܡܠܦܢܐ ܠܚܘܕܝܗ ܘܪܕܐ		ܡܠܦܢܐ ܠܚܘܕܝܗ ܘܪܕܐ
84.	ܦܪܬܐ ܕܫܘܒܚܐ ܝܩܕܠܗ ܗܦܝܟ. ܘܚܫܠܗ ܘܢܓܗ ܡܬܕܘܒܪ ܗܦܝܟ.		ܠܚܘܕܝܗ ܘܪܕܐ		ܠܚܘܕܝܗ ܘܪܕܐ
85.	ܦܥܒܝܢ ܥܒܕܥܕܢܐ ܦܠܠܓܝܢ. ܕܐܠܗܫܘܕܪܘܣ ܡܬܥܫܝܢ ܐܟܠܐ ܥܢܒܐ		ܡܠܦܢܐ ܘܪܕܐ		ܡܠܦܢܐ ܘܪܕܐ
86.	ܬܪܥܢܐ ܕܟܠ ܚܝܕܬܐ. ܦܬܒܘܓܬܐ ܕܓܡܝܫܬܐ	*	ܘܪܕܐ	ܡܠܦܢܐ ܠܚܘܕܝܗ ܕܡܬܩܪܐ ܘܪܕܐ	ܘܪܕܐ
87.	ܦܬܘ ܡܬܟܣ ܦܓܪܐ. ܦܪܬܐ ܠܝܒܢܐ ܡܚܕܐ ܒܠܒܠܐ		ܘܪܕܐ		ܘܪܕܐ
88.	ܠܐܓܥܬܐ ܕܫܘܒܚܐ ܝܠܕܬ. ܦܬܟܘܪܬܐ ܕܒܢܐ ܫܦܝܪ		ܡܪܝ ܢܗܘܕܪܐ		ܡܠܦܢܐ ܡܪܝ ܢܗܘܕܪܐ

		M1 1483	M2 1541	B1 1550	D1 1565
89.	ܗܘ ܕܠܝܬ ܣܘܟܐ ܥܘܬܪܗ. ܠܟܠܗ ܕܠܐ ܒܘܪܟܝ ܗܘܕܐ		ܡܪܝ ܐܦܪܝܡ ܒܪ ܡܫܝܚܐ		ܡܪܝ ܐܦܪܝܡ ܒܪ ܡܫܝܚܐ
90.	ܐܠܗܐ ܐܒܘܢ ܡܠܟܐ. ܥܡܗ ܥܡ ܐܒܘܗܝ ܒܐܒܗܘܬܐ		*		*
91.	ܐܘܪܚܗ ܕܒܪܐ ܚܣܝܢܐ. ܠܐ ܡܬܕܪܟܐ ܠܟܠܗܘܢ ܒܢܝܢܐ	ܕܝܠܗ	ܘܪܕܐ	ܘܪܕܐ	ܠܚܘܕܝܗ ܘܪܕܐ
92.	ܥܡܗ ܕܐܒܐ ܠܥܠܡ ܢܘܗܪܐ. ܠܥܠܡ ܡܢ ܢܘܗܪܐ ܘܗܘ ܠܢܘܗܪܐ	ܡܠܦܢܐ ܠܚܘܕܝܗ ܘܪܕܐ	ܠܚܘܕܝܗ ܘܪܕܐ	*	ܠܚܘܕ. ܘܪܕܐ
93.	ܦܬܐ ܠܬܘܕܝܬܗ ܕܟܝܢ ܚܣܝܐ. ܘܥܠܡ ܡܬܬܪܡ ܠܥܕܢ ܥܡܢܐ	ܚܡܝܣ	ܡܠܦܢܐ ܚܡܝܣ	ܗܕܐ ܚܡܝܣ	ܡܠܦܢܐ ܚܡܝܣ
94.	ܥܒܕܐ ܕܐܪܥܐ ܡܫܥܡܢܐ. ܐܡܪܐ ܡܫܡܠܝܐ ܡܫܬܚܢܐ ܡܫܠܡܢܐ		ܡܠܦܢܐ ܠܚܘܕܝܗ ܘܪܕܐ		ܡܠܦܢܐ ܠܚܘܕܝܗ ܘܪܕܐ
95.	ܥܒܝܕܝܢ ܘܡܥܒܕܝܢ ܐܢܘܢ. ܥܒܕܐ ܥܒܕܝ ܘܡܘܕܝܢ ܠܟܠܗܘܢ		ܠܚܘܕܝܗ ܘܪܕܐ	ܘܪܕܐ	ܡܠܦܢܐ ܠܚܘܕܝ [sic] ܘܪܕܐ
96.	ܥܒܕܐ ܕܐܘܪܚܝܢ ܠܥܡܘܕܝܗ ܕܥܒܕܐ. ܘܗܘܝ ܠܥܠܡܐ ܕܡܝܢ ܒܢܝܢܐ	*	ܠܚܘܕܝܗ ܘܪܕܐ	ܡܠܦܢܐ ܠܚܘܕܝܗ	ܠܚܘܕܝܗ ܘܪܕܐ
97.	ܡܢܘ ܗܟܢ ܕܚܝܠܬܐ. ܢܬܪܝܡ ܠܟܠܢ ܡܪܢܐ ܡܠܟܐ	ܘܪܕܐ	ܘܪܕܐ	*	ܘܪܕܐ
98.	ܢܝܚܘܬܐ ܕܠܟܐ ܐܝܟ ܗܘ. ܥܡܗ ܐܢܫܐ ܡܢܝܢ ܡܫܩܠܗܘܢ	*	ܘܪܕܐ	*	ܘܪܕܐ
99.	ܥܡܪܐ ܠܗ ܠܗܘ ܝܠܕܐ. ܘܗܘܐ ܩܘܡܐ ܘܩܠܝܠ ܣܓܝܐܐ	ܘܪܕܐ	ܘܪܕܐ	*	ܘܪܕܐ
100.	ܗܘ ܡܠܟܐ ܕܥܠܡܐ. ܘܡܪܐ ܕܥܠܡܐ ܘܕܢܛܪܐ	*	ܘܪܕܐ	ܘܪܕܐ	ܠܚܘܕܝܗ ܘܪܕܐ
101.	ܥܒܕܐ ܕܡܠܟܐ ܡܥܘܠܝܬܐ. ܒܐܪܥܐ ܘܠܝ ܐܝܟ ܡܫܡܫܢܐ	ܘܪܕܐ	ܘܪܕܐ	ܡܠܦܢܐ ܠܚܘܕܝܗ	ܘܪܕܐ
102.	ܡܘܡܐ ܐܘ ܢܟܝܢܐ ܚܫܝܒܬܐ. ܢܬܬܥܒܪܘ ܘܥܡܝ ܢܥܝܢܬܐ	ܘܪܕܐ	ܠܚܘܕܝܗ ܘܪܕܐ	ܕܝܠܗ	ܠܚܘܕܝܗ ܘܪܕܐ
103.	ܐܡܢܐ ܕܐܝܬ ܠܗ ܫܘܒܚܐ. ܩܘܫܬܐ ܘܠܐ ܠܡܫܒܚܐ	ܘܪܕܐ	ܘܪܕܐ	*	ܘܪܕܐ
104.	ܠܢܟܝܬ ܕܝܕܥܐ ܢܟܠܐ ܗܘܢܐ. ܡܬܕܟܝܢܘܬܐ ܢܬܢܐ ܚܘܢܐ ܗܘܢܐ		ܡܠܦܢܐ ܘܪܕܐ	*	ܠܚܘܕܝܗ ܘܪܕܐ
105.	ܠܦܪܘܩܢܐ ܐܢܫܝܐ. ܕܢܝܚ ܒܝܘܡܗ ܒܪܐ ܚܣܝܢܐ		ܘܪܕܐ	ܘܪܕܐ	ܘܪܕܐ
106.	ܐܠܗܐ ܕܝܢ ܐܢܫܐ. ܒܪܗ ܥܠܝܗ ܢܦܠ ܠܦܘܪܩܢ ܐܢܫܐ		ܗܘܡܪܐ		ܗܘܡܪܐ
107.	ܐܡܢܐ ܕܠܟܐ ܐܝܟ ܐܡܘܬܗ. ܠܐ ܡܐܟܠܐ ܐܝܟ ܐܝܟ ܢܝܫܘܬܗ	ܘܪܕܐ	ܘܪܕܐ	ܠܚܘܕܝܗ	ܘܪܕܐ
108.	ܗܘ ܢܛܠܝܐ ܝܘܡܐ ܘܡܥܒܕܐ. ܕܐܡܪ ܥܒܕܝ ܒܢܝ ܦܠܝܓܐ	*	ܘܪܕܐ	ܘܪܕܐ	ܘܪܕܐ
109.	ܝܡܝܢܗ ܕܐܒܐ ܡܬܘܦܪܐ ܠܥܡ ܒܫܠܡܘܬܗ ܦܪܝܫܐ ܢܠܟܐ	ܘܪܕܐ	ܘܪܕܐ	ܘܪܕܐ	ܘܪܕܐ
110.	ܡܫܝܚܐ ܡܠܟܐ ܕܫܘܒܚܐ. ܘܡܠܟܝܢ ܡܠܟܐ ܕܡܫܝܚܘܬܐ	*	ܘܪܕܐ	ܡܠܦܢܐ ܠܚܘܕܝܗ	ܘܪܕܐ
111.	ܐܘ ܕܡܫܒܠܝܢ ܠܟܠ ܢܦܫܗܘܢ.. ܘܡܫܬܒܗܪܝܢ ܠܟܠ ܠܡܫܪܪܗܘܢ	ܘܪܕܐ	ܘܪܕܐ	ܘܪܕܐ	ܘܪܕܐ
112.	ܢܫܒܚܐ ܡܪܢܐ ܕܒܪܝܬܐ. ܘܒܠܒܢ ܕܢܪܥܡܐ ܢܫܒܚܬܐ		ܘܪܕܐ	ܠܚܘܕܝܗ	ܘܪܕܐ

		M1 1483	M2 1541	B1 1550	D1 1565
113.	ܢܦܫܐ ܡܢܟܦܐ ܒܝܒܢܝܐ. ܒܓܠܠ ܢܟܦܐ ܚܘܒ ܚܘܒܬܢܐ		ܠܚܘܕܝܗ ܘܪܕܐ	*	ܠܚܘܕܝܗ ܘܪܕܐ
114.	ܡܠܟܐ ܕܫܡ ܥܒܕܐ. ܕܒܥܒܕܝܢܐ ܘܠܐ ܗܘܐ ܕܦܠܚܐ	*	ܠܚܘܕܝܗ ܘܪܕܐ	ܘܪܕܐ	ܠܚܘܕܝܗ ܘܪܕܐ
115.	ܐܘ ܣܓܝܐܐ ܦܪܘܩܢܐ. ܐܘ ܝܗܒܘ ܡܚܝܠܗ ܕܒܣܝܡܐ	ܘܪܕܐ	ܘܪܕܐ	ܘܪܕܐ	ܘܪܕܐ
116.	ܒܘܗܪܐ ܒܪܐ ܟܠ ܒܘܗܪܝܢ. ܕܪܘܡܐ ܡܚܘܦܫܐ ܒܐܝܕܗ ܠܟܝܢܢ	*	ܘܪܕܐ	ܘܪܕܐ	ܘܪܕܐ
117.	ܡܪܚܡܢܐ ܡܟܪܗ ܕܡܪܚܡܢܐ. ܕܝܠܝܕܘܬܗ ܡܢ ܟܠ ܪܡܐ	*	ܘܪܕܐ	ܘܪܕܐ	ܘܪܕܐ
118.	ܡܠܦܢܐ ܐܠܗܝܐ. ܡܢܐ ܕܒܢܝܐ ܐܠܗܝܐ	*	ܘܪܕܐ	ܘܪܕܐ	ܡܠܦܢܐ ܠܚܘܕܝܗ ܘܪܕܐ
119.	ܐܘ ܓܒܪܐ ܒܝܕ ܛܒܘܬܐ. ܟܠܗܝܢ ܗܦܟܘܢ ܡܟܝܢܘܬܐ		ܠܚܘܕܝܗ ܘܪܕܐ		ܘܪܕܐ
120.	ܒܣܝܡܐ ܕܠܓܠ ܓܒܪܐ ܕܠܓܒܪ ܝܗܒܗ ܠܓܝܘܣ ܠܗ ܒܪܐ	*	ܘܪܕܐ	ܡܠܦܢܐ ܠܚܘܕܝܗ	ܡܠܦܢܐ ܘܪܕܐ
121.	ܡܠܟܐ ܘܡܪܐ ܕܟܠ ܡܠܟܐ. ܕܒܓܒܪܘܗܝ ܐܬܦܝ ܟܠܗܘܢ ܡܠܟܐ	*	ܘܪܕܐ	ܡܠܦܢܐ ܘܪܕܐ	ܘܪܕܐ
122.	ܡܠܟܐ ܕܪܘܡܐ ܝܟܝܐ. ܕܐܬܐ ܕܢܦܪܘܩ ܠܐܕܡܝܐ	*	ܡܠܦܢܐ ܘܪܕܐ	ܘܪܕܐ	ܘܪܕܐ
123.	ܡܪܚܡܢܐ ܡܟܪܗ ܕܡܪܚܡܢܐ. ܗܘ ܕܐܝܠܝܕܘܬܗ ܡܢ ܟܠ ܪܡܐ		ܘܪܕܐ	*	ܠܚܘܕܝܗ ܘܪܕܐ
124.	ܡܪܐ ܕܟܘܟܒܐ ܘܕܝܠܝܬܐ. ܐܦ ܬܪܥܐ ܕܟܠ ܐܝܠܢܐ	*	ܠܚܘܕܝܗ ܘܪܕܐ	ܘܪܕܐ	ܘܪܕܐ
125.	ܡܟܘܢܐ ܕܟܠ ܒܪܝܬܐ. ܢܚܬ ܪܒܐ ܡܠܐ ܢܬܠܟܬܐ	*	ܘܪܕܐ	ܡܠܦܢܐ ܘܪܕܐ	ܡܠܦܢܐ ܘܪܕܐ
126.	ܐܬܝܐ ܕܪܘܡܐ ܒܝܕ ܫܠܝܚܘܗܝ ܐܬܐ ܠܐܪܥܐ ܕܢܐܣܐ ܠܟܪܝܗܘܗܝ	*	ܘܪܕܐ		ܡܠܦܢܐ ܘܪܕܐ
127.	ܥܡܝܢܐ ܠܗ ܠܐ ܝܕܥܬܐ. ܘܓܒܪܐ ܡܬܚܡܝܢ ܟܠ ܒܢܝܢܐ		ܡܠܦܢܐ ܠܚܘܕܝܗ ܘܪܕܐ		ܘܪܕܐ
128.	ܢܘܪܐ ܡܝܬܐܬܝܐ ܠܐܠܗܘܬܗ. ܘܦܪܩܗ ܠܓܢܣܢ ܓܒܪܐ ܕܝܠܢ		*		*
129.	ܡܪܝ ܓܢ ܒܝ ܡܬܠܒܒ ܗܘܐ. ܕܥܡܓܒܗ ܠܫܠܝܚܘܗܝ ܒܫܘܐ ܗܘܐ		ܠܚܘܕܝܗ ܘܪܕܐ		ܓܘܪ [sic]
130.	ܝܗܒܗ ܕܐܓܐ ܡܓܘܦܝܐ ܕܝܗܒ ܐܠܗܘܬܗ ܥܡܐ ܒܐܘܪܚܐ		ܘܪܕܐ		ܘܪܕܐ
131.	ܐܝܬܝܐ ܕܝܗܒ ܡܬܦܠܓ ܒܝܣܘܦܗ ܒܪܝ. ܘܐܝܬܝܐ ܠܟܝܢܐ ܢܘܓܠܝ		*		*
132.	ܥܟܝܣ ܘܡܪܡܟܝܬ ܡܪܝܐ ܟܠ. ܘܓܒܪܐ ܒܣܘܟܗ ܡܢܗܪܗ ܠܓܢܣܢ		ܪܒܢ ܠܒܪܝܫܘܥ ܒܪ ܥܒܕܐܗ		ܪܒܢ ܠܒܪܝܫܘܥ ܕܡܢ ܒܝܬ ܥܒܕܐܗ
133.	ܒܪܝܟ ܗܘ ܡܫܝܚܐ ܡܚܝܢܢ. ܐܒܘܗܝ ܘܪܘܚܐ ܕܦܪܩܢ ܘܦܪܩܢ		*		*
134.	ܒܪܝܟܘ ܡܫܝܚܐ ܡܫܠܠܢܢ. ܐܒܘܗܝ ܘܪܘܚܐ ܕܫܠܝܢ ܡܚܝܢܢ		*		*
135.	ܒܟܠ ܥܕܢܝܢ ܘܒܟܠ ܙܒܢܝܢ. ܠܟܐ ܘܠܒܪܐ ܠܗܘܢ ܡܫܝܚܐ ܡܪܝ		*		ܡܪܝ ܠܝܫܘܥ ܡܬܪܓܡܢܘܬܐ ܕܒܝܬ ܠܪܡܐ

		M1 1483	M2 1541	B1 1550	D1 1565
136.	- ܫܘܒܚܐ ܙܡܪܝ ܒܪܘܡܐ. ܒܪܘܡܐ ܕܠܥܠ ܡܢܘܬܐ ܕܠܒܫܗ..... - ܫܡܝܐ. ܘܐܪܥܐ ܗܠܝܢ ܡܠܝܢ ܕܚܕܘܬܐ		* ܚܕܐ ܒܪ ܫܡܫܐ ܡܕܢܚܝ		*
137.	ܐܘ ܡܪܝܐ ܚܣܝܢ ܒܟܠ ܥܒܕܐ. ܐܘ ܡܪܝܐ ܢܗܝܪ ܒܪܐ ܥܒܕܐ		*		
138.	ܡܢܚܡ ܠܚܝܐ ܐܘܪܚܐ. ܒܝܘܦܛܡܘܢ ...ܕ ܡܢܐ	ܠܒܕܐܝܬ ܡܫܬܪܥܠܝܢܐ ܕܡܘܬܐ			
139.	ܒܪܐ ܕܐܬܝܠܕ ܡܬܡܛܝܢܐ. ܕܒܪܐ ܒܪܬܐ ܡܢ ܫܘܪܝܐ	*		ܡܠܟܐ ܠܚܘܕܝܗ	
140.	ܒܪܝܬܐ ܡܫܒܚܐ ܦܪܘܩܢ. ܕܒܪܝܟ ܚܘܒܗ ܐܘܪܝܒ ܘܢܗܪ			ܘܪܒܐ	
141.	ܒܐܘܪܚܐ ܕܩܕܝܫܐ ܪܚܡ ܚܘܒܟܘܢ. ܘܝܘܡܢܐ ܒܪܐ ܕܒܝܫܬܐܘܗܝ			ܘܪܒܐ	
142.	ܒܫܡܐ ܡܠܟܐ ܕܒܫܡܝܐ. ܕܫܘܠܛܢ ܗܠܝܢ ܫܡܝ ܒܫܒܝܬܐ			ܕܠܗ ܗܘ ܕܝܠܗ	
143.	ܐܘ ܢܘܗܪܐ ܒܫܠܝܚܘܬܐ. ܘܢܘܗܪܐ ܒܪܘܚܬܐ			ܗܟܢܐ ܫܡܝܗ ܒܪ ܡܪܝܡ	
144.	ܐܘ ܡܫܝܚܐ ܫܡܝܢܝܐ. ܝܗܒܬ ܒܝܫܝܐ ܘܚܠܝܡܐ			ܡܫܝܚܐ ܐܢܫܐ ܫܒܝܚܐ	
145.	ܟܠ ܫܡܝܢܐ ܢܗܪܝܢ. ܐܦܠܐ ܒܥܡܠܐ ܢܗܘܪܐ			ܡܠܟܐ ܠܚܘܕܝܗ ܡܣܝܒܪܘܠܝܛܐ ܕܟܠܗ	
146.	ܫܪܒܐ ܕܡܠܐ ܫܘܒܚܐ. ܦܠܛ ܒܗ ܒܪܥܐ ܕܝܩܢܬܐ			ܕܠܗ ܗܘ ܕܝܠܗ	
147.	ܫܡ ܗܝܡܢ ܡܪܝ ܠܥܘܠ ܢܦܫܐ. ܐܫܐ ܡܘܬܐ ܘܗܝܟܠܐ			*	
148.	ܢܪܝܫ ܒܢܟܐ ܒܢܝܫܘܬܐ. ܕܦܪܩܢܐ ܕܐܘܪܚܐ ܫܒܝܚܬܐ			*	
149.	ܢܘܢ ܦܘܡܐ ܡܢ ܡܠܟܐ. ܘܐܫܬܡܥ ܒܟܠܗ ܒܬܫܒܘܚܬܐ				
150.	ܐܘ ܢܨܝܒܐ ܝܬܝܪܐ. ܫܘܠܛܢܗ ܕܐܒܘܗܝ ܘܗܝܐ				
151.	ܫܘܒܚܐ ܠܩܢܘܡܐ ܦܪܘܩܢ. ܕܒܪ ܝܗܒ ܚܘܒܐ ܕܡܫܟܚܐ ܠܟܝܢܢ				
152.	ܠܫܒܚܐ ܝܡܝܐ ܡܫܒܚܬܐ. ܒܐܘܠܨܢܐ ܕܢܝܚܐ ܘܫܘܒܚܬܐ				
153.	ܐܘܢܝܬܐ ܢܦܫ ܒܟܠ. ܒܕܘܒܪܝ ܝܘܡܐ ܕܦܪܘܩܢ				
154.	ܒܢܝܪܗ ܡܫܝܚܐ ܕܡܠܝܬܐ. ܝܫܬܡܥ ܩܠܐ ܕܟܢܫܐ ܠܢܝܫܐ				
155.	ܘܠܘܬ ܗܘ ܡܫܝܚܐ ܕܝܗܒ ܝܘܡܐ. ܐܦ ܠܓܒܪܐ ܕܝܫܬܘܚܪ				
156.	ܝܘܡܐ ܘܢܗܘܪܗ ܫܡܫܐ. ܝܬܬܚܒܪܘ ܘܢܬܢܗܪܘܢ ܐܘ ܡܫܒܚܐ				
157.	ܡܪܐ ܕܩܢܝܐ ܘܫܡܝܐ. ܘܒܠܒ ܒܩܢܘܡܐ ܡܫܝܚܐ ܕܚܝܐ				

		M1 1483	M2 1541	B1 1550	D1 1565
158.	ܡܪܝ ܕܫܠܡܐ ܠܥܡܡܐ. ܒܪܘܚܐ ܕܦܠܛܘܬܐ ܠܟܠܗ				
159.	ܫܡܐ ܠܥܘܕܪܢܐ ܢܒܥܐ ܦܪܘܩܐ. ܚܢܢܐ ܦܫܛܐ ܡܪܘܡܐ ܘܡܫܒܚܐ				
160.	ܥܘܕܪܢܐ ܠܢܘܟܪܝ ܦܪܘܩ ܚܝܐ ܫܒܝܚܐ ܡܪܚܡܢܘܬܟ				

Table 7B

		C1 1568	C2 1568	D2 1575	B2 1581
1.	ܦܬܚܘ ܬܪܥܝܟܝ ܡܠܟܝܢ ܥܡܡܐ. ܠܡܠܟܐ ܫܠܝܚܐ ܕܪܘܚܢܝܐ		ܡܠܟܐ ܠܚܘܕܪܐ ܡܕܢܚܐ	ܡܠܟܐ ܠܚܘܕܪܐ ܡܕܢܚܐ	*
2.	ܫܠܡܐ ܕܫܠܡ ܠܫܠܡܘܗ ܘܟܢܫܐ. ܘܟܠ ܚܝܐ ܡܫܒܚܝܢ ܘܟܠ ܢܫܡܬܐ		ܡܠܟܐ ܠܚܘܕܪܐ ܡܕܢܚܐ	ܡܠܟܐ ܠܚܘܕܪܐ	ܡܠܟܐ ܠܚܘܕܪܐ ܡܕܢܚܐ
3.	ܡܢ ܩܕܡ ܠܗ ܠܡܪܝܡܬܟ. ܚܪܐ ܕܐܠܗܐ ܡܠܘܚܡܪܝܡܬܟ		ܡܕܢܚܐ	ܡܕܢܚܐ	ܡܕܢܚܐ
4.	ܫܡܥܘ ܐܚܝ ܦܬܓܡܘܗܝ. ܕܒܐܬܐ ܢܒܝܐ ܕܟܠ ܚܕ ܡܢܗܘܢ		ܠܚܘܕܪܐ ܡܕܢܚܐ	ܠܚܘܕܪܐ ܡܕܢܚܐ	ܠܚܘܕܪܐ ܥܘܡܪܐ ܕܡܕܢܚܐ
5.	ܦܘܫܐ ܡܪܝܡ ܠܡܘܬܐ. ܘܡܠܟ ܒܥܘܠܡܐ ܦܪܘܩܐ ܕܒܫܐ		ܡܠܟܐ ܠܚܘܕܪܐ ܡܕܢܚܐ	ܡܠܟܐ ܠܚܘܕܪܐ ܡܕܢܚܐ	ܡܠܟܐ ܠܚܘܕܪܐ ܡܕܢܚܐ
6.	ܟܠ ܥܡܡܐ ܫܪܝܪܬܐ. ܕܝܢܐ ܩܢܘܡܐ ܕܐܪܥܢܐ ܒܟܢܘܫܬܐ		ܡܠܟܐ ܠܚܘܕܪܐ ܡܕܢܚܐ	ܡܠܟܐ ܠܚܘܕܪܐ ܡܕܢܚܐ	ܠܚܘܕܪܐ
7.	ܒܠܡܐ ܡܫܝܚܐ ܕܫܠܝܛ. ܚܝܠܗ ܩܠܐ ܘܡܬܒܪܝܢ ܠܥܠܡܐ		ܠܚܘܕܪܐ ܡܕܢܚܐ	ܠܚܘܕܪܐ ܡܕܢܚܐ	ܠܚܘܕܪܐ ܡܕܢܚܐ
8.	ܒܪܐ ܕܫܡܥܢ ܒܗ ܗܝܡܢܬܐ. ܕܡܠ ܡܫܩܠܬܐ ܘܫܢܝܬܗܐ		ܡܕܢܚܐ	ܡܕܢܚܐ	ܡܕܢܚܐ
9.	ܒܝܬܐ ܕܫܡܝܐ ܗܘ ܕܝܠܗ ܐܝܬ. ܘܟܕ ܡܫܬܒܚ ܗܘ ܡܬܝܕܥ ܐܝܬ	ܠܚܘܕܪܐ ܡܕܢܚܐ	ܠܚܘܕܪܐ ܡܕܢܚܐ	ܠܚܘܕܪܐ ܡܕܢܚܐ	ܠܚܘܕܪܐ ܡܕܢܚܐ
10.	ܡܢ ܡܬܠ ܕܟܬܒܐ ܝܠܕܬܐ. ܐܘ ܕܟܠܗܘܢ ܢܦܠܛ ܡܝܬܘܬܐ	ܡܕܢܚܐ	ܡܕܢܚܐ	ܡܕܢܚܐ	ܡܕܢܚܐ
11.	ܐܝܟܢܐ ܚܝܐ ܡܪܐ ܚܝܐ. ܚܢܢܐ ܠܥܒܘܕܐ ܦܫܛܐ ܘܫܠܛܐ	*	*	*	*
12.	ܦܬܚܘ ܫܠܝܚܐ ܦܫܠܡܝܢ. ܕܐܠܗܘܬܗ ܡܫܘܚ ܬܪܥܝܟ ܥܡܡܝܢ	ܗܢ ܥܘܡܪܐ ܠܚܘܕܪܐ ܡܕܢܚܐ	ܗܢ ܥܘܡܪܐ ܠܚܘܕܪܐ ܡܕܢܚܐ	ܗܢ ܥܘܡܪܐ ܠܚܘܕܪܐ ܡܕܢܚܐ	ܗܢ ܥܘܡܪܐ ܠܚܘܕܪܐ ܡܕܢܚܐ
13.	ܦܠܚܘܗ ܦܪܝܩܐ ܒܥܘܡܪܐ. ܫܦܪܘ ܥܘܗ ܗܕܝܐ ܕܪܘܚܐ ܡܥܘܪܐ	ܡܠܟܐ ܠܚܘܕܪܐ	ܡܠܟܐ ܠܚܘܕܪܐ	ܡܠܟܐ ܠܚܘܕܪܐ	ܡܠܟܐ ܠܚܘܕܪܐ
14.	ܐܘ ܚܒܝܒܝ ܦܫܝܛܝܢ. ܢܦܫ ܥܘܕܪܢܐ ܫܠܝܚܐܝܬ	ܣܗܕ ܕܒܝܬ ܡܪܐ	ܣܗܕ ܕܒܝܬ ܡܪܐ	ܣܗܕ ܕܒܝܬ ܡܪܐ	ܣܗܕ ܕܒܝܬ ܡܪܐ
15.	ܚܝܠܐ ܕܦܠܛܘ ܒܢܗܪܐ. ܡܪܕܘܬ ܡܢܐ ܡܢ ܫܪܪܐ	ܠܚܘܕܪܐ ܡܕܢܚܐ	ܠܚܘܕܪܐ ܡܕܢܚܐ	ܠܚܘܕܪܐ ܡܕܢܚܐ	ܠܚܘܕܪܐ ܡܕܢܚܐ
16.	ܐܘ ܚܒܝܒܝ ܝܗܒܬ ܒܟܘܪܣܝܗܘܢ. ܕܐܢܫܐ ܫܠܝܚܐ ܩܕܝܫܘܗܝ ܕܡܫܝܚܐ	*	*	*	*
17.	ܐܘ ܚܒܝܒܝ ܝܘܡܐ ܥܕܬܐ. ܒܕܘܟܪܢܗܘܢ ܕܫܠܝܚܐ ܩܕܝܫܘܗܝ ܕܡܫܝܚܐ	*	*	*	*
18.	ܒܫܩܩܐ ܪܘܚܐ ܕܫܠܝܚܘܬܐ ܕܩܠܗܘܢ ܦܪܝܢ. ܫܠܝܚܐ ܐܒܐ ܦܬܓܡܐ ܘܦܝܫܘ	*	*	*	*
19.	ܡܢ ܫܡܝܐ ܕܡܫܝܚܐ. ܬܠܡܝܕܘ ܠܟܘܠܗ ܐܘ ܗܘܝܐ	*	*	*	*

		C1 1568	C2 1568	D2 1575	B2 1581
20.	[illegible]	*	*	*	
21.	[illegible]		[illegible]		
22.	[illegible]	*			*
23.	[illegible]	ܗܪܟܐ ܡܠܦܢܐ ܗܟܢ ܢܘܗܪܐ	ܗܪܟܐ ܡܠܦܢܐ ܗܟܢ ܢܘܗܪܐ	ܗܪܟܐ ܡܠܦܢܐ ܗܟܢ ܢܘܗܪܐ	ܗܪܟܐ ܡܠܦܢܐ ܗܟܢ ܢܘܗܪܐ
24.	[illegible]	ܗܪܟܐ	ܗܪܟܐ	ܗܪܟܐ	ܗܪܟܐ
25.	[illegible]	ܠܚܘܕܝܗ ܗܪܟܐ	ܡܠܦܢܐ ܠܚܘܕܝܗ ܗܪܟܐ	ܡܠܦܢܐ ܠܚܘܕܝܗ ܗܪܟܐ	ܡܠܦܢܐ ܠܚܘܕܝܗ ܗܪܟܐ
26.	[illegible]	*	ܠܚܘܕܝܗ ܗܪܟܐ	ܡܠܦܢܐ ܠܚܘܕܝܗ ܗܪܟܐ	ܠܚܘܕܝܗ ܗܪܟܐ
27.	[illegible]	*	ܗܪܟܐ	*	ܗܪܟܐ
28.	[illegible]	ܡܠܦܢܐ ܠܚܘܕ [sic]	ܡܠܦܢܐ ܠܚܘܕܝܗ	ܡܠܦܢܐ ܠܚܘܕܝܗ	ܡܠܦܢܐ ܠܚܘܕܝܗ
29.	[illegible]	ܟܠܗ ܡܢ ܟܠܗ	ܟܠܗ ܡܢ ܟܠܗ	ܟܠܗ ܡܢ ܟܠܗ	ܟܠܗ ܡܢ ܟܠܗ
30.	[illegible]	[illegible]	[illegible]	[illegible]	[illegible]
31.	[illegible]	ܡܠܦܢܐ ܠܚܘܕܝܗ ܗܪܟܐ	ܡܠܦܢܐ ܠܚܘܕܝܗ ܗܪܟܐ	ܡܠܦܢܐ ܠܚܘܕܝܗ ܗܪܟܐ	ܡܠܦܢܐ ܠܚܘܕܝܗ ܗܪܟܐ
32.	[illegible]	ܠܚܘܕܝܗ ܗܪܟܐ	ܠܚܘܕܝܗ ܗܪܟܐ	ܠܚܘܕܝܗ ܗܪܟܐ	ܠܚܘܕܝܗ ܗܪܟܐ
33.	[illegible]	ܗܪܟܐ	ܗܪܟܐ	ܗܪܟܐ	ܗܪܟܐ
34.	[illegible]	ܡܠܦܢܐ ܗܪܟܐ	ܗܪܟܐ	ܗܪܟܐ	ܗܪܟܐ
35.	[illegible]	ܗܪܟܐ	ܗܪܟܐ	ܗܪܟܐ	ܗܪܟܐ
36.	[illegible]	ܟܠܗ ܡܢ ܟܠܗ	ܟܠܗ ܡܢ ܟܠܗ	ܟܠܗ ܡܢ ܟܠܗ	ܟܠܗ ܡܢ ܟܠܗ
37.	[illegible]	ܗܪܟܐ	ܗܪܟܐ	ܗܪܟܐ	ܗܪܟܐ
38.	[illegible]	ܗܟܢ ܢܘܗܪܐ	ܗܟܢ ܢܘܗܪܐ	ܗܟܢ ܢܘܗܪܐ	ܗܟܢ ܢܘܗܪܐ
39.	[illegible]	ܟܠܗ ܡܢ ܟܠܗ	ܟܠܗ ܡܢ ܟܠܗ	ܟܠܗ ܡܢ ܟܠܗ	ܟܠܗ ܡܢ ܟܠܗ
40.	[illegible]	ܗܟܢ ܢܘܗܪܐ	ܗܟܢ ܢܘܗܪܐ	ܗܟܢ ܢܘܗܪܐ	ܗܟܢ ܢܘܗܪܐ
41.	[illegible]	ܡܠܦܢܐ ܠܚܘܕܝܗ	ܡܠܦܢܐ ܠܚܘܕܝܗ	ܡܠܦܢܐ ܠܚܘܕ [sic]	ܡܠܦܢܐ ܠܚܘܕܝܗ
42.	[illegible]	ܗܪܟܐ	ܗܪܟܐ	ܗܪܟܐ	ܗܪܟܐ

		C1 1568	C2 1568	D2 1575	B2 1581
43.	ܠܡܪܗ ܢܗܘܐ ܫܘܒܚܐ ܕܪܘܚܐ. ܠܟܝܢ ܡܠܦܢܐ ܗܟܝܢ ܗܘܠܟܝܢ	ܡܠܦܢܐ ܓܝܘܪܓܝܣ ܘܪܕܐ	ܡܠܦܢܐ ܓܝܘܪܓܝܣ	ܡܠܦܢܐ ܓܝܘܪܓܝܣ	ܡܠܦܢܐ ܓܝܘܪܓܝܣ
44.	ܠܥܡܐ ܕܫܠܝܚܐ ܡܫܝܚܝܬܐ. ܢܥܕܐ ܕܡܠܟܐ ܥܠ ܡܫܝܚܝܬܐ	ܕܝܠܗ ܗܘ ܕܝܠܗ	ܕܝܠܗ ܗܘ ܕܝܠܗ	ܕܝܠܗ	ܕܝܠܗ ܗܘ ܕܝܠܗ
45.	ܝܘܡ ܐܠܗܐ ܕܩܕܝܫܬܐ. ܘܝܘܡ ܡܫܝܚܐ ܕܥܡܝܩܬܐ	ܓܝܘܪܓܝ [sic]	ܘܪܕܐ	ܡܠܦܢܐ ܓܝܘܪܓܝܣ	ܘܪܕܐ
46.	ܝܘܡ ܢܒܝܐ ܡܠܟܐ ܝܫܝܥܬܐ ܘܝܘܡ ܡܪܘܡܘܬܐ ܡܠܟܐ ܡܪܘܡܬܐ	ܡܠܦܢܐ ܓܝܘܪܓܝܣ ܘܪܕܐ	ܡܠܦܢܐ ܓܝܘܪܓܝܣ ܘܪܕܐ	ܡܠܦܢܐ ܓܝܘܪܓܝܣ ܘܪܕܐ	ܡܠܦܢܐ ܓܝܘܪܓܝܣ ܘܪܕܐ
47.	ܣܓܝܕ ܘܡܫܒܚ ܡܠܟ ܣܓܝܐ ܐܢܐ. ܡܠܟ ܣܓܝܐ ܐܢܐ ܐܦ ܡܫܝܚܐ ܐܢܐ	ܕܝܠܗ ܗܘ ܕܝܠܗ	ܕܝܠܗ ܗܘ ܕܝܠܗ	ܕܝܠܗ ܗܘ ܕܝܠܗ	ܕܝܠܗ ܗܘ ܕܝܠܗ
48.	ܒܪܝܟ ܕܒܗ ܒܡܪܢܘܬܗ ܠܐ ܒܗܪܝ. ܐܠܐ ܐܦܝܣ ܡܠܟܐ ܒܗܪܝ	ܕܝܠܗ ܗܘ ܕܝܠܗ	ܕܝܠܗ ܗܘ ܕܝܠܗ	ܕܝܠܗ ܗܘ ܕܝܠܗ	ܕܝܠܗ ܗܘ ܕܝܠܗ
49.	ܒܪܝܟ ܕܒܗ ܒܝܬ ܡܥܡܪ ܓܒܒܢ. ܒܚܝܠܗ ܢܣܟܝ ܓܒܒܝ	ܘܪܕܐ	ܘܪܕܐ	ܘܪܕܐ	ܘܪܕܐ
50.	ܐܘ ܡܫܒܚܐ ܫܡܟ ܡܬܝܕܥܢܘ. ܘܫܡܟ ܡܠܟܐ ܕܪܘܚܐ ܕܩܘܕܫܐ	*	*	*	*
51.	ܫܡܟ ܡܬܝܕܥܢܘ ܦܪܘܩܐ. ܡܠܟܐ ܗܘܝܬ ܡܫܒܚܢ ܡܠܟ ܪܘܚܐ	ܐܦܪܝܡ ܡܠܦܢܐ	ܐܦܪܝܡ ܡܠܦܢܐ	ܐܦܪܝܡ ܡܠܦܢܐ	ܐܦܪܝܡ ܡܠܦܢܐ
52.	ܒܝܫܐ ܒܡܘܕܝܢ ܠܟܘܢ. ܡܛܠ ܡܠܟ ܠܡܫܝܚܟܘܢ	ܐܠܝܐ ܡܝܛܪܦܘܠܝܛܐ ܕܨܘܒܐ	ܐܠܝܐ ܡܝܛܪܦܘܠܝܛܐ ܕܨܘܒܐ	ܐܠܝܐ ܡܝܛܪܦܘܠܝܛܐ ܕܨܘܒܐ	ܐܠܝܐ ܡܝܛܪܦܘܠܝܛܐ ܕܨܘܒܐ
53.	ܒܗ ܗܝܡܢܘ ܐܢܫܐ ܒܒܪܝܬܐ. ܡܬܦܪܥܘ ܠܟܠܗܘܢ ܥܡܡܐ	ܡܠܦܢܐ ܘܪܕܐ	ܓܝܘܪܓܝܣ ܘܪܕܐ	ܡܠܦܢܐ ܘܪܕܐ	ܓܝܘܪܓܝܣ ܘܪܕܐ
54.	ܡܢܘ ܕܢܦܫܗ ܒܟܠ ܫܥܝܢ. ܘܡܢܘ ܝܕܥܐ ܐܦ ܝܠܕܐ ܟܠܗܝܢ	ܡܠܦܢܐ ܓܝܘܪܓܝܣ	ܡܠܦܢܐ ܓܝܘܪܓܝܣ	ܘܪܕܐ	ܡܠܦܢܐ ܓܝܘܪܓܝܣ
55.	ܐܢܘ ܕܢܦܫܗ ܕܝܢܐ. ܦܪܝܫܐ ܕܚܝܠܐ ܘܢܝܚܐ ܗܘܐ	ܘܪܕܐ	ܘܪܕܐ	ܘܪܕܐ	ܘܪܕܐ
56.	ܐܘ ܡܫܝܚܐ ܡܪܐ ܡܠܟܐ. ܐܘ ܡܦܪܩܢ ܡܪܐ ܡܢܝܚܢ	ܘܪܕܐ	ܡܠܦܢܐ ܓܝܘܪܓܝܣ ܘܪܕܐ	ܡܠܦܢܐ ܓܝܘܪܓܝܣ	ܡܠܦܢܐ ܓܝܘܪܓܝܣ
57.	ܐܘ ܢܘܗܪܐ ܡܪܐ ܒܪܝܫ. ܘܡܪܐ ܗܝܟ ܝܢܝܩ ܘܡܪܐ ܡܪܒܝܢܝ	ܘܪܕܐ	ܘܪܕܐ	ܘܪܕܐ	ܘܪܕܐ
58.	ܐܘ ܫܘܒܚܐ ܕܒܝܠܕܗ. ܘܫܘܒܚܐ ܕܒܝܠܕܗ	ܡܪܝ ܫܠܝܡܘܢ ܕܦܪܬ ܡܝܫܢ	*	*	*
59.	ܡܪܐ ܕܟܠ ܡܪܘܬܐ. ܐܦ ܢܗܘܪܐ ܕܟܠ ܡܪܘܬܐ	ܡܠܦܢܐ ܓܝܘܪܓܝܣ ܘܪܕܐ	ܡܠܦܢܐ ܓܝܘܪܓܝܣ ܘܪܕܐ	ܡܠܦܢܐ ܓܝܘܪܓܝܣ ܘܪܕܐ	ܡܠܦܢܐ ܓܝܘܪܓܝܣ ܘܪܕܐ
60.	ܡܠܟܐ ܕܡܠܟܘܬܐ. ܡܥܒܕܐ ܐܒܗܘܗܝ ܒܥܒܕܘܬܐ	ܘܪܕܐ	ܘܪܕܐ	ܘܪܕܐ	ܘܪܕܐ
61.	ܒܪܐ ܕܠܐ ܒܘܗ ܠܗ ܫܘܠܛܢܐ. ܘܝܗܒ ܒܗܘܠܟܐ ܡܠܟ ܡܠܟܘܬܐ	وردا[33]	ܘܪܕܐ	ܘܪܕܐ	ܘܪܕܐ
62.	ܒܫܘܒܚܐ ܕܡܫܝܚܐ ܡܪܐ ܢܘܗܪܐ. ܘܒܫܠܝܚܘܗܝ ܢܘܗܪܐ ܢܘܗܪܐ	ܡܠܦܢܐ ܓܝܘ ܗܘܝ ܛܘܒܢܐ [sic]	ܡܠܦܢܐ ܓܝܘܪܓܝܣ ܗܘܝ ܛܘܒܢܐ	ܡܠܦܢܐ ܓܝܘܪܓܝܣ ܗܘܝ ܛܘܒܢܐ	ܡܠܦܢܐ ܓܝܘܪܓܝܣ ܛܘܒܢܐ [sic]
63.	ܡܠܟܐ ܕܡܠܟܐ ܠܗ ܦܠܚܝܢ. ܘܫܝܡܢܐ ܠܫܡܗ ܡܫܡܫܝܢ	ܡܠܦܢܐ ܓܝܘ [sic]	ܡܠܦܢܐ ܓܝܘܪܓܝܣ	ܡܠܦܢܐ ܓܝܘܪܓܝܣ	ܡܠܦܢܐ ܓܝܘܪܓܝܣ
64.	ܒܫܡ ܐܠܗܐ ܕܫܡܝܐ. ܕܒܐܠܗܘ ܕܒܪܐ ܐܠܗܘܬܐ	ܓܝܘܪܓܝܣ ܘܪܕܐ	ܘܪܕܐ	ܘܪܕܐ	ܘܪܕܐ
65.	ܒܟܠܡܐ ܡܪܐ ܫܡܝܐ ܘܐܪܥܐ. ܒܪܘܚܐ ܕܩܘܕܫܐ ܘܡܪܐ	ܘܪܕܐ	ܘܪܕܐ	ܘܪܕܐ	ܘܪܕܐ

[33] The name Wardā is written in Arabic.

		C1 1568	C2 1568	D2 1575	B2 1581
66.	ܒܚܘܒܐ ܕܒܪܐ ܫܡܥܘܢ ܗܦܟܘ. ܕܡܠܠ ܫܢܐ ܒܠܒܟ ܠܘܩܒܠܗ	ܥܡܐ	*	ܡܠܦܢܐ ܠܚܘܕܝܗ	*
67.	ܒܬܪ ܕܐܬܚܙܝܘ ܡܕܝܢܬܐ. ܦܬܚ ܫܘܦܪܐ ܕܝܘܡܐ ܕܐܬܐ	ܠܚܘܕܝܗ ܥܡܐ	ܠܚܘܕܝܗ ܥܡܐ	ܠܚܘܕܝܗ ܥܡܐ	ܠܚܘܕܝܗ ܥܡܐ
68.	ܡܪܝܡܘ ܐܝܟ ܕܝܢܝܬܐ. ܒܫܦܝܪܘܬܐ ܕܡܫܝܚܘܬܐ	*	*	*	*
69.	ܢܫܒܚ ܟܠܗ ܠܟ ܗܘܢܐ. ܡܫܒܚܘ ܢܦܫܐ ܡܫܪܝܗ ܢܦܫܐ	ܥܡܐ	ܥܡܐ	ܥܡܐ	ܥܡܐ
70.	ܐܘ ܕܠܥܠܡܝܢܫܝܐ ܕܟܠܢ. ܡܠܬܟܠܬܗ ܡܣܪܣܪܢ	ܥܡܐ	*	*	*
71.	ܐܘ ܒܝܬܐ ܡܢ ܟܠ ܕܠܗ ܠܟܠܐ ܟܠ. ܟܠ ܡܣܟܢܐ ܠܟܠ ܡܢܘܬܐ ܠܟܠ	ܥܡܐ	ܥܡܐ	ܥܡܐ	ܥܡܐ
72.	ܒܬܪ ܒܪܘܟܘܬ ܕܡܫܝܚܐ. ܕܗܘܝܘ ܒܬܪܐ ܠܥܠܡܐ ܒܬܪܐ	ܡܠܦܢܐ ܠܚܘܕܝܗ ܥܡܐ	ܡܠܦܢܐ ܠܚܘܕܝܗ	ܡܠܦܢܐ ܠܚܘܕܝܗ	ܡܠܦܢܐ ܠܚܘܕܝܗ
73.	ܐܘ ܐܝܟ ܡܚܒܪܐ ܒܗ. ܒܝܘܡܐ ܢܘܟܪܝܐ ܡܫܪܐ ܠܗ	*	*	*	*
74.	ܡܥܝܢܐ ܫܪܝܪܐ ܕܡܫܝܚܘܬܐ. ܗܡܠܠܗ ܕܐܠܗܐ ܡܠܟܐ	ܗܟܢܐ ܐܡܪ ܒܪ ܦܠܓܘܬ ܥܡܐ	ܗܟܢܐ ܐܡܪ ܒܪ ܦܠܓܘܬ ܥܡܐ	ܗܟܢܐ ܐܡܪ ܒܪ ܦܠܓܘܬ ܥܡܐ	ܗܟܢܐ ܐܡܪ ܒܪ ܦܠܓܘܬ ܥܡܐ
75.	ܫܢ ܠܗ ܠܬܚܬ ܢܦܫܐ ܒܬܪ. ܫܢܐ ܕܒܪܐ ܠܕܪܝ ܒܫܡܐ ܥܠܝܟ	ܥܡܐ	ܥܡܐ	ܥܡܐ	ܥܡܐ
76.	ܡܪܐ ܕܡܟܢܐ ܠܟܠܗܘܢ. ܕܡܘܬܐ ܡܚܘܫܢܐ ܠܚܢܢ ܒܬܪܗ	ܠܚܘܕܝܗ ܥܡܐ	ܠܚܘܕܝܗ ܥܡܐ	ܠܚܘܕܝܗ ܥܡܐ	ܠܚܘܕܝܗ ܥܡܐ
77.	ܡܢ ܟܠ ܫܢܝ ܠܐܬܪܥܝܬܐ. ܕܢܫܠܡ ܒܬܪܐ ܝܘܡܐ ܕܢܦܩܬ	ܠܚܘܕܝܗ ܕܡܫܡܫܢܐ ܥܡܐ	ܠܚܘܕܝܗ ܥܡܐ	ܠܚܘܕܝܗ ܥܡܐ	ܠܚܘܕܝܗ ܥܡܐ
78.	ܦܠܓܐ ܕܡܢܟܐ ܘܡܢܟܝܬܐ. ܕܠܥܠܡܐ ܟܠ ܗܝܟ ܠܗ ܡܒܪܟܬܐ	ܠܚܘܕ ܥܡܐ [sic]	ܠܚܘܕܝܗ ܥܡܐ	ܠܚܘܕܝܗ ܥܡܐ	ܠܚܘܕܝܗ ܥܡܐ
79.	ܒܝܬܗ ܕܫܡܝܐ ܗܝܟ ܢܗܪܐ. ܡܢܝܢ ܥܘܬܪܐ ܠܟܢܫܐ ܡܠܟܐ	ܥܡܐ	ܥܡܐ	ܥܡܐ	ܥܡܐ
80.	ܒܫܡܗ ܕܐܒܐ ܚܢܢܐ. ܘܒܗ ܐܠܗܐ ܘܫܠܡܐ ܥܡܢ	ܥܡܐ	ܥܡܐ	ܥܡܐ	ܥܡܐ
81.	ܒܢܘܗܪܐ ܢܘܗܪܐ ܕܩܘܕܫܐ. ܝܒܐ ܒܪܬܐ ܕܒܪܐ ܟܠܗܘܢ	ܥܡܐ	ܥܡܐ	ܥܡܐ	ܥܡܐ
82.	ܒܪܐ ܫܠܡܐ ܢܒܚܐ. ܠܒܝܬܗ ܠܦܓܪܐ ܕܩܕܫܐ	ܥܡܐ	ܥܡܐ	ܥܡܐ	ܥܡܐ
83.	ܐܒܐ ܗܘܝ ܠܟ ܡܬܢܒܪܐ. ܒܪܐ ܢܚܘܬܐ ܗܘܝ ܡܬܦܠܓܐ	ܥܡܐ	ܡܠܦܢܐ ܠܚܘܕܝܗ ܥܡܐ	ܡܠܦܢܐ ܠܚܘܕܝܗ ܥܡܐ	ܡܠܦܢܐ ܠܚܘܕܝܗ ܥܡܐ
84.	ܒܪܬܐ ܕܫܘܒܚܐ ܫܡܥܠܗ ܗܦܟܘ. ܘܒܫܠܡܗ ܘܢܬܠܗ ܡܬܡܪܘܡ ܗܦܟܘ.	ܠܚܘܕܝܗ ܥܡܐ	ܠܚܘܕܝܗ ܥܡܐ	ܠܚܘܕܝܗ ܥܡܐ	ܠܚܘܕܝܗ ܥܡܐ
85.	ܒܥܕܗ ܥܒܕܩܘܐ ܦܬܠܝܗ. ܕܐܬܚܫܒܘܢ ܡܥܡܘܕܝܢ ܗܟܠܗ ܥܡܝ	ܥܡܐ	ܡܠܦܢܐ ܥܡܐ	ܡܠܦܢܐ ܥܡܐ	ܡܠܦܢܐ ܠܚܘܕܝܗ ܥܡܐ
86.	ܬܪܘܢܐ ܕܟܠ ܢܒܝܝܐ. ܘܡܢܒܝܐ ܕܒܝܫܬܐ	ܥܡܐ	ܥܡܐ	ܥܡܐ	ܥܡܐ
87.	ܦܪܘ ܡܥܡܕ ܕܢܝܚܐ. ܒܪܬܐ ܠܚܝܢܐ ܡܚܝܢܐ ܒܠܒܟܠ	ܥܡܐ	ܥܡܐ	ܥܡܐ	ܥܡܐ
88.	ܠܥܠܡܐ ܕܫܘܒܚܐ ܢܠܟܗ. ܘܡܫܘܒܚܐ ܕܒܪܐ ܫܡܝܐ	ܥܡܐ	ܗܢܐ ܒܥܘܬܐ	ܡܠܦܢܐ ܗܢܐ ܒܥܘܬܐ	ܗܢܐ ܒܥܘܬܐ
89.	ܐܘ ܟܠܗ ܢܘܦܪܐ ܥܡܚܝܐ. ܠܐܠܗܐ ܟܠܐ ܒܪܘܚܐ ܗܘܐ	ܟܗܢ ܡܠܦܢܐ ܐܟܚܕܐ ܥܡ ܡܫܡܫܢܐ	ܟܗܢ ܡܠܦܢܐ ܐܟܚܕܐ ܥܡ ܡܫܡܫܢܐ	ܟܗܢ ܡܠܦܢܐ ܐܟܚܕܐ ܥܡ ܡܫܡܫܢܐ	ܟܗܢ ܡܠܦܢܐ ܐܟܚܕܐ ܥܡ ܡܫܡܫܢܐ

		C1 1568	C2 1568	D2 1575	B2 1581
90.	ܐܠܗܐ ܐܝܬܝܗ ܡܠܬܐ. ܫܘܐ ܥܡ ܐܒܘܗܝ ܒܐܝܬܘܬܐ	*	*	*	*
91.	ܐܘܪܚܗ ܕܒܪܐ ܚܒܝܒܐ. ܠܐ ܡܬܕܪܟܐ ܠܥܝܪܘ̈ܗܝ ܒܩܢܘܡܐ	ܗܕܟܐ	ܗܕܟܐ	ܗܕܟܐ	ܗܕܟܐ
92.	ܐܝܟܢܐ ܕܒܢܝܐ ܠܒܝܬ ܐܒܘܗܝ. ܠܒܝܬ ܡܢ ܐܒܘܗܝ ܘܐܦ ܠܐܒܘܗܝ	ܗܕܟܐ	ܠܚܘܕܝܗ ܗܕܟܐ	ܠܚܘܕܝܗ ܗܕܟܐ	ܠܚܘܕܝܗ ܗܕܟܐ
93.	ܩܡ ܠܐܒܘܗܝ ܒܐܝܕܐ ܦܪܘܩܐ. ܘܥܠܡܐ ܡܬܦܪܩ ܠܟܠܗ ܥܡܡܐ	ܡܠܦܢܐ ܚܡܫܐ	ܡܠܦܢܐ ܚܡܫܐ	ܡܠܦܢܐ ܚܡܫܐ	ܡܠܦܢܐ ܚܡܫܐ
94.	ܥܒܕܐ ܕܥܒܕܗ ܡܫܝܚܐ. ܐܡܪ ܡܫܝܚܐ ܡܫܡܫܢܐ ܡܢܠܬܐ	ܡܠܦܢܐ ܠܚܘܕܝܗ ܗܕܟܐ	ܡܠܦܢܐ ܠܚܘܕܝܗ ܗܕܟܐ	ܡܠܦܢܐ ܠܚܘܕܝܗ ܗܕܟܐ	ܡܠܦܢܐ ܠܚܘܕܝܗ ܗܕܟܐ
95.	ܥܒܝܕܝܢ ܦܬܓܡܝܢ ܐܠܗܝܐ. ܥܒܕܐ ܥܒܕܝ ܘܡܕܒܪܝܢ ܠܟܠܗܝܢ	ܡܠܦܢܐ ܠܚܘܕܝܗ ܗܕܟܐ	ܠܚܘܕܝܗ ܗܕܟܐ	ܡܠܦܢܐ ܠܚܘܕܝܗ ܗܟܢ ܢܘܣܚܐ	ܠܚܘܕܝܗ ܗܕܟܐ
96.	ܥܡ ܐܒܘܗܝ ܒܒܪܝܬܐ ܕܥܠܡܐ. ܘܗܘ ܠܥܠܡ ܩܝܡ ܒܒܝܬܐ	ܠܚܘܕܝܗ ܗܕܟܐ	ܠܚܘܕܝܗ ܗܕܟܐ	ܠܚܘܕܝܗ ܗܕܟܐ	ܠܚܘܕܝܗ ܗܕܟܐ
97.	ܡܢܗ ܗܘܐ ܕܝܫܘܥ ܡܫܝܚܐ. ܢܫܬܒܚ ܒܟܠܗܝܢ ܡܠܟܐ ܕܡܠܟܐ	ܗܕܟܐ	ܗܕܟܐ	ܗܕܟܐ	ܗܕܟܐ
98.	ܐܢܫܐ ܕܒܠܥܕ ܐܒܘܗܝ. ܒܗ ܐܬܒܪܝ ܟܠ ܕܐܝܬܘܗܝ	ܠܚܘܕܝܗ ܗܕܟܐ	ܗܕܟܐ	ܗܕܟܐ	ܗܕܟܐ
99.	ܥܒܕܢܐ ܠܗ ܠܗܘ ܚܝܠܐ. ܘܐܝܟ ܕܐܝܬܘܗܝ ܘܫܒܝܚ ܚܝܠܐ	ܗܕܟܐ	ܗܕܟܐ	ܗܕܟܐ	ܗܕܟܐ
100.	ܗܘ ܡܠܟܐ ܕܥܠܡܐ. ܘܡܪܐ ܕܒܪܝܬܐ ܘܕܟܠܗܝܢ	ܠܚܘܕܝܗ ܗܕܟܐ	ܗܕܟܐ	ܗܕܟܐ	ܗܕܟܐ
101.	ܥܒܕܐ ܕܡܠܟܐ ܡܫܡܠܝܢܐ. ܒܒܪܬܐ ܘܠܐ ܐܝܟ ܡܬܥܒܕܐ	ܗܕܟܐ	ܗܕܟܐ	ܗܕܟܐ	ܗܕܟܐ
102.	ܣܘܥܪܢ ܐܘ ܠܒܝܬܗ ܐܝܬܘܗܝ. ܐܬܬܚܙܝ ܕܥܒܕ ܒܐܝܬܘܬܐ	ܠܚܘܕܝܗ ܗܕܟܐ	ܠܚܘܕܝܗ ܗܕܟܐ	ܠܚܘܕܝܗ ܗܕܟܐ	ܠܚܘܕܝܗ ܗܕܟܐ
103.	ܐܝܟܢܐ ܕܐܝܬ ܠܗ ܡܫܡܫܢܐ. ܕܫܡܝܐ ܘܐܪܥܐ ܠܡܫܡܫܢܐ	ܗܕܟܐ	ܗܕܟܐ	ܗܕܟܐ	ܗܕܟܐ
104.	ܠܐܠܗܐ ܕܝܠܗ ܝܠܕ ܒܪܗ. ܡܬܬܝܕܥܐ ܒܝܕ ܚܝܠܐ ܒܪܝܬܐ	ܡܠܦܢܐ ܗܕܟܐ	ܡܠܦܢܐ ܗܕܟܐ	ܡܠܦܢܐ ܗܕܟܐ	ܡܠܦܢܐ ܗܕܟܐ
105.	ܠܡܫܒܚܘ ܐܠܗܘܬܐ. ܦܪܝܩ ܒܝܕܗ ܒܪܐ ܚܒܝܒܐ	ܡܠܦܢܐ ܠܚܘܕܝܗ ܗܕܟܐ	ܗܕܟܐ	ܗܕܟܐ	ܗܕܟܐ
106.	ܐܠܗܐ ܕܐܝܬ ܐܒܐ. ܒܪܗ ܥܠܝܗ ܐܬܐ ܠܡܘܕܝܘ ܐܒܐ	ܚܣܝܪܐ	ܚܣܝܪܐ	ܚܣܝܪܐ	ܚܣܝܪܐ
107.	ܐܝܟܢܐ ܕܠܒܗ ܐܝܟ ܐܝܬܘܬܗ. ܠܐ ܡܬܦܠܓܐ ܐܝܬ ܐܝܟ ܡܬܚܫܒܐ	ܗܕܟܐ	ܗܕܟܐ	ܗܕܟܐ	ܗܕܟܐ
108.	ܗܘ ܚܝܠܐ ܕܝܠܗ ܐܒܘܗܝ. ܕܐܒܐ ܥܡܗ ܒܪܐ ܦܠܓܐ	ܗܕܟܐ	ܗܕܟܐ	ܗܕܟܐ	ܗܕܟܐ
109.	ܐܝܬܝܗ ܕܐܒܐ ܡܬܩܢܝܐ ܠܥܡ ܒܝܠܕܘܬܗ ܦܪܘܩܐ ܐܠܗܐ	ܗܕܟܐ	ܗܕܟܐ	ܗܕܟܐ	ܗܕܟܐ
110.	ܦܪܘܩܐ ܒܠܗ ܕܡܘܬܐ. ܘܡܢܝܢ ܒܠܗ ܕܒܝܬܘܬܐ	ܗܕܟܐ	*	ܗܕܟܐ	ܗܕܟܐ
111.	ܐܘ ܕܐܬܝܠܕ ܒܟܠ ܚܝܠܘܗܝ. ܘܡܬܦܪܫܝܢ ܒܟܠ ܒܥܒܕܘܗܝ	ܗܕܟܐ	ܗܕܟܐ	ܗܕܟܐ	ܗܕܟܐ
112.	ܐܬܐܒܐ ܡܕܝܢܐ ܕܒܪܝܬܐ. ܘܒܟܠܗ ܕܐܪܥܐ ܐܬܐܒܝܬܐ	*	ܗܕܟܐ	ܗܕܟܐ	ܗܕܟܐ
113.	ܢܦܫܐ ܡܬܚܝܐ ܒܝܘܡܢܐ. ܐܬܒܠܐ ܢܦܫܐ ܚܘܒ ܒܡܘܬܐ	ܠܚܘܕܝܗ ܗܕܟܐ [sic]	ܠܚܘܕܝܗ ܗܕܟܐ	ܠܚܘܕܝܗ ܗܕܟܐ	ܠܚܘܕܝܗ ܗܕܟܐ

		C1 1568	C2 1568	D2 1575	B2 1581
114.	ܦܠܚܐ ܕܫܡܐ ܥܒܕܐ. ܕܒܩܘܫܬܐ ܘܠܐ ܗܘܐ ܕܦܠܚܬܐ	ܠܚܘܕܝܗ ܡܪܒܐ	ܠܚܘܕܝܗ ܡܪܒܐ	ܡܪܒܐ	ܠܚܘܕܝܗ ܡܪܒܐ [sic]
115.	ܐܘ ܣܓܝܐܐ ܦܪܘܫܐ. ܐܘ ܐܝܟܘ ܦܪܝܫܘ ܕܝܠܝܕܐ	ܡܪܒܐ	ܡܪܒܐ	ܡܪܒܐ	ܡܪܒܐ
116.	ܢܘܗܪܐ ܕܢܚ ܥܠ ܢܘܗܪܝܢ. ܕܐܘܡܢ ܡܫܘܡܠܐ ܒܡܝܬܘ ܠܚܝܝܢ	ܡܪܒܐ	ܡܪܒܐ	ܡܪܒܐ	ܡܪܒܐ
117.	ܡܕܢܚܐ ܦܫܝܛܘ ܕܡܕܢܚܐ. ܕܒܠܝܕܘܬܗ ܦܢ ܥܠ ܐܘܡܐ	ܡܠܦܢܐ ܠܚܘܕܝܗ ܡܪܒܐ	ܡܪܒܐ	ܡܪܒܐ	ܡܪܒܐ
118.	ܦܠܦܠܐ ܐܠܗܝܐ. ܡܝܐ ܕܪܚܡܐ ܐܠܗܝܐ	ܡܪܒܐ	ܡܪܒܐ	ܡܠܦܢܐ ܠܚܘܕܝܗ ܡܪܒܐ	ܡܪܒܐ
119.	ܐܘ ܕܒܪܐ ܒܢܝܢ ܠܫܡܝܐ. ܠܠܚܐ ܐܪܝܘܗܝ ܡܫܝܚܐ	ܠܚܘܕܝܗ ܡܪܒܐ	ܠܚܘܕܝܗ ܡܪܒܐ	ܠܚܘܕܝܗ ܡܪܒܐ	ܠܚܘܕܝܗ ܡܪܒܐ
120.	ܝܚܝܕܝܐ ܕܠܒܠ ܒܪܐ ܕܠܒܪ ܡܢܗ ܠܐܒܘܗܝ ܠܗ ܒܪܐ	ܡܠܦܢܐ ܠܚܘܕܝܗ ܡܪܒܐ	ܡܪܒܐ	ܡܠܦܢܐ ܡܪܒܐ	ܡܪܐ [sic]
121.	ܡܠܟܐ ܘܡܪܐ ܕܟܠ ܡܠܟܐ. ܕܒܐܝܕܘܗܝ ܐܢܘܢ ܟܠܗܘܢ ܡܠܟܐ	ܡܪܒܐ	ܡܪܒܐ	ܡܪܒܐ	ܡܪܒܐ
122.	ܡܠܟܐ ܕܐܘܡܐ ܝܩܝܪܐ. ܕܐܬܐ ܕܢܦܪܘܩ ܠܐܪܡܝܐ	ܡܠܦܢܐ ܡܪܒܐ	ܡܠܦܢܐ ܡܪܒܐ	ܡܠܦܢܐ ܡܪܒܐ	ܡܠܦܢܐ ܡܪܒܐ
123.	ܡܕܢܚܐ ܦܫܝܛܘ ܕܡܕܢܚܐ. ܗܘ ܕܐܝܬܘܗܝ ܦܢ ܥܠ ܐܘܡܐ	ܡܪܒܐ	ܡܪܒܐ	ܠܚܘܕܝܗ ܡܪܒܐ	ܡܪܒܐ
124.	ܡܪܐ ܕܒܪܝܬܐ ܘܕܒܢܝܐ. ܐܦ ܬܘܕܝܬܐ ܕܟܠ ܐܢܫܝܢ	ܠܚܘܕܝܗ ܡܪܒܐ	ܠܚܘܕܝܗ ܡܪܒܐ	ܠܚܘܕܝܗ ܡܪܒܐ	ܠܚܘܕܝܗ ܡܪܒܐ
125.	ܦܪܘܩܐ ܕܟܠ ܝܠܝܕܬܐ. ܢܡܐ ܕܒܪܐ ܡܠܝܐ ܢܨܝܚܬܐ	ܠܚܘܕ ܡܪܒܐ[sic]	ܡܪܒܐ	ܡܠܦܢܐ ܡܪܒܐ	ܡܪܒܐ
126.	ܐܢܫܐ ܕܐܘܡܐ ܒܢܝ ܩܝܡܬܗܘܢ ܐܬܐ ܠܐܪܥܐ ܕܢܦܫܐ ܠܦܪܩܗܘܢ	ܡܠܦܢܐ ܡܪܒܐ	ܡܪܒܐ	ܡܠܦܢܐ ܡܪܒܐ	ܡܪܒܐ
127.	ܥܒܕܢܐ ܠܗ ܠܗܝ ܝܠܕܬܐ. ܕܒܪܬ ܡܢܗܘܢ ܥܠ ܒܝܬܗܐ	ܡܠܦܢܐ ܠܚܘܕܝ [sic]	ܡܠܦܢܐ ܠܚܘܕܝܗ ܡܪܒܐ	ܡܠܦܢܐ ܠܚܘܕܝܗ ܡܪܒܐ	ܡܠܦܢܐ ܠܚܘܕܝܗ ܡܪܒܐ
128.	ܢܘܪܐ ܡܬܚܙܝܐ ܠܐܠܗܘܬܗ. ܕܦܪܥܬ ܠܚܝܐ ܒܒܪܐ ܕܝܢܢ	*	*	*	*
129.	ܡܪܝ ܕܝܢ ܟܕ ܐܬܚܙܝ ܗܘܐ. ܕܥܒܕܝܗ ܠܩܕܝܫܘܗܝ ܒܫܘܪܐ ܗܘܐ	ܡܠܦܢܐ ܠܚܘܕܝܗ ܡܪܒܐ	ܠܚܘܕܝܗ ܡܪܒܐ	ܡܠܦܢܐ ܠܚܘܕܝܗ ܡܪܒܐ	ܠܚܘܕܝܗ ܡܪܒܐ
130.	ܝܡܝܢܗ ܕܐܒܐ ܡܬܦܩܕܐ ܕܒܗ ܐܠܗܘܬܗ ܥܡܐ ܒܐܘܟܠܐ	ܡܪܒܐ	ܡܪܒܐ	ܡܪܒܐ	ܡܪܒܐ
131.	ܐܒܗܬܐ ܕܝܢ ܡܬܗܦܟ ܕܒܝܘܡܝܗ ܒܪܝ. ܘܐܒܩܪܐ ܠܥܒܕܐ ܢܘܟܪܝ	*	*	*	*
132.	ܥܒܝܕ ܘܡܪܡܪܡ ܡܪܐ ܥܠ. ܕܚܙܐ ܒܝܘܡܗ ܡܢܡܪܗ ܠܚܝܐ	ܕܝܢ ܠܥܒܕܝܢܢ ܒܪ ܥܒܕܪܗ	ܕܝܢ ܠܥܒܕܝܢܢ ܒܒܪ ܥܒܕܪܗ	ܕܝܢ ܠܥܒܕܝܢܢ ܒܪ ܥܒܕܪܗ	ܕܝܢ ܠܥܒܕܝܢܢ ܒܪ ܥܒܕܪܗ
133.	ܒܪܝܟ ܗܘ ܡܥܒܕ ܡܢܝܚܢܐ. ܐܒܘܝ ܘܡܪܐ ܕܦܪܩܢ ܡܢܟܝܢ	ܡܪܝ ܫܒܪܝܫܘܥ ܕܒܗ ܡܡܐ	ܡܪܝ ܫܒܪܝܫܘܥ ܕܒܗ ܡܡܐ	ܡܪܝ ܫܒܪܝܫܘܥ ܕܒܗ ܡܡܐ	ܡܪܝ ܫܒܪܝܫܘܥ ܕܒܗ ܡܡܐ
134.	ܒܪܝܟܘ ܡܥܒܕ ܡܬܠܠܢܝ. ܐܒܘܝ ܘܡܪܐ ܕܟܠܢ ܡܢܝܚܢ	*	*	*	*
135.	ܒܪܟ ܡܢܢ. ܡܒܪܟ ܕܡܢ. ܠܒܪܐ ܘܐܟܝܕܐ ܠܗܘܢ ܡܥܒܕ ܡܪܝ	*	*	*	*
136.	- ܥܘܒܕܐ ܘܡܪܝ ܝܕܥܬܐ. ܠܒܪܐ ܕܠܚܝܠ ܡܝܬܪܐ ܕܠܚܣܐ..... - ܗܡܝܢܐ . ܡܟܬܒ ܗܠܝܢ ܡܪܝ ܕܝܫܘܥ	*	*	*	*
137.	ܐܘ ܚܟܝܡܐ ܣܓܝ ܒܥܘܬܐ ܗܘܐ. ܐܘ ܚܟܝܡܐ ܦܪܝܫ ܒܪܥܐ ܗܘܐ	*	*		*

		C1 1568	C2 1568	D2 1575	B2 1581
138.	ܡܫܝܚܐ ܠܚܕܐ ܐܦܢܝ. ܒܐܘܢܓܠܝܘܢ ܡܪܝܐ ܕ...				
139.	ܒܪܐ ܕܐܠܗܐ ܡܬܘܕܝܢܐ. ܕܒܪܐ ܒܟܝܢܐ ܡܢ ܫܘܪܝܐ				
140.	ܒܟܝܢܗ ܡܫܝܚܐ ܦܪܘܩܢ. ܕܝܠܕ ܚܘܒܗ ܐܘܪܚ ܩܢܘܡܗ				
141.	ܒܐܘܪܚܐ ܕܩܠܝܠܐ ܪܕܘ ܚܘܫܒܝܢ. ܘܚܘܪܝ ܟܪܟܐ ܕܒܢܝ ܫܢܝܢܗܘܢ				
142.	ܒܫܡܐ ܦܠܛܗ ܒܫܠܡܐ. ܕܫܘܠܛܢ ܗܠܝܢ ܫܢܝܢ ܠܫܢܬܐ				
143.	ܐܘ ܦܘܪܩܢܐ ܒܬܫܒܘܚܬܐ. ܦܘܪܩܢܐ ܒܪܘܚܬܐ				
144.	ܐܘ ܚܒܝܒܝ ܫܡܥܘܢ. ܫܒܝܚܐ ܒܫܡܝܐ ܘܒܐܪܥܐ				
145.	ܟܠ ܒܢܝܢܫܐ ܦܪܝܩܐ. ܐܦܟܠ ܒܢܘܟܪܝܐ ܦܪܝܩܐ				
146.	ܫܪܒܐ ܕܡܠܟܐ ܕܪܘܚܐ. ܦܠܓ ܒܗ ܒܪܝܬܐ ܕܝܩܢܐ				
147.	ܕܝ ܗܠܝܢ ܡܪܝ ܠܒܪ ܦܫܛܐ. ܐܝܟ ܦܘܩܕܐ ܘܫܠܝܚܐ				
148.	ܫܪܝܪ ܒܫܡܐ ܒܫܘܠܛܢܐ. ܕܟܠܗܝܢ ܕܦܘܡܐ ܠܫܡܝܐ				
149.	ܢܦܩ ܦܘܩܕܢܐ ܡܢ ܡܠܟܐ. ܘܐܬܚܙܝ ܠܗܘ ܒܬܫܒܘܚܬܐ	*			
150.	ܐܘ ܚܒܝܒܝ ܝܬܝܪܐ. ܒܝܠܕܗ ܕܐܒܘܗܝ ܘܐܚܐ	*		*	
151.	ܫܘܒܚܐ ܠܒܪܝܫܝܬ ܦܪܘܩ. ܕܝܗܒ ܚܝܐ ܚܘܒܐ ܕܡܫܝܚܐ ܠܥܠܡ			ܡܪܝ ܝܘܚܢܢ ܐܠܗܐ ܡܬܩܠܣܐ ܗܪܟܐ	
152.	ܠܒܝܬ ܝܕܥܐ ܡܫܪܪܐ. ܒܫܠܡܐ ܕܒܗ ܘܫܘܒܚܐ			ܡܪܝ ܫܠܝܡܘܢ ܡܬܪܦܠܓܐ ܕܦܪܩ ܡܢܢ	
153.	ܐܘܪܚܐ ܢܦܩ ܒܠܝ. ܒܪܘܚܝ ܢܦܫܝ ܕܦܪܘܩ			*	
154.	ܒܢܝܪܗ ܡܫܝܚܐ ܕܫܠܝܚܐ. ܢܬܚܙܐ ܦܠܓ ܕܡܪܝ ܠܥܠܡ			ܡܠܟܐ ܠܡܪܟܘܣ ܚܘܝܢܐ	
155.	ܘܠܗܘ ܗܘ ܦܘܩܕܐ ܕܝܬܒܐ. ܐܦ ܫܡܐ ܕܝܬܒܐ			ܡܪܝ ܡܪܢܫܡܐ ܡܬܩܠܣܐ ܦܠܪܢܘܣ ܚܫܝܫܐ ܕܡܬܒܥ ܒܪܐ ܡܫܝܚܐ	
156.	ܝܗܒܘ ܘܝܬܢܛܠܘ ܫܡܥܘܢ. ܐܬܬܠܒܪܘ ܘܝܬܢܦܩܘ ܐܘ ܚܛܝܬܐ		*	*	*
157.	ܡܪܐ ܕܒܪܝܐ ܘܫܡܝܐ. ܘܫܠܚ ܒܪܚܡܝܗ ܦܘܩܕܐ ܕܝܢܐ			ܡܪܝܫܡܐ ܐܦܣܩܘܦܐ ܡܛܪܦܘܠܝܛܐ ܕܐܬܪܐ ܕܒܪܘܐܪ	
158.	ܡܪܝ ܕܫܠܝܡ ܠܫܡܥܘܢ. ܒܪܘܚܐ ܕܦܠܛܝܐ ܠܟܠܢ				

		C1 1568	C2 1568	D2 1575	B2 1581
159.	ܛܘܒܐ ܠܡܫܝܚܐ ܢܒܥܐ ܬܪܘܨܐ. ܚܝܐ ܓܗܝܐ ܡܘܡܐ ܘܡܫܒܠܢܐ				
160.	ܫܘܒܚܐ ܠܣܘܓܐܝ ܦܪܘܩܢ ܚܠܐ ܗܘܝܐ ܡܪܚܡܢܘܬܟ				

Table 7C

		M3 1586	G1 1300-1400	D3 1400-1600
1.	ܦܫܝܛ ܐܪܚܐ ܘܡܘܥܝܢ ܫܒܝܠܐ. ܠܡܦܩ ܡܠܟܐ ܕܪܘܚܡܢܐ	ܡܠܦܢܐ ܓܘܪܓܝܣ ܘܪܕܐ		ܡܠܦܢܐ ܓܘܪܓܝܣ ܕܡܬܩܪܐ ܘܪܕܐ
2.	ܢܠܒܫ ܕܟܝܐ ܠܢܠܒܘܗ ܙܒܢܐ. ܘܠܐ ܚܫܐ ܡܬܚܡܐ ܘܠܐ ܐܪܥܐ	ܡܠܦܢܐ ܓܘܪܓܝܣ ܘܪܕܐ	ܡܠܦܢܐ ܓܘܪܓܝܣ ܘܪܕܐ	ܡܠܦܢܐ ܓܘܪܓܝܣ ܘܪܕܐ
3.	ܡܢ ܡܟܐ ܠܗ ܠܐܪܥܘܗܝ. ܒܪܐ ܕܠܠܗܐ ܘܠܒܫܐܪܘܗܝ	ܘܪܕܐ		ܘܪܕܐ [sic]
4.	ܫܡܝܢ ܐܪܥ ܬܪܥܝܗܘܢ. ܕܐܢܫܐ ܚܝܐ ܕܟܠ ܒܪ ܐܪܥܗܘܢ	ܓܘܪܓܝܣ ܘܪܕܐ		ܓܘܪܓܝܣ ܘܪܕܐ
5.	ܦܬܚ ܘܪܡܐ ܠܦܘܩܕܢܐ. ܘܟܠ ܒܡܫܝܚܐ ܦܪܘܩܐ ܕܥܠܡܐ	ܡܠܦܢܐ ܓܘܪܓܝܣ ܘܪܕܐ	ܡܠܦܢܐ ܓܘܪܓܝܣ ܘܪܕܐ	ܡܠܦܢܐ ܓܘܪܓܝܣ ܘܪܕܐ [sic]
6.	ܟܠ ܫܡܝܐ ܫܒܚܝܢܝ. ܚܢܢܐ ܛܝܒܘܬܐ ܕܐܪܥܐ ܒܡܫܝܚܘܬܐ	ܡܠܦܢܐ ܓܘܪܓܝܣ ܘܪܕܐ	ܡܠܦܢܐ ܓܘܪܓܝܣ ܘܪܕܐ	ܡܠܦܢܐ ܓܘܪܓܝܣ ܘܪܕܐ
7.	ܒܢܝ ܕܐܪܥܐ ܡܫܒܚܐ ܕܠܠܒܟ. ܫܒܚܘ ܟܠܐ ܕܡܪܢ ܠܒܝܬܐ	ܓܘܪܓܝܣ ܘܪܕܐ		ܓܘܪܓܝܣ ܘܪܕܐ
8.	ܒܪܐ ܕܒܬܘܠܐ ܒܗ ܫܒܚܬܐ. ܘܟܠ ܚܝܠܘܬܐ ܘܕܢܚܐ	ܘܪܕܐ		ܘܪܕܐ
9.	ܒܢܝܐ ܕܡܫܬܐ ܗܘ ܪܘܚܐ ܩܕܫܐ. ܘܒܚܘܫܒܘܢܐ ܗܘ ܡܫܡܫܢ ܩܕܫܐ	ܓܘܪܓܝܣ ܘܪܕܐ	ܡܠܦܢܐ ܓܘܪܓܝܣ ܘܪܕܐ	ܓܘܪܓܝܣ ܘܪܕܐ
10.	ܡܢ ܢܫܡܬ ܕܒܚܝܠܗ ܢܬܒܪܟܐ. ܐܘ ܒܪܚܡܘܗܝ ܫܒܝܠܐ ܘܢܫܬܒܚܐ	ܘܪܕܐ	ܘܪܕܐ	ܘܪܕܐ
11.	ܐܝܬ ܚܕܐ ܘܒܪ ܚܕܐ. ܚܝܐ ܠܚܝܘܬܐ ܓܗܝܐ ܘܠܠܒܐ	*		*
12.	ܦܫܝܛ ܫܠܡܘܬܐ ܫܠܡܝܢ. ܕܐܠܗܘܬܗ ܘܫܘܒ ܐܪܚܐ ܫܒܝܠ	ܗܘܢ ܢܘܗܪܐ ܓܘܪܓܝܣ ܘܪܕܐ	ܗܘܢ ܢܘܗܪܐ ܓܘܪܓܝܣ ܘܪܕܐ	ܗܘܢ ܢܘܗܪܐ ܓܘܪܓܝܣ ܘܪܕܐ
13.	ܦܠܓܘܗ ܕܒܪܐ ܒܘܟܪܐ. ܫܒܘ ܗܘܘ ܥܒܕܐ ܕܪܘܚܐ ܘܫܘܪܐ	ܡܠܦܢܐ ܓܘܪܓܝܣ ܘܪܕܐ		ܡܠܦܢܐ ܓܘܪܓܝܣ
14.	ܐܘ ܡܫܝܚܐ ܦܘܪܩܢܢ. ܢܫܡ ܫܘܒܚܐ ܫܠܝܚܘܬܟ	ܣܗܕܐ ܕܟܠܗ ܡܪܐ		ܣܗܕܐ ܕܟܠܗ ܡܪܐ
15.	ܚܝܠܐ ܕܦܐܝܐ ܒܢܒܝܐ. ܘܢܦܩ ܡܢܐ ܡܢ ܓܒܪܐ	ܓܘܪܓܝܣ ܘܪܕܐ	ܓܘܪܓܝܣ ܘܪܕܐ	ܓܘܪܓܝܣ ܘܪܕܐ
16.	ܐܘ ܡܫܝܚܐ ܫܠܝܚܐ ܒܠܘܗܝܗܘܢ. ܕܒܢܝܐ ܫܠܝܚܐ ܩܕܝܫܘܗܝ ܕܡܫܝܚܐ	*	*	*
17.	ܐܘ ܡܫܝܚܐ ܦܘܩܕ ܫܘܒܚܐ. ܠܘܒܝܠܗܘܢ ܕܫܠܝܚܐ ܩܕܝܫܘܗܝ ܕܡܫܝܚܐ	*	*	*
18.	ܒܦܩܕܐ ܪܘܚܐ ܕܡܠܟܘܬܗ ܕܦܘܠܘܣ ܪܒܐ. ܫܠܝܚܐ ܓܒܪܐ ܦܛܪܘܣ ܘܦܘܠܘܣ	*	*	*
19.	ܡܢ ܢܫܝܗ ܕܡܫܝܚܐ. ܢܠܒܫܘ ܚܘܒܐ ܐܘ ܗܘܒܐ	*	*	*
20.	ܫܡܥܘܢ ܦܛܪܘܣ ܘܦܘܠܘܣ ܒܗ ܚܘܒܐ. ܘܡܫܠܡ ܠܟܠܢ ܕܟܠܢ ܦܪܘܩܢ	*		*

		M3 1586	G1 1300-1400	D3 1400-1600
21.	ܐܘ ܡܫܒܚܐ ܒܟܠ ܬܘܕܝܬܐ. ܘܡܬܩܢܐ ܒܟܠ ܬܫܒܘܚܬܐ			
22.	ܛܘܒܐ ܠܣܒܠܐ ܡܢܝܫܬܗܘܢ. ܕܦܘܠܐ ܘܩܢܐ ܘܡܘܒܠܐ	*		
23.	ܡܫܒܚܬܐ ܕܫܒܝܚܬܐ. ܘܡܬܕܪܫܬܐ ܕܡܫܝܚܬܐ	ܘܪܕܐ ܡܠܦܢܐ ܗܟܢ ܒܗܘܪܐ		
24.	ܡܢ ܒܥܒܕܐ ܕܦܘܩܕܢܐ ܡܢܗ ܘܐܬܬܠܝܬܐ ܕܒܢܝܐ ܒܝܢܬ	ܘܪܕܐ		
25.	ܡܢ ܢܦܫ ܢܘܢ ܡܢ ܢܘܢܐ. ܐܘܠ ܠܒܝܬܐ ܐܝܟ ܦܘܡܪܐ	ܡܠܦܢܐ ܓܝܘܪܓܝܣ ܘܪܕܐ		
26.	ܐܘ ܢܦܫܐ ܕܐܬܦܢܝܬ ܡܢ ܟܠ. ܡܢܘ ܢܦܢܘܢ ܦܢܝܬ ܡܢ ܟܠ	ܓܝܘܪܓܝܣ ܘܪܕܐ	ܡܠܦܢܐ ܓܝܘܪܓܝܣ ܘܪܕܐ	
27.	ܐܘ ܕܒܝܬܐ ܢܘܗܪܐ. ܘܐܝܟ ܕܒܝܬܕܐ ܕܡܢܐ ܒܡܕܒܪܐ	ܘܪܕܐ		
28.	ܒܥܘܬܝ ܫܡܥ ܐܠܗܐ ܠܝ. ܘܡܪܐ ܕܡܫܝܚܐ ܡܬܦܪܥ ܐܢܐ ܠܝ	ܡܠܦܢܐ ܓܝܘܪܓܝܣ	ܕܝܠܗ	
29.	ܠܡܝܬ ܒܡܠܘܟ ܕܡܠܟܘܬܗ. ܝܬܝܒ ܕܐܡܝܢ ܥܡ ܡܠܟܘܬܗ	ܕܝܠܗ ܥܡ ܕܝܠܗ	ܕܝܠܗ ܥܡ ܕܝܠܗ	
30.	ܛܘܒܐ ܠܩܕܝܫܐ ܡܪܝܡ. ܕܦܪܝܫܐ ܠܢܦܫܗ ܐܘܡܢܐ	ܐܪܡܠܬܐ ܣܒܝܬܐ ܘܐܚܪܬܐ ܡܐܪܚܡܢܘܬܐ ܣܦܝܚܐ ܪܒܐ ܡܐܪܐ ܕܡܬܡܢܝܢ ܒܒܪ ܡܫܝܚܐ		
31.	ܬܪܐ ܕܢܒܝܘܬܐ. ܕܠܗ ܘܬܪ ܕܗܘܐ ܢܒܝܘܬܐ	ܡܠܦܢܐ ܓܝܘܪܓܝܣ ܘܪܕܐ	ܡܠܦܢܐ ܓܝܘܪܓܝܣ ܘܪܕܐ	
32.	ܛܘܒܗ ܗܘܐ ܠܒܢܝ ܒܫܪܐ. ܕܠܦܪܐ ܥܠ ܗܘܘ ܢܨܠܘܬܐ	ܓܝܘܪܓܝܣ ܘܪܕܐ		
33.	ܐܠܗܐ ܠܒܝܬܐ ܘܦܫܛ. ܒܢܝܐ ܡܕܝܢܬܐ ܘܡܫܒܠܢܐ	ܘܪܕܐ		
34.	ܬܪܝܢ ܕܝܪܝ ܒܫܠܝܘܬܗ. ܘܐܡܘܪ ܦܪܘܫܘܬܗ	ܘܪܕܐ		
35.	ܒܫܘܒܐ ܕܫܘܠܐ ܢܦܫܐ ܐܢܐ. ܒܠܘܡܝܐ ܕܫܡܝܐ ܗܘ ܢܘܗܪܐ ܐܢܐ	ܘܪܕܐ	ܘܪܕܐ	
36.	ܬܪܝ ܡܫܝܚܐ ܕܢܐܬܐ ܢܣܒܝ. ܘܢܬܠܠܝ ܒܦܫܛܐ ܢܐܬܝ	ܕܝܠܗ ܥܡ ܕܝܠܗ		
37.	ܐܘ ܕܐܡܪܐ ܒܬܠܝܬܝܬܐ. ܦܪܘܩ ܢܦܫܢ ܐܝܟ ܕܒܫܘܒܬܐ	ܘܪܕܐ		
38.	ܢܨ ܩܝܡܬܐ ܕܦܩܕܐ ܠܢܐ ܠܗ. ܬܗܘܡܐ ܕܫܘܒܐ ܕܠܐ ܡܬܕܪܟܐ ܠܗ	ܗܟܢ ܒܗܘܪܐ		
39.	ܬܪܐ ܝܠܕܬ ܕܡܫܝܚܐ. ܣܓܝܐ ܘܫܡܥܐ ܘܢܦܫ ܢܝܢܝܢ	ܕܝܠܗ ܥܡ ܕܝܠܗ		
40.	ܬܪܐ ܕܒܩܘܫܬܐ ܢܡܘܣܐ. ܘܒܠܒܘܬܗ ܦܪܘܩܐ ܠܢܦܫ	ܗܟܢ ܒܗܘܪܐ		
41.	ܢܘܒܪ ܥܡܢ ܘܢܒܝܐ ܡܢ ܟܠ. ܡܠܟܐ ܡܫܝܚܐ ܕܡܫܠܛ ܒܟܠ ܟܠ	ܡܠܦܢܐ ܓܝܘܪܓܝܣ	ܡܠܦܢܐ ܓܝܘܪܓܝܣ	
42.	ܠܒܪܐ ܠܡܝܬ ܒܬܠܝܬܝܬܐ. ܝܕܥܝܢ ܕܐܝܟ ܒܬܪܝܢܘܬܐ	ܘܪܕܐ		
43.	ܠܡܪܗ ܢܩܡܢ ܘܫܠܗ ܕܫܠܝܐ. ܠܗܘܢ ܡܫܠܡܢܐ ܗܝܢ ܗܘܡܢܝܢ	ܡܠܦܢܐ ܓܝܘܪܓܝܣ		

		M3 1586	G1 1300-1400	D3 1400-1600
44.	ܠܥܒܕܐ ܚܣܝܐ ܘܡܗܝܡܢܐ. ܥܘܠ ܕܥܘܠ ܥܡ ܒܬܘܠܬܐ	ܕܒܠܗ ܡܢ ܕܒܠܗ		
45.	ܟܡܐ ܓܠܠܐ ܕܥܠܝܡܘܬܐ. ܘܟܡܐ ܦܣܩܘܠܐ ܕܥܒܕܘܬܐ	ܘܕܐ		
46.	ܟܡܐ ܟܪܐ ܡܠܐ ܝܬܝܪܬܐ ܘܟܡܐ ܦܪܨܘܦܐ ܡܠܐ ܦܪܨܘܦܐ	ܡܠܦܢܐ ܠܫܘܪܝܗ ܘܕܐ		
47.	ܣܓܝܢ ܘܢܣܓܘܢ ܡܐܘܬ ܣܓܝܐ ܐܢܐ. ܡܐܘܬ ܣܓܝܐ ܐܢܐ ܐܦ ܦܣܓܐ ܐܢܐ	ܕܒܠܗ ܡܢ ܕܒܠܗ	ܕܒܠܗ ܡܢ ܕܒܠܗ	
48.	ܒܪܝܟ ܕܡܢ ܒܦܪܨܘܦܘܗܝ ܠܐ ܟܦܪ. ܐܠܐ ܐܘܕܝ ܦܠܓܝܗ ܟܦܪ	ܕܒܠܗ ܡܢ ܕܒܠܗ	ܕܒܠܗ ܡܢ ܕܒܠܗ	
49.	ܒܪܝܟ ܕܡܢ ܠܟܝܢ ܘܒܦܪ ܠܚܝܢ. ܟܝܢܗ ܐܫܟܚ ܠܚܝܢ	ܘܕܐ	ܘܕܐ	
50.	ܐܘ ܢܘܗܪܐ ܥܒܪܘ ܘܢܬܒܪܘ. ܘܟܠܗ ܥܠܐ ܕܪܘܚܐ ܕܩܘܕܫܐ	*		
51.	ܥܒܪܘ ܘܢܬܒܪܘ ܩܕܡܝܐ. ܘܐܠܐ ܬܘܒ ܬܬܟܠܘܢ ܥܠܝ ܪܘܚܐ	ܐܩܪܝܢ ܡܠܦܢܐ		
52.	ܒܝܘܡܐ ܕܐܘܕܝܘ ܠܒܪܝ. ܟܕ ܘܢܦܩ ܠܡܫܝܚܘܬܗ	ܐܠܐ ܡܬܪܓܡܢܝܬܐ ܕܝܘܢܝܐ		
53.	ܡܢ ܫܡܝܐ ܐܢܬܐ ܒܪܝܟܬܐ. ܡܬܬܩܪܝܐ ܠܝܘܡܐ ܦܪܘܩܬܐ	ܠܫܘܪܝܗ ܘܕܐ	ܘܕܐ	
54.	ܡܢܗ ܕܢܦܫܗ ܟܠ ܫܘܒܚ. ܘܡܢܗ ܝܗܒܬ ܐܦ ܝܠܕܐ ܠܟܠܢ	ܡܠܦܢܐ ܠܫܘܪܝܗ	ܡܠܦܢܐ ܠܫܘܪܝܗ	
55.	ܐܝܟܘ ܕܒܫܠܗ ܕܠܝܠܝܐ. ܦܓܪܐ ܦܪܥܐ ܘܢܦܫܐ ܩܘܡܐ	ܘܕܐ	ܘܕܐ	
56.	ܐܘ ܦܪܘܩܢ ܡܪܐ ܦܪܘܩ. ܐܘ ܡܢܗܘܢ ܡܪܐ ܦܪܘܩ	ܡܠܦܢܐ ܠܫܘܪܝܗ	ܡܠܦܢܐ ܠܫܘܪܝܗ	
57.	ܐܘ ܢܘܗܪܗ ܡܪܐ ܒܪܝܟ. ܘܡܪܐ ܗܝܟܠ ܫܡܝܐ ܘܡܪܐ ܡܪܝܡܐ	ܘܕܐ	ܘܕܐ	
58.	ܐܘ ܥܘܬܪܐ ܕܡܠܟܘܬܐ. ܘܡܫܟܚܢܐ ܕܫܠܝܚܘܬܐ	*	*	
59.	ܡܪܐ ܕܟܠ ܡܪܘܬܐ. ܐܦ ܢܘܗܪܐ ܕܟܠ ܥܘܬܪܐ	ܠܫܘܪܝܗ ܡܠܦܢܐ ܘܕܐ	ܡܠܦܢܐ ܠܫܘܪܝܗ ܘܕܐ	ܡܠܦܢܐ ܠܫܘܪܝܗ ܘܕܐ
60.	ܡܠܟܐ ܕܫܒܝܚܘܬܐ. ܡܫܝܚܐ ܐܠܗܘܢ ܒܪܝܟܘܬܐ	ܘܕܐ		ܘܕܐ
61.	ܒܪܐ ܕܐܠܗܐ ܠܟܠ ܥܘܬܪܐ. ܢܘܗܪܐ ܒܥܠܡܐ ܐܠܐ ܡܪܘܬܐ	ܘܕܐ		ܘܕܐ
62.	ܒܥܩܒܝ ܕܪܘܚܐ ܡܪܐ ܟܘܠܗ. ܘܥܠܬܗܘܢ ܡܠܟܘܬܐ ܟܘܠܗ	ܡܠܦܢܐ ܠܫܘܪܝܗ	ܡܠܦܢܐ ܠܫܘܪܝܗ ܗܟܢ ܒܬܘܪܐ	ܡܠܦܢܐ ܠܫܘܪܝܗ ܗܟܢ ܒܬܘܪܐ
63.	ܡܠܟܐ ܕܡܠܟܐ ܠܗ ܦܠܚܝܢ. ܘܪܘܚܢܐ ܠܪܘܡܗ ܡܫܒܚܝܢ	ܡܠܦܢܐ ܠܫܘܪܝܗ	ܡܠܦܢܐ ܠܫܘܪܝܗ	ܡܠܦܢܐ ܠܫܘܪܝܗ
64.	ܒܝܬ ܠܚܡܐ ܐܘܪܫܠܡ. ܕܟܪܝܗܘܢ ܕܝܢܐ ܠܐܘܪܫܠܡ	ܘܕܐ	*	ܘܕܐ
65.	ܒܠܠܡܐ ܡܪܐ ܫܪܪ ܐܘܪܫ. ܕܝܠܘܦܘܬܐ ܡܫܝܚܐ ܐܘܪܫ	ܘܕܐ		ܘܕܐ
66.	ܒܪܘܬܐ ܕܡܪܐ ܫܡܥܬ ܫܡܥܐ. ܕܟܠܗ ܡܪܐ ܒܠܒܗ ܠܫܡܥܐ	*	ܘܕܐ	*
67.	ܒܪܝܟ ܕܒܪܘܟܘ ܡܒܪܟܐ. ܟܪܝܟ ܫܘܒܚܐ ܕܟܢܫܐ ܕܟܢܫܐ	ܠܫܘܪܝܗ ܘܕܐ	ܠܫܘܪܝܗ ܘܕܐ	ܠܫܘܪܝܗ ܘܕܐ

		M3 1586	G1 1300-1400	D3 1400-1600
68.	ܡܪܘܡܘ ܐܚܝ ܒܬܫܒܚܬܗ̇. ܒܬܫܒܘܚܬܐ ܦܪܝܫܬܐ	*	*	*
69.	ܢܬܦܐ ܝܟܠܘ ܠܟ ܗܘܢܐ. ܘܐܬܒܗܘ ܢܦܫܐ ܘܐܬܕܟܝܘ ܐܘܪܚܐ	ܘܪܕܐ	ܘܪܕܐ	
70.	ܐܘ ܕܐܬܥܬܝܩܬܐ ܕܐܠܝܢ. ܘܐܬܥܢܝܢܬܐ ܕܡܬܪܓܪܓܝܢ	*	*	*
71.	ܐܘ ܒܩܝܐ ܡܢ ܟܠ ܕܠܗ ܠܟܠܐ ܟܠ. ܟܠ ܕܡܬܚܙܐ ܠܟܠ ܘܚܙܐ ܠܟܠ	ܘܪܕܐ	ܘܪܕܐ	ܘܪܕܐ
72.	ܒܢܝ ܐܒܪܗܡ ܪܘܚܢܐ. ܕܗܘܘ ܒܢܝܢܐ ܠܥܕܬܐ ܚܕܬܐ	ܡܠܦܢܐ ܓܝܘܪܓܝܣ	ܡܠܦܢܐ ܓܝܘܪܓܝܣ	ܡܠܦܢܐ ܓܝܘܪܓܝܣ
73.	ܗ̇ܘ ܐܚܝ ܕܐܬܬܪܝܡ ܒܗ. ܒܪܘܚܐ ܕܓܠܐ ܕܐܬܪܡܐ ܠܗ	*	ܘܪܕܐ	*
74.	ܡܫܝܚܐ ܡܪܢ ܕܡܬܥܒܕܬܐ. ܘܡܠܟܘ ܕܐܠܗܐ ܡܠܟܬܐ		ܦܛܪܝܪܟܘܬ ܒܪ ܦܘܠܘܣ ܩܘܪܝܠܐ	ܦܛܪܝܪܟܘܬ ܒܪ ܦܘܠܘܣ ܩܘܪܝܠܐ
75.	ܗ̇ܘ ܠܗ ܠܐܒܘܗܝ ܕܥܠܡܐ ܒܪܐ. ܗܢܐ ܕܒܪܐ ܠܐܕܡ ܒܥܠܡܐ ܚܕܬܐ	ܘܪܕܐ	ܘܪܕܐ	ܘܪܕܐ
76.	ܦܠܐ ܕܐܬܐ ܠܡܠܘܗܝ. ܕܪܘܚܐ ܘܡܫܝܚܐ ܡܫܒܚܝܢ ܒܗ̇ܝ	ܓܝܘܪܓܝܣ ܘܪܕܐ	ܓܝܘܪܓܝܣ ܘܪܕܐ	ܓܝܘܪܓܝܣ ܘܪܕܐ
77.	ܡܢ ܟܠ ܡܪܝ ܠܐܘܪܫܠܡ. ܕܢܦܩܘ ܒܢܝܐ ܕܝܠܗ ܕܢܦܩܘ	ܓܝܘܪܓܝܣ ܘܪܕܐ	ܓܝܘܪܓܝܣ ܘܪܕܐ	ܓܝܘܪܓܝܣ ܘܪܕܐ
78.	ܟܠܗ̇ ܕܟܪܝܐ ܘܟܪܝܗܘܬܐ. ܕܠܥܠܡܐ ܟܠ ܗܘܐ ܠܗ ܡܟܝܠܘܬܐ	ܓܝܘܪܓܝܣ ܘܪܕܐ	ܡܠܦܢܐ ܓܝܘܪܓܝܣ	ܓܝܘܪܓܝܣ ܘܪܕܐ
79.	ܒܝܬܗ ܕܡܪܝ ܗܘܐ ܒܝܬܐ. ܐܝܟ ܕܗܘܐ ܠܟܢܫܐ ܐܢܫܐ	ܘܪܕܐ	ܡܠܦܢܐ.....[34]	ܘܪܕܐ
80.	ܒܩܘܫܬܐ ܕܟܪܐ ܚܝܕܐ. ܢܒܥ ܐܪܥܐ ܘܪܘܚܐ ܒܥܘܬܐ	ܘܪܕܐ	ܘܪܕܐ	ܕܝܠܗ ܗܘ ܕܝܠܗ
81.	ܒܝܕܥܬܐ ܢܗܝܪܐ ܦܘܩܕܢܐ. ܝܗܒ ܬܪܘܢܐ ܕܟܪܐ ܐܠܗܐ	ܘܪܕܐ	ܘܪܕܐ	ܘܪܕܐ
82.	ܒܪܐ ܡܠܟܐ ܝܚܝܕܐ. ܐܬܝܗ ܠܦܓܪܐ ܐܕܡܝܐ	ܘܪܕܐ	ܘܪܕܐ	ܘܪܕܐ
83.	ܐܢܬ ܗܘܝܬ ܠܟ ܡܥܒܕܢܐ. ܒܪܐ ܝܚܝܕܐ ܗܘܝܬ ܡܥܒܕܢܐ	ܡܠܦܢܐ ܓܝܘܪܓܝܣ ܘܪܕܐ	ܡܠܦܢܐ ܓܝܘܪܓܝܣ ܘܪܕܐ	ܡܠܦܢܐ ܓܝܘܪܓܝܣ ܘܪܕܐ
84.	ܟܪܟܐ ܕܫܘܒܚܐ ܫܡܥܬ ܗܘܬ. ܘܒܚܝܠܗ ܘܢܝܚܗ ܘܡܬܪܘܪܒ ܗܘܬ.	ܓܝܘܪܓܝܣ ܘܪܕܐ	ܓܝܘܪܓܝܣ ܘܪܕܐ	ܓܝܘܪܓܝܣ ܘܪܕܐ
85.	ܟܢܫܗ ܥܒܕܬܐ ܦܠܚܝܢ. ܕܐܠܚܫܒܘܢܘܬ ܘܢܦܫܝܢ ܗܟܢܐ ܥܠܝܢ	ܡܠܦܢܐ ܘܪܕܐ	ܡܠܦܢܐ ܘܪܕܐ	ܡܠܦܢܐ ܘܪܕܐ
86.	ܬܪܘܢܐ ܕܟܠ ܒܪܝܬܐ. ܘܡܒܪܝܢܐ ܕܒܪܝܬܐ	ܘܪܕܐ	ܓܝܘܪܓܝܣ	ܘܪܕܐ
87.	ܦܪܘܩ ܡܫܝܚܐ ܕܒܪܝܬܐ. ܟܪܟܐ ܠܒܢܝܐ ܘܡܠܟܐ ܒܥܠܡܐ	ܘܪܕܐ		ܘܪܕܐ
88.	ܠܐܬܪܐ ܕܫܘܒܚܐ ܢܠܟܝ. ܦܪܘܩܘܬܐ ܕܟܠ ܥܠܡܐ	ܚܢܢ ܢܘܗܪܐ	ܚܢܢ ܢܘܗܪܐ ܓܝܘܪܓܝܣ ܐܪܒܠܝܐ	ܚܢܢ ܢܘܗܪܐ
89.	ܗ̇ܘ ܡܠܟ ܝܘܡܢܐ ܥܘܒܕܐ. ܠܐܠܗܐ ܟܠܗ ܒܪܘܚܐ ܩܘܕܫܐ	ܪܒܢ ܡܐܪܝ ܐܪܒܝܠܝܐ ܒܪ ܡܫܝܚܐ		ܪܒܢ ܡܐܪܝ ܐܪܒܝܠܝܐ ܒܪ ܡܫܝܚܐ
90.	ܐܠܗܐ ܐܝܬܘܗܝ ܡܠܟܐ. ܥܡܗ ܟܠܗ ܐܒܘܗܝ ܒܐܝܬܘܬܐ	*		*

[34] The word after this is illegible.

		M3 1586	G1 1300-1400	D3 1400-1600
91.	ܐܘܪܚܗ ܕܒܪܐ ܚܒܝܒܐ. ܠܐ ܡܬܕܪܟܐ ܠܟܠܗܘܢ ܒܪ̈ܝܬܐ	ܘܪܕܐ	ܘܪܕܐ	ܘܪܐ [sic]
92.	ܢܝܫܐ ܕܐܢܫܐ ܠܒܝܬ ܓܙܪܐ. ܠܒܝܬ ܡܢ ܓܙܪܐ ܘܦܩ ܠܓܙܪܐ	ܠܡܘܪܠܡܣ ܘܪܕܐ	*	ܠܡܘܪܠ ܕܘܪܕܐ [sic]
93.	ܦܬܚ ܠܐܠܗܐ ܚܙܐ ܓܙܐ. ܘܗܠܟ ܡܬܚܙܐ ܠܥܩܒ ܥܡܢܐ	ܡܠܟܬܐ ܚܡܝܣ	*	ܡܠܟܬܐ ܚܡܝܣ
94.	ܡܪܐ ܕܐܠܗܐ ܘܕܥܡܢܐ. ܐܡܪ ܡܬܡܠܟܐ ܡܬܚܣܐ ܡܬܠܠܢܐ	ܡܠܟܬܐ ܠܡܘܪܠܡܣ ܘܪܕܐ		ܡܠܟܬܐ ܠܡܘܪܠܡܣ ܘܪܕܐ
95.	ܥܒܝܕܝܢ ܘܡܬܒܝܢ ܐܕܡܐ. ܡܪܝܐ ܡܪܝ ܘܐܘܪܒܝܢ ܠܟܘܢܝ	ܠܡܘܪܠܡܣ ܘܪܕܐ		ܠܡܘܪܠܡܣ ܘܪܕܐ
96.	ܡܢ ܕܐܘܪܒܝܢ ܠܒܪܘܗܝ ܕܡܪܝܐ. ܘܗܘܐ ܠܦܠܚܐ ܕܡܝܢ ܥܒܕܐ	ܠܡܘܪܠܡܣ ܘܪܕܐ	ܘܪܕܐ	ܠܡܘܪܠܡܣ ܘܪܕܐ
97.	ܡܢܘ ܗܟܢ ܕܒܝܠܗ. ܝܬܝܪܐ ܠܟܠܝܢ ܡܪܝܐ ܡܠܟܐ	ܘܪܕܐ	ܘܪܕܐ	ܘܪܕܐ
98.	ܢܬܒܪܐ ܕܠܗ ܐܒܘܗܝ. ܒܗ ܐܕܡܐ ܦܓܪ ܡܬܦܢܝܢܗ	ܘܪܕܐ	*	ܘܪܕܐ
99.	ܥܘܒܕܐ ܠܗ ܠܗܘ ܚܘܒܐ. ܗܠܝܢ ܕܚܙܐ ܘܥܒܝܕ ܚܘܒܐ	ܘܪܕܐ	*	ܘܪܕܐ
100.	ܗܘ ܡܠܟܐ ܕܥܠܡܝܢ. ܘܡܪܐ ܕܒܪܝܬܐ ܘܕܦܠܓܘܬܐ	ܘܪܕܐ	*	ܘܪܕܐ
101.	ܡܪܐ ܕܡܠܟܐ ܡܥܘܠܝܬܐ. ܒܐܪܥܐ ܗܘܠܝ ܐܝܟ ܡܫܡܫܢܐ	ܘܪܕܐ	*	ܘܪܕܐ
102.	ܡܘܬܐ ܐܘ ܠܒܝܬܐ ܚܝܠܬܐ. ܐܬܐܬܒܪܘ ܕܩܕܫ ܒܬܘܠܬܐ	ܠܡܘܪܠܡܣ ܘܪܕܐ	ܘܪܕܐ	ܠܡܘܪܠܡܣ ܘܪܕܐ
103.	ܐܡܪܐ ܕܐܬܐ ܠܗ ܡܫܬܥܝܢ. ܕܘܫܢܐ ܘܠܐ ܠܘܬܟܘܢ	*		ܘܪܕܐ
104.	ܠܐܠܗܐ ܕܝܠܕܬܐ ܝܠܕܬ ܗܘܝܬ. ܘܡܬܒܢܝܢ ܒܬܢܐ ܚܘܒܐ ܗܘܝܬ	ܡܠܟܬܐ ܘܪܕܐ	ܣܘܡܩܐ ܠܡܘܪܠܡܣ	ܡܠܟܬܐ ܘܪܕܐ
105.	ܠܦܪܘܩܢܐ ܐܟܘܢܐ. ܕܝܢܝ ܒܝܠܕܗ ܒܪܐ ܚܒܝܒܐ	ܘܪܕܐ	*	ܘܪܕܐ
106.	ܐܠܗܐ ܕܝܢ ܐܢܫܐ. ܒܪܗ ܥܠܝܢ ܓܒܪ ܠܦܘܪܩܢ ܐܢܫܐ	ܣܘܡܩܐ	ܣܘܡܩܐ	ܣܘܡܩܐ
107.	ܐܡܪܐ ܕܠܗ ܐܝܟ ܐܡܘܬܗ. ܠܐ ܘܐܦܠܐ ܐܬܐ ܐܝܟ ܢܝܚܘܬܗ	ܘܪܕܐ	*	ܘܪܕܐ
108.	ܗܘ ܚܢܟܐ ܝܘܡܐ ܕܥܒܝܕܬܐ. ܕܐܡܪ ܡܪܝ ܒܢܝ ܦܠܚܐ	ܘܪܕܐ	*	ܘܪܕܐ
109.	ܝܡܝܢܗ ܕܐܒܐ ܡܬܦܩܕܐ ܠܥܡ ܒܝܬܗ ܦܓܪܐ ܓܠܝܐ	ܘܪܕܐ	ܠܡܘܪܠܡܣ	ܘܕܕܐ [sic]
110.	ܡܥܘܕ ܟܠܗ ܕܥܘܠܬܐ. ܘܡܟܝܢ ܟܠܗ ܡܕܝܢܘܬܐ	ܘܪܕܐ	ܘܪܕܐ	ܘܪܕܐ
111.	ܐܘ ܕܡܬܒܠܥܝܢ ܒܟܠ ܚܝܠܘܗܝ. ܘܡܥܬܕܝܢ ܒܟܠ ܒܘܣܡܝܗ	ܘܪܕܐ	ܘܪܕܐ	ܘܪܕܐ
112.	ܢܒܝܐ ܡܪܝܐ ܕܒܪܝܬܐ. ܘܒܟܢܝܐ ܕܝܕܥܘܢ ܢܒܝܘܬܐ	ܘܪܕܐ	ܘܪܕܐ	ܘܪܕܐ
113.	ܢܦܫܐ ܡܒܝܐ ܒܝܒܝܢܐ. ܢܘܠܐ ܝܐܝܐ ܚܘܒ ܒܘܝܢܐ	ܠܡܘܪܠܡܣ ܘܪܕܐ		ܠܡܘܪܠܡܣ ܘܪܕܐ
114.	ܡܠܟܐ ܕܝܢ ܥܩܒܬܐ. ܕܒܬܠܟܢܐ ܘܠܐ ܗܘܐ ܕܦܠܓܬܐ	ܠܡܘܪܠܡܣ ܘܪܕܐ		ܠܡܘܪܠܡܣ ܘܪܕܐ

		M3 1586	G1 1300-1400	D3 1400-1600
115.	ܐܘ ܡܫܝܚܐ ܦܪܘܩܢܐ. ܐܘ ܢܘܗܪܐ ܦܬܓܡܗ ܕܡܫܒܚܐ	ܘܪܕܐ	ܘܪܕܐ	ܘܪܕܐ
116.	ܢܘܗܪܐ ܕܕܪܐ ܡܢ ܢܘܗܪܝܢ. ܕܪܡܙܐ ܘܬܘܕܝܬܐ ܒܐܝܕܗ ܠܒܢܝܢ	ܘܪܕܐ	ܘܪܕܐ	ܘܪܕܐ
117.	ܡܪܢܝܬܐ ܦܬܓܡܗ ܕܡܪܢܝܬܐ. ܕܐܬܒܪܘܠܗ ܡܢ ܡܢ ܪܡܐ	ܘܪܕܐ	ܘܪܕܐ	ܘܪܕܐ
118.	ܦܠܚܢܐ ܐܠܗܝܐ. ܡܢܐ ܦܪܫܐ ܐܠܗܝܐ	*[35]	ܘܪܕܐ	ܘܪܕܐ
119.	ܐܘ ܦܪܘܩܐ ܕܢܒܐ ܠܥܠܡܐ. ܚܠܦܝܢ ܚܛܗܝܢ ܘܣܟܠܘܬܢ	*[36]	*	ܠܓܝܘܪܓܝܣ ܘܪܕܐ
120.	ܚܣܝܕܐ ܦܠܚܐ ܟܪܡܐ ܦܠܚܐ ܫܪܝܗ ܠܐܟܪܗ ܠܟܘ ܒܪܐ	*[37]	ܠܓܝܘܪܓܝܣ ܘܪܕܐ	ܘܕܕܐ [sic]
121.	ܦܠܚܐ ܘܪܕܐ ܕܡܢ ܦܠܚܐ. ܕܦܠܚܘܗܝ ܐܢܘܢ ܒܠܗܘܢ ܦܠܚܐ	ܘܪܕܐ		ܘܪܕܐ
122.	ܦܠܚܐ ܕܪܘܚܐ ܚܟܝܡܐ. ܕܐܬܐ ܕܢܦܪܘܩ ܠܐܪܥܢܐ	ܡܠܦܢܐ ܘܪܕܐ	*[38]	ܡܠܦܢܐ ܘܪܕܐ
123.	ܡܪܢܝܬܐ ܦܬܓܡܗ ܕܡܪܢܝܬܐ. ܗܘ ܕܐܬܒܪܘܗ ܡܢ ܡܢ ܪܡܐ	ܘܪܕܐ	ܠܓܝܘܪܓܝܣ	ܘܪܕܐ
124.	ܡܪܐ ܕܦܪܘܩܐ ܘܦܠܚܢܐ. ܐܦ ܢܦܩܐ ܕܡܢ ܐܠܗܝܐ	ܠܓܝܘܪܓܝܣ ܘܪܕܐ	ܗܟܢ ܢܘܗܪܐ ܐܪܒܠܝܐ	ܠܓܝܘܪܓܝܣ ܘܪܕܐ
125.	ܦܪܘܩܢܐ ܕܡܢ ܚܕܝܘܬܐ. ܢܦܫܐ ܪܒܐ ܡܠܟܐ ܢܛܪܬܐ	ܘܪܕܐ	ܘܪܕܐ	ܘܪܕܐ
126.	ܐܚܝܢܐ ܕܪܘܚܐ ܒܗܢ ܩܕܝܫܘܬܐ ܐܬܐ ܠܐܪܥܐ ܕܢܐܚܐ ܠܦܠܚܘܗܝ	ܘܪܕܐ	ܘܪܕܐ	ܘܪܕܐ
127.	ܒܪܘܟܝܐ ܠܗ ܠܗܘ ܚܝܠܬܐ. ܕܒܪܝܗ ܡܫܬܡܥ ܡܢ ܟܢܫܬܐ	ܡܠܦܢܐ ܠܓܝܘܪܓܝܣ ܘܪܕܐ		ܡܠܦܢܐ ܠܓܝܘܪܓܝܣ ܘܪܕܐ
128.	ܢܘܪܐ ܡܝܬܠܦܬ ܠܐܠܗܘܬܗ. ܕܦܪܕܝܣ ܠܟܝܢܐ ܟܪܒܐ ܕܚܝܝ	*		*
129.	ܡܪܝ ܕܝܢ ܡܢ ܐܢܫܐ ܗܘܐ. ܕܒܪܘܟܝܗ ܠܩܕܝܫܘܬܗ ܒܫܘܐ ܗܘܐ	ܠܓܝܘܪܓܝܣ ܘܪܕܐ		ܠܓܝܘܪܓܝܣ ܘܪܕܐ
130.	ܢܦܫܗ ܕܐܢܫܐ ܡܬܦܩܕܐ ܕܝܢܐ ܢܠܦܘܗ ܒܪܐ ܒܐܘܟܢܐ	ܘܪܕܐ	ܠܓܝܘܪܓܝܣ ܘܪܕܐ	ܘܪܕܐ
131.	ܐܝܟܢܐ ܕܡܢ ܡܬܠܐ ܦܪܘܩܗ ܒܪܝ. ܘܐܝܟܢܐ ܒܥܝܢܐ ܢܘܦܠ	*		*
132.	ܒܪܝܟ ܦܪܘܩܢܐ ܡܪܐ ܡܢ. ܕܝܗܒ ܒܫܘܒܚܗ ܡܢܗܪܗ ܠܟܝܢܐ	ܒܪ ܩܪܕܚܗ		ܕܡܪ ܥܒܕܝܫܘܥ ܒܪ ܩܪܕܚܗ
133.	ܒܪܝܟ ܗܘ ܡܫܝܚܐ ܡܢܝܫܢܝ. ܐܢܘܢ ܘܗܘܐ ܕܦܪܩܢܝ ܘܦܪܩܢܝ	ܡܪܝ ܥܒܕܝܫܘܥ ܕܒܝܬ ܨܘܒܐ		ܡܪܝ ܥܒܕܝܫܘܥ ܕܒܝܬ ܨܘܒܐ
134.	ܒܪܝܟܘ ܡܫܝܚܐ ܡܫܠܡܢܝ. ܐܢܘܢ ܘܗܘܐ ܕܟܠܝ ܘܦܢܫܝ	*	*	*

[35] In this manuscript this hymn is without title, a space was left empty to be filled with title afterwards.

[36] In this manuscript this hymn is without title, a space was left empty to be filled with title afterwards.

[37] In this manuscript this hymn is without title, a space was left empty to be filled with title afterwards.

[38] The name is illegible.

		M3 1586	G1 1300-1400	D3 1400-1600
135.	ܒܟܠ ܩܢܘܡܝ ܘܒܟܠ ܦܓܪܝ. ܒܟܠ ܘܓܝܐ ܠܗܘܢ ܡܫܝܚܐ ܡܪܝ	*		*
136.	- ܫܘܒܚܐ ܙܡܪܝ ܢܓܢܐ. ܠܒܪܐ ܕܠܐܠܗ ܘܠܒܪܐ ܕܠܐܠܗܘܬܗ..... - ܗܘܝܬܐ. ܘܒܗܠܐ ܘܠܟܝ ܡܪܝ ܕܒܢܐ			*
137.	ܐܘ ܒܪܬܐ ܚܒܝܒ ܡܠܟܐ ܗܘܐ. ܐܘ ܒܪܬܐ ܓܒܝܐ ܓܒܪܐ ܗܘܐ	*		*
138.	ܗܝܕܝܢ ܠܚܕܐ ܐܘܪܝܬܐ. ܒܢܝܘܦܣܛܘܣ ܕ ܘܕܢܐ...			
139.	ܒܪܐ ܕܢܗܘܐ ܡܛܘܠܬܐ. ܕܒܪܐ ܒܪܢܫܐ ܡܢ ܫܘܪܝܐ			
140.	ܒܪܝܟ ܡܫܝܚܐ ܦܪܘܩܢ. ܕܒܝܬ ܚܘܒܗ ܐܘܪܚ ܘܢܦܪ			
141.	ܒܐܘܪܚܐ ܕܩܘܫܬܐ ܪܕܘ ܚܘܫܒܐ. ܘܚܘܒܗ ܓܪܒܐ ܕܢܝܫܬܗܘܢ			
142.	ܒܥܕܬܐ ܩܕܝܫܬܐ ܒܢܫܡܬܐ. ܕܫܘܠܛܢ ܗܠܐ ܫܢܝ ܠܫܢܬܐ			
143.	ܐܘ ܓܘܪܢܐ ܒܠܚܘܕܝܬܐ. ܦܪܘܢܐ ܒܪܥܘܬܐ			
144.	ܗܘ ܢܒܝܐ ܓܘܢܝܐ. ܝܗܒܝܐ ܒܝܬܢܐ ܘܠܠܢܝܐ			
145.	ܟܠ ܚܒܝܒܐ ܦܘܬܝܐ. ܐܦܟܠ ܒܚܒܝܟܠ ܦܘܬܝܐ			
146.	ܓܪܒܐ ܙܡܝܠ ܚܪܝܘܬܐ. ܦܟܪ ܒܢ ܒܪܬܐ ܕܝܩܢܬܐ			
147.	ܚܕ ܗܝܡ ܡܪܝ ܠܪܥ ܦܝܫܐ. ܐܚܐ ܩܘܡܐ ܘܫܠܒܐ			
148.	ܢܪܝܫ ܒܢܫܐ ܒܢܝܚܘܬܐ. ܕܩܠܢܐ ܕܗܘܢܐ ܚܢܝܬܐ			
149.	ܢܦܫ ܦܘܩܕܢܐ ܡܢ ܡܠܟܐ. ܘܐܫܬܡܥ ܠܟܠܗ ܒܐܬܘܬܐ			
150.	ܗܘ ܢܒܝܐ ܝܫܥܝܐ. ܚܝܠܬܗ ܕܐܠܗܐ ܘܗܘܐ			
151.	ܫܘܒܚܐ ܠܡܫܝܚܐ ܦܪܘܩܢ. ܕܚܕ ܝܘܡܐ ܚܘܒܝ ܕܐܫܬܕܪ ܠܟܝܢܢ			
152.	ܠܘܬܟܘܢ ܝܘܡܐ ܡܚܪܒܬܐ. ܒܬܘܠܬܐ ܕܒܝܬܐ ܘܦܪܝܫܬܐ			
153.	ܗܘܝܬܐ ܢܦܫ ܒܟ. ܒܕܘܟܝ ܝܘܡܐ ܕܦܘܪܩܢ			
154.	ܒܢܝܪܗ ܡܕܝܢܬܐ ܕܥܠܝܬܐ. ܝܫܬܡܥ ܩܠܐ ܕܠܚܡܝ ܠܢܦܫܟ			
155.	ܘܠܗܪ ܗܘ ܦܘܠܚܐ ܕܝܠܕܝܐ. ܐܦ ܠܟܐ ܕܝܫܬܚܝܐ		ܡܪܝ ܦܘܪܥܢܟ ܦܠܓܘܬܐ ܫܡܝܢܐ ܕܡܬܬܪܒܐ ܒܚܪܐ ܡܫܝܚܐ	
156.	ܝܘܡܐ ܘܢܫܬܒܚ ܫܡܝܢܐ. ܢܬܬܠܒܫ ܘܢܬܢܦܫ ܐܘ ܠܒܝܬܝܐ		*	
157.	ܡܪܐ ܕܢܩܫܐ ܘܦܬܚܐ. ܘܒܠܒ ܒܩܫܬܐ ܦܘܠܚܐ ܕܒܝܬܐ			

		M3 1586	G1 1300-1400	D3 1400-1600
158.	ܡܪܝ ܕܫܠܡܬ ܠܥܡܡܐ. ܒܪܘܚܐ ܕܦܠܛܝܐ ܠܟܠܐ	ܡܒܪܝܫܝܬ ܒܪ ܦܠܛܘ ܡܢܝܠܐ		
159.	ܬܘܐ ܠܥܘܒܕܐ ܐܒܗܐ ܬܪܘܢܐ. ܒܢܝܐ ܓܫܐ ܘܐܪܥܐ ܦܣܓܠܐ			ܪܒ ܬܟܘܬ ܕܣܒܪܐ
160.	ܥܘܒܢܐ ܠܣܘܦܝ ܬܪܘܡ ܒܥܕܐ ܗܓܝܢܐ ܡܪܫܥܘܬܟ		*	

TABLE 8: PUBLISHED HYMNS FOUND IN THE BOOK OF WARDĀ

1. In the Liturgical Books[39]

Ḥūdrā[40] of the Chaldean Church 1886, 1938[41]						
	Author	Occasion	The Hymn	Vol.	Pages	Table 6
1		ܕܥܕܢܐ ܕܫܠܝܚܐ ܩܕܡܝܐ ܕܩܝܛܐ ܫܒܝܚܬܐ ܚܢܢܬܐ	ܒܝܡ ܢܘܪܐ ܩܕܫܐ ܡܕܒܚܐ. ܚܙܘ ܢܝܫܐ ܗܒܝܫܐ ܡܬܒܥܐ(*)[42]	vol. I	ܫܝܐ - ܫܝܕ 311-314	
2		ܕܥܕܢܐ ܕܡܬܒܪܟܝܢ ܢܠܦܝܢ ܢܝܫܐ ܩܕܝܡ	ܒܢܘܗܪܐ ܕܫܘܒܚܐ ܗܘ ܕܡܢ ܐܒܐ. ܘܒܡܫܝܚܘܬܗ ܗܘܐ ܡܬܓܠܐ ܐܒܐ	vol. I	ܫܣܐ — ܫܣܗ 361-365	9
3		ܕܥܕܢܐ ܕܝܠܕܐ ܕܡܠܟܘܬܐ	ܒܠܒܘܫ ܦܓܪܐ ܥܒܕܗ ܡܬܓܠܝܢܘܬܗ. ܦܓܪܗ ܦܓܪܘܗ ܒܝܘܡܐ ܕܗܠܝܢ(*)	vol. I	ܫܥܚ — ܫܥܛ 378-379	
4		ܒܥܐܕܐ ܕܒܪܘܟܬܗ ܕܡܪܢ	ܒܕܒܚܘ ܕܡܠܟܐ ܒܢܝܢܘܗܝ. ܡܢܚܐ ܒܟܘܪܗܘܢ ܒܕܒܚܬܐ(*)	vol. I	ܫܦܚ — ܫܨ 388-390	
5		ܒܥܐܕܐ ܕܕܢܚܐ ܕܕܝܢܝܗ ܕܡܪܢ	ܫܒܚܘܗܝ ܠܢܘܗܪܐ ܚܢܢܐ. ܗܘ ܕܒܓܠ ܠܢܘܗܪܐ ܡܬܓܠܝܢܐ(*)	vol. I	ܬܙ — ܬܝ 407-410	
6		ܒܥܐܕܐ ܕܡܪܢ ܡܥܠܝ ܩܕܡܬܐ	ܚܢܢܐ ܕܡܠܟܐ ܒܢܝܢܐ. ܡܢܕܝܢ ܡܢܐ ܡܢ ܫܡܝܐ.	vol. I	ܬܠܘ — ܬܡ 436-440	15
7		ܕܥܕܢܐ ܕܢܒܝܐ ܕܐܘܪܫܠܡ	ܒܝܬܩܢܐ ܕܝܘܡܐ ܕܡܠܟܘܬܗ ܕܡܠܟܐ ܕܝܢܐ. ܥܠܝܢܐ ܫܡܝܐ ܩܕܝܫܐ ܘܩܕܝܫܐ.	vol. I	ܬܢܗ — ܬܢܙ 455-457	18
8		ܕܥܕܢܐ ܕܩܕܫ ܕܐܘܠܦܢܐ	ܒܥܕܢܐ ܟܠ ܡܢ ܡܠܐ ܩܘܡܘ. ܩܕܫܐ ܫܡܝܐ ܕܐܬܓܠܝ ܡܢܗ(*)	vol. I	ܬܥܐ 471	
9		ܕܥܕܢܐ ܕܡܠܟܘܬܐ ܢܘܗܪܐ	ܡܫܒܚܐ ܡܠܟܐ ܘܡܢܗ ܒܝܬ ܚܘܒܐ. ܡܫܒܚܝܢ ܠܡܪܢ ܕܩܡ ܒܥܕܢܗ	vol. I	ܬܦܗ — ܬܦܙ 485-487	20
10		ܕܥܕܢܐ ܕܡܠܟܘܬܐ ܗܘܕܝܐ ܡܕܝܢܬܐ	ܥܡܪ ܡܬܓܠܝܢܘܬܗ ܩܕܡܝܐ. ܡܠܐ ܗܘܐ ܫܘܒܚܗ ܡܠܟܐ ܕܝܘܡܐ.	vol. I	ܬܨܚ — ܬܩܐ 498- 501	51
11		ܕܥܕܢܐ ܕܚܕ ܩܕܝܫܐ	ܒܕܒܚܘ ܡܫܝܚܐ ܕܒܪܐ ܫܒܚܘܗܝ. ܐܘܕܝ ܡܢܗ ܡܢ ܕܥܕܢܝܗ(*)	vol. I	ܬܩܝܘ — ܬܩܝܚ 516-518	
12		ܕܥܕܢܐ ܕܚܕ ܩܕܝܫܐ	ܡܠܟܐ ܕܫܒܝܚܬܐ. ܡܫܝܚܐ ܐܒܘܗܝ ܒܥܕܢܗ.	vol. I	ܬܩܝܚ — ܬܩܟܐ 518-521	60
13		ܒܥܐܕܐ ܕܡܠܟܘܬܗ ܕܡܪܢ ܠܥܠܡܐ	ܐܒܘܢ ܚܢܢܐ ܘܒܪ ܚܢܢܐ. ܚܢܢܐ ܠܟܠܗ ܥܠܡܐ ܘܥܠܡܐ.	vol. I	ܬܩܠܙ — ܬܩܠܚ 537-538	11
14		ܒܥܐܕܐ ܕܥܐܕܐ	ܒܝܘܡܗ ܕܡܪܢ ܗܘܐ ܚܕܘܬܐ. ܘܒܝܬ ܩܘܕܫܐ ܠܟܠܗ ܥܠܡܐ	vol. II	ܫܥܘ — ܫܦ 376-380	79
15		ܒܥܐܕܐ ܕܥܡܕܐ ܕܡܪܢ	ܒܥܐܕܐ ܕܩܕܝܫܐ ܒܥܕܢܗ ܗܘܐ. ܘܡܫܝܚܐ ܘܢܘܗܪܐ ܡܬܓܠܝܢܐ ܗܘܐ.	vol. II	ܬܠܓ — ܬܠܘ 433-436	84
16		ܒܥܐܕܐ ܕܕܢܚܐ ܕܗܘܠܕܗ ܕܡܪܢ	ܐܘܕܝܘ ܩܕܡܐ ܡܫܝܚܐ. ܠܐ ܡܬܓܠܝܐ ܠܥܠܡܐ ܒܪܢܫܐ.	vol. II	ܬܩܐ — ܬܩܓ 501-503	91

[39] In what concern the hymns in the book of prayers ܓܙܐ Gazzā, See A. Pritula, *The Wardā*, pp. 15-81.

[40] It is one of the liturgical books used during the year in the Assyrian and Chaldean churches.

[41] *Breviarium Chaldaicum*, vol. I-III.

[42] In what concern the Ḥūdrā books, the hymns marked with star (*) are those found in the Ḥūdrā and might not belong to Wardā, but these hymns are to be sang with the melody of ܒܝܘܡ ܠܟ ܒܥܕܢܐ which is also used in the Book of Wardā, we opted to add them in this table just for knowledge. The first column of this table indicates the name of the author of the hymn if it is given in the Ḥūdrā. To check the author of a hymn, See Table 7.

17		ܥܐܕܐ ܕܩܝܡܬܐ ܕܡܪܢ ܡܫܝܚܐ	ܦܬܚ ܡܫܝܚܐ ܒܩܝܡܬܗ. ܬܪܥܐ ܠܒܢܝܢܫܐ ܘܚܝܐ ܠܟܠܢ.	vol. II	ܬܩܢܛ — ܬܩܣܐ 559-561	87
18		ܕܘܟܪܢܐ ܕܩܕܫܐ ܦܛܪܘܣ	ܐܘ ܡܠܟ ܝܘܩܪܐ ܥܘܕܪܢܐ. ܠܐܠܗܐ ܡܠܟܐ ܕܥܘܠܡܝܢ ܫܘܒܚܐ.	vol. II	ܬܩܥܓ — ܬܩܥܗ 573-575	89
19		ܕܘܟܪܢܐ ܕܐܣܛܦܢܘܣ ܘܕܝܘܢܝܐ	ܡܪܢܐ ܡܪܝ ܘܐܠܗܝ. ܕܐܒܘܟ ܫܡܝܐ ܢܘܗܪܐ ܕܥܠܡܝܢ(*)	vol. II	ܬܩܦܙ — ܬܩܦܚ 587-588	
20		ܕܘܟܪܢܐ ܕܩܕܫܐ ܥܪܘܒܬܐ ܡܗܠܟ ܕܐܒܗܬܐ ܘܕܝܢܐ	ܡܢ ܡܫܝܚܐ ܕܒܫܒܘܚܬܐ ܝܗܒܢܐ. ܐܘ ܕܒܣܘܡܟܐ ܢܦܠܟ ܡܝܬܝܐ.	vol. II	ܬܩܨܙ — ܬܪ 597-600	10
21		ܥܐܕܐ ܕܥܢܕܐ ܕܩܕܫܐ ܥܪܘܒܬܐ ܠܟܠ ܫܠܝܚܐ	ܒܢܝܢܗ ܡܫܝܚܐ ܕܫܠܝܚܐ. ܝܗܒ ܫܠܡ ܕܢܗܘܐ ܠܚܝܐ.	vol. III	ܬܡܘ — ܬܡܛ 446-449	7
22		ܥܐܕܐ ܕܩܕܫܐ ܦܛܪܘܣ ܘܦܘܠܘܣ	ܐܘ ܚܒܝܒܐ ܕܫܠܝܚܐ ܕܢܘܗܪܐ ܕܘܡܝܟ	vol. III	ܬܣܒ — ܬܣܗ 462-465	16
23		ܕܘܟܪܢܐ ܕܩܕܫܐ ܡܪܝ ܬܐܘܡܐ ܕܒܗܢܕܘ ܫܠܝܚܐ	ܢܦܩ ܩܘܡܪܝܐ ܡܢ ܫܡܝܐ. ܘܡܫܝܚܐ ܫܠܚܗ ܒܟܪܝܗܘܬܐ.	vol. III	ܬܦܛ — ܬܨ 489-490	149
24		ܥܐܕܐ ܕܡܪܝ ܫܡܥܘܢ ܕܦܐܦܐ	ܡܪܝ ܥܡ ܟܠ ܩܕܝܫܝܟ ܗܢܐ. ܕܥܒܕܘ ܠܫܠܝܚܘܗܝ ܒܩܘܫܬܐ ܗܘܘ.	vol. III	ܬܩܐ — ܬܩܕ 501-504	129
25		ܥܐܕܐ ܕܡܪܝ ܩܘܪܝܩܘܣ ܕܩܕܫܐ ܥܪܘܒܬܐ	ܡܢ ܡܫܝܚܐ ܕܒܫܒܘܚܬܐ ܝܗܒܢܐ. ܐܘ ܕܒܣܘܡܟܐ ܢܦܠܟ ܡܝܬܝܐ.	vol. III	ܬܩܝܘ — ܬܩܝܚ 516-518	10
26		ܥܐܕܐ ܕܡܪܝ ܓܝܘܪܓܝܣ ܕܩܕܫܐ ܥܪܘܒܬܐ	ܕܒܢܐ ܘܐܝܟ ܠܒܢܝܐ. ܘܒܠܐ ܒܩܘܫܬܐ ܡܢܗܘܢ ܕܒܗ.	vol. III	ܬܩܟܚ — ܬܩܠ 528-530	5
27		ܥܐܕܐ ܕܡܪܝ ܓܝܘܪܓܝܣ ܕܩܕܫܐ ܥܪܘܒܬܐ	ܒܪܐ ܕܒܬܘܠܬܐ ܒܗ ܗܝܡܢܘܬܐ. ܕܟܠ ܝܘܡܐ ܘܕܝܢܗ.	vol. III	ܬܩܠ — ܬܩܠܒ 530-532	8
28		ܥܐܕܐ ܕܐܠܝܐ ܡܫܝܚܐ	ܐܘ ܕܒܪܐ ܒܢܝ ܐܢܫܐ. ܢܟܠܐ ܗܕܡܘܗܝ ܘܩܝܡܬܗ.	vol. III	ܬܩܡܘ — ܬܩܡܚ 546-548	119
29		ܕܘܟܪܢܐ ܕܩܕܫܐ ܢܫܘܥ ܡܫܝܚܐ	ܒܝܬܗ ܥܒܕ ܡܪܐ ܘܐܠܗܝ. ܕܢܬܪܥܒܕܘܢ ܘܢܚܘܢ ܗܟܢܐ ܥܡܢ.	vol. III	ܬܩܣܒ - ܬܩܣܗ 562-565	85

Ḥūḏrā of the East-Syriac Churches 1960/1961[43]						
	Au-thor	Occasion	The Hymn	Vol.	Pages	Table 6
1	ܓܝܘܪܓܝܣ ܘܪܕܐ	ܩܕܡܝܬܐ ܕܣܘܒܪܐ	ܡܫܝܚܐ ܢܘܗܪܐ ܕܥܠܡܐ. ܩܘܠܐ ܕܒܫܪܬܐ ܡܢܐ ܫܡܥܢܐ.	vol. I	ܫܘ — ܫܚ 306-308	
2	ܓܝܘܪܓܝܣ ܘܪܕܐ	ܬܠܝܬܝܬܐ ܕܣܘܒܪܐ	ܡܢ ܕܒܪܐ ܕܒܘܩܪܐ ܡܪܝܡ. ܘܡܬܝܠܕܐ ܕܒܬܐ ܕܝܠܗ	vol. I	ܫܠܙ - ܫܠܛ 337-339	24
3	ܓܝܘܪܓܝܣ ܕܐܪܒܝܠ	ܬܠܝܬܝܬܐ ܕܣܘܒܪܐ	ܐܠܗܐ ܐܠܗܝܢ ܠܥܠܡ ܫܡܝܢ. ܕܝܠܕܬܐ ܗܘܬ ܡܫܒܚܬܐ.	vol. I	ܫܡܓ 343	
4		ܬܠܝܬܝܬܐ ܕܣܘܒܪܐ	ܠܟܘܠܗ ܠܥܠܡܐ ܢܘܗܪ ܕܢܚܬ. ܡܫܒܚܐ ܕܝܠܕܬܐ ܕܒܬܘܠܘܬܐ(*)	vol. I	ܫܣܕ - ܫܣܙ 364-367	
5		ܪܒܝܥܝܬܐ ܕܣܘܒܪܐ	ܐܘ ܕܡܫܝܚܐ ܡܫܒܚܐ. ܘܡܢ ܕܒܢܫܡܬܐ ܕܡܪܢ ܒܦܘܡܟܘܢ.	vol. I	ܬܕ - ܬܘ 404-406	27
6		ܪܒܝܥܝܬܐ ܕܣܘܒܪܐ	ܡܪܝ ܕܒܥܘܬܐ ܒܝܬ ܢܘܗܪܐ. ܕܒܢܐ ܡܫܒܚܐ ܟܠܗ ܡܕܒܪܢܐ(*)	vol. I	ܬܘ — ܬܚ 406-408	
7		ܪܒܝܥܝܬܐ ܕܣܘܒܪܐ	ܝܘܡܢ ܫܡܥܢܐ ܘܒܫܪܬܐ. ܡܠܐܟܐ ܕܒܫܪܗ ܗܘ ܢܘܗܪܐ(*)	vol. I	ܬܠ — ܬܠܕ 430-434	

---

[43] T. Darmo, ed. *Ḥūḏrā* ܚܘܕܪܐ [The Cycle], vol. I-III.

8	ܡܛܠ ܥܢܝܕܐ ܕܫܢܬܐ ܕܡܝܬ	ܐܪܓܘܢܐ ܕܟܬܢܝܬܐ	ܠܐ ܬܫܡܫ ܐܘܠܦܢܐ. ܘܡܫܒܚܢܐ ܕܫܠܡܘܬܐ.	vol. I	ܗܠܕ - ܗܠܙ 434 - 437	58
9		ܕܥܐܕܥܐܕܐ ܕܡܪܝܐ ܡܫܝܚ	ܒܝܘܡܐ ܕܫܒܬܐ ܗܘ ܕܝܠܗ ܐܢܐ. ܘܒܫܘܒܚܐ ܗܘ ܡܫܒܚ ܐܢܐ.	vol. I	ܗܨܒ - ܗܨܘ 592-596	9
10		ܕܥܐܕܥܐܕܐ ܕܡܪܝܐ ܡܫܝܚܐ ܡܪܢܝܬܐ	ܫܠܡܐ ܕܡܠܟܐ ܒܪܒܐ. ܡܢ ܕܝܢ ܡܢܐ ܡܢ ܢܗܪܐ.	vol. I	ܗܪܣܙ - ܗܪܥ 667 - 670	15
11		ܕܥܐܕܥܐܕܐ ܕܡܪܝܐ ܦܠܚܘܬܐ ܘܦܘܠܚܢܐ	ܐܘ ܫܒܝܚܐ ܝܬܝܪ ܒܡܘܠܕܗ. ܕܚܙܝܢ ܥܠܝܢܐ ܫܘܒܚܗ ܕܡܫܝܚܐ.	vol. I	ܗܪܨܒ - ܗܪܨܗ 692-695	16
12		ܕܥܐܕܥܐܕܐ ܕܐܪܒܥܐ ܕܥܢܝܢܐ	ܐܘ ܫܒܝܚܐ ܝܘܡܐ ܗܢܐ. ܒܡܘܠܕܗ ܕܥܠܝܢܐ ܫܘܒܚܗ ܕܡܫܝܚܐ.	vol. I	ܗܫܝܒ - ܗܫܝܕ 714-712	17
13		ܕܥܐܕܥܐܕܐ ܕܐܪܒܥܐ ܕܥܢܝܢܐ	ܒܝܘܡܐ ܗܢܐ ܕܡܠܟܘܬܗ ܕܡܫܝܚܐ ܪܒܐ. ܥܠܝܢܐ ܘܬܚܬܝܐ ܗܘܘ.	vol. I	ܗܫܝܕ - ܗܫܝܙ 714-717	18
14		ܕܥܐܕܥܐܕܐ ܕܡܪܝܐ ܕܡܠܟܘܬܐ	ܒܡܘܠܕܗ ܟܠ ܡܢ ܟܠ ܒܪܝܬܐ. ܡܠܐ ܫܡܝܐ ܘܐܪܥܐ ܬܫܒܘܚܬܐ(*)	vol. I	ܗܫܠܒ - ܗܫܠܓ 732-733	
15		ܕܥܐܕܥܐܕܐ ܕܡܠܟܐ ܡܫܝܚܐ	ܡܠܟܐ ܫܡܝܢܝܐ ܘܬܚܬܝܐ ܫܡܐ ܚܕܬܐ. ܡܫܒܚܝܢ ܠܡܪܢ ܘܡܘܕܝܢ ܠܒܪܝܟܘܬܗ	vol. I	ܗܫܢ - ܗܫܢܒ 750-752	20
16	ܡܪܝ ܐܦܪܝܡ	ܕܥܐܕܥܐܕܐ ܕܡܠܟܐ ܡܘܠܕܗ	ܡܫܒܚ ܡܫܝܚܐ ܒܡܘܠܕܗ ܦܘܪܩܢܐ[44] ܡܢ ܐܒܐ ܡܫܝܚܐ ܡܠܟܐ ܕܝܢܐ.	vol. I	ܗܫܣܛ - ܗܫܥܒ 769-772	51
17		ܕܥܐܕܥܐܕܐ ܕܒܝܬ ܦܪܨܘܦܐ	ܒܐܝܕܘ ܡܫܝܚܐ ܕܚܕܫܘܬܐ. ܐܘܕܝ ܡܠܟܐ ܗܢܐ ܕܥܐܕܐ(*)	vol. I	ܗܫܨܒ - ܗܫܨܕ 792 - 794	
18		ܕܥܐܕܥܐܕܐ ܕܒܝܬ ܦܪܨܘܦܐ	ܡܠܟܐ ܕܫܡܝܐ. ܡܫܝܚܐ ܐܒܘܗܝ ܒܪܝܬܗ.	vol. I	ܗܫܨܕ - ܗܫܨܙ 794-797	60
19	ܠܡܘܢܠܝܬ ܕܐܪܥܐ	ܝܠܕܬܐ ܕܡܫܝܚܐ ܕܒܝܬܐ ܕܒܬܘܠܬܐ	ܡܪܝܐ ܥܡܝ ܡܠܟܝ. ܐܦ ܟܠ ܥܡܝ.	vol II	ܩܨܐ-ܩܨܒ 191-192	
20	ܕܡܘܕܐ	ܒܪܟܬܐ ܐܪܒܥܐ	ܒܝܘܡܐ ܕܡܪܝ ܗܘܐ ܫܒܚܐ. ܘܡܢ ܐܘܪܚܐ ܠܥܠܡܐ ܘܐܢܫܐ.	vol. II	ܗܩܝܒ - ܗܩܝܗ 512-515	79
21		ܠܐܘܪܚܐ ܕܡܘܕܝܢܐ	ܐܪܥܐ ܕܡܫܝܚܐ ܝܠܕܬܗ ܗܘܬ. ܘܫܠܝܚܐ ܘܐܬܝܐ ܡܠܟܘܬܐ ܗܘܬ.	vol. II	ܗܩܥܛ - ܗܩܦܒ 579-582	84
22	ܠܡܘܢܠܝܬ ܡܘܕܐ	ܡܘܠܕܗ ܕܡܪܝ	ܐܘܪܚܐ ܕܐܒܐ ܫܒܝܚܐ. ܟܠ ܡܫܒܚܝܢ ܠܡܠܟܘܬܗ ܒܫܡܝܐ.	vol. II	ܗܪܣܘ - ܗܪܣܚ 666-668	91
23		ܕܥܐܕܥܐܕܐ ܕܡܢܚܬܗ ܘܕܡܝܬܐ	ܒܡܘܠܕܗ ܘܡܠܟܘ ܝܠܕܬܐ. ܒܝܘܡ ܕܥܐܕܥܐܕܐ ܕܡܘܠܕܗ ܕܒܬܘܠܬܐ(*)	vol. III	ܬܢܐ - ܬܢܓ 351-353	
24		ܕܥܐܕܥܐܕܐ ܕܡܪܝ ܡܘܕܝܢܘܬܐ ܘܦܘܠܚܢܐ ܕܡܘܬܐ	ܐܘ ܡܠܟ ܠܐ ܒܢܝ ܝܠܕܬܐ. ܝܘܡܐ ܕܒܪܝܟܘܬܐ ܠܡܫܝܚܐ(*)	vol. III	ܗܪܢܒ - ܗܪܢܕ 652-654	
25		ܕܥܐܕܥܐܕܐ ܕܡܪܝ ܡܘܕܝܢܘܬܐ	ܢܦܩ ܒܘܨܪܐ ܡܢ ܡܠܟܐ. ܘܡܫܒܚܢܐ ܝܠܕܬܐ ܒܬܘܠܬܐ.	vol. III	ܗܪܡܕ-ܗܪܡܘ 644-646	149
26	ܕܡܘܕܐ	ܕܡܠܟܘܬܗ ܕܡܪܝ	ܡܪܝ ܕܡܢ ܡܢ ܐܪܥܐ ܗܘܐ. ܕܡܘܠܕܗ ܠܫܘܒܚܗ ܥܡܗ ܗܘܐ.	vol. III	ܗܪܥܐ - ܗܪܥܕ 671-674	129
27	ܕܡܘܕܐ	ܒܪܐ ܕܐܠܗܐ ܡܫܝܚܐ	ܠܐ ܐܒܐ ܒܢܝ ܝܠܕܬܐ. ܡܠܟܐ ܗܪܘܕܣ ܘܡܫܝܚܐ.	vol. III	ܗܫܘ - ܗܫܙ 706-707	119
28		ܒܪܐ ܕܐܠܗܐ ܡܫܝܚܐ	ܒܡܠܟܘܬܗ ܕܝܢ ܡܫܝܚܐ. ܕܐܒܐ ܗܘܐ ܐܪܥܐ ܡܢܗ ܗܘܐ ܠܡܘܠܕܗ(*)	vol. III	ܗܫܝ - ܗܫܝܐ 710 - 711	
29		ܒܪܐ ܕܐܠܗܐ ܡܫܝܚܐ	ܝܠܕܬܐ ܕܐܠܗܐ ܒܬܘܠܬܐ. ܠܡܠܟܐ ܡܫܝܚܐ ܡܘܠܕܗ ܕܒܝܬܗ(*)	vol. III	ܗܫܟܓ - ܗܫܟܘ 723-726	
30		ܕܥܐܕܥܐܕܐ ܕܡܪܝ ܒܬܘܠܬܐ ܡܫܝܚܐ	ܒܬܘܠܬܐ ܥܠܡܐ ܡܪܝ ܡܠܟܐ. ܕܐܠܗܘܬܗ ܘܡܫܝܚܐ ܐܠܗܐ ܥܡܢ.	vol. III	ܗܫܢ - ܗܫܢܓ 750-753	85

44 The last two stanzas of this hymn in the Ḥūdrā are not similar to what is in the manuscripts. See for example Mardin 41 [f. 108v].

ܬܘܪܓܡܐ Tūrgāmē[45] 1983, 2001					
				Pages	Table 6
1	ܠܡܘܪܝܠܡܐ ܘܪܕܐ	ܝܠܕܐ ܕܝܠܕܬܐ	ܝܠܕܐ ܕܠܒܫ ܠܝܠܕܗ ܙܒܢܐ. ܘܠܐ ܚܣܝܐ ܘܝܬܝܪܐ ܘܠܐ ܒܨܝܪܐ.	ܩܝܚ - ܩܟ 118-120	2
2	-	ܝܠܕܐ ܕܗܘܟܡܬܐ	ܐܘܪܚܗ ܕܒܪܐ ܚܣܝܢܬܐ ܠܐ ܡܬܕܪܟܐ ܠܟܠܗܘܢ ܒܪ̈ܝܬܐ	ܩܦܗ-ܩܦܘ 185-186	91

2. Other Publications

	Year	Author	Title	Pages	Trans.	Table 6
1	1852 1987	George Percy Badger	*The Nestorians and Their Rituals*, vol. II.			
			ܡܢ ܡܥܒܕܢ ܕܡܫܝܚܐ ܡܫܒܚܐ. ܠܗ ܕܡܥܡܕܢܐ ܡܫܠܡ ܘܡܫܡܠܝܐ.	51-57	English	10
2	1873	Theodor Nöldeke	*"Zwei syrische Lieder auf die Einnahme Jerusalems durch Saladin,"* in *Zeitschrift der Deutschen Morgenländischen Gesellschaft* 27.	489-510		
			ܡܫܝܚܐ ܝܠܕܐ ܡܫܬܥܝܢܐ. ܕܡܢ ܡܕܡ ܫܠܡܐ ܕܠܐ ܥܘܕܪܐ.	495-505	German	
			ܦܬܘ ܕܫܠܡ ܠܐ ܝܚܝܕܐ. ܘܡܢܘ ܕܫܠܡ ܠܐ ܣܥܪ.	505-510	German	
3	1875	Gabriel Cardahi	*Liber thesauri de arte poetica Syrorum : nec non de eorum poetarum vitis et carminibus.*			
			ܒܪܐ ܕܩܕܡ ܒܗ ܗܝܡܢܘܬܐ[46] ܕܥܠ ܝܘܩܢܐ ܦܪܨܘܦܗ.	51-53	No trans.	8
4	1895	Aladár Deutsch	*Edition dreier Syrischen Lieder nach einer der Berliner Königlichenn Bibliothek.*			
			ܥܒܕ ܐܠܗܐ ܘܡܫܝܚ ܦܪܩܢ.. ܘܐܬܒܪܝ ܦܓܪܐ ܠܦܘܠܚܢܐ ܕܒܢܝ..	15-22	German	

[45] It is a book of prayers used only during the mass.

[46] Anton Pritula mentioned in his book that Cardahi published two hymns one is complete and the another in part, but actually Cardahi published parts of one hymn from the beginning, the middle and the end, it is Hymn (8) Table (6). However, to point the verses I used Mardin 41. Cardahi published from the verse ܒܪܐ ܕܩܕܡ ܒܗ ܗܝܡܢܘܬܐ [f. 23v] till the verse ܕܝܢܐ ܗܘ ܕܒܪܐ ܦܪܘܩܐ ܡܫܒܚܘܬܗ [f. 24v] then from the verse ܝܗܒܝܢ ܢܘܗܪ ܦܪܘܩܐ [f. 25v] till the verse ܠܟܠ ܠܗ ܒܡܠܟܘܬܗ ܡܢܗܪܐ [f. 25v], and the last part of the hymn ܥܡܕ ܗܘܐ ܠܗ ܦܘܪܩܢܐ [f. 27r] till the verse ܠܝ ܥܘܕܪܢܐ ܕܠܟܠ ܕܐܦܝܐ ܠܝ [f.27v]. See: Anton Pritula, *The Wardā*, p. 2.

			ܒܗ ܒܫܒܬܐ ܕܦܢܩܝܬܐ ܡܪܢܐ. ܘܫܒܚܢܬܐ ܕܢܒܝܐ ܒܝܢܢ.	22-25	German	24
			ܒܗ ܢܦܫ ܢܘܚ ܗܘ ܢܘܚܐ. ܐܘܠ ܠܒܝܬܐ ܐܝܟ ܦܘܡܪܐ.	25-29	German	25
5	1896	Isak Folkmann	*Ausgewählte nestorianische Kirchenlieder über das Martyrium des heil. Georg von Giwargis Warda.*			
			ܟܠ ܒܓܘܢܐ ܡܕܝܢܬܐ. ܐܦܟܠ ܒܫܡܟ ܦܪܘܫܬܐ	1-17	German	145
			ܡܪܝܐ ܡܪܝ ܒܗܢܐ ܒܐܝܕܐܘܗܝ. ܘܟܠܠܐ ܡܢ ܡܠܟ ܠܗ ܡܠܘܟܗ.	18-22	No trans.	
			ܐܘܪܘ ܐܚܝ ܘܫܠܡܘ ܘܡܪܚܡܘ. ܘܩܠܐ ܕܬܘܕܝܬܐ ܕܪܚܡܘ.	22-29	German	
			ܗܘ ܚܘ ܠܦܠܚܝܢ ܕܡܫܠܡܐ. ܚܠܡ ܘܢܨܚ ܠܫܠܛܢܘܗܝ ܡܠܟܘܗܝ.	29-34	No trans.	
			ܦܬܘ ܢܚܘܫ ܕܢܚܝܪܐ. ܓܒܪܐ ܠܚܝܠܬܐ ܘܚܝܠܐ ܒܟܝܠܟ.	34-41	No trans.	87
			ܠܓܒܪܐ ܕܦܘܩܕܐ ܢܨܚ. ܘܒܥܘܕܪܢܐ ܕܬܪܐ ܦܩܕ.	42-50	No trans.	88
			ܚܘܒܫܐ ܠܫܠܡܐ ܚܫܝܢܐ. ܕܟܠܒܐ ܘܚܒܪ ܠܬܒܪܐ ܗܢܐ.	50-55	No trans.	
6	1898	Y. Qelaytā	ܡܟܢܫܢܐ ܕܦܬܬܘܬܐ [The Book of Crumbs]	ܪܣܗ - ܪܥܕ 265-274		
			ܒܥܘܪܐ ܕܬܪܐ ܦܩܕ ܗܘܢܐ. ܕܝܠܕ ܦܬܐ ܒܠܒܐ ܕܘܟܝܐ.	ܪܣܙ — ܪܥܕ 267-274	No trans.	66
7	1901	Jacques Eugène Manna	المروج النزهية في آداب اللغة الآرامية *Morceaux choisis de littérature araméenne*, vol. II.	ܪܨܗ-ܫܟܒ 295-322		
			ܒܝܘܡܐ ܕܫܒܬܐ ܗܘ ܪܘܡܐ ܐܬܐ. ܘܒܦܘܩܕܢܗ ܗܘ ܡܫܟܚ ܐܬܐ	ܪܨܘ — ܫܐ 296-301	No trans.	9
			ܢܠܟܐ ܕܟܠܗ ܠܢܠܟܗ ܘܟܬܐ. ܘܟܠ ܚܕܐ ܘܢܦܫܗ ܘܟܠ ܢܦܫܐ	ܫܒ - ܫܙ 302-307	No trans.	2
			ܒܟܪܝܬܐ ܚܠܩܬܐ ܘܚܕܪܐ ܚܠܗ ܒܪܝܬܐ ܢܗܝܪܐ.[47]	ܫܙ - ܫܟܒ 307-322	No trans.	
8	1903	Henri Pognon	*Une version syriaque des aphorismes d'Hippocrate*, vol. II.			
			ܒܥܘܪܐ ܕܬܪܐ ܦܩܕ ܗܘܢܐ. ܕܝܠܕ ܦܬܐ ܒܠܒܐ ܕܘܟܝܐ.	VII-IX	French	66

[47] For a complete translation of this hymn Cf. Philippe Gignoux, "Un poéme inèdit sur l'homme-Microcosme de Guiwarguis Wardā (13ème siècle)," *Ressembler Au Monde* (1999): pp. 95-189.

9	1904	Heinrich Hilgenfeld	*Ausgewählte Gesänge des Gewargis Warda von Arbel.*			
			ܡܢܘ ܕܢܟܝܬ ܠܟ ܫܒܩܢ. ܘܡܢܘ ܢܦܩܐ ܐܦ ܢܐܠܐ ܠܟܘܢ.	23-28	German	54
			ܐܝܟܘ ܕܐܝܬܠܗ ܕܠܡܢܐ. ܦܪܝܫܐ ܦܪܫܬܐ ܘܐܘܝܬ ܗܘܢܐ.	29-35	German	55
			ܐܘ ܦܬܓܡܝܟ ܡܢܐ ܦܫܩܝܢ. ܐܘ ܡܕܡܝܬܟ ܡܢܐ ܦܚܡܝܢ..	36-43	German	56
			ܐܘ ܢܘܗܪܟ ܡܢܐ ܚܒܝܒ. ܘܡܢܐ ܗܝܟܢ ܢܚܢܢ ܘܡܢܐ ܡܫܒܚܝܢ.	44-49	German	57
			ܥܢܐ ܐܝܟ ܘܡܢܘܚ ܡܢܝ.. ܘܐܪܒܥܝܢ ܦܬܓܡ ܠܦܠܚܐ ܕܢܘܗܝ..	49-59	German	
			ܐܘ ܡܠܟܐ ܣܓܝܐ ܟܝܢܐ ܗܘܝܐ. ܐܘ ܡܠܟܐ ܦܪܝܫ ܫܪܒܐ ܗܘܝܐ.	60-65	German	137
			ܚܝܠܐ ܕܦܠܓܐ ܒܐܪܥܐ. ܘܐܪܒܥ ܡܢܬܐ ܡܢ ܓܒܪܐ.	65-74	German	15
			ܓܒܪܐ ܕܫܘܒܚܐ ܫܦܝܪ ܗܘܐ. ܘܕܚܠܬ ܘܬܚܬ ܡܬܚܪܘܬ ܗܘܐ.	74-79	German	84
			ܫܡܝܐ ܥܠܡܢܐ ܦܬܓܡܝܢ. ܕܐܠܗܘܬܗ ܡܫܡܫܝܢ ܟܠܗ ܥܡܝܢ.	80-86	German	85
10	1905	A. J. MacLean	*Rituale Armenorum.*	300-388		
			ܫܡܝܐ ܘܐܠܗܐ ܦܬܓܡܝܢ. ܕܐܠܗܘܬܗ ܘܡܘܬ ܐܪܥܐ ܥܡܝܢ	325-327	English	12
			ܥܒܝܕܝܢ ܦܬܡܝܢ ܐܢܫܝ. ܡܪܝܐ ܡܪܝ ܘܡܪܢ ܠܟܠܗܘܢ	327-330	English	95
			ܐܘ ܚܝܒܐ ܢܘܗܪܝܗ. ܐܝܟ ܥܡܘܕܐ ܕܠܒܐܝܬ	350-352	English	14
11	1907	Bernhard Vandenhoff	*Vier geistliche Gedichte in syrischer und neusyrischer Sprache : aus den Berliner HSS. Sachau 188 u. 223 mit Erklärenden Anmerkungen.*			
			ܡܢ ܦܩܘܕ ܠܗ ܠܒܪܝܬܐ. ܒܪܐ ܕܐܠܗܐ ܘܡܠܘܟܐ ܕܡܪܝܐ.	ܐ – ܝܕ 1-14	No trans.	3
12	1924	Y. Qelaytā	ܡܪܓܢܝܬܐ [The Pearl].			
			ܥܘܡܩܐ ܘܡܢܝ ܡܢܘܢ. ܚܟܡܬܐ ܕܠܝܬ ܡܫܘܚܬܐ ܕܠܡܫܚܐ	ܨܓ – ܨܙ 93-97	No trans.	136
13	1937	S. Aṣ-Ṣāʾiġ	”شاعر العذراء، كيوركيس وردا الأربيلي“ [The Poet of the Virgin: Gīwargīs Wardā of Erbil], in *Al-Naǧm* 9.	321-326		
			ܒܪܝܟ ܕܫܘܒܚܐ ܗܘ ܕܡܢ ܐܒܐ. ܘܬܫܒܘܚܬܐ ܗܘ ܡܫܒܚ ܐܒܐ.	322-326	Arabic	9

14	1949	A.–M. Massonnat, O.P.	"Marie dans la Liturgie Chaldénne." In *Maria Études sur la Sainte Vierge.*	341-351		
			ܒܟܢܫܐ ܕܫܘܒܚܐ ܗܘ ܐܝܟܐ ܐܢܐ. ܘܒܡܫܬܘܬܐ ܗܘ ܡܫܬܟܚ ܐܢܐ.[48]	345-347	French	9
			ܐܡܐ ܘܐܡܬܐ ܠܡܪܢܐ. ܗܘܟܠܒ ܒܩܘܫܡܝ ܦܪܝܟܐ ܕܚܕܐ.[49]	349	French	5
15	1950	Paul Mouterde	"Une invocation au Cœur de Jésus dans le Livre de Warda." In *AB* 68.	305-309		
			ܦܬܚܘ ܕܢܦܫܗ ܚܠܠ ܫܘܒܚܝ. ܘܡܚܝܗ ܢܦܩܐ ܐܦ ܝܠܕܐ ܚܠܠܗ.[50]	307-309	French	54
16	1957	Paul H. Bachi	"Marie dans la doctrine de Ghiwarghis Warda a'prés les manuscrits syriaques de la Bibliothèque Vaticane. Étude historique et doctrinale."			
			ܐܡܐ ܘܐܡܬܐ ܠܡܪܢܐ. ܗܘܟܠܒ ܒܩܘܫܡܝ ܦܪܝܟܐ ܕܚܕܐ.	296-320	French	5
			ܒܬܘܠܬܐ ܡܕܝܢܬܐ ܕܠܠܒܟܐ ܐܬܬܦܝܣ ܩܠܐ ܕܫܒܩܐ ܠܝܠܝܐ.[51]	321-340	French	7
			ܒܪܐ ܕܦܫܘܡ ܝܗ ܗܝܡܢܘܬܐ. ܕܟܠ ܡܫܩܠܐ ܘܕܝܢܘܬܐ.	341-367	French	8
			ܒܟܢܫܐ ܕܫܘܒܚܐ ܗܘ ܐܝܟܐ ܐܢܐ. ܘܒܡܫܬܘܬܐ ܗܘ ܡܫܬܟܚ ܐܢܐ.	368-392	French	9
			ܦܢ ܡܬܒܥ ܕܒܦܘܕܥܐ ܝܗܒܬܐ. ܐܘ ܕܒܦܘܡܐ ܢܦܠܠ ܘܡܬܦܠܐ.	393-421	French	10
			ܒܫܡ ܐܒܐ ܘܒܪܐ ܘܪܘܚܐ ܕܩܘܕܫܐ. ܚܕ ܐܠܗܐ ܫܒܝܚܐ ܡܫܒܚܐ.[52]	422-437	French	

[48] Only some selected stanzas were translated.
[49] Only some selected stanzas were translated.
[50] This hymn was translated till stanza [11].
[51] According to the manuscripts used in this work, we found two hymns that begin with ܒܬܘܠܬܐ ܡܕܝܢܬܐ ܕܠܠܒܟܐ but one of them its second verse has ܥܡܗ ܡܠܐ ܕܫܡܝܐ ܠܚܝܐ this hymn is found in different manuscripts and it is attributed to Gīwargīs Wardā (cf. Hymn (7), Table 6), while the other hymn its second verse has ܐܬܬܦܝܣ ܩܠܐ ܕܫܒܩܐ ܠܝܠܝܐ and it is found only in D2, f37v (cf. Hymn (145), Table 6) and it belongs to Gīwargīs of Adiabene. It seems many authors had confused between the titles of the two hymns.
[52] I'm not sure if this hymn belongs to Gīwargīs Wardā but it is found in the Chaldean Ḥūḏrā. See *Breviarium Chaldaicum*, vol. I, p. ܪܝܐ [211].

17	1991	G. Gharib	"Giorgio Warda (c. 1175-1236)." In *Testi mariani del primo millennio, IV Padri e altri autori orientali* 4.	370-397		
			ܩܝܡܐ ܘܐܢܫܐ ܠܒܪܢܫܐ. ܗܘܟܢ ܒܩܝܡܬܢ ܦܪܝܩܐ ܕܩܝܡܐ.	373-377	Italian	5
			ܒܢܝܢܐ ܡܕܝܢܬܐ ܕܡܠܟܘܬܐ ܝܥܒܘܕ ܗܝܟܠܐ ܕܡܠܟܐ ܠܝܠܕܬܐ	378-381	Italian	7
			ܒܪܐ ܕܒܬܘܠܬܐ ܒܗ ܗܝܡܢܘܬܐ. ܕܡܠ ܝܗܒܬܐ ܦܪܘܩܘܬܐ.	381-386	Italian	8
			ܒܝܘܡܐ ܕܫܘܒܚܐ ܗܘܐ ܩܝܡܐ ܐܒܐ. ܦܪܘܣܛܘܠܐ ܗܘܐ ܡܬܒܥܐ ܐܒܐ.	386-390	Italian	9
			ܦܢ ܡܥܡܝܢ ܕܒܦܘܪܫܢܐ ܝܗܒܬܐ. ܐܘ ܦܪܩܘܡܐ ܢܦܩܬ ܘܡܥܒܕܬܐ.	390-396	Italian	10
			ܦܬܚܘ ܕܢܩܒܠ ܚܠܠ ܫܘܒܚܐ. ܘܡܚܘ ܝܒܝܐ ܐܦ ܝܠܕܐ ܚܠܝܐ.[53]	396-397	Italian	54
18	1991	Gerrit Jan Reinink	"Ein syrisches streitgespräch zwischen tod und Satan." In *Dispute Poems And Dialogues In The Ancient And Mediaval Near East OLA* 42.	135-152		
			ܦܡ ܗܝܠܐ ܦܬܝܪ ܠܡܘܬܐ ܦܫܩܐ. ܐܡܪ ܡܘܬܐ ܘܣܛܢܐ.	143-152	German	147
19	1999	Philippe Gignoux	"Un poème inédit sur l'homme-Microcosme de Guiwarguis Wardā (13ème siècle)." In *Ressembler Au Monde*.	95-188		
			ܥܒܝܕ ܦܪܨܘܦܐ ܘܡܬܚܙܐ ܒܥܠܡܐ. ܕܡܢ ܟܠ ܠܟܠ ܘܒܗܘܢ ܡܢ ܟܠ.	100-189	French	
20	1999	ʾAndrāws Ṣanā	"قصيدة لكيوركيس وردا في قيامة المسيح" [A Hymn of Gīwargīs Wardā on the resurrection of Christ.' In *Nağm Al Mašriq* 17.	44-47		
			ܒܩܝܡܬܗ ܕܡܪܢ ܡܫܝܚܐ. ܩܡ ܠܐܒܐ ܘܐܬܚܙܝ ܥܡܢܐ.	46-47	Arabic	80
21	2000	S.P. Brock	"Two Syriac Dialogue Poems on Abel and Cain." In *Le Musèon*.	333-375		
			ܦܪܬܐ ܕܗܒܝܠ ܘܩܐܝܢ ܐܚܘܗܝ. ܩܛܠܗ ܒܗ ܒܪܘܚܐ ܕܩܢܝܢܐ.	367-373	English	146

[53] Only twelve stanzas are translated from this hymn.

22	2004	Anton Pritula	"An Autobiographic Hymn by Givargis Warda." In *Syriaca II*.	229-241		
			ܓܝܪ ܫܢܝܐ ܣܓܝܐ ܝܬܒܬ. ܘܓܝܪ ܦܪܨܘܦܐ ܣܓܝܐ ܦܪܨܦܬ.	234-241	English	46
23	2005	Anton Pritula	"A Hymn by Givargis Warda on the Childhood of Christ." In *Die Suryoye und ihre Umwelt* 4.	423-451		
			ܡܢ ܫܡܫ ܠܗ ܠܒܪܝܬܗ. ܒܪܐ ܕܐܠܗܐ ܘܐܝܬܘܬܗ.	433-451	English	3
24	2006	Anton Pritula	"Из истории восточносирийской литургической поэзии: заключительное песнопение моления ниневитян" [From the History of Eastern Syriac Liturgical Poetry: the Final Hymn "A Prayer of the Ninevians"]. In *ВГ* [Magic Mountain] 12.	147-159		
			ܐܘ ܡܫܡܫܢܐ ܕܬܠܡܝܕܐ. ܦܘܫܩܢܐ ܕܬܢܘܬܐ.	151-159	Russian	58
25	2006/12	Dahlia Khay Azeez	"قصيدة عن ميلاد الكلمة في الزمن للشاعر كيوركيس وردا (القرن 13)" [A Poem about the Nativity of the Word in the Time, by the Poet Gīwargīs Wardā (Cen. 13)]. In *Nağm Al Mašriq* 48.	470-475		
			ܝܠܕܐ ܕܒܪܐ ܠܝܠܕܗ ܙܒܢܐ. ܘܠܐ ܚܣܪ ܘܐܦܩܗ ܘܠܐ ܝܬܝܪ.[54]	470-475	Arabic	2
26	2007	Anton Pritula	"Песнопение Гиваргиса Варды о гробе" [A Hymn by Giwargis Warda about the coffin]. In *ВГ* [Magic Mountain] 14.	92-102		
			ܐܘ ܢܦܫܐ ܕܣܒܪܬ ܡܢ ܟܠ. ܡܢܘ ܢܓܕܘܢ ܦܪܫܢ ܡܢ ܟܠ.	96-102	Russian	26

[54] This hymn was translated till stanza [31].

27	2009	Anton Pritula	“Гимн о неравенстве в человеческом обществе из восточно-сирийского сборника ‘Варда’” [A Hymn about Human Inequality in Easter Syriac Miscellaneous ‘Warda’]. In *ВГ* [Magic Mountain] 15.	122-135		
			ܒܥܠܡܐ ܗܢܐ ܚܙܝܬ ܗܘܝܬ. ܘܦܠܓܘܬܐ ܡܫܚܠܦܬܐ ܗܘܬ.	128-135	Russian	65
28	2009	Anton Pritula	“Восточносирийские песнопения (ʿониты) и гомилии Нарсая: шесть гимнов из сборника ‘Варда’” [Eastern Syriac Hymns (ʿonita) and Homilies by Narsaj: Six Hymns from the Collection ‘Wardā’]. In *Символ* [Symbol] 55.	152-253		
			ܡܢ ܒܢ̈ܝܢܐ ܕܦܪ̈ܨܘܦܐ ܡܫܝܢܐ. ܘܡܬܟܢܝܬܐ ܕܒܢ̈ܝܢܐ ܒܝܢܝ.	166-177	Russian	24
			ܡܢ ܢܦܫ ܢܘܚܡ ܗܘ. ܢܘܪܐ. ܐܙܠ ܠܒܝܬܐ ܐܝܟ ܦܘܡܦܐ.	178-192	Russian	25
			ܢܚܘ ܕܐܒܗܬܗ ܕܟܢܫܐ. ܘܕܝܢܐ ܦܪܝܩܐ ܘܢܘܚܐ ܗܘܢܐ.	193-210	Russian	55
			ܐܘ ܢܘܩܦܝ ܩܕܐ ܒܝܬܝ. ܘܩܕܐ ܫܝܢ ܚܝܝ ܘܩܕܐ ܡܪܝܪܝ.	211-224	Russian	57
			ܐܘ ܪܒܪܐ ܒܢܝ ܥܠܡܘܬܐ. ܟܠܠܩܐ ܬܪܥܘܗܝ ܘܒܝܬܝܟܬܐ.	225-238	Russian	119
			ܡܢ ܫܒܝܘ ܐܢܫܐ ܒܒܪܝܬܐ. ܘܐܬܦܪܥܘ ܠܬܘܠܝ ܦܪܥܘܢܝܬܐ.	239-253	Russian	53
29	2010	Anton Pritula	“Восточносирийский гимн о Детстве Христа и прозаические (сиро- и арабоязычные) параллели” [An Eastern Syriac Hymn about the Childhood of Christ and its (Syriac and Arabic) Parallels in Prose]. In *Символ* [Symbol] 58.	229-267		
			ܟܕ ܦܫܛ ܠܗ ܠܪܒܘܬܟ. ܒܪܐ ܕܐܠܗܐ ܘܠܒܪܢܫܘܬܟ.	239-267	Russian	3

30	2010	Rony Patrous	"سبي كرمليس لكيوركيس وردا الأربيلي" [The Capture of Karmlīs for Gīwargīs Wardā of Erbil]. In *Sīmtā* 14.	102-114		
			ܥܢܝܬ ܐܪܒܠ ܘܢܝܫܝܗ ܗܕܘܢ.. ܘܐܬܒܢܝܬ ܦܫܝܛܐ ܠܡܠܟܐ ܕܝܗܘ..	104-114	No trans.	
31	2010	Alessandro Mengozzi	"A Syriac Hymn on the Crusades from a Warda Collection." In *EVO* 33.	187-203		
			ܡܫܝܚܐ ܡܠܟܐ ܡܗܝܡܢܐ. ܕܥܡ ܡܢܝܢ ܚܠܩܝܢ ܕܟܠ ܫܘܪܝܐ.	194-201	English	
32	2010	Pier Giorgio Borbone	"Due Episodi Delle Relazioni Tra Mongoli e Siri Nel XIII Secolo Nella Storiografia e Nella Poesia Siriaca." In *EVO* 33.	205-228		
			ܥܢܝܬ ܐܪܒܠ ܘܢܝܫܝܗ ܗܕܘܢ.. ܘܐܬܒܢܝܬ ܦܫܝܛܐ ܠܡܠܟܐ ܕܝܗܘ..	208-218	Italian	
33	2011	Rony Patrous	"تبليس (تفليس) عاصمة جورجيا" [Tbilisi (Tiflis) the Capital of Georgia]. In *Sīmtā* 16.	180-189		
			ܒܥܝܬܐ ܦܠܚܝܬ ܒܝܬܗ. ܕܫܘܠܛܢ ܗܠܝܢ ܫܢܝ ܒܥܝܬܗ.	182-188	Arabic	142
34	2012	Anton Pritula	"The Last Hymn of the Praying (Rogation) of the Ninevites." In *Orientalische Christen und Europa.*	173-186		
			ܐܘ ܬܫܒܘܚܬܐ ܕܨܠܘܬܐ. ܦܘܫܩܠܐ ܕܢܝܢܘܝܬܐ.	177-186	English	58
35	2012	Anton Pritula	"A Hymn on Tiflis from Wardā Collection: A Transformation of the Muslim Conquerors into Pagans." In *Caucasus during the Mongol Period – Der Kaukasus in der Mongolenzeit.*	217-237		
			ܒܥܝܬܐ ܦܠܚܝܬ ܒܝܬܗ. ܕܫܘܠܛܢ ܗܠܝܢ ܫܢܝ ܒܥܝܬܗ.	224-236	English	142

36	2013	ʿImād Dāwd	"ترتيلة عن الميلاد الزمني ل'الله الكلمة"" [A Hymn about the Nativity of the Word in the Time]. In *Nağm Al Mašriq* 76.	444-447		
			ܐܠܗܐ ܕܐܠܝܐ ܠܐܒܠܟܘܗܝ ܙܕܩܐ. ܘܠܐ ܚܙܐ ܘܦܬܚܗ ܘܠܐ ܐܦܬܚܐ.	444-445	Arabic	2
37	2014	Anton Pritula	"The Wardā Hymnological Collection and Šlēmōn of Aḫlāṭ (13th Century)." In *Scrinium* 10.	149-207		
			ܐܠܗܐ ܕܐܠܝܐ ܠܐܒܠܟܘܗܝ ܙܕܩܐ. ܘܠܐ ܚܙܐ ܘܦܬܚܗ ܘܠܐ ܐܦܬܚܐ.	167-180	English	2
			ܠܦܪܘܫܘܬܐ ܐܠܗܝܬܐ. ܦܪܝܫ ܒܝܬܗ ܒܪܐ ܡܫܝܚܐ.	181-191	English	105
			ܚܝܠܐ ܕܫܠܝܛ ܒܢܘܗܪܐ. ܘܡܕܒܪ ܡܢܐ ܡܢ ܓܒܪܬܐ.	192-206	English	15
38	2014	Rony Patrous	ܟܘܢܫ ܡܙܡܘܪܬܐ ܕܓܝܘܪܓܝܣ ܘܪܕܐ ܐܪܒܝܠܝܐ [A Collection of Hymns of Gīwargīs Wardā].			
			ܦܬܚܘ ܬܪܥܝܢ ܘܐܬܬܪܝܡܘ ܥܠܡܐ. ܠܡܠܟܐ ܡܠܟܐ ܕܬܫܒܘܚܬܐ.	27-32	No trans.	1
			ܐܠܗܐ ܕܐܠܝܐ ܠܐܒܠܟܘܗܝ ܙܕܩܐ. ܘܠܐ ܚܙܐ ܘܦܬܚܗ ܘܠܐ ܐܦܬܚܐ.	33-38	No trans.	2
			ܡܢ ܩܕܡ ܠܗ ܠܥܠܡܐ. ܒܪܐ ܕܐܠܗܐ ܘܐܬܓܠܝ ܒܣܘܦܐ.	39-47	No trans.	3
			ܝܘܡܐ ܘܪܡܫܐ ܠܘܩܒܠܢ. ܘܫܠܡ ܒܩܘܫܛܐ ܫܘܬܦܐ ܕܝܘܡܐ.	48-53	No trans.	5
			ܟܠ ܥܕܬܐ ܬܫܒܘܚܬܐ. ܢܙܡܪ ܗܘܢ ܕܡܪܥܝܬ ܦܬܓܡܐ.	54-58	No trans.	6
			ܒܢܝ ܐܕܡ ܡܫܝܚܐ ܕܡܠܒܠܐ. ܥܡܗ ܡܠܟܐ ܕܠܒܫܝܢ ܠܫܠܝܐ.	59-63	No trans.	7
			ܒܪܐ ܕܐܒܘܢ ܒܗ ܗܝܡܢܬܐ. ܕܠܐ ܢܫܠܡܬܐ ܘܕܢܦܩܬܐ.	64-70	No trans.	8
			ܒܢܝܬܐ ܕܫܘܒܚܐ ܗܘܐ ܪܒܐ ܐܝܬ. ܘܒܦܫܥܘܬܐ ܗܘܐ ܡܬܦܢܐ ܐܝܬ.	71-77	No trans.	9
			ܡܢ ܡܥܒܕ ܕܒܦܘܠܚܢܐ ܝܗܒܝܗ. ܘܐ ܕܒܠܘܡܐ ܢܦܠܠ ܘܝܥܩܒܐ.	77-84	No trans.	10
			ܐܝܬܝ ܚܝܐ ܘܒܪ ܚܝܐ. ܒܢܝܐ ܠܟܝܢܐ ܦܫܝܐ ܘܫܠܝܐ.	85-87	No trans.	11
			ܦܬܚܝ ܗܠܠܗܟܐ ܘܗܠܠܗܝ. ܕܐܠܗܝܘܬܗ ܘܗܘܐ ܒܪܝܬ ܥܡܝ.	88-92	No trans.	12
			ܦܠܥܒܘܗܝ ܦܓܪܐ ܒܘܪܟܐ. ܗܦܟܘ ܗܘܘ ܗܕܡܐ ܕܪܘܚܐ ܘܢܘܪܐ.	93-95	No trans.	13
			ܚܝܠܐ ܕܫܠܝܛ ܒܢܘܗܪܐ. ܘܡܕܒܪ ܡܢܐ ܡܢ ܓܒܪܬܐ.	96-101	No trans.	15

			ܗܘ ܡܫܝܚܐ ܕܐܬܦܫܩ ܒܛܘܦ̈ܣܘܗܝ. ܕܢܒ̈ܝܐ ܫܠܝܚ̈ܐ ܐܣܝܘܗܝ ܕܡܫܝܚܐ.	102-105	No trans.	16
			ܗܘ ܡܫܝܚܐ ܝܘܡܢܐ ܥܡܢܐ. ܒܕܘܒܪ̈ܝܗܘܢ ܕܫܠܝܚ̈ܐ ܐܣܝܘܗܝ ܕܡܫܝܚܐ.	106-107	No trans.	17
			ܒܫܦܝܘܬ ܪܘܚܐ ܕܬܠܡܝܕܘܬܗ ܕܫܡܥܘܢ ܟܐܦܐ. ܫܠܝܚܐ ܓܒܝܐ ܦܛܪܘܣ ܘܦܘܠܘܣ.	108-112	No trans.	18
			ܡܢ ܢܒܝܘܬ ܕܡܫܝܚܐ. ܬܫܒܘܚܬ ܠܒܪܐ ܐܘ ܫܘܒܚܐ.	113-117	No trans.	19
			ܥܘܡܪܐ ܠܢܣܟܐ ܡܢ ܩܕܝܫܘܗܝ. ܕܦܘܩܕܢܐ ܘܩܢܐ ܘܡܕܒܪ̈ܢܐ.	118-124	No trans.	22
			ܦܓܪ̈ܢܝܬܐ ܕܢܨܚܢ̈ܘܬܐ. ܘܡܬܓܪ̈ܘܬܐ ܕܥܡܠ̈ܐ.	125-129	No trans.	23
			ܗܢ ܒܥܒܕܐ ܕܦܘܪܩܢܐ ܡܪܢܐ. ܘܬܫܡܫܬܐ ܕܢܟܣ̈ܐ ܒܝܫܐ.	130-133	No trans.	24
			ܗܢ ܒܓܘ ܢܘܢ ܡܢ ܒܘܢܐ. ܐܝܟ ܠܒܝܘܬܐ ܐܝܟ ܦܘܡܕܐ.	134-138	No trans.	25
			ܐܘ ܒܢ̈ܝܐ ܕܫܒܝܚ ܡܢ ܟܠ. ܡܢܘ ܕܡܫܒܚ ܦܢܝܢ ܡܢ ܟܠ.	139-142	No trans.	26
			ܐܘ ܕܒܥܝܬܐ ܕܫܒܝܚܐ. ܘܐܝܟ ܕܒܢܝܬܐ ܕܘܟܐ ܒܦܘܪܩܢܐ.	143-145	No trans.	27
			ܒܥܘܡܪܝ ܫܒܚܐ ܐܬܐ ܠܒ. ܘܐܘܠܐ ܕܡܫܒܚܐ ܡܬܥܒܕ ܐܢܐ ܠܒ.	146-148	No trans.	28
			ܠܥܒܕ ܒܥܠܘܗܝ ܕܐܠܗܘܬܗ. ܢܥܒܕ ܕܐܡܝܢ ܒܗ ܦܠܚܝܢܬܗ.	149-151	No trans.	29
			ܦܬܐ ܕܫܒܝܚܘܬܐ. ܕܠܗ ܘܡܢ ܕܘܝܕ ܡܫܒܚܘܬܐ.	152-157	No trans.	31
			ܥܒܕܗ ܗܕܐ ܒܠܒܘܟ ܒܥܕܐ. ܕܠܦܪܘܩܐ ܒܠ ܗܘܘ ܫܠܝܚܘܬܐ.	158-161	No trans.	32
			ܐܠܗܐ ܠܥܒܘܕܐ ܘܡܫܚܐ. ܒܢܝܐ ܡܫܡܫܢܐ ܘܡܬܠܠܢܐ.	162-164	No trans.	33
			ܦܬܚ ܕܪܫܝ ܒܫܘܒܚܗ. ܘܢܥܡܪ ܡܫܒܚܘܬܗ.	165-167	No trans.	34
			ܒܗܘܢܐ ܕܡܠܟܐ ܢܦܩܬ ܐܢܐ. ܒܒܘܥܝܐ ܕܫܘܒܚܐ ܗܘ ܡܫܝܚ ܐܢܐ.	168-170	No trans.	35
			ܦܬܝ ܡܫܝܚܐ ܕܐܬܬܦܫܩܬ. ܘܡܫܠܡ ܒܦܘܫܩܐ ܕܐܬܬܠܝܬ.	171-173	No trans.	36
			ܐܘ ܕܪܡܝܐ ܒܫܘܒܚܬܐ. ܦܬܘܪ ܡܫܒܚܐ ܐܝܟ ܕܒܗܘܢܬܐ.	174-176	No trans.	37
			ܢܗܘ ܩܫܝܐ ܕܦܓܪܐ ܠܒܗ ܠܗ. ܬܗܘܡܐ ܕܫܘܒܚܐ ܕܠܐ ܡܬܒܕܩ ܠܗ.	177-179	No trans.	38
			ܦܬܐ ܕܠܒܝܒ ܕܡܫܒܝܢ. ܣܓܝܐܐ ܘܫܒܚܐ ܘܡܫܒܚ ܡܫܒܚܝܢ.	180-182	No trans.	39
			ܦܬܐ ܕܒܩܘܫܬܐ ܕܢܨܚܢ. ܘܡܬܬܒܘܬܗ ܦܪܘܩܗ ܠܟܠܗܘܢ.	183-185	No trans.	40
			ܢܥܒܕ ܥܡܢܐ ܘܡܫܒܚ ܡܢ ܟܠ. ܦܠܚܐ ܡܫܝܚܐ ܕܡܫܬܠܚ ܠܟܠ ܟܠ.	186-188	No trans.	41
			ܓܒܪܐ ܠܥܒܕ ܒܬܫܒܘܚܬܐ. ܝܕܥܢ ܕܐܒܝܢ ܒܓܒܪܘܬܐ.	189-191	No trans.	42

			ܠܡܪܢ ܢܩܘܫ ܘܢܦܠܘ ܪܘܚܢ. ܠܝܢ ܡܘܠܦܢܐ ܗܝܢ ܗܘܕܝܢܐ.	192-194	No trans.	43
			ܠܡܪܢ ܦܨܝܚܘܬܐ ܘܫܘܒܚܬܐ. ܢܐܡܪ ܪܡܝܐ ܥܠ ܫܘܒܚܬܐ.	195-197	No trans.	44
			ܥܡ ܐܠܦܐ ܕܩܠܝܬܐ. ܘܥܡ ܦܣܩܘܠܐ ܕܥܡܝܩܬܐ.	198-200	No trans.	45
			ܥܡ ܟܘܪܐ ܡܠܐ ܝܩܝܪܬܐ ܘܥܡ ܦܪܡܘܕܬܐ ܡܠܝܐ ܦܪܡܘܕܐ.	201-203	No trans.	46
			ܚܝܢܐ ܘܐܚܝܕܝܢ ܡܬܘܒ ܚܝܠܐ ܐܢܐ. ܡܬܘܒ ܚܝܠܐ ܐܢܐ ܐܦ ܦܚܝܠܐ ܐܢܐ.	204-206	No trans.	47
			ܒܪܝܟ ܕܡܢ ܒܪܝܢܘܗܝ ܠܐ ܦܫܪ. ܐܠܐ ܐܘܣܦ ܘܠܒܫ ܒܫܪ.	207-209	No trans.	48
			ܒܪܝܟ ܕܡܢ ܚܝܠ ܘܝܒܪ ܐܠܗܢ. ܦܪܘܩܢ ܐܢܫܐ ܐܠܗܢ.	210-212	No trans.	49
			ܗܘ ܡܫܒܚܐ ܫܡܗ ܘܢܬܪܡܡܘ. ܘܦܬܓܡܗ ܡܠܟܐ ܕܪܘܚܐ ܕܩܘܕܫܐ.	213-215	No trans.	50
			ܟܠ ܒܢܬܐ ܡܕܝܢܬܐ. ܐܦܠܐ ܒܡܟܠܐ ܦܘܩܕܢܐ.	216-230	No trans.	145
			ܒܢ ܗܠܝܢ ܐܝܬܐ ܒܒܪܝܬܐ. ܘܢܬܦܪܥܘܢ ܠܟܠܗܘܢ ܦܘܪܥܢܘܬܐ.	231-235	No trans.	53
			ܡܢܘ ܕܢܦܩܗ ܚܠܦ ܥܡܡܝܢ. ܘܡܢܘ ܝܗܒܗ ܐܦ ܝܠܕܐ ܚܠܦܝܢ.	236-239	No trans.	54
			ܐܢܘ ܕܐܝܬܠܗ ܪܘܚܢܬܐ. ܘܕܝܢܐ ܦܪܘܩܐ ܘܐܘܪܚܐ ܗܘܐ.	240-244	No trans.	55
			ܐܘ ܦܫܝܛܘܬܟ ܡܢܐ ܦܨܝܚܐ. ܐܘ ܡܟܝܟܘܬܟ ܡܢܐ ܦܠܝܐܝ.	245-250	No trans.	56
			ܐܘ ܢܘܚܡܟ ܡܢܐ ܒܣܝܡ. ܘܡܢܐ ܗܝܢ ܚܢܢܝܢ ܘܡܢܐ ܡܪܚܡܢ.	251-255	No trans.	57
			ܐܘ ܫܡܝܥܬܐ ܕܐܠܗܘܬܐ. ܘܡܫܘܚܠܦܬܐ ܕܐܢܫܘܬܐ.	256-263	No trans.	58
			ܡܪܐ ܕܟܠ ܒܪܝܬܐ. ܐܦ ܢܘܗܪܐ ܕܟܠ ܦܘܪܩܢܐ.	264-266	No trans.	59
			ܦܠܛܢܐ ܕܦܫܝܛܘܬܐ. ܡܥܒܕܢܐ ܐܝܬܘܗܝ ܒܥܒܕܘܬܐ.	267-271	No trans.	60
			ܒܪܐ ܕܐܠܗܘܗܝ ܠܒܫ ܡܘܟܟܐ. ܘܢܦܩܘ ܒܡܘܠܕܐ ܘܠܐ ܡܙܘܓܝܐ.	272-276	No trans.	61
			ܒܫܦܝܪܘ ܪܘܚܐ ܡܪܐ ܗܘܢܐ. ܘܒܡܠܟܘܗܝ ܫܠܡܘܬܐ ܗܘܢܐ.	277-281	No trans.	62
			ܦܠܚܐ ܕܦܠܚܬܐ ܠܗ ܦܠܚܝܢ. ܘܩܘܫܬܐ ܠܪܡܘܗܝ ܡܫܡܫܝܢ.	282-286	No trans.	63
			ܒܪܝܟ ܕܒܝܘܡܗ ܡܕܝܢܬܐ. ܦܪܩ ܫܘܒܚܗ ܕܝܘܡܐ ܕܐܢܫܐ.	287-291	No trans.	67
			ܡܪܘܡܡ ܐܚܝ ܕܡܫܝܚܝܐ. ܒܡܫܝܚܘܬܐ ܦܪܘܩܘܬܐ.	292-295	No trans.	68
			ܢܩܫܐ ܝܠܗ ܠܝ ܗܘܢܐ. ܘܢܘܚܗ ܚܕܐ ܘܢܕܝܚܗ ܝܕܥܐ.	296-300	No trans.	69
			ܐܘ ܕܠܥܡܡܝܢܬܐ ܪܫܝܢ. ܘܠܡܫܒܚܢܬܐ ܡܬܪܒܝܢ.	301-304	No trans.	70
			ܐܘ ܡܫܐ ܡܢ ܥܠ ܕܠܗ ܐܠܐ ܥܠ. ܟܠ ܡܬܚܘܐ ܠܟܠ ܘܚܘܐ ܠܟܠ.	305-307	No trans.	71

			ܒܢܝ̈ ܐܪܥܬܗ ܕܘܫܢܐ. ܕܗܘܘ ܒܢܝ̈ܢܐ ܠܥܒܕܐ ܚܢ̈ܢܐ.	308-310	No trans.	72
			ܗܘ ܐܝܬ ܢܗܦܟ ܒܗ. ܒܝ ܘܡܢܐ ܢܦܩܠܐ ܢܚܚܘ ܠܗ.	311-314	No trans.	73
			ܒܝܬ ܟܡܐ ܕܘܫܢܐ. ܕܝܠܟܪܬܗ ܕܒܪܐ ܟܪܣܛܝܢܐ.	315-318	No trans.	64
			ܗܝ ܕܝܠܗ ܠܘܬܝܢ ܕܡܫܐ ܒܝܬ. ܗܢܐ ܕܒܐ ܠܟܘܪ ܒܫܐ ܥܠܝܬ.	319-322	No trans.	75
			ܦܐܪܐ ܕܪܘܚܐ ܠܢܟܦܘܬܗ. ܕܐܘܣܝܐ ܘܡܘܣܝܐ ܒܚܝܕܝܢ ܒܐܝܕܗ.	323-327	No trans.	76
			ܡܢ ܒܬܠ ܐܝܟ ܠܐܦܪܥܝܬ. ܕܡܠܟ ܢܒܝ̈ܐ ܝܕܥ ܕܒܝܬ.	328-331	No trans.	77
			ܦܠܓܐ ܕܓܝܕܐ ܘܦܘܪܥܢܐ. ܕܠܡܪܐ ܡܠ ܗܘܐ ܠܗ ܡܚܝܕܬܐ.	332-335	No trans.	78
			ܒܝܬܗ ܕܡܪܝ ܗܘܐ ܝܢܩܐ. ܘܐܝܟ ܦܗܪܐ ܠܐܝܩܪܐ ܘܐܢܫܐ.	336-341	No trans.	79
			ܒܡܘܬܗ ܦܓܪܐ ܚܝܕܐ. ܙܟܝ ܐܪܟܐ ܘܫܠܠܝ ܥܡܢܐ.	342-344	No trans.	80
			ܒܝܕܥܬܐ ܢܘܡܐ ܦܩܕܐ. ܝܒܐ ܬܪܘܢܐ ܦܓܪܐ ܢܠܡܐ	345-348	No trans.	81
			ܒܪܐ ܝܠܬܐ ܒܝܕܥܬܐ. ܠܒܢܗ ܠܦܬܪܐ ܐܪܥܐ	349-353	No trans.	82
			ܐܦܐ ܗܘܝ ܠܟ ܡܦܪܩܢܐ. ܒܪܐ ܝܚܝܕܐ ܗܘܝ ܡܢܚܡܢܐ	354-358	No trans.	83
			ܦܪܚܐ ܕܫܘܪܐ ܦܬܚܬ ܗܘܬ. ܘܕܝܠܗ ܘܙܟܬ ܘܬܦܪܗܒ ܗܘܬ.	359-362	No trans.	84
			ܦܥܠܝ ܥܒܕܬܐ ܘܬܠܝܢ. ܕܐܠܗܘܬܗ ܘܡܪܝܢ ܗܟܢ ܥܒܕ	363-367	No trans.	85
			ܬܪܥܐ ܕܒܬ ܢܘܗܪܐ. ܘܡܢܗܪܬܐ ܕܒܬܘܠܬܐ	368-371	No trans.	86
			ܦܬܚ ܝܡܐ ܕܒܗܝܐ. ܦܬܚܐ ܠܚܝ̈ܐ ܘܝܗܒܐ ܠܟܠܢ	372-375	No trans.	87
			ܠܐܓܘܢܐ ܕܫܘܪܐ ܝܠܗ. ܘܒܥܘܪܬܗ ܐܪܐ ܫܘܚ	376-380	No trans.	88
			ܐܠܗܐ ܐܝܬ ܝܠܬܐ. ܥܡܐ ܒܗ ܐܒܘܗܝ ܒܐܝܬܘܬܐ.	381-386	No trans.	90
			ܐܘܪܚܗ ܦܓܪܐ ܚܝܕܐ. ܠܐ ܡܬܦܪܫܐ ܠܥܠܡܝܢ ܒܪܢܐ.	-390387	No trans.	91
			ܝܡܐ ܕܐܒܐ ܝܚܝܕ ܡܢ[55] ܐܒܘܗܝ. ܝܚܝܕ ܡܢ ܐܒܘܗܝ ܘܫܘܐ ܠܐܒܘܗܝ.	-395391	No trans.	92
			ܗܢܐ ܕܐܪܥܐ ܘܫܡܝܐ. ܐܬܐ ܡܦܢܝܐ ܡܢܝܚܐ ܡܢܗܪܢܐ.	396-400	No trans.	94
			ܥܒܝܕܝܢ ܦܬܚܝܢ ܐܢܫܝܢ. ܗܪܟܐ ܗܢܝ ܘܐܘܪܚܝܢ ܠܚܝܝܢ.	401-407	No trans.	95
			ܗܢܐ ܐܘܪܚܝܢ ܒܫܘܠܗ ܕܡܪܢ. ܘܗܘܐ ܠܫܠܡ ܐܘܪܚ ܒܢܝܢ.	408-412	No trans.	96
			ܡܢܘ ܗܦܟ ܕܒܝܠܬܐ. ܝܗܒܐ ܠܠܒܐ ܡܪܝܐ ܝܠܬܐ.	413-417	No trans.	97

[55] In some manuscripts ܡܢ is omitted.

			ܓܡܝܪܐ ܕܠܝܬ ܐܝܟܘܬܗ. ܒܗ ܐܬܒܪܝܬ ܟܠܗ ܡܬܩܢܘܬܗ.	427-430	No trans.	98
			ܡܘܕܝܢܐ ܠܗ ܠܗܘ ܚܢܢܐ. ܦܠܓ ܕܡܫܚܐ ܘܫܒܝܚ ܚܝܠܐ.	431-436	No trans.	99
			ܗܘ ܡܠܟܐ ܕܥܠܡܐ. ܘܡܪܐ ܕܒܪ̈ܝܬܐ ܘܕܦܓܪ̈ܐ.	437-441	No trans.	100
			ܡܪܐ ܕܡܠܟܘܬܐ ܘܫܘܠܛܢ̈ܐ. ܒܪܝܬܗ ܗܘ ܐܝܟ ܕܨܒܐ.	442-443	No trans.	101
			ܫܘܒܚܐ ܠܗ ܠܫܡܝܐ ܒܫܘܒܚܬܐ. ܝܗܒܘܢ ܕܥܠܡܐ ܒܬܫܒ̈ܚܬܐ.	444-447	No trans.	102
			ܐܢܫܐ ܕܐܝܬ ܠܗ ܡܫܡܫܢܐ. ܪ̈ܘܚܢܐ ܘܠܐ ܓܘܫܡܢܐ.	448-451	No trans.	103
			ܠܐܠܗܐ ܕܝܗܒ ܚܝ̈ܐ ܠܗܘܢ. ܘܡܬܒܝܢܐ ܒܝܕ ܚܘܒܐ ܗܘܢܐ.	452-457	No trans.	104
			ܠܡܪܢܐ ܐܠܗܝܢ. ܕܢܝܚ ܒܝܘܡܗ ܒܪܐ ܡܫܝܚܐ.	458-461	No trans.	105
			ܐܠܗܐ ܡܢܗ ܐܬܐ. ܒܪܗ ܥܠܝܗ ܐܬܪ ܠܡܘܪܝܐ ܐܬܐ.	462-464	No trans.	106
			ܐܢܫܐ ܕܠܝܬ ܐܝܟ ܐܢܫܘܬܗ. ܠܐ ܘܐܦܠܐ ܐܝܬ ܐܝܟ ܝܘܡܬܗ.	465-468	No trans.	107
			ܗܘ ܚܢܢܐ ܝܘܡܐ ܡܥܒܕܢܐ. ܕܐܡܪ ܡܪܢ ܒܟܠ ܦܠܓܘܬܐ.	469-472	No trans.	108
			ܝܗܒܗ ܕܐܒܐ ܡܫܡܫܢܐ ܠܟܠ ܕܡܫܡܫܢܘܬܗ ܦܓܪܐ ܠܒܫܐ.	473-477	No trans.	109
			ܡܫܝܚ ܡܠܟܐ ܕܫܘܒܚܐ. ܘܡܠܟ ܡܠܟܐ ܕܫܒܝܚܘܬܐ.	478-480	No trans.	110
			ܐܘ ܕܡܫܒܚܝܢ ܟܠ ܚܝܠܘ̈ܗܝ.. ܘܡܫܬܥܒܕܝܢ ܟܠ ܥܘܡܪ̈ܘܗܝ..	481-484	No trans.	111
			ܒܡܠܟܐ ܡܪܢܐ ܕܒܪܝܬܐ. ܘܒܝܘܡܐ ܕܡܪܕܘܬ ܒܫܡܝ̈ܬܐ.	485-487	No trans.	112
			ܢܦܫܐ ܡܫܒܚܐ ܒܫܡܝܢ̈ܐ. ܒܟܠ ܝܘܡܐ ܡܢ ܒܢܝ̈ܢܫܐ.	488-490	No trans.	113
			ܡܠܟܐ ܪܒܐ ܥܦܝܪܐ. ܕܒܪ̈ܝܬܐ ܘܠܐ ܗܘܐ ܕܦܠܓ̈ܐ.	491-494	No trans.	114
			ܐܘ ܚܝ̈ܠܐ ܘܪ̈ܘܚܐ. ܗܘ ܝܘܡܐ ܡܫܠܡ ܕܒܚܝ̈ܐ.	495-500	No trans.	115
			ܒܗܘܢܐ ܒܪܐ ܟܠ ܒܗܘܢܝ. ܕܪܘܡܐ ܘܡܘܡܬܐ ܒܐܝܕܗ ܠܟܠܝܢ.	501-503	No trans.	116
			ܡܫܒܚܐ ܘܒܪܗ ܕܡܫܒܚܐ. ܕܐܠܝܢܘܬܗ ܡܢ ܟܠ ܕܡܐ.	504-507	No trans.	117
			ܒܫܠܡܐ ܗܘܐ ܚܕܗ ܗܘܝܘ. ܘܒܫܘܒܚܐ ܡܫܒܚܐ ܗܘܝܘ.	508-511	No trans.	65
			ܒܝܘܡܐ ܕܒܗ ܩܡܬ ܗܘܬ. ܕܡܫܠܡ ܡܢܐ ܒܠܝܠ ܫܘܒܚܐ.	512-519	No trans.	66
			ܡܠܟܐ ܐܠܗܐ. ܡܪܐ ܕܒܢܝܐ ܐܠܗܝܢ.	520-523	No trans.	118
			ܐܘ ܕܒܪܐ ܒܢܝ ܫܡܝܐ. ܟܠܗܘܢ ܒܪ̈ܘܚܐ ܘܒܢܝܫܬܐ.	524-527	No trans.	119
			ܚܢܢܐ ܕܠܒܠ ܒܪܐ ܕܠܒܪ ܡܢܗ ܠܐܒܘܗܝ ܠܗ ܒܪܐ.	528-531	No trans.	120

			ܫܠܡܐ ܘܫܪܪܐ ܕܟܠ ܫܠܡܐ. ܕܫܬܪܪܘܗܝ ܐܝܟ ܟܠܗܘܢ ܫܠܡܐ.	532-535	No trans.	121
			ܫܠܡܐ ܕܪܘܡܐ ܠܟܠܢ. ܕܐܬܐ ܕܢܦܪܘܩ ܠܐܢܫܝܐ.	536-541	No trans.	122
			ܡܫܝܚܐ ܦܪܩܗ ܕܡܫܝܚܐ. ܗܘ ܕܐܬܓܠܝ ܡܢ ܟܠ ܪܘܚܐ.	542-545	No trans.	123
			ܥܕܬܐ ܕܩܕܘܫܐ ܘܕܒܢܝܢ. ܐܦ ܢܝܦܩܐ ܕܟܠ ܐܬܠܬܐ.	546-549	No trans.	124
			ܫܒܘܚܬܐ ܕܟܠ ܝܡܬܐ. ܢܡܪܐ ܕܒܪܐ ܡܠܟܐ ܢܦܠܚܬܐ.	550-554	No trans.	125
			ܐܡܢܐ ܕܪܘܡܐ ܥܡ ܩܝܣܘܗܝ ܐܬܐ ܠܐܪܥܐ ܕܢܐܡܐ ܠܒܢܝܢܗܘܢ.	555-558	No trans.	126
			ܚܘܒܫܐ ܠܗ ܠܗܘܢ ܝܚܝܕܬܐ. ܕܒܝܬܐ ܘܢܬܐܡܢ ܟܠ ܒܢܝܬܐ.	559-563	No trans.	127
			ܩܕܡ ܕܝܢ ܥܡ ܐܬܓܠܝܒ ܗܘܐ. ܕܚܘܒܝܗ ܠܩܝܣܘܗܝ ܚܫܘܐ ܗܘܐ.	564-567	No trans.	129
			ܝܡܝܢܗ ܕܐܒܐ ܡܬܦܩܕܐ ܕܒܝܬ ܢܠܡܕܗ ܚܡܐ ܒܠܘܚܝܐ	568-572	No trans.	130
			ܢܘܪܐ ܘܝܫܬܦܘܕ ܠܐܠܗܘܬܗ. ܕܦܪܡܗ ܠܟܝܢܗ ܒܒܪܐ ܕܝܘܡ.	573-575	No trans.	128
			ܐܝܟܢܐ ܕܝܢ ܡܬܦܫ ܕܚܘܫܟܗ ܒܪܝ.. ܘܐܝܩܪܐ ܚܩܝܩܐ ܢܘܪܝ.	576-580	No trans.	131
			ܚܘܒܫܐ ܙܡܪܝ ܒܪܬܐ. ܚܕܬܐ ܕܟܠܝܠ ܘܝܕܥܬܐ ܕܠܒܫܗ.	581-585	No trans.	136
			ܚܘܒܫܐ ܠܗ ܠܟܒܪܐ ܐܝܟܢܐ. ܘܐܬܚܙܝܬܐ ܒܪܐ ܡܬܦܩܕܐ.	586-594	No trans.	
			ܒܪܝܟ ܗܘ ܡܥܝܢܐ ܡܢܝܫܢܐ. ܐܚܘܝ ܘܗܢܐ ܕܦܪܚܐ ܘܦܘܪܥܢܐ.	595-597	No trans.	133
			ܒܪܝܟܘ ܡܥܝܢܐ ܡܓܠܠܢܐ. ܐܚܘܝ ܘܗܢܐ ܕܓܒܝܐ ܘܢܝܫܐ.	598-600	No trans.	134
			ܒܟܠ ܥܕܢ ܘܒܟܠ ܕܥܕ.. ܠܟܐ ܘܬܓܪܐ ܠܗܘܢ ܡܥܝܢܐ ܥܕܝ..	601-604	No trans.	135
			ܥܢܗ ܐܠܦ ܘܢܝܫܐ ܥܠܐ.. ܘܐܪܒܥܝܢ ܦܬܓܡ ܠܫܠܡܐ ܕܢܐ..	605-611	No trans.	
			ܒܥܢܝܬܐ ܫܠܝܡ ܒܝܬܐ. ܕܚܘܠܡ ܗܠܡ ܚܝܝ ܒܥܝܬܐ.	612-617	No trans.	142
			ܐܘܕܝܬܐ ܢܦܫ ܟܠ. ܒܕܘܒܪܐ ܝܩܪܗ ܕܦܪܘܩ.	618-620	No trans.	153
			ܐܡܝܢܘܢ ܐܝܟ ܒܪܒܝܬܗܘܢ.. ܕܒܐܬܐ ܢܩܢܐ ܕܒܟܠ ܒܪ ܥܕܬܗܘܢ..	621-627	No trans.	4
			ܩܕܝܫܐ ܦܐܝܢܐ ܘܡܪܢܝܢ ܓܢܐ ܚܘܒܐ. ܘܝܥܕܕܐ ܠܥܕܢ ܕܦܩܕ ܒܡܥܒܕܢܗ.	628-632	No trans.	20
			ܫܠܡܐ ܕܟܠܗܘܢ ܒܢܝܬܐ. ܐܦ ܢܗܘܦܟܐ ܕܟܠ ܟܢܫܐ.	633-646	No trans.	
			ܥܕܬܐ ܥܕܝ ܚܕܐ ܒܐܝܬܘܗܝ ܝܗܒ ܐܒܘܗܝ. ܚܝܒܐ ܕܝܢ ܫܠܝܚܐ ܟܠܗ ܩܕܝܫܘܗܝ ܕܒܝܬܐ ܠܗܘܢ.	647-648	No trans.	
			ܒܪܝܟܘ ܡܥܝܢܐ ܕܒܪܟܬܗ. ܦܪܘܩ ܠܒܢܝܢ ܡܢ ܚܘܒܬܗ.	649-652	No trans.	
			ܫܡܘ ܝܥܩܘܒ ܕܒܝܬܐ. ܕܘܟܪܐ ܒܡܟܝܐ ܪܘܫܝܬܐ.	653-666	No trans.	

			ܒܓܒܝ ܫܡܝܢܐ ܡܫܬܒܚܐ. ܒܟܪܘܒܘܬܐ ܕܠܘܩܒܠ ܢܗܪܐ.	667-677	No trans.	
			ܥܢܢ ܐܝܟ ܘܡܢܗܪܢܐ ܥܡܝ. ܕܐܝܟܫܝܕܘܬ ܘܡܢ ܦܬܟܪܝ.	678-682	No trans.	
			ܡܥܝܢܐ ܦܬܝܚܐ ܕܡܥܡܘܕܝܬܐ. ܦܬܚܬܗ ܕܐܠܗܐ ܡܠܟܐ.	683-686	No trans.	74
			ܟܥܢܢ ܐܝܟ ܘܡܥܡܕܝܢܐ. ܦܬܟܪܐ ܕܡܠܟܐ ܢܘܪܢܐ.	687-689	No trans.	
			ܥܠܡ ܠܥܠܡܝܢ ܐܡܝܢ. ܕܐܥܡܪ ܥܠܡܐ ܘܡܠܐ ܒܡܝܢ.	690-693	No trans.	
			ܟܠܗ ܗܘܐ ܦܢܝܢ ܐܡܝܢ. ܠܟܢ ܒܡܘܠܕܐ ܟܡܢ ܡܢܝܢ.	694-696	No trans.	
			ܥܘܒܕܐ ܠܣܘܓܐ ܡܦܘܩܢܐ. ܕܐܝܟܐ ܦܪܩܐ ܒܕܡܗ ܐܟܢܢ.	697-699	No trans.	
			ܒܝܠܕ ܒܬܘܠܬܐ ܦܪܘܩܢ. ܢܝܠܕ ܘܢܬܕ ܠܡܣܝܒܪܢ..	700-702	No trans.	52
			ܒܝܠܕ ܐܠܗܘܬܐ ܐܒܘܢ . ܢܝܠܕ ܦܩܘܕ ܠܡܣܝܒܪܢ..	703-705	No trans.	
			ܡܥܝܢܐ ܒܕܝܚܝܢ ܕܡܢ ܐܠܗܐ. ܣܘܟܠܗ ܠܐܒܪܝ ܟܕ ܐܬܐ.	706-707	No trans.	
			ܥܘܒܕܐ ܠܕܝܚܝܢ ܦܬܘܠ. ܕܦܩܕ ܕܐܝܠܝܢ ܦܥܒܝܢ.	708-710	No trans.	
			ܡܥܝܢܐ ܢܦܩ ܡܕܝܚܢܐ. ܗܘܦܟܐ ܕܟܠ ܡܠܟܐ ܫܘܒܚܐ.	711-713	No trans.	
			ܥܘܒܕܐ ܠܕܝܚܝܢ ܥܦܪܢܐ. ܡܥܝܢܐ ܦܠܚܐ ܡܠܟܐ ܒܬܘܕܝܬܐ	714-716	No trans.	
			ܐܘ ܢܥܝܡܝ ܝܬܝܪܘܬ. ܒܠܒܗ ܕܐܒܘܝ ܘܐܡܝ.	717-724	No trans.	150
			ܥܝܢܐ ܦܬܘܚܐ ܘܢܒܥܐ ܒܥܠ. ܕܡܢ ܟܠ ܒܥܒܘ ܦܬܚܐ ܡܢ ܟܠ.	725-742	No trans.	
			ܐܝܬܝܐ ܦܫܝܛܐ ܕܐܬܚܙܝ ܒܐܝܠܝܢ. ܕܐܬܚܙܝ ܒܐܝܠܝܢ ܒܦܓܪܐ ܐܝܠܢܐ.	743-745	No trans.	
			ܐܢܬ ܠܝ ܐܒܐ ܠܝ ܐܒܪܐ ܗܘ ܠܝ. ܕܒܪܐ ܗܘ ܠܝ ܘܐܚܝ ܐܟܐ ܠܝ.	746-749	No trans.	
			ܐܘ ܢܒܝܐ ܫܡܥܘܢ. ܢܫܘܐ ܥܘܒܕܐ ܠܐܠܗܝܢ.	750-756	No trans.	14
			ܒܪܦܬܐ ܠܝܫܘܥ ܡܫܘܕܥܐ ܐܝܟ ܐܒܐ. ܦܩܝܕܐ ܠܗ ܢܡܘܣ ܡܫܝܚܐ.	757-761	No trans.	
			ܡܥܝܢܐ ܢܠܕܐ ܡܦܘܩܢܐ. ܕܡܢ ܡܪܝܡ ܟܠܗܘܢ ܕܟܠ ܥܘܕܪܢܐ.	762-767	No trans.	
			ܦܬܘ ܕܡܠܟܝܢ ܟܠ ܡܚܕܐ. ܦܬܘ ܕܡܠܟܝܢ ܟܠ ܡܢܝܢ.	767-769	No trans.	
			ܐܘ ܡܫܐ ܣܒܝܒ ܡܠܟܐ ܗܘܐ. ܘܦܩܕ ܦܬܝܚ ܦܬܚܐ ܗܘܐ.	770-772	No trans.	137
			ܐܦܪܘ ܦܪܝܫ ܘܦܝܠܘ ܘܦܬܚܘ. ܘܦܐܪܐ ܕܐܘܪܚܐ ܦܬܚܘ.	773-777	No trans.	
			ܣܘܪ ܠܦܠܓܝܢ ܕܡܠܟܐ ܢܟܝܡ. ܘܦܢܝܢ ܠܗܘܢ ܕܐܝܬ ܫܒܚܐ	778-781	No trans.	
			ܥܘܒܕܐ ܠܡܠܟܐ ܥܦܪܢܐ. ܕܢܒܐ ܘܦܕܐ ܠܢܦܪܐ ܗܘܐ.	782-784	No trans.	

			ܐܘ ܕܗܘܘ ܒܢܝܢܐ ܡܬܘܡܝܢܐ. ܘܡܟܝܟܬܐ ܘܕܘܫܐ ܗܘܝܐ ܦܘܬܢܝܬܐ.	785-788	No trans.	
			ܐܘ ܚܒܝܒܝ ܝܘܡܢܐ ܥܘܒܕܐ. ܒܟܝܢܐ ܦܪܝܫܐ ܕܚܘܒ ܕܘܒܪܝܗ.	789-793	No trans.	17
			ܢܦܩ ܦܘܩܕܢܐ ܡܢ ܡܠܟܐ. ܘܐܬܐܡܪ ܠܟܠܗ ܒܐܬܘܬܐ.	794-796	No trans.	149
			ܡܢ ܟܠ ܐܬܪܐ ܕܡܘܕܝܢܐ. ܕܢܝܬܘܢ ܗܘܝܐ ܡܬܡܪܐ ܕܪܘܡܝܐ.	797-800	No trans.	
			ܡܪܝܐ ܕܐܪܥܐ ܘܫܡܝܐ. ܐܡܪ ܡܬܒܠܥ ܡܢܝܢ ܡܬܢܠܢܐ.	801-805	No trans.	94
			ܡܫܝܚܐ ܢܦܩ ܦܪܘܩܐ. ܠܗܘܦܟܐ ܥܒܕܐ ܡܠܟܐ ܚܘܒܬܐ.	806-808	No trans.	
			ܝܘܠܦܢ ܢܡܘܣܐ ܘܢܒܝܐ. ܒܪܬܐ ܕܢܦܠ ܘܡܢܬܚܒܬܐ.	809-811	No trans.	
			ܡܫܝܚܐ ܢܦܩ ܡܪܚܡܢܐ. ܕܢܦܠ ܕܚܘܒܐ ܘܚܘܒܐ.	812-814	No trans.	
			ܒܟܝܢܐ ܕܟܢܝܫܐ ܗܘ ܕܒܢܝܗ. ܕܟܢܝܫܐ ܐܠܗܘܢ ܐܦ ܝܒܢܝܗ.	815-816	No trans.	
			ܢܦܩ ܕܐܘܪܚܐ ܘܫܘܒܚܐ. ܦܪܘ ܒܥܘܠ ܦܠܓܢܐ.	817-818	No trans.	
			ܠܡܠܟܝ ܐܒܘܝ ܐܝܬܝܐ. ܠܡܠܟܝ ܐܘܪܚܗ ܕܢܒܝܐ ܡܫܝܚܐ.	819-821	No trans.	
			ܥܘܒܕܐ ܠܢܦܫܐ ܘܠܒܗܬܐ. ܦܪܘܩܐ ܒܘܚܪܗ ܕܟܢܝܫܐ.	822-824	No trans.	
			ܥܘܒܕܐ ܠܢܦܫܐ ܕܠܒܝ ܒܘܚܪܗ. ܘܟܒܪܐ ܕܦܪܘܩ ܠܚܝܘܬܗ.	825-827	No trans.	
			ܦܪܘܩܐ ܦܪܘ ܚܝܐ ܒܠܒܘܬܗ. ܦܠܓܘ ܡܢ ܟܠ ܢܦܫ ܢܠܦܘܬܗ.	828-830	No trans.	
			ܐܘ ܡܫܝܚܐ ܢܒܝܐ ܢܒܝܘܬܐ. ܕܠܦܘܪܩܢ ܕܝܢ ܗܘܐ ܡܢܝܬܐ.	831-833	No trans.	
39	2015	Anton Pritula	*The Wardā: An East Syriac Hymnological Collection Study and Critical Edition.*			
			ܢܠܟܐ ܕܟܠܗ ܠܢܠܟܝܗ ܘܒܢܝܐ. ܘܠܐ ܚܕܐ ܡܢܝܢܗܝ ܘܠܐ ܢܓܒܢܐ.	170-183	English	2
			ܡܢ ܦܩܘܕ ܠܗ ܠܐܠܗܘܬܗ. ܒܪܐ ܕܐܠܗܐ ܘܠܘܬܗܘܢ.	184-204	English	3
			ܒܢܝܢܐ ܡܕܒܪܬܐ ܕܠܒܠܝܟ. ܝܚܒܘܗ ܦܟܐ ܕܡܒܪܝ ܠܢܦܫܐ.	204-215	English	7
			ܒܢܝܢܐ ܕܫܘܒܚܐ ܗܘܐ ܕܡܢܐ ܐܢܐ. ܘܒܡܫܝܚܘܬܐ ܗܘܐ ܡܬܒܪܟ ܐܢܐ.	216-230	English	9
			ܥܘܡܪܐ ܠܩܕܝܫܝ ܦܪܘܩܢ. ܕܒܪ ܝܚܐ ܚܘܬܝ ܕܡܫܬܒܚ ܠܝܠܝܢ.	230-237	English	151
			ܚܝܠܐ ܕܡܠܟܐ ܒܢܬܐ. ܘܢܦܪܘܩ ܡܢܢ ܡܢ ܡܠܟܬܐ.	238-251	English	15
			ܦܘܠܚܢܐ ܕܚܠܝܡܘܬܐ. ܘܡܬܒܪܟܝܢ ܕܫܒܝܚܘܬܐ.	252-264	English	23
			ܒܝ ܒܚܕܪܐ ܕܦܘܩܕܢܐ ܡܪܢܐ ܘܡܫܡܠܝܢܐ ܕܥܡܐ ܒܝܬܐ.	264-273	English	24

			ܒܪ ܢܟܦܐ ܢܘܗܪ ܡܢ ܢܘܗܪܐ. ܐܙܠ ܠܥܠܡܐ ܐܝܟ ܦܘܩܕܢܐ.	274-284	English	25
			ܐܘ ܢܟܦܐ ܕܐܬܝܠܕ ܡܢ ܟܠ. ܡܢܘ ܢܫܬܥܐ ܫܪܒܗ ܡܢ ܟܠ.	284-293	English	26
			ܗܕܐ ܕܢܟܬܒܘܬܐ. ܕܠܗ ܘܗܕܐ ܕܩܝܡ ܕܢܬܡܗܘܬܐ.	294-310	English	31
			ܥܡܠܗ ܗܘܐ ܠܟܠܗܘܢ ܥܡܡܐ. ܕܠܗܕܐ ܠܟܠ ܗܘܘ ܫܠܝܚܐ.	310-319	English	32
			ܫܥܝܬܐ ܫܠܝܡ ܒܝܫܬܐ. ܕܥܘܠܐ ܗܠܝܢ ܥܒܕ ܫܥܝܬܐ.	320-335	English	142
			ܝܘܡ ܚܕܐ ܡܠܟܐ ܝܬܝܒܬܐ ܘܝܘܡ ܚܕܡܘܕܝܬܐ ܡܠܟܐ ܚܕܡܕܝܬܐ.	336-342	English	46
			ܣܠܩ ܘܐܣܬܠܩ ܘܗܘܐ ܣܠܩܐ ܐܢܐ. ܘܗܘܐ ܣܠܩܐ ܐܢܐ ܐܦ ܡܣܠܩܐ ܐܢܐ.	342-349	English	47
			ܒܕܝܢ ܕܟܕ ܒܝܢ ܘܒܪܐ ܫܠܝܚܐ. ܫܡܥܘ ܕܝܠܝ ܫܠܝܚܐ.	350-355	English	49
			ܒܪ ܐܠܗܐ ܐܝܟܐ ܒܒܪܝܬܐ. ܘܐܬܦܪܥܘ ܠܗܘܢ ܡܫܡܫܢܘܬܐ.	356-366	English	53
			ܡܢܘ ܕܢܦܩ ܒܟܠ ܫܘܒܚܐ. ܘܡܢܘ ܝܕܥܐ ܐܦ ܝܗܠܐ ܟܠܗ.	366-376	English	54
			ܐܝܟܘ ܕܐܬܬܠܝ ܕܒܢܝܐ. ܕܒܟܐ ܫܒܚܐ ܘܐܘܕܝ ܗܘܢܐ.	376-388	English	55
			ܐܘ ܡܫܝܚܐ ܡܪܐ ܡܪܢ. ܐܘ ܡܕܒܪܐ ܡܪܐ ܡܠܟܐ..	388-402	English	56
			ܐܘ ܢܘܗܪܐ ܡܪܐ ܒܝܬܝ. ܘܡܪܐ ܗܝܡ ܚܝܝܢ ܘܡܪܐ ܡܕܒܪܢ.	402-414	English	57
			ܐܘ ܚܡܝܡܐ ܕܩܠܝܬܐ. ܘܡܫܡܠܝܐ ܕܬܚܬܝܬܐ.	414-424	English	58
			ܐܘ ܚܡܝܡܐ ܕܩܠܝܬܐ. ܘܡܫܡܠܝܐ ܕܬܚܬܝܬܐ.	424-435	English	
			ܡܠܟܐ ܕܫܒܝܚܬܐ. ܡܫܝܚܐ ܐܬܝܗܒ ܒܥܕܢܘܬܐ	436-445	English	60
			ܡܠܟܐ ܕܡܠܟܐ ܠܗ ܦܠܚܝܢ. ܘܟܘܫܪܐ ܠܫܡܗ ܡܫܡܫܝܢ.	446-456	English	63
			ܒܟܠܡܐ ܗܘܐ ܚܕܐ ܗܘܝܐ. ܘܒܝܕܘܗܝ ܝܬܒܬܐ ܗܘܝܐ.	456-464	English	65
			ܒܪ ܟܠ ܡܕܝ ܠܐܘܪܫܠܡ. ܕܫܠܚ ܢܒܝܐ ܥܠܝܗ ܕܢܬܠܡ.	464-474	English	77
			ܒܥܘܬܗ ܕܟܠܐ ܣܒܪܬܐ. ܙܟܝ ܐܕܡܐ ܘܕܟܠܝ ܥܡܢܐ.	474-482	English	80
			ܠܐܒܘܢܐ ܕܡܫܒܚ ܝܫܘܥ. ܘܒܪܘܚܐ ܕܩܘܕܫܐ ܩܢܘܡ.	482-494	English	88
			ܗܕܐ ܕܐܕܟܐ ܘܫܡܝܐ. ܐܡܪ ܡܫܡܫܢ ܡܫܒܚܝܢ ܡܠܐܟܐ.	494-505	English	94
			ܠܟܕܡܥܐ ܐܠܗܢܐ. ܕܢܬܒ ܒܚܝܘܬܗ ܒܕܐ ܣܒܪܬܐ.	506-516	English	105
			ܐܘ ܚܝܠܐ ܝܘܬܐ ܐܬܥܒܕܬܐ. ܕܐܡܪ ܡܪܝ ܒܝܬ ܩܠܝܬܐ.	516-525	English	108
			ܡܫܝܚ ܒܠܗ ܕܡܘܬܐ. ܘܡܠܟ ܒܠܗ ܡܠܝܟܘܬܐ.	526-533	English	110

			ܟܘܟܒܐ ܡܕܢܚ ܕܒܪܝܬܐ. ܦܪܨܘܦܗ ܕܐܒܘܗܝ ܟܠܗ̇ ܒܪ̈ܝܬܐ.	534-540	English	112
			ܦܠܚ̈ܐ ܐܠܗܝ̈ܐ. ܡܢܐ ܕܒܢ̈ܝܐ ܐܠܗܝ̈ܐ.	540-550	English	118
			ܐܘ ܕܟܪܐ ܒܢܝ ܡܠܟܘܬܐ. ܫܠܝܚ̈ܐ ܬܪ̈ܥܣܪ ܘܡܫܝܚܘܬܐ.	550-559	English	119
40	2016	Polīs Ḥabīb	"قصيدة مديح للعذراء مريم للشاعر المشرقي الكبير كيوركيس وردا" [A Praising Hymn for the Virgin Mary of Gīwargīs Wardā the Great Eastern Poet]. In *Nağm Al Mašriq* 87.	245-249		
			ܒܢܝܢ ܕܫܘܒܚܐ ܐܘ ܕܟܪܐ ܐܒܐ. ܦܪܘܫܘܬܐ ܐܘ ܡܫܒܚܐ ܐܒܐ.	246-247	Arabic	9
41	2016	Maroš Nicák	*"Konversion" im Buch Wardā: Zur Bewältigung der onversions-fragein der Kirche des Ostens.*			
			ܐܘ ܚܕܐ ܚܒܝܒ ܫܠܝܚܐ ܗܘܐ. ܐܘ ܚܕܐ ܦܪܝܫܐ ܒܪܝܐ ܗܘܐ.	153-170	German	137
42	2019	Joshua K. Hood	"Songs of Supplication and Penitence: ʿOnyātā from the Wardā Collection in Mingana Syr 214."			
			ܦܬܓܡ̈ܐ ܕܟܬܒܢܝܬܐ. ܘܡܬܓܘܡ̈ܐ ܕܫܒܝ̈ܚܬܐ.	82-88 226-237	English	23
			ܒܗ ܒܬܕܟܪܐ ܕܦܘܩܕܢܐ ܡܪܢܐ ܘܡܫܬܠܡܢܘܬܐ ܕܝܘܡܬܐ ܒܪܢܫ.	88-92 237-246	English	24
			ܒܗ ܢܦܫ ܢܘܚܝ ܡܢ ܢܘܚܐ. ܐܝܟ ܠܚܝܘܬܐ ܐܢܝ ܦܘܪܩܢܐ	92-97 246-255	English	25
			ܐܘ ܢܦܫܐ ܕܚܝܒܬ ܡܢ ܟܠ. ܡܛܠ ܓܒܪܘܬܟ ܫܒܩܬ ܡܢ ܟܠ	97-102 255-264	English	26
			ܐܘ ܕܒܝܬܐ ܢܚܒܒܬܐ. ܘܐܝܟ ܕܒܝܬܗܕܐ ܕܘܪܐ ܒܫܒܝܠܐ	103-106 264-270	English	27
			ܒܘܗܕܝ ܫܘܒܚܐ ܐܝܬܐ ܠܟ. ܘܬܘܕܝܬܐ ܕܡܫܒܚܝܢ ܡܬܒܪܟ ܐܒ̄ܐ ܠܟ	106-110 270-276	English	28
			ܠܥܠܡ ܒܚܠܘܦ ܕܒܟܝܢܘܬܗ. ܒܥܘܬ ܕܐܢܫܝܢ ܒܡܢ ܡܬܥܒܕܢܘܬܗ	110-114 276-282	English	29
			ܡܪܝܐ ܕܢܚܒܬܐ. ܕܠܗ ܘܟܕ ܕܘܒܪ ܟܢܫܘܬܐ.	114-124 282-295	English	31
			ܢܦܫܗ ܗܕܐ ܒܠܒܘܢ ܚܛܝܐ. ܕܠܦܘܬܐ ܒܠ ܗܘܐ ܫܠܝܘܬܐ.	124-129 295-303	English	32
			ܐܠܗܐ ܠܚܒܝܒܐ ܘܦܪܘܩܐ. ܒܢܝܐ ܡܕܝܢܬܐ ܘܡܫܒܠܢܐ	129-133 303-305	English	33
			ܡܪܝܐ ܕܒܪܟ ܒܚܢܢܘܬܗ. ܘܐܢܫܝܢ ܟܢܘܫܬܐ ܫܘܒܚܘܬܗ	133-136 305-310	English	34

			ܒܥܘܬܐ ܕܡܘܬܐ ܢܦܝܠ ܐܢܐ. ܒܟܘܪܗܢܐ ܕܚܛܗܐ ܗܐ ܟܪܝܗ ܐܢܐ.	137-140 310-316	English	35
			ܡܪܝ ܡܫܝܚܐ ܕܐܬܬܚܝܬ. ܘܐܬܠܠܬ ܒܦܘܡܐ ܐܬܐܠܝܬ.	140-144 316-321	English	36
			ܐܘ ܕܪܘܡܐ ܒܬܠܝܬܝܘܬܐ. ܦܪܘܩ ܚܛܝܐ ܐܝܟ ܕܒܪܘܫܝܬܐ.	144-147 321-326	English	37
			ܢܗ ܬܝܒܘܬܐ ܕܩܪܒܐ ܠܘܬ ܠܗ. ܐܘܪܚܐ ܕܝܘܡܐ ܕܟܠ ܡܬܕܪܫ ܠܗ.	147-150 326-332	English	38
			ܩܪܐ ܐܠܗܐ ܕܦܠܝܛܝܢ. ܫܘܒܚܐ ܘܫܘܟܪܐ ܘܐܝܩܪܐ ܠܥܠܡܝܢ.	150-154 332-334	English	39
			ܩܪܐ ܕܒܪܫܝܬܗ ܐܬܚܙܝ. ܘܒܚܪܬܗ ܦܪܘܩ ܠܟܠܢ.	154-157 334-336	English	40
			ܢܦܠ ܥܡܐ ܘܕܒܪ ܗܘ ܟܠ. ܦܠܚܐ ܡܫܝܚܐ ܕܦܠܚܝܢ ܒܟܠ ܟܠ.	157-161 336-342	English	41
			ܐܪܥܐ ܠܥܡܐ ܒܬܘܠܬܐ. ܝܘܠܕܗ ܕܐܒܘܗܝ ܒܬܪܝܢܘܬܐ.	162-165 342-348	English	42
			ܠܗܢܐ ܢܩܫ ܘܦܠܚ ܕܪܘܚܐ. ܠܝܫ ܡܬܦܩܕ ܗܝܟ ܗܘܟܢܐ.	165-169 348-354	English	43
			ܠܥܡܐ ܚܣܝܢܐ ܘܗܢܘܢܐ. ܢܦܫ ܕܡܠܟܐ ܟܠ ܗܢܘܢܐ.	169-173 354-360	English	44
			ܒܗ ܐܠܗܐ ܕܒܠܝܬܐ. ܘܒܗ ܦܪܘܩܘܬܐ ܕܥܡܝܬܐ.	173-176 360-362	English	45
			ܒܗ ܟܪܐ ܡܠܟܐ ܝܫܘܥܐ ܘܒܗ ܦܪܘܩܘܬܐ ܡܠܟܐ ܦܪܘܩܝܐ.	176-180 362-369	English	46
			ܣܓܝܐ ܘܡܣܓܝܐ ܡܘܬܒ ܣܓܝܐ ܐܢܐ. ܡܘܬܒ ܣܓܝܐ ܐܢܐ ܐܦ ܦܣܝܓܐ ܐܢܐ.	181-184 369-371	English	47
			ܒܪܝܟ ܕܒܗ ܒܦܪܨܘܦܗ ܠܐ ܒܗܬ. ܐܠܐ ܐܘܬܒ ܦܠܝܓ ܒܗܬ.	185-188 372-378	English	48
			ܒܪܝܟ ܕܒܗ ܚܝܐ ܘܢܦܫ ܚܠܦܝ. ܚܣܝܕܘ ܢܦܫܝ ܚܠܦܝ	188-192 378-383	English	49
			ܒܗ ܗܟܝܠ ܐܢܫܐ ܒܒܪܝܬܐ. ܘܢܬܦܪܩ ܠܬܘܬܝ ܦܪܘܩܘܬܐ	192-198 383-393	English	53
			ܡܢܘ ܕܢܦܩܘܗ ܚܠܦ ܫܘܒܚܐ. ܘܡܢܘ ܝܗܒ ܐܦ ܝܗܒ ܚܠܦ	198-204 393-402	English	54
			ܐܢܘ ܕܐܬܐܠܗ ܕܥܡܢܐ. ܘܕܡܐ ܦܪܘܩܐ ܘܢܘܗܪܐ ܕܘܒܪܐ	204-211 402-413	English	55
			ܐܘ ܦܫܝܛܘܬܐ ܩܪܐ ܦܢܝܢ. ܐܘ ܡܪܘܡܘܬܐ ܩܪܐ ܦܠܝܓܐ	211-218 413-426	English	56
			ܐܘ ܢܘܩܫܐ ܩܪܐ ܒܥܒܝ. ܘܩܪܐ ܗܝܟ ܫܦܝܪ ܘܩܪܐ ܡܪܚܡܢ	218-224 426-435	English	57
43	2020	Rony Patrous	"قصيدة عيد الميلاد للشاعر كيوركيس وردا" [A Hymn on Nativity by the Poet Gīwargīs Wardā]. In *Church of beth Kokheh Journal* 8.			
			ܒܥܝܢܐ ܢܪܢܡ ܘܡܪܢܝܡ ܥܡܢܐ. ܠܥܘܕܐ ܦܠܚܐ ܕܪܘܚܩܢܐ	-	Arabic	1

44	2021	Adam Carter Bremer-McCollum	"Prose, Poetry, and Hagiography. The Martyrdoms of Jacob the Persian and Tahmizgard in Syriac Story and Song." In *Syriac Hagiography, Texts and Studies in Eastern Christianity* 20.[56]			
			ܦܬܚܝ ܥܕܬܐ ܦܘܡܟܝ. ܕܬܫܒܚܝܢ ܘܬܘܕܝܢ ܠܟܠ ܥܕܢ	234-238	English	85
			ܛܒܒܐ ܕܩܘܪܐ ܝܥܩܘܒ ܗܘܦܐ. ܘܕܚܠܬܐ ܘܪܚܡܬܐ ܘܬܘܕܝܬܐ ܗܘܦܐ.	232, 241, 243-244	English	84
45	2021	Andrew Palmer and Anton Pritula	"From the Nile to Mount Izlā and Tigris George." In *Den Orient erforsschen, mit Orthodoxen leben.*	505-540		
			ܢܘܕܐ ܘܢܫܒܚ ܠܐܠܗܘܬܟ. ܕܥܒܕܬ ܠܓܝܘܪ ܓܒܪܐ ܕܡܝܢܝ.	520-528	English	128

[56] Only few stanzas of these hymns are published in this article.

Complete Bibliography

Including both works cited and other sources of relevance

1. Manuscripts

Mardin Chald. 43; 1483 CE, Mardin Chaldean Cathedral. (VHMML no. CCM 00406)[1]
Mardin Chald. 41; 1541 CE, Mardin Chaldean Cathedral. (VHMML no. CCM 00405)
Cambr. Add. 1983; 1550 CE, Cambridge University Library.
Diyarbakir 78; 1565 CE, Mardin Chaldean Cathedral. (VHMML no. CCM 00407)
Vat. Syr. 567; 1568 CE, Vatican Library.
Vat. Syr. 184; 1568 CE, Vatican Library.
Diyarbakir 84; 1575 CE, Mardin Chaldean Cathedral. (VHMML no. CCM 00423)
Baghdad Chaldean 492; 1581 CE, currently in ʿAinkawā – Erbil, monastery of S. Hūrmīzd.
Mardin Chald. 42; 1586 CE, Mardin Chaldean Cathedral. (VHMML no. CCM 00412)
Mingana Syr. 505; 14th-15th centuries, Birmingham, University Library.
Diyarbakir 85; 1400-1500 CE, Mardin Chaldean Cathedral. (VHMML no. CCM 00396)

2. Catalogues

ASSEMANI, J.S. *Bibliotheca Orientalis clementino-Vaticana*. Vol. I-III. Rome: Typis Sacrae Congregationis de Propaganda Fide, 1719-1728.

——— and S.E. ASSEMANI. *Bibliothecæ apostolicæ Vaticanæ codicum manuscriptorum catalogus*. Vol. I/3. Paris: Maisonneuve Frères, 1926.

HADDAD, P. and J. ISAAC. *المخطوطات السريانية والعربية في خزانة الرهبانية الكلدانية في بغداد*, Syriac and Arabic Manuscripts in the Library of the Chaldean Monastery. Vol. III/1. Baghdad: Al-Majmaʿ al-ʿIlmī al-ʿIrāqī, 1988.

MINGANA, A. *Catalogue of Mingana Collection of Manuscripts*. Vol. I. Cambridge: W. Heffer and Sons, 1933.

SCHER, A. "Notice sur les manuscrits syriaques et arabes conservés dans la bibliothèque de l'évêché chaldéen de Diarbékir." *JA* 10 (1907): 6-82.

[1] By using this number the manuscript can be found on https://www.vhmml.org/.

———. "Notice sur les manuscrits syriaques et arabes conservés dans la bibliothèque de l'évéché chaldéen de Mardin." *Revue des Bibliothèques* (1908): 64-94.

VAN LANTSCHOOT, A. *Inventaire des manuscrits syriaques des fonds Vatican (490-631) Barberini oriental e neofiti*. Vatican: Bibliotac Apostolica Vaticana, 1965.

WRIGHT, W. *A Catalogue of the Syriac Manuscripts Preserved in the Library of the University of Cambridge*. Vol. I-II. Cambridge: Cambridge University Press, 1901.

3. SOURCES AND STUDIES[2]

ABRAMOWSKI, L., and A.E. GOODMAN, eds. *A Nestorian Collection of Christological texts*. Vol. I-II. Cambridge: Cambridge University Press, 1972.

ABOUNA, A. *أدب اللغة الآرامية* [Literature of the Aramaic Language]. Beirut: Dār al-Mašriq, 1996.

———. *تاريخ الكنيسة السريانية الشرقية من العهد المغولي إلى مطلع القرن التاسع عشر* [History of East Syriac Church from the Mongol era until the Beginning of the Nineteenth Century]. Vol. III. Beirut: Dār al-Mašriq, 1993.

———. *ديارات العراق* [Monasteries of Iraq]. Baghdad: no place, 2006.

Al-ARBALĪ, Ḥ.D.Ḫ. *المفصّل في تاريخ إربل، قصة المدينة حتى تسوية مشكلة الموصل (1926م)* [The History of Erbil in detail, the Story of the City until Resolving the Problem of Mosul (1926)]. Erbil: Al-Tafseer, 2020.

———. *إربل تحت الأنظار، أشهر ما تعرضت له المدينة على مدار أدوارها التاريخية من سرجون الأكدي حتى الاحتلال الإنكليزي سنة 1918* [Erbil under the Spotlight, the Most Renowned that the City was Expose to during its Historical Roles since Sargon the Akkadian till the British Invasion 1918]. Erbil: Al-Tafseer, 2021.

———. *القال والقيل في سلطان أربيل، قراءة جديدة لسيرة حياة السلطان مظفر الدين كوكبوري* [Tittle-tattle about the Sultan of Erbil, A New Reading of the Biography of Sultan Muẓaffar ad-Dīn Gukbūrī]. Erbil: Al-Tafseer, 2022.

Al-ʿABŪD, ʿA.T. *الشعر العربي في العراق من سقوط السلاجقة حتى سقوط بغداد* [Arabic Poetry in Iraq from the Fall of Seljuks until the Fall of Baghdad]. Baghdad: Dār al-Ḥuriyah, 1976.

Al-FALLĀḤĪ, ʾA.ʿA.ʾI. "أثر الحياة الاجتماعية في وجهة الشعر في إربل في القرن السابع الهجري" [The Influence of Social Life on the Tendency of Poetry in Erbil in the Seventh Century of Hijra]. *Magazine of Arts and Human Sciences* 16 (1016): 120-153.

Al-MUḤĀMĪ, ʿA.ʿA. *تاريخ العراق بين احتلالين: حكومة المغول 1258-1338م* [History of Iraq between two Invasions: The Government of Mongols 1258-1338 CE]. Vol. I. Beirut: Al-Dār al-ʿArabyiah lil-Mausūʿāt, 2004.

ARTHUR, ROSEMARY A. *Pseudo-Dionysius as Polemicist: The Development and Purpose of the Angelic Hierarchy in Sixth Century Syria*. Ashgate New Critical Thinking in Religion. Theology and Biblical Studies. Aldershot: Ashgate, 2008.

AṢ-ṢĀʾIĠ, S. "شاعر العذراء كيوركيس وردا الأربيلي" [The Poet of Mary, Gīwargīs Wardā the Erbilian]. *An-Nağm* 9 (1937/9): 321-326.

———. "الشاعر المداح للعذراء في الكنيسة المشرقية" [The Praising Poet of the Virgin]. *An-Nağm* 5 (1954/14): 193-201.

[2] For more detailed bibliography about the hymns from the Book of Wardā published by different authors, see Table 8.

AZEEZ, D.K. "قصيدة عن ميلاد الله الكلمة في الزمن للشاعر كيوركيس وردا (القرن 13)" [A Hymn on the Temporal Nativity of "God the Word" by the Poet Gīwargīs Wardā (13th century)]. *Nağm al-Mašriq* 48 (2006/12): 470-475.

ʾAMĪN, Ḥ. *تاريخ العراق في العصر السلجوقي* [The History of Iraq in the Seljuks' Era]. Baghdad: Al-ʾIršād, 1965.

ʾIBN AL-AṮĪR. *الكامل في التاريخ* [The Complete History]. Vol. XI-XII. Edited by C.J. Tornberg. Beirut: Dār Ṣādir- Dār Beirut, 1966.

ʾIBN ḪALAKĀN. *وفيات الأعيان* [The Deaths of the Notables]. Vol. IV. Beirut: Dār Ṣādir, 1978.

ĪŠŌʿYĀHB III. *رسائل البطريرك إيشوعياب الثالث الحديابي* [The Letters of the Patriach ʾĪshoʿyāb III of Adiabene]. Translated by A. Abouna. Erbil: Chaldean Diocese of Erbil, 2020.

ʿABDĪŠŌʿ BAR BRĪḪĀ. ܡܪܓܢܝܬܐ: ܕܥܠ ܫܪܪܐ ܕܟܪܣܛܝܢܘܬܐ [The Pearl: on the truth of Christianity]. Edited by Y. Qelaytā, Mosul: Ancient Church of the East Press, 1924².

———. ܡܐܡܪܐ ܕܟܬܒ̈ܐ ܕܥܒܕܝܫܘܥ ܕܨܘܒܐ, *Catalogus Auctorum Abdišoʿ Sob. (1318+)*. Translated and edited by Yūsif Ḥabbī. Baghdad: Al-Mağmaʿ al-ʿIlmī al-ʿIrāqī, 1986.

———. *كتاب فرائد الفوائد في أصول الدين والعقائد: خطبة في التثليث والتوحيد. أمانة مار عبديشوع*, *Testi teologici di Ebedjesu*. Translated and edited by G. Gianazza. *PCAC* 15, Bologna: CreateSpace Independent Publishing, 2018.

———. *كتاب أصول الدين*, *I fondamenti della religione*. Translated and edited by G. Gianazza. *PCAC* 14, Bologna: CreateSpace Independent Publishing, 2018.

ʿIMĀD, D. "ترتيلة عن الميلاد الزمني لله الكلمة" [A hymn on the temporal Nativity of God the Word]. *Nağm al-Mašriq* 67 (2013/19): 444-447.

ʿĪSĀ, S. *العراق في التاريخ* [Iraq in History]. Baghdad: Dār al-Ḥuriyah, 1983.

BĀBĀI. ܟܬܒܐ ܕܚܕܝܘܬܐ [The Book of the Union]. Translated and edited by A. Vaschalde as *Babai magni: Liber de unione*. *CSCO* 79, Syr. 34, Paris: J. Gabalda; Bibliopola, 1915.

BACHI, P.H. "Marie dans la doctrine de Ghiwarghis Warda d'aprés les manuscrits syriaques de la bibliothèque Vaticane: Étude historique et doctrinale." PhD diss., Rome: Università Propaganda Fide, 1957.

BADGER, G.P. *The Nestorians and Their Rituals*. Vol. I-II. London: Joseph Masters: 1852.

BADR, M.Ṭ. *مغول إيران بين المسيحية والإسلام* [The Mongols of Iran between Christianity and Islam]. Beirut: Dār al-Fikr al-ʿArabī, 2001.

BAR ʿEBRĀYĀ. *كتاب الحمامة*, *The Book of the Dove*. Translated by Zakka Iwaṣ, Tripoli: Mağmaʿ al Luġah al-Siryānīah, 1983².

———. ܡܟܬܒܢܘܬ ܙܒܢ̈ܐ [The Chronography]. Translated by E.A.W. Budge as *The Chronography of Bar Hebraeus*. Vol. I. London: Oxford University Press, 1932.

———. ܟܬܒܐ ܕܐܩܠܝܣܝܣܛܝܩܘܢ [The Ecclesiastical Chronicle]. Translated by D. Wilmshurst as *Bar Hebraeus: The Ecclesiastical Chronicle*. *GECS*, Piscataway, NJ: Gorgias Press, 2016.

BARṢŪM, ʾI.ʾA. *اللؤلؤ المنثور* [The Scattered Pearls]. Translated by Matti Moosa as *The Scattered Pearls: History of Syriac Literature and Sciences*. Piscataway, NJ: Gorgias Press, 2004².

BAUM, W. and WINKLER, D.W. *The Church of the East: A Concise History*. Translated by Miranda G. Henry. London and NY: Routledge Curzon, 2003.

BAUMER, C. *The Church of the East: An Illustrated History of Assyrian Christianity*. London: I.B. Tauris, 2006.

BAUMSTARK, A. "B- Besprechungen." In *Essays on Eastern Christianity*, OC 4, edited by Anton Baumstark, 204-209. Piscataway, NJ, USA: Gorgias Press, 1904.

———. *Geschichte der syrischen literatur: Mit ausschluss der Christlich-palästinensischen texte*. Bonn: A. Marcus and E. Webers, 1922.

BORBONE, P.G. "Due episodi delle eelazioni tra Mongoli e Siri nel XIII secolo nella storiografia e nella poesia Siriaca." *EVO* 33 (2010): 205-228.

BOTTINI, L. "Due lettere inedite del patriarca mār Yhabhallāhā III 1291-1317." *RSO* 66, fasc. 3-4 (1992): 239-257.

BREMER-McCOLLUM, A.C. "Prose, Poetry, and Hagiography: The Martyrdoms of Jacob the Persian and Tahmizgard in Syriac Story and Song." In *Syriac Hagiography, TSEC* 20, edited by S. Minov and F. Ruani, 223-256. Leiden: Brill, 2021.

Breviarium iuxta ritum Syrorum Orientalium id east Chaldaeorum. Vol. I-III. Paris: Via Dicta de Sèvres 95, 1886.

BROCK, S.P. "Clothing Metaphors as a Means of Theological Expression in Syriac Tradition." *EB* 4 (1982): 11-40.

———. "Syriac dialogue poems: marginalia to a recent edition." *Le Muséon* 97 (1984): 29-58.

———. "The Christology of the Church of the East in the Synods of the Fifth to Early Seventh Centuries. Preliminary Considerations and Materials." Aksum-Thyateira. A Festschrift for Archbishop Methodius of Thyateria and Great Britain, Athens (1985): 125-142.

———. "A Dispute of the Months and Some Related Syriac Texts." *JSS* 30 (1985): 181-211.

———. "Dramatic Dialogue Poems." *OCA* 229 (1987): 135-147.

———. "The Sinful Woman and Satan: Two Syriac dialog poems." *OC* 72 (1988): 21-62.

———. "Syriac Poetry on Biblical Themes: 1. The prophet Elijah and the widow of Sarepta." *The Harp* 3 (1990): 75-86.

———. "Syriac Dispute Poems: The Various Types." *OLA* 42 (1991): 109-119.

———. "Syriac Poetry on Biblical Themes, 2. A Dialogue Poem on the Sacrifice of Isaac (Genesis 22)." *The Harp* 7 (1994): 55-72.

———. *A Brief Outline of Syriac Literature*. Kottayam: SEERI, 1997.

———. "The Robe of Glory: A Biblical Image in the Syriac Tradition." *The Way* 39 (1999): 247-259.

———. "Two Syriac Dialogue Poems on Abel and Cain." *Le Muséon* 113 (2000): 333-375.

———. "The Dispute Poem: From Sumer to Syriac." *HJSS* 5:2 (2002): 169-193.

———. "The Dialogue Between the two Thieves (Luke 23:39-41)." *The Harp* 20 (2006): 151-170.

———. *Bride of Light: Hymns on Mary from the Syriac Churches*. Kottayam – India: St. Joseph's Press, 1994.

———. "Gewargis of Arbela: Pseudo (9th cent.?)." In *GEDSH*, edited by Sebastian Brock, Aaron M. Butts, George A. Kiraz, Lucas Van Rompay, 176-177. Piscataway, NJ: Gorgias Press, 2011.

———. *Mary and Joseph and other Dialogue Poems on Mary*. Piscataway, NJ: Gorgias Press, 2011.

BROCKELMANN, C. تاريخ الأدب العربي [History of Arabic Literature]. Vol. V. Translated by Ramaḍān ʿAbd al-Tawāb. Cairo: Dār al-Mʿārif, 1977.

BUNDY, D. "Georges Warda." *Dictionnaire d'histoire et de Géographie Ecclésiastiques* 20 (1912): 668-669.

———. "George Warda as Historian and Theologian of the 13th Century." *AOB* 7 (1992): 191-200.

———. "Interpreter of the Acts of God and Humans: George Warda, historian and theologian of the 13th century." *The Harp* 6 (1993): 7-20.

———. "The Syriac and Armenian Christian Responses to the Islamification of the Mongols." *MCPI* 10 (1996): 33-53.

———. "Interpreter of the Acts of God and Humans: George Warda, Historian and Theologian of the 13th century." *The Harp* 10 (1997): 19-32.

CARDAHI, G. الكنز الثمين في صناعة شعر السريان وتراجم شعرائهم المشهورين, *Liber thesauri de arte poetica Syrorum nec non de eorum poetarum vitis et carminibus*. Rome: Ex typographia Polyglotta, 1875.

Cause of all Causes: Book 7 - ܡܐܡܪܐ ܕܥܠܬܐ ܕܟܠ ܥܠܠܬܐ ܕܥܒܕܐ. based upon C. Kayser, ed. *Das Buch von der Erkenntniss der Wahrheit oder der Ursache aller Ursachen*. Leipzig: J.C. Hinrichs'sche Buchhandlung, 1889. https://syriaccorpus.org/512 [Accessed 30 September 2021].

CHABOT, J.-B. *Littérature syriaque*. Paris: Librarie Bloud et Gay, 1934.

CONYBEARE, F.C., and MACLEAN, A.J., ed. *Rituale Armenorum: Being the Administration of the Sacraments and the Breviary Rites of the Armenian Church; Together with the Greek Rites of Baptism and Epiphany Edited from the Oldest Mss. And the East Syrian Epiphany Rites*. Oxford: Clarendon Press, 1905.

DARMO, T. ed. *Ḥūḏrā* ܚܘܕܪܐ [The Cycle]. Vol. I-III. Trissur: Narsai Press, 1960-1962.

DELLY, E. "كيوركيس الملقب وردا محب العذراء مريم وشاهد كوارث أربيل" [Gīwargīs the so-called Wardā the Adorer of the Virgin Mary and the Witness of Erbil's Disasters]. *Naǧm Al-Mašriq* 36 (2003/9): 522-515.

DEUTSCH, A. *Edition dreier Syrischen lieder nach einer handschrift der Berliner königlichen bibliothek*. Berlin: Itzkowski, 1895.

DUVAL, R. *Syriac Literature: An English Translation of la littérature Syriaque*. Translated by tr. O. Holmey. Piscataway, NJ: Gorgias Press, 2013.

ḌAYF, Š. تاريخ الأدب العربي [History of Arabic Literature]. Vol. I-II. Cairo: Dār al- Mʿārif, 1963.

EBEID, B. "La Cristologia del catholicos Mar Georgis I: Un'analisi della sua lettera a Mina." *OCA* 298 (2015): 203-219.

———. "The Christology of the Church of the East: An Analysis of Christological Statements and Professions of Faith of the Official Synods of the Church of the East before A.D. 612." *OCP* 82 (2016): 353-402.

ĒLĪĀ II. *كتاب أصول الدين للبطريك إيليا الثاني (1131+)* [The Book of Foundations of Religion by the Patriarch Ēlīā II (1131 +)]. Edited by G. Gianazza. PAC 17-18, Beirut: CEDRAC, 2005.

ĒLĪĀ III Abū Ḥalīm. *التراجيم السنيّة للأعياد المارانية*, *Discours Religieux*. Vol. I. Mossul: Dominican Fathers Press, 1901.

ĒLĪĀ OF NISIBIS. *تفسير الأمانة الكبيرة*, Elias of Nisibis: Commentary on the creed (Tafsīr al-Amānah al-Kabīrah). Translated and edited by B. Ebeid, *SSA* 9, Cordoba: UCO-Press, 2018.

FIEY, J.M. *Jalons pour une histoire de l'église en Iraq*. *CSCO* 310, SS 36, Louvain: Secrétariat du CorpusSCO, 1970.

———. *Chrétiens syriaques sous les Mongols (Il-Khanat de Perse, XIIIe-XIVe S.)*. *CSCO* 362, SS 44, Louvain: Secrétariat du CorpusSCO, 1975.

———. *Chrétiens syriaques sous les Abbassides surtout à Bagdad 749-1258*. *CSCO* 420, SS 54, Louvain: Secrétariat du CorpusSCO, 1980.

FOLKMANN, "I. Ausgewählte Nestorianische kirchenlieder über das martyrium des H. Georg von Giwargis Warda mit einleitung, anmerkungen und deutscher übersetzung." PhD diss., Kirchhain: Zahn & Baendel, 1896.

FRISHMAN, J. "Narsai's Christology According to his homily 'On the Word Became Flesh'." *The Harp* 8/9 (1995/96): 289-303.

GHARIB, G. "Giorgio Warda (c. 1175-1236)." In *Testi Mariani del primo millennio, padri e altri autori orientali*. Vol. IV. Rome: Città nuova (1991): 370-397.

GIGNOUX, PH. "Un poème inédit sur l'homme-microcosme de Guiwarguis Wardā (13ème siècle)." *RM* (1999): 95-189.

———. "Giorgio Warda." In *Storia della scienza – Treccani, 1. La Scienza Siriaca,* edited by J. Teixidor and R. Contini, (2001) 52–53. https://www.treccani.it [Accessed 15 January 2020].

GRILLMEIER, A., and T. HAINTHALER, *Christ in Christian Tradition*. Vol. I-II. Translation by John Bowden. Westminster: John Knox Press, 1975.

GUTAS, D. *Greek Thought, Arabic Culture: The Graeco-Arabic Translation Movement in Baghdad and Early ʿAbbâsid Society (2nd-4th/8th-10 centuries)*. London – New York: Routledge, 1998.

HALTON, T.P. *The Fathers of the Church: St. Cyril of Alexandria Letters 1-50*. Translated by J.I. McEnerney. Vol. LXXVI. Washington: Catholic University of America Press, 1987.

HILGENFELD, H. *Ausgewählte gesänge des Gīwargīs Wardā von Arbel: Herausgegeben mit übersetzung, einleitung und erklärung*, Leipzig: Otto Harrassowitz, 1904.

———. "Giwargis Warda." *ZWT* 47 (1904): 269-272.

HOOD, J.K. "Songs of Supplication and Penitence. ʿOnyātā from the Warda Collection in Mingana Syr 214." PhD diss., The Catholic University of America, Washington D.C., 2019.

ḤABĪB, P. "قصيدة مديح للعذراء مريم للشاعر المشرقي الكبير كيوركيس وردا" [A Praising Hymn for Mary of Gīwargīs Wardā the Great Oriental Poet]. *Nağm al-Mašriq* 87 (2016/3): 245-249.

ḤADBŠABBĀ, Š.Ī., ed. ܚܡܝܣ ܒܪ ܩܪܕܐܚܐ [Ḫāmīs bar Qardāḥē]. Nūhadrā: Nisibin Press, 2002.

ḤUSAYN, M.M. أربيل في العهد الأتابكي [Erbil during the Atabeg Era]. Erbil: Al-Tafseer, 2014.

ḪAṢBĀK, Ğ.Ḥ. العراق في عهد المغول الأيلخانيين [Iraq in the Time of the Il-Ḫānate Mongols]. Baghdad: Al-ʿĀnī, 1968.

IRENAEUS. *The Five Books of Saint Irenaeus Bishop of Lyons Against Heresies*. Vol. IV. Translated by J. Kebel. London: Rivingtons, 1872.

JACOB OF SERUGH. *On the Mother of God*. Translated by Mary Hansbury. Crestwood – NY: St Vladimir's Seminary, 1998.

JOSEPH, E. "Mary as Portrayed in the Hymns of George Warda in the 13th Century." *JCSSS* 9 (2009): 43-53.

KARUKAKALATHIL, T. "Christ's Humanity in the Christological Homilies of Narsai: Influence of the Antiochean and the Syriac Heritage; A Theological and Historical Analysis." PhD diss., Rome: Pontificio Istituto Orientale, 2013.

Ktābā d-Tūrgāmē ܟܬܒܐ ܕܬܘܪܓܡܐ [The Book of Interpretations]. Baghdad: Church of the East Press, 1983.

Le COZ, R. *Histoire de l'église d'Orient*. Vol. I-II. Translated by A. Abouna. Erbil: no place, 2020.

MANNA, J.E. المروج النزهية في آداب اللغة الآرامية *Morceaux choisis de littérature Araméenne*. Mosul: Dominican Fathers Press, 1901.

MARTIN, F. "Homélie de Narses sur les trois docteurs nestoriens." *JA* 9.14 (1899): 446-493.

MASSONNAT, A.-M. "IV. Marie dans la liturgie Chaldéenne." *Maria, études sur la sainte Vierge* II (1949): 341-351.

MENGOZZI, A. "A Syriac Hymn on the Crusades from a Warda Collection." *EVO* 33 (2010): 187-203.

———. "Giwargis Warda (13th cent.?)." In *GEDSH*, edited by Sebastian Brock, Aaron M. Butts, George A. Kiraz, Lucas Van Rompay, 176-177. Piscataway, NJ: Gorgias Press, 2011.

———. "The Book of Khamis bar Qardaḥe: History of the Text, Genres, and Research Perspectives." *SEECS* 20 (2015): 415-436.

McGUCKIN, J.A. *St. Cyril of Alexandria: The Christological Controversy; Its History, Theology, and Texts*. Leiden – NY: St Vladimir's Seminary, 2004.

McLEOD, F.G., ed. *Narsai's Metrical Homilies on the Nativity, Epiphany, Resurrection and Ascension. PO* 40, Turnhout: Brepols, 1979.

MISSICK, S.A. "The Assyrian Church in the Mongolian Empire as Observed by World Travelers in the Late 13th and Early 14th Centuries." *JAAS* 13 (1999): 85-102.

MOFFETT, S.H. *A History of Christianity in Asia: Beginnings to 1500*. Vol. I. Maryknoll – NY: Orbis Books: 1998, 2006[2].

MOUTERDE, P. "Une invocation au cœur de Jésus dans le livre de Warda." *AB* 68 (1950): 305-309.

MURRAY, R. *Symbols of Church and Kingdom*. New York: T&T Clark International, 2004.

NAṢRĪ, P. *ذخيرة الأذهان في تواريخ المشارقة والمغاربة السريان*, *Histoire des églises chaldéenne et syrienne*. Vol. I-II. Mosul: Dominican Fathers Press, 1905.

NESTORIUS. ܬܓܪܬܐ ܕܗܪܩܠܝܕܘܣ [The Treatise of Heracleides]. Translated and edited by P. Bedjan as *Le livre d'Héraclide de damas*. Paris – Leipzig: Otto Harrassowitz, 1910.

NICÁK, M. "Der Mongoleneinfall in Karmeliš auf dem forschungshintergrund des liturgischen Buches Wardā" [The Invasion of the Mongols in Karmeliš on the scientific Background of the Liturgical Book Wardā]. *TT* 7:2 (2013): 199-223.

———. "Fenomén konverzie a boj za zachovanie náboženskej identity v 'Knihe Wardā'." [The Conversion Phenomenon and the Fight for Preservation of the Religious Identity in the 'Book Wardā]. *Teologická Reflexe* (2013): 147-158.

———. "Zeugenschaft und emotion in der ostsyrischen poesie des 13. Jahrhunderts." [Testimony and Emotion in the Eastern Syriac Poetry of the 13th Century]. *Begegnungen in Vergangenheit und Gegenwart: Beiträge dialogischer Existenz, Theologie* 112 (2015): 123-128.

———. "The Figure of Mary in Understanding of Warda in its Historical Context." *PDO* 40 (2015): 303-320.

———. "Interkonfessioneller dialog in der Ostsyrischen poesie." [Interreligious Dialogue in the Eastern Syriac Poetry]. *Informationes Theologiae Europae: internationales ökumenisches Jahrbuch für Theologie,* (2015): 151-166.

———. *"Konversion" im Buch Wardā*: Zur bewältigung der konversionsfrage in der kirche des Ostens. Wiesbaden: Otto Harrassowitz, 2016.

———. "The Direct Speech of John the Baptist and Liturgical use of the Book of Wardā." *Take Another Scroll and Write, Studies in the Interpretative After life of Prophets and Prophecy in Judaism, Christianity and Islam*, (2016): 325-338.

———. "Penitential Theology and Optative form of Remission of Sin in the Liturgical Book of the Rose." *The Harp* 31 (2016): 329-340.

———. "Bildersprache und symbolik der feinde der kirche des Ostens im liturgischen buch Wardā." [Language of Images and Symbolism of the Enemy of the Eastern Church in the Book *Wardā*]. *Syrische Studien: Beiträge zum 8. Deutschen Syrologie-Symposium in Salzburg 2014*, *OPO* 10, (2016): 323-340.

———. "The Theological Perspective on Adam and the Inclination Toward Sin in the Book of the Rose." *Studies in the Reception History of the Bible* 8 (2017): 185-198.

———. "Symbolický obraz ako artikulačný prostriedok hymnologickej zbierky Wardā." [Symbolic Image as an Interpretative Means in the Hymn Collection Wardā]. *TT* 11:2 (2017): 69-83.

———. "Špecifiká východosýrskej teológie v hymnologikej zbierke Wardā (13. Stor)." [Specific Features of the Eastern Syriac Theology in the Hymn Collection Wardā (13th cent.)]. *O filozofii a viere* (2018): 63-80.

NÖLDEKE, T. "Zwei Syrische lieder auf die einnahme Jerusalems durch Saladin." *ZDMG* 27 (1873): 489-510.

PALMER, A. and A. PRITULA. “From the Nile Delta to Mount Izlā and the Tigris Gorge: A Hymn by Gīwargīs Wardā on Mār Āwgēn’s Family of Monks.” *Den Orient erforschen, mit Orthodoxen leben*. Wiesbaden: Harrassowitz Verlag, 2021.

PATROUS, R. “سبي كرمليس لكوركيس وردة الأربيلي” [The Capture of Karmlīs by Gīwargīs Wardā the Erbilian]. *SĪMTĀ* 14 (2010): 102-114.

———, ed. ܟܘܢܫ ܡܘܫܚܬܐ ܕܓܝܘܪܓܝܣ ܘܪܕܐ ܐܪܒܝܠܝܐ [A Collection of Hymns of Gīwargīs Wardā the Erbilian]. Vol. I-II. Duhōk: Dār al-Mašriq, 2014.

———. “ميامر كيوركيس وردا الأربيلي في حوذرا كنيسة المشرق الآشورية” [The Homilies of Giwargis Warda the Erbilian in the Ḥūdrā of the Assyrian Church of the East]. *Beth Kokheh* 8 (2020): 1-4. https://bethkokheh.assyrianchurch.org [Accessed 12 November 2020].

———. “قصيدة عن الميلاد للشاعر كيوركيس وردا الأربيلي” [A hymn on Nativity by the Poet Gīwargīs Wardā the Erbilian]. *Beth Kokheh* 8 (2020): 1-12. https://bethkokheh.assyrianchurch.org [Accessed 10 March 2020].

POGNON, H. *Une version syriaque des aphorismes d’Hippocrate*. Leipzig: J.C. Hinrichs’sche Buchhandlung, 1903.

PRITULA, A. “An Autobiographic Hymn by Givargis Warda.” In *Beiträge zum 3. Deutschen Syrologen-Symposium in Vierzehnheiligen, Studien zur Orientalischen Kirchengeschichte 33, Syriaca II*, edited by Martin Tamcke, 229-241. Münster: LIT Verlag, 2004.

———. “A Hymn by Givargis Warda on the Childhood of Christ.” *Die Suryoye und ihre Umwelt, Studien zur Orientalischen Kirchengeschichte 36*, (2005): 423-451.

———. “Из истории восточносирийской литургической поэзии: заключительное песнопение моления ниневитян.” [From the History of Eastern Syriac Liturgical Poetry: The Final Hymn ‘A prayer of the Ninevians’]. *ВГ* [Magic Mountain] 12 (2006): 147-159.

———. “Песнопение Гиваргиса Варды о гробе” [Song of Gīwargīs Wadā about the Coffin]. *ВГ* [Magic Mountain] 14 (2007): 93-102.

———. “Восточносирийские песнопения (ʿониты) и гомилии Нарсая: шесть гимнов из сборника “Варда”” [Eastern Syriac Hymns (ʿOnita) and Homilies by Narsaj: Six Hymns from the Collection ‘Wardā’]. *Символ* [Symbol] 55 (2009): 152-253.

———. “Гимн о неравенстве в человеческом обществе из восточно - сирийского сборника “Варда”” [A Hymn about Human Inequality in Easter Syriac Miscellaneous ‘Wardā’]. *ВГ* [Magic Mountain] 15 (2009): 167-178.

———. “Восточносирийский гимн о Детстве Христа и прозаические (сиро- и арабоязычные) параллели” [An Eastern Syriac Hymn about the Childhood of Christ and its (Syriac and Arabic) Parallels in Prose]. in *Символ* [Symbol] 58 (2020): 229-267.

———. “A Hymn on Tiflis from Warda Collection: A Transformation of the Muslim Conquerors into Pagans.” In *Caucasus during the Mongol Period-Der Kaukasus in der Mongolenzeit*, edited by J. Tubach and S.G. Vashalomidze and M. Zimmer, 217-237. Wiesbaden: Reichert, 2012.

———. "The Last Hymn of the Praying (Rogation) of the Ninevites." In *Orientalische Christen und Europa. Kulturbegegnung zwischen Interferenz, Partizipation und Antizipation. Göttinger Orientforschungen. I. Reihe: Syriaca*, edited by M. Tamcke, 173-186. Wiesbaden: Harrassowitz, 2012.

———. "Die hymnensammlung Wardā und die homilien Narsais: Wege der Syrischen dichtung im 13. Jahrhundert." In *Orientalische Christen und Europa. Kulturbegegnung Zwischen Interferenz, Partizipation und Antizipation. Göttinger Orientforschungen. I. Reihe: Syriaca* 41, edited by M. Tamcke, 159-171. Wiesbaden: Harrassowitz, 2012.

———. "The Wardā Hymnological Collection." In *Syrians and the Others: Cultures of the Christian Orient in the Middle Ages, Scrinium* 9, edited by Basil Lourié and Nikolai N. Seleznyov, 309-365. Piscataway, NJ: Gorgias press, 2013.

———. "The Wardā Hymnological Collection and Šlemon of Ahlat (13th century)." In *Syrians and the Others: Cultures of the Christian Orient in the Middle Ages, Scrinium* 10, edited by Basil Lourié and Nikolai N. Seleznyov, 148-207. Piscataway: Gorgias press, 2014.

———. *The Wardā: An East Syriac Hymnological Collection; Study and Critical Edition.* Wiesbaden: Harrassowitz Verlag, 2015.

PROVERA, M.E. *Il Vangelo arabo dell'infanzia: Secondo il Ms Laurenziano Orientale (n. 387)*. Jerusalem: Franciscan Printing Press, 1973.

QELAYTĀ, Y., ed. ܟܬܵܒܵܐ ܕܦܸܬܘܵܬܹ̈ܐ: ܗܵܘ ܕܝܼܢ ܡܢܵܘܵܬܹ̈ܐ ܡܟܲܢܫܵܬܹ̈ܐ ܡܼܢ ܟܬ݂ܵܒܹ̈ܐ ܕܐܲܒ݂ܵܗܵܬ݂ܵܐ ܣܵܦܪ̈ܵܝܹܐ ܘܡܲܠܦܵܢܹ̈ܐ ܣܘܼܪ̈ܝܝܹܐ. ܥܲܡ ܡܲܘܕܥܵܢܘܼܬܵܐ ܩܲܠܝܼܠ ܕܥܲܠ ܚܲܕ ܚܲܕ ܡ̣ܢ ܡܣܲܝܡܵܢܘܗܝ. [The Book of Crumbs: i.e. Collected Parts from Books of Syriac Scribal Fathers and Teachers With note on Each one of Their Composers]. Urmi: Archbishop of Canterbury's Mission, 1898.

RASSAM, S. *Christianity in Iraq: Its Origins and Development to the Present Day*. Leominster, UK: Gracewing, 2010.

RASSI, S. "Justifying Christianity in the Islamic Middle Ages: The Apologetic Theology of ʿAbdīshōʿ bar Brīkhā (d. 1318)." PhD diss., Oxford: University of Oxford, 2015.

REININK, G.J. "Ein Syrisches streitgespräch zwischen tod und Satan." In *Dispute Poems and Dialogues in the Ancient and Mediaval Near East, Forms and Types of Literary Debates in Semitic and Related Literature, OLA* 42, edited by G.J. Reinink and H.L. Vanstiphout, 135-152. Leuven: Peeters, 1991.

———. "Man as Microcosm: A Syriac Didactic Poem and its Prose Background." In *Calliope's Classroom. Studies in Didactic Poetry from Antiquity to the Renaissance*, edited by G.J. Reinink and A. Harder and A.A. MacDonald, 123-152. Leuven, Paris, Dudley, MA: Peeters, 2007.

———. "George Warda and Michael Badoqa." In *The Syriac Renaissance, ECS* 9, edited by H. Teule and C.F. Tauwinkl and B. Ter Haar Romeny and J. Van Ginkel, 65-74. Leuven, Paris, Walpole, MA: Peeters, 2010.

RICCIOTTI, G., ed. *Inni alla Vergine*: di S. Efrem Siro. Rome: Federazione Italiana Uomini Cattolici, 1925.

SACHAU, E., ed. *Theodori Mopsuesteni fragmenta Syriaca*. Leipzig: Engelmann, 1869.

SETTON, K.M., ed. *A History of the Crusades*. Vol. I-VI. Madison: University of Wisconsin Press, 1969-1985.

SCHER, A. *سيرة أشهر شهداء المشرق القديسين* [Biography of the Most Famous Holy Martyrs of the East]. Vol. II. Erbil: Dār ʾĀrās, 2009[2].

SCIPIONI, L.I. *Ricerche sulla Cristologia del 'Libro Eraclide' di Nestorio: La formulazione teologica e il suo contesto filosofico*. Freiburg: University Edition, 1956.

ṢALĪBĀ BIN YŌḤANNĀ AL-MAWṢILLĪ. *كتاب أسفار الأسرار*, *I Libri dei Misteri*. Translated and edited by G. Gianazza. Rome: Aracne editrice, 2017.

ṢĀLIḤ, ʿA.A. *أربيل مدينة الأدب والعلم والحضارة* [Erbil the City of Literature, Science and Civilization]. Erbil: Dār ʾĀrās, 2009.

ṢANĀ, A. "قصيدة لكوركيس وردة في قيامة المسيح" [A Hymn of Giwargis Warda on the Resurrection of Christ]. *Naǧm al-Mašriq* 17 (1999/5): 44-47.

TAMCKE, M. "Bemerkungen zu Giwargis Warda's ʿOnita über die katholikoi des Ostens." In *Beiträge zum 3. Deutschen Syrologen-Symposium in Vierzehnheiligen, Studien zur Orientalischen Kirchengeschichte 33, Syriaca II*, edited by Martin Tamcke, 203-227. Münster: LIT Verlag, 2004.

———. "Remarks Concerning Giwargis Warda's ʿOnita about the Catholicoi of the East." *The Harp* 18 (2005): 115-123.

———. "Die Islamische zeit in Giwargis Warda's ʿOnita über die katholikoi des Ostens". In *The Encounter of Eastern Christianity with Early Islam. The History of Christian - Muslim Relations* 5, edited by E. Grypeou and M. Swason and D. Thomas, 139-152. Leiden, Boston: Brill, 2006.

———. "How Giwargis Warda Retells Biblical Texts: Some Remarks." In *Rewritten Bible Reconsidered*: Proceedings of the Conference in Karkku, edited by A. Laato and J. Van Ruiten, 249-269. Finland: Ābo Akademi University, 2008.

———. "Leben aus den ursprüngen: zur funktion des lesens und schriftlicher überlieferung bei Giwargis Warda." in *The Syriac Renaissance, ECS* 9, edited by H. Teule and C.F. Tauwinkl and B. Ter Haar Romeny and J. Van Ginkel, 53-63. Leuven, Paris, Walpole, MA: Peeters, 2010.

TEULE, H. "A Theological Treatise by Išoʿyahb bar Malkon Preserved in the Theological Compendium Asfār al-Asrār." *JECS* 58 (2006): 235-252.

———. *Les Assyro-Chaldéens: Chrétiens d'Irak, d'Iran et de Turquie. fils d'Abraham*. Turnhout: Brepols, 2008.

———. "The Syriac Renaissance." In *The Syriac Renaissance ECS* 9, edited by H. Teule and C.F. Tauwinkl and B. Ter Haar Romeny and J. Van Ginkel, 1-30. Leuven, Paris, Walpole, MA: Peeters, 2010.

———. "Christian Spiritual Sources in Bar Hebraeus' Ethicon and the Book of the Dove." *ECS* 10 (2011): 333-354.

———. "Christian-Muslim Religious Interaction 1200-1350: A Historical and Contextual Introduction." In *Christian-Muslim Relations A Bibliographical History* 4 (1200-1350), edited by D. Thomas and A. Mallett, 1-16. Leiden: Brill, 2012.

———. "George Bar ʿEbrōyō and ʿAbdishoʿ bar Brikhā: Similar but Different." *OC* 70 (2013): 544-551.

———. "The Synod of Timothy II, 1318." In *West and East-Syriac Canons*, edited by E. Ishaq, Bologna (forthcoming).

———. "The Syriac Renaissance and Inner-Christian Relations." In *La Teologia Orientale Bilancio e prospettive*, edited by C.G. Conticello, M. Fédou, Rome (forthcoming).

THEODORE OF MOPSUESTIA. *Theodori Mopsuesteni fragmenta exegetica et dogmatica.* PG 66, lib. xv, 992 BC. https://www.roger-pearse.com/weblog/patrologia-graeca-pg-pdfs [Accessed 20 October 2021].

———. *Theodori Mopsuesteni Fragmenta Syriaca: E Codicibus Musei Britannici Nitriacis.* Edited and translated by E. Sachau. Lipsiae: Engelmann, 1869.

TŌMĀ d-MARGĀ. ܬܫ̈ܥܝܬܐ ܘܡܕܒܪ̈ܢܘܬܐ ܕܐܒܗ̈ܬܐ ܩܕ̈ܝܫܐ ܕܡܢ ܥܘܡܪܐ ܩܕ̈ܝܫܐ ܘܡܣܬܒܪ̈ܢܐ ܕܗܘܘ ܒܕܪ ܒܕܪ ܒܥܘܡܪ̈ܐ ܩܕ̈ܝܫܐ ܕܕܝܪܐ ܟܬܒܐ ܕܐܬܟܬܒ ܠܡܪܝ ܥܒܕ ܬܐܘܡܐ ܐܦܝܣܩܘܦܐ ܕܡܪܓܐ, *The Book of Governors. The Historia Monstica of Thomas Bishop of Margâ A.D. 840.* Translated and edited by E.A.W. Budge. Vol I-II. London: Kegan Paul, Trench, Trübner & Co. LTD, 1893

VANDENHOFF, B. *Vier geistliche gedichte in Syrischer und Neusyrischer sprache. Aus den Berliner HSS. Sachau 188 u. 223 mit erklärenden anmerkungen.* Leipzig: Verlag nicht Ermittelbar, 1908.

VAN VOSSEL, V. *ثيودوروس المعلم الكبير* [Theodore the Great Teacher]. Baghdad: Aṭ-Ṭaif, 2004.

———. *مدرسة أنطاكيا* [The School of Antioch]. Baghdad: Aṭ-Ṭaif, 2007.

———. *مدرسة الإسكندرية* [The School of Alexandria]. Baghdad: Aṭ-Ṭaif, 2008.

VÖÖBUS, A. *History of Asceticism in the Syrian Orient: A Contribution to the History of Culture in the Near East.* Vol. I. *CSCO* 184, SS 14, Louvain: Secrétariat du CorpusSCO, 1958.

WILMSHURST, D. *The Ecclesiastical Organisation of the Church of the East 1318-1913. CSCO* 582, SS 104, Lovanii: Secrétariat du CorpusSCO, 2000.

———. *The Martyred Church: A History of the Church of the East.* London: East & West Publishing Ltd, 2011.

WRIGHT, W. *A Short History of Syriac Literature.* London: Wipf and Stock, 1894.

ZACHARIA, S., ed. *The Acts and Decrees of the Synod of Diamper 1599.* Kerala: Indian Institute of Christian Studies, 1994.

ZAYĀT, H. *الصليب في الإسلام* [The Cross in Islam]. Lebanon: Saint Paul Press, 1935.

4. TOOLS

ABOUNA, A. *قواعد اللغة الآرامية* [Grammar of Aramaic Language]. Erbil: Dār ʾĀrās, 2001.

Al-ḤAMAWĪ, YĀQŪT. *معجم البلدان* [Dictionary of Countries]. Vol. II. Beirut: Dār Ṣādir, 1977.

Al-ZARKALĪ, Ḫ. *الأعلام: قاموس تراجم لأشهر الرجال والنساء من العرب والمستعربين والمستشرقين* [Celebrities: Dictionary of Biography of the Most Famous Men and Women of Arabs, Arabized and Orientalists]. Beirut: Dār al-ʿIlm lil-Malāīīn, 1986.

BROCK, S.P. and A.M. BUTTS and G.A. Kiraz and L. Van Rompay. *Gorgias Encyclopedic Dictionary of the Syriac Heritage.* Piscataway, NJ: Gorgias Press, 2011.

DUVAL, R. *Lexicon Syriacum Auctore Hassano Bar Bahlule.* Paris: Leroux, 1901.

GIBB, H.A.R., J.H. Kramers, E. Lévi-Provençal and J. Schacht eds. *The Encyclopedia of Islam*. Leiden: Brill, 1986.

KIRAZ, G.A. *A Computer-Generated Concordance to the Syriac New Testament*. Leiden: Brill, 1993.

———. *Comparative Edition of the Syriac Gospels Aligning the Sinaiticus, Curetonianus, Peshîṭtâ and Ḥarklean Versions*. Vol. IV. Leiden: Brill, 1996.

MOSS, C., *Catalogue of Syriac Printed Books and Related Literature in British Museum*, London, British Museum 1962.

Multiple lexicons: http://www.dukhrana.com/lexicon/search.php.

SMITH, R.P. *Thesaurus Syriacus*. Oxford: Clarendon Press, 1879.

SMITH, J.P. ed., *A compendious Syriac dictionary founded upon Thesaurus Syriacus of R. Payne Smith*. Oxford: Clarendon Press, 1903.

SOKOLOFF, M. *A Syriac Lexicon: A Translation from Latin, Correction, Expansion, and Update of C. Brockelmann's Lexison Syriacum*. Winona Lake, Indiana: Eisenbrauns; Piscataway, NJ: Gorgias Press, 2009.

The Concordance to the Peshitta Version of the Aramaic New Testament. Edited by The Way International Research Team. New Knoxville, Ohio: American Christian Press, 1986.

Ter Haar Romeny, R.B, and W. Th van Peursen and B. Albrektson, and Konrad Dirk Jenner eds., *The Old Testament in Syriac According to the Peshiṭta Version*. Leiden: Brill, 1987.

APPENDIX I

Greek words found in the hymns translated in the third chapter

Syriac	In Greek	Number of the hymn and stanza
ܐܐܪ	ἀήρ	14.(96)[14d]
ܐܓܘܢܐ	ἀγών	5.(67)[36c]
ܐܘܢܓܠܝܘܢ	εὐαγγέλιον	In the heading: 14.(96), 17.(109), 18.(121)
ܐܘܣܝܐ	οὐσία	7.(72)[8c], 11.(91)[2b], 20.(130)[1b]
ܐܘܩܝܢܘܣ	ὠκεανός	1.(12)[24c]
ܐܟܣܢܝܐ	ξενία	5.(67)[16d]
ܐܣܘܛܘܬܐ	ἄσωτος	4.(59)[12a]
ܐܣܛܠܐ	στολή	2.(13)[1d]
ܐܣܟܡܐ	σχῆμα	15.(97)[6d]
ܐܣܦܪܐ	σφαῖρα	20.(130)[8d]
ܐܣܛܪܐ	στατήρ	18.(121)[23b, 24a, 24c, 25c, 28d, 29c, 31d]
ܐܦܣܘܢܝܬܐ	ψώνια	19.(127)[21a]
ܐܦܝܣܩܘܦܐ	ἐπίσκοπους	19.(127)[20b]
ܐܪܟܘܣ	ἀρχή	11.(91)[18d], 13.(95)[47c], 16.(106)[10d], 19.(127)[27a]
ܐܬܘܢܘܣ	θόναι	16.(106)[9b]
ܓܢܣܐ	γένος	1.(12)[3d], 2.(13)[12d], 5.(67)[1b], 10.(86)[27e], 11.(91)[20b, 38d], 12.(92)[1a], 19.(127)[31c]
ܕܝܢܪܐ	δηνάριον	16.(106)[13b]
ܗܕܝܘܛܐ	ἰδιώτης	8.(75)[31d], 16.(106)[15c]
ܗܘܦܕܝܩܢܐ	ὑποδιάκονος	19.(127)[30d]
ܛܘܟܣܐ، ܛܟܣܝܢ	τάξις	12.(92)[38d], 19.(127)[23d]
ܟܘܡܘܣ	κυμός	16.(106)[10b]
ܟܪܘܙܘܬܐ	κήρυξ	1.(12)[35b], 2.(13)[6d], 11.(91)[13d], 12.(92)[32a]

ܟܪܝܣܛܘܣ	χρηστός	1.(12)[1d], 16.(106)[9d]
ܟܪܣܛܝܢܐ	χριστιανός	8.(75)[19d]
ܢܘܣܐ	ναός	13.(95)[52c], 20.(130)[29b]
ܢܡܘܣܐ	νόμος	8.(75)[24]
ܦܛܪܝܪܟܐ	πατριάρκης	19.(127)[10a]
ܦܢܛܩܘܣܛܐ	πεντηκοστή	In the heading:13.(95) + [53], 14.(96), 16.(106)
ܦܢܛܣܝܐ	φαντασία	5.(67)[29d]
ܦܪܘܣ	πρός	16.(106)[9c]
ܦܪܨܘܦܐ	πρόσωπον	In the heading:4.(59), 17.(109)[5b, 13b, 16d]
ܦܪܩܠܛܐ	παράκλητος	14.(96)[6c, 26c]
ܩܝܛܘܢ	χοιτών	13.(95)[2b]
ܩܠܝܡܐ	κλίμα	19.(127)[26c]
ܛܓܡܐ	τάγμα	14.(96)[36b], 19.(127)[3b, 4a, 11a, 17a, 19a, 20c, 22a, 23a, 24a, 25a, 26a, 27a, 29a, 31a, 32b]

APPENDIX II

Because of the poetical nature of the Book of Wardā the poet never gives literal quotations from the Bible but only more or less direct reference.

Old testament		New Testament	
Gen	1:6-10; 2:7; 3:6; 7:1-23; 18:1-8.	Matt	2:1; 2:15; 3:3; 3:9; 3:10; 3:11; 3:12; 3:16; 3:17; 4:1; 4:2; 4:3; 4:4; 4:5; 4:6; 4:7; 4:8; 4:9; 4:10; 4:11; 14:14; 16:19; 16:21; 17:1-13; 17:23; 17:24; 17:25; 17:27; 20:20-21; 23:37; 24:3-14; 24:1-31; 24:45-51; 24:64; 25:31; 26:17; 26:51; 27:52; 28:1; 28:8; 28:9; 28:16.
Exod	12:3; 12:29-32; 15:1-21; 16:35; 17:1-7; 17:10; 32:4; 34:33.	Mark	1:3; 1:7; 1:8; 1:10; 1:11; 1:12; 1:13; 6:23; 9:2-13; 10:35; 10:51; 13:4; 13:3-27; 14:12; 14:15; 14:47; 16:2; 16:7; 16:9; 16:10; 16:12; 16:19.
Num	11:13; 20:2-9, 11; 22:28.	Luke	1:28; 1:31; 1:32; 1:34; 1:35; 1:53; 2:14; 3:1; 3:4; 3:8; 3:9; 3:16; 3:17; 3:22; 4:1; 4:2; 4:3; 4:4; 4:5; 4:7; 4:9; 4:10; 4:11; 4:13; 9:3; 9:12; 9:28-36; 12:37; 12:41-48; 13:34; 18:41; 21:5-28; 22:7; 22:12; 22:49; 24:7; 24:10; 24:13; 24:18; 24:36; 24:37; 24:38; 24:39; 24:40; 24:42; 24:49; 24:50; 36:24.

Old testament		New Testament	
Deut	6:16.	John	1:14; 1:23; 1:27; 1:32; 1:33; 4; 4:6; 4:7; 4:9; 4:10; 4:11; 4:12; 4:13; 4:14; 4:15; 4:16; 4:17; 4:18; 4:19; 4:20; 4:21-23; 4:24; 4:25; 4:28; 4:29; 4:30; 5:25; 6:33-35; 6:49; 6:51-58; 9:1; 9:6; 9:10; 9:16; 9:18; 9:19; 9:20; 9:21; 9:24; 9:27; 9:28; 10:33-36; 11:16; 11:39; 13; 14:15-16; 14:17; 14:25-28; 16:6-8; 16:13; 16:15; 17:23; 18:10; 20:11; 20:14; 20:18; 20:19; 20:21; 20:22; 20:23; 20:24; 20:25; 20:26; 20:27; 20:28; 20:29; 21:1; 21:2; 21:15.
Josh	19:22.	Acts	1:3; 1:8; 1:9; 1:11; 1:13; 2:1-12; 2:3; 2:1-5; 2:6; 2:7; 2:8; 5:15; 7:56; 14:11.
1 Kgs	16:30; 18:4; 19:1-3; 21.	1 Cor	8:12; 15:6, 8; 15:40.
2 Kgs	5:10.	2 Cor	4:4.
Ezek	10:1; 10:21.	Gal	1:16.
Neh	9:15.	Eph	1:21; 3:10; 4:8.
Job	34:15.	Phil	2:7.
Ps	7:10; 36:8; 45:7-8; 45:9; 51:17; 91:11; 92:5, 6; 104:15; 105:40; 110:1; 111:2; 119:156; 145:3; 147:5.	Col	1:15; 1:16.
Prov	17:3; 30:19.	1 Thess	4:16.
Isa	6:1; 6:2; 6:3; 6:5-7; 9:6; 38:21-22.	1 Tim	2:14.
Jer	1:5; 11:20; 17:10.	Heb	1:3; 1:8; 1:13; 9:14; 13.
Dan	6:23; 7:10, 13, 22.	1 Pet	3:19-20; 4:6.
Hos	11:1.	Rev	2:23.

MANUSCRIPTS

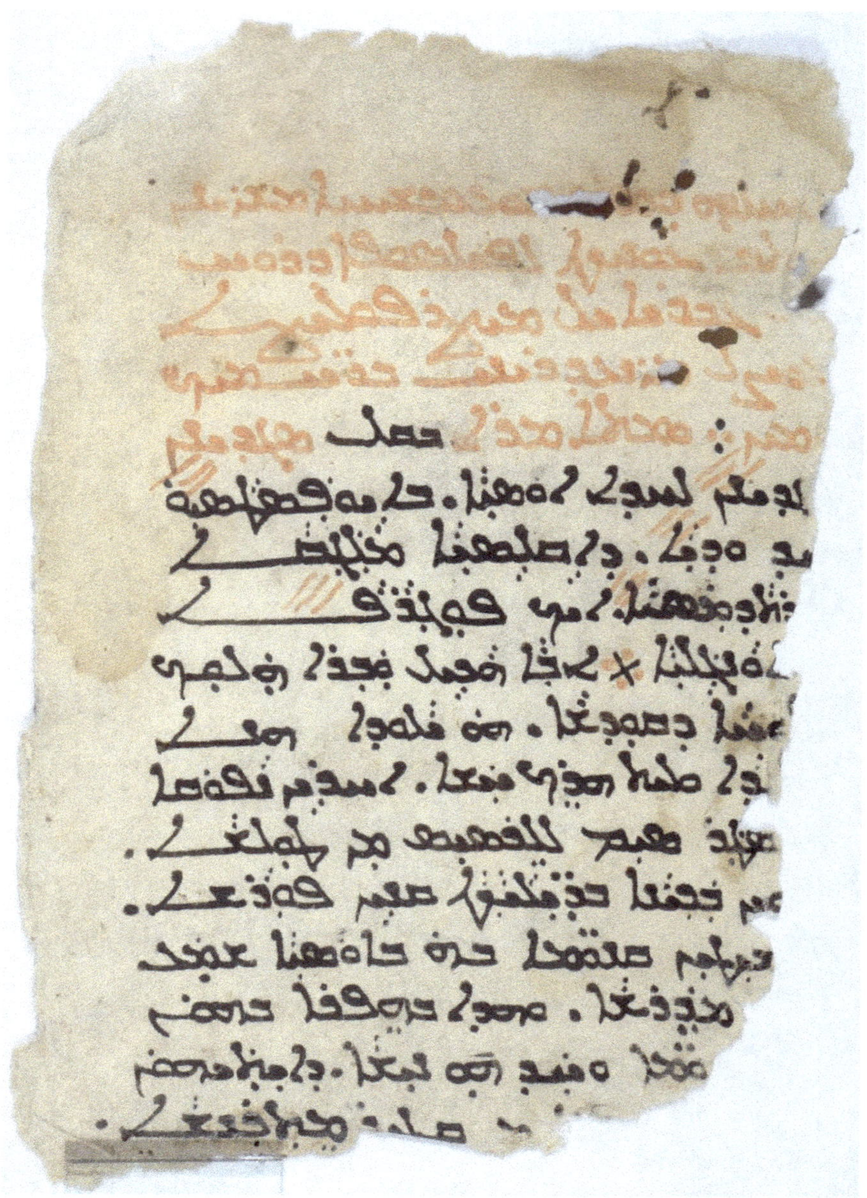

Mardin Chaldean 43, f1v. CCM_00406
https://w3id.org/vhmml/readingRoom/view/132525

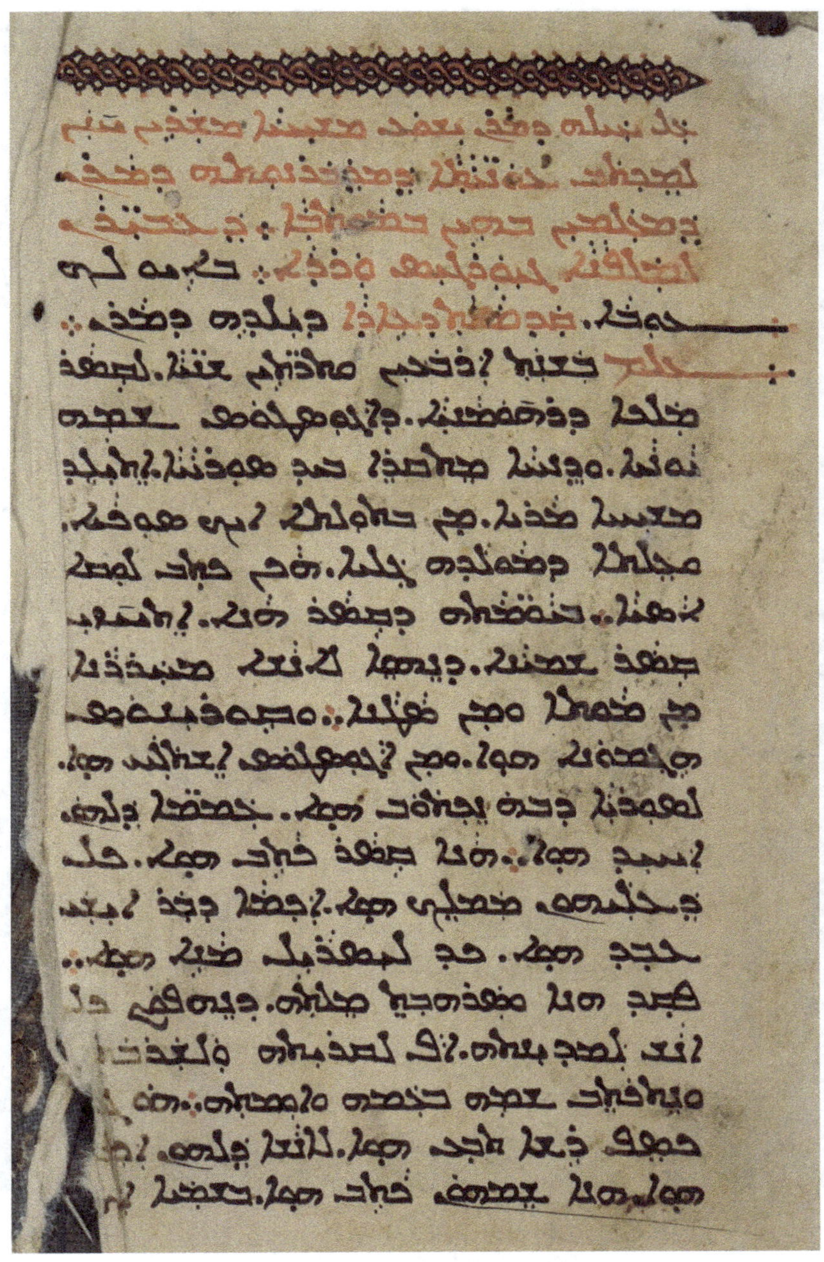

Mardin Chaldean. 41, f1v. CCM_00405
https://w3id.org/vhmml/readingRoom/view/132524
Image courtesy of Mar Hirmiz Keldani Kilisesi, Mardin, Turkey and the Hill Museum & Manuscript Library. Published with permission of the owners.

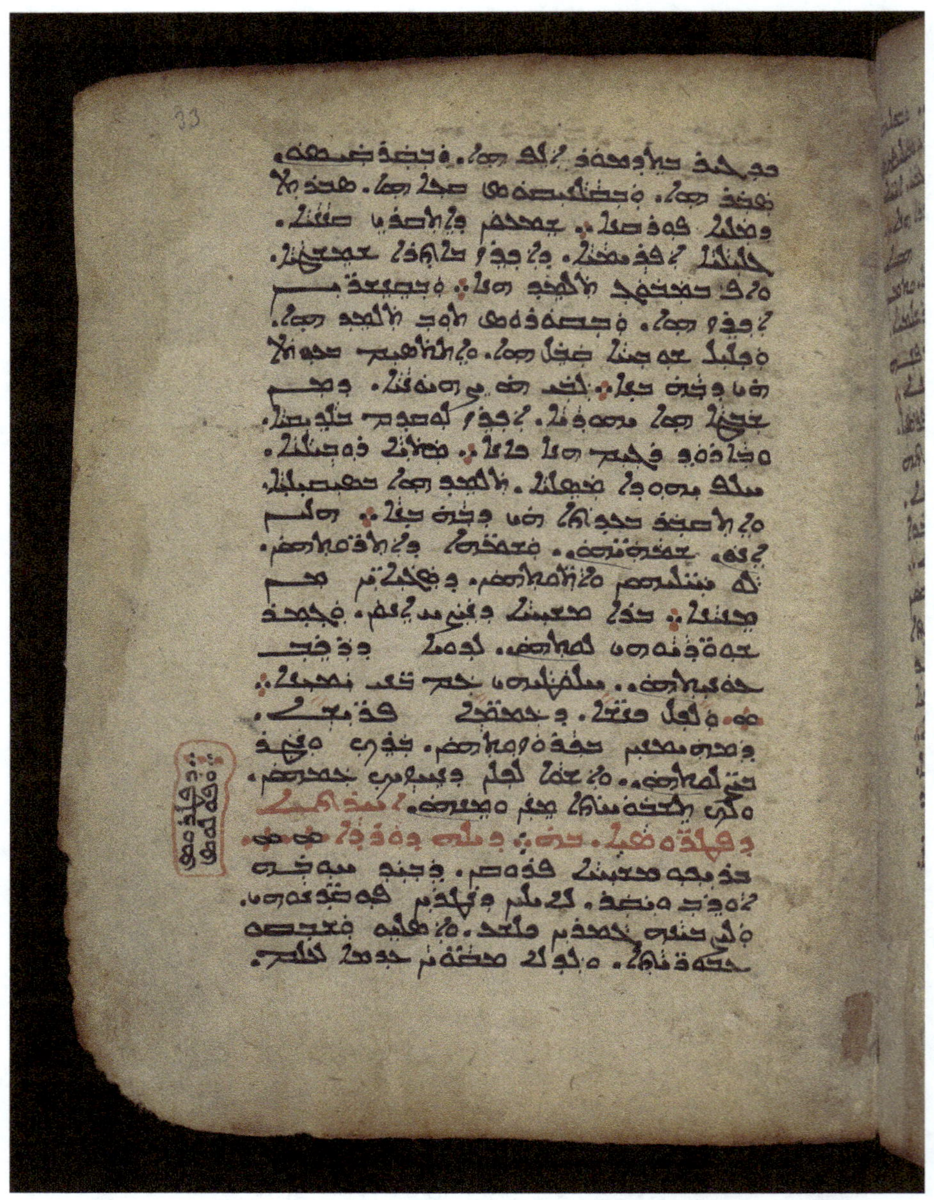

Cambridge University Library Add. 1983, f33r
Used with permission of the Syndics of Cambridge University Library.

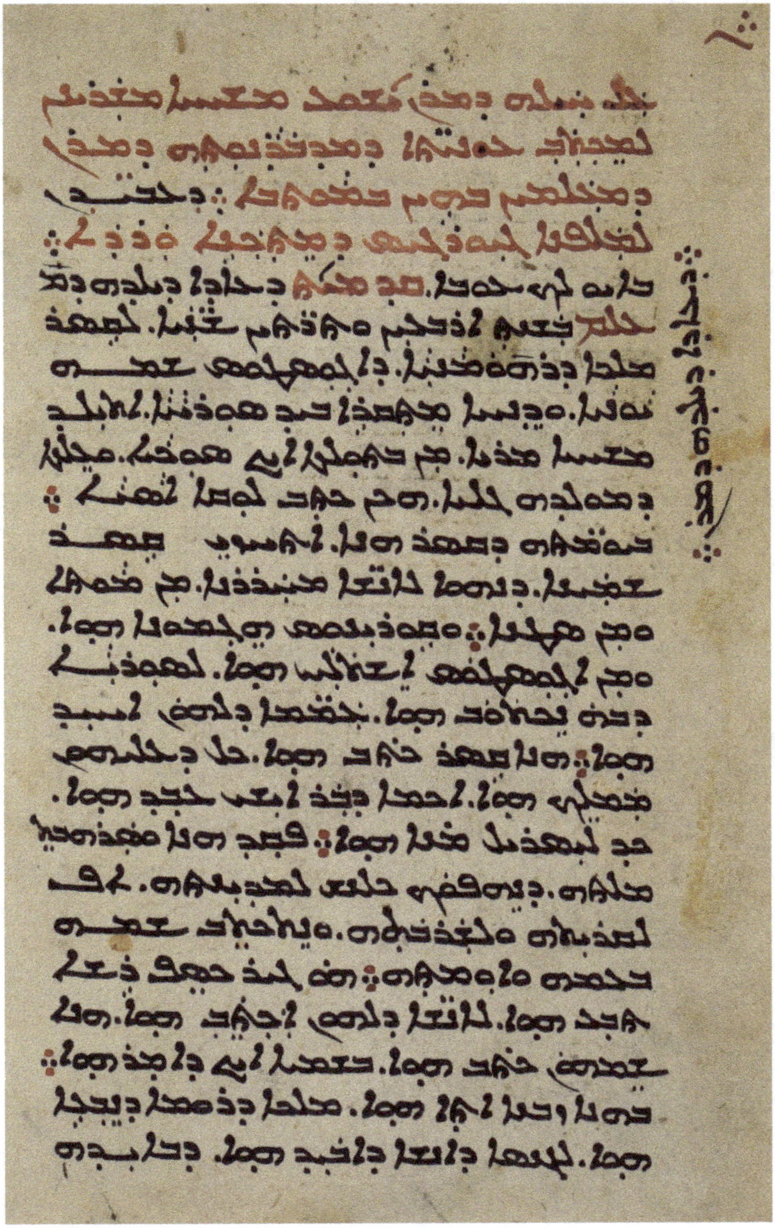

Diyarbakir 78, f2v. CCM_00407
https://w3id.org/vhmml/readingRoom/view/132526
Image courtesy of Mar Hirmiz Keldani Kilisesi, Mardin, Turkey and the Hill Museum & Manuscript Library. Published with permission of the owners.

Diyarbakir 84, f1v. CCM_00423
https://w3id.org/vhmml/readingRoom/view/132542

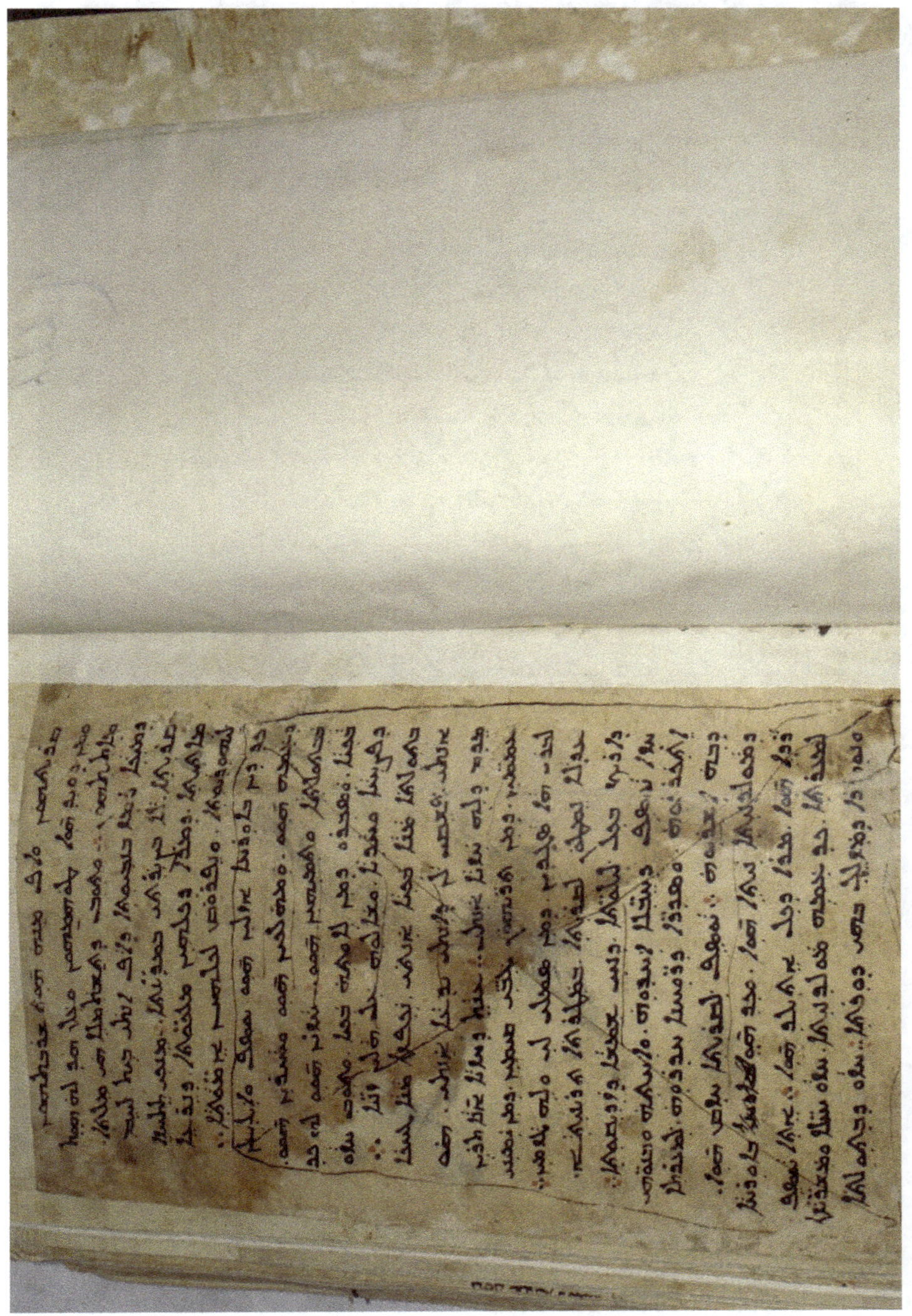

Baghdad Chaldean 492, f1. Chaldean Patriarchate, Library of Scriptorium Syriacum. Used by permission.

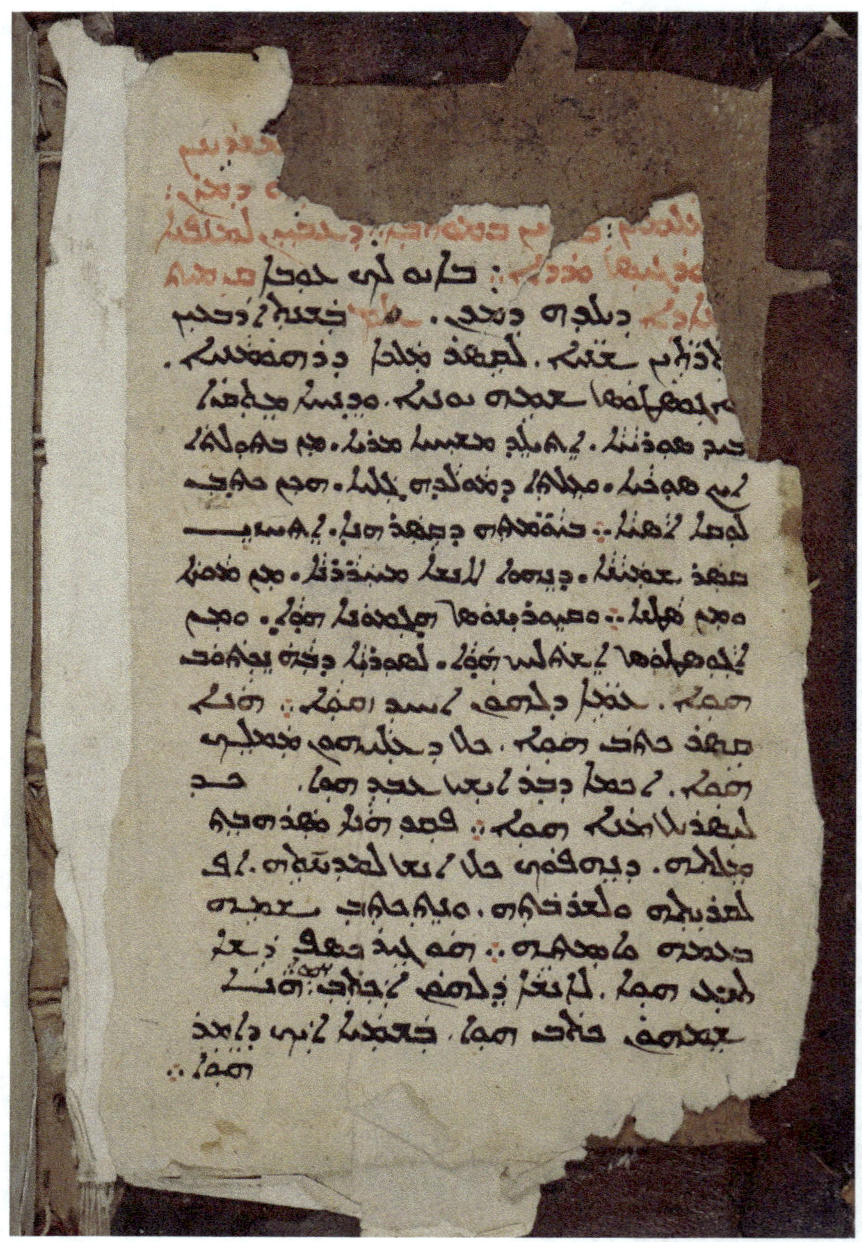

Mardin Chaldean 42, f1v. CCM_00412
https://w3id.org/vhmml/readingRoom/view/132531
Image courtesy of Mar Hirmiz Keldani Kilisesi, Mardin, Turkey and the Hill Museum & Manuscript Library. Published with permission of the owners. All rights reserved.

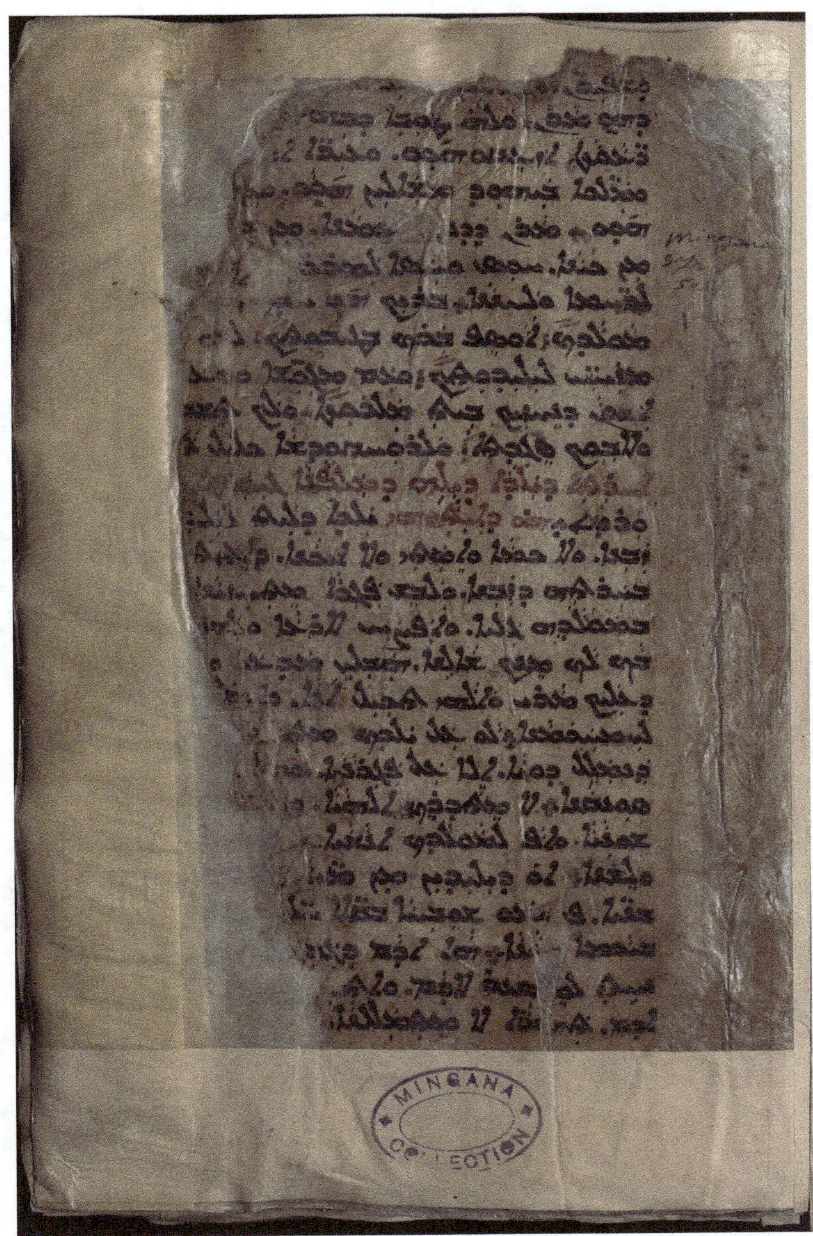

Mingana Syr. 505, f1v
Used with permission of the Cadbury Research Library:
Special Collections, University of Birmingham.

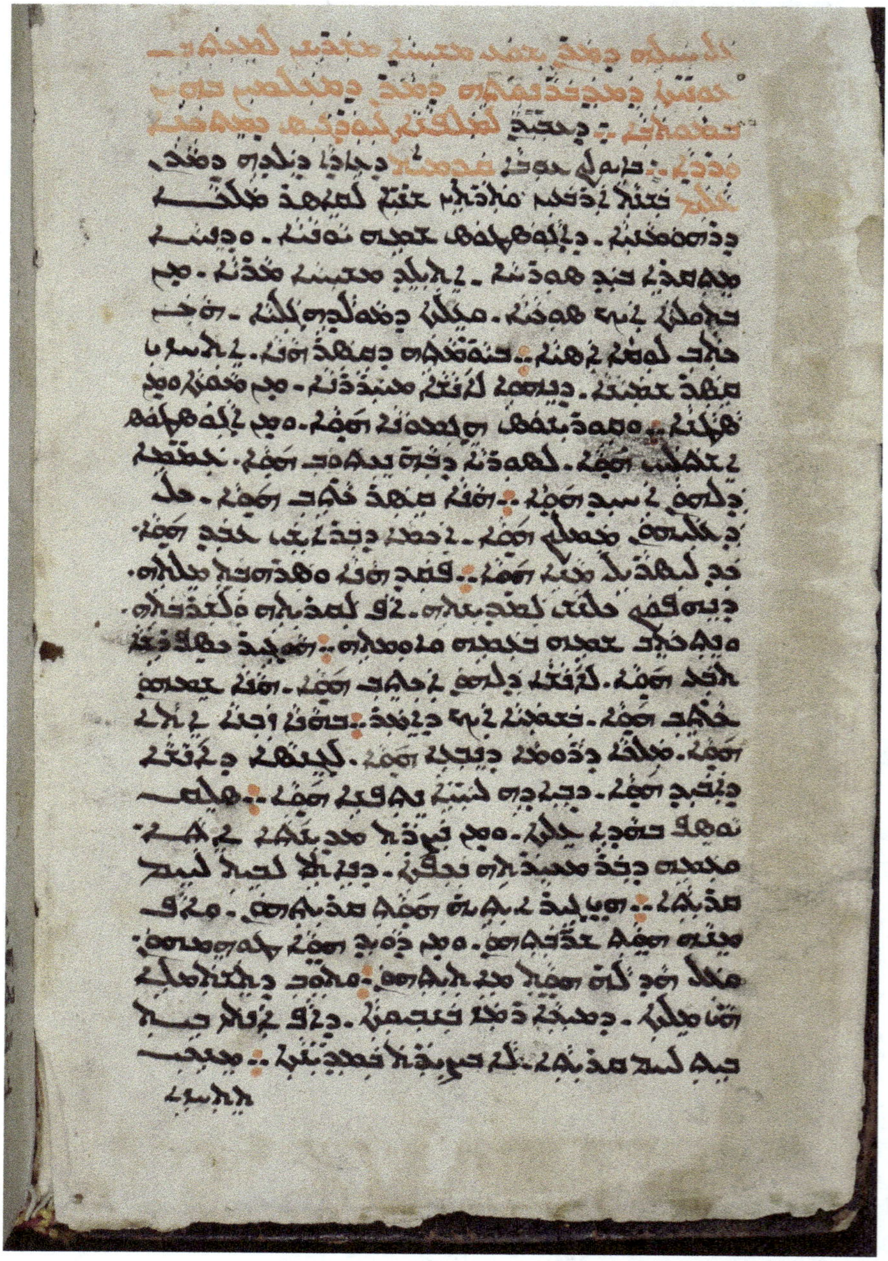

Diyarbakir 85, f1v. CCM_00396
https://w3id.org/vhmml/readingRoom/view/132515
Image courtesy of Mar Hirmiz Keldani Kilisesi, Mardin, Turkey and the Hill Museum & Manuscript Library. Published with permission of the owners. All rights reserved.

INDICES

GENERAL INDEX

INDEX OF THEOLOGICAL EXPRESSIONS